Founding the Fathers

DIVINATIONS: REREADING
LATE ANCIENT RELIGION

Series Editors:
Daniel Boyarin, Virginia Burrus, Derek Krueger

A complete list of books in the series
is available from the publisher.

FOUNDING
THE FATHERS

Early Church History and Protestant Professors
in Nineteenth-Century America

ELIZABETH A. CLARK

PENN

UNIVERSITY OF PENNSYLVANIA PRESS

PHILADELPHIA · OXFORD

Published by
University of Pennsylvania Press
Philadelphia, Pennsylvania 19104-4112
www.upenn.edu/pennpress

Printed in the United States of America
on acid-free paper

10 9 8 7 6 5 4 3 2 1

ISBN 978-0-8122-4319-2

A Cataloging-in-Publication Record is Available
from the Library of Congress

For Patricia Cox Miller
who many years ago attempted to teach me about
American history
and who since then has taught me much else

To [the American of the year 2000] the nineteenth century would stand on the same plane with the fourth,—equally childlike,—and he would only wonder how both of them, knowing so little, and so weak in force, should have done so much.

—Henry Adams, *The Education of Henry Adams*

CONTENTS

x   Contents

Introduction: Higher Education and Religion in Nineteenth-Century United States

> The question is, What is involved in the transformation of
> a field of studies into a discipline?
>
> —Hayden White (1982)

Founding the Fathers explores how the study of early Christian history and theology became instantiated as a discipline in four nineteenth-century Protestant seminaries in the United States: Princeton Theological Seminary, Harvard Divinity School, Yale Divinity School, and Union Theological Seminary.[1] Although these four began in differing degrees as sectarian outposts—Princeton, Union, and Yale variously represented the Reformed (i.e., Calvinist) branch of Protestantism, while renegade Harvard "defected" from Congregationalism to Unitarianism early in the century—they functioned for most of this period as America's closest equivalent to graduate schools in the Humanities.[2] I track their hesitant transition from institutions of ministerial training to distinguished centers of advanced education that pioneered scholarship on early Christianity.

Founding the Fathers is based on the documentary records and published writings of six nineteenth-century professors of church history: Samuel Miller of Princeton; Henry Smith, Roswell Hitchcock, and Philip Schaff of Union; George Fisher of Yale; and Ephraim Emerton of Harvard. Their and their students' class notes, an underutilized resource, reveal the infrastructural and pedagogical difficulties they faced: inadequate textbooks and libraries, students untutored in history, few colleagues (from zero to four) with whom to organize a theological curriculum, and new methods of instruction that challenged their knowledge and their institutions' resources. The creation of early Christian history as a scholarly discipline—then little known and even less appreciated—took place concomitantly with academic institution-building in the United States. When Samuel Miller began his teaching career at the Theological Seminary in Princeton in 1813, America had few colleges, a mere handful of seminaries, and nothing that could be called a university. Moreover, "religion" was not an academic subject. During the decades covered in this book, vast changes at all levels of American education were to take place.

Protestant professors in America used the term "patristics" (if they used it at all) in a much looser sense than did their Roman Catholic or Anglican counterparts in Europe: there, "patristics" denoted a theologically oriented discipline centered on those designated as "Church Fathers," who wrote from the second to the sixth centuries. It also suggested a heavy respect for ancient ecclesiastical tradition. In America, this book argues, the Fathers' writings were not cordoned off as a separate discipline, but were incorporated into a broader study that took its bearings from the historical, rather than from the strictly theological, arena. Borrowing much from the striking development of church history as a subject in the Protestant universities of nineteenth-century Germany, the professors in the four institutions I survey incorporated the writings of the Fathers into a historically oriented curriculum. Scholars in North America today who have witnessed changes in late twentieth-century nomenclature—from "Patristics" to "Early (or "Late Ancient") Christian Studies"—may find surprising the relatively little emphasis these nineteenth-century Protestant forerunners placed on theology per se. The latter instead stressed institutional developments, early Christianity's relations with Judaism and various forms of Greco-Roman religion and philosophy, and what we might label "social history," as evidenced by their discussions of marriage, slavery, wealth and poverty, and ethnicity.[3] The nineteenth-century professors, all of whom belonged to denominations deriving from Calvinism, rued early liturgical developments that savored of "high church" practices of their own time. They displayed relatively little interest in Trinitarian theology after the Council of Nicaea or in the Christological controversies; the New Testament, containing all the truth Christians needed, required only minimal theological elaboration through the centuries. "Patristics" in the European sense, some might argue, never *did* become established as a separate discipline in the very seminaries that would soon be at the forefront of promoting the study of post-New Testament early Christianity. Nevertheless, the Fathers *were* founded in America insofar as they were assigned a humble place in the broader sweep of the study of Christianity's history. Like those other, eighteenth-century "founders" whom American schoolchildren are taught to revere, the nineteenth-century professors I here discuss created from the materials offered by the Old World something peculiarly American. Perhaps we cannot assert, without considerable nuance and elaboration, that it was entirely "Bye, Bye Patristics," as Charles Kannengiesser ruefully put it.[4]

In nineteenth-century America, to be sure, the study of early Christian history and theology was not pursued as an end in itself. Appeal to the Church Fathers assumed a highly ideological cast: they were enlisted as allies or opponents in contemporary denominational battles over religious belief and practice and in the culture wars of the day. With time, the study of early Christian history shed enough (although by no means all) of its sectarian biases to take its place in departments of Religious Studies in colleges and universities. The early stages of the dismantling are signaled in this book. Only when this process had made substantial headway, Conrad Cherry argues, could a new academic discipline—Religion—be born from the old "womb of theological studies."[5] Along the way, expectations regarding professorial roles and duties changed, as did understandings of what constituted scholarship. *Founding the Fathers* moves from a broader consideration of how the study of Christian history developed in these four pioneering institutions, through the infrastructural difficulties and intellectual challenges the professors faced, to specific topics of early Christian history that intersected with various religious, social, and cultural issues in an America that was becoming less "Protestant."

In this narrative, Germany plays a double leading role, as tutor and as villain. Throughout most of the nineteenth century, bright young American males who desired (and could afford) post-collegiate education were shipped abroad, largely to Germany.[6] ("What," Edward Robinson asked in 1831, "has England to offer in comparison with the host of learned theologians who now fill the German chairs of instruction?"[7]) To place the arrival of the "German" model of graduate education on American shores only with the founding of John Hopkins University in 1876 overlooks the large number of American theological students in Germany during the early and middle decades of the century—students who returned home to teach and to preach.[8]

Between 1815 and 1914, nearly ten thousand Americans studied in Germany; before 1850, about one-quarter of them were in Protestant theology faculties.[9] In the decades between 1830 and 1860, 30 percent of *all* university students in Germany pursued theology—a figure that dropped rapidly as medicine, the sciences, and the humanities rose to prominence.[10] For evangelically inclined American theological students making their way to Germany, the University of Halle was the institution of choice, whose Pietistic emphases countered the radical scholarship of Tübingen.[11] Only toward the turn to the twentieth century did Germany's appeal begin to wane, as Americans developed their own graduate schools. While not all American professors were enamored of German university education,[12] five of the six surveyed in this book were strongly marked by their own studies in Germany and by German scholarship.

These five not only studied in Germany, but also continued to engage German scholarship throughout their careers. The Union and Yale professors in particular struggled to tame troubling German criticism—biblical and philosophical—to fit American evangelical convictions.[13] The disturbing depictions of earliest Christianity offered by David Friedrich Strauss, Ernest Renan, and Ferdinand Christian Baur and the Tübingen School, so foreign to the confessional, precritical approaches of American evangelical churchgoers, demanded serious scholarly response. At stake was the understanding of Jesus' role in Christianity's formation—indeed, the reconstruction of the first two Christian centuries.

The Princeton, Union, and Yale professors understood the Gospels to provide eyewitness accounts of the Savior, who had founded a spiritual Kingdom that reached to the present. They believed that the New Testament books—all written within the first century and many authored by Paul—exhibited no disharmonies. For these professors, the Church Fathers stood on the far side of a great divide that separated "inspired" from "uninspired" books. European scholarship, insofar as it ignored that divide, must be refuted or at least be rendered palatable for American evangelical Protestants. In addition, forms of Hegelianism emanating from Germany had to be carefully monitored so as to forestall a deadly Pantheism that gave no privilege to Christianity's uniqueness, or an equally unchristian Materialism that downplayed the role of mental and spiritual factors in historical interpretation. Such movements betokened "Infidelity," against which the Professors warned. As we shall see, of the six professors here considered, Samuel Miller alone, who died in 1850, remained oblivious to these challenges. Later in the century, the Unitarian Ephraim Emerton manifested little interest in the doctrinal and philosophical issues in the fight against German "radicalism" that so absorbed the four Union and Yale professors. Miller and Emerton remain the outliers who frame my book.

Germany, whatever its alleged dangers, nevertheless offered the professors new notions of historical development that derived from Romanticism and Idealism. These notions would, in time, prompt two changes to the study of early Christianity. First, professors—gradually and often reluctantly—came to concede that *as historians*, they could not privilege the New Testament as a static and untouchable divine revelation, exempt from scrutiny by the historical-critical methods applied to other ancient literatures. Only then could New Testament and patristic literature be linked as sources for the development of early Christianity.

Second, the traditional Protestant assumption that the early church had suffered grievous decline between the apostolic and the Reformation eras collided with theories of historical development that encouraged a more sympathetic assessment of early and medieval Christianity and a cautious celebration of *difference* among ethnic groups.[14] While championing Christianity's historical development was necessary for according signal importance to the Protestant Reformation, exhibiting sympathy with Christianity's distant past, however, became ever more difficult for American Protestant professors in an era of increasing Roman Catholic presence, one that saw the promulgation of Vatican decrees on the Immaculate Conception of Mary (1854), the Syllabus of Errors (1864), and Papal Infallibility (1870)— and unprecedented Catholic immigration to American shores. Steering an uneasy course between "decline" and "development," these professors provided a (limited) counterbalance to American Protestants' hostility to Roman Catholicism in the present and to periods of history perceived as "Catholic," the patristic era in particular.[15] The professors' attempts at tolerant understanding, however strained, coupled with their knowledge of German scholarship and interest in new methodologies of historical practice, distinguished them from many evangelical Protestants of their time.

In particular, the rise of asceticism in early Christianity and its persistence into the present presented a major conceptual stumbling block to the professors' sympathetic assessment of Roman Catholicism. The professors argued that since Jesus had gloriously raised women, marriage, and family from their allegedly demoralized status in ancient paganism and Judaism, proponents of asceticism grievously misinterpreted his intentions. Yet in pitting the Protestant idealization of family against the Roman Catholic promotion of celibacy, the professors confronted a new challenge: advocates of women's rights who demanded—often with an appeal to New Testament teachings—equal opportunities in church and society. Ancient and modern ascetic devotees, on the one side, and American supporters of women's suffrage, on the other, posed intellectual and social challenges to the Protestant professors' reconstruction of early Christianity and its authority for the present.

Last, I suggest how these professors accorded Protestants' favorite Church Father—Augustine—surprisingly rough treatment, even as they mined his writings for their own purposes. For Union and Yale professors, a more mellow form of Calvinism was in the making, one that mitigated the harsher implications of Augustine's theory of original sin. Unbaptized babies were not to be automatically consigned to hell, and adult Christians, however "innately depraved," were still deemed capable of righteous living. Moreover, the professors argued that Augustine's collusion with state authorities in the persecution of Donatists laid the foundation for later religious repression—from which America, so "exceptional" in its (alleged) separation of church and state, had struggled free. Yet, on the side of appropriation, these same scholars borrowed Augustine's explication of the early chapters of Genesis that detailed the development of human "races" to construct a "Christian" racial theory.

As students of American religion will readily observe, this book does not explore *religion* in nineteenth-century America, nor even nineteenth-century *Protestantism*. There is scarcely a Baptist or a Methodist in sight on these pages.[16] Jews (except as biblical characters) and women (except as mothers, wives, and daughters) are likewise absent.[17] Contemporary Roman Catholics are cast largely, although not exclusively, in the role of antagonists. "Others," such as "Hindoos" or "Mohammedans," are variously the objects of anthropological curiosity, of Protestant derision, or of missionizing concern.

This limitation is unsurprising, considering the identity of the figures under consideration. The professors at two of the schools, Union and Yale, called themselves evangelicals, but this designation must be distinguished from its present customary usage.[18] By "evangelical," these professors self-identify as proponents of theologies derived from the Reformed (i.e., Calvinist) branch of Protestantism, softened by influences stemming from German Pietism, from latter-day proponents of Jonathan Edwards's theology, and from American religious enthusiasm of a more decorous variety.[19]

Manifesting little association with the more celebrated revivalist emphases of their time,[20] they can be styled (in Curtis D. Johnson's classification) "Formalists": their notion of "orderly faith" required "consistent doctrine, decorum in worship, and biblical interpretation through a well-educated ministry."[21] Unlike their Princeton colleagues, however, the Union and Yale professors largely discarded Scottish Common Sense philosophy in favor of approaches touched by German Idealism and Romanticism.[22] Yet also unlike the Unitarians at Harvard, they staunchly upheld doctrines of the Trinity and the divinity of Jesus, and a high view of biblical accuracy, which (so they claimed) conformed comfortably to scientific discoveries.[23]

Colleges and the Study of Religion

Religion and history, the two disciplines that today frame the study of ancient church history, had an uncertain start in the American academy. In early American colleges, religion was considered a "frame of reference," not "a subject for scientific study"[24]: religion was assumed, not taught. The lack of instruction in subjects pertaining to religion may puzzle, since American colleges founded before, and well into, the nineteenth century were largely religious in nature,[25] often functioning as "the intellectual arm of American Protestantism."[26]

The lack of academic coursework in religion, to be sure, did not leave students religion-less. In the eighteenth century, undergraduates—those at Yale, for instance—devoted some hours on Friday and Saturday to "divinity."[27] Until the late nineteenth century, college seniors, even at the newer, state-supported public institutions,[28] customarily took a required course entitled "Evidences of Christianity" ("natural theology" or "mental and moral philosophy"), often taught by the president of the college.[29] This course, James Turner argues, "the chief curricular fallout" from Scottish Common Sense philosophy, was "a hodgepodge of intellectual flotsam and jetsam . . . from political economy to the origin of language to animals' rights."[30] "Evidences" was usually students' *only* actual course on religion. In the early 1870s, however, "Evidences" began to lose favor: Columbia discontinued it in 1871,[31] Harvard in 1872.[32] Other institutions followed.

Historians note the dramatic change in American higher education—an explosion in breadth, depth, and numbers—between 1860 and 1900.[33] Writing at the turn to the twentieth century, Henry Adams observed: "America had made so vast a stride to empire that the world of 1860 stood already on a distant horizon somewhere on the same plane with the republic of Brutus and Cato, while school-boys read of Abraham Lincoln as they did of Julius Caesar."[34] The academic study of religion likewise experienced unprecedented change and growth during this period, as evidenced not only in seminaries, but also in colleges. As late as 1885, Yale College offered only three courses related to religion, but fifteen years later, more than fifty. By the early twentieth century, new fields such as comparative religion and psychology of religion had found their way into university curricula. At the University of California-Berkeley, for example, two courses in Asian religions were added in 1900, and in 1904, a course entitled "The Religious Practices and Beliefs of Non-literary Peoples."[35] In sum, something approaching Religious Studies was in the making.[36]

Even "Biblical Literature" was not a common collegiate offering until the late nineteenth century.[37] William Rainey Harper (shortly to become founding President of the University of Chicago) introduced the study of the English Bible at Yale College in 1886. The trend soon spread.[38] Indeed, "Bible" remained the staple of many college Religion Departments into the mid-twentieth century. The American Academy of Religion was originally named the "National Association of Biblical Instructors" and continued under that rubric as late as 1964.[39] That the emphasis on "Bible" was not merely Christian, but resolutely Protestant, is a fact not always fully registered.[40]

From Harper's time onward, professors of a liberal stripe could treat the English Bible, and more broadly, religion, less as a "deposit of revelation" than as an aspect of culture. As such, its study was gathered into the new division of Humanities that had arisen to fill the void left by the declining emphasis on Greek and Latin.[41] Humanities, Jon Roberts and James Turner argue, assured university leaders (and doubtless, parents) that "the essence of religion could survive the loss of an explicitly Christian framework of knowledge."[42] Yet, with some exceptions, only in the late 1920s and thereafter were Departments of Religion established in private colleges and universities[43]—and a half-century more would pass before organizations such as the National Endowment for the Humanities and the American Council of Learned Societies recognized religion as a distinctive academic subject.[44]

Universities, Seminaries, and the Study of Religion

Harvard, Princeton, and Yale, as much as Amherst and Bowdoin, remained "colleges" for the greater part of the nineteenth century: the United States *had* no universities on the European model until late in the century.[45] Mid-century critics of American education, such as Henry Tappan, incoming President of the University of Michigan, complained that America lacked even the basic necessities—adequate libraries and sufficient professors—for establishing a university. American colleges, Tappan alleged, were at present merely elementary preparatory schools.[46] He pleaded for the development of at least one great university, preferably in New York, that could vie with European institutions.[47] Although Tappan believed that a university should be free from ecclesiastical control and "sectarian partialities," he nevertheless assumed that Christianity would be acknowledged as the only true religion and the Bible as divinely inspired.[48]

Distinctive approaches to religion in seminary, college, and university education unfolded gradually and somewhat uncertainly. From the early nineteenth century onward, theological education in the United States (unlike Germany and England) found its institutional home in the theological seminary.[49] Many scholarly studies of graduate education in North America, however, focusing on the late nineteenth century and especially on the founding of Johns Hopkins University, fail to register *seminaries'* pioneering role. "The scholarly elite of theologians has been so well hidden from the general study of American history," Gary Pranger claims, "that it has often been thought not to exist."[50]

To be sure, the "graduate" character of the early seminaries was dubious. Extremely limited in resources, they had few students and even fewer faculty. According to a report compiled in 1832, *no* Protestant seminary in America then employed more than four professors.[51] By 1844, 39 such seminaries existed, each enrolling from fewer than ten to 150 students. By 1855, even the largest seminaries boasted only five professors, and the smaller, only two or three.[52] By 1869, the 48 Protestant seminaries then in existence were competing with each other for denominational support, funds, and students. This proliferation of institutions, most with scanty resources, worked against educators' desire to provide advanced training.[53] A statistic cited in 1844 brings home the point: the *combined* libraries at the *nine* leading American seminaries of the era contained fewer than one-quarter of the volumes available to theologians at Munich or Paris.[54]

Moreover, seminaries did not originally require a bachelor's degree for entrance (Harvard Divinity School was the first, but only in the 1890s[55]) nor did students always remain in residence for three years.[56] At mid-century, Union Seminary attempted to remedy this problem by requiring "non-collegiate students" soon after arrival to pass a Greek examination based on the first two books of Xenophon's *Anabasis*.[57] As the century progressed, college graduation as a prerequisite for seminary study was more often the norm.[58] Professional schools in other fields, to be sure, were no stricter in this respect.[59] These caveats registered, theological seminaries, as I shall argue, pioneered graduate education of the Humanities-type in the United States.

Only at century's turn did universities begin to supplant seminaries as the main conduit of advanced scholarship in religion. Then, Bruce Kuklick claims, divinity schools "collapsed" as purveyors of graduate education,[60] largely remaining content to steer students toward various university departments for further study.[61] At the seminaries featured in this book, connections with a university would become increasingly important for the development of graduate programs in religion.

The Seminary Curriculum: Church History

In America's early Protestant seminaries, academic emphasis lay squarely on the Bible, biblical languages, and systematic theology, not on historical studies of Christianity's development. As late as 1889, Union's Philip Schaff remarked that in America the serious study of church history had hardly begun. Some seminaries still have *no* professor of the subject, Schaff remarked ruefully, and others regard it merely as a supplement. Although some boast two or three professors of Bible, none employ more than one church historian. What a contrast with Germany, he bitterly exclaimed![62] Yet, since America is "destined to be the main theatre of the future history of the world and the church,"[63] the study of church history, he prophesied, would eventually flourish on these shores. Schaff's hopes accorded well with his colleagues' belief in America's "exceptional" status.[64]

Even with the development of seminaries in the United States, however, church history was deemed somewhat dangerous: confronting the diversity of beliefs, outright errors, and rancorous divisions of the Christian past could undermine a student's faith. At Andover, generally conceded to be America's first independent Protestant seminary, church history was postponed until late in the senior year, by which time students had presumably been fortified against the theological threat that might arise from confronting the vicious clash of opinions throughout Christian history.[65]

Yet seminary officials should have had little cause for fear: church history was readily corralled to prove the antiquity of one's own denominational polity and to connect the founding moments of Christianity with later "Protestantizing" developments. The Church Fathers were deployed to batter down claims regarding doctrine and polity made by competing Christian groups. Debates over the "original" polity of the early church, for example, provided ammunition for the nineteenth century's culture and religion wars. Here, the discovery of new manuscripts—Syriac versions of some of Ignatius' letters, as well as the *Philosophumena* and the *Didache*—fueled Protestant professors' zeal to claim *their* denomination's governance as faithful to that of the apostolic era.[66] The Fathers could also be cited to prove how soon in Christian history a "decline" had set in that led precipitously toward Roman Catholicism. The Bible, sacrosanct and "undeveloping," remained the touchstone against which all subsequent ecclesiastical developments were judged.[67] Augustine, Jerome, and the earlier Fathers, Robert Baird wrote at mid-century, "important in their places, are regarded as of small importance in comparison with the questions, What saith the Scripture? What did Christ and the Apostles teach?"[68] In Protestant America, appropriating the Church Fathers was always a negotiation with what interpreters believed were the authentic words of a Jesus who could be cordoned off from subsequent Christian history.

Factors for Change in Higher Education: The Case of Religion

Specialization and Professionalization

What prompted the change in the study of religion? Increased specialization was one factor. Today, it is startling to realize that until the 1880s, research played almost no role in the lives of college and seminary teachers.[69] Indeed, the professoriate began to be recognized as a distinct profession only circa

1840; earlier, college teaching had not been considered a "career."[70] The few faculty employed by any institution taught whatever was necessary—and since instruction ("not designed to promote inquiry") was by recitation from a textbook, the teacher need not be expert in the subject.[71] Tracing the development of the American college, George Marsden claims that before mid-century, most faculty were generalists who could "teach almost anything."[72] Moreover, "specialization" to some early nineteenth-century ears (such as those of historian George Bancroft) sounded "commercial": young men were being trained to "sell" their Greek and Latin.[73] Elitist notions that higher education ought to be economically useless—its purpose being to form the mind and character of select youths—worked *against* the development of specialization.

In Germany, by contrast, professors were expected to develop, and devote themselves to, a circumscribed field. There, the subject area (classics, for example) would be construed—as Carl Diehl puts it—less like "a public park in which anyone is free to wander as he wishes," and more like "some kind of restricted collective farm, owned and intensively cultivated by a select group of inhabitants."[74] In America, proponents of the "restricted collective farm" model of the professoriate, such as President Charles Eliot at Harvard, waged an upward struggle against those who preferred a leisurely Sunday outing in the college park, available to all whose class background allowed them to dress and speak "decently."

Professors at American theological seminaries fared only somewhat better than their counterparts at colleges. A telling example is provided by the career of Philip Schaff, unarguably nineteenth-century America's most distinguished church historian. When Schaff arrived at Union Theological Seminary in 1870 after his tenure at Mercersburg Seminary in Pennsylvania, he was first given a chair in "Theological Encyclopedia and Christian Symbolics" (i.e., an introductory outline of the various theological subdisciplines, plus the study of Christian creeds). From there, he transferred to the chair in Hebrew; next, to the chair in New Testament Exegesis; and at last, in 1887, a few years before his death, to the chair of Church History. This example illustrates how fungible were the categories of theological teaching—and how central the study of the Bible remained. In addition, the fact that Union, like other seminaries, employed only *one* professor of church history suggests how wide that professor's chronological reach would need to be.

A second step toward specialization is signaled by the creation in the

1890s of departments as organizational units within colleges and universities: here, the University of Chicago provided the model. Previously, the cluster of instructors in any subject was insufficient to constitute a department. Until 1870–1871, the Harvard College catalogue listed course offerings by which *classes* of students (first-year, second-year, and so on) enrolled in them, not by the *departments* offering them.[75] Only in 1891, for example, were there enough history teachers at Harvard to constitute an official History Department.[76] With professors grouped with (allegedly) likeminded colleagues, the self-identification of the professoriate by *discipline* could not but become stronger.

The rise of professional societies at the end of the nineteenth century is a third indicator of increased academic specialization.[77] Although the American Philosophical Association was founded in 1743, most professional societies in the Humanities were products of the nineteenth century: the American Oriental Society was founded in 1842; the American Philological Association, in 1869; the Modern Language Association, in 1883; the American Historical Association, in 1884.[78] The Society of Biblical Literature and Exegesis, the first professional society devoted to a specialized area of religious studies, dates to 1880,[79] and the American Society of Church History (to be discussed in Chapter 1), to 1888. The new professional associations, Jurgen Herbst argues, worked to "weaken the claim of a college as the locus of professional identity, and to give the scholar a new *persona* as a practitioner of his discipline. Thus he began to think of himself less as a teacher, and more as a historian, a biologist, or an anthropologist."[80]

Only from the 1880s onward did professionalization enable historians in America to distinguish themselves from lay amateurs and become (as Gabriele Lingelbach puts it) "self-referential." Now, a man—I use the term advisedly—might strive for prestige and recognition within his own disciplinary community through research and publication.[81] Research was increasingly imagined as *producing* knowledge, as posing and attempting to answer questions, not merely passing down commentary on older texts.[82]

Likewise, the founding of university presses (Johns Hopkins boasted the first, in 1891[83]) and field-specific journals prompted greater professional specialization.[84] In 1825, Charles Hodge of the Theological Seminary at Princeton founded the *Biblical Repertory*[85]; this journal, along with Andover's *Bibliotheca Sacra*, established in 1843, served as important conduits for theological scholarship in mid-nineteenth century America.[86] The *New Englander* (later to become the *Yale Review*), founded in 1843, disseminated the "New Haven Theology," while the *Mercersburg Review* (established in 1849 and managed by Philip Schaff and John W. Nevin) served as the conduit for the "Mercersburg Theology."[87] The *American Theological Review*, which began publication in 1851 and whose editors often included Union Seminary professors, went through several name-changes as it furthered the views of the New School wing of the Presbyterian Church. Later in the century (1881) appeared the first issue of the *Journal of Biblical Literature*.[88] William Rainey Harper, as President of the University of Chicago, encouraged each department to publish a field-specific journal. In the first year of the University's operations (1892), *Biblical World* and the *American Journal of Semitic Languages and Literatures* were established, and in 1897, the *American Journal of Theology*, which later combined with *Biblical World* to form the *Journal of Religion*.[89] These journals, from earliest to latest, were important stimuli to creating a sense of a discipline (albeit broadly defined) and of their readers as "professionals."

Growth in faculty numbers and in specialized publication spurred the enlargement of seminary and university libraries, which nevertheless developed much more slowly than professors desired: seminary boards of directors frequently underestimated the cost of providing an ever-increasing supply of books and journals, most of which were produced in Europe.[90] The difficulties of establishing adequate seminary libraries will be detailed in Chapter 2.

Still another sign of specialization was the institution of sabbatical leaves, initiated at Harvard in 1880: the shrewd President Charles Eliot hoped that offering sabbaticals might lure outstanding professors from other institutions to Cambridge.[91] Yet even earlier, we may note, seminaries were granting professors time away from teaching duties, with financial assistance for travel and study, as is evidenced by the careers of the Union Seminary professors in particular. These points will be illustrated in the chapters that follow.

The Elective System and the Seminar Method

Two other developments within American colleges and universities in the mid-to-late nineteenth century also contributed to more advanced study in all fields, including religion: the elective system and the seminar method.

For much of the century, all students took the same prescribed curricu-

lum throughout their college careers. Introducing a curriculum in which
students were given at least some choice in their courses—the elective system—was hotly contested. Electives, promoted by President Eliot of Harvard in 1869,[92] allowed for greater specialization than had the prescribed
curriculum. In Eliot's view, they made "scholarship possible," for not all
subjects would be taught at the elementary level.[93] The elective principle, in
effect, allowed colleges to become universities.[94]

Detractors of the elective system, however, argued that American youth
entering college were not sufficiently prepared to make an elective system
feasible.[95] Admitting that American education was not yet equal to its German or British counterparts, President James McCosh of Princeton claimed
that forcing a European model on America would only worsen the situation.[96] Electives, some feared, might encourage students to abandon rigorous work in languages and mathematics.[97] McCosh charged that the elective
system allowed students to slack off, choosing easy courses and professors.
(As examples of such at Harvard, McCosh singled out music, art, French
plays and novels.[98]) Students, he insisted, need discipline to keep them from
going to ruin.[99] If we cannot prevent the evils of the elective system at
Harvard, he exhorted, "we may arrest it in the other colleges of the country."[100] Yet McCosh conceded that *some* few undergraduate students with
strong preparation might benefit from elective work in specialized subjects,
such as Sanskrit.[101] By the 1890s, however, enthusiasts of the new order
deemed a regimen of required courses a remnant of "mediaeval" times,
whose partisans, to be consistent (one writer claimed) should "only ride in
stage coaches and read by tallow drips."[102]

The introduction of the seminar method—developed first in classical
philology in Germany and passing to History—similarly afforded opportunities for more advanced instruction in a field.[103] The customary methods
(student recitation of textbook material, or professors' lectures) had not
encouraged student initiative or research. The historical seminar was introduced to America in 1869 by Charles Kendall Adams at the University of
Michigan and was adopted by Henry Adams at Harvard in 1871.[104] Thereafter, the seminar became especially associated with the Johns Hopkins University.[105] Entrepreneurial historian Herbert Baxter Adams traced the
evolution of the modern seminar from scholastic methods, elaborating its
growth "from a nursery of dogma into a laboratory of scientific truth."[106]
Praising seminar arrangements at German universities, Baxter Adams was
afire with a "scientific" vision of history: he likened seminars to laboratories

and books to mineralogical specimens.[107] By this standard, teaching by text-book and class recitation seemed hopelessly antiquated.[108] The introduction of seminar teaching in church history will be discussed in Chapter 2.

Graduate Education and the Ph.D.

Still another marker of increasing academic specialization was the creation of the graduate school.[109] Instituting graduate studies in America had been a topic of discussion since the 1830s, with no positive results.[110] The college retained its place as the distinctive institution of American education.

Of key importance for the development of graduate education in America was the creation of fellowships to fund advanced study, the impetus for which was spurred by the British university system. A great impact was apparently made by Charles Astor Bristed's book of 1852, *Five Years in an English University*. Bristed claimed that advanced study at Cambridge and Oxford had been enabled by the fellowships those universities offered.[111] In the early 1870s, Princeton, Columbia, and Harvard began to encourage and subsidize foreign study for their especially promising graduates; Johns Hopkins would make such study systematic.[112]

Here again, seminaries appear in the forefront: American seminaries, Natalie Naylor argues, pioneered the provision of financial aid for post-collegiate study.[113] Providing students with financial assistance for seminary education constituted a first step toward a system of graduate fellowships.[114] As for post-seminary education, Yale by 1876 was offering graduate scholarships for further study at its seminary or in Europe or Palestine.[115] In 1877, Union Seminary established two "Prize Fellowships" enabling some graduates to continue their studies in Germany. The first recipient was Francis Brown, later to serve as Professor and then as President at Union.[116] Other notable recipients of Union's "Prize Fellowships" included Edward Caldwell Moore (a student notetaker in Roswell Hitchcock's classes), who won the award in 1884, spent two years in Germany, and eventually became a professor at Harvard Divinity School; and Arthur Cushman McGiffert, who received the fellowship in 1885 for doctoral work with Adolf von Harnack in Marburg, and who succeeded Philip Schaff as Professor of Church History at Union.[117]

Newly minted theology professors returning from Germany began to organize seminars, urge the study of primary sources, and assign research papers—all considered novel moves. As early as 1850–1851, Henry Smith at Union Seminary reported that the seniors in his church history class had been assigned "two or three subjects for special investigation"; in 1852, "each student had prepared three dissertations upon assigned topics."[118] Although these "dissertations" were surely not very advanced, they constituted a step toward the research model.[119] Some decades later, the church historian at Harvard, Ephraim Emerton, listed paper topics from which his students might choose; his approach, and his students' efforts, are detailed in Chapter 2.

The first Ph.D.s in any subject awarded in America were at Yale in 1861.[120] The Yale doctorate required candidates to pursue two extra years of study beyond the completion of the Bachelor's degree, with high attainment in two different fields.[121] Twenty years later, Johns Hopkins raised the bar by requiring at least *three* years of post-collegiate study for the doctorate.[122] Between 1870 and 1900, the number of students in American graduate programs increased from 50 to about 6000.[123] This dramatic statistic illustrates in the academic arena Henry Adams's claim that these decades largely changed the face of American life. It is nevertheless sobering to note that as late as 1884, only 19 members of Harvard's entire faculty of 189 held the Ph.D.[124]

Doctoral programs in religion or theology in the United States, however, were products largely of the twentieth century. Seminaries were slower than universities in offering doctoral work under their own auspices— although the titles of some early university dissertations suggest that students wrote theses on topics pertaining to religion under the supervision of other departments.[125] At Yale, for example, such students received their degrees through the Departments of Semitics or Philosophy.[126] Of the schools featured in this study, Harvard Divinity School began to grant a Th.D. in 1914 or 1915, Union Theological Seminary in 1917 (no degree was actually awarded until 1924), and Princeton Theological Seminary in 1940.[127]

Yale's situation was complex. Unlike some other seminaries, the Divinity School at Yale never offered a Th.D. At some point the Divinity School began to award the Ph.D., administered by faculty holding rank in the Divinity School and the Graduate School.[128] In the 1920s, a Department of Religion within the University was established, a move apparently linked with the Yale Corporation's decision no longer to require compulsory chapel.[129] When a graduate program within the Department of Religion was established in 1963, M.A. and Ph.D. work was repositioned under the auspices of the (renamed) Department of Religious Studies.[130]

University Ph.D. programs in religion at Princeton date to 1955, and at Columbia, to 1946.[131] Of schools I hope to consider in a further study, the University of Chicago inaugurated a Ph.D. in religion in 1892, and the Catholic University of America, founded as a research university, offered a S.T.D. in 1889 and a Ph.D. in 1940.[132]

By 1971, the American Council of Learned Societies (ACLS) study *Graduate Education in Religion*, commonly known as the "Welch Report," counted 52 Ph.D. programs in religion in the United States and Canada, of which 20 had been established since the 1960s. The decline of the divinity school as a center of graduate education was evident: by 1970, 41 percent of Ph.D. students in religion held no professional degree.[133] The seminary was losing its preeminence as the conduit to the Ph.D.

Seminaries, despite their obvious defects, were the first purveyors in the United States of post-collegiate education in *any* Humanities-oriented subjects.[134] Amid lack of funds, buildings, faculty, books, and libraries; with programs that scarcely differentiated elementary from advanced work; with poorly prepared students; and with denominational leaders aggressively seeking to control educational programs and oversee the rectitude of faculty and students, seminary professors forged ahead.[135] Their effort to found the discipline of early church history on American shores is the subject of the chapters that follow.

PART I

The Setting: Contextualizing the Study
of Early Christianity in America

CHAPTER 1

The Institutions and the Professors

The American universities were not constructed from
blueprints shipped over on the Hamburg line.
—Carl Diehl (1978)

And what is this Maine, which produces men like these?
—August Tholuck (1850s?)

The Institutions

For my study, I have selected four seminaries or "theological departments"
founded in the first half of the nineteenth century that later developed into
major centers of graduate education: those at Princeton, Harvard, Yale, and
Union.[1] These institutions' importance in pioneering the study of Christian
history in nineteenth-century America renders them central to my project.
Each, we shall see, had its own denominational and doctrinal allegiances—
allegiances that sometimes provoked clashes among them.

Theological study at Yale and Harvard began within their respective
colleges and later moved into distinctive theological schools or "departments." At Princeton, by contrast, the Theological Seminary was established as an independent institution in part to counter the allegedly
deficient teaching of Christianity at Princeton College. Union also was
founded as a free-standing seminary and had no original connection to any
college or university.[2] Some important early nineteenth-century seminaries,
I readily admit, are absent from this book: despite their significance for
ministerial training, they did not develop into major centers of graduate

education in the twentieth century. Of these, three deserve special (albeit brief) mention.[3]

Andover, the second oldest seminary in America,[4] was founded in 1808 to serve as a Congregationalist "Maginot line against Unitarianism."[5] Home to the renowned scholar Moses Stuart, Andover produced over a thousand graduates by 1860.[6] As noted in the Introduction, the study of church history had a rocky start at Andover. Although James Murdoch was appointed to teach the subject in 1819, he was forced out in 1828 and the position was redefined as "Pastoral Theology and Ecclesiastical History."[7] Church history never received the favor at Andover that it did at Union. Although some of its graduates (including Roswell Hitchcock, later professor at Union, and George Fisher, later professor at Yale) pursued post-seminary study, by century's end Andover's pre-eminence had faded, its enrollment dwindling to 23 students.[8]

The General Theological Seminary, founded in 1817 and reorganized in the 1820s,[9] continued the Anglican tradition's devotion to patristics. (One of its graduates, Arthur Cleveland Coxe, later Bishop of Western New York, served as editor of the American version of the Ante-Nicene Fathers series: we shall encounter him later.[10]) Within two decades of its founding, the Seminary was deemed the bastion of high-church Episcopalianism,[11] "the Oxford of American Anglicanism."[12] General Seminary established a Th.D. program in 1926 and has remained an important force in the Episcopal Church, but it did not become a major center for doctoral education.[13]

A third nineteenth-century seminary—that of the German Reformed Church at Mercersburg, Pennsylvania—was renowned more for its two controversial professors than for the numbers of its graduates. In 1844, Philip Schaff arrived in America to teach at Mercersburg, where he joined John Williamson Nevin in promoting a "high" ecclesiology sympathetic to early Christian history.[14] Throughout his career at both Mercersburg and Union Seminaries (whose faculty he joined in 1870), Schaff emphasized Christianity's grounding in the institutional church. Despite its signal importance in American theology, Mercersburg, given its small size, German-language orientation, and geographical location, did not grow into a doctoral-granting institution.[15]

Although the four institutions I have chosen for my study represent only a small slice of Protestantism in nineteenth-century America, their educational and intellectual importance in the early development of theological (and later, religious) studies in America remains unrivalled. That

Presbyterians, Congregationalists, and (in New England) Unitarians were leaders in education more generally has often been noted. The professors at these schools were in discussion mainly among themselves, with leaders of their respective denominations, and (apart from Samuel Miller) with European, especially German, colleagues. Other, rapidly expanding sects and denominations made little or no mark on them or their seminaries. Indeed, many of the newer Protestant groups rejected the requirement of an educated ministry so essential to Presbyterians, Congregationalists, and Unitarians. As late as 1880, the lecturer in Ecclesiastical History at Harvard Divinity School could sneer at his institution's appointment of a *Baptist*— Crawford Howell Toy—whose denomination had "discarded" him for his liberal views on biblical criticism.[16]

In this chapter, I first sketch the institutions on which my study focuses and their provision for the teaching of early church history. Next, I offer more detailed accounts of the professors who taught the subject. Subsequent chapters probe the emphases of their teaching and writing.

The Theological Seminary at Princeton and Princeton University

The College of New Jersey (Princeton) was founded in 1746 by evangelical New Side Presbyterians who desired a more experiential, less doctrinally rigid, approach to Christianity. A Professorship in Divinity was established twenty-one years later.[17] In 1812, the General Assembly of the Presbyterian Church, seeking to upgrade the customary apprenticeship model of ministerial training, voted to establish a seminary at Princeton—a first for its denomination.[18] The Seminary's founders, Mark Noll claims, believed that they faced a multi-faceted crisis: a short supply of Presbyterian ministers, rampant "infidelity," and "the unprecedented dissemination of deistic, immoral, and unsound speculation." The Seminary, they hoped, would provide a stable bulwark in the face of religious, social, and political turmoil.[19]

Equally important, the Seminary's founders doubted that true Christian principles were being taught at Princeton College. In particular they suspected the orthodoxy of its President, Samuel Stanhope Smith, whom they forced out of office in 1812.[20] Noll argues that Samuel Miller and Ashbel Green (who would shortly replace Smith) had schemed since late 1808 to found an *undergraduate* "theological academy" that would render the College "entirely superfluous for the theological training of Presbyterians."[21] Instead of an undergraduate institution, however, Presbyterians opted for a seminary. The College's administrators agreed not to hire a professor of theology as long as the Seminary remained in Princeton.[22] This agreement perhaps delayed the creation of a separate Department of Religion within Princeton University, an event that did not occur until 1946.[23]

A Professorship of Ecclesiastical History, paired with Church Government, was slated as one of the first three appointments for the new Presbyterian seminary. In 1813, Samuel Miller, minister of the Wall Street Church in New York and a promoter of the Seminary, was appointed to fill this post.[24] The Seminary, Miller claimed, was carrying on the work of early Christian scholars Pantaenus, Clement, and Origen in the Alexandrian "seminary" [the so-called "catechetical school"] that served as "a nursery of the church." He exulted that American Presbyterians, at last awakened from their sleep, with "tardy" but "heaven-directed steps" were following not only these ancients, but also other denominations in America that had already founded seminaries.[25] Miller was the professor of church history at the Seminary from 1813 to 1849. After he retired, a succession of relatively undistinguished scholars filled the church history post.[26] From its founding until 1870, the Seminary at Princeton was under the immediate direction of the General Assembly of the Presbyterian Church. The Plan of the Seminary required professors to subscribe to the Confession of Faith and Catechisms of the Presbyterian Church U.S.A., pledging not to "inculcate, teach, or insinuate" anything contrary to that Confession or oppose any fundamental principle of Presbyterian polity.[27] By the late 1830s, the Seminary had positioned itself on the conservative, Old School wing of Presbyterianism, rejecting the "softer" Calvinist tenets that were embodied in New School Presbyterianism and the New Haven Theology, as well as cooperation with other Protestants in voluntary societies.[28] Old School and New School Presbyterians remained formally separated from 1837 until 1870. Bruce Kuklick argues that Princeton by mid-century had become "the arch-symbol of conservative philosophy and theology."[29] (Samuel Miller, for example, deplored the "semi-Pelagian" spirit of Yale, charging that its students lacked "the meek, humble, devout spirit of the Gospel."[30]) Over the course of the nineteenth century, the Seminary's conservatism manifested itself in its friendliness to Southern values and its opposition to both the New Haven Theology and Charles Finney's brand of revivalism.[31]

Of students from the first decade of the Seminary's existence, 25 became professors and 15, college presidents—a testimony, variously, to the Seminary's scholarly reputation, to the lack of opportunities for Presbyterian ministerial training elsewhere, and to the few men in America with sufficient education to assume a college presidency. In 1855, Princeton stood as the largest of America's 45 theological seminaries.[32] Soon, however, its enrollment was outstripped by Union's.[33]

Development of graduate education at the institutions here studied remains somewhat confused: on this point, Princeton was not alone. Princeton University established graduate programs in various fields in 1877, with the first doctorates awarded in 1879.[34] Only in the early twentieth century, however, did Princeton Seminary advertise a "post-graduate department" that allowed seminary graduates to continue their studies with concentration in particular areas, including church history.[35] The Th.D. program established at the Seminary in 1940 was changed to a Ph.D. in 1973. As noted above, the University Ph.D. program in religion was added in 1955.[36]

Harvard Divinity School and Harvard University

In 1805, Unitarian-leaning Henry Ware was appointed Hollis Professor of Divinity in Harvard College, an event that spurred more traditional Calvinists to found Andover Theological Seminary.[37] In 1819, "Divinity" branched off into a separate "Theological Department" (i.e., what became the Harvard Divinity School).[38] Decades later, President Charles Eliot claimed that the founding of the Divinity School showed Harvard's commitment to "unbiased investigation": teachers and students were not required to subscribe to "the peculiarities of any denomination."[39]

Church history, however, remained an "orphan discipline" at the Divinity School[40]—despite Harvard College's establishment of the first professorship of history in the United States.[41] The original plan for the School called for a position in ecclesiastical history (and four others), but no funds for this appointment were forthcoming. Some limited provision was made for instruction in the subject, but the proposed professorship languished.[42] Over the years, church history was taught by Henry Ware, Charles Follen, Convers Francis, Frederic H. Hedge (1857- 1878[43]), and Joseph Henry Allen (1878–1882).[44]

In 1854, the report of a Visiting Committee appointed by the Harvard College Overseers noted that the Divinity School had only two (over-worked) Professors, one in "Pulpit Eloquence and the Pastoral Care" (with church history as a minor sideline[45]), and the other in "Hebrew and Other Oriental languages"/"Biblical Literature." The committee recommended the establishment of two more professorships, including one in ecclesiastical history. Yet again, no professorship was forthcoming. The Visiting Committee's report nevertheless confidently announced that divinity students were advancing from "loose and unsettled notions to a well-grounded and stable faith." The course of study, it concluded, is "well ordered, systematic, impartial, and full."[46] "Full" might not be the word that springs to present-day readers' minds, given the School's inadequate staffing.

Throughout mid-century, the School remained small and somewhat lackluster. Between 1840 and 1880, Sydney Ahlstrom admits, its scholarship did not keep pace with the standards of the day.[47] When Thomas Hill was sworn in as President of Harvard in 1863, he rhetorically asked in his inaugural address: "Our Divinity School prepares its scholars to take charge of parishes; but where are our young men coming simply as lovers of truth, simply as scholars, for aid in exploring the highest realms of human thought?"[48] Apparently nowhere.

The Divinity School's change of fortune came with Charles Eliot's appointment as President of Harvard in 1869. Eliot, so an enthusiast later claimed, planned "to make this a university school of theology instead of a drill-shed for Unitarian ministers."[49] In his *Annual Report* for 1874–1875, Eliot scored the state of Divinity at Harvard.[50] Four years later, he led a campaign to endow five new professorships for the School, to be filled by scholars trained in historical and critical methods.[51] At Harvard, Eliot insisted, there should be a nondenominational theological school positioned *within* the university, offering courses to all students, not only to future ministers.[52] This arrangement, he argued, would ensure that ministerial training upheld the "standards in truth-seeking which modern science has set up."[53] Reorganizing the Divinity School as effectively undenominational, Eliot later claimed, was one of the most important accomplishments of his forty-year presidency.[54]

At last, in 1877, the Divinity School received a gift for the endowment of the Winn Professorship in Ecclesiastical History;[55] in 1882, it was awarded to Ephraim Emerton. Emerton, a layman who had earned his Ph.D. at Leipzig in 1876,[56] was then teaching history in Harvard College. As Winn

Professor, Emerton was charged with introducing new methods, including the seminar, to the study of church history, and opening church history courses to non-Divinity students.[57]

Others were less pleased with Eliot's plan, including the disappointed candidate, Joseph Henry Allen, who had provided instruction in ecclesiastical history since 1878. Although gracious in public about not receiving the coveted Professorship, Allen confided to several correspondents that Eliot arranged to pay Emerton only his regular salary as instructor in history, thus saving the Winn funds ("at a stroke $2000") for other purposes at the University.[58] Moreover, Eliot's promotion of "scientific theology" (in Allen's view) was fatuous: he had no understanding of what that phrase meant.[59]

According to Harvard catalogs from the 1880s and 1890s, Emerton taught all periods of church history through the seventeenth century. Now, historical approaches to divinity subjects become standard at Harvard. In 1896, John Winthrop Platner, a graduate of Union Seminary, was also appointed to a position in church history at Harvard, but after a few years he decamped for Andover.[60] Platner had little praise for Emerton's approach. On one occasion, inviting Arthur Cushman McGiffert of Union Seminary to lecture at Harvard in order to "arouse more interest in the study of Church history here," he commented that *they don't even know what it means. . . .* Regard the trip somewhat in the light of missionary work."[61]

By 1886–1887, the Divinity School counted six resident graduate students among its total student population of 21; by the early twentieth century, more than half the School's students were considered graduate students. At first, Master's and Ph.D. degrees were awarded through agreement with the University Graduate School, but in 1914–1915 the Divinity School received permission to offer the Th.D. A Ph.D. in Religion, offered by the University, was added in 1934.[62]

Yale Theological Department, Yale Divinity School, and Yale University

At Yale, as at Harvard, church history was first taught within the College. In 1778, Ezra Stiles was designated "Professor of Ecclesiastical History," a post he retained throughout his Presidency of Yale until his death in 1795.[63]

In the 121 years between the College's founding in 1701 and the organization in 1822 of the "Theological Department" (which became the Divinity School), Yale emerged as a distinguished center of theological studies, with Jonathan Edwards just one of its stars.[64]

The creation of the Theological Department in 1822 was prompted by fifteen students' petition to remain at Yale College after their graduation to receive further instruction. To meet their needs, churches contributed funds to secure a new professor in theology, and some members of the existing College faculty were reassigned to divinity.[65] Historians of Yale credit both the disestablishment of Congregationalism in Connecticut in 1818 and the religious revival at Yale College in 1820 with fostering the desire for theological study.[66] A college degree (or even college attendance) was not a strict requirement for admission, and many students did not stay three years. As at other institutions, awarding the Bachelor of Divinity degree at Yale came later: in 1867.[67]

The Yale Theological Department was relatively conservative in comparison to Harvard and Union.[68] Its conservatism matched that of the College as portrayed in the famous Yale Report of 1828. Called "the most influential educational statement of the antebellum period" by historian Julie Reuben, the Yale Report defended the classically oriented curriculum against proposed changes. The purpose of a Yale education, the Report claimed, was to "discipline" mental faculties and to form character, not to impart knowledge or enlarge the mind's "furniture."[69]

Theological study at Yale (as at Harvard) faltered in the mid-nineteenth century. Whereas circa 1840 the enrollment in the Theological Department had stood at about 87, by 1858 it had fallen to 22[70]—in contrast to Princeton's 130, Andover's 123, and Union's 114 in the same period.[71] Professorial replacements were stalled and financial difficulties abounded;[72] student interest had shifted from theology, formerly Yale's special glory, to biblical studies, a subject not yet prominent at Yale.[73] The School nearly closed after the Civil War, but was saved by the fund-raising activities of the younger Timothy Dwight.[74] And with the arrival of *Wünderkind* William Rainey Harper at Yale in 1886, biblical studies were invigorated.[75]

Nineteenth- and twentieth-century commentators alike note the neglect of church history at Yale.[76] Although in the College, history had been made a separate subject in 1847 and a professorship established in 1865, the Divinity School lacked a permanent position in the subject.[77] Finally, despite the hardships of the Civil War era, gifts enabled the establishment in 1867 of a chaired professorship in church history, named for Titus Street.[78] The focus of Yale Divinity education now shifted from theology to biblical and historical studies, deemed the "best preparation against infidelity of the day."[79] George Fisher, who had been appointed in 1854 as College Pastor and Professor of Divinity, assumed the new Street Professorship of Church History.[80] When Fisher retired in the early twentieth century, he was succeeded by Williston Walker, who had received his Ph.D. from Leipzig.[81]

The development of graduate education beyond ministerial training at the Yale Theological Department, as at other seminaries, came late—especially considering that the first Ph.D.s awarded in America were at Yale (1861).[82] By 1876, graduate scholarships had been instituted to provide for a year of post-ministerial study at the Seminary or abroad. Professors, however, were unclear what role this extra year should play. That they still thought of these students as ministers rather than as future scholars is suggested by their questions: would churches wish their ministers to have a fourth year of education, and if so, who would pay for it?[83]

The awarding of doctorates in religion at Yale, as noted above, had a complex history. At some point, faculty from the Divinity School and the Graduate School began to offer the Ph.D. under the auspices of the Divinity School, but when a graduate program within the University Department of Religious Studies was established in 1963, M.A. and Ph.D. work was repositioned there.[84]

Union Theological Seminary

Union Theological Seminary, founded in 1836, offered a more liberal brand of Presbyterianism (New School) than Princeton's.[85] Less tied to a hardened Calvinism and willing to work with other Protestants, especially Congregationalists, for religious and social improvement in America and beyond, New School Presbyterians found their views supported in Union's charters. The Seminary's Plan and Constitution stated that it would be open to "all men of moderate views and feelings, who desire to live free from party strife, and to stand aloof from all extremes of doctrinal speculation, practical radicalism, and ecclesiastical domination."[86] Qualified men from "every denomination of evangelical Christians" were invited to attend.[87] In the Seminary's first year, 23 students enrolled; by its fourth year, enrollment had grown to 120.[88]

Although some critics deemed a large city an inappropriate location for a seminary,[89] a plot of land was leased in what is now the area around New York University—"well uptown," a contemporary commentator wrote, "quite on the outskirts of the city."[90] It was not a propitious moment to found a seminary in New York: the Great Fire of 1837 rendered would-be patrons unable to meet their financial commitments.[91] Moreover, unlike Harvard and Yale, Union was not affiliated with a university.

New York City in the mid-nineteenth century was awash in social change. Not only had the population grown tenfold in the century's first sixty years;[92] "new money" had also arisen to challenge the hegemony of a homogeneous upper class who had previously imagined themselves the city's cultural legislators. Union, Thomas Bender argues, set out to exploit the opportunities of a metropolis, capitalizing on the financial and intellectual life of the city.[93] The Seminary profited from large gifts given by business entrepreneur James Roosevelt (father of Franklin D.) and from banker James Brown (of the family that would later merge businesses to become Brown Brothers Harriman), establishing chaired professorships in Theology, Hebrew and Cognate Languages, Sacred Literature, Sacred Rhetoric and Pastoral Theology, Church Polity, and Mission Work.[94] As the Seminary grew, it sought larger quarters. With the financial assistance of New York's wealthy, it moved progressively uptown: first, in 1884, to buildings on Park Avenue between Sixty-Ninth and Seventieth Streets, and then, in 1910, to its present location on Morningside Heights.[95]

Union's professors, whose meager salaries—allegedly $2500 per year, but often less, or occasionally nothing[96]—distinguished them from the moneyed elite, nevertheless benefited from their relationships with businessmen and entrepreneurs. Seminary professors elsewhere joked that their colleagues in New York "lived among millionaires."[97] Despite their relative penury, the Seminary's professors were considered sufficiently genteel to associate with the Dutch aristocrats of old New York (the Schuylers),[98] and be financially assisted by capitalists (Charles Butler) and commercial publishers (Charles Scribner).[99] Philip Schaff was so well connected that W. H. Vanderbilt's son-in-law, Eliott Shepard, threw a party in 1882 at his new mansion on Fifth Avenue and Fifty-Second Street for members of the American Bible Revision Committee (of which Schaff was chair) and 300 or so "friends" to celebrate the Revision's publication.[100] Some Union faculty enjoyed membership in the Century Club, "headquarters for a clubbish, genteel culture."[101] They were invited to lunches that included thirteen

artery-numbing courses[102] and to dinners at Delmonico's, the favored res-
taurant of New York elites.[103] Even professors who lived in rented houses
had spacious enough quarters to entertain 125 of the delegates to the Evangelical Alliance meeting in 1873.[104] Intellectual and cultural capital, it
appears, compensated for the professors' lack of cash. Many wealthy New
Yorkers were then invested in the relatively liberal brand of Protestantism
that Union represented.

Unsupported by a university or a denomination, Union's earliest years
were ones of grave financial difficulty; in 1839–1840 the professors had for
the most part gone unpaid. Financial agents were employed to drum up
monies from various constituencies.[105] New York ministers who favored the
Union experiment (such as George Prentiss, later to join Union's faculty)
exhorted their congregations to give to Union—perhaps even to mortgage
their church buildings.[106] Prentiss sensed that potential patrons might deem
the subjects studied at Union arcane: some, he rhetorically declaimed, will
doubtless scoff, "What is the use of Hebrew roots, of Greek and Latin
erudition . . . of the history of obsolete dogmas, and dead heresies, and
extinct or corrupt churches, in our new and busy world of the Future? . . .
'Let the dead bury their dead!'" Prentiss vigorously argued the necessity of
these studies for fostering a strong pastorate. He compared nostalgia for a
time before there were professors of "Sacred Philology and Ecclesiastical
History and Exegesis" to that for an era before the invention of railroads
and steamboats.[107]

The first three professorial appointments at Union were in theology,
biblical literature, and pastoral theology and church government.[108] There
was no permanent professor in church history until 1850,[109] when Henry
Smith joined the faculty. Earlier, Samuel Cox, a prominent local pastor and
father of Arthur Cleveland Coxe, covered the subject (badly, judging from
student notes).[110]

In November 1849, Albert Barnes, who chaired a committee on faculty
appointments, reported to Union's Board of Directors that a permanent
position in church history was much needed. Barnes conceded that often
the subject was taught in a "repulsive" fashion. But this need not be the
case if the professor included "the history of doctrine, the development of
the Christian spirit and the religious life of the church." The chair, in
Barnes's view, should be filled by a man with "ample learning, a philosophical mind, and a knowledge of German."[111]

Henry Smith, selected for the new position, took up his post in the winter of 1850. He had not been especially trained in church history, although he had achieved some national renown in what we would today call philosophy of religion and philosophy of history.[112] Having studied in Germany, Smith brought to Union the German organization of church history that incorporated historical theology and history of doctrine.[113] Some worried that Smith's German training might lead him astray; rumors circulated that he had "publicly testified his reverence for the name of Schleiermacher." Indeed, he had: in a lecture delivered in 1849, before joining the Union faculty, Smith praised Schleiermacher for leading the return of German theology from cold rationalism to "the fervent and almost mystic love to Christ."[114] Although Union had waited fourteen years after its inception to establish a Professorship in Church History (albeit not endowed until 1855), Yale waited longer—and Harvard, over a quarter of a century longer.

Smith, however, held the Professorship in Church History for less than four years before assuming the Roosevelt Professorship of Theology.[115] Upon Smith's transfer, Roswell Hitchcock was awarded the post in church history, now endowed as the Washburn Professorship.[116] Hitchcock remained at Union for 33 years until his death, the last seven serving as President.[117] Only in 1870 was a distinguished church historian—Philip Schaff—appointed to the Union faculty, but Schaff assumed the Professorship of Church History only in 1887, after Hitchcock's death.[118] Upon Schaff's retirement and subsequent death in 1893, he was succeeded by his former student, Arthur Cushman McGiffert.[119] By the early twentieth century, the historical method reigned in all fields at Union.[120]

Graduate education at Union developed as slowly, and with as much complication, as at other institutions. Catalogs from the 1860s list "resident licentiates," later called "graduate students."[121] Yet no courses were instituted especially for them. By 1879, some Union graduates were remaining for another year of study.[122] These students were to take five hours of "exercises" (classes) every week; in 1889–1890, the requirement was added to "carry on special research in some branch of theological science, under the direction of the faculty." Five years later, the number of required courses was raised to eight, three of which (if students so desired) could be taken at area universities.[123] (By 1892, Union had made arrangements with Columbia and the University of the City of New York [NYU] that allowed "superior" Union students to enroll in certain courses, without fees, at those institutions.[124]) A Union circular from 1905, announcing graduate offerings for that year, listed three options: the History of Christian Thought; a Historical Training Class; and a Historical Seminar.[125]

Union, like other institutions, had a rather confused history of conferring degrees. For most of the century, until 1890, no official degrees were offered. On April 1, 1890, an agreement between the University of the City of New York and Union stipulated that NYU would award a B.D. to Union students who were recommended by the Union faculty—a provision that would enable the nonsectarian NYU to offer this degree without having to mount a theology school.[126] The arrangement lasted only six years, during which time *not one* B.D. degree was awarded. The President of Union, Thomas S. Hastings, in 1896 informed Henry MacCracken, Chancellor of NYU, that the present arrangement should end: either the New York State Regents would grant the B.D. or Union itself would ask for the power to confer it.[127] In 1917–1918, the D.D. (then an earned degree at Union) was changed to a Th.D., requiring at least three years of residency, rigorous language study, and "publication of a substantial book." During the 1920s, when both Columbia University and Union Seminary were well established on Morningside Heights, arrangements were made whereby Columbia would grant the M.A. in "the literature and religion of the Bible, the comparative study of Christianity and other religions, and (by 1930) Christian education."[128] Columbia instituted a Ph.D. program in religion in 1946.[129] At Union, the Th.D. was changed to a Ph.D. in 1974.[130]

Such were the beginnings of church history and the degrees offered at the four institutions here studied. I turn now to the six major professors who developed the subject at their respective institutions.

The Professors: A Sketch

The six professors who are the focus of my study, and around whom the subsequent chapters of this book are organized, need to be introduced. Celebrated in their day not only as professors of church history but also as public figures, they shaped the study of their subject for much of the nineteenth century. The surviving information on these men, however, is unequal: about some, a great deal is known, while about others, much less.

Biographies of three of the six (Samuel Miller of Princeton, Henry Smith of Union, and Philip Schaff of Mercersburg and Union), written by well-informed—if partial—family members, incorporate letters, journal entries, and other documents highly useful to the historian. Since no such biographies exist for Roswell Hitchcock of Union, George Fisher of Yale, or Ephraim Emerton of Harvard, their lives are less fully documented. Moreover, the lengthy tenures of Miller at Princeton and Fisher at Yale place disproportionate attention on *one* professor's shaping of early church history at his institution—in contrast with the *three* church history professors at Union during that period (Henry Smith, Roswell Hitchcock, and Philip Schaff).

Class notes and other archival materials, as well as print sources, however, remain for all six. Yet even here, there is an unavoidable disproportion: the course notes given by three of the professors (Samuel Miller, Henry Smith, and Roswell Hitchcock) are far more abundant than those of George Fisher and Ephraim Emerton. As for Philip Schaff, although class notes remain in the archives at both Lancaster and Union Seminaries, he wrote so constantly and used his class preparations so extensively as aids to his published works that the extant material threatens to drown the historian. The coverage I give the six is, then, admittedly unequal.

The professors present disparate careers in other respects as well, as the following chapters will detail. Samuel Miller at Princeton and Ephraim Emerton at Harvard are in a sense outliers, with experiences and concerns different from the four professors at Union and Yale. Miller, whose long tenure at Princeton Seminary ended just as that of some of the other professors was beginning, remained untouched by German education, philosophy, and theology. He represents a distinctive Princeton approach to theological studies, inflected by Scottish Common Sense philosophy. By an accident of professional longevity, Miller kept the teaching of church history at Princeton Seminary in an older style than might otherwise have been the case.

The Unitarian Ephraim Emerton of Harvard, on the other end—the only one of the six to earn a German Ph.D. in history entirely apart from seminary training—evinced little interest in theology or biblical studies per se, unlike the Union and Yale professors. His occupation of the Winn Professorship meant that a man with quite different historical interests from those of his Union and Yale counterparts would train students at Harvard.

The rapid growth of Union in particular from mid-century onward, however, ensured that a newer understanding of church history—evangelically pious, yet colored by German historiographical and philosophical assumptions—was offered to hundreds of prospective ministers and (even) a few scholars. By the time of Philip Schaff's death in 1893, Union was well on the way to forging a theological *persona* that would mark American liberal Protestantism in the early twentieth century.

Samuel Miller (1769–1850)

Born in Delaware, Miller was educated at home in Greek and Latin by his father and graduated from the University of Pennsylvania at nineteen as salutatorian. He then studied theology privately in 1791–1792 with Charles Nisbet, the first Principal of Dickinson College.[131] From 1793 to 1813, Miller served as minister at the Presbyterian Church in Wall Street (New York), during which time he wrote his most famous work, *A Brief Retrospect of the Eighteenth Century*.[132] Miller's placement in New York afforded him frequent opportunity for criticizing Episcopalians' "immense wealth," "arrogant claims and high-church principles."[133] As a professor of church history, his assaults on Episcopalians took the form of battles over the "original" church polity. Miller's polemicizing against all groups except his own brand of Presbyterianism was not modified by any seeming acquaintance with German theology or philosophy.[134]

Although Miller's training in church history was nearly nonexistent, during his years in New York he had been active in the New-York Historical Society, for which organization he collected information on the early history of New York State and its environs. His questions to correspondents manifest his interest in social, cultural, and technological developments. To one correspondent, Miller explained that although his questions seemed "trifling," they might help to uncover information from documents "indirectly gathered . . . which they were not designed originally to convey."[135] His "nose" for historical investigation was perhaps better than his later deployment of patristic texts to rail against Episcopalians and other groups would suggest.

Miller agonized over leaving the active ministry to become a professor. At the time of his call to Princeton, he had already rejected the presidency of three colleges.[136] He confessed to his New York congregation that the constant exertion of a New York City pastorate made him fear for his health: apparently he imagined that a professorship would be less demanding.[137] His salary at Princeton was to be $1800 a year plus the use of a house.[138]

In 1813, Miller joined the new Presbyterian Seminary as its second professor, with an appointment in Ecclesiastical History and Church Government. This position he held for 36 years.[139] Although he claimed to keep the two subjects of his professorship separate,[140] his teaching of church history focused strongly on polity: he aimed to show that the Presbyterian form of church government was in place at Christianity's inception.[141] Miller's slant on church history was suggested in his inaugural address, a "Sketch of the . . . Witnesses for the Truth During the Dark Ages." These "witnesses"—Trinitarians, Calvinists, and Presbyterians, among others— prove that "doctrines of grace were the genuine doctrines of God's Word."[142] Miller's long tenure at Princeton set the tone for the teaching of church history in that institution. When Miller stepped down in 1850, he was not replaced with a professor of note.[143]

Although others praised Miller as exhibiting "a ripe scholarship, a minute acquaintance with the annals of the early Church, and a capacity to vindicate the primitive form of ecclesiastical government,"[144] Miller himself was keenly aware of his inadequate preparation. Having accepted the Princeton position, he confessed in his diary that his heart sank when he contemplated the appointment. I do not have "the appropriate qualifications," he wrote; "I have not the talents; I have not the varied furniture; especially I have not the mature spiritual wisdom and experience, which appear to be indispensable."[145] (Whether training in church history was among the missing "furniture" is not stated.[146]) His election, he mused, was by default, so lamentably scarce were Presbyterian ministers who had turned their attention to the study of church history. Years later, as an experienced professor, he acknowledged how "very raw, and very poorly prepared" he had been. Since he had not started his studies in church history until he was forty-four, he conceded that he would never be as qualified as those who had undertaken them in their youth.[147]

In the Seminary's opening year, 1813, Miller and his colleague Archibald Alexander taught 24 pupils.[148] Miller was responsible for organizing the curriculum in church history. That Miller was not enamored of patristics in general is suggested by his critique of the "addiction" of Episcopalians and "their Papal exemplars" to the "Fathers."[149] Nevertheless, he thought that budding Presbyterian ministers should know "the opinion and practice of our Fathers in all past ages."[150]

An unidentified (and seemingly unsympathetic) reviewer of the junior Samuel Miller's two-volume biography of his father describes the senior

Miller as not brilliant, nor a man of "great powers," but an enthusiastic plodder who by "constant and methodical working" became a prominent scholar in his denomination. Miller, the reviewer concedes, possessed a "much larger spirit" than did many Old School Presbyterians.[151] Nevertheless, he like other "Princeton gentlemen" had succumbed to the pressures from "the extreme and anathematizing party . . . rather than lose their positions or abandon the old views."[152] The reviewer pokes fun at Miller's now-dated condemnation of dancing, novel-reading, and the shocking "New Haven view" that the six days of creation were not strictly "days."[153]

In addition to his famed *Brief Retrospect of the Eighteenth Century* and numerous published articles and sermons, Miller wrote (among other books) *Letters on Unitarianism* (1821); *Letters on Clerical Manners and Habits* (1827); *Letters Concerning the Constitution and Order to the Christian Ministry* (1807, 1830); *An Essay on the Warrant, Nature and Duties of the Office of the Ruling Elder* (1831); and *Presbyterianism: The Truly Primitive and Apostolical Constitution of the Church of Christ* (1840).

Henry Boynton Smith (1815–1877)

Henry Boynton Smith was the first full-time professor of church history at Union Theological Seminary.[154] A native of Maine, Smith attended Bowdoin College, Andover Theological Seminary, and Bangor Seminary.[155] In 1834, he converted from Unitarianism to Congregationalism.[156] (His zeal as a convert is amply on display in the chapters that follow.) At Bangor, Smith was instilled with an enthusiasm for German literature by his teacher Leonard Woods, Jr., son of his Andover professor.[157] In late 1837, he crossed the Atlantic, studying first in Paris. Arriving in Germany in spring 1838, three years after David Friedrich Strauss's *Leben Jesu* had shaken the Christian world, he pursued work at the Universities of Halle and Berlin until 1840.[158] An American fellow student at Halle later recalled their "anxious consultation" in which Smith worried whether "he could be a student or not."[159] Apparently he decided he could.

Smith's German was strong enough to follow professors' lectures, although the occasional sketchiness of his extant notes, now in the Union Seminary archives, suggests that he occasionally lost his way. These notes focus largely on lectures given by August Tholuck, who became a good friend—the only person in Germany who called him by his first name, "Henry," Smith plaintively wrote to his parents.[160]

Smith's letters from Germany also describe August Neander's lectures on the "History of Christian Doctrines."[161] He styles the erudite Neander (exhibiting a "decidedly Jewish" face) a living source of Christianity, "the father of a new era in church history." Neander, he reports, is considered "the best exegetical lecturer in Germany"; more auditors flock to him than to any other German theologian.[162] In Berlin, Smith heard Leopold von Ranke's lectures on the Calvinist Reformation and studied Hegel with Friedrich Trendelenberg.[163] Later in his life, Smith made three return trips to Europe. On the last, he spent a year and a half in Germany, Italy, and "the lands of the Bible."[164]

The German university experience shaped Smith's life and work. He, like other American students, was warmly welcomed by several German professors.[165] In Berlin, Smith was invited to dine with Neander and to meet with Hegel's widow. At Halle, Tholuck explicated Hegel to him during their customary walks and took him along on a vacation trip.[166] Professor of Philosophy Hermann Ulrici, in whose home Smith lived for a time, also developed a warm relationship with Smith.[167] When Smith returned to America, he kept in touch with both Tholuck[168] and Ulrici.[169] Professor Isaak Dorner also praised Smith: "einen der ersten, wenn nicht als ersten Amerikanischen Theologen der Gegenwart angesehen; festgegründet . . . in philosophischen Geistes und für systematische Theologie ungewöhnlich begabt."[170] Smith had, it is clear, made a deep impression on German professors and their wives.

His German education in place, Smith returned to America but had difficulty finding a permanent post. He was turned down for a chair in literature at Bowdoin; at Dartmouth for a professorship of divinity; and even at a girls' school—and so he became a pastor by default.[171] Yet even then, Smith pursued German scholarship, translating ten German articles for *Bibliotheca Sacra* during these years.[172] In 1847, Smith became Professor of Mental and Moral Philosophy at Amherst College, where he taught Mill, Hume, Scottish and English philosophy, logic, and the Baconian method.[173] The philosophy he had imbibed in Germany, it appears, had not yet secured a place in American college curricula.

In 1850, Smith was offered the Professorship of Church History at Union. He doubted the wisdom of accepting the appointment: he was not a historian by training, considered himself unsuited for a "theological institution," and worried about Union's viability. Pondering the offer, he wrote to a friend, "the literary character of the seminary is slight, its zeal in theological science is little, the need of a comprehensive range of theological studies and of books thereto has got to be created."[174] He accepted Union's offer, but a few years later (1854/1855) transferred to the Chair in Theology.

Despite Smith's preference for theology and philosophy over history, George Bancroft—then considered America's premier historian—praised Smith's "Oration on the Problem of Philosophy of History" (presumably his Phi Beta Kappa address at Yale College in 1853[175]). This excellent speech, Bancroft claimed, shows how the scholarly study of history can help uncover "the unity and harmony of all truth," in which God is "always and everywhere" seen as present.[176] After Smith's death, Bancroft wrote to Elizabeth Smith, praising her late husband as "the best teacher we ever had of the philosophy of history."[177] Indeed, Bancroft earlier had lauded Smith: "In Church history, you have no rival on this hemisphere, and you know I am bound to think history includes dogmatics and philosophy and theology."[178] Smith's teaching of church history characteristically infused the subject with a substantial dose of doctrinal history and philosophy.[179]

From 1866 to 1870, Smith was Chair of the Executive Committee of the American branch of the Evangelical Alliance, an international Protestant organization formed in London in 1846. In 1867, his "Report on the State of Religion in the United States of America" to the Alliance's Conference in Amsterdam argued (among other points) that slavery, although now abolished, had been the one great hindrance to the realization of America's ideal.[180] A decade earlier, Smith had written the "Resolution on Slavery" adopted by the Presbytery of New York, denouncing slavery as "a system which is essentially opposed to the rights of man, to the welfare of the Republic, to the clear position of our Church, and to the principles of the Christian religion."[181]

At Union, Smith became active in the (New School) Presbyterian Church USA. He served as Moderator of its General Assembly in 1863 and was hailed as mediator in reuniting Old and New School Presbyterians in 1870.[182] His address as retiring moderator to the General Assembly in 1864 ("Christian Union and Ecclesiastical Reunion") warned against the "infidelity" of recent social philosophy and historical criticism, including the British *Essays and Reviews*, Bishop John Colenso's books on the Old Testament, Renan's *Life of Jesus*, and Strauss's new version of his *Life of Jesus*; these works, Smith posited, mark the mere beginnings of a contest long foreseen, with Christianity at stake.[183] Smith's critiques of these topics I shall detail below.

In addition to these activities and his teaching, from 1859 to 1874 Smith edited the *American Theological Review*, a journal that changed names several times during its history.[184] He was awarded honorary doctorates by the University of Vermont in 1850 and by Princeton in 1869. As librarian at Union Seminary, he presided over the Van Ess collection, brought from Europe to form the core of the Seminary's library.[185] (The library's growth will be charted in Chapter 2.) Always in poor health, Smith resigned his chaired professorship in 1874 (although he continued teaching) and died in 1877 at the age of 62.[186] At the time of his death, he was preparing lectures for a course on evolution.[187] His interest in politics may also be noted: he wrote searing essays against the Confederacy and against Great Britain's sympathy (which he attributed to financial interests) for the southern cause.[188]

Although Smith wrote frequently for journals, he did not publish many books during his lifetime. His most notable work, *History of the Church of Christ in Chronological Tables* (1859), however, displays his (by then) considerable knowledge of church history.[189] He also translated Gieseler's *Church History* and Hagenbach's *Textbook of the History of Doctrine*.[190] Smith's posthumous volume of speeches and essays, *Faith and Philosophy*, edited by his colleague George Prentiss, contains much of interest pertaining to church history. Former student William S. Karr of Hartford Theological Seminary also prepared three volumes for publication after Smith's death, based largely on his lectures: *Apologetics* (1882), *Introduction to Christian Theology* (1883), and *System of Christian Theology* (1884).[191] Reviewing Elizabeth Smith's biography, one commentator wrote, "His [Smith's] industry was not as marvelous as that of Origen, who is said by Jerome to have written more than any other man could read; but it was almost as incessant." Origen, however, had composed many more lines that the reviewer deemed ripe for erasure.[192]

After Smith's death, his nephew, Munroe Smith—later a professor of law at Georgetown and Columbia Universities—wrote to his aunt, Elizabeth Smith, commenting on details of his uncle's life that he had gleaned from her biography. Never before, the young man wrote, had he ever comprehended "the utter and absurd inadequacy of the *material* reward" which those of "rare intellectual power" receive. Smith was at the head of his profession, a great success, yet the recompense he received for his work was "to put it bluntly—not enough to live on! I never understood before that the extra work under which Uncle Henry broke down was largely mere bread-and-butter work, to which he was forced by the inadequacy of his professional salary." It is a "crying shame," the nephew exclaimed, that in America a man who devotes himself to professional pursuits is not "freed from the sordid anxiety in the struggle for physical existence. The scholar must have *skolê*."[193] Indeed, we know that Smith and other early professors at Union were very poorly paid—sometimes payday brought "no pay"[194]— and that he spent many Sundays preaching to supplement his income. Three boxes of Smith's sermons (some quite erudite, on a par with his classroom lectures) are extant in Union's archives; his marginal notes indicate that many were delivered multiple times. His active Sunday mornings doubtless testify to the state of his finances as well as to his piety.[195]

Some two decades after Smith's death, Yale historian George Park Fisher declared that no thinker in the "New England School" since the time of the elder Edwards had surpassed Smith in learning and philosophical ability.[196] Years later, those who had known Smith wished fervently that another like him could be appointed at Union after the retirement of the hard-line (and rather unsympathetic) Calvinist theologian W. G. T. Shedd in 1890.[197]

Roswell Dwight Hitchcock (1817–1887)

With Smith's transfer to the chair in theology at Union, the way was open to appoint a new church historian. This post fell to Roswell D. Hitchcock. Born in Maine in 1817, Hitchcock graduated from Amherst College in 1836 and Andover Theological Seminary in 1841, meanwhile serving as a tutor at Amherst. The next years he spent as a Congregationalist minister. In 1847– 1848, Hitchcock studied at Halle and Berlin.[198] Of his student days, no records are extant.

After his stint as a pastor and three years as Collins Professor of Natural and Revealed Religion at Bowdoin College (1852–1855), Hitchcock assumed the Washburn Professorship of Church History at Union, a position that he held until his death.[199] At the time of his appointment, an anonymous referee wrote that Hitchcock had a "decided historical tendency,—much beyond what is usual in these days," and that he possessed a "familiar and accurate acquaintance with the facts, the doctrines, and the great teachers, both of the earlier periods of the Christian Church and of the times of the

Reformation."[200] When some members of the Board and faculty opposed his appointment, Hitchcock withdrew his candidacy, but in the end, all came around and Hitchcock assumed the position.[201] Indeed, Hitchcock became President of Union Seminary in 1880, a position that he occupied until his unexpected death in 1887.

Hitchcock became a life trustee of Amherst in 1869, and was elected President of the Palestine Exploration Society in 1871, a post he held for several years.[202] He received D.D. degrees from Bowdoin (1855) and the University of Edinburgh (1855), and L.L.D. degrees from Williams College (1873) and Harvard University (1886).[203] He served as editor of the *American Theological Review* from 1863 to 1870, overlapping a few years with Henry Smith. During his time at Union, he made three return trips to Europe and the Middle East.[204]

Hitchcock was widely respected for his excellent teaching, as will be detailed below. He also had wide interests in social movements, advocating civil service reform[205] and attacking the "Tweed ring."[206] During the Civil War, he used his "forcible and living oratory" in support of the Union cause.[207] According to one memorialist, he had great influence on "some of the wealthiest and most beneficent Christian gentlemen of New York"— including, apparently, ex-governor Edwin D. Morgan, who during Hitchcock's presidency contributed $100,000 toward the purchase of a new site for the Seminary on Park Avenue.[208] On his death, Hitchcock left money to establish a prize to be awarded to a member of the senior class at Union for excellence in church history.[209]

The anonymous editor of Hitchcock's sermons reports that Hitchcock destroyed the greater part of his manuscripts. Attempting to explain Hitchcock's low scholarly production given his acknowledged brilliance, the editor wrote,

> his mind was always so active, and he was so constantly giving out fresh thoughts to stimulate others, that he left himself little space to revise and elaborate for the press. . . . His intellect was so original and powerful that it could not be confined; and the store of knowledge which it absorbed, instead of being so much dead learning, only fed and stimulated its activity. He was always making new acquisitions.[210]

Hitchcock was dedicated to Union. On the 48th anniversary of the Seminary, recalling some moments in its history, he expressed his pride in this

"School of the Prophets." Union had "began in poverty and weakness, praying almost day by day for its daily bread. The planting of it in this whirling metropolis of commerce, was against all our American traditions."[211] Yet the Seminary had not merely survived, but grown preeminent.

Apart from some articles on the patristic era, Hitchcock left no books on that topic except the edition and translation (with introduction and notes) of the *Didache* that he produced with his Union colleague Francis Brown.[212] Among his other publications are book reviews of works on Zoroastrianism and Confucianism;[213] a book, *Socialism*; an "anthropological" treatment of race theory entitled *Laws of Civilization*; a *Complete Analysis of the Holy Bible, or the Whole of the Old and New Testaments Arranged According to Subjects in Twenty-Seven Books*; and a memorial volume he wrote with Henry Smith, *The Life, Writings and Character of Edward Robinson*.[214] In addition, a volume of his often scholarly sermons, *Eternal Atonement*, was published after his death.

Philip Schaff (1819–1893)

As nineteenth-century America's most famous church historian and "public theologian," Philip Schaff has been the subject of several biographies. The first, written by his son David and published in 1897,[215] has been joined in the twentieth century by those by George Shriver,[216] Gary K. Pranger,[217] and Stephen R. Graham.[218] In addition, Klaus Penzel has contributed a long biographical essay[219] and a monograph on the intellectual and religious climate of Schaff's early years in Switzerland and Germany.[220]

Philip Schaff—founder of the American Society of Church History, founding member of the Society of Biblical Literature, editor of the Nicene and Post-Nicene Fathers series, head of the American Committee for the Authorized Revision of the Bible, leader of the American branch of the Evangelical Alliance—was Union Theological Seminary's most distinguished nineteenth-century professor of church history. As a reviewer of the sixth volume of Schaff's monumental *History of the Christian Church* noted, if he had lived in the Middle Ages, he would have been called "Philip the Indefatigable."[221] After Schaff's death, a colleague claimed, "Work was his element, out of which he was as ill at ease as a fish out of water."[222]

Schaff's self-assessment was modest: "I am no genius, no investigator, no great scholar, and all the distinction I can aspire to is that of a faithful and, I trust, useful worker in biblical and historical theology."[223] He appropriated the title "*pontifex*," "bridge-builder," to suggest his role in bringing together German and more generally, European, scholarship with America's fledgling endeavors in the field.[224] Later in life, Schaff reflected that if he had stayed in Europe, he might have had "a more comfortable literary life and perhaps accomplished more in the line of mere scholarship"—but now he had become "an American by the call of Providence and by free choice." America, he believed, "the land of freedom and the land of promise," awaits the "brightest future."[225]

Born in Switzerland in 1819 and educated at Tübingen, Halle, and Berlin, Schaff was called to America in 1844 to serve as professor at the Theological Seminary of the German Reformed Church in Mercersburg, Pennsylvania.[226] On the way to America, he spent six weeks in England, improving his English.[227] In Pennsylvania, he soon found himself charged with heresy by his co-religionists for his alleged Romanizing tendencies, but emerged unscathed from these investigations. During the Civil War, the Mercersburg Seminary, near the Gettysburg battlefield, was transformed into a hospital for captured Confederate soldiers and temporarily suspended operations.[228] Schaff and his family moved to New York, where he first worked as secretary for a committee attempting to enforce stricter Sabbath observance,[229] before being invited to join the faculty of Union Seminary—named not, however, to the chair of church history, but (as detailed above) first to one in "Theological Encyclopedia and Christian Symbolics"; then to the chair in Hebrew; third, to the chair in Sacred Literature-New Testament Exegesis; and last, only upon Roswell Hitchcock's death in 1887, to the Washburn Chair of Church History.[230] This list affords an insight into the highly generalized approach to theological study in nineteenth-century America. As German historian Adolf Harnack remarked upon Schaff's death in 1893, he was the last great "generalist" of church history.[231] Schaff himself modestly believed that the next generation of church historians would throw his own "preparatory labors into the shade." He was confident that church history would be for them "the favorite branch of theological study."[232]

In poor health the last years of his life, Schaff delivered his resignation letter in March 1893. In it he wrote:

Teaching has been my life for more than fifty years. . . . The growing importance of the department of Church history requires the undivided attention of a first-class scholar. The Seminary . . . must make satisfactory provision for the next years. The interests of an institution are far more important than those of any individual. The workmen will die, but the work must go on.[233]

Schaff received honorary degrees from the University of St. Andrews, Marshall College, the University of the City of New York, Amherst, and the University of Berlin. Schaff's former pupil, Arthur Cushman McGiffert, was appointed to fill the Washburn Professorship of Church History in his place, to carry on the work when "the workmen die."

Among Schaff's voluminous publications are (to sample some of the most important): *The Principle of Protestantism* (1845); *What Is Church History?* (1846); *History of the Apostolic Church* (1854); *America: A Sketch of the Political, Social, and Religious Character of the United States of North America* (1855 [1854]); *Bibliotheca Symbolica Ecclesiae Universalis: The Creeds of Christendom* (3 volumes, 1877); *The Revision of the English Version of the Holy Scriptures* (1873, 1877); *Through Bible Lands* (1878); *The Person of Christ* (1882); *The* (Schaff-Herzog) *Religious Encyclopediae* (3 vols., 1882–1884, 1887)[234]; A *Companion to the Greek Testament and the English Version* (1883); *St. Augustine, Melanchthon, Neander* (1886); *History of the Christian Church* (7 volumes, 1882–1892); and *Theological Propaedeutic* (2 parts, 1892). "The Reunion of Christendom" (1893) was delivered as Schaff's last major public appearance at the World's Parliament of Religions: Christian reunion had been a theme dear to his heart throughout his entire life.[235] Schaff's activities aside from teaching were so numerous that I here wish to highlight a few of the most important.

SCHAFF AND THE EVANGELICAL ALLIANCE

Schaff was active in both the American and international branches of the Evangelical Alliance.[236] The Constitution of its American wing, dated 1870, declares that the aim of the Alliance was to promote evangelical union, "to counteract the influence of infidelity and superstition, especially in their organized forms"; to promote religious freedom everywhere and observance of the Lord's day; to give supreme authority to the Bible; and to "correct immoral habits of society."[237] Although this statement does not target Roman Catholicism explicitly, it nevertheless makes clear the Alliance's Protestant allegiance.[238] Later, Schaff strongly denied that the Alliance was an "anti-popery society"; to the contrary, he claimed, it champions religious liberty wherever that is threatened.[239]

The records of the New York branch from November 1868 onward show that its organizers hoped to sponsor an international conference on American soil—the first such—as early as autumn 1869, but the Franco-Prussian War and other events precluded this date.[240] With Schaff as organizer, the New York meeting was finally held from October 2 to 12, 1873. Schaff journeyed to Europe to solicit participation and ease Europeans' anxiety about venturing across the ocean to the unknown wilds of America. On home soil, he took charge of most of the arrangements.[241] Schaff considered the conference the high point of his life.[242] Official delegates numbered 516, of whom 294 were from the United States.[243] Fifteen thousand lay people and clergy attended various sessions. The conference was a major media event; even secular newspapers provided almost verbatim coverage.[244] A large volume of conference papers, *Evangelical Alliance Conference, 1873*, edited by Schaff and S. Irenaeus Prime (former editor of the *New-York Observer* and co-organizer of the conference) was published in 1874.[245]

SCHAFF AND THE AMERICAN SOCIETY OF CHURCH HISTORY

The American Society of Church History was founded on March 23, 1888 in Schaff's home. He was elected the Society's first President, serving until his death in 1893. Addressing the first general meeting of the Society on December 28, 1888, Schaff declared that ASCH was formed "for the purpose of cultivating church history as a science." He hoped that the Society would be "catholic and irenical," bringing together scholars who would aid "the cause of Christian union."[246] "The Society," he wrote (prophetically) to his son after the meeting, "may become an important training school for rising historians."[247] On learning of the Society's founding, Adolf von Harnack claimed that "America has put us in Europe to shame."[248] ASCH established a prize essay in Schaff's honor ("The Schaff Prize in Church History"),[249] and in December 1892 formally feted Schaff as the one to whom the Society owed its existence.[250]

An experimental union of ASCH in its early years with the American Historical Association was short-lived.[251] J. Franklin Jameson later explained one reason for the failed merger: the Smithsonian, linked to the AHA, feared that Congress would not publish the *Annual Reports of the AHA* (what would become the *Journal of the American Historical Associa-*

tion) at government expense if Christian theological materials were included.[252] Church historians, one suspects, were too confessional for historians at colleges and universities who were struggling to establish their discipline in the academy as a science. In any event, the two societies broke official ties in 1906, and ASCH was reconstituted as an independent organization.[253]

Schaff and the Nicene and Post-Nicene Fathers Series

In the 1880s, Schaff undertook to organize and edit two series of the Nicene and Post-Nicene Fathers. Schaff planned to bring out about twenty-five volumes with the Christian Literature Company of Buffalo, the company that had earlier published the Ante-Nicene Fathers series edited by Arthur Cleveland Coxe.[254] Schaff hoped to use some translations from the Tractarians' Oxford Library of the Fathers, although he also solicited many new translations. Schaff himself was actively involved in Series 2 of NPNF only through Volume 2.[255]

The object of the series, Schaff wrote, "is historical, without any sectarian or partisan aim"[256]—unlike the Oxford Library, which had "an apologetic and dogmatic purpose" (namely, "to furnish authentic proof for the supposed or real agreement of the Anglo-Catholic school with the faith and practice of the ancient church before the Greek schism"[257]). In the promotional advertisement for the series, Schaff stated that the volumes would sell for $3.00 apiece.[258]

In 1885, Schaff solicited British and American contributors[259] and devised a "Preliminary Prospectus." He asked potential contributors to declare which patristic texts they proposed to translate afresh or to rework from earlier translations. Schaff allowed five years for the contributors to complete their tasks, but hoped for an earlier publication date. With the "Prospectus," he enclosed a letter from the Christian Literature Company stating financial arrangements for the contributors.[260] The "Prospectus" reveals that several patristic writers that Schaff had intended to include never made the Series (e.g., Cyril of Alexandria, Maximus Confessor, and Photius).[261]

Schaff originally hoped that (for example) Arthur Cleveland Coxe would take the Canons of the Ecumenical Councils and Vincent of Lerins's *Commonitorium*; Benjamin B. Warfield would tackle Theodore of Mopsuestia; William Sanday, Hilary and Lucifer of Cagliari; and H. B. Swete, some of the Cappadocians' treatises and John of Damascus' *On the Orthodox Faith*.[262] Schaff asked John Henry Newman to revise and edit his translation of Athanasius for the American series; Newman responded that his failing eyesight would not permit his participation.[263] In the end, new contributors had to be solicited, as some of those whom Schaff had originally approached either declined or failed to fulfill their obligations.

The first series, featuring works by Augustine and Chrysostom, appeared between late 1886 and 1889 in 14 volumes.[264] Schaff himself wrote the "Prolegomena" to Augustine and to Chrysostom.[265] Although he used some of the Oxford Library of the Fathers' translations of Chrysostom's writings,[266] he solicited new translations of Chrysostom's *On the Priesthood*, *The Fallen Theodore*, and *Letters, Tracts, and Special Homilies*.[267] Schaff also paid his son Anselm, who apparently lacked other remunerative employment, to read proof in 1887—the "best work I can provide for him," Schaff wrote to his more scholarly son, David.[268]

The second series followed, with Schaff's pupil (and soon-to-be successor) Arthur Cushman McGiffert contributing the first volume on Eusebius.[269] Schaff confided to McGiffert that he had taken on "this elephant" in part as a way "to give some of our most promising students useful work and a chance to build up a literary reputation and to get an historical professorship"[270]: Schaff here covertly signaled McGiffert himself.

On leave in Europe in 1890, Schaff kept abreast of publication details.[271] By 1892, he reported, the first series was now complete, and four volumes of the second series published.[272] In the end, the publisher would not let Schaff have the fifteen volumes he wanted for the second series, but only thirteen.[273]

Along the way, the project encountered financial problems. In 1888, Schaff feared that the publisher would "break down," having spent "$100,000 with little prospect of a speedy return."[274] The next year saw Schaff asking colleagues to invest in the Christian Literature Company (his requests apparently produced few or no results).[275] In June 1889, Schaff decided that he himself should "give pecuniary aid to the publisher to enable him at least to publish the Greek historians."[276] He contributed $5000 of his own money for the series—a large sum for a professor at that time—so as not to "disappoint or break faith with the contributors."[277] Whatever Schaff's deficiencies as a creative scholar, his service to the field was remarkable.

Volumes of the Nicene and Post-Nicene Fathers series were widely hailed in the press. To give just one example: the reviewer for the Boston *Zion's Herald*, commenting on the volume containing Augustine's *Homilies on the Gospel of John, Homilies on I John, and the Soliloquies*, wrote, "The American Church can never discharge its obligation to Philip Schaff for the work of authorship which he has wrought, inspired, and edited." His erudition is especially valuable, the reviewer continued, in that "he has no tendency either to ecclesiastical narrowness or theological hobbies."[278]

Schaff Eulogized

After Schaff's death in 1893, George Park Fisher of Yale recalled his "unfailing vivacity, his amiable temper, his generous recognition of contemporary scholars in the same field with himself, and his loyal friendship." Schaff was "a living, visible link, binding us to Germany, the land of scholars, the country which to many of us is an intellectual fatherland." Fisher praised Schaff for his catholic spirit—and for remaining "an historian, not an antiquary." Noting Schaff's willingness to take on large projects even later in life (including the NPNF series), Fisher predicted that Schaff's *History of the Church* would stand as "the most lasting monument of a scholar who served his generation in the use of remarkable powers and with unwearied industry."[279]

Schaff's Union colleague Marvin Vincent eulogized Schaff in a talk at the Century Club in New York—the locale itself an indicator of Schaff's prestige among wealthy and influential New Yorkers. Vincent claimed that it was due to Schaff that "a broader learning and a bolder and more independent thinking are fast becoming at home amid conditions where they originally appeared as dangerous novelties, were eyed with suspicion, or fought with dogged persistence of ignorance."

At the time of Schaff's arrival in the United States, Vincent continued, the influence of the German school was scarcely felt here—but men like Schaff and Henry Smith, German-trained, kept "steady hands on the floodgates through which, a little later, the tide of German thought came pouring into the square enclosures of New England metaphysics and theology."[280] In other words, Schaff and Smith moderated the entrance of contemporary German thought into American intellectual life so as to preserve traditional Christian interests.[281]

At the December 27, 1893 meeting of the American Society of Church

History, representatives from various confessions (including the Roman Catholic[282]) praised Schaff's accomplishments. Methodist Bishop John Fletcher Hurst compared Schaff's efforts to unite Teutonic and Anglo-Saxon theology to Jerome's linking of East and West and to Origen's union of three continents (Schaff however, unlike Origen, mercifully had "no touch of Oriental fancy"). Schaff, Hurst proclaimed, will be remembered as "the first to bring to the Anglo-Saxon mind the treasures of the Father-land."[283]

George Park Fisher (1827–1909)

George Fisher—whom historian Roland Bainton describes as a "mellowed Puritan"[284]—was born in Massachusetts in 1827, graduating from Brown in 1847. At Brown he was introduced to historical studies by Professor William Gammell, under whose tutelage he wrote a paper on Roger Williams, based on manuscripts of Williams's correspondence that had recently come to the Rhode Island Historical Society.[285] After one year in the Yale Theological Department, he decamped to Andover Seminary, graduating in 1851. He then went to Germany, studying at Halle in 1852–1853. From Germany, he was called back to a position at Yale.[286] His entire subsequent career was spent at New Haven.

Fisher kept a travel diary (now in the Yale Divinity School archives) detailing his year in Europe. Arriving in Halle in June 1852, he learned that the university had only recently "recovered" from the prevailing Rational-ism of German universities. Earlier, anyone who showed a leaning toward Christianity, he was told, had been deemed a fanatic.[287]

Fisher began attending lectures at Halle a few days after his arrival. He confessed in his diary that he "understood precious little"—but within a week or so, he was able to catch an idea here or there.[288] He steadily improved in the coming months, eventually translating German texts for American audiences. One example is his translation of an article by August Neander ("The Relation of the Grecian to Christian Ethics"), prefaced by a long introduction that Fisher offered as "a contribution to Christian evi-dences."[289] After Fisher assumed the chair of Ecclesiastical History at Yale, the number of books by German scholars that students in the Theological Department checked out from the library increased significantly.[290]

Many aspects of German university education—for example, the lack of examinations—required adjustment on Fisher's part.[291] Several professors at Halle, however, befriended him and helped him to understand the German system. One of these, Heinrich Leo, liked to discuss all things American with him,[292] while August Tholuck, as was his custom with American students, went on walks during which he explained the mysteries of theological parties in Germany.[293] In 1853, Tholuck gave Fisher letters of introduction to professors in Rome, Basel, Bern, Heidelberg, and Bonn.[294] In Germany, Fisher, like other American evangelical students, developed a suspicion of "Pantheism" and the Tübingen School that remained with him in later years, as did a general distaste for radical biblical criticism.

In December 1853, President Theodore Dwight Woolsey of Yale invited Fisher to accept a position in theology. Woolsey bluntly admits that there had been a delay with the appointment because a few professors were "somewhat reluctant to call a man not a graduate of the College," but all now seemed ready to concur. The post involved offering instruction in "Natural Theology and the Evidences"; in addition, Fisher would preach and serve as pastor of the university church, officiating at least once a week at prayers. He would receive $1300 annually—and salaries are soon to be raised to $1500 ("beyond a question," Woolsey assures him). Woolsey claims the faculty's agreement to Fisher's appointment shows that Providence must be at work![295]

Fisher's appointment came over the objections of Noah Porter, who for two decades had taught courses in "Natural Theology and Evidences of Christianity" in the College. Porter reasoned that since Fisher had no particular philosophical training, he should not be allowed to teach theology.[296] (Porter apparently suspected Fisher of wanting to teach philosophy—his own turf.[297]) Both appealed to President Woolsey. Fisher hotly rejected Porter's implication that he was to be "merely like a city missionary or tract-distributor in college—prevented from guiding by thorough and careful discussions the religious opinions of the students—prevented from assailing 'philosophical' and all other unbelief." It appears that Fisher won this dispute, as the catalogue for 1855–1856 lists him as teaching "Natural Theology and Evidences of Christianity" to the senior class.[298] In 1858–1859, Fisher is listed as the Livingston Professor of Divinity,[299] and in 1861 he was awarded the new Street chair in Ecclesiastical History.[300] With this appointment, Fisher resigned his position as pastor of the university church, although he continued to preach throughout the difficult years of the Civil

War.[301] In 1895, Fisher became Dean of the theological faculty (i.e., the Divinity School), a post he held for five years.[302]

Upon Fisher's retirement in 1900–1901, the Yale Corporation noted that he had given Yale more years of service—forty-six—than any other professor (excepting the "elder Silliman") since the College had been founded, and praised his "expansive learning," "truly Catholic spirit," and "temperate attitude as a Theologian."[303] He had taught (after his seven years in the College) in the Theological Department from 1861 to 1901.[304] His writings, one commentator claims, "struck the theological and apologetic note, with which was combined the historical approach."[305] After Fisher's death in December 1909,[306] a memorial window was dedicated in his honor. At the dedication ceremony, he was described as neither a liberal nor a conservative, but a middle-of-the-roader.[307] Indeed, compared with the other professors here described, he seems rather bland. Since there is no biography of him, we lack details of his life and work that would have sharpened our picture.

Fisher was esteemed outside Yale as well. In 1873, he was invited to become a member of the Philosophical Society of Great Britain.[308] He received seven honorary degrees.[309] (President Charles Eliot of Harvard himself wrote to convey Harvard's wish to confer an honorary D.D. on him during its 250th anniversary celebration.[310]) In 1897, Fisher served as President of the American Historical Association, delivering an address on "The Function of the Historian as a Judge of Historic Persons."[311]

Fisher also was an editor of *The New Englander*, which advertised itself as disavowing "allegiance to any party in theology or politics." Although the editors claimed that the journal would discuss issues of "public interest in literature, science, and philosophy" beyond the realm of theology, they also assured readers that it "will not be inattentive to the various assaults of rationalism against revealed religion, or to the position of the Roman Catholic Church in the United States."[312] Several of Fisher's essays were published in this journal.

Fisher wrote many lengthy serial articles, some of which, when combined, constitute book-length treatises. Of his published books, I here note the following: *Essays on the Supernatural Origins of Christianity* (1865);[313] *The Beginnings of Christianity with A View of the State of the Roman World at the Birth of Christ* (1877); *Discussions in History and Theology* (1880, a collection of his essays); *The Grounds of Theistic and Christian Belief* (1883, another collection of essays); *Outlines of Universal* History (1885); *History of the Christian Church* (1887);[314] *A Brief History of the Nations and of Their Place in Civilization* (1896); and *History of Christian Doctrine* (1896). Several of his scholarly articles, more than his textbooks, show his interest in the Jewish streams of early Christianity and in combating modern German criticism; these essays shall be considered in the chapters that follow.

Colleagues elsewhere knew Fisher as a hard and rapid worker. James B. Angell, President of the University of Michigan, wrote to Fisher that his *Outlines of Universal History* (1885) has "work enough in it to break the back of a horse. Where under the sun do you find time to turn off books so fast? And when do you get the patience to accomplish such a job as this?"[315] Daniel Gilman of Johns Hopkins deemed Fisher's *History of Christian Doctrine* his best book, and wondered how its author had found time to write it, since Fisher had other duties associated with "an important chair."[316] Likewise, A. M. Fairburn of Mansfield College, Oxford wrote that the *History of Christian Doctrine* was "the best book in English on the subject, and for students altogether suitable"—adding his relief that Fisher had "departed from the bad example set by Harnack."[317]

Ephraim Emerton (1851–1935)

Ephraim Emerton, the son of a pharmicist,[318] was born in 1851 in Massachusetts, graduated from Harvard College in 1871, and attended Harvard Law School. He served for a time as secretary to the mayor of Boston, Henry L. Pierce, and worked as a reporter for the *Boston Advertiser* to earn money for study in Germany. He received his Ph.D. from the University of Leipzig in 1876. While in Germany, he attended the (senior) Droysen's "practice-course" (or seminar) in Berlin on historical method, in which, he later reported, students engaged in "unrestrained criticism" of each other's papers "to the verge of savagery."[319] Returning from Europe, he was made Instructor of German (1876–1878) and History (1878–1882) in Harvard College. Emerton's specialization was early medieval history, not then a typical subject at American colleges. In 1882, he was plucked from his duties in the College by President Charles Eliot to be the Winn Professor of Ecclesiastical History at Harvard Divinity School, a post he held until his resignation in 1918.[320]

Emerton was a founding member of the American Historical Association; at its organizational meeting in 1884, he was one of only nine men present who held the rank of "Professor of History."[321] A Fellow of the American Academy of Arts and Sciences, Emerton also served as President of the American Society of Church History in 1921.[322] Since no biography remains of Emerton, many personal details of his life and teaching remain unknown.

Among Emerton's writings are an interesting essay on "The Practical Method in Higher Historical Instruction" (1883); a textbook entitled *An Introduction to the Study of the Middle Ages (375–814)* (1888, 1896); *Medieval Europe* (1893); *Unitarian Thought* (1911, a scathing reflection on evangelicals); and a book of essays recounting aspects of his life as a professor of history, *Learning and Living: Academic Essays* (1921). His medieval and early modern interests came more prominently to the fore in his mature years, with books entitled *Desiderius Erasmus of Rotterdam* (1899); *Beginnings of Modern Europe (1250–1450)* (1917); the *Defensor Pacis of Marsiglio of Padua* (1920); *Humanism and Tyranny* (1925); and an edition and translation of the *Correspondence of Pope Gregory VII* (1932)—works whose subjects indicate that even by the early twentieth century, scholarship on history was not yet strictly regulated by specialization. It is notable that Emerton is the only one of the professors here discussed who did not attend divinity school and who, as a Unitarian, stood outside the evangelical nexus of Presbyterians and Congregationalists.[323]

These six professors pioneered the teaching of church history in America. The problems they encountered in developing a field that was new to Americans and that lacked most of the supports that professors today take for granted are the subject of the next chapter, on the material "infrastructure" (more precisely, on the lack of it) that attended the teaching of church history in nineteenth-century America.

CHAPTER 2

Infrastructure: Teaching, Textbooks, Primary Sources, and Libraries

> What professors actually told students, what students heard
> professors say (rarely the same thing!), what purposes
> professors believed their courses served, what methods they
> used to achieve these goals—the data bearing on such
> questions remain as pristine as if the archives were in
> Albania.
>
> —James Turner (1982)

Teaching Church History
in Nineteenth-Century America

Before exploring the professors' theoretical approaches to and assumptions about history, I examine the (woefully inadequate) academic "infrastructure"—the material conditions of knowledge production and transmission—that attended the teaching of church history in early and mid-nineteenth-century America. Suitable textbooks seemed nonexistent, let alone anthologies of primary sources in translation. Libraries, conceived as book depositories for (shockingly) small collections, were open only a few hours a week. As the century progressed, new methods of teaching placed greater demands on professors: they could no longer simply listen to students recite from textbooks, but must prepare lectures and guide advanced students in seminars that required independent investigation.[1] The challenges facing professors of church history in nineteenth-century America

were daunting. In this chapter, I first examine assumptions about and practices of teaching, then turn to examine the textbooks the professors chose,
the accessibility of primary sources, and the development of institutional
and personal libraries.

Samuel Miller: The Theological Seminary at Princeton

Samuel Miller, coming of age before the development of theological seminaries in America, received one year of post-collegiate training via private
study with an accomplished minister. When he assumed his professorship
of church history at the newly established Theological Seminary at Princeton
in 1813–1814, he had had no seminary experience. With no advanced education or access to textbooks he thought appropriate for Presbyterian students,[2] Miller was responsible for developing the curriculum in church
history at the new Presbyterian Seminary at Princeton.

At the Seminary's inception, church history was taught only in the second year;[3] later, in the first and third years as well. Some two decades after
he began his Princeton career, Miller described his teaching regime: he met
the senior class three times a week; middlers, twice; and juniors, once, on
Saturday afternoons, each class running about 75 minutes.[4] Miller's teaching notes, even late in his career, give little attention to European scholarship. They also reveal that he never changed his method of teaching or
approach to church history in his 36 years as professor. Miller, in any case,
deemed church history of less importance than biblical studies and "didactic and polemick [sic] theology."[5]

In 1813, the recitation method of instruction was still commonly used,
supplemented by professors' comments. Miller's class notes, preserved in
the Princeton Seminary archives, suggest that he examined his class on a
few points at the beginning of the session, then turned to lecture.[6] Relying
on the lecture method alone, Miller thought, assumes that students are "an
ear"; they hear the lecture only once and have no chance to review it. But
recitation alone, on the other hand, does not "awaken and excite the
mind." A combination of both methods works best.[7] Miller's son reports
that his father, who claimed that lectures alone make students too dependent on the professor, combined the two methods throughout his teaching
career.[8]

The professor's duty, Miller believed, was "to excite [students] to think," to examine opinions on their own, and "to state leading facts, rather than the minuter items of history."[9] Thinking, to be sure, existed within a Presbyterian framework: it should not lead students to be "corrupted" by "philosophical unbelievers" such as Hobbes, Hume, Voltaire, Rousseau, and Byron. In Miller's view, "a rage for *novelty*, an ardent love of *originality*" are among the "most unhappy symptoms" that could afflict a prospective minister.[10]

A goodly sample of Miller's lecture notes, running from 1814 to 1843, for his courses in ecclesiastical history and church government are extant. Dates on some notes indicate that Miller gave the same lecture up to six times. Miller responded to students' questions in the following class session, allowing himself time to consult his books for appropriate answers:[11] this practice suggests both his relative lack of expertise in church history and an admirable honesty in admitting this lack to his students.

During recitations, Miller asked questions, the correct answers to which he had written out in his notes. For example:

Question: "Whence did this superstition [of celibacy] arise?"
Answer: "From the *Gnostic* notions of the *malignity of matter*, and the best means of counteracting its influence."[12]

Miller's recommendation that students take notes on their reading and make abstracts of important points suggests that notetaking was not then a customary practice in colleges. Above all, he opposed "mere speculative and unsanctified learning": remember that you must die, he warned his students.[13]

Henry Smith: Union Theological Seminary

Before Henry Smith arrived at Union in 1850 to teach church history, the subject was (minimally) covered by a local pastor, Samuel Cox. Cox lectured once a week on church history—while Hebrew grammar received five hours, and "Harmony of the Gospels," three. In the 1840s, Edward Robinson, Union's famous professor of biblical studies, also offered some lectures on church history in the first three (or perhaps five) centuries.[14]

From a letter Cox addressed to Smith before the latter joined the Union faculty, we get a taste of his style and approach. Cox sees himself as preparing the way for Smith, "by outline and generality, not ambiguity, respecting the grand vertebral column of history, its osteology and *loca majora*." He continues:

> They [the students] have been very attentive, and I have endeavored to affect them with a sense of the *sine-qua-non* importance to ministers of its thorough and scientific acquisition. . . . I go on the principle that premises must be before inductions, and hence that without knowing facts, dates, places, men, relations, and some circumstances, they are not prepared for philosophizing as historians. Hence, I teach them the elements, the what, where, when, who, why, how, and the connections, consequences, antecedents, and motives, as well as we can know them, in order [*sic*] to their masterly use of them in their subsequent lucubrations. But I prefer the grand to the minor relations and matters of history; suppose Church History to be *in re* so connected with secular history, since the Church and the world mutually affect and modify each other, that the former cannot be understood without the latter; and so endeavor to fix in consecutive order, in their minds, those great events, which, when well understood are seen to regulate the others, and at once to stimulate the student, and direct him, in his later researches.

Despite his grandiose tone and condescending assurance to Smith that he will counsel the Union community to make allowance for Smith's inadequate preparation and greenness as a teacher, Cox himself (judging from student lecture notes) did not have a strong grasp of the subject.[15]

Smith served as Professor of Church History only until 1855, when he transferred to the Professorship of Theology. In his first half-year at Union, Smith lectured to the seniors four hours a week, covering the ecclesiastical and doctrinal history of the first six centuries, and gave fifteen lectures on "theological encyclopedia,"[16] an introduction to the theological curriculum derived from German university practice.

Still under discussion in Smith's era was the question of the best means of preparation for would-be ministers: private instruction or theological seminary? Private instruction for the ministry is peculiar to America, Smith told his class; in Europe, schools of theology date back for centuries—think of Iona, founded around 521. Jumping to the eighteenth century, Smith described ministerial training in colonial America. After college the student would spend about a year with a minister of note who provided practical training and whose small salary was supplemented by student fees. Some distinguished northeastern clergymen in the course of their careers trained up to 60 ministerial students apiece. A half century ago, Smith mused, ministers were usually more cultivated than their congregations, but with the rise in the general level of lay education, that situation no longer always obtains.[17] Students must prepare well to keep up.

Seminary education, however, was better than private instruction. Although critics charge that seminaries do not prepare men for the pastoral life, are "injurious to piety," and easily spread doctrinal corruption, Smith countered that in a group setting, students learn to critique each other's views and are less likely to become "tinctured" by one person's peculiarities. Moreover, seminaries provide a complete course of instruction that individual ministers cannot replicate. The greatest works in all branches of theology have been produced by scholars at seminaries, Smith claimed.[18]

Despite Smith's reputation as a progressive, his approach to church history often seems both adversarial and apologetic. On the progressive side, Smith advocated "a broader theological culture," in part because students who are to be ministers need to understand the sects and controversies of America. To this "broader culture," church history contributes by making ministers more careful in their choice of language and more averse "to the petty and easy art of the unscrupulous polemic." It teaches them not to stress minor points of difference.[19]

This broader view, however, was still circumscribed. Ministerial students, in Smith's view, needed to be fortified to defend and advance their Presbyterian beliefs and polity against the claims of other Christian groups, not just those of "infidels." Progress in theology, he claimed, consists in "giving the truth a new form adapted to the new *warfare* it is called to meet." Students must learn how to refute the views and practices of others (for example, Roman Catholic approaches to Scripture) and to adjudicate competing theories about the consequences of the Fall for the human race.[20] Although intra-Protestant controversies, in Smith's view, pale beside those between Protestants and Catholics, only by studying history can Rome's claims be understood.[21] Striking what he imagined as a sound mean, Smith recommended that theological education should be "conservative without bigotry and progressive without lawlessness."[22]

In his class on "Theological Encyclopedia," Smith advised students on their course of study. First, they should pursue a broad program, with philology as a foundation. Historical studies come second. Natural science is important for addressing questions of biblical interpretation on such topics as "controversies concerning the races of men" and the resurrection of the body. Philosophy teaches students to analyze, construct arguments, and answer objections. "Master Plato, or some of the works of Aristotle," Smith urged; learn both the history of philosophy and modern philosophy. Psychology and ethics also should not be neglected; for "mental philosophy," "Reid's as good as any."[23]

Smith recommended that once every six or eight weeks, students should put "all [their] strength into some sermon or essay," a recommendation implying that students were not accustomed to writing papers. "Have some independent definite investigation," Smith counseled. Every student should have two or three theological "hobbies," so that he can be a "terror" to his friends on these points. Students should stay abreast of contemporary history by reading newspapers; when perusing foreign ones, they should keep a map in hand.[24] Smith also tried to stimulate his students by organizing an essay competition, offering a first prize of $50 and a second of $25—but only one senior opted to enter.[25]

Archival materials provide a warm portrait of Smith as a teacher. The professor, he thought, should expound points according to students' needs. If the relation between teacher and student does not remain open, the teacher will become dogmatic and the student will copy his dogmatism. Each student should be encouraged and "brought out through the medium of a free discussion." New School Presbyterian teachers and ministers, Smith asserted—implying a contrast with the Old School Presbyterians of Princeton—enjoy freedom of explanation; they understand that modern philosophy and theology should work together, rather than in opposition. Intellectual stumbling blocks should not be deemed irreconcilable.[26] Smith's (Hegelian-inspired) vision of the harmonious unity of knowledge is here in evidence. The unity, nevertheless, is constructed around Christian confession.

Smith's former student Thomas S. Hastings, later President of Union, recalled his impression of Smith's teaching. His approach to church history, Hastings testified, "was so different from anything we had known before—so much more scientific and thorough, that he awakened our enthusiasm and stimulated us to the uttermost." Students tried to take down Smith's every word: indeed, the extant student notes on Smith's lectures often seem verbatim. "We wrote with intense effort," Hastings confessed, "but always, in our weariness at the close of the lecture-hour, we felt we had lost much because we had not secured all that he had said." Students deemed remarkable Smith's ability to answer their questions on the spot—suggesting that most professors (*pace* Samuel Miller) were not able to do so. Hastings added:

> No question surprised him; his answers dissected the subject so thoroughly that it seemed as if he had specially prepared himself for each question. He made us work harder than we had ever done before. He marked out courses of reading sufficient to occupy us for years, and *seemed* quietly to take it for granted that we would accomplish it all in a few weeks.[27]

Smith mainly lectured to his classes, as the many student course notebooks housed in the Union Seminary archives show. Abandoning the still-customary recitation method of teaching, Smith proposed topics for student investigation.[28] Clearly he was a pedagogical pioneer.

Roswell Hitchcock: Union Theological Seminary

Roswell Hitchcock was likewise widely respected for his excellent teaching. He held the Washburn Professorship of Church History at Union from 1855 (when Smith transferred to Theology) until his death in 1887; by then, 1400 living former students could count him as their professor. Hitchcock's list of courses included Biblical and Apostolic History; General Church History; Sacred History; Old Testament History; The Life of Christ and Apostolic History; General Church History from the Second Century; The History of the World Before Christ; and History of Doctrines.[29] This list shows the prominence of "biblical history." There remain three sets of student notes for each of Hitchcock's courses on "Church History, 100–323 [or 325]," "Church History, 323 [or 325] to 800,"[30] and "The Apostolic Church"; two sets on "The Life of Christ"; and one set each for "The History of the World Before Christ," "Church History, 800–1294," and "Church History, 1517–1884." Hitchcock largely taught by the lecture method. Since Hitchcock never published a *Church History*, as Philip Schaff had urged,[31] his approach to the subject must be gleaned largely from these fourteen extant sets of class notes taken by his students, supplemented by his articles and sermons.

Hitchcock's lectures on ancient church history follow a pattern. First comes a lengthy "Introduction," in which Hitchcock describes, inter alia, church history, its "uses," sources, and the auxiliary studies needed for its pursuit. Turning to the "First Period" (ante-Nicene), Hitchcock gives a general overview and describes its "external history" (Judaism and the Roman Empire) and Christianity's interactions with this larger world (historical, intellectual, philosophical, moral). Next comes "polity" (including the rise of "sacerdotalism"); then councils; schisms; the life and worship of the church (including its piety; asceticism; domestic, social, and public life, with considerable attention to the subjects of marriage, family, and slavery); and sacred days and services (including discussion of the sacraments). A next heading is "doctrine," under which rubric Hitchcock expounds his notion of dogmatic development, and describes various authors, writings, and "heresies" (including Gnosticism and Manicheanism). He then takes up apologetics, the Rule of Faith, the canon, and inspiration of the Bible (and lack thereof in post-biblical writings). The last major topic, theology, includes discussion of the Trinity, "anthropology," Christology, soteriology, ecclesiology, the sacraments (again), and eschatology. This schema is also largely followed in Hitchcock's discussion of the Nicene and post-Nicene periods, with appropriate modifications for the changed historical situation. Although Hitchcock lists no category of "social history," one former student described how he wove contemporary issues pertaining to war, law, medicine, and science into his lectures on church history.[32] Judging from class notes and incidental writings, Hitchcock gave more than usual attention to what today we would call "history of religions" and "theory" in religious studies. Both Hitchcock and Smith, it may be noted, showed more interest in the political events and social movements of their time in America than did Schaff, whose life was devoted to more strictly Christian causes.

Hitchcock declared that although it was "a luxury to learn," that of teaching was even greater. The teacher must himself keep on learning, "have something fresh to communicate"—and when he does not, it is time to resign. Antiquarianism, Hitchcock claimed, should be relegated to the museum.[33] Former students confirmed the "careful research" that went into Hitchcock's teaching: "he did not weary of fresh investigations, even on familiar topics."[34] A friend claimed, "Who that ever heard him lecture in his class-room on Ecclesiastical History can forget his masterly picture of the past; how he made the great figures of the Apostolic age to live again. . . . He believed in the Holy Catholic Church and in the Communion of Saints."[35] Students testified that Hitchcock never gave the same lecture in two different classes, but always updated his presentations with the latest research.[36] Student notes from his courses over the years cast doubt on the strict accuracy of this claim, although Hitchcock clearly continued to read and report on new works.

Shortly after Hitchcock's sudden death in 1887, Philip Schaff described him as "a brilliant scholar and lecturer, with an absolute command of language"—but one whose publication record was scanty, since he considered authorship "intolerable drudgery." In his own inaugural lecture later that year, Schaff claimed that his predecessor "always spoke like a book," thus sparing himself the trouble of writing them.[37] Another memorialist claimed that Hitchcock's students took down what he said, "word for word," helped by the fact that he spoke slowly and precisely—and some very detailed student notes suggest that this was not an overly extravagant claim. "He was," the memorialist asserts, "the master of the terse, crisp, epigrammatic, condensed speech."[38]

As noted above, Hitchcock left money in his will to establish a prize for excellence in church history, to be given to a member of the senior class at Union.[39] This prize was sometimes used by the recipient to continue studies abroad. The Hitchcock Prize in Church History is still awarded at Union Seminary.

George Fisher: Yale Theological Department and Yale University

In his history of Yale Divinity School, Roland Bainton comments that from George Fisher's published historical writings (which he praises as "impartial"), readers would never guess that he was a witty and vivacious conversationalist and teacher. So engaging was his manner of speech that some might receive the misimpression that he had fallen prey to "secularization."[40] Upon Fisher's death, one memorialist commented, "So delightful was Professor Fisher's personality, so nimble his wit, so genial his spirit, that it was not always easy to remember that he was one of the foremost scholars of his time."[41]

From class notes taken by undergraduate Bernadotte Perrin, later a professor of Greek at Yale, it appears that Fisher largely taught by the lecture method. Perrin's notes, however, do not convey the witty, vivacious spirit here suggested. Indeed, Fisher's genial classroom style apparently suffered in his later years. By then, students complained that he simply repeated the contents of his textbooks. One student allegedly sat with the textbook open, occasionally adding a note should Fisher ever offer anything new.[42]

Bainton praises Fisher for his attempt to modernize the study of theology in the broader sense, working scientific advances into both apologetics and older theories of design.[43] In general, Fisher thought that historical studies needed more emphasis on "modern" (i.e., post-476) history. Books on "universal history," he advised, should devote more attention to history since the Roman Empire's "fall"—an event he nevertheless deemed the most "stupendous" change in history from that time to the present. In his own *Brief History of the Nations*, he sought to give more space to medieval and modern history than was then customary, ancient history still dominating history textbooks.[44] Fisher's complaint suggests that as late as the 1890s, ancient history received disproportionate attention—and that covering "universal history" was deemed viable.

To acquire a vivid picture of church history, Fisher insisted, the student must know sources—not only written sources such as letters and monastic Rules, but also the evidence derived from coins, art, and other artifacts. He needs the "*ipsissima verba*" of the actors to get a sure grip on truth.[45] The one set of lecture notes on Fisher's course that remains does not reveal how he introduced students to primary sources or aspects of material culture, if in fact he did so.

Despite Fisher's alleged attempt to modernize the study of Christian history, his treatment remained largely conservative as well as derivative. Many of his scholarly essays, we shall see, were devoted to warding off the assaults of more radical German scholarship.

Philip Schaff: Mercersburg and Union Theological Seminaries

Philip Schaff in his youth had served as a *Privatdozent* at the University of Berlin, offering lectures on the Catholic Epistles, the Gospel of John, the theology of Schleiermacher, and the doctrinal history of Protestantism.[46] During his years at Mercersburg, Schaff taught courses on early, medieval, and Reformation church history, and on dogmatics—indeed, historian George Shriver reports, for one period, he taught the entire seminary curriculum. On the basis of remaining lecture notes, Shriver infers that Schaff used his class preparation as an opportunity to develop material that he would incorporate into his multivolume *History of the Christian Church*.[47]

Joining the Union Seminary faculty in 1870, Schaff was granted the Professorship of Church History only after Roswell Hitchcock's sudden death in June 1887. In his "Autobiographical Reminiscences for My Children," Schaff confessed, "I naturally shrank from the drudgery of preparing several courses of new lectures, and from the difficulty of filling the chair of so brilliant a lecturer as Dr. Hitchcock." But he "had to obey," and was inaugurated on September 22, 1887. He hoped that his move to the historical chair would enable him to finish his *History of the Christian Church*.[48]

Schaff faulted the dry and lifeless way in which church history was taught in seminaries, often approached as if it were merely a "curiosity shop."[49] "Intellectual education alone may be a curse," he warned, as the examples of Voltaire, Rousseau, and D. F. Strauss show.[50] Explaining the German educational system to American audiences, Schaff praised the "seminary" method (i.e., the seminar) as one of the most important innovations at Berlin and other German universities; he planned to introduce the method at Union.[51]

Schaff frequently wrote about the teaching of church history. In the last years of his life, he composed a *Theological Propaedeutic*, designed for beginning-level theology students, which illuminates his approach to the various subdisciplines of theological studies. The book, he claimed, is "the first original work on *Propaedeutic* in America," aimed to serve for American students the same purpose as K. R. Hagenbach's *Encyclopädie und Methodologie* in Germany. Although many seminaries treat church history as a mere "appendix" to other subjects, Schaff argued that it, like biblical studies, should run through all three years of coursework. Schaff advised beginners to acquire "some knowledge of the primary sources"—advice again suggesting that primary source reading was not usually the focus of regular coursework. Yet so vast are the sources, Schaff conceded, that even the greatest historians must depend on the collections, digests, and specialized monographs produced by others.[52] In this concession, Schaff surely included himself, for his lengthy volumes on the history of Christianity are not always grounded in primary source investigation.

Unsurprisingly, Schaff retained a pietistic orientation in his teaching, attempting to inculcate faith as well as to provide information. He opened his lectures with a prayer: "Sanctify us by the truth; Thy Word is Truth. Amen."[53] The first hour of the day, he counseled students, before they commence their academic work, should be given over to prayer and devotion. Students are being trained as theologians, not as philosophers: they should not be encouraged to doubt everything. A special danger lies in the "pseudo-theology of rationalism—the chief tempter of the student of the present day," meeting him at "every step in exegesis" from Genesis to Revelation. The spiritual, for Schaff, takes precedence over the purely intellectual.[54] Schaff's pious approach to academic study emulated that of evangelical German professors Neander and Tholuck.[55]

Which areas of concentration are most important for seminary students? Schaff advised that after the Bible, students should study Reformation history, followed by the history of their own denomination. They should choose one particular period or aspect for more exhaustive work. Note that Schaff does not here identify the patristic era as worthy of this concentrated study: it is "of far more consequence to know the exact teaching of Christ and the Apostles than that of the Fathers, Reformers and Councils," he wrote.[56]

Schaff also offered practical advice to American seminarians, who were often scarcely twenty years old and still unsettled in their habits. Study systematically, Schaff urged, since time cannot be replaced. Leave light reading, such as newspapers, for the afternoon or evening. Don't sleep more than is necessary for your health. Take exercise. Keep your body clean and vigorous; does not sound Christianity teach that "cleanliness is next to godliness"? Our model, Christ, manifested no trait of "ascetic austerity and self-mortification," but rather was "healthy, serene, and hopeful."[57]

On the academic side, Schaff urged the student to acquire a good library. He should read the Bible daily in Hebrew and Greek, making use of commentaries by Chrysostom, Augustine, and Protestants from the Reformation era to the present. Master ancient and modern philosophy, the orators, the classical poets, Schaff counseled. But don't be a bookworm: study also the book of Nature and "the book of society." Students should cultivate their hearts as well as their heads, and keep guard over their morals.[58]

Schaff's generous spirit is revealed in the financial support he offered promising students in church history. In the 1880s, he gave copies of his books to Mercersburg Seminary (then relocated at Lancaster) to serve as prizes for student essays on church history. In 1889, he endowed a Teaching Fellowship at Union.[59] Soon thereafter, he contributed half the funds for a prize essay in church history offered by the American Society of Church History.[60] Late in life, he employed a junior colleague, Francis Brown, soon to be a noted scholar of the Hebrew Bible and later President of Union, to act as his assistant, paying him $1500 out of his own salary.[61] And when Schaff's favorite student, Arthur Cushman McGiffert, who succeeded him as Washburn Professor, encountered financial difficulties while studying in Germany, Schaff sent him money and encouragement.[62] As noted earlier, he contributed $5000 to rescue the Nicene and Post-Nicene Fathers Series from collapse.[63] After Schaff's death, 1800 of his books went to the Union Seminary library.[64]

That Schaff was a beloved teacher seems clear from the tributes of former students. During his time at Mercersburg, Schaff—on the model of German professors—invited students to his home one evening a week, encouraging them to ask questions and join in free discussion.[65] One former student, U. H. Heilman, reminisced that such evenings "reminded one of Socrates gathering around him some of the young men of Athens, asking and answering questions."[66] Joseph Henry Dubbs (later Professor of History at Franklin and Marshall College) recalled both pleasant evenings at the Schaffs' home and his trips accompanying Schaff when he preached in surrounding communities. Teacher-student relations, Dubbs observed, then were "more free and unconventional" than in later times. Schaff's students largely continued to follow the lines of thought that they had learned from him.[67]

Frederick A. Gast, who later taught Hebrew at Lancaster, testified that Schaff gave him his first lessons in that language, "when it seemed to me a wild dream that I should myself be called to teach others, however imperfectly, the principles of the language of Moses and the prophets." But his obligation to Schaff preceded his seminary days: even before he had met Schaff, Gast reported, Schaff's *Principle of Protestantism* showed him "a new standpoint from which to survey the whole realm of truth," namely, that Christ is the principle of the entire cosmos, not only of Christianity. Moreover, the book convinced Gast that he could maintain an unshaken faith while adjusting to new truths: "I came to know what life and history might mean."[68]

All three Union professors here surveyed, it is clear, made indelible impressions on their students. In student notes and tributes, as well as in their published writings, they stand out as lively characters.

Ephraim Emerton and Predecessors: Harvard Divinity School and Harvard University

Before Ephraim Emerton assumed the Winn Professorship of Ecclesiastical History at Harvard in 1882, various instructors connected with the theological faculty taught the subject.[69] At least two of them, although not specialists in church history, had studied in Germany: Charles Follen and Frederic Hedge.[70] Emerton's immediate predecessor in a temporary appointment was Joseph Henry Allen (the grandson of Henry Ware), a firm Unitarian who had strongly desired the chaired professorship that Emerton received.[71]

In his inaugural speech as Lecturer in Ecclesiastical History in 1878, Joseph Allen expressed hope for the day when there would be an entire department of church history at Harvard enjoying equal rank with other departments. While a full staff at Harvard pursues the study of ancient Greece and Rome, one man—namely, himself—is expected to cover the entire 2000 years of Christianity. Allen outlined his proposed teaching method. He will look to the original sources when possible, "listen to the voice of the man himself." He will combine weekly lectures with student reports on special topics and with recitation. Among the textbooks he will use are Philip Smith's (with first-year students),[72] Gieseler's and Neander's *Histories*, Henry Milman's *Latin Christianity*, and Thomas Greenwood's *Cathedra Petri* (with second-and third-year students).[73]

As he began teaching, Allen described his academic routine to a correspondent. He spent two hours a week with each class, he reported, striving to keep up "the tone of the study." The juniors (i.e., the first-year class) cover to 800; the middlers, to 1500; and the seniors, to the present. Allen listed twenty-seven lectures he was preparing, extending from "Christ" down to "German Theology," "Unitarians," and "Present Prospects."[74]

To another correspondent, Allen complained that the History Department at Harvard did not encourage appeals to the imagination, sympathy, or moral judgment, approaches that he favored. He intends to introduce a new teaching method: to pair off the students in the first-year class (all ten of them), asking one to prepare a presentation based on the writings of an Apostolic Father, and the other to present material about the same Father derived from other sources. This procedure will be experimental, as "most men know very little how to go to work." He hoped to engage the students with the primary sources rather than have them rely exclusively on "patch-work" compilations and digests.[75] Although Allen's approach may strike the modern reader as an advance beyond recitation and lecture, his "non-scientific" notions of history, lack of German education, and strong Unitarian commitments probably ruled him out of Charles Eliot's consideration for the new Winn professorship.[76]

Ephraim Emerton was hired from his Ph.D. work at Leipzig to be an Instructor in History and German at Harvard College before Eliot selected him for the Professorship in Ecclesiastical History.[77] He confessed that at the time he began teaching in the Divinity School, he had "only a very loose connection with a religious organization" and had made no special study of the history of doctrines or of ecclesiastical institutions.[78]

Both in student notes from Emerton's class and in his own later reflections on the teaching of history, his less confessional approach is apparent. A chief satisfaction of teaching, he thought, was to see students "lose their childish faith in the printed word" and develop "a fair critical temper." Since the (German) method of learning by research was still new in America, professors who adopt it must struggle against "the mental apathy" that other methods of teaching history have induced. Although advocating the German approach, Emerton, like an older generation of American professors, also believed that the study of history should train the mind and encourage better citizenship.[79]

Emerton was quick to decry the earlier neglect of historical study in America. Writing circa 1920, he cited the example of Henry Adams who, although lacking academic training in history, was appointed to an Assistant Professorship of History at Harvard in 1871. When Adams protested that he knew little history, especially of the period he was expected to teach, President Eliot rejoined that if he were aware of anyone who knew more, he would appoint him. There were then no specially trained historians in America, Emerton claimed, but that situation, he is glad to report, had now changed.[80] Indeed, writing in 1883 on "The Historical Seminary in American Teaching," Emerton had painted a picture nearly as bleak as that facing Henry Adams—but even then he was filled with enthusiasm for raising the status of history to that of a "science," of turning at least a few of "our boys" into "manly" historians.[81]

Assuming the Winn Chair in 1882, Emerton titled his inaugural address

"The Study of Church History." In the past, he noted, the *history* of most academic subjects was sadly neglected. Even today, there are only a half-dozen colleges in America at which "any adequate provision for an independent department of history has been made." But a new era of study based on source criticism and archival research has begun, in which men search for the truth of their subject, not touting their own biases, as do those who assume they have "missions." America, Emerton ruefully admitted, remains very backward in this respect.[82]

Of various branches of history, that of the church is even farther behind in its methods and approaches. In this field, Emerton charged, scholars who readily applied new methods of research to the Ancient Near East, "shrank from the unpopular task of submitting the Christian record to similar tests"—and the scanty sources for earliest Christianity left abundant room for "devout imagination" to do its work. The farther back in time historians probe, the more they tend to adduce supernatural causes for events. Here, theology has been greatly to blame. But now, Emerton approvingly noted, historical criticism "has laid an unsparing hand upon the early records of Christianity."[83]

Catalogues from the Harvard Divinity School reveal that after Emerton became Winn Professor of Ecclesiastical History in 1882 he regularly taught courses (or ones similarly titled) on "The Conflict of Christianity with Paganism to about A.D. 800," "History of the Protestant Reformation and the Roman Catholic Reaction," "History of Christian Doctrine," "Medieval Church," and "General Church History," as well as an advanced seminar on medieval "Church-State Relations." As noted above, in 1896 he acquired a Union-trained colleague, John Winthrop Platner, who had greater expertise in patristic literature.[84] Platner, however, stayed at Harvard only a short time before moving to Andover Seminary.[85]

Emerton geared his class lectures in early Christianity around what he knew best: over a three-week period, he gave students 27 pages of notes on the barbarian groups, their "invasions," and settlements (29 pages, if we count a lecture on Ulfila and his Gothic Bible)—while making one brief reference to Athanasius and skipping lightly over doctrinal developments. The Church Fathers in general, he told students, form a "curious and not uninteresting" subject—a rather cool recommendation for early church history! For Emerton, unlike the more evangelical professors, the life of Jesus did *not* form part of church history.[86]

Although he clearly lacked interest in doctrine,[87] Emerton showed considerable concern for the teaching of history. He wrote little pertaining to late antiquity and the early Middle Ages, but in 1888 published an *Introduction to the Study of the Middle Ages (375–814)*. He also contributed to a volume on *Methods of Teaching History*, and published several essays of methodological interest in his collection, *Learning and Living* (1921). As noted in Chapter 1, he published much more on the High and Late Middle Ages and early modernity in his mature years.[88]

Emerton was determined that under his tutelage at Harvard, ecclesiastical history would be viewed as "a department of historical rather than of theological science." In his inaugural address, he declared that students would learn to do independent historical work, seeking to find *ideas* under the bare "facts." They will, he claimed, study the church as "a great human institution"; any approach that strays beyond the realm of the human flirts with "philosophic speculation." He will teach the history of church doctrines without regard to their truth or falsity, their orthodoxy or heterodoxy. He intends to offer a seminar in which students will learn "by practical experience something of the rules and limitations of independent historical research and criticism." In brief, the study of church history should employ the same methods and rules of evidence that have now become the accepted norm in all other branches of historical research.[89] Elsewhere, Emerton wrote that historians need "not miracles nor inspirations, nor revelations, nor the dictations of any authority whatsoever, but more documents and better authenticated ones."[90] More than the other professors here surveyed, Emerton moved the study of church history away from its confessional orientation.

Among the documents in the Harvard Divinity School archives is a list compiled by Emerton, dating to the late 1880s, of forty-six topics from which students in "History of the Early Church" might choose to write papers. The topics range from "The Roman State-religion at the time of Christ" through the Apostolic Fathers, Apologists, Montanism, Gnosticism, the persecutions, issues of canon, episcopate, and "the legend of the 'Petrine Supremacy'," to Constantine, Julian, and Theodosius, with around a dozen options regarding "barbarians" (Ostrogoths, Visigoths, Huns, Franks, Lombards; their migrations, religion, and settlements). Despite Emerton's avowed lack of interest in doctrine, he offers a few options on "The Arian Controversy to the close of the Council of Nicaea," "The Council of Chalcedon," and "The Augustinian-pelagian controversy."[91]

Also among the paper topics were "The Origin and Development of the

Monastic Principle," and "The Life and Work of Ulfilas, the Visigoth." On these, there remain papers (43 and 45 pages, respectively) written by the student who took the one set of extant notes from Emerton's ecclesiastical history class, Earl Morse Wilbur.[92] These and other papers ("theses") Wilbur wrote for Emerton[93] show that Emerton instructed the students to preface their papers with a bibliography of relevant books and articles in several modern languages. (Wilbur included a second list of "more easily accessible" works he consulted, including a few in German.) Even though Wilbur listed many primary sources in his bibliography, most of his references to patristic authors are taken from such secondary works as Schaff's *Histories*, a point suggesting that Emerton relegated work in the primary sources to higher-level seminars.[94]

In his paper on "The Life and Work of Ulfilas, the Visigoth," Wilbur noted the paucity of sources for his topic. His bibliography cited Georg Waitz's *Über das Leben and die Lehre des Ulfilas* (1840) and the later (and better, so he observed) study by W. Bessel, *Über das Leben des Ulfilas* (1860). Most of Wilbur's actual references, however, were taken from works in English. Wilbur the Unitarian was not disturbed by scholars' charge that Ulfilas' Bible was "tainted with Arianism." He placed Ulfilas' contribution in the context of Germanic philology: just as scholars now study Sanskrit to probe the background of Indo-European languages, so the Gothic Bible remains a monument of Germanic literature, whose birth lay seven centuries before the Scandinavian Eddas, five centuries before the *Niebelungen Lied*, and three centuries before the "Paraphrase" of Caedmon.[95]

Despite Wilbur's inattention to primary sources, his papers are of high quality for a first-year student in church history. It does not surprise that Wilbur later studied in Berlin (where he confessed disappointment that that the lectures were "only a review of what I had already had at Harvard"), taught courses at Meadville Seminary, and was the organizer of a new divinity school (the Pacific Unitarian School for the Ministry) at Berkeley, of which he later served as President.[96] There he wrote his pamphlet, "The First Century of the Liberal Movement in American Religion."[97]

From Samuel Miller's recitation method to Emerton's assignment of term papers, the teaching of church history in America evolved considerably in seventy-five years. The change in pedagogy reflects both the professors' greater expertise and the availability of books. Here, as we shall shortly see, the growth of seminary library collections was key. Students by century's end were no longer tied to one textbook, as was largely the case with

Miller's students at Princeton. In addition, the diminution of denominational polemic meant that various topics pertaining to early Christianity might be explored for their own historical interest, not primarily as weapons drawn from a textual arsenal with which to batter those whose doctrine and polity might differ.

Introducing Seminar Teaching in Church History

By the 1870s, the "seminary method" (i.e., the seminar) had been adopted in a few university history departments. As noted above, the seminar was introduced to American education by historian Charles Kendall Adams at the University of Michigan in 1869, was taken up by Henry Adams at Harvard in 1871,[98] and in the later nineteenth century became especially associated with Johns Hopkins.[99] Henry Adams later reflected that, ignorant of medieval history, he had introduced the seminar so that he and his students should learn together about Anglo-Saxon and medieval law; the boys, he reminisced, "worked like rabbits, and dug holes all over the field of archaic society."[100] That this method should be utilized in courses on church history was a recommendation frequently advanced by seminary professors from the 1880s onward.

For example, a handbook by Frank Hugh Foster, Professor of Church History at the Theological Seminary in Oberlin, published in 1888, illustrated how the seminar could be used in the study of church history. Foster admitted that students would need guidance in this new method, since they were accustomed to "dependent study."[101] They should learn that the study of history involves explanation, the analysis of causes and effects—not merely knowing facts. Although Foster praised Neander's and Schaff's volumes on ancient church history as the best of their kind, he argued that such manuals would not give students any sense of how to do history for themselves. They must work with original sources, such as are found in the volumes of Migne and Mansi, and the Ante-Nicene Fathers series.[102] Although, Foster admitted, America lacks the archives necessary for original research in (for example) medieval history, the historian of Christian antiquity is in a better position since the Greek and Latin sources are available in print. Foster reported that at Oberlin, one seminar was organized around various topics pertaining to Augustine, such as "Augustine's View of the Constitution of the Human Mind." Other subjects Foster suggested for a "practice" seminar in early church history include "The Council of Nice" and "Hippolytus and his Conflict with the Bishops of Rome." Foster advised professors to propose a large project, then divide the work among the students in a team effort.[103]

At the schools here surveyed, seminars were offered at Harvard and probably at Union. Schaff in 1886 praised the "seminary" method (i.e., seminar) as one of the most important innovations at Berlin and other German universities. German seminars, Schaff reported, cover topics in exegesis, history, and theology. Neander in his seminar would select a particular patristic work to be read and explained, for example, Origen's *Against Celsus,* Tertullian's *Apology,* or Augustine's *Confessions.* One *Privat-dozent* had chosen the (newly discovered) *Didache.* Schaff urged American theological institutions to introduce the seminar, adding that he expected to do so at Union the following winter.[104] (Whether or not Schaff himself did, there is evidence for seminars offered by his successor, Arthur Cushman McGiffert.[105]) Schaff's comments once more suggest that close attention to primary sources in the classroom had not been a central feature of church history courses in mid-nineteenth-century America.

Ephraim Emerton developed the seminar method for "higher instruction" in church history at Harvard. He gave due credit to Ranke, the elder and younger Droysen, and various French historians for their work in instituting the "practice-seminar."[106] German historical scholarship, Emerton remarked, broke the eighteenth-century approach to history, with its "partisan purpose" and "rhetorical elaboration." He had nothing but scorn for the older recitation method used in American colleges: for "an educated man to listen to such repetition is an actual loss to science," he exclaimed. Relying on a textbook does not deepen students' mental capacities. Although the lecture method has its purposes if artfully organized, often a student can get the same information much faster from a book.[107] Genuine historical scholarship requires "independent, individual effort," and this is what seminar work teaches. The point of the seminar, Emerton asserted, is to lead students back from a completed work to the primary sources. In America, professors face a challenge in combating the "mental apathy" engendered by older methods of studying history. Students must read the primary sources in order to "rise out of the state of blind receptivity into that of vigorous and independent action."[108]

In a seminar, Emerton claimed, the student should learn to take nothing on faith or authority, but rather look for "evidence of probability," even if "proof" is lacking. The professor's role is to assist students in developing a "critical temper" and in judging evidence.[109] He is an "overseer guiding the action of intelligent workers." For those engaged in seminar work, the library becomes a laboratory, not a mere storehouse for books.[110]

Emerton conceded that history had been so neglected in students' pre-collegiate education that they would arrive as freshmen with "colossal igno-rance" of the subject—yet documents lie at hand all over America on which students could go to work. Emerton was pleased that he had made some progress in introducing the seminar method at Harvard.[111] Indeed, the Har-vard Divinity School catalogues show that Emerton often taught such a "practice-course" on "Church and State in the Age of Hildebrand" (vari-ously, "in the Eleventh Century").[112] As noted above, Herbert Baxter Adams of Johns Hopkins praised Emerton's seminars (including those offered at the "Harvard Annex," i.e., what became Radcliffe) on "the Papacy and the German Empire, the origin of mediaeval institutions, the rise of French communes, etc." Baxter Adams praised Emerton for incor-porating "the most modern views of mediaeval history and the relations of church and state," views he had learned from his study in Germany with J. G. Droysen.[113]

Church History Textbooks
in Nineteenth-Century America

American Professors and German Textbooks

An ongoing problem for the American professors was the lack of appro-priate textbooks. The texts in translation they most frequently used were Johann L. Mosheim's eighteenth-century *Ecclesiastical History*; Johann Gie-seler's *Text-Book of Ecclesiastical [Church] History*, written and revised sev-eral times in the 1820s and 1830s; Karl von Hase's *History of the Christian Church*; and (sometimes) Augustus Neander's volumes on the history of early Christianity.[114]

It is noteworthy that the American professors did not select books writ-ten by British or Scots authors. George Fisher, for example, faulted Mil-man's *History of Latin Christianity* for the author's lack of sympathy with figures whose piety exceeded the "limit of Anglican moderation," especially any form of devotion that displayed extravagant "austerities." This lack,

Fisher charged, constitutes an "involuntary disrespect" and colors Milman's entire portrait.[115] Even Samuel Miller, who had *not* studied in Germany, chose a text (admittedly by default, we shall see) by a German author, Mosheim. For all of them, Germany represented the gold standard of scholarship.[116]

JOHANN MOSHEIM'S TEXTBOOK

Johann Mosheim's ecclesiastical history, composed in Latin in the 1750s, was available in English translation by the early nineteenth century. Despite Mosheim's general popularity in America—a "Von Mosheim Society" was founded in 1789 to perpetuate German language and culture[117]—his text was not favored by Protestant professors of a warmly evangelical stripe.

When Samuel Miller began teaching at the Theological Seminary at Princeton in 1813, only Mosheim's *Church History* was available in translation. Miller was aware that students would prefer something smaller and of a "different character," but he judged no other book to be "equally eligible." Works that might be preferable were not available, whereas Miller could obtain copies of Mosheim for his students. Mosheim, he conceded, provides the "best skeleton of a course of Ecclesiastical History that is anywhere within our reach." As for other historians who wrote church history books, "Dupin, Fleury, Baronius were all *Catholics*!" Miller exclaimed—apparently feeling no need to explain what would be wrong with consulting works by these authors. Miller confessed that he had not discovered *any* textbook of ecclesiastical history suitable for Calvinist and Presbyterian students.[118]

Miller, who used Mosheim throughout his teaching career,[119] informed his "young gentlemen" that he would be stressing Mosheim's faults: Mosheim entertains unsatisfactory notions of the true church, devotes too much time to politics, and is defective in "portrait painting." Miller deemed Mosheim "a coldblooded low Arminian—an enemy to vital piety."[120] Mosheim's history was not "religious,"[121] exhibiting "very inadequate ideas of the true church" and concentrating on its "secular and political" manifestations. Moreover, Mosheim finds truth even among heretics, while scarcely noting the "pouring out of the spirit" in religious revivals. He gives too much attention to "the Romish church," dwelling "unnecessarily and tediously on the Popes." As a Lutheran, Mosheim was not friendly to Calvinism, the reigning theology at Princeton. The students can supplement the defects of Mosheim (whom Miller nevertheless considered a "learned German") by comparing his work with that of other writers.[122] Yet this was the textbook available for use.

Nor was Mosheim in good favor with the Union and Yale professors. Henry Smith, attempting to liven up the subject of church history, abandoned the use of Mosheim "and all that lumber."[123] Roswell Hitchcock faulted Mosheim's division by "centuries" as untrue to the messier flow of events.[124] George Fisher, while claiming that Mosheim had initiated a new "scientific spirit" in ecclesiastical historiography, criticized that author's commonplace style, lack of "philosophical insight," arrangement of material by "centuries," and "sabbath school tone"—an interesting critique, given that others faulted Mosheim's alleged rationalism. Mosheim's text, in Fisher's view, had been rendered obsolete by Neander, Gieseler, and Baur.[125]

Schaff too abandoned Mosheim's *Ecclesiastical History* ("dry and undigestable") in favor of English translations of Neander's and Gieseler's books.[126] Mosheim's "freedom from passion," in Schaff's view, almost borders on "cool indifferentism."[127] At mid-century, he decried the fact that theological schools in England and America, including Princeton, had for a hundred years been content to use Mosheim,[128] whose text had been "shelved" at least fifty years ago in Germany.[129] Schaff imagined that the long-dead Mosheim would himself be displeased if he could know that in English and American seminaries, the study of church history had not gone a step beyond him in the whole intervening century, students still mechanically memorizing his textbook.[130]

Schaff believed that a good church history textbook, unlike Mosheim's, "should unite in proper harmony a thorough use of original sources, clear apprehension, organic development, lively and interesting delineation, strong but liberal and universal church feeling, and fruitfulness in the way of practical edification."[131] The work must not be overly long: what student can get through the forty volumes of Baronius, Schaff asked, or even Henry Smith's *History of the Church of Christ in Chronological Tables*, the pages of which are "too large for convenient use"?[132] By Schaff's time, English translations of other German *Church Histories* made better textbook options available.

Johann Gieseler's Textbook

An alternative to Mosheim's *Ecclesiastical History* was Johann Gieseler's *Lehrbuch der Kirchengeschichte* (1824ff.), the first English translation of which was published in 1836.[133] In the mid-1850s, Henry Smith of Union Seminary, desiring an updated version,[134] undertook a new translation based on the fourth German edition (1844–1857).[135] That Smith, always in precarious health and overworked, judged it a good use of his time to translate this multivolume work suggests the desperate need for adequate textbooks.

The great virtue of Gieseler's *Text-Book* was its inclusion of copious extracts from the primary sources. Moses Stuart of Andover Seminary, among others, praised the book for placing the reader "in a better condition to judge for himself,"[136] while George Fisher styled it a "library of authorities."[137] Philip Schaff also praised the *Text-Book*'s inclusion of primary source extracts,[138] and Roswell Hitchcock assigned it as "collateral reading."[139] In the absence of anthologies of primary sources, Gieseler's work was highly valued.

Yet much was wrong with Gieseler's text in the eyes of the American professors. Too synoptic, "history, it is not," one reviewer complained.[140] Even Henry Smith found it unsatisfactory and extremely "dry."[141] Smith praised Gieseler's spirit of charity in assessing which groups might count as "Christian"[142] and his copious citation of original sources "such as can nowhere else be found." Yet he found the book "cold, but cautious . . . more rational than sympathetic; it has not the warmth of Neander's incomparable work" nor "the vividness of Hase's delineations." Particularly to be faulted, in Smith's view, was Gieseler's sketchy and biased treatment of the first century; nevertheless, this omission can easily be remedied by students, since "the source for correcting [Gieseler's] opinions is near at hand"[143]— namely, the New Testament. Moreover, Gieseler emphasized (to Smith's discomfort) patristic writers' distortion of truth through ignorance, credulity, party-spirit, or "even intentional dishonesty."[144]

Philip Schaff likewise criticized Gieseler's *Text-Book* for failing to "reach the inward life and spiritual marrow of the church of Christ," scarcely rising above "jejeune rationalism"; Gieseler writes with the "indifference of an outside spectator." Yet, in Schaff's view, Gieseler had a better appreciation of history than did his Rationalistic predecessors. In the last year of his life, and with his own *Histories* behind him, Schaff generously claimed that Giesler and Neander had not yet been superseded.[145]

Karl von Hase's Textbook

A third text sometimes used in church history classes was Karl von Hase's *History of the Christian Church*, originally published in 1834 and translated into English in 1856.[146] The great virtues of Hase's text for class use were that the section on early Christianity was manageably short, under 200 pages—a virtue noted by Henry Smith[147]—and that Hase provided colorful depictions of the era's leading figures.[148]

Hase aimed to present the "living freshness" of the original documents, even as he condensed their contexts. He confessed his regret that in his coverage of the patristic era, he had failed to prune unnecessary description of minor points, thus obscuring the "freshness" of the sources.[149] Elsewhere, avoiding "useless verbiage," he had endeavored to "let the facts of the narrative speak for themselves." Conceiving his volume as a workable textbook, he encouraged instructors to enlarge on whichever points they chose.[150]

In his early teaching career at Mercersburg Seminary, Schaff claimed that of the available textbooks, Hase's, with its fine "graphic miniature sketches," was the best for American seminary students. Despite being "not altogether sound," Hase's text avoids Rationalism.[151] In default of anything better, Hase's text was at least short and comprehensible to students.[152] Too sketchy to warrant much praise from the scholarly perspective, Hase's *Church History* was admittedly useful in the classroom.

August Neander's Histories

A fourth possibility: the various histories by Augustus Neander. Neander, a Jew who converted to evangelical Protestantism in young adulthood,[153] was acclaimed as the most distinguished German church historian of the mid-nineteenth century.[154] Indeed, British historian Lord Acton called Neander "probably the best-read man living towards 1830."[155] Neander held the Professorship of Church History at Berlin during the period when Henry Smith, Roswell Hitchcock, and Philip Schaff were students in Germany. At the time of Neander's death in 1850, memorial notices proclaimed him a "Father of the Church for the church of the nineteenth century" who combined exhaustive learning with "sound and sober criticism."[156]

Neander's historical perspective well suited the American Protestant professors, although they sometimes (as we shall see) disagreed on specific points and deemed his books too large and dense to serve as useful textbooks.[157] In the early 1860s, Smith told students that he considered Neander's "the greatest theological discussion of this century."[158] The *American Theological Review*, edited by Smith and others, remarked on Neander's almost incredible (to them) achievement: he allegedly had read "every page of the ante-Nicene Fathers."[159]

Although Hitchcock critiqued Neander's failure to provide sufficient extra-ecclesial context, he nevertheless in 1858 assigned the senior class at Union "collateral reading" in Neander's *Church History*—but complained that the students were unable to complete the assignment because they were so burdened with work outside of school to support themselves.[160] An earnest student in Hitchcock's class at Union in 1876–1877, Samuel Jackson, struggled for several months to read his copy—now in the Union library—of the first volume of Neander's *General History*. He penned in at the end, "A great work. But on the whole very like the Sahara desert—mostly very dry, although here and there an oasis of interest."[161] That Jackson owned a copy of Neander shows that at least one student managed to do the "collateral reading" for Hitchcock's courses.

Philip Schaff deemed Neander the most accomplished German church historian of the nineteenth century.[162] He preferred texts by Neander and Gieseler for advanced students, but conceded that the best shorter manuals (presumably for less advanced students) were those by Hase and Kurtz. As the "father of modern church history," Neander, in Schaff's view, had rescued that subject "from the icy grasp of rationalism, infused into it the warm love of Christ." Before Neander, church history "had been degraded by German Rationalism into a godless history of human errors and follies," but Neander made the "dreary desert" of church history into "a garden of God."[163] The patristic period was the area of his greatest scholarly competence. His vision of church history as "a continuous revelation of Christ's presence and power in humanity" suited Schaff well. Schaff liked to repeat Neander's pietistic motto: "*Pecus est quod theologum facit*": "It is the heart that makes a theologian."[164]

Yet Union and Yale professors had many criticisms of Neander's histories. Hitchcock, Schaff, and Fisher all charged Neander with indifference to the secular and political setting of church history (i.e., with failure to contextualize).[165] Moreover, they criticized Neander's writing for lack of dramatic power, as stylistically "diffuse and monotonous," "colorless."[166] Although Hitchcock urged Americans to emulate Neander's historical sympathy—he could bind himself to future Christian ages "because he joined himself so genially to all the Christian past"—he came to think that Neander exhibited *too* great a "catholicity," verging on Latitudinarianism. More of a Christian than a Protestant, Neander, in Hitchcock's view, found sainthood "wherever it was."[167] Yet compared to both Gibbon and "Ultra polemical Protestants," Neander appeared to Hitchcock as an historian who "struck [a] medium."[168]

For Schaff's tastes, Neander was often too lenient toward "heretical aberrations."[169] Schaff also faulted Neander for conceding too much to modern biblical criticism, for doubting points of Gospel history and the "genuineness" of certain canonical books.[170] Fisher, similarly, abhorred Neander's tendency to treat the Gospels as books "to be criticized like any other histories."[171] In addition, Schaff faulted Neander's somewhat antinomian, "spiritualized" view of Christianity as implying that the "church" must inhabit some realm different from, and almost opposing, "Christianity." Schaff's critique reveals his own more "churchly" orientation: there *is* no Christianity apart from the church. Although Schaff in 1889 conceded that Harnack—then only 38 years old—was the leading German scholar of early Christianity, with a fresh and bold approach, he confessed his preference for the older (and more piously evangelical) generation of Neander and Tholuck.[172]

At Yale, Fisher toward the end of his teaching career replaced German-authored textbooks by one that he himself had written. Schaff liked features of Fisher's "manual" of church history (Fisher's *History of the Christian Church*). In 1889, Schaff reviewed the book, claiming that up to now, Americans had been dependent on German works that were poorly translated and not improved as new editions appeared in German. Fisher's book, he believed, met a need for coverage of English and American church history that the German-authored books failed adequately to provide. Schaff's praise appears a bit muted—perhaps because Fisher had borrowed so much from Schaff's own work?[173]

At Harvard, before a chaired professorship was established, Mosheim's and, later, Gieseler's texts were used by instructors of church history.[174] A list of readings for church history at Harvard dating to the 1860s reveals that in addition to Gieseler, an instructor used (among other works) Neander's *Church Histories*, Milman's *Latin Christianity*,[175] Mosheim's *Commentaries*, Joseph Bingham's *Antiquities of the Christian Church* [*Origines Ecclesiasticae*], Hagenbach's *History of Christian Doctrines*, Julius Müller's *Christian Doctrine of Sin*, and Isaak Dorner's *History of the Doctrine of the Person of*

Christ.[176] The authors listed are for the most part those being read in more evangelically oriented theological institutions of the period, suggesting that Unitarian professors, like colleagues elsewhere, considered these the best works for their courses.

Ephraim Emerton, however, the first Professor of Ecclesiastical History, in the late 1880s made no mention of Neander in his class lectures.[177] He rather recommended that students use Philip Smith's *Student's Church History* (as noted above, a work largely dependent on Schaff[178]), Schaff's *History of the Christian Church*, and Fisher's recently published *History of the Christian Church*. Emerton mentioned several times in his lectures that for the Roman Catholic viewpoint, students might consult "Blane's *Church History*," a work I have not been able to locate.[179] Emerton's approach on this point contrasts with that of Samuel Miller earlier in the century, who assumed it unnecessary even to explain why books by Roman Catholic authors would be inappropriate.

The professors here discussed found problematic the German historians' lack of familiarity with Christianity in America.[180] Henry Smith complained that "German divines are far better acquainted with the obscurest heresy of remote antiquity, than with the teeming life of America."[181] Smith especially faulted Gieseler for dwelling on the (to him) bizarre behavior displayed at "camp meetings" as if it characterized all American Protestantism.[182] Moreover, Gieseler stressed the poor opportunities for theological education in America, mentioning only the German Lutheran and German Reformed seminaries,[183] with nary a word for Yale, Princeton, Harvard, Andover—or Union.

Philip Schaff agreed with Smith that at present there existed no adequate history of the American church. German works, he thought, were "well-nigh worthless" on the topic,[184] their authors either ignorant of American church history or distorting it so as to be unrecognizable. Gieseler, Schaff charged, leaves European readers with many misconceptions, for example, that "love of money, cold selfishness, hypocritical piety, overweening conceit, and contempt for everything European" were the chief attributes of the American character, especially of Yankees, New Yorkers, and Pennsylvanians! His biased view was common thirty or forty years ago on the Continent, Schaff added.[185] At that time, to most German historians, "America was a *terra incognita*, or known only from vague and conflicting reports of travelers." "American church history," Schaff concluded, "remains to be written." Is not America "the land of freedom and of the future," where church-state separation flourishes?[186]

As the above summary makes evident, the professors deemed no textbook fully adequate for American Protestant students' use. Some texts by German authors were lacking in evangelical piety; almost all were too long for beginning students. The problem of textbooks was compounded by the lack of student access to primary sources.

Primary Sources

One feature obvious to readers today is the relative lack of primary source study in nineteenth-century American classrooms. Although the professors frequently urged their students to read various early Christian writings, the class presentation did not revolve around study and discussion of the sources. When, for example, Samuel Miller wished to impress upon his students the "decline" that soon infected the early church, he exhorted them, "Read Cyprian! Read Origen! Read Eusebius!"[187]—but there is no suggestion that these authors were required reading for the class, nor, for that matter, that students had access to these texts.

Roswell Hitchcock taught his Union students the distinction between monumental sources and written sources.[188] He offered suggestions on where to find the primary written sources—civil laws, councils, papal bulls, the monastic Rules, liturgies, hymns, catechisms and confessions, in addition to theological writings. Among secondary sources, Hitchcock listed church histories from the second century onward, biographies of and monographs on famous figures in church history, including the *Acta Sanctorum*, of which he owned an entire set.[189] Many "auxiliary studies" should also be consulted.[190] One wonders if Hitchcock's students were discouraged by his rather comprehensive list—if they were, they give no sign of it in their notes. As Hitchcock's recommendations show, by his time contextualization had come to be a desideratum for the student of the early church.

Despite his admonition to students to consult the sources so they might judge the impartiality of historians, Hitchcock nevertheless conceded that the use of primary sources is "absolutely indispensable" only for those who teach and write church history. Yet even these do not always ground their works in the primary sources; in Germany, as well as in (admittedly deficient) England and America, many write on the basis of secondary accounts, using "the labor of others." Even the best writers (Mosheim,

Neander, Gieseler, Baur, and Niedner) sometimes quote ancient authors without verifying the citations. No one, Hitchcock added, can feel certain, relying only on secondary sources. With the materials now available, students can at least make a beginning in primary-source study.[191]

Philip Schaff, for his part, urged beginning students to acquire "some knowledge of the primary sources"—an admonition that once more suggests that such study was not the task of regular coursework. He noted the Edinburgh edition by Roberts and Donaldson of the *Ante-Nicene Christian Library*, and its American reprint. (Schaff in the 1880s instigated the publication of the *Nicene and Post-Nicene Fathers* series, as discussed in Chapter 1.) Yet he conceded that the sources are so vast that even the greatest historians must depend on the work of others, using collections, digests, and specialized monographs.[192] One reviewer of Schaff's *History of the Christian Church*, Volume 1, declared that Schaff himself "makes no pretension to an exclusive or even primary dependence upon the original sources," although [in a concession startling to historians today] he uses them "whenever he deems it necessary."[193]

By the early 1890s, the patristic works that Schaff especially recommended to divinity students were largely available in either the *Ante-Nicene Fathers* series or the first volumes of the *Nicene and Post-Nicene Fathers*: namely, the *Didache*, *I Clement*, Polycarp's *Epistle*, Ignatius' *Epistles*, the *Epistle to Diognetus*,[194] Justin Martyr's *Apologies*, Tertullian's *Apology*, Cyprian's *Unity of the Church*, Origen's *Against Celsus*, Eusebius' *Church History*, Augustine's *Confessions* and *City of God*, and some of John Chrysostom's *Homilies*.[195] The list makes evident that the ante-Nicene Fathers were considered more essential reading for divinity students than the post-Nicene: the former were closer to the inspired source, the New Testament, and were written before the church became immersed in intricate doctrinal tangles and elaborate ritual, beholden to ecclesiastical hierarchy. Characteristically, the Protestant professors devoted little or no time to the Cappadocian Fathers, perhaps because their writings were not readily available in translation, but also because their theology and rhetoric represented a "decline" from primitive simplicity.

More Primary Sources: The Ante-Nicene Fathers Series

The publication of the American edition of the Ante-Nicene Fathers series was such a welcome event for American seminary professors and students that it deserves mention here, even though its editor, Arthur Cleveland Coxe, was not a professor but a cleric.[196] Coxe's series was largely a reprint from the Edinburgh edition of the Ante-Nicene Christian Library,[197] with a different ordering of the texts.[198] As Richard Pfaff notes, the neutral quality of the Edinburgh edition was "completely submerged" by Coxe's strong theological [i.e., anti-Catholic] views,[199] which he expressed in his additional footnotes and "Elucidations." It also differed from the patristic series edited by the Tractarians, the *Library of the Fathers*, which had focused on Christian writers of the fourth through sixth centuries.

Coxe deemed the Edinburgh editors of the Ante-Nicene Fathers guilty on several points: overly literal as translators,[200] they failed to correct possible Romanizing interpretations,[201] incautiously ascribed schismatic or heretical views to various Church Fathers,[202] organized and printed their source materials in volumes inappropriate in terms of date and subject-matter,[203] and were tone-deaf to liturgical usage.[204] Their lack requires a supplement, which Coxe was happy to provide.

His additions, Coxe wrote, aim "to note such corruptions or distortions of Patristic testimony as has been circulated, in the spirit of the forged Decretals, by those who carry on the old imposture by means essentially equivalent. Too long have they been allowed to speak to the popular mind as if the Fathers were their own."[205] Elsewhere he claimed that "garblings of patristic authorities" recently appearing in America render "an accurate and intelligent study of the *Ante-Nicene Fathers* a necessity for the American theologian."[206] Indeed, "the aggressions of an alien element" (i.e., Roman Catholics) now force scholars of Christianity to renew their study of "that virgin antiquity which is so fatal to its pretensions."[207] In the eight volumes to be published, Coxe was sure that the student would find "all that is needful to disarm Romanism," to refute those "pretensions," and to direct "honest and truth-loving spirits in the Roman Obedience" to a reformed Catholicism such as was represented by J. J. I. Döllinger and the "Old Catholics."[208] Coxe believed that the Apostolic Fathers and Scripture, taken together, supply "a succinct autobiography of the Spouse of Christ for the first two centuries." Volume I was to provide the "supplement" (to the Scriptures) that should be "indispensable" to every scholar and all libraries.[209]

Coxe imagined the day when in the vast and still-unnamed regions of America, beautiful critical editions of the Ante-Nicene Fathers would be available—unlike the careless, inaccurate, and inelegant volumes of the

Patrologia Migne.[210] His series, Coxe believed, would simultaneously enlighten Episcopalians about their origins and provide a bulwark against the evils of Roman Catholicism, past and present: for him, the ante-Nicene Fathers remain the standard by which all subsequent Christian history is to be judged.

Coxe's introductions, notes, and "Elucidations" provide a fascinating window onto American social and intellectual life in the mid- to late nineteenth century. To name just some of his favorite topics: home, family, children, motherhood and women's roles[211] (often in opposition to Roman Catholic praise of celibacy[212]); immigrants to America[213] ("vast and mongrel"[214]); and the evils of German scholarship that lead to unbelief.[215] Whatever the deficiency of Coxe's series, at least it provided numerous primary source texts for American students.

Libraries

If such were the difficulties that the lack of textbooks and primary source collections posed for teaching early Christian history, the libraries at various American seminaries proved similarly problematic. Several of the professors here studied served as their institution's "librarian," gathering statistics on their collections for annual reports—and making heartfelt pleas to trustees for more library funds. Trustees, who had been enthusiastic to found a seminary or "theological department," often seemed oblivious to the sums required annually to maintain and increase a collection.

The American professors frequently expressed the disheartening contrast between their access to books and that of their European counterparts. In their publications, personal correspondence, and travel diaries, they often noted the size of European university and national libraries, as well as of professors' personal collections.[216] They recorded their efforts to buy books for themselves and their seminaries during their trips abroad. To American professors who had seen European libraries, the conditions in their own country appeared discouraging.

For example, George Fisher, studying in Germany in 1852–1853, registered amazement that Tholuck owned around 5000 books. (Apparently the library's size deterred Tholuck from retiring to Switzerland: how to transport the collection over the Alps?)[217] In 1860, Henry Smith reported that

Alexander von Humboldt by the end of his life had amassed about 10,000 volumes for his personal library.[218]

The size of major European libraries was a source of wonder and envy to the American professors. In 1862, Henry Smith noted that the Imperial Library in Paris [the Bibliothèque Nationale] had 1,800,000 volumes and seventeen miles of shelves to house them. Two years later, he reported that the British Museum in London had just spent 75,000 pounds ($477,500, he calculated), adding 107,784 items to the library alone. Even in Spain—not known by Protestant professors as a center of distinguished recent scholarship—the government contributed about six and a half million dollars in gold for its national libraries annually.[219] America was clearly lacking.

American Professors' Personal Libraries

Given the small number of library books available to the American professors and students when seminaries first opened, professors accrued as many books as they could for their personal collections, which they sometimes shared with students. For two of the professors, Samuel Miller and Roswell Hitchcock, interesting data remain regarding their personal libraries.

Princeton Theological Seminary Archives has an undated "Catalogue of Dr. Miller's Library" (consisting of around 2400 items) found at his death.[220] The list, organized by title, sometimes preceded by the author's name, reveals that among the patristic sources he possessed were William Wake's translation of *The Genuine Epistles of the Apostolical Fathers* in its 1810 edition; the *Epistles* of Ignatius; the collected works of Irenaeus, Tertullian, Cyprian, Athanasius, and Augustine; Chrysostom's *On the Priesthood*; Eusebius' *Ecclesiastica Historia*; Gregory Nazianzus' *Querela*;[221] and Origen's *Contra Celsum*. Of secondary works, Miller owned a number of *Church Histories* by Baxter, Campbell, Dupin, Gedder, Haweis, Milner, Mosheim (in two different translations, by McLaine and by Murdock); *Histories of Christianity* by Benson and several by Neander in translation; Clarkson's *Primitive Episcopacy*; two unspecified volumes on Arianism; a book on the *Apostolic Church*; Bower's *History of the Popes*; Ludovici's *History of the Council of Nicaea* (in Latin); Jowett's *Christian Researches*; Cave's *Lives of the Apostles*; the Magdeburg *Ecclesiastical History*;[222] Jansen's *Augustinus*, plus Bibles, biblical reference works, and a few books on ancient Judaism.

Miller's library is notable in several respects. First, students marveled at its size, considered extraordinary by those who had never seen a larger private collection.[223] Second, the catalog shows that German scholarship—such as Neander's writings—had migrated to Miller's study only in English translation: the day of German-language scholarship was yet to come. Third, the catalog also suggests that many of the patristic writings that Miller cited in his polemics against Episcopalians and others were derived not from first-hand knowledge of the primary sources, but from secondary accounts.

Roswell Hitchcock, more fortunate in his personal library collection than most seminary teachers in America, owned the entire *Acta Sanctorum* (of which there were then only three or four sets in America), 34 volumes of the Baronius-Raynaldi *Ecclesiastical Annals*, and 22 volumes of Herzog's *Encyclopedia*, in addition to 7000 or so other books.[224] At his death, he left between 3000 and 4000 volumes to Union, including an edition of Du Cange's seventeenth-century glossary of medieval and late Latin. His set of Lange's 25-volume *Commentary* on the Bible and twenty-two volumes of Herzog's *Encyclopedia* went to Bangor Theological Seminary; and a complete set of 40 volumes of *Bibliotheca Sacra* was shipped to the Syrian College at Beirut. Some books were also left to his son-in-law, Professor Samuel Emerson, who taught Greek, modern languages, and history at the University of Vermont.[225]

As noted above, 1800 volumes from Philip Schaff's personal library went to the Union Seminary library upon his death.[226] In 1873, a few years after he began teaching at Union, Schaff bought for his own library a set of Migne's *Patrologia* from (a not otherwise identified) Mrs. French in New Haven.[227] Some professors, it appears, were able to compensate for their institution's lack of books with their personal collections.

Seminary Libraries

Various seminaries built their collections by buying the libraries of retired or deceased European—largely German—professors. In 1856, Harvard Divinity School acquired 4000 volumes from the library of Professor Friedrich Lücke of Göttingen.[228] By the early 1880s (so Hitchcock told his students), Thilo's library had gone to New Haven, that is, to Yale; Niedner's, to Andover Seminary; and Hengstenberg's, to the Baptist seminary in Chicago. Neander's library, secured by the Baptist Theological Seminary in

Rochester,[229] was disappointingly small, but Hitchcock explained that Neander did not need to own many books himself because he had access to the excellent libraries in Berlin.[230] The collection that grounded Union's library will be discussed below.

The professors were also delegated to buy books for their institution's library on trips abroad. Letters and notes in their travel diaries detail how much they spent—often more than they had been allotted—and sometimes, what they had been able to buy. In 1826, for example, the young Charles Hodge in Europe was delegated by Seminary officials at Princeton to deal with European booksellers.[231] In 1866, on a European trip, Smith purchased $600 worth of books for the Union library.[232] Philip Schaff on his many trips abroad bought books in London, Rome, and Germany for the libraries at Mercersburg and later at Union.[233] In June 1890, the president of Union wrote to Schaff in Europe to restrain his book-buying: "I hope you will not be tempted to run us into debt."[234]

In 1832, of seminary libraries in America, Andover had the largest collection (10,000 volumes), followed by Princeton (6000 volumes).[235] In 1844, The Society of Clergymen noted that all seminary libraries in the United States held collectively about 130,000 volumes; how much better (they argued) it would be if there were fewer seminaries with more books for each. They contrasted the paltry state of American libraries with those in Berlin (over 500,000 volumes), Göttingen (nearly 300,000), Munich and Paris (nearly 800,000 each). As noted earlier, the combined collections of the nine most important theological libraries in America, the clergymen reported, contain fewer than one-quarter of the volumes available at Munich or Paris.[236]

Henry Smith, who served as the librarian at Union Seminary for much of his career, was keenly interested in the size of collections. As the editor of the "Theological Intelligence" column of the *American Theological Review*,[237] he garnered information on libraries from various journals to report in his column. In the mid-nineteenth century, university libraries and public libraries vied with each other in terms of their holdings. For example, in 1860 Smith noted that the Astor Library in New York—the largest public library in the country, which provided the foundation for the New York Public Library—housed 80,000 books, topping Harvard University's 74,000 volumes.[238] At Columbia in 1876, by contrast, the library contained only about 25,000 volumes, and was open for one and a half hours a day for books to be checked out.[239] Smith's statistics also suggest that the

1860s, despite the nation's massive problems during and after the Civil War, were years of library expansion.

THE SEMINARY LIBRARY AT PRINCETON

Although the founders of the Theological Seminary at Princeton in 1812 hoped to establish a large theological library, they faced the same difficulties that other seminaries soon would. The first professor at the Seminary, Archibald Alexander, served as librarian and kept the Seminary's books in his house. By 1817, however, the collection had received its own new building and acquired a deputy librarian.[240] As Samuel Miller complained to his students, we lack books, and public libraries are few.[241] Miller expressed regrets to his students that many books he would recommend were not obtainable, so we must "grope our way as well as we can." Americans (he told students at some unspecified date) are hindered from securing many useful books from abroad, due to "the state of our foreign relations"—perhaps the aftermath of the War of 1812?[242]

A report by an unidentified author in 1822 regarding the Seminary at Princeton remarks that the present library was "very small and imperfect." It then contained "comparatively few of the books which are most indispensable to Theological Students," and even the ones it did own were in single copies, thus not adequate for student needs.[243] A fireproof building was a chief desideratum: the writer reminded his audience that the greater part of the Princeton College library had been destroyed by fire in 1802.[244] By 1823, eleven years after the Seminary's founding, the library had amassed about 4000 volumes.[245] This number grew in the years to come: by 1830, to over 6000 volumes;[246] by 1850, to 9000; by 1879, to over 31,000 books and 8500 pamphlets; and by 1900, to 64,544 books and nearly 27,000 pamphlets.[247]

In the early days of American seminaries, it was not imagined that libraries were places where students would work; rather, libraries were repositories from which students might retrieve books for use in their own rooms. This situation is reflected in the hours during which seminary libraries were available to professors and students. As late as the 1850s, the library at Princeton Seminary opened its doors just twice a week for the borrowing of books; after 1868, it was open two hours every weekday.[248] In the 1870s, Cornell University's decision to keep its library open from 8 a.m. till 6 p.m. was considered a major innovation.[249] Given these conditions, it is not surprising that writers commenting on German seminars often marvel that students have their own work-spaces in rooms where books and journals are readily available for their use.

THE LIBRARIES AT HARVARD

In 1816, George Ticknor, one of the first American scholars to study in Germany, complained to the steward of Harvard College's meager library that the 20,000 volumes at Harvard paled before the 200,000 at Göttingen. Libraries are what make a university, he indignantly asserted.[250] In the decades to come, Harvard's libraries would become the envy of many theological institutions.

In the mid-1820s, as work was started on Divinity Hall at Harvard, the Trustees of the Theological Education Society and the Corporation of the College appropriated $2000 to acquire books for the Theological Institution: this marked the beginning of the Harvard Divinity School library.[251] By mid-century, the theological library at Harvard had grown, despite the dwindling student population. By 1870, it had 16,000 volumes,[252] and was declared by Edward Everett Hale to be "the best and largest theological library in the country."[253] (Apparently Hale did not know that by then, Union Seminary's library topped Harvard Divinity School's.) Yet the library was cramped, not fireproofed, and open only two hours a day for dispensing books. Although a permanent librarian was hired, when he died in 1876, the faculty was forced to resume the librarian's duties.[254] For seminar work in history to be developed, libraries had to be reconceived as "laboratories" (as Ephraim Emerton put it), not merely as storehouses for books—and hence be open for students to consult many books at a time.[255] In the early twentieth century, the Andover Seminary library, which had been the envy of other developing seminaries a century previous, was merged with the library of the Harvard Divinity School.[256]

THE LIBRARY AT UNION THEOLOGICAL SEMINARY

When in 1837 Edward Robinson accepted the appointment in biblical studies at the newly founded Union Seminary, he argued that the fledgling Seminary's library should have "a complete series of the work of the Fathers, so called, in the best editions, and with the proper apparatus," as

well as the best editions of Greek and Roman writers.[257] Some years passed
before this desideratum was filled.

The development of the Union Seminary library benefited from the
secularization of the religious houses in Germany, most notably, the Benedictine Monastery of St. Mary at Paderborn. In response to political turmoil
and anticipating the dissolution of their monastery during the Napoleonic
Wars, the monks divided the library collection among themselves. About
13,000 volumes[258] were placed in the safekeeping of a monk whose family
name was Leander Van Ess. Van Ess took the volumes with him when he
became a professor at the University of Marburg in 1812, and upon retirement, offered his library for sale. Apprised of this opportunity, Edward
Robinson, on a trip to Europe and Palestine, was commissioned by the
Directors of Union to buy the Van Ess collection, which became the nucleus
of the Union library. The total cost upon the books' arrival in New York
was $5070.08.[259] Some years later, Roswell Hitchcock suggested to his stu-
dents that the Van Ess Library at Union—so much richer than the "disap-
pointing" collection of Neander's library at Rochester—had ushered in a
new era in scholarship.[260]

In May 1866, the librarian at Union reported that the library now had
about 25,000 books.[261] A few years later, the library received about 4000
volumes of British history and theology from David H. McAlpin, which
became a new collection of its own.[262] From an unidentified and undated
clipping in Schaff's scrapbooks at Union, we learn that the Seminary had
received a gift of nearly 7000 volumes from Dr. Edwin Hatfield's library
and around 250 books on philology (especially Indo-European linguistics)
from Professor Benjamin W. Dwight.[263] In May 1875, librarian Henry Smith
reported that the library had now amassed about 33,500 volumes and was
"the most valuable in the country."[264] In 1877–1878, just after Smith's death,
Union tried to raise $5000 by subscription to acquire his personal library.
This attempt appears not entirely successful, for the Board finally purchased
Smith's collection—but paid only $2500.[265]

The professor in charge of the library—Edward Robinson from 1841 to
1850, Henry Smith from 1850/1851 to 1876, and Charles Briggs from 1876 to
1883[266]—had to solicit the Board every year for funds, apparently not a
standard budget item. In October 1851, for example, the library committee
asked for $150 to buy "German works on Church History." Board members
hesitated due to the Seminary's impoverished condition, but "Professor
Smith forced [their] hand." In May 1853, the Board voted to compensate

Smith $500 "for general and special services as librarian during the present year."[267]

Professors at Union often complained that it was easier to convince the Board of Directors to establish a new professorship than it was to secure adequate funds for books. Throughout the 1850s, the professors decried the state of the library, despite the installation of gas lights in 1853.[268] Along the way, New York ministers who favored the Union experiment delivered heart-rending pleas to their congregations to give until it hurt: the man who could give $100,000 for "a theological library worthy of New-York" would build an enduring monument for himself, Reverend George Prentiss claimed.[269]

Throughout the 1860s, faculty constantly pressed for more library funds. The librarian in his report of May 1863 requested an endowment for the library equal to a professorship, asking the Board to find a benefactor.[270] Over the years, Smith besieged Union officials to build a fireproof library, claiming that some parts of the collection could not be replaced at all, and other parts only at great expense.[271] Finally, in 1880 ex-Governor Edwin D. Morgan gave $100,000, part of which was designated for a fireproof building.[272]

THE LIBRARY AT THE YALE THEOLOGICAL DEPARTMENT

In 1829 the theological library at Yale was open once a week for one hour (Thursday afternoons from 2 to 3, except during vacations). Students were allowed to take out two books once every two weeks.[273] In 1830, the theological division had increased its holdings to more than 6000 volumes;[274] by 1861 to 67,000 volumes plus around 7000 pamphlets, with 1800 more books and pamphlets at the American Oriental Society, headquartered at Yale. Moreover, the library had by 1861 been allotted around $1500 per year for books, then considered a princely sum, and $25,000 has been set up as a permanent fund to increase the college library.[275] That George Fisher's assumption of the Chair of Ecclesiastical History had made an impact is shown by the increase in books by German church historians—Hagenbach, Neander, Mosheim, Gieseler—that students now checked out of the library.[276]

A new building planned for the Theology Department in 1868–1869 was to have a "large library and reading room," the latter of which was to be kept open at all hours for the use of seminary students. In 1870 a "Reference

Library" was established, modeled after the British Museum reading room, open three hours in the afternoons. A newspaper article announcing the Reference Library exclaimed that it would be almost as if "each [student] had such a library in his own room."[277]

Thus from small beginnings, "infrastructural" resources grew along with the seminaries. Nevertheless, it is sobering to recall the scanty resources with which the professors in America worked as they aimed to create theological education for a new age and a new country. The inadequacy of the material conditions under which they taught students and wrote their books and articles renders poignant Henry Adams's claim in the frontispiece of his book: that Americans of the year 2000 might wonder how their counterparts of the nineteenth century, as childlike, ignorant, and weak in force as men of the fourth, should have done so much.[278] How they did, and the intellectual, theological, and philosophical problems they faced, are the subjects of the next chapters.

PART II

History and Historiography

CHAPTER 3

Defending the Faith: European Theories
and American Professors

What a sequel and summing up of the history of
Christianity would that be, to say that "God sent his Son
into the world," "that the world through him might be
saved," but the Tübingen School and British "Essays and
Reviews" defeated that purpose, and it had to be
abandoned?

—Frederic Hedge (1864)

Although nineteenth-century American seminary professors looked to
Europe for scholarship, textbooks, and teaching methods, they recognized
not only the differences between European universities and American colleges and seminaries, but also the dangers—most keenly felt by the professors at Union and Yale—to which American evangelical piety might be
exposed by contact with them.[1] These perceived dangers centered on Infidelity (often linked to Pantheism, an offshoot of Hegelian philosophy) and
Materialism (largely Comtian Positivism), as well as on a more radical biblical criticism than most American teachers could countenance.[2] Although
Germany was the site from which the alleged dangers most notably ema-
nated, Britain contributed its share by way of *Essays and Reviews* and
Bishop J. W. Colenso's books.[3] The professors' approach to early Christian
history was decisively shaped by their reaction to these larger critical currents, attempting to appropriate what was "good" in them, while decisively
rejecting aspects that might lead American Protestants astray.[4]

The professors stood at a crossroads: themselves educated under the

assumptions of British empiricism and Scottish Common Sense Philosophy—as noted above, Smith taught these subjects—they now encountered
German metaphysics and French social theory.[5] Whereas (in E. Brooks Holifield's words) "Scottish philosophy seemed tailor-made for a theology that
would show the rationality of faith while preserving the necessity for revelation,"[6] Continental approaches might pose more intellectual difficulties.
Nineteenth-century evangelicals of an intellectual cast, George Marsden
notes, seemed unaware that their theoretical assumptions, often unexam-
ined, would soon be rendered dubious.[7] Positioned between "Scotland"
and "Germany," in effect, the Union and Yale professors responded ambig-
uously both to philosophical challenges and to those regarding the authorship, dating, context, and significance of the New Testament and other
early Christian writings. For them, the category of inspiration decisively
separated the Church Fathers from the writers of the New Testament books.

   In the next sections, I selectively cite examples from those professors
who dealt most fully with these issues.

Infidelity, Pantheism, and Materialism

Henry Smith at Union and George Fisher at Yale, in particular, were wary
that European Pantheism, Infidelity, and Materialism might undermine
their students' faith.[8] Well known in America for his expertise in Continental philosophy, Smith had attended lectures in Germany given by Hegel's
noted expositor, Friedrich Trendelenberg. Smith's articles in the *New American Cyclopaedia* on Kant, Hegel, Schelling, and Pantheism impressed
American colleagues.[9] Indeed, the charge to Smith at his inauguration as
Professor of Theology at Union explicitly cautioned him against displaying
any favor to Skepticism, Radicalism, Romanism, Materialism, and Pantheism.[10]

   In Smith's view, modern Infidelity—covering both skepticism and
unbelief—assumed three forms: in England, Rationalism; in France, Atheism; and in Germany, Pantheism. The subtle and persuasive "weapons"
and "arts" of Infidelity, especially in its German guise, must be studied
carefully by Christians who wish to mount a challenge:[11] mere denuncia-
tion, "the indiscriminate censure of all that is German," will not suffice.[12]
Labeling philosophies "German and transcendental" does not defeat them.

Challengers must, Smith insisted, demonstrate that the *ideas* are "radically unsound" and "essentially unphilosophical."[13]

Smith believed that Christianity in Germany was facing its "fiercest assault": Pantheism had promoted "Revolutionary democratic opinions, and foul-mouthed blasphemy."[14] He worried that "applauded schemes of infidelity . . . assume that the age of theology is past. . . . They give what they call a philosophical sense to the Christian doctrines, turning realities into fictions, and destroying all in Christianity that has been the source of its life and power."[15]

Ancient methods of apologetics, Smith insisted, were too feeble to answer modern philosophical problems. Students must not imagine that Butler's *Analogy*—the text used in courses on Christian apologetics—could meet "the questions raised by Hegel and Bauer, by Darwin and Spencer."[16] Nor is the ancient orthodox Trinitarianism that condemned Arianism, Sabellianism, and tritheism sufficient to demolish the "humanitarian view" associated with Pantheism. Although Christianity is stronger now than ever, Smith claimed, its "assailants" are likewise more powerful.[17]

The conflict with Pantheism remained Smith's special concern.[18] Pantheism he defined as "that modification of religious belief, or philosophical speculation, which affirms that God is all; 'all' being here taken as the unity, which underlies, and is expressed in, individual, multiple existences." Pantheism claims that there is "but one substance, or spirit, in the universe, which alone has real and permanent being."[19] Hegelian philosophy was the central culprit.[20] Smith cited Hegel's claims that the highest problems of philosophy and theology are the same; that his system was merely biblical theology in a new guise; that to know God—"Absolute Spirit"—is to know Hegelian philosophy. Pantheism as the "absolute philosophy," Smith objected, asserts that it contains the truth of Christianity—but all other truth as well.[21]

Despite Smith's sometimes more generous reading of Hegel, he registered many criticisms of Hegel's system. First, it has no true doctrine of creation. "Negation," a moment in the dialectic, is not a productive force. It is incapable of showing how matter came to be. The creation of the "real world," Smith insisted, requires "power-force." Pantheism teaches emanation, not creation.[22]

Second, Hegel discounts the uniqueness of Christianity and the Christian understanding of deity. For Hegel, Smith charged, Christianity becomes the mere "flower" that is developed out of all religions, not "a new and divine and supernatural order of things." Pantheism concedes that Christianity is true *only* if it is taken philosophically. God is accorded no existence apart from the world, finding his "consciousness" only in man.[23] The Incarnation is not uniquely located in Jesus, but in the "generic unison of divinity and humanity, found in the race as a whole," while the Trinity is the "rational process" of God's development.[24] "It is *atheism* itself," Smith claimed, "for it virtually denies the *being*, the *power*, the *providence of God*."[25] Is God just "another name for the Absolute Unknown?"[26] As a system, he concluded, Pantheism is complete—and dangerous.[27]

Pantheism's consequences for ethics likewise troubled Smith. On the theoretical level, he claimed, it denies human freedom ("because all is development"), individual immortality (because only the race survives), and the reality of sin. On the practical level, Pantheism, in the company of materialistic and socialistic philosophy, teaches that this present life and the pursuit of happiness is all. Allegedly the "most ideal of systems," Pantheism produces sensual men. In practice, it is a new form of Epicureanism. It encourages humans to aim for a "high social state," rather than to concede that earthly life is simply "the portal to another world."[28] Elsewhere, Smith more generously admitted that *some* "infidels" are moral and embrace "natural religion"—without acknowledging its source in the Bible, as they should.[29]

Materialism, that is, Positivism, was also of grave concern to Smith.[30] In 1868, Union sponsored James McCosh's (subsequently published) Ely Lectures on "Christianity and Positivism."[31] Smith had warned students and readers against Materialism (holding that "mind is a modification of matter"[32]) even before McCosh's lectures roused greater interest. As a philosophical theory, Smith claimed, Materialism is atheistic in its practical results. Identified with "the Compte [*sic*] school," Materialism "asserts that all facts, events, and laws can be ultimately explained by matter and its modifications." Spirit, in this view, is merely a "mode of matter." The soul is conceived as a material entity that "comes and goes with the body." For Materialists, Smith charged, sensation alone is the source of knowledge; the moral law, only a modification of natural phenomena; and God, simply the name for the ultimate unconscious power of nature.[33]

Against these Materialist assumptions, Smith armed his students with Idealist rebuttals. Matter, the substratum of all phenomena, he told them, is "itself an idea of the mind," the latter being the productive "power-force" of creation. Materialism fails in that it cannot explain the phenomenon of life, of "living organism." Christians, by contrast, reject the notion that the human soul and mind are simply modifications of matter.[34]

George Fisher of Yale likewise warned students and readers against a Pantheism that "hypostatizes" the laws of nature "as if they were a self-active being" and resolves history into "the movement of a great machine."[35] Pantheism, he charged, obviates the notion of a personal God. It denies humanity's distinctiveness (resolving "personal being into a . . . transient phase of an impersonal essence") and the notion of mind as "a separate, substantial, undivided entity." Pantheists and atheistic Rationalists rashly claim that they alone own science, assuming that the "supernatural is unhistorical."[36] Moreover, Pantheism undermines morality by dissolving the "absolute antithesis between good and evil," "the bonds of obligation."[37] Fisher cautioned his audience against trying "to evolve the Christian religion out of consciousness," as do German Pantheists: Christianity's distinctive essence cannot be identified with "a process of thought."[38]

Philosophical Materialism had a stormy history at Yale. In the 1870s, President Noah Porter protested Professor William Graham Sumner's teaching of Herbert Spencer and Comte; he specifically objected to Sumner's use of Spencer's *Study of Sociology* as a textbook.[39] Although Sumner was an ordained Episcopal priest, he deemed Spencer's book, despite its religious implications, the best available for teaching the new subject of sociology. The controversy escalated in the public press and became a major moment in the struggle for professorial freedom.[40] Fisher apparently sided with the conservative Yale President. The best refutation of Materialism ("a gloomy and unnatural creed"), Fisher advised, simply attends to "the agency of mind" and registers human moral feelings of compassion, self-forgetfulness, obligation, conscience, guilt, and remorse, which, he claimed, cannot be accounted for on Materialist grounds.[41] If Materialism were to prevail, then (as with Pantheism) sensual appetite and "earthly passions" could "gain an undisputed ascendancy, and overturn at last the social fabric." Fisher charged that Comte, an "avowed Atheist," deems religion a delusion stemming from humanity's "childhood," a faltering, primitive attempt to understand nature. Comte thus overlooks the deep power that religion has exerted in human history, its innate and ineradicable presence in human souls. Fisher, however, cautioned ministers against launching diatribes against "materialistic infidelity" that make Christianity seem in need of elaborate defense: Christianity can stand on its own. Knowledge of physical discoveries and speculation, he counseled, is "not indispensable" for a preacher.[42] Arguing with Comtians is simply counter-productive.

With these charges, the American professors defended the unique status of Christianity: it did not evolve from "lower" religions nor can it be derived from mental processes. They merged traditional Christian notions of revelation and creation with an Idealist vision of human nature as spiritual and "mental," against the claims of Materialism and Positivism. These views comprised one aspect of the professors' "defense of the faith" that informed their teaching of history.[43]

Biblical Scholarship

For the professors, an equally important danger posed by European scholarship lodged in the Higher Criticism of the Bible, especially that of the New Testament. Surveying biblical scholarship in nineteenth-century America, Mark Noll calls the early Protestant seminaries (Andover, Princeton, Yale) "centers of advanced study designed to de-fang criticism and to absorb the new facts into orthodoxy."[44] Although Noll's claim may overstate the motivation for the founding of those seminaries—to Samuel Miller of the Theological Seminary at Princeton, for example, "biblical criticism" was a seemingly unknown category[45]—it perceptively describes how the nineteenth-century professors, "post-Miller," operated.

While the American professors appropriated some few aspects of European criticism, they vigorously attacked points they found offensive to the evangelical sympathies still dominant in mid-nineteenth century America. Although they had gleaned the notion of historical development from German scholars, they shied from applying it to New Testament texts. Development, they believed, should be limited to the study of post-New Testament Christianity.[46]

That the Gospels were not composed by eyewitnesses to Jesus' life, that Paul did not write the Pastoral Epistles, that the New Testament was to be studied not as a divine, incomparable revelation, but (merely) as a source for the history of the first and second centuries: these propositions were strongly rejected by professors in America. Although German criticism was the central offender, the British scholars who compiled *Essays and Reviews* and Bishop J. W. Colenso also troubled American sensibilities. While the larger public became more cognizant of changed approaches to the Bible only in the 1870s and 1880s,[47] the Union and Yale professors recognized the new critical treatment of the Bible earlier—even as they strove to fend off its most damaging effects.

German Universities and American Professors

The Union and Yale professors of church history spent much of their scholarly careers attempting to counter the alleged dangers and excesses of German biblical criticism. German was, of course, Philip Schaff's native tongue,[48] yet the other professors, as students in Germany, soon became sufficiently fluent to translate, appropriate, and critique German scholarship.

Here we should recall the professors' early encounters with Germany. Of the three on whom I shall here focus, Henry Smith studied at Halle and Berlin from 1838 to 1840;[49] Philip Schaff, at Tübingen, Halle, and Berlin from 1837–1842 (from 1842–1844, serving as a *Privatdozent* in Berlin);[50] and George Fisher, at Halle from 1852 to early 1854.[51] There they encountered German biblical criticism (especially that of the Tübingen School) and theories of Christianity's historical development.

At mid-century, of the German Protestant universities, Halle—where Smith, Schaff, and Fisher studied—boasted the largest number of theology students.[52] Early in the century, Halle had renounced its Pietistic origins and embraced Rationalism; it was later alleged that only five out of 900 students in that era affirmed the divinity of Christ.[53] (As late as 1852, August Tholuck of Halle told George Fisher that if a decade earlier he had preached the sermon on the devil that he had just delivered, he would have been pelted.[54]) Piety at Halle slowly revived, influenced by Friedrich Schleiermacher's theology and August Neander's historical studies.[55] At mid-century, the newly pious atmosphere of Halle and its evangelically inclined professors—especially Tholuck—suited American students well.[56]

Halle's piety, however, was offset by the radical criticism emanating from Tübingen's David Friedrich Strauss and Ferdinand Christian Baur, whose views were strongly opposed by the American professors.[57] Back in America, some years later, they also took up scholarly arms against Ernest Renan's *Vie de Jésus*. Their conservative approach to the New Testament sat uncomfortably alongside their more sympathetic assessment, nurtured in Germany, of historical development in *post*-New Testament Christianity.

The New Testament, they averred, was not to be subjected to the same critical scrutiny as other ancient texts, such as those of the patristic era. Only at century's end would more critical treatments receive a friendlier reception in America. First, to the "radical" criticism.

Strauss, Baur, and Renan

In 1835, David Friedrich Strauss's *Leben Jesu* and in 1863, Ernest Renan's *Vie de Jésus* shook traditional Christian approaches to the Gospels. Translations made these works available to the larger reading public: Strauss's book was translated into English (by George Eliot) in 1846; Renan's, in 1864.[58] F. C. Baur's writings, however, tended to remain the purview of scholars, although the professors that I here consider introduced his theories to a wider audience.

DAVID FRIEDRICH STRAUSS

Strauss's *Leben Jesu* was one of the most-criticized books of the nineteenth century[59]—indeed, it cost its author his position as a *Privatdozent* at Tübingen.[60] As Karl Barth comments, *Leben Jesu* made Strauss "at once and for many years to come the most famous theologian in Germany and ensured that he would never in his life be considered for any post in the church or in the academic world."[61]

Adopting a Hegelian framework, Strauss acknowledged religion—especially Christianity—as a perception of truth, not in the form of Idea (as in philosophy), but in images.[62] Supermundane beings and a heavenly afterlife are not religion's true province, but present spiritual realities as moments in the eternally pulsating life of the Divine Spirit. The *essence* of the Christian faith, in his view, exists independently of biblical criticism and is not shaken by it; the miracles, for example, convey eternal truths, not historical facts.[63]

Strauss's "mythical" approach to the life of Jesus was influenced by studies on myth in various non-Christian religions. Myth, according to Strauss, relinquishes the historical reality of the Gospel narratives in order to preserve their inherent spirit and truth.[64] Albert Schweitzer explains Strauss's concept:

> It is nothing else than the clothing in historic form of religious ideas, shaped by the unconsciously inventive power of legend, and embodied in a historic personality. . . . we are almost compelled to assume that the historic Jesus will meet us in the garb of Old Testament Messianic ideas and primitive Christian expectations.[65]

After listing various "negative" and "positive" factors that contribute to the mythic quality of a narrative, Strauss concluded that when several of these factors converge, the account is probably unhistorical.[66]

In *Leben Jesu*, Strauss appropriated the Hegelian dialectic to map modern scholarship on the Gospels: the "thesis" of the supernaturalistic explanation met its "antithesis" in a naturalistic or rationalistic explanation, the two canceling each other out and making way for a new "synthesis," the mythical.[67] Whereas Rationalist scholars such as H. E. G. Paulus had affirmed the historicity of the Gospel narratives but devised naturalistic explanations for them (a procedure, in Barth's view, that rendered "things a trifle shabby"), Strauss questioned their historical reliability.[68] In addition, Strauss faulted Rationalist scholars' depiction of Jesus: the Jesus who is (merely) a "distinguished man" is not the Christ in whom the church believes.[69] Strauss found Kant's approach to Christianity as a system of morals—offering devotees only "obligation," not "consolation"—deeply unsatisfying.[70]

The Gospel writers, Strauss claimed, although not eyewitnesses to the events of Jesus' life, should not be charged with fraudulent intent. They simply filled up historical gaps with imaginary circumstances.[71] Strauss takes aim especially at Schleiermacher's belief that John, the most important Gospel, was written by an eyewitness:[72] for Strauss, the discourses assigned to Jesus in the Fourth Gospel are sheer fabrications. John's inclusion of such unlikely scenes as the resurrection of Lazarus should convince readers of the Gospel's "unauthenticity."[73]

Much myth in the Gospels, Strauss argued, stemmed from the Evangelists' desire to make Jesus' words and deeds echo, but surpass, heroes of the Hebrew Bible such as Moses and Elijah. Strauss sharply rebuked theologians (especially Schleiermacher) who divorced Jesus from his Jewish milieu.[74] The miracle stories, for example, should be understood as the Gospel writers' need to depict Jesus as conforming to Old Testament types. Jesus himself, Strauss argued, did not give much weight to miracles: did he not declare, "no sign is to be given to this generation"? This claim, when coupled with the silence regarding Jesus' miracles in Acts and Paul's epistles, should cast doubt on the historicity of the miracle stories.[75]

Likewise, Strauss argued against both the miraculous explanation of Jesus' resurrection and the Rationalist claim that Jesus had not died, but merely returned after a few days' disappearance. On Strauss's reading, the story was devised to fulfill Isaiah's notion of the Suffering Servant and such Old Testament verses as "God will not leave his soul in Hell [Sheol]." By "resurrection," Jesus meant that his cause would continue after his death, but his disciples misunderstood his words to imply a corporeal resuscitation.[76] Although Strauss attributed a messianic consciousness to Jesus from the time of his baptism, he also claimed that divinity is instantiated in the human race as a whole, not in Jesus alone.[77]

Horton Harris, historian of the Tübingen School, argues that Strauss's *Leben Jesu* made possible that School's development: the book changed Tübingen overnight "from a centre of orthodoxy into a centre of heresy."[78] Tübingen, we shall see, stood as a blight on American piety.

Ferdinand Christian Baur and the Tübingen School

If Strauss's mythical (and later, Renan's novelistic) approach could be dismissed as deeply unhistorical, the arguments of Ferdinand Christian Baur and his followers more seriously disturbed American scholars. Tübingen studies of early Christianity were centered in Baur. The Tübingen School, Harris claims, was "the most important theological event in the whole history of theology from the Reformation to the present day," in two decades changing the entire course of critical study of the New Testament. All nineteenth-century theologians, regardless of which stripe, lived under its shadow.[79]

Baur posed an even more ominous threat than Strauss or Renan, given his more detailed scheme for relating the New Testament to the emerging Christian church. Already in 1831, Baur had startled readers with his initial investigations into the parties that had warred in the Corinthian church, their slide into opposing Pauline and "Jewish" factions, and their reconciliation in the developing Catholic church of the late second and early third centuries.[80] In the next years, Baur continued to ruffle traditional Christian scholars with his claims regarding the "tendencies" that divided the early Christian communities and his insistence that Paul did not write the Pastoral Epistles.[81] He investigated Gnosticism and Manicheanism, as well as the

New Testament books (most of which he dated later than did traditional scholars) and developments in post-biblical Christian history.[82] Baur shattered Christians' assumptions regarding the harmony of the early Christian church and its narrators.

Although Baur's *Church History of the First Three Centuries* (1853) was translated into English only in 1878, the American professors here considered were familiar with his writings on the New Testament and early Christianity long before.[83] Despite their denunciations, Baur set their agenda: in reaction, they defended traditional views of the dating and authorship of the New Testament books and the development of second-century Christianity. In fact, Schaff's *History of the Apostolic Church* has been called "a conservative rebuttal to the Tübingen School's rival interpretation of apostolic Christianity."[84]

Baur's working assumptions were anathema to American evangelicals. In effect, he broke down the protective barrier cordoning off the study of church history from general history[85]—and the New Testament from other early Christian literature. He assumed that for scholarly purposes, the New Testament and second-century literature should be examined together as a source for understanding Christianity's early development. He explicitly contested the claim that second-century Christian texts differed qualitatively from the canonical books: the only people who could think this, he remarked, are "those who hold the most extravagant view of the inspiration of the whole canonical collection."[86] ("Those," it would appear, include the evangelical church historians here considered.) On Baur's reading, the New Testament, from an academic perspective, was simply a source for the historical study of primitive Christianity.

A second assumption that disturbed the American professors was Baur's insistence that a historical interpretation of the Bible should exclude all supernatural or miraculous elements.[87] To take Jesus' birth and incarnation as miracle, Baur argued, is to step "outside all historical connection": "miracle" is not a historical category. Jesus' resurrection thus "lies outside the sphere of historical inquiry"—although Baur conceded that the disciples' *belief* in his return was necessary for Christianity's development.[88]

Third, Baur posited a strong element of conflict in primitive Christianity. The earliest Jewish followers of Jesus, he argued, soon engaged in battle with Paulinists; only through concessions on each side were the two approaches reconciled in the Catholic Church in the late second century.[89] The Jewish element, in Baur's view, remained dominant for a long time.

Although the "mythico-historical" tradition from Acts through the first Christian centuries portrayed Peter and Paul as inseparable even in death, its picture was unconvincing, given the strong evidence for conflict between their respective parties.[90] Baur's scheme of conflict and belated resolution read early Christianity through the lens of the Hegelian dialectic: thesis and antithesis were resolved in a higher synthesis.[91]

Baur's narration of early Christian development played havoc with the traditional dating of New Testament books: aside from the four Pauline epistles that he considered genuine, the only other New Testament book composed before 70 C.E., he argued, was the Apocalypse.[92] (Baur held that only Romans [minus the last two chapters], Galatians, and I and II Corinthians were genuinely Pauline,[93] exhibiting the signs of Jewish-Gentile conflict that he considered hallmarks of the earliest Christian communities.[94]) Baur dated the Pastoral Epistles—which most Christians then ascribed to Paul—to the late second century, when Gnosticism and Marcionism were present dangers and church offices more fully developed.[95]

The Gospels, Baur claimed, reflect the (later) period in which they were written, not the time of Jesus. Their "tendencies" assist in their dating.[96] Among the four canonical Gospels, Baur granted priority and general trustworthiness to Matthew, whose original Jewish version he placed at the end of the first century.[97] Mark is indebted to Matthew; Luke, imbued with Paulinism, cannot be regarded as an independent source.[98]

Furthermore, Baur stood against the Protestant predilection for making the Gospel of John the key to the other three. Attempting to harmonize the Synoptics' depiction of Jesus with John's exalted representation requires abandoning "all historical treatment of gospel history." John, he argued, is not historical even in the "limited sense in which the Synoptics can be called historical." As for authorship, Baur held that the "John" of Revelation was a Jewish-oriented follower of Jesus, a "pillar-apostle" who opposed Paul and became influential in Asia Minor. The Gospel of John, by contrast, written in the later second century, shows evidences of Gnosticism, Montanism, Greek thought (e.g., in the *Logos* doctrine), and the controversy over Passover—and is "conciliatory" in the dispute between Pauline and Jewish Christianity.[99] This Gospel, in Baur's view, expresses the Western, Roman church's position that the Last Supper was *not* a Passover meal: here, the breach with Judaism is complete. Despite the Fourth Gospel's lack of historicity, Baur (like many Protestants of his time) called it "the purest expression of that higher form of the Christian consciousness."[100] Thus for Baur

the "higher form" is far from the earliest and cannot be claimed as historical. Origins do not imply value.

Baur also challenged the reliability of the book of Acts as a historical
source, except insofar as it shows the developing conflict between Jewish
and Gentile versions of Christianity, signaled by the account of Stephen.[101]
Baur explained why the author of Acts passed over the split in parties after
the Jerusalem Council: he could not reconcile the opposition between Peter
and Paul with the harmonizing tendency that suffuses his book.[102]

Reconciliation of these opposed parties came gradually, in Baur's view.
Pauline universalism at length overcame Jewish "particularism." The first
practice to give way in "the absolute power of Judaism" was circumcision,
replaced by baptism. Baur paralleled the tendency toward universalism that
developed in the Roman Empire with Christianity's attempt to overcome
"all religious particularism." Not only external factors, such as Roman
transportation routes, "prepared" for Christianity. There were more "intimate" connections: in the Empire, "the barriers raised by national sentiment had been broken down" both inwardly and outwardly. The
universalism of Christianity enabled it to be considered (in Hegelian parlance) the "Absolute Religion," "elevated above the defects and limitations,
the one-sidedness and finiteness, which constitute the particularism of
other forms of religion."[103]

Christianity, Baur noted, had neither the many gods of pagan polytheism, nor the "outward rites and ordinances" to which both paganism and
Judaism gave great attention. Nor did Christianity "identify itself with the
positive authority of a purely traditional religion," namely, Judaism. (Judaism's role in the larger scheme of things, Baur bluntly stated, was to "fill
up an interval.") Although *all* religions seek communion with the supernatural, Christianity differs in its "spirituality," its freedom from "everything
merely external, sensuous, or material." Nevertheless, it was important for
Christianity's historical development, in Baur's view, that its "spiritual contents" were "clothed in the concrete form" of Jewish Messianic ideas.[104]
Baur's scheme emphasizes the all-important role of Judaism in primitive
Christianity, but holds that the true, spiritual, essence of Christianity tran-
scends all Jewish particularity. Christianity could become the "absolute,"
universal religion when the Pauline "tendency" overcame some features of
Jewish Christianity, and both were raised in a higher synthesis of the Catholic Church.

Biblical books that appear neutral in the struggle between Jewish and

Gentile factions (such as the Gospels of Mark and John, and the letters of Ignatius) must, in Baur's view, be dated late in the second century, because no such conciliatory stance was possible until then.[105] The stages of reconciliation are shown in Hebrews and James (which represent a freer, more spiritual form of Jewish Christianity), while Ephesians and Colossians exhibit modifications from the Pauline side.[106] Conciliation in the form of Catholicism's development, Baur claimed, came only when the church faced dangers from outside.[107]

Baur on Early Christian Literature Outside the New Testament. The Pseudo-Clementine literature served as a centerpiece for Baur's argument that in the second century, opposition still raged between Petrine ("Jewish") and Pauline ("Gentile") Christianity.[108] Baur claimed that the *Clementine Homilies*, written by an Ebionite author about 170 C.E., stood as an attack on the Pauline party, Paul being represented by the figure of Simon the Magician.[109]

In addition, Baur maintained that the letters of Ignatius were later second-century productions, since they contain no traces of party conflict. Baur entered the dispute over the longer and shorter Greek and the Syriac recensions of the Ignatian letters.[110] His book, *Die ignatianischen Briefe* (1848), argued that the historical data in the Ignatian letters did not represent circumstances at the turn to the second century. Among other points suggesting late authorship, in Baur's view, are the letters' seeming knowledge of Valentinian Gnosticism and their references to the episcopate, an institution that Baur believed developed only in the mid-second century. The three Ignatian letters found in Syriac (those to Polycarp, the Ephesians, and the Romans) that some scholars alleged were the only "genuine" ones were, in Baur's opinion, just as "ungenuine" as the other four.[111]

The second-century Quartodeciman controversy, another area of debate, centered on the Gospels' discrepant dating of the Last Supper in relation to Passover,[112] and the proper timing for the celebration of Easter. Should other Christians, with the Quartodecimans, calculate the date of Easter in relation to the 14th of Nissan (Passover), regardless of the day of the week on which it might fall; or should Easter always be celebrated on a Sunday, the day of resurrection, without regard to the timing of Passover? For Baur, the Fourth Gospel's silence regarding the Last Supper as a Passover meal was an implicit repudiation of Quartodeciman practice. Baur's conclusion: the Gospel of John was not composed by Jesus' disciple, but was a late second-century production.[113]

In other second-century literature as well, Baur argued, the Jewish-Christian and Gentile-Christian divisions play out, with the *Epistle of Barnabas* and the (pseudo-) Ignatian epistles representing the Jewish-Christian side, and *I Clement* and the *Epistle of Polycarp*, the Gentile-Christian. Mediating such divisions are the *Shepherd of Hermas* and Justin Martyr.[114] With Irenaeus, Tertullian, Clement, and Origen the mediation seems complete. Rome now claims *both* Peter and Paul as its own: to the church at Rome, Baur argued, belongs the merit for first having made good "the essential condition of Catholicism," namely, the representation of Peter and Paul in brotherly unity.[115]

Now, those who stubbornly clung to an older Jewish Christianity were branded "Ebionites," heretics. Now, the Catholic Church stood poised to mediate between the extremes of a more "universalistic" Gnosticism and a more "Jewish" Montanism.[116] The development of the episcopate, Baur claimed, alone rendered possible "the historical development of Christianity and prepared its way to a world-historical future."[117]

The American Professors and Baur. The American professors protested many of Baur's theses: that Jewish Christianity was the original form of the religion; that conflict was the motor driving early Christianity; that arguments from silence were admissible; that writings could be dated by ascertaining what signs of struggle (or lack of it) between Jewish and Gentile "tendencies" they exhibited. Moreover, Baur's scheme implied that early Christian belief and practice remained highly unsettled until much later than these professors were prepared to accept.

In addition, the American professors sharply rejected Baur's dating of many New Testament texts to the second century: they dated *all* New Testament books to the first century. For them, the Pastoral Epistles show the harmonious development of the church out of primitive Christianity. Moreover, their interest in (and alarm over) issues posed by the *Clementine Homilies*, the Ignatian letters, and the Quartodeciman controversy—about which they wrote in more detail and passion than we might expect—appear to have been fueled by Baur.

Despite their many criticisms, the Americans garnered two important points from Baur. The first, quite simply, was an appreciation for development in early Christianity—although in their eyes, Baur had let development run riot. Baur forced historians of early Christianity to ask, "How did it happen?", a question that had been asked before, but with preconceived ideas that prevented its implications from being clearly understood.[118] The Americans, as we shall see in Chapter 5, admitted development in church history from the second century onward—but only as guided by the providential hand of God.

Second, Baur's praise for the alleged universalism and spirituality that developed in Catholic Christianity (despite his assertion of the Judaizing character of the primitive movement) was one to which the evangelical Americans could warm. To be sure, German Protestantism since the time of Luther had often stressed the inwardness and spirituality of true Christianity, as contrasted with the "externalism" of Roman Catholicism (and ancient Judaism). Baur gave striking expression to this view, in new form, for the nineteenth century.

ERNEST RENAN

Later in the century came Ernest Renan's wildly popular *Life of Jesus*. Whereas, one commentator argued, "The German historian represents the early history of the Church as a succession of metaphysical and philosophical theories, and the world in which they are propounded also as a world of theories," here at least was history as *narrative*.[119] Evangelical scholars denounced Renan's book as a piece of romantic—albeit dangerous—fluff. Some more positive critics claimed that Renan had rescued Christians from Strauss: he presented a *historical*, not a *mythical*, Jesus. But, objectors countered, it was not a Jesus who was God Incarnate. Appealing to "the whole cultured world," Renan's book went though eight editions in three months.[120]

Renan styled the Gospels—which he considered in "flagrant contradiction" with each other—"legendary biographies." Steeped in miracles and the supernatural, they resemble the "Legends of the Saints" or the "Life of Plotinus."[121] The discourses of Jesus in Matthew and Mark's "collection of anecdotes and personal reminiscences" [of Peter] form the original core documents.[122] Renan recognized the very different style of John, and bluntly wrote: "If Jesus spoke as Matthew represents, he could not have spoken as John relates." And if the son of Zebedee *did* write Jesus' speeches in the Fourth Gospel, he appears to have "forgotten the Lake of Gennesareth, and the charming discourses which he had heard upon its shores."[123] Yet John's

Gospel seems necessary for composing the story of Jesus' life, especially in its last months.[124] Despite proclaiming the four canonical Gospels, on the whole, "authentic,"[125] Renan nevertheless remained skeptical about their factuality and wary of harmonizing the Synoptics with John—yet harmonization seemed necessary for the complete story of Jesus.

Renan aimed to write an historical account of the *human* Jesus. His seeming exclusion of Jesus' divine nature, as pronounced by the Council of Chalcedon and later Christians, unsurprisingly, incurred the wrath of the pious. Renan styled Jesus a "noble initiator," in the "first rank" of those who "felt the Divine within themselves." Jesus is divine, he conceded, insofar as he enabled humans to advance toward their own divinity.[126]

Jesus, in Renan's scheme, amid the beauties of the Galilean countryside (as well as of Nazarene females), grew up in happy "poetic ignorance" of the outside world—of Greek science, of the political events of his time.[127] His religion, based on feeling, was devoid of priests and external observances; it brought devotees into direct relation with God the Father and promoted purity of heart and human brotherhood.[128] In Renan's anti-Jewish narrative, Jesus, representing a "rupture with the Jewish spirit," recognized that the sway of Judaism was over, that the Law was to be abolished.[129]

Renan believed that some aspects of Jesus' teaching and practice, not wearing well over time, were to be cast off. For example, Jesus had appealed to the lower classes with a gospel of "pure Ebionism"; "the poor" alone were his concern. This "exaggerated taste for poverty," in Renan's view, could not last, nor could the apocalyptic vision of the end-time. "Let us pardon him his hope," Renan condescendingly wrote.[130] In addition, the accounts of Jesus' miracles—a violence perpetrated on him by the expectations of his era—were merely an accommodation to the masses' avidity for spectacles: he either had to renounce his mission or become a *thaumaturgus*.[131]

As Jesus approached his end, his teaching grew darker; he forgot life's pleasures and loves. (Renan suggested that Jesus' mind might have become unbalanced.[132]) Convinced that his death would save the world, Jesus gave himself up to it. On the cross, after moments of doubt, he recalled his mission. The disciples believed in Jesus' resurrection because they loved their Master so deeply.[133] Albert Schweitzer pithily depicted Renan's representation of the death scene:

He is dead. Renan, as though he stood in Père Lachaise, commissioned to pronounce the final allocution over a member of the

Academy, apostrophizes Him thus: "Rest now, amid Thy glory, noble pioneer. Thou conqueror of death, take the sceptre of Thy Kingdom, into which so many centuries of Thy worshippers shall follow Thee, by the highway which Thou hast opened up."[134]

Renan tellingly confessed his own religious position: to write about a religion, one must first have believed it, and then, believe it no longer.[135] That this claim expressed his own situation was patently clear to the evangelical professors—to whom "belief" was an all-important criterion for religious allegiance. Although some readers may have deemed Renan's picture of Jesus as truly human more satisfactory than Strauss's mythical Jesus, it hardly represented the divinely ordained Jesus of Christian belief.

American Professors and New Testament Scholarship

Without doubt, German criticism set much of the teaching and research agenda for the American professors. Although they appropriated some themes for their own narratives of early Christianity, their reactions remained largely negative.[136] Not until this conservative approach to the Bible was quietly (or sometimes, not so quietly) abandoned could views of historical development—*also* imbibed from Germany—be allowed to stretch back to the earliest days of the "Jesus movement." Only then (at least in the classroom) did professors abandon the supernaturalistic approach that precluded studying the Bible as an ancient text like others.

Here, I shall focus on Henry Smith and Philip Schaff of Union and George Fisher of Yale as examples of the professors' strategy.[137]

HENRY SMITH

Henry Smith's studies in Germany shaped his mental universe.[138] He advised Americans to be tolerant of German philosophy and theology: "orthodoxy can afford to be just, to be generous."[139] He yearned for theology and church history to assimilate all that was good in German *Wissenschaft*.

In addition to his critique of Hegelian-inspired Pantheism, Smith attacked aspects of European biblical criticism.[140] Scholarship should not lead Christians to doubt the "genuineness" and "authenticity" of the New

Testament, or prompt skepticism about Christianity's historical foundations, as (Smith warned) the theses of Baur and the Tübingen School did.
Baur's detachment of the "Christian system" from the person of Christ
himself subverts its historical basis and finds Christianity's truth only in
abstract principles. He charged the Tübingen School in effect with reviving
Gnosticism, with implying that Jesus was "the greatest of imposters."[141]

Smith attacked more radical European biblical criticism in a variety of
venues. In a sermon delivered in 1855, "The Inspiration of the Holy Scriptures," Smith claimed to eschew "Bibliolatry," rather seeking the Bible's
"spirit." Decrying "rationalistic infidelity," he declared that Protestants'
according supreme authority to the Bible "stands or falls with the evidence
for its infallibility." To avoid Straussian skepticism and to acknowledge
God's omnipotence, Christians must admit "the possibility of inspiration."[142]

In the first 1600 years of Christian history, Smith continued, even
though no developed theory then existed, only a few—for example, Theodore of Mopsuestia, Abelard, and the fourth-century Anomoeans—rejected
the plenary inspiration of Scripture. Now, however, German Rationalists'
claim that Scripture contains errors has "infected" modern German theology; even Neander and Tholuck admit there are mistakes (albeit limited to
"trivial details"). Smith conceded that the Bible has "human elements," but
its truth is reinforced by modern archeology.[143] The chief proof of the Old
Testament's veracity comes from Jesus and the Apostles, who refer to these
writings as Scripture.[144] What authority do Carlyle, Strauss, and Theodore
Parker have compared to the heroes of the Bible, Smith pointedly asked?[145]

Smith rehearsed such views not only in sermons before laymen innocent of recent biblical criticism. He also, as retiring Moderator of the General Assembly of the Presbyterian Church USA in May 1864, cautioned
Presbyterian clergy against the Materialism and Pantheism manifest in the
Essays and Reviews (to be discussed below) and the Colenso controversy in
England, in Renan's Life of Jesus, and in Strauss's recent popularized version
of the Life of Jesus.[146] Historical Christianity and the doctrines of faith are
at stake, Smith warned. Is the Bible to be thought of the same way as other
books?[147] These movements dissolve Christianity's "facts into myths, . . . its
doctrines into ideas, its God-man into a vague moral hero." The contest
against Infidelity in Biblical studies looms large, as does the contest against
Romanism.[148]

In print venues as well, Smith endorsed conservative principles of biblical criticism. In 1874, reviewing Strauss's *The Old Faith and the New*, Smith downplayed the importance of the author's earlier *Leben Jesu* (in any case, superseded by Tübingen School criticism). Strauss in this new book, composed in his old age, mocks American democratic institutions with his pro-monarchy and anti-republican views.[149] Yet Strauss's book presents readers with a stark choice, an either/or: they must choose between Atheism and Christianity, or, what here seems the same to Smith, between Darwin and God.[150] Strauss's "unhistoric" account, Smith claimed, is refuted by Christianity's foundation on historic facts. In the last analysis, Strauss's theory combines the theses of Feuerbach (religion is derived from human wishes) and Schleiermacher (religion amounts to a mere "feeling of dependence on the Universe"). Strauss's views only further encourage the materialistic greed of American culture. If they prevail, nothing will remain sacred: institutions of church and state will be, if not destroyed, at least reshaped; and among the masses will emerge "a fierce struggle for wealth and power and pleasure, with the survival of the strongest." Yet because religion is an essential element of human nature, it cannot ultimately be obliterated.[151]

Smith sharply critiqued Tübingen scholars' claim that the church precedes the Bible and that New Testament books represent conflicting "tendencies" in Christianity's development. Such Pantheistically inspired critics deny that "the higher" can stand first, not merely evolve through a process of development. Although Smith conceded that the Tübingen School had stimulated closer study of primitive Christian history, its influence, he assured readers, is declining.[152]

Moreover, Tübingen scholars' ascription of pseudonymous authorship and late dating to various New Testament books, and their emphasis on partisan strife ("*Tendenz*") within early Christianity, were disturbing to the evangelical Smith. Ministers who endorse the views of Hegel and the "infidel" Baur, Smith claimed, should be relieved of their pulpits.[153] Smith's earlier plea for a spirit of charity toward German scholarship appears to have vanished.

Infidelity also had marked French spiritual life, with Renan the villain. In his "Theological Intelligence" column, Smith noted whenever Renan's *Life of Jesus* received "a good criticism"[154] and emphasized Renan's anti-democratic, elitist theories.[155] He reported (with seeming pleasure) that although Renan had been nominated for a professorship at the Collège de France, his lectures were suspended when he allegedly expressed skepticism regarding Jesus' divinity.[156] In the classroom as well, Smith faulted Baur,

Strauss, and Renan: the first two evince Pantheism, and Renan's system, "as far as he has any," is similarly derived from Hegel.[157]

In January 1864, Smith reviewed Renan's *Life of Jesus*, the seventh French edition of which had been translated in 1863. Renan, Smith charged, makes Jesus into a Romantic hero. Placing Renan's book among the Apocryphal Gospels—as Smith first suggested—rates it too highly: at least the authors of those Gospels believed in God! Indulging in a "poetic pantheism," Renan treats the "records of our faith" as if naturalism does not differ from supernaturalism, as if nothing changed when God became incarnate in history. If Christ's life can be understood "on the basis of naturalism, . . . then the battle of infidelity is substantially gained," Smith alleged.[158]

Only "the low estate of Biblical criticism" in France, Smith charged, allowed Renan's book to achieve such success there. A quarter-century behind, Renan exhibits no knowledge of German scholarship of the last thirty years.[159] Catholic clergy denounce the work, but have not the means to counter it. Renan's approach, Smith concluded, makes the central event in human history "a mockery and a delusion," offering only a "theology of despair."[160]

Smith on the New Testament and Earliest Christianity. In response to more radical European critics, Smith defended the authenticity and "genuineness" of the New Testament books—"genuine," if written by those whose names they bear.[161] As Christ's "companions," the Apostles had "ample opportunities to know the facts of his life." The "common copies" we have of the New Testament, Smith insisted, contain "what was originally written."[162] He appears to register only two categories of assessment: the New Testament books are either "genuine" or "forgeries."

Here, Smith's view of the utility of patristic literature comes to the fore: the Church Fathers authenticate the "genuineness" of the New Testament books. Yet, even if we were to grant that the Fathers were inspired (which Smith did not), we would concede only that they offer "inspired *testimony*." Appealing to the Fathers as "witnesses" who show which books were then received as carrying "divine warrant" differs from according them authority.[163] The Fathers may be considered a "sign-post" showing the way to a city, but are not the city itself.[164]

What reliance, then, should Protestants place in the testimony of these uninspired Church Fathers? Smith's answer: only so far as they give "credible witness" to which books Christ and the Apostles recognized, received, and issued as having divine authority.[165] The best Fathers (for example, Tertullian and Irenaeus) always made Scripture the final appeal; Polycarp, too, calls it the rule of faith.[166] The integrity of the New Testament sources is reinforced by the Fathers' citation of the Scriptures as "genuine."[167] The writings of Barnabas and Clement [of Rome[168]], Smith claimed, "fellow-laborers with the Apostle Paul," repeatedly refer to and quote from the Gospels as Scripture.[169] Irenaeus, Tertullian, and Clement of Alexandria refer to the Four Gospels, Acts, thirteen Pauline Epistles (including the Pastorals), I Peter, I John, and Revelation as "genuine." (Although Revelation's "genuineness" was contested, the book was received by Papias and Justin.) Some early Christian writers expanded the New Testament canon: Clement of Alexandria and Origen, for example, cite the *Epistle of Barnabas*, *I Clement*, and the *Shepherd of Hermas* as Scripture—but these works were later deemed not "genuine" (Smith referred students to Eusebius, *Church History* 3.12).[170] Tertullian's writings, Smith posited, "probably contain more and longer quotations from the N[ew] Testament" than all the citations from Cicero in later classical sources. Smith told his audience,

> In the third century we find numerous authors commenting upon the Scriptures; and still more in the fourth century, with catalogues of the number of Scripture books, translations made of them, harmonies, and commentaries published. So numerous were the citations, that from the Christian literature of that period, the whole, or nearly so of the N[ew] Testament could be recomposed from it. . . . *Why then doubt* the truth of God's word?[171]

Moving to a later period, Smith cited Augustine's statement that he would not have believed the Scriptures without the authority of the church. What did Augustine mean? *Not* that "the church gave authority to the Scriptures, but [rather] gave to Augustine his authority for receiving them."[172] This convoluted interpretation diminishes the role of the church's authority in the matter and allows the Scriptures to stand on their own authority. For Smith, that the New Testament canon was largely agreed upon and its books abundantly cited by the Church Fathers guaranteed the truth of its contents.

Another source of verification for the Scriptures' "genuineness" to which Smith alludes rests with pagan authors of the era: ancient historians

(Tacitus, Suetonius, and Pliny) "confirm the fact of the genuineness of the Scriptures." Even

> the early enemies of Christianity, Celsus, Porphyry, and Julian, acknowledge the existence, and the genuineness of the Christian Scriptures; adverting to them in their writings, and quoting them for the purpose of controversy and ridicule. No person in his right mind has any doubt of Homer's or Virgil's works being theirs; by reason of the constant testimony of Greeks concerning the one, and of Latins concerning the other.[173]

Our confidence in the "genuineness" of works by the pagan Homer and Virgil should prompt ready assent to that of the Christian Scriptures.

In contrast to "genuineness" stands "forgery." To suppose that the Bible is a forgery, Smith argued, "implies a greater miracle than anything recorded in the Book itself."[174] Although scribal errors may have entered in the transcription of manuscripts, even the most faulty manuscripts do not "pervert one article of our faith," and early biblical manuscripts substantially agree with the received text. Smith found a different, and advantageous, meaning to the German critics' claim that Christian parties warred against each other soon after Jesus' death: namely, they kept a "jealous eye" on each other so that no group could alter the sacred text.[175]

Smith nevertheless admitted that some period of time passed before the New Testament canon was established. Many early Christian writers, he alleged, quote more extensively from the Old Testament than from the New because the latter canon was "still somewhat disputed." He conceded that only with the heretic Marcion do we find "the first trace of a collection" of New Testament books, namely, the Pauline Epistles and one Gospel.[176]

Despite Smith's criticisms of Hegel and the Tübingen School's narrative of early Christianity, he appears to have adopted their approach on one point. He taught students that in early Christian history there is a movement from thesis to antithesis to synthesis: a Jewish form of Christianity (represented by Peter, the Ebionites, the Nazarenes, and the Pseudo-Clementine literature) met a form influenced by Greco-Roman movements such as Gnosticism. The resolution of these currents in Catholic Christianity, according to Smith, came *after* the Constantinian settlement. Only then does the Catholic Church emerge, that is, "the Apostolic Church so unfolded as to meet the wants of the Greek and Roman world."[177] Here, Smith sounded more "German."

PHILIP SCHAFF

Although we identify Philip Schaff chiefly as a church historian, we should recall that he lectured on the Catholic Epistles and the Gospel of John at the University of Berlin,[178] taught Bible (as well as several other subjects) at Mercersburg, and held positions in Hebrew Bible and in New Testament at Union Seminary before assuming the Washburn Professorship of Church History.[179] His approach to biblical scholarship remained conservative throughout his life.[180] His work on the American Committee on Bible Revision (i.e., revision of the King James Version), however, was not the arena in which his conservatism most fully emerged.

Schaff and Biblical Revision. Schaff served as President of the American Committee on Bible Revision in the 1870s and 1880s.[181] Joining British scholars, he and his colleagues labored for nearly a decade on this project. Schaff argued that a clear, dignified English translation would be a powerful check on "infidelity among the English-speaking nations." Had the Roman Catholic Church allowed the Bible to circulate freely, Schaff claimed, it would now be "better fortified against the assaults of skepticism and infidelity."[182]

The Revisers assigned to the New Testament began their task in June 1870.[183] Schaff's letters and diaries from the period detail numerous problems: difficult dealings with University Press officers in Britain; questions regarding copyright; strained relations with the British Committee; and, always, concerns about money (whereas the University Presses paid the expenses of the British revisers, the Americans enjoyed no such support). Schaff, as chief organizer of the American Committee, kept the Protestant reading public in America updated through speeches and newspaper articles.[184] In 1878, as his *Diary* charts, he traveled across America to drum up enthusiasm and funds for the project.

In May 1881, the Authorized Revised Version of the New Testament appeared, that of the Old Testament following four years later. Its publication was a media event: two days after the manuscript was received in America, newspapers in Chicago published the entire text that had been transmitted by telegraph from New York—the largest dispatch that had then ever been sent over the wires.[185] (The editors assured readers that "there is no change in the plot."[186]) On May 20 alone, 200,000 copies were sold in New York;[187] in all, almost three million.[188]

Schaff deemed the Revision "the noblest monument of Christian union and co-operation in this nineteenth century."[189] The American Committee had agreed not to publish for twenty years an American edition that would incorporate the textual changes rejected by their more conservative British colleagues. Schaff hoped (in vain) to live long enough to see the American edition.[190] His dedication to the Revision, however, did not lessen his conservative approach to New Testament criticism.

Schaff and Biblical Criticism. Schaff, like Smith, proposed only two categories for assessing biblical books: "genuine" and "fraudulent."[191] "Genuine" meant that the books were written by those whose names stand on them—for the Gospels, the immediate disciples of Jesus. To posit that the Gospels were composed later, by non-apostolic authors, would be to dismiss them as "frauds," a willful deceit perpetrated on believers. For Schaff (again like Smith), patristic writers' citation of or allusion to New Testament passages testifies to the "genuineness and integrity of the apostolical writings" and proves that the content of the books is trustworthy.[192] Christianity's "historical foundations" as given in the New Testament are "immovable."[193]

Schaff appealed to various factors to claim the Gospels' "genuineness." One rests on the claim that Jesus and his first followers knew Greek: hence there is no reason to doubt the apostolic authorship of the Gospels and the veracity of Jesus' words therein.[194] Jesus, Schaff claimed, spoke Greek, "though not exclusively," and the Apostles "wrote it with naturalness and ease."[195] If Jesus' disciples, "unlettered fishermen of Galilee," knew Greek [because they wrote the Gospels], why should not Jesus?[196] Greek served the apostolic mission well—like French in our day, Schaff added. To be sure, the Greek of the New Testament was designed for the common people, but this lower style was supremely proper for a "universal religion." No doubt is cast on the faith, Schaff insisted, because we lack writings by Jesus, although writing was not beneath his dignity: did not God himself write the Two Tables [the Ten Commandments]? "We do not crave a book-writing Christ, but one of sympathy and love," he concluded.[197] Thus Schaff sought to guarantee the "genuineness" of dominical and apostolic voices.

The "genuineness" of the New Testament books might also be called into question by the relative lateness of the manuscripts on which the received text was based. The oldest manuscripts, Schaff conceded, date only to the fourth century; we lack the Apostles' "original writings."[198] Schaff offered a piously ingenious explanation for why no "originals" remain: by divine arrangement, the New Testament books were first composed on papyrus (a material of short life-span) so that the loss of "the autographs of the apostles" would stimulate enquiry and prompt "a more thorough search for the spirit and reading of the text."[199] On this explanation, "genuineness" is not cast in doubt.

Affirming all New Testament books as datable to the first century also helped to secure their "genuineness." Schaff held that Matthew, Mark, Luke, Acts ("the best as well as the first manual of church history"[200]), James, I Peter, Jude, the Pastorals and (other) epistles of Paul were composed before 70;[201] only Revelation and the Gospel and Epistles of John were composed after that date.[202] Dating most New Testament books this early allowed Schaff to link them tightly to the inspired apostolic era.[203]

Schaff considered the Gospels "the inspired biographical memoirs of Jesus Christ"; his disciples' "reports" recounted "actual facts."[204] The Evangelists, as objective historians, he claimed, refrained from intruding their own views; they "modestly abstained from adding their own impressions to the record of the words and acts of the Master."[205]

Yet Schaff admitted that the orthodox theory of verbal inspiration could not account for the discrepancies among the Gospels.[206] These he explained as deriving from the Gospels' status as not "full biographies," but as "memoirs." Each Evangelist had selected certain features of Jesus' life and work "as best suited his purpose and the class of his readers." John, for example, omits many points (such as an imminent eschatology) that the other Evangelists include: he did not need to, since these were already familiar.[207] The four canonical Gospels thus present a harmonious picture of Jesus' life and teachings.

Schaff also affirmed the unity of the Johannine corpus and its authorship by the disciple John. John wrote the Apocalypse first, then the epistles, and late in the first century, the Gospel ("God's Love Letter to Man"); all share the same theology and Christology.[208] Were it not for John's writings, the period between 70 and 100 A.D. would be nearly blank. Some nineteenth-century critics, Schaff protested, have assailed the "citadel" (i.e., the disciple John's authorship of the Fourth Gospel): this for Schaff is "a question of life and death between constructive and destructive criticism." No second-century writer (such as Strauss and Baur had proposed) could have produced this "marvelous book," he argued. Are we to imagine that for 1800 years, deluded Christians have mistaken "a Gnostic dream for the genuine history of the Saviour of mankind . . . drinking the water of life from the muddy source of fraud"?[209] Such is unthinkable for Schaff.

Schaff, like most other Protestant colleagues of his day, downplayed the status of Jesus and the disciples as Jews. Schaff's Jesus is distinctly non-Jewish: he had no "repugnant or exclusive" Jewish characteristics that would mar his proclamation of a universal religion.[210] Paul, for his part, led congregations away from "the darkness of heathen idolatry and Jewish bigotry to the light of Christian truth and freedom."[211] As Chapter 7 will document, Schaff and the other professors held that Judaism and Roman Catholicism shared various features—an "externality," a reliance on ceremony and priesthood—that the spiritual, universal religion of Jesus displaced. Schaff's anti-Jewish tone, however, is bested by that of George Fisher of Yale, as we shall shortly see.

Schaff: Faulting European Criticism. Schaff urged professors to fortify their students against "the attacks of the infidel and semi-infidel criticism of the age."[212] He faulted the reconstructions of primitive Christianity by Renan and Strauss as "imaginative": early Christianity, he protested, was born into "a critical and philosophical age," not one (like the nineteenth century) of "imagination."[213]

Schaff generously credited Baur with revolutionizing the history of apostolic and post-apostolic Christianity, despite his overvaluing "tendencies" and undervaluing "persons and facts." Baur, in Schaff's judgment, had reduced early Christianity's "rich spiritual life" into conflicting tendencies of Petrinism and Paulinism, resolved in a Hegelian synthesis.[214] Baur and his followers, Schaff charged,

> ignore the supernatural element of inspiration, lack *spiritual* sympathy with the faith of the apostles, overstrain his [Paul's] antagonism to Judaism . . . , and confine the authentic sources to the four anti-Judaic Epistles to the Galatians, Romans, and Corinthians, although recognizing in the minor Epistles the *"paulinische Grundlage."*[215]

Unlike August Neander,[216] the Tübingen critics have no sense of a "living, practical Christianity." Baur, Schaff concluded, is "too philosophical to be a true historian and too historical to be an original philosopher." His school makes the history of doctrine nothing more than a dialectical process of thought that runs into Hegelian Pantheism, sundering early Christian thought from its "religious life-ground."[217] In Schaff's eyes, Baur made early Christianity seem merely like a form of Judaism.

Schaff objected particularly to Baur's acknowledgment of only four genuine Pauline letters,[218] his claim that Acts misrepresents Paul, and his dating of John to the mid-second century.[219] Tübingen scholars, in Schaff's opinion, "show great want of spiritual discernment in assigning so many N.T. writings, even the Gospel of John, to the borrowed moonlight of the post-apostolic age."[220] Radical biblical critics (like Baur) could never get a chair in America, "not even in the Divinity School of Harvard University," Schaff exclaimed—whereas they win professorships in Germany, Switzerland, and Holland.[221]

Nevertheless, Schaff, like Smith, adopted (in modified form) the claim of both F. W. J. Schelling and the Tübingen School that Petrine and Pauline strains of Christianity were united in Johannine theology.[222] Schaff's modification de-emphasized the motif of conflict and the notion of development *within* the New Testament books. Since Schaff believed that all New Testament books had been composed within about a thirty-five-year period, there was not much chronological room for development, in any event. Differences among New Testament authors do not reflect development, but only slightly varying viewpoints on the same historical given, the life and teachings of Jesus.

Both Smith and Schaff, however, extracted the Tübingen critics' theme of historical development for the study of *post*-New Testament Christianity. Schaff later credited Baur (whose lectures on history of Christian doctrine and on symbolics he had attended as a student) for first stimulating his thinking about historical development. Despite Schaff's rejection of Baur's views on the New Testament, he judged him the most able modern opponent of traditional Christianity.[223]

George Fisher

George Fisher of Yale took a more generous view of acceptable approaches to the Bible than many Protestants of his time: those who espouse Christianity's essential truths should not be "denied the title of Christian" on the grounds of their beliefs concerning biblical inspiration. Deviant opinions, however wrong or ill-founded, do not warrant expulsion from the fold of any who claim the name Christian.[224]

Rather surprisingly, Fisher argued that the Old Testament—"an earlier stage of revelation"—was *not* Christian Scripture. By accenting the "difference in times" between ancient Israel and the early Christian era, he avoided the need to explain, or explain away, what he considered the theological, ethical, and scientific "embarrassments" of the Old Testament[225]—but he hastened to add that he does not aim to detract from the dignity of the Old Testament. Revelation being progressive, Christians today can admit that the ancients had but limited knowledge. The New Testament remains "the touchstone": "the law was given by Moses, but grace and truth came by Jesus Christ," Fisher concluded, citing John 1:17.[226]

Jesus' first Jewish followers, like their ancestors, went astray on several points. They misguidedly looked for the Second Coming of Jesus[227] and his establishment of an earthly Kingdom. Jewish notions of the Kingdom encompassed an "externality" that later believers were "destined to outgrow, and finally to shuffle off."[228] Only later could the Kingdom be correctly conceived as a "community . . . bound together by a moral and spiritual bond of union," rooted in the human heart.[229] Fisher worried that the growing popularity enjoyed by the study of comparative religions might mistakenly lead his contemporaries to place Christianity on "the level of the Jewish or even the ethnic systems."[230] All in all, Fisher's downplaying of the Old Testament and "Jewish systems" seems in accord with his anti-Jewish remarks that will be detailed in Chapter 5: his notion of early Christianity's decline was strongly linked to factors he associated with Jewishness. The negative characteristics he ascribed to ancient Jews remained stamped on their descendants in his own day.

Fisher on the New Testament. The Gospels for Fisher are truthful but incomplete "memoirs," not "formal histories."[231] Fisher's approach to Jesus—one that seemingly owes much to Schleiermacher—appeals strongly to the subjective impression that Jesus made on believers over the centuries. The unity and harmony of his character convinces them that the Gospels' image is "substantially faithful."[232] That Jesus exhibited no consciousness of guilt, for example, prompts Christians to affirm that he was sinless, that he stood in a singular relationship to God.[233] Fisher, unlike Schaff, did not here appeal so much to biblical "facts" as to the subjective impression that the

Gospel accounts made, and still make, on the minds of receptive readers and hearers.

Like Smith, Fisher rested his case regarding the "genuineness" of the Gospels (especially the Synoptics) on their reception history: they were accorded exclusive authority in the church by the later second century, accepted as ancient and "genuine" by Irenaeus, Justin Martyr, Papias, and the author of the Muratorian Canon.[234] The similarities in the first three Gospels can be attributed to the Evangelists' "interdependence," and by acknowledging the priority of Mark. "German" views such as these are gaining ground even among the more conservative English, Fisher assured his readers.[235] Hence *some* German scholarship does not obstruct the faith of Christians.

Of particular interest to Fisher are the New Testament miracles. This subject had commanded considerable attention in college courses on "Christian Evidences": Jesus' miracles supplied (so it was thought) proof of his divinity and of Christianity's supernatural origin. Yet, as the treatment of miracles by Hume, later skeptics, and Rationalist New Testament critics became more widely registered, a more sophisticated defense was needed. Here, although Fisher joined his German-educated colleagues in calling for better "weapons," he appealed more readily to strands of German theology influenced by Schleiermacher.

As a student in Germany, Fisher had translated for publication an article by August Neander, prefaced by his own introduction, conceived as "a contribution to Christian evidences."[236] Reflecting Schleiermacher's more liberal approach to Jesus' miracles,[237] Fisher here posited that their chief value lies in calling attention to "the system of truth of which they are the heralds . . . confirming a belief which has been established by other sources of truth": miracles, in other words, do not *in themselves* establish the truth of Christianity, but support other "evidences." Indeed, Fisher claimed, few believers in *any* age were converted primarily on the basis of miracles; rather, they were first—and even now—won by the "person of Christ and the irresistible power of his presence." Jesus' miracles, "the natural and appropriate *symbols*" of his majestic doctrine, confirm belief arrived at by other means.[238]

Decades later, ensconced in his professorial chair at Yale, Fisher wrote several essays on this theme, including a four-part series for the *Princeton Review* on "The Historical Proofs of Christianity."[239] Fisher apparently wished to reformulate the teaching of "Christian Evidences," still a curricular staple in many American colleges. Although now espousing more traditional views on miracles, and critiquing the disbelief of Renan, Strauss, and some of their predecessors,[240] he continued to endorse themes from liberal German theology. The miracles, he here claimed, are of one piece with Jesus' teaching; although not standing as proofs on their own, they complement the "internal evidence" for Christianity's supernatural origin, namely, the consciousness of early believers.[241] The disciples' trust in Jesus' resurrection, he argued, cannot be explained in any other way than by an appeal to miracle: out of "the depths of despondency" they were transformed into "courageous heralds," willing to risk their lives to proclaim what they had witnessed.[242]

In addition, Fisher continued to emphasize that historians of Christianity study not the events "as they actually happened," but rather the *subjective consciousness of the believer*. Here, unlike Smith and Schaff, Fisher rejected attempts to argue for Christianity's historicity by appeal to the "genuineness and credibility of the Gospels." Rather, he claimed, *whoever* wrote the Gospels, we should look first to the *effects* of Jesus and his message, and second, to the internal cohesion of the details presented.[243]

Fisher acknowledged that although these arguments would not convince determined atheists, they might convince less implacable skeptics.[244] On this point, at least, he had gone some way toward "Germany." Yet he stalled in his treatment of European biblical criticism. Here, he appears as conservative as Smith, Schaff, and other colleagues.

Fisher and Modern Biblical Criticism. That Fisher was well schooled in what is now called "lower [i.e., textual] criticism" is evident from his 1881 essay, "How the New Testament Came Down to Us," a popular piece published in *Scribner's Monthly*. "Textual criticism has become a science," he wrote. In the last three centuries, scholarship in this area has advanced as much as in astronomy and botany.[245] With the forthcoming publication of the Authorized Revision of the New Testament in mind, Fisher explained to lay readers how the biblical text was assembled. He assured them that few textual changes—although some errors in transcription—entered after the late second century. Textual criticism leaves intact, indeed, supports, all the doctrines and precepts of Christianity. Fisher described Tischendorf's contribution, passing over any discrediting explanation of how that scholar managed "to carry away the precious discovery [the Codex Sinaiticus] as a present to the Czar Alexander."[246] In this popular essay, Fisher apparently chose *not* to instruct his readers on the "Higher Criticism" of the Bible, as developed by 1881.

Fisher on Strauss and Renan. Seventeen years earlier, in four long articles in the *New Englander* (1864) grouped under the general title, "The Conflict with Skepticism and Unbelief," Fisher had addressed the "Higher Criticism." The date of 1864 for these essays is no accident: that year, the first English translation of Renan's *Life of Jesus* appeared, as well as [in German] Strauss's *Life of Jesus for the German People*, a popular account that was published in English in 1865. Fisher's articles provided a basis for his book, *Essays on the Supernatural Origin of Christianity, with Special Reference to the Theories of Renan, Strauss, and the Tübingen School* (1866). He also rehearsed these themes in popular lectures at the Lowell Institute in 1876 that appeared the next year as *The Beginnings of Christianity*.[247] Thus in both scholarly and popular formats, he drew attention to the dangers of European biblical criticism.

Like Smith and Schaff, Fisher defended the "genuineness" of the canonical Gospels against Strauss.[248] Responding to Strauss's claim that stories of Jesus' miracles were myths arising from Jewish Messianic expectations, Fisher argued (somewhat inconsistently) that Jesus could not have been acknowledged as Messiah *without* them—but that insufficient time had elapsed between Jesus' death and the composition of written Gospels for a cycle of myths to gain ground.[249] Perhaps borrowing a point from Schaff, Fisher insisted that Jesus' era was devoted to history, a devotion underscoring the Gospels' credibility. Strauss's theory, he charged, cannot explain the Apostles' faith in Jesus' resurrection, and hence the rise of Christianity.[250]

Unsurprisingly, Fisher also took aim at Renan's *Life of Jesus*, which the reading public had devoured.[251] The "infidel" Renan, Fisher charged, makes Jesus a deceiver: "When the light coating of French varnish is rubbed off, it is a picture of degrading duplicity that is left."[252] Renan treats the Gospel narratives as comparable to "the lives of Francis of Assisi and other mediaeval saints." Conceding that Renan is "brilliant" and "not deficient in learning," Fisher faulted his "imaginative" presentation, "torpidity" of moral feeling, and failure to sense "the *holiness* of the sacred authors and of the revealed system of religion." Renan's *Saint Paul* is similarly deemed "full of vivacity"—but abounds in "numerous unverified assertions and conjectures."[253]

Renan, Fisher charged, skews the representation of Jesus and his teachings. He falsely claims that Jesus "enjoined"—not just "counseled"—poverty and celibacy. Fisher counter-argued: riches alone to do not condemn (Dives's fault lay not in his wealth) and Matthew 19's injunction to "become eunuchs for the Kingdom of Heaven" does not advise castration, but merely admits the lawfulness of celibacy when "spontaneously practiced" (Origen's interpretation and alleged deed is a "revolting absurdity"). Like other nineteenth-century Protestant advocates of "domestic Christianity," Fisher insisted that the Gospels uphold marriage and the family as "sacred." To imagine Jesus commanding his disciples to forsake parents is "preposterous."[254] Renan, in Fisher's eyes, has made Christianity's message repugnant, not attractive.

Fisher on Baur and Tübingen. Against Baur and his followers, Fisher's tone was sharp:

> It is very doubtful whether the individuals of our Teutonic race who attack the Christian religion [presumably Strauss and Baur] would know their letters, or would be possessed of any vehicle for expressing their ideas except in an oral form, if it had not been for the heroic missionaries of that religion which is thought to be so deleterious in its influence.[255]

Against these "Teutons," Fisher upheld traditional evangelical views on authorship and dating of New Testament books. The written accounts of Jesus' life, Fisher claimed, existed within twenty or so years of his death.[256] Downplaying differences among New Testament books and authors,[257] he denied that James and Peter were steeped in Judaizing tendencies. He cited ancient historians' (alleged) love of truth, the soul's innate desire for God, and humans' conviction of freedom and sin, as testimonies to the New Testament's historical veracity.[258]

Fisher vigorously upheld Acts as a reliable historical source, rejecting Tübingen's "strange, morbid suspicion" that discrepancies between Acts and other books reveal a conscious authorial design ("tendencies"). The strong moral spirit pervading the book of Acts, he claimed, supports the book's historical accuracy.[259] Tübingen scholars' penchant for pitting Paul's letters against Acts in order to question the latter's veracity is "without foundation," for Luke-Acts substantially accords with Galatians and other Pauline epistles. The Tübingen School's appeal to "tendencies" and "theological bias," Fisher declared, has now been rejected by critics of an "independent spirit," who affirm the trustworthiness of Acts.[260]

Fisher also scored the Tübingen scholars for decoupling Jesus from a "universalizing" Paulinism. They represent Jesus' teaching as so Jewish that it is scarcely distinguishable from Ebionitism.[261] Fisher countered that "Judaic Christianity" had been outgrown even by the time of John's Gospel and Epistles: "the teachings of Jesus had broken the chain of bondage to the Old Testament system."[262] Fisher also challenged Baur's theory that the Judaizing party discredited Paul's writings, which were rehabilitated only a century later. This scenario—derived, Fisher claimed, from an over-reliance on "the spurious Clementine Homilies"—could not have occurred without attracting the notice of Irenaeus, Tertullian, and Clement of Alexandria, all of whom appeal to an unbroken tradition of teaching.[263]

A third point of Fisher's critique concerned Baur's treatment of the Gospel of John. That Fisher deemed this topic worthy of special consideration is clear from his 1881 essay, "The Genuineness of the Gospel of John," well over a hundred pages long.[264] His interest in this Gospel is also exhibited in his later essay on the "obscure and insignificant" second-century sect, the Alogoi[265]—the *only* ancient group, he claimed, that rejected the Gospel of John.[266] Fisher, like his Union colleagues, held that the apostle John wrote the book of Revelation twenty or thirty years earlier (68–70 A.D.) than he did the Gospel and First Epistle.[267]

Baur had dated the Gospel of John to the late second century and understood it as a testimony to the reconciliation of earlier Jewish and Gentile "tendencies."[268] Opposing this late dating that implied the Gospel's "inauthenticity," Fisher looked to patristic "witnesses" to assist his case. A key element is provided by Polycarp: if Polycarp knew John, and Irenaeus ("no dreamer") knew Polycarp, then the chain of witnesses is assured.[269] Even opponents of Christianity (Celsus, Marcion, Basilides, Valentinus[270]) testify to the Fourth Gospel, while the Gnostic Heracleon wrote a commentary on it. If *they* acknowledged the Gospel, how, Fisher rhetorically asked, can *we* doubt? If the Fourth Gospel was *not* written by John, it must be considered a "pious fraud."[271] But the "sound ethical feeling" of that Gospel stands against this explanation. No post-apostolic text, Fisher claimed, can match John's Gospel, which "fills up the gaps in the Synoptical tradition." Its vigor and power, entirely lacking in the "languor" of the Apostolic Fathers or the feebleness of *I Clement*, shows that it dates to the first century.[272]

Fisher devoted much of his scholarly writing to the Judaizing parties (Ebionites and Nazarenes) in second-century Christianity. Baur's reliance on the Clementine literature had led him to imagine that a Judaic, anti-Pauline theology was then prevalent. In Fisher's view, Ebionitism—"an obsolescent system" that was struggling to maintain itself—had to be overcome, since it robbed Christianity of its "universal character and world-wide destination."[273] Since God's plan extends to all humans of every age,[274] a Jewish orientation had to be discarded. Baur's representation of early Christianity, Fisher charged, is no "historical divination," but an "arbitrary, artificial construction."[275]

Although Continental, largely German, scholarship on early Christianity received the professors' largest consideration, they also noted the major controversy that marked British theological discussion of their day: the controversy over *Essays and Reviews*.

Essays and Reviews

It was not only Continental scholars who incurred the wrath of traditional Christians. In March 1860, the publication of a volume of essays by seven British (mainly Oxonian) writers unleashed what has been called "the greatest religious crisis of the Victorian era."[276] Entitled—innocuously—*Essays and Reviews*,[277] the book provoked hostile rejoinders and occasioned two well-publicized trials. Of the American professors, Henry Smith of Union Seminary was the most invested in the dispute: he responded with a lengthy essay, "The New Latitudinarians of England,"[278] and often noted the book in the journal he edited, then titled the *American Theological Review*.

Published less than a year after Darwin's *Origin of Species* and in reaction to the Oxford Movement, *Essays and Reviews* raised troubling questions about the Genesis accounts of creation. Those to whom Darwin's tome remained impenetrable could understand the import of *Essays and Reviews*. The book also called for the established (i.e., Anglican) Church to loosen its grip on the universities of Oxford and Cambridge.[279] Many readers of *Essays and Reviews* thought its authors had undermined the truth of Anglicanism from within its fold.[280]

The controversy was fueled in part by the prominent positions held by several essayists: Frederick Temple was Chaplain in Ordinary to the Queen and Head Master of the Rugby School; Rowland Williams was Vice-Principal and Professor of Hebrew at St. David's College, Lampeter; Baden Powell was Savilian Professor of Geometry at Oxford; Mark Pattison was Rector of Lincoln College, Oxford; and Benjamin Jowett was Regius Professor of Greek at Oxford. Six of the seven were clergymen of the Church of England. Although several bishops called to judge the work proclaimed their high regard for the book's authors, the latter could not stand unchastised. Despite the writers' claim that each was responsible only for his own essay,[281] reviewers and bishops alike deemed the book part of an insidious cabal against Christianity's basic tenets. By early 1862, with many thousand copies in print, more than 8500 clergy petitioned Lambeth against the book, and by 1864, 11,000 had signed the protest; the Upper and Lower Houses of the Anglican Church met to judge the work and hand down condemnations.[282] The essayists, in the end, were saved by the Privy Council's decision that there should be freedom of opinion on matters about which the Anglican Church had prescribed no rule. It was, in effect, the state that rescued the authors from the church.[283]

The essays were widely believed to introduce dangerous German ideas—near-atheism, Rationalism, and Hegelian Pantheism—into the bosom of English Christianity. In addition, the essayists also raised questions about the scientific and historical validity of Genesis, the doctrines of atonement and eternal punishment, and biblical infallibility more generally.[284] Ieuan Ellis, historian of the controversy, argues that for many British readers, the novel aspect of the book was the centrality accorded to historical method: it was "a religious counterpart of those historically dominated studies (Buckle, Maine, etc.) which proposed to explain society and its institutions by their historical origins, an evolutionary process from lower to higher." This historical treatment "put the traditional doctrine of revelation in a new and unflattering light." Yet, Ellis notes, despite the essayists' appeal to history and development, they remained curiously traditional in affirming notions of eternal, unchanging truths and a static human nature.[285]

Today, scholars of New Testament and early Christianity might deem the essays rather harmless and less "Germanizing." For example, Temple claimed in his essay, "The Education of the World," that since Christians had now reached "manhood," they should decide for themselves the meaning and limits of biblical inspiration and the degree of authority to be ascribed to various books of the Bible. Temple also warned readers not to shy from the findings of geology, even if they implied that the opening chapters of Genesis could not be taken literally.[286]

The appeal to science also marked Baden Powell's essay, "On the Study of Evidences of Christianity"—the only essayist who explicitly evoked Darwin's *Origin of Species*. This author counseled Christians to divorce their understanding of truth from "physical things": in centuries past, astronomy had jarred Christians' understanding of the universe; more recently, geology; and now, theories of the antiquity of the human race and the development of the species. Modern Christians, Powell advised, might better abandon the scientific views of biblical writers, who did not rise above "the prepossessions and ignorance of their times."[287]

A third essayist, Henry Bristow Wilson, argued that neither the Scriptures nor the earliest patristic writings contain the doctrines set forth in the Nicene and Athanasian Creeds. The Church of England, Wilson claimed, leaves its devotees free to interpret Scripture literally or allegorically, as poetry or as parable, and to decide for themselves how to understand stories in which serpents tempt or asses speak.[288]

Some critics deemed Benjamin Jowett's essay, "On the Interpretation of Scripture," the most damaging. As a noted scholar of classical Greek, Jowett could authoritatively address New Testament philology. Yet he argued that textual problems (e.g., questions of variations) were *not* the troubling issue; more frequently, problems stem from interpreters' deployment of the text as a "weapon" for their party's view, or attempt to make the Bible speak according to modern critical standards.[289] As for recent scientific and historical discoveries, Jowett pointedly remarked, "the same fact cannot be true in religion when seen by the light of faith, and untrue in science when looked at through the medium of evidence or experiment." He counseled readers to abandon "a losing battle" over the creation of the world or human origins; they imperil religion by resting it on false geological or philological views. How, he bluntly asked, can religious truths, so important to human life, depend on "the mere accident of an archaeological discovery"? "Interpret the Scripture like any other book," he advised, and distinguish interpretation, the province of the few, from application, which even the uneducated can appropriate. He urged that study of the Scripture, just as of the classics, should be part of a liberal education. Unfortunately, ministerial students are mainly schooled to reconcile discrepancies or (in a jab at Tractarians) to adopt the "fancies and conjectures" of the Fathers—an unprofitable exercise, in Jowett's view.[290]

Critics were hostile: *Essays and Reviews* was deemed "a radical subversion of the faith of the Church of England," "infidelity made easy."[291] Critics veered precipitously between charging that the book's ideas were "old" (so no cause for excitement) or "new" (thus very dangerous, especially to the young).[292] Most commentators, whatever their line, accused the authors of adopting German historical and biblical criticism.

For example, the staunchly High-Anglican scholar Edward Pusey charged the authors with "random dogmatic skepticism" stemming from "foreign sources of unbelief," namely, "German unbelievers" of thirty years ago.[293] An editor (or contributor), writing in the *British and Foreign Evangelical Review* and signing himself "S.," claimed that *Essays and Reviews*, a "manifesto," had alarmed Anglicans more than any book since Strauss's *Life of Jesus* a quarter-century earlier. The essays are not "English," "S." complained. Hanging "like a portentous cloud over the Anglican church, blackening her whole horizon," the essays represent "the destructive theology of Germany, and the Hegelian philosophy on which the former rests." They are "tainted with the school of Tübingen, which may be called the Medusa head that threatens to turn Oxford into stone."[294] The essays cannot even be called "Christian," for the theory of development they contain lies "outside the pale of Christianity." "S." accused the essayists of jettisoning the truth of Scripture in favor of a (Hegelian) "ideal," of endorsing Pantheism (the human race, not Christ alone, is deemed divine), and of implying that the doctrine of the Trinity is not biblical. These "hollow and arrogant speculations of Hegelianism," "S." observed, were a reaction to the Tractarian movement's exaltation of the early church and "hoar [*sic*] antiquity."[295] In this latter claim, at least, "S." appears correct.

Henry Smith reviewed the book (in its second American edition) in his *American Theological Review*. Although Smith treats the essayists' arguments more fully than does "S.," his assumptions and major criticisms are largely the same. For Smith, Christianity, whatever internal developments have shaped it,

> has always aimed to be a specific, divine revelation, supernatural in its origin, announced in prophecy, attested by miracles, recorded in inspired Scriptures, centering in the person and work of the God-man, and having for its object the redemption of the world from sin. It presupposes a personal God, and anticipates a future state of reward and punishment.[296]

Like "S.," Smith linked the essayists with Hegelianism, German thought, Tübingen, and Pantheism; they repay "the debt which German rationalism owed to that English deism, from which it received its impulse." Yet while the essayists don German garb, they err in not pressing further, so as either to accept the radical conclusions of certain German authors or to discover how other German scholars had already answered their questions. The essayists had not worked through to a "positive position."[297] They had not, in effect, passed from thesis and antithesis to synthesis.

The Christian system, Smith argued, "as a supernatural and historic revelation," requires miracles.[298] The "philosophic unbeliever" (presumably like the essayists), by contrast,

> resolves revelation into intuition, miracles into the course of nature *plus* myths, inspiration into genius, prophecy into sagacious historic conjectures, redemption into the victory of mind over matter, the incarnation into an ideal union of humanity with divinity realized in no one person, the Trinity into a world-process, and immortal life into the perpetuity of spirit bereft of personal subsistence.[299]

Especially disturbing to Smith was the essayists' claim that the Bible should be "interpreted just like any other book," for example, a work of classical literature. Thus Jowett's essay, which Smith deemed the most "ingenious and subtle," is the most insidious: in the guise of rescuing Scripture "from arbitrary and dogmatic interpretations," Jowett "equally undermines all positive faith, not only in creeds, but also in the inspired authority of the sacred Scriptures."[300] Other essays (those by Temple and Pattison in particular) aim to show

> that the external evidences of Christianity are insufficient; that its sacred books are not specifically inspired; that the histories contained in these Books are to be judged as we would any other histories, and in many parts are incredible; and that the doctrines of historic Christianity are to be resolved into more general truths, into more philosophic and rational formulas.[301]

Smith also emphasized the tendentious relation between the essayists and the Oxford Movement. This book, he (correctly) claimed, represents a different Oxford from that "most opposed to Protestantism and Rationalism," that is, Tractarianism. Much of the "force and influence" of the essays "are found in their constant opposition to the revival of patristic, and even mediaeval authority in the teachings of this [Oxford] university. . . . Reason revenges itself for the degradation, which tradition would fain impose upon her."[302] Smith concluded,

> We must go forward with the church, or outside of it. We must press through the diversity to a higher unity. . . . For he who believes in a personal God cannot doubt the possibility of revelation, inspiration, incarnation and redemption, in their specific Christian import: he cannot believe that natural law is all, and that supernaturalism is a fiction.[303]

Smith's *American Theological Review* printed assessments—largely negative—of the *Essays and Reviews* with seeming enthusiasm. First announcing the work in February 1860, Smith tracked the discussion over the next years.[304] As his own lengthy review makes evident, his biblical conservatism could only minimally incorporate the Higher Criticism. Yet Smith cleverly turned Hegelian principles against the authors of *Essays and Reviews*: if they had pushed on through "negativity," they could have reached a higher synthesis.

Conclusion

Despite the American professors' own German educations and reading, they incorporated only limited aspects of European philosophy and biblical criticism into their teaching and writing. They remained biblically centered, evangelical Protestants. Considering their vigorous attack on much European criticism, it is notable (as later chapters will illustrate) that they accepted the Tübingen School's argument that early Christianity developed—yet they limited that development to post-New Testament writings. For them, the New Testament remained a static and unchanging foil, an "undeveloping" text, against which development in patristic Christianity was charted;[305] it occupied an entirely different category from that of the writings of the Church Fathers. The Fathers' importance rather lay in their "witness" to the "authenticity" of the New Testament books.

Today, biblical scholars would scarcely claim that Strauss, Renan, and

Baur were entirely "right" and the more confessional American professors, entirely "wrong." It is prudent to remember that in *their* time these professors were regarded as progressive, even dangerous, church historians. The history of the patristic era, to be sure, awaited a better integration with studies of the "Jesus movement" and earliest Christianity.

CHAPTER 4

History and Church History

It is sometimes said, that of all historical studies that of
Ecclesiastical History is the most repulsive.
                                        —Arthur Penrhyn Stanley (1862)

The winning of ecclesiastical history for science by
Protestant scholarship has been one of the triumphs of the
nineteenth century.
                                        —G. P. Gooch (1913)

Historical Studies
in Nineteenth-Century America

History as a distinctive academic subject, we shall shortly see, had a slow
and uncertain entry to American academia.[1] Hence it is not surprising that
its incorporation into the seminary curriculum was similarly halting. The
spirit of evangelical piety that so colored its teaching renders dubious the
above claim that "science"—in the German sense of *Wissenschaft*—had
"triumphed." Although most of the American professors here considered
had imbibed some newer, "German" (largely Romantic and Hegelian)
approaches to history, these they interpreted through the lens of God's
providential design. Moreover, older assumptions lingered on: that history
contributed to the formation of character and good citizenship, that it provided useful warnings against possible future missteps.

In this chapter, I first detail the development of historical instruction in
the American academy and seminary,[2] then turn to discuss how German

approaches to history inflected the teaching of early church history in the United States. In the next chapter, I elaborate how the contrasting themes of historical decline and development co-inhabited—somewhat uneasily— the professors' historical imaginaries. The professors, we shall see, straddled older and newer approaches to church history in ways that often appear quite contradictory.

History in the Academy

History as a subject was largely nonexistent in American college curricula until the later nineteenth century. Often relegated to an hour or so on Saturdays, instruction in history was organized around recitation from a textbook.[3] No advanced training was required: any teacher (indeed, any "cultivated gentleman"[4]) might listen to students recite.[5] As late as the 1880s, some college teachers considered a professorship in history a wasteful luxury; the subject, they argued, could easily be handled by an instructor in another field, such as classics.[6]

Nor was historical study, such as it existed, strongly differentiated by chronological period or geographical region. For example, the course that Jared Sparks initiated in 1840 for Harvard juniors on "modern history to the close of the American Revolution" covered the entire period from 476 to 1791[7]; its subject matter was largely restricted by geographical area to Europe and colonial America. (Regarding American history, which was largely neglected in the college curriculum, Harvard's Ephraim Emerton claimed that "one might suppose a knowledge of [it] to form a part of those innate ideas some philosophers tell us about, for all the effort visible to compass it by way of education."[8]) Special training in history and the entry of the historical monograph lay in the future of American education.[9]

At the American Historical Association's founding in 1884, only 15 Full Professorships and five Assistant Professorships in History could be identified in all United States' colleges and universities.[10] In that year, the reforming President of Harvard, Charles Eliot, speaking at Johns Hopkins University, decried the lack of attention to history in the academy. The great majority of the 400 American colleges then in existence, Eliot claimed, still had no admission requirement in history; indeed, most had "no teacher of history whatever." This situation obtained not only at "inferior colleges": prestigious Dartmouth had no instructor of history at *any* academic rank, while Princeton, with three professors of Greek, employed just one professor of history who also taught political science.[11]

The dearth of professional historians entailed intellectual isolation for history graduates seeking their fortunes. Across America, the students of Herbert Baxter Adams at the beginning of their careers were often the sole historians at their institutions.[12] In 1887, a newly minted historian teaching at the University of California imagined that he was living among the Huns and the Slavs, "the brethren of Genghiz, Kublai, Timour, et al."[13] A decade later, another former student of Baxter Adams reported from his post at the University of Kansas that he was trying to keep up his studies (and enthusiasm) "in this land of beef, corn, and hogs."[14] Just prior to World War I, Harvard's History Department—then the largest in America—still claimed only six Full Professors, three Assistant Professors, and two Instructors.[15]

The teaching of history was scarcely more specialized by the late nineteenth century than when Jared Sparks assumed his professorship at Harvard. At the University of Wisconsin in 1890, neophyte instructor Frederick Jackson Turner reported to his mentor that he was teaching courses on the French Revolution, Primitive Society, Dynastic and Territorial History of the Middle Ages, Constitutional History of the United States, and a seminar ("seminary") on the History of the Northwest.[16]

Until graduate education in history developed in America, would-be historians usually went to Germany for post-collegiate training. Late in life, Ephraim Emerton recalled his "shock of listening for the first time, as I did in Germany, to teachers of History who actually knew what they were talking about."[17] Younger generations, he mused, could scarce imagine the amazement of "an eager youth familiar only with the dreary routine of an American recitation-room [and Emerton had graduated from Harvard!] at finding himself day after day, face to face with scholars like Leopold von Ranke, Theodor Mommsen, Johann Gustav Droysen, Heinrich von Sybel, and Wilhelm von Giesebrecht."[18] The methods of instruction and general goals of the American college, especially in the teaching of history, would be challenged by German advanced education.[19]

The heavy stress on classical studies, including ancient history, in nineteenth-century American education has often been noted.[20] For example, students seeking admission to Harvard College in 1886 were expected to be familiar with Greek history to the death of Alexander and Roman history to the death of Commodus.[21] Not all institutions, to be sure, mounted such requirements: at the University of Wisconsin in 1891, the young Charles Homer Haskins learned to his chagrin that undergraduates were sorely ignorant of ancient history; most knew no Latin, and "Greek is of course out of the question with nearly all of them."[22] Although academic historians today may rue the prolonged stress on ancient history and the lateness of modern history's arrival in the American college curriculum,[23] this emphasis doubtless benefited students contemplating seminary study.[24] Moreover, since classics entailed work with primary sources, "going to the sources" was incorporated earlier in the study of ancient than of modern history.[25]

Church History in America

A church historian was not customarily among the first faculty appointees at early nineteenth-century Protestant seminaries in America.[26] Although the Seminary at Princeton hired a professor of ecclesiastical history and church government in 1813,[27] Union Seminary instituted such a professorship only in 1850, fourteen years after its founding (in 1855, endowed as the Washburn Professorship);[28] at Yale, the Titus Street Chair in Ecclesiastical History was founded in 1861;[29] and at Harvard, the Winn Professorship of Church History in 1882.[30] Lack of funds stands as only a partial reason for the delay. The subject, as noted above, was deemed dangerous, since it might lead Christian youth to doubt.[31] In addition, from around 1840 onward, the study of Christian antiquity was seen as troublingly linked to the Tractarian movement: over-attention to the Church Fathers seemed "Catholicizing" and could prompt "defections" to Rome.[32] At Andover Seminary, skeptics of history's value objected, how could "the mere *opinions* of fallible men [determine] the sense of the inspired volume [i.e., the Bible]?"[33] As we shall see in Chapter 5, competing notions of the church's decline from apostolic purity and of her subsequent development were uneasy bedfellows in the American professors' historical imaginary.[34]

History and Church History: From Germany to America

German Church Historians

As Chapter 2 detailed, the American church historians here studied—even Samuel Miller—used textbooks written by German scholars.[35] These German historians lauded the use of "original records," a practice not always in evidence in their day.[36] They stressed that historians must be impartial, must guard against bias in the sources, must be unwaveringly attached to truth[37]—although they need not abandon a "truly religious spirit."[38] (Impartiality, August Neander claimed, does not require the historian to "turn himself into a *tabula rasa*."[39]) From Mosheim onward, German church historians argued that scientific history links facts to causes, seeks connections and explanations.[40] Their desire to be scientific, however, did not preclude displays of Christian piety.

Neander most centrally stressed the theme dear to the evangelical Americans: that history, although a "purely human" phenomenon, reveals the "eternal and divine," the "higher government of the world," amid "the vicissitudes of Time."[41] History is not "merely the sport of human caprice"; "trivial causes" cannot explain great events and men.[42] The church historian must search everywhere for the "rays of light scattered through the darkness"—"darkness," since the Holy Spirit's operations in history are always obscured through their mixture with "carnal and undivine" elements.[43] Neander believed that too great a stress on the individual, the "great man"—or worse, on material factors—shortchanged the role of Providence in history.[44] But many decades would pass before historians became interested in the "little people."

Although Ferdinand Christian Baur praised the advances that German ecclesiastical historiography had made from Mosheim onward,[45] he criticized his fellow-countrymen's untheorized and pious approach. In his *Epochen der kirchlichen Geschichtsschreibung* (1852), he charged historians ancient and modern with inattention to the "*how* of historiography," and ecclesiastical historians, with a static reading of the church through time.[46] Most had no sense of an "inner principle" guiding historical change.[47] For example, Johann Gieseler and Karl von Hase, Baur alleged, had not kept up with philosophical developments (signaled by the movement from Kant to Schelling) that would have prompted them to look for the (Hegelian) "Idea"; their church histories lack a universal guiding principle that creates a unified vision by connecting and controlling the particulars.[48]

Neander's supernaturalistic notion of historical development, in Baur's judgment, failed on this point as well.[49] Citing Neander's motto, that "the heart . . . makes a theologian," Baur charged that his histories rest on a theology of feeling.[50] Historians must rather rise above "feeling" to the level of "Idea" if they would see the particular in the universal and the universal in the particular, the true theme of historiography.[51] For Baur, the very definition of church history is "the process of the self-actualization of its *Sache*, the Idea of Christianity."[52]

American Church Historians

American church historians absorbed a mixture of these notions from their German models and mentors. In Germany, the American professors-to-be learned that history as representation differs from "the past." They learned the importance of contextualization—although, to be sure, contextualization often provided the means to explain away disturbing features of early Christianity. Distancing themselves from a "great man" historiography, they still cherished older notions of history's utility in providing moral examples. Most centrally, they absorbed German notions of history's development, conceived on the analogy of a naturally developing organism that is impelled by its own inward structure. This view of history allowed them to argue that Providence (i.e., God) was always with the church: even the less salutary features of Christian history had some larger purpose. Amid the darkness, some light always shone.[53]

"Real historians," the professors learned, relied on primary sources, although primary-source analysis was not standard in American classrooms until late in the century. Also late was the introduction of the "seminary" (i.e., seminar) method for teaching advanced classes. The Union and Yale professors (although not Ephraim Emerton at Harvard) favored the German incorporation of history of dogma—that is, of ideas and doctrine as well as of institutions and events—into church history.[54] Last, from German scholars, the professors-to-be absorbed notions of Caucasian superiority that celebrated the Teutons in the westward march of civilization—a march that they extended so far west as North America.[55] Here, a theological notion of Providence joined smoothly with Americans' vision of their country's special destiny. The professors did not hesitate to embrace America's "exceptional" status.[56]

The following sections detail the assumptions regarding history in general and ecclesiastical history in particular that professors at Princeton, Union, Yale, and Harvard held and taught their students.

Samuel Miller at the Theological
Seminary at Princeton

Samuel Miller advised the "young gentlemen" at the Theological Seminary at Princeton not to underestimate, as many do, either the importance of church history or the time required to know the field; two or three months of leisure-time reading will not suffice.[57] How wrong are the secular men who imagine that a cursory examination of Mosheim or Milner might suffice for a minister's knowledge of church history![58]

"History," Miller taught his students, "is nothing but the *combined* and *transmitted* memory of a number of individuals—a memory, *defective*, indeed, and often *unfair*, but still a repository of information inestimably valuable." Ecclesiastical history in particular is "the record of [God's] Providence,"[59] the "development of the *prophecies* and *promises* of Scripture."[60] History, he claimed, is centrally important because it brings conviction that Christianity's origins are "real."[61] The Union and Yale professors, we shall see, likewise held that history is providential, and that church history should build on that uniquely privileged text, the Bible.

Henry Smith at Union Theological Seminary

Henry Smith, absorbing German intellectual currents, pioneered a new approach to church history in American seminary education. Smith argued that eighteenth-century Rationalism had exhibited a "contempt of history" against which nineteenth-century historians (himself included) were reacting.[62]

Smith in Germany. Smith's lecture notes from his studies at the University of Halle/Wittenberg[63] and the Kaiser Wilhelm University of Berlin in 1838–1840 are in the Union Seminary archives.[64] Although none focus on patristics per se, they reveal how in Germany the study of the early Christian era was integrated into the broader theological curriculum.[65] The primary expertise of Smith's favorite professor, the Pietistic August Tholuck of Halle, lay not in church history, yet Tholuck addressed some approaches to historiography that the young American would carry home.[66]

In Tholuck's lectures on "Theological Encyclopedia"—an introduction to all areas of theological study—Smith encountered the German organization of the theological curriculum. (Smith, Schaff, and others were to make versions of "Theological Encyclopedia" a mainstay of American seminary education.) Here, Tholuck defined church history as "the representation of the development of the church of Christ."[67] From this definition, Smith appropriated two important themes: that historians deal with representation, and that the church's history has shown development.

Church history, Tholuck taught students, should be considered an aspect of world history. He recommended wide reading in authors from Plutarch, Diodorus Siculus, Tacitus, and Josephus to works on the French Revolution; he praised Neander's *Kaiser Julian* as a model monograph. In addition to their study of languages, hermeneutics, philology, and geography, Tholuck advised students to learn something of anthropology (as then construed) and psychology (for example, Mesmer's magnetism). He also discussed books—such as Strauss's *Leben Jesu*—of which students should be aware, but which he strongly criticized.[68] We later hear echoes of Tholuck's approach in Smith's recommendation to his own students that they should study archeology as an aid to history, and read secular historians such as Ranke[69] and Gibbon (whose summary of the Christological debates Smith deemed "able"[70]), along with works by German historians Gieseler and Neander.[71]

When Tholuck arrived at the sub-field of patristics, he recommended that to learn the "spirit of the oldest Christian communities" students should read Tertullian's *Apology*; Minucius Felix's *Octavius*; the *Epistle to Diognetus*; Justin Martyr; Clement of Alexandria's *Who Is the Rich Man Who Will Be Saved?*; John Chrysostom's *On the Priesthood*; and (unspecified) works of Augustine. (That primary sources from the first three centuries are favored is typical of nineteenth-century Protestant curricula in both Germany and America.) Tholuck also advised students to read (in German) Neander's *Life of Chrysostom* and *Antignostikus* (largely on Tertullian); Carl Ullman's *Gregory of Nazianzus*; and Johann Möhler's *Life of Athanasius*.[72]

Tholuck's lectures on "Christliche Sittenlehre" ("Christian Ethical Teaching") also treated patristic authors. Smith learned that the ethics of Clement of Rome, Polycarp, and Irenaeus, albeit undeveloped, were "purely Biblical"; with the *Shepherd of Hermas*, however, "impure elements" enter Christian moral teaching. The Church Fathers' approach, Tholuck admitted, was "one-sided," since they had "first [to] concentrate on bringing down paganism"; thus their diatribes against the theatre and gladiatorial games, deemed the *pompa diaboli*. On these topics, Tholuck recommended that students read Tertullian's *De spectaculis* and Salvian's

De gubernatione Dei to understand the ethical problems that early Christian writers faced in combating paganism.[73] From Tholuck, Smith also learned a theory of the early church's decline, a topic to be considered in the next chapter.

Smith in America. Smith pioneered the importance of church history, which had been subordinated to theology and biblical studies, as a seminary discipline in America. "History to us [Americans]," Smith wrote, "is the driest of studies that we appropriate by rote learning; and the history of the church is the driest of the dry." He hoped to counter this impression. Rather than focusing on names and dates, "kings and wars," Smith claimed that history should be approached as "the unfolding of the moral, the political, the artistic, the social, and the spiritual progress of the human family."[74] Smith's successor, Roswell Hitchcock, later testified that Smith taught history "as it was then taught nowhere else among us."[75]

Smith recognized his students' ignorance of historical study. Americans, he charged, approach history only for its utility rather than for its "inherent worth."[76] He complained to a correspondent, "I do not believe that one in ten of the graduates of our colleges knows any historical facts under the true idea of such facts, or, in other words, knows what makes a fact to be historical." He hoped "to habituate the students to proper historical investigations."[77] Smith's assessment of his students' lack of preparation reflects the weak state of historical studies in mid-nineteenth-century American colleges.

Smith introduced his course in church history with a larger question: What is history? His discussion reveals the influence of his German education and reading. The word "history," he told his students, can be taken in two senses, as the events themselves, or as the *narration* of deeds and events, which involves "criticism of the sources and examination of authorities." To construct a history in the largest sense, one must know the facts, their causes, and the results stemming from them:[78] only then can church history be considered a science.[79] Many philosophies of history fail because the authors advance their own theories rather than letting history "explain itself."[80] Competing assumptions underlie Smith's words: the newer scientific approach to history that uncovers laws and causes is joined with a narrative history that "explains itself." Moreover, the high point of historical study appears to be the "philosophy of history."[81]

Smith's approach to history was thoroughly pious. "History," he wrote, "is the ever unfolding providence of God."[82] Through it, "we trace the finger of God, which overrules all events that transpire on the earth; and discover what he does through the free agency of man." From the records of the past, the student "gains an exalted idea of the Supreme Ruler, who displays his perfections in his dealings with the sinful children of men."[83] Affirming manifestations of reason and progress in history's course is essential for the vindication of Providence, of convincing even skeptics that "history has a guiding hand."[84] As "the very theodicy of God," human history is the greatest apology for the Christian faith, "the record of the progress of the kingdom of God, intermingling with and acting upon all the other interests of the human race, and shaping its destiny."[85] Smith's strong Christocentrism led him to view all human history as revolving around Jesus.[86] When viewed correctly, the "genius of human history is identical with the genius of Christianity." Besides, through historical study the student may absorb some of the wisdom of great men who have "performed their important parts on the great theater of life."[87] History is thus conceived as an enterprise directed by God, who enlists free human agents to carry out a divine plan.

Given this approach, it does not surprise that Smith sharply criticized John William Draper's *History of the Intellectual Development of Europe* (1862), a book that achieved considerable fame in that era.[88] Smith charged that Draper, like Henry Thomas Buckle, espoused a Positivist, Materialist approach to history, assigning all progress to natural forces, especially to human physiology. Draper, he protests, subordinates moral themes, restricts development to humans' physical condition, and imagines that this earthly life is all, thus discounting God and immortality.[89] Histories of human development, in Smith's view, should rather focus on matters of the spirit.

The purpose of the church's history, Smith held, is salvific: to bring the human race "back to union with God" after 6000 years of human "travail."[90] The church is the manifestation of God's Kingdom on earth, "a visible organization united for the worship of God and having the sacraments," "the economy for the redemption of mankind established in the world by the death of Christ." Smith stressed the institution of sacrifice as linking the Old Dispensation to the New, preparatory for the church.[91]

Scriptures, however, remained for Smith the norm by which developments in church history are assessed.[92] Since doctrine is derived from Scripture, doctrinal history's task is "to show how the contents of S[acred]

S[cripture]" have been reproduced in the church's history—in its heart, mind, and life—to meet its "wants." The history of doctrines reveals how far each system has progressed toward the "perfect reproduction of the substance of Revelation."[93] Although this goal has never been fully reached, progress consists in "giving the truth a new form adapted to the new warfare it is called to meet." In addition, doctrinal history enables us to compare systems, assessing whether our own confession's doctrine (i.e., Presbyterianism) is "better or worse than others:"[94] comparison enables judgment. As this book amply illustrates, the professors considered the delivering of value judgments an essential aspect of studying church history. For Smith, "systems" derived from Calvinist principles doubtless trumped all others.

Although studying church history (the record of her "rise and progress and various fortunes") is valuable for its own sake, Smith taught his students, it is also a "practical necessity" for those laboring on her behalf: it leads to a deeper conviction of past truths and forearms against heresies. It combines fixedness with liberality of mind, indispensable qualities for the theological student and minister. The subject may also aid in the reunion of the church's now-separated parts. Last, church history, he argued, may provide "right ideas of the true nature of Christianity."[95] Here, history serves as a key to essence.

Smith was particularly keen to convince seminary students that history of doctrine—or dogma, as the Germans called it—should be considered part of church history. Doctrine, more than institutions and leaders, expresses "the life and nature of the Church itself." This categorization of dogma, he informed students, was recently adopted in the German theological curriculum. Patristics and the study of the creeds are now deemed a subsection of church history.[96] The history of doctrine, in fact, is the "more important portion" of church history, giving us "the real internal life of the church"—although Smith conceded the importance of attending to the church's "external" condition (by studying, for example, geography, chronology, archeology, polity, discipline, church-state relations, and statistics regarding the church's growth).[97] Smith's emphasis on "doctrine," appropriated from Germany, reveals his Idealist understanding of Christian studies.

When Smith transferred to the Roosevelt Chair in Theology at Union, he argued that instruction in theology should be historically oriented: "We need more of the historical element," Smith told students in his systematic theology class. By studying the *history* of the Westminster Confession of 1648, for example, we come to understand its meaning for Presbyterians today.[98] History and theology should go "hand in hand." Reframing a Kantian aphorism, Smith argued that "theology divorced from history runs into bare abstractions; history separated from theology becomes naturalistic or humanitarian merely."[99]

In Smith's lectures and writings, we see newer "German" notions of historiography and the study of church history blended with the confessional, supernaturalistic approach characteristic of American Protestant devotion.

Roswell Hitchcock at Union Theological Seminary

Hitchcock on History. Roswell Hitchcock, who assumed the newly established Washburn Professorship of Church History at Union Seminary in 1855, was less philosophically oriented than his predecessor Henry Smith. He had, however, borrowed Herder's theme that each ethnic group had its own particular and ineradicable genius:[100] the Teutons were spiritual,[101] the Chinese, "intensely materialistic and utilitarian."[102] Hitchcock's classroom lectures were studded with statistics, with references to world issues, "other" religions, and social concerns of the day. He emphasized the conditioning (we might say contextualization) of various early Christian doctrines and thinkers. To understand church history, he told his students, you must know something about race, law, constitutions, economics, letters, arts, and more.[103] He also cautioned against the "doctrinal bias" that influences the interpretation of early Christian texts: "every man will find what he carries."[104]

History, Hitchcock claimed, is the problem of the modern age. Considered a science, that is, a body of knowledge subject to ascertainable laws, history is "our coming culture," evidence of a now-mature civilization. By modern standards, all ancient church historians fall short, being "deficient in scientific method." A scientific approach also excludes the "panorama" approach to history, so delightful to children. History for adults requires something better, which Hitchcock aimed to provide. His recommendation of scientific history sat somewhat uncomfortably with his belief that God is manifest in *all* history, thus making world history in its entirety sacred.[105] Describing Hitchcock's contributions, Philip Schaff claimed that "history to him was not a heap of dry dates and facts, but a development of the plan of redemption. . . . He found the footsteps of the Redeemer in all ages and denominations."[106]

In a wider sense, history according to Hitchcock is "the report of an evolution"; more narrowly, a report of *"human evolution."* Although the word "evolution" belongs to the vocabulary of organic life, he conceded, it can fruitfully be applied to historical studies as well.[107] History as evolution led Hitchcock to a consideration of historical development,[108] a topic discussed more fully in Chapter 5.

In his inaugural address as Washburn Professor, Hitchcock affirmed history as a solely human endeavor, pertaining to what is "free and finite." Crystals and "germs" of life are uni-directional, existing without conflict or the ability to pursue any different end: they *have* no history. Nor can God have a history. Rather, history necessarily implies development and a "law of freedom," in contrast to the law of nature, associated only with fate.[109] In zoology, a germ, a "something"—Hitchcock noted debates on whether an atom or a cell—determines what the animal shall be. But the distinguishing characteristic of humans, absent from lower forms of nature, is freedom, the moral factor.[110] Although humans lost some portion of this freedom as a result of Adam's Fall, enough remains to assign individual responsibility and blame. In sum, history is "the *report* of human development in all its stages, before and after the Fall."[111] Development, Hitchcock emphasized, characterizes *human* life, not God or inorganic matter—and history provides its narrative.

Human history, however, does share one characteristic with the inorganic planets: it proceeds through cycles. Governments, Hitchcock held, exhibit a cyclic development. "When despotism becomes extreme it goads men to revolt and evolution dissolves in anarchy and anarchy gives place again to despotism" (French history stands as a noteworthy example). In the religious sphere, cycles also obtain. Ancient faith decays into formalism, formalism provokes infidelity, infidelity by a violent reaction produces mysticism, and mysticism returns "to a sober robust faith." In human history, the circuits are all spirals, society advancing "like a screw."[112]

Although Ecclesiastes proclaims that there is nothing new under the sun, history's spiral movement *does* produce the new, under God's impetus. Hitchcock was confident that his audience would agree (since he was "not addressing atheists") that the law of history is one of progress. The Kingdom established 1800 years ago with Christianity has steadily grown, aiming toward "the promised millennium's" arrival.[113] Here, notions of historical

development met the millenial hopes of many American Protestants—
expectations that they strongly associated with God's favoring of the
"American experiment." Despite downward lapses in history's course,
Hitchcock argued, an upward turn prevails.

If development is one key historical principle for Hitchcock, crystallization is another. In the process of crystallization, Hitchcock explained to his
students, "certain substances under certain conditions arrange themselves
in mathematical forms—all that is needed is a nucleus." This law holds true
(albeit not so firmly) in human history as well: "the marshalling of men or
events about a strong will or a word."[114] The force of great men, however is
not predetermined—and always under the sway of Providence. Hitchcock's
efforts to espouse scientific history here appear to have succumbed to a
"great man" model popular in American schoolrooms for allegedly building character in youth. Yet, given his (and the other American church historians') stress on pre-modern history and ancient literary sources, it would
be unrealistic and anachronistic to expect from them a social history of
Christianity from the "bottom up." Providence, however pious a theme,
does temper a focus on "great men."

Given his emphasis on human will, it is not surprising that Hitchcock
favored historians who emphasized moral causation in history: Thucydides,
Tacitus, and Livy rather than Herodotus. Gibbon, he charged, although
"the greatest of historians," fails to expound the *moral* causes that sapped
the strength of the Roman Empire. By skimming over divine Providence
and grace, while "ingeniously" emphasizing the secondary causes of Christianity's success, Gibbon lends a "false perspective" to the record.[115]

Despite Hitchcock's more expansive approach and wider-ranging interests, his views on Providence and meaning in history were as confessionally
oriented as Smith's. Even so-called secular history, he informed his students, does not exclude God, for history is "God's day of judgment." Since
"all history has some Christ in it," God is in secular history "providentially"
and in sacred history "graciously, redemptively."[116]

In contrast to secular history stands truly "profane" history that
opposes Christian principles. Henry Thomas Buckle's *History of Civilization*
stands as an example. Hitchcock faulted Buckle for reasons similar to those
Smith alleged against Draper. For Buckle, Hitchcock charged, history is a
mere sequence of external phenomena, devoid of Providence. Eschewing
God, Buckle is left with only man and nature.[117] Indeed, many aspects of
Buckle's work might understandably rouse Hitchcock's ire: his insistence

that historians must look first to the influence of material (such as climate, food, and soil) rather than mental factors;[118] that the diffusion of knowledge, not spiritual forces, best promotes enlightened tolerance;[119] that Adam Smith's *Wealth of Nations* is "probably the most important book that has ever been written"; that Christian governments, through their "literary police," have helped to destroy freedom of press, squelching free expression on political and religious issues; that skepticism should be promoted to reduce superstition and intolerance.[120]

Hitchcock, a Yankee patriot, addressed American history and destiny as well. Once again, his views of national genius and race theory are on display. He accorded America a unique place in the grand sweep of the world's development. By the decree of Providence, he wrote, Americans are "in charge of the final theatre and the final problems of history."[121] Although geology holds that North America was one of the first continents to be heaved up from the ocean bed, it was "the last to be used in history." Why did Providence wait so long?

> Plainly it was not meant for those Indian tribes that were found in possession of it. They were not such lords of the forest as romance has delighted to picture them, but worn out Asiatics, who were here by sufferance to fulfill a temporary purpose, and then to pass away. Not by an eastward, but by a westward migration; not by Asia, but by Europe, was the continent to be taken and made a theatre for new experiments in history, to be accomplished by a new mixing of the human races.[122]

We now have in America, Hitchcock claimed, a new people to evangelize and a "new, vast Continent to subdue and save." This is our gigantic task, and we must not shrink from it.[123]

But will America last? Although the presumption has been that nations, like individuals die, Hitchcock claims, this is not necessarily the case. Nations are organisms, not masses of men, and none has ever died of old age. There may be some now in existence, he hinted, that may not die— unless they commit suicide. The conditions under which nations may go on living are four: they must have enough land in a temperate climate, be racially favored, of high morality, and have Providence, God's "good and gracious will," on their side. Then there is hope.[124] Clearly, the United States lay at the center of Hitchcock's hope for a nation that would neither die nor "commit suicide."

Hitchcock admitted that America, so recent, had been "unhistoric." Lack of books had discouraged the study of church history, directing American professors' reliance on German scholarship. But now—1856— Hitchcock claimed, America had advanced far enough that no special advocacy for historical studies was needed.[125] The United States had a grand role to play in human history *and* in the history of Christianity's westward march.

Hitchcock on Church History. Of world history, Hitchcock taught his students, church history is the "most vital part."[126] In his inaugural address, he warned that a professor might sink beneath the burden of teaching such a "multitudinous and rich" subject. Yet church history, Hitchcock claimed, is not chaos, but cosmos; simple laws govern it. Sacred history takes its starting point in the story of humans' Fall, which is not speculation or allegory, but "a well authenticated report of an actual occurrence." For more than 5000 years [i.e., since the time of the Fall], human ingenuity has fruitlessly exhausted itself in striving for self-redemption.[127] Atheism (in the form of "Chaldaic idolatry") provoked the Deluge, and this descent from true religion continued in the pantheisms of India, China, Greece, and Rome. Yet God worked throughout this history to prepare the world for the coming of Christ and his Kingdom, now "the grand and central reality of history."[128] As is evident, the far longer sweep of human history that soon would disturb the world views of evangelical Christians had not, in 1856, presented itself as the serious challenge that it would shortly become.

Church history, Hitchcock continued, seeks out the facts of this development, exploring how the church "turned away from the smoking ruins of the Holy City" [Jerusalem's defeat in 70 C.E.] only to encounter persecution by pagans. It looks for developments in polity, as the church "passed from Apostolic simplicity to the scarlet flauntings of the Papacy," from "unstudied prayer, to the Church of surpliced priests, and tinkling bells, and swinging censers." The Presbyterian Hitchcock concluded that Christianity's most "mature" and "best expression" to date is found in the Westminster Confession and Catechisms.[129] Despite Hitchcock's profession of scientific history, Presbyterianism trumps all other Christian groups.

In lectures on post-biblical Christianity, Hitchcock applied the exhortation to eschew bias in a novel way: by bias, he signaled an excessive favoring of *patristic* Christianity.[130] "We must not be deterred [from seeing the defects] by glamour," he warned. The glories of the church of the first three centuries, often considered its "heroic age," have been exaggerated. While Roman Catholics favor the first *five* centuries, Anglo-Catholic "Puseyites" rest content with the first *three*. Yet patristic Christianity in its entirety, Hitchcock argued, falls *below* present-day Protestantism in its biblical exegesis, its piety regarding the Person of Christ, and its knowledge of Hebrew.[131] Scholarly forms of evangelical Protestantism—especially the Presbyterian requirement of Hebrew study for ministers—chasten Roman Catholics' and "Puseyites'" misplaced reverence for the Fathers.

Despite his view that church history requires no special pleading, Hitchcock offered various reasons for why Christians *need* church history. As "religion teaching by examples,"[132] church history has a moral end. It is also necessary for a correct understanding of confessional theology, showing how creeds and doctrines were formed. Further, church history is essential for training missionaries for the Orient and for evangelizing "Heathen, Moslems, and Jews."[133]

On another level, Hitchcock claimed, church history serves a social-theological function: it puts us amid the communion of saints, the holy ones of former ages. It profoundly expresses the biblical claim [Gen. 2:18] that it is not good for man to be alone, as the sour and fanatical desert hermits of Egypt so vainly imagined. Having an ample charity toward earlier times will not make us "less Protestant," Hitchcock averred, but it surely will make us "all the more Christian." He urged American Protestants to emulate the example of August Neander, who could bind himself to future Christian ages "because he joined himself so genially to all the Christian past."[134] Christians of the present, in Hitchcock's view, can understand the social quality of their humanity more fully through a study of the church's history.

George Fisher at the Yale Theological Department

Fisher on History. George Fisher, while confessing history's providential design, emphasized its societal component more emphatically than did some of his colleagues. History, he declared, narrates the past events in which humans have participated,[135] reporting "the rise and progress of *culture* and *civilization*," the mutual relations of nations.[136] History differs from mere chronicle in emphasizing connections, causes, and effects.[137]

Faulting the older "artistic" version of historiography, Fisher noted that a newer sociological approach had been gaining ground, spurred by the French Revolution and the methods of natural science.[138]

Fisher attempted to accommodate the social approach to history by critiquing an excessive emphasis on the individual: Athanasius and Augustine, he argued, should not be taken as lonely geniuses, but "stand as representatives of tendencies of thought inherent in the nations or races to which they respectively belong."[139] (As with Hitchcock, Fisher's absorption of nineteenth-century race theory here worked to limit the appeal of "great man" approaches to history.) In contrast to biography, history focuses on individuals *only* to the extent that they show "the character and the progress of the community as a whole."[140] As "the biography of Society," history rightly portrays society as "the natural state of man, *contra* Rousseau and other eccentric philosophers."[141] Yet eminent men, such as Cromwell and Michelangelo, must be given their due; general laws cannot account for the historical force they exerted.[142]

While somewhat accepting of the newer historiographical trends, Fisher nevertheless retained a highly theological framework in which social history could be placed. Material and physical factors should not be so emphasized as to detract from this theological framework. Like his predecessor Smith, Fisher faulted Draper's *Intellectual History of Europe* for bypassing the "providential order and plan in history, which gives it its highest, its religious interest."[143] He opposed both Draper and Henry Thomas Buckle for their seeming denial of free will and Providence, and their over-emphasis on physical factors such as climate and food—in Fisher's view, the mere "machinery of physical laws."[144] Despite his critique, Fisher occasionally stressed geography's role in the determination of events: for example, had there been no Alps, ancient Rome could not have built up and retained its dominion.[145]

By contrast, a Christian view of history affirms a personal God who will establish a Kingdom on earth. It stands against not only Buckle and Draper, but also against the Pantheistic visions of Herder, Schlegel, and Hegel. Even *atheists*, Fisher claimed, admit some plan in human history, more wondrous than the order of the natural world. An example: Providence is visible in the Roman Empire's preparing the way for modern Christian civilization.[146]

Fisher circumspectly applauded German scholars' approach to history. They have taught historians how to connect "a thorough historical and critical survey of the field . . . with the opinions which [the author] himself propounds, and the arguments by which he supports them."[147] "Real historians," in other words, must advance and defend their own ideas, not simply repeat textbook accounts. They must weigh evidence, distinguish fact from hypothesis, and detect authorial bias.[148] In his inaugural address as the President of the American Historical Association in 1899, Fisher pictured the historian with the scales of justice in hand, quite literally weighing evidence.[149]

The study of the past, Fisher assured his students, is not an antiquarian operation.[150] Students of history must learn to judge people and events in relation to times past—but for Fisher this appears to mean that historians should make allowances for humans' conditioning by their times and circumstances. Old Testament laws, for example, should be evaluated in terms of the "obtuse moral perceptions" and the "debased condition" of people in that era.[151]

Today, Fisher claimed, scholars can better judge the sources for themselves: archives are open, documents are in print, and historians are more "dispassionate," "in quest of truth alone."[152] Yet historians' judgments are all too easily perverted by hero-worship (and its opposite, the desire to topple heroes); by their eagerness to offer something novel, even "sensational"; and by their lack of "imaginative sympathy" with the characters and events they study. Historians should seek to build up, not simply to criticize.[153] The high office of historian rescues those who have been unjustly defamed and strips the laurels from the unworthy: Fisher cites Tacitus, *Annales* 3.66 to underscore this point.[154]

Fisher appeals to race theory to provide illumination for humanity's historical development. Since history deals with human change, "savage peoples" who (to Fisher's mind) exhibit no change offer little material on which the historian can work. History requires records, whether written or monumental, and the "savages" who lack records are better considered under the rubric of anthropology.[155] Moving up the ethnographical ladder, Fisher accorded lowly status even to old civilizations such as China, whose denizens, in his view, exhibit an "ingrained, excessive veneration for the past" and are resistant to change. Up to the present, he wrote, the Caucasian "variety" of humankind has played the most important part in history; in the main, civilization and progress are the creation of "this dominant race."[156]

How did Caucasians come to embody the best? Adopting approaches to world history savoring of Hegel and Herder, Fisher posited that Oriental kingdoms, in which despotism held sway, allowed individuals no freedom to develop. Only on European soil, taking its cue from Greece, could the "true idea of liberty, and a type of mankind much closer to the ideal," arise. When we pass from Asia to Greece, Fisher wrote, "we feel the influence of the spirit of *humanity*"; it is from Greece that modern culture principally developed. Christianity represents a higher stage; by teaching humans to give their chief allegiance to God rather than to rulers unmindful of divine law, it indirectly sowed "the germs of liberty."[157] Yet all who believe in Providence hold that God's plan "extends over all of mankind and embraces all the ages of man's existence on the earth."[158] No one, in any era, is bereft of God's foresight and care.

Providence, for Fisher as for the other Protestant historians, was key: through it, order is made to emerge from events and "a worthy goal" attained, despite the "disorder introduced by human perversity." Like Hitchcock, Fisher affirmed that history's movement was that of "a spiral rather than a straight line"; some nations regress, sinking back into a lower stage of development. The meaning of history in the larger sense, he conceded, is not entirely manifest; affirming Jesus' centrality, however, gives to the whole whatever meaning humans can discern.[159]

Fisher on Church History. The task of church history, Fisher asserted, is "to describe the rise and progress of that community which had its beginnings in Palestine more than eighteen centuries ago, and of which Jesus of Nazareth was the founder." It recounts "the effects wrought by the religion of Christ in successive ages in the world of mankind." Church history, however, must be put into context, since secular and sacred history form "inseparable parts of one whole." Fisher claimed that he attempted to give a fuller secular, especially political, contextualization in his own *History of the Christian Church* than was usual in church history texts of his era.[160]

Fisher has little to offer on the historiography of early Christianity. Random comments on the topic are scattered throughout his writings. For example: the early Christian movement was greatly conditioned by the circumstances in which it began, namely, ancient Israel.[161] Eusebius was a truthful, if not especially critical, historian.[162] Recent historians rank above earlier ones in overcoming "party prejudice"; they no longer brand heretics "with epithets appropriate to thieves and robbers."[163] Apparently borrowing from Schaff the parables of the Mustard Seed and the Leaven as foretelling Christianity's development,[164] Fisher tentatively advanced an "organic" notion of church history, as will be described in Chapter 5. Throughout his very long term at Yale, however, he retained older views of history's providential design. The social and secular contextualization of church history must always be kept within a theological framework.

PHILIP SCHAFF AT MERCERSBURG AND UNION THEOLOGICAL SEMINARIES

Schaff on History. Philip Schaff was doubtless the most notable church historian in nineteenth-century America, yet in his fifty-year career, he passed from being hailed as an innovator to being faulted as unscientific. As modern historical criticism became more widely practiced in America, Schaff's confessional approach seemed (so Gary Pranger puts it) anachronistic.[165] His opposition to a naturalistic historiography that aligned history with the empirical sciences, Henry Bowden adds, was outdated by the 1880s, when historians in the wider profession were discarding spiritual considerations as inappropriate to historical study. By the time of Schaff's death, Bowden claims, confessional church history no longer commanded scholars' respect.[166]

Although Schaff conceived church history to be a science, his understanding of "scientific history" differed from that of empirically minded historians who dominated the profession by century's end. Church history, he wrote, emerged as a science when the church came "to reflect upon herself," a reflection prompted by the Reformation's critical assessment of ecclesiastical development.[167] History was scientific, in his view, if it traced a phenomenon back to its origins so as to locate its "essence" or "life force," and then chronicled its subsequent development.[168] A philosophical Idealist, Schaff believed that in the last instance, *"ideas* only" rule the world's history.[169] New historiographical currents that emphasized economics, statistics, and material factors he found wanting in "soul" and "idea." Schaff favored an older narrative-style historiography (with generous attention to God's providential design) rather than the analytic, problem-oriented history that was coming to the fore among European historians in the late nineteenth century.

Schaff (like Fisher) defined history as "the biography of the human race."[170] He was, however, warmer towards the "artistic" dimension of history-writing. The historian's task, Schaff explained to divinity students, is to "reproduce the movements of the past, clothe the actors with flesh and blood, and make them live their lives over again"—without turning history into a romance. As an artist, the historian relies on imagination as well as "critical acumen"; he "must look the actors in the face, and feel the pulse of events." History being "stranger than fictions," the historian should also develop a style that tells his story with "vivacity and freshness."[171]

Schaff's avowedly confessional approach to history was inflected with the coloring of Hegel and Schelling: history is "a *self-evolution of God* in the course of *time*,"[172] "the evolution of God's thoughts and purposes,"[173] "the ever-opening sense of eternal thoughts." Such views, Schaff believed, would gradually conquer the "revolutionary and negative spirit" characteristic of eighteenth-century historiography and "restore a sense of respect for the church and its history."[174]

Schaff's confessionalism did not, to be sure, preclude his endorsing the thesis that history concerns representation. History, he wrote, has an objective sense (the "what happened") and a subjective sense,

> the apprehension and representation in language of what has thus taken place in the course of time. [The historian must] surrender himself wholly to his object . . . reproduce it in a living way in his own mind, and thus become a conscientious organ, a faithful mirror of the past, making the representation exactly answerable to the actual occurrences.[175]

While embracing representation, Schaff seemingly assumed that the historian has independent access to the reality to which his representation should conform. Here, he did not reveal *how* the historian should become "a faithful mirror of the past," aside from endorsing older calls for the historian's truthfulness and fidelity:[176] he cites Tacitus' line that the historian must be "*sine ira et studio*."[177] "The historian's duty," Schaff wrote, "is not to make the facts, but to discover them, and then to construct his theory wide enough to give them all comfortable room."[178] Since facts are "out there," the historian embarks on a voyage of exploration.

For Schaff, sacred history should control its secular counterpart:[179] Christianity "forms the turning point of the world's history."[180] All events occurring before Jesus' birth were preparation for his coming, and all "history after his birth [shows] a gradual diffusion of his spirit and progress of his kingdom," the "development of the divine principle of life, which he

has introduced into human nature."[181] "My highest ambition in this skeptical age," Schaff professed, "is to strengthen the faith in the immovable
historical foundations of Christianity and its victory over the world."[182]
Secular history, he claimed, is "the theatre of Elohim, . . . the Father of
Gentiles as well as Jews," while sacred history is "the sanctuary of Jehovah,
the God of the covenant, the Lord of a chosen people."[183] "History is the
epos of God; Church History the epos of Christ."[184]

Despite such assertions, Schaff aimed to distance himself from a super-
naturalist history. Such a history rejects the idea of development, avowing
that doctrine was forever fixed in the Bible. Schaff, by contrast, pictured
the history of the world on the analogy of a living, developing organism.
He attributed the notion of history as *"living spirit,"* as a process of *"organic
development,"* to Herder and Hegel[185]—a topic to be explored further in
Chapter 5. Although Schaff disavowed certain aspects of Hegel's philosophy
of development, he acknowledged that it best expressed the notion of an
"interior organism" of history, of history as "the self-evolution of the absolute spirit." The guidance of *Geist,* which Schaff links with divine Providence, means that history is rational throughout.[186] Although humans do
not always comprehend the meaning of historical events, Christians should
believe that an intelligent design lies behind them.

Although this Christianized form of the Hegelian dialectic suggests an
optimism regarding historical development, Schaff conceded that along the
path of Spirit's unfolding, there were "many obstructions, retrogressions
and diseases caused by sin and error." Deviations occur because human
nature is "fallen"—and human nature remains essentially the same in its
fallenness through time. Throughout human history, Satan maintains his
role as antagonist, but is "always defeated in the end by the superior wisdom of God."[187]

Like Hitchcock and Fisher, Schaff linked nineteenth-century race theory
with a notion of Caucasian America's high role in human history. Not all
ethnic groups, he wrote, enjoy nationality, in that they lack the necessary
"community of rights and duties, of laws and institutions . . . of literature
and art, of virtue and religion."[188] Some cannot even be considered historical: Hottentots, Caffrarians, Negroes, and New Zealanders, in Schaff's reckoning, have to date "played no part whatever in the grand drama of
history." Endorsing Herder's theme that history and individuals develop
through the same stages, Schaff believed that the Oriental world, under
absolute power, corresponds to a person's childhood. Greece, with its free-

dom, represents youth, while Rome, "full of calculation and action," manhood. The era since the advent of Christianity, old age, surpasses all others
in reason and virtue.[189] History, Schaff claimed, "pursues the course of the
sun from East to West." Rising in the Orient, it marched on to Greece and
Rome; then, during the Reformation, to Germany and England; and last,
to the "Northern portion of the New World." History—now hypostasized
as an actor—proceeds with foresight, preparing future developments before
it abandons the old ones; thus Europe, although "weary of life," still lives
on to send forth her people to America.[190] Adopting Herder's notion of the
genius of particular peoples, Schaff proclaimed that America, too, was set
to develop its own nationality.[191] America, he believed, is "Immanuel's land
for all time to come."[192]

Schaff on Church History. The church's history, like history generally, exhibits an organic development.[193] The task of church historians is to display,
with artistry, this organic development as a "living process," to bring out
the "soul" of their subject. Studying church history, Schaff believed, has the
same effect as foreign travel: it "destroys prejudice, enlarges the horizon,
liberalizes the mind, and deepens charity."[194] Church history offers a "running commentary on Christ's twin parables of the mustard seed and the
leaven (Matt. 13: 31–33), and of his parting promise to his disciples, 'Behold,
I am with you all the days even unto the end of the world' (Matt. 28:20)."[195]

Schaff's optimistic view was counterbalanced by his claim that the history of Christianity also includes the history of Anti-Christ—yet, in the
end, all corruptions would surely be made to serve the cause of truth and
holiness.[196] This conviction underlay Schaff's oft-stated claim that Providence (i.e., God) brings good out of seemingly evil historical events. Examples of this claim are abundant in the chapters to follow.

Church history is confessionally and theologically defined for Schaff.[197]
It "exhibits the rise and progress of the kingdom of God from the beginning
to the present time." It is "the backbone of theology on which it rests, and
the storehouse from which it derives its supplies." Among its practical values is its ability to warn, encourage, console, and counsel; it reveals that
Christ is continually present with his people.[198]

The best scholarship on church history, Schaff held, exhibits a "spirit of
catholicity," an "*impartiality* and *freedom from prejudice*" that rises above
"*party or confession.*" Impartiality, however, is not "indifferentism."[199]
Adapting Terence's line to a Christian purpose, Schaff urges church histori-

ans to declaim, *"Christianus sum, nihil Christiani a me alienum puto."* Unbelievers who write church histories, in Schaff's view, produce a "repulsive caricature," "at best a lifeless statue." To understand historical development correctly, historians must wholeheartedly espouse "a right view of positive Christianity."[200] Here, German Protestants have taken the lead. Indeed, for the last three centuries, they have been the primary authors of church history manuals.[201] Although Schaff faulted the new German scholarship as "often arbitrary and untenable"—he appears to have in mind the Tübingen School—it had, he admitted, "done good service by removing old prejudices." It offered "a comprehensive and organic view of the living process and gradual growth of ancient Christianity in its distinctive character."[202]

"Partisan and sectarian interests," to be sure, have distorted and misrepresented the church's history from early times. In Christian antiquity, orthodox and heretical historians rarely did justice to each other's positions. In recent centuries, the "war between Romanists and Protestants" is reflected in their historiography. One exception escapes Schaff's critique: the New Testament as a historical source does not distort. The Gospels and Acts of the Apostles—"the best as well as the first manual of church history"—provide a true picture of primitive Christianity.[203] It is not merely that the New Testament should be spared the kind of historical criticism employed in studying other ancient documents: Schaff implies that even if critical scholars *were* so impious as to lay hands on those inspired Scriptures, they would conclude that there is nothing to critique.

Americans, in Schaff's view, had struggled to develop skills that might feebly approximate—although they could not rival—those of European historians. He blamed Americans' deficient knowledge of history largely on their Puritan heritage, "unhistorical in its very constitution."[204] If Ambrose, Athanasius, Cyprian, Irenaeus, Clement, and Polycarp could rise from their graves and be transported to Puritan New England, he imagined, they would not recognize the Christianity they there encountered. In fact, they would think it more congenial to the heretics and schismatics of their own time than to the orthodox![205]

Schaff acknowledged that historians have differing talents: some, he wrote, are miners, others are manufacturers, and still others are retailers who popularize.[206] He does not here reveal in which occupational stratum he placed himself, although he never claimed to be a "miner," digging out hitherto unknown sources. It is rather his important services as a "manu-facturer" or a "retailer" that we appreciate still today.

EPHRAIM EMERTON AT HARVARD DIVINITY SCHOOL

Church History at Harvard Before Emerton. Before Ephraim Emerton assumed the Winn Professorship of Ecclesiastical History at Harvard in 1882, various instructors connected with the theological faculty taught the subject. His immediate predecessor, Joseph Henry Allen, claimed that history mainly concerned "moral forces, . . . ethical passion." Allen eschewed newer currents that stressed either philosophy of history or (alternatively) history as a science, since these omit the most important factor, "the lives and thought of individual men." History studied as science, he charged, "tends to degenerate to anthropology." The value of history as a subject rather lies in "its appeal to the imagination," in "its education of the moral sense."[207]

With Emerton's appointment, President Charles Eliot of Harvard hoped to establish the study of church history on a new basis at that institution.[208] Indeed, of the major professors I here discuss, only Emerton eschewed a confessional approach,[209] doubtless influenced both by his Unitarianian-ism[210] and by his German doctoral training as a medieval historian, not as a theologian.[211] Unlike the Union and Yale professors, Emerton never attended divinity school. His appointment as Winn Professor of Ecclesiastical History, moreover, was meant to serve the wider University, not Divinity students alone.

Emerton on History. Emerton endorsed J. G. Droysen's claim that the object of historical study is "to understand by investigation" ("forschend zu verstehen").[212] History should *not* be approached as the "story of the Divine Revelation." History, he told his students, "concerns itself *only* with human actions, motives and interpretations."[213] History teaches us about "causal sequence," about "the absolute certainty of cause and effect." Not "a recital of marvels, it is the unfolding of a law." Historians, he insisted, do not need miracles or revelations, or "the dictations of any authority whatsoever, but more documents and better authenticated ones."[214]

Emerton also critiqued the "big break" approach to history, which plots dramatic and sudden changes. Rather, movements gather force because a receptivity is present. Luther, for example, was not "the originator of the reforming impulse but . . . its mouthpiece." It would greatly advance the study of church history, Emerton stated, if historians looking at crisis moments gave "due weight to those conditions of receptivity in the community at large by which the success of the new idea has been determined."[215]

Emerton on Church History. Emerton defined church history, a subdivision of general history, as "the record of the actions of men grouped together under the form of the Christian Church." Although traditional Christians consider church history "a record of the divine dispensation," they think this of *all* human history; the history of the church offers nothing special. Although, Emerton announced, he would teach his students about the history of the church from the human point of view, he nevertheless granted that any who wished might "reverence its divine origin."[216] Emerton's fellow church historians had sometimes voiced similar sentiments, but they did not (as we have seen) often incorporate them in practice. With Emerton, the limitation of church history to the realm of human forces is better realized. Here, "historical consciousness"[217] is more fully displayed, as Providence makes an exit.

The Christian church as an organization, Emerton insisted, must be judged by the same rules as all other organizations. Church history, like all history, studies its subject as an *institution:*[218] thus Emerton signaled his interest in institutions, not doctrine. He advised his students to read Edwin Hatch's Bampton lectures of 1880, *The Organization of the Early Christian Churches*, a work that stressed the derivation of early ecclesiastical organization largely from secular models.[219] So strong was Emerton's sense of institutional history that he tended to dismiss the writings of the first three centuries of Christianity ("pre-Eusebius") as *not* church history, but simply as doctrinal literature. Yet even Eusebius and his successors, he claimed, wrote "very poor histories, inaccurate, prejudicial tomes and narrow."[220]

Emerton was more sensitive than his counterparts to the bias of ancient writers. Much of our knowledge of Roman antiquity, he told students, is taken from literary texts written by the upper classes. "Is it safe to trust what the best minds of any age say about the state of religion among the masses," he asked? Cicero, Tacitus, Pliny look on religion with elite scholarly eyes, representing it as in "deep decay." They mock the practices of Roman religion, such as augury, as well as its mythology. If we were to derive our view of Roman religion from such writers alone, Emerton claimed, we would deem it "pretty thoroughly undermined." Monuments, inscriptions, and other material remains provide a different picture. Trusting Roman moralists' depictions of social conditions at the time of Christianity's inception is not judicious. As for the history of ancient Judaism, only recently, he noted, has that subject begun to be studied with the same assumptions and methods as other branches of history.[221]

Emerton rejected the older moralizing view that Christianity came into a pagan world teeming with superstition and sin. In his account, that world was rather "teeming with efforts after spiritual religion." Early Christianity should be pictured as "one among a group of rival claimants for the allegiance of an eagerly expectant world"; the "age of Justin Martyr," he reminded his audience, "was the age also of Marcus Aurelius." He set himself against the theory of the "great man or movement" that brings forth something completely unknown and unanticipated. In brief, the study of church history should employ the same methods and rules of evidence that Emerton claimed had now become the accepted norm in all other branches of historical research.[222]

Despite his Unitarian allegiance, Emerton took a sympathetic approach to those early Christians (such as the Stylites) who engaged in practices that he and others of his day would scorn: "We must try to judge men and institutions by the use they had in the day in which they belonged, not by the use they might have for us in these better times," he advised.[223] "Function" here appears to be the operative concept.

Emerton claimed that historical studies, after biblical studies, were the most important aspects of theological education. Only by these, he advised, can the Protestant ministry "prepare itself for the insidious attacks of an aggressive institutionalism on the one hand [presumably Roman Catholicism] and a self-sufficient individualism on the other."[224] *All* branches of theological study are to be considered historical, including language study and theology, since every theology is "*somebody's* theology."[225]

In his inaugural address ("The Study of Church History") as Winn Professor in 1882,[226] Emerton challenged those (such as, we might note, professors at Union) who have adopted the German model of subsuming church history under the rubric of historical *theology*: is not history an independent subject on its own? Emerton wished that under his tutelage, ecclesiastical history at Harvard would be viewed as "a department of historical rather than of theological science." One sign that church historians were theologians in disguise was their penchant for tracing the beginnings of the church from the ancient Jews to the New Testament: this chain of reasoning, Emerton objected, is theological, not historical.[227] Church history, he claimed, does *not* encompass the Bible—especially not the portions devoted to the ancient Hebrews.

Late in life, as President of the American Society of Church History, Emerton summarized his guiding approach to the subject. In church history, one does not get to the "thing itself," something superhuman or miraculous: such are theological confessions. Rather, the church historian studies "the *experiences of men* organized under the form of the Christian Church"—that is, human beliefs and practices.[228] Church history, he claimed, is "one chapter in that continuous record of human affairs," of history in general. He gently mocked those who imagined that at some moment time stood still, Christianity entered, and then time moved on "under radically new conditions." He cited an unnamed church historian who declared that at the decisive moment of Christianity's origin, "the controlling hand intervened"—to which Emerton wryly asked, "whose hand was managing the universe in the off times?" That pilloried author, who understood the church historian's task as following "the golden thread of the divine presence in all Christian ages," must (in Emerton's view) have fancied his occupation to be "not that of the investigator, but that of the certified pilot." Emerton himself confessed ignorance of that "golden thread of the divine presence"; just tally up all the rival claims for identifying that "thread," he advised.[229]

More than the other professors here surveyed, Emerton moved the study of church history from its confessional orientation to an academic discipline that began to resemble the History of Christianity. That he wrote little about early Christian history is to be regretted by those (such as myself) seeking to chart the development of a discipline in American academia.[230]

Conclusion

Given the state of historical instruction and the inadequacy of books and libraries in America, forging new approaches to historical study in American seminaries was difficult. German scholarship had taught the five professors, "post-Miller," to look to primary sources and contextualization, to view history as an organic process, to engage the past with intellectual sympathy. These currents grated uneasily against notions dear to American Protestants regarding the incomparability of the New Testament and the fixity of Christian truth from the time of Jesus and the Apostles. The professors likewise (Emerton excepted) assumed that the New Testament was not a text that could be compared with any other: as the inspired Word of God, it retained a unique status. Only Christian history after the New Testament developed in the sense of being liable to change. The traditional Protestant assumption that the pure religion of Jesus had suffered a decline from the first century to the sixteenth was challenged by notions of the church's "organic development." The professors' attempt to reconcile decline and development in history is the topic to which I next turn.

Development and Decline: Challenges to Historiographical Categories

Piety is always declining.

—Roswell D. Hitchcock (1883)

If you wish . . . to understand German thought I will furnish
you a key to it in one word. The word is "*Entwicklung*"
—DEVELOPMENT.

—August Tholuck to George Prentiss (1839)

Did the early church develop or did it decline? This question occupied nineteenth-century German and American church historians years before Charles Darwin and Herbert Spencer were to trouble their intellectual worlds with other, but similarly disturbing, notions of development.[1] Decline, on the other hand, was a theme to which American Protestants warmed: the post-apostolic church had abandoned Jesus' lofty spiritual message with distressing alacrity. Since the New Testament stood as the apex of Christianity, how could the patristic era *not* represent decline? Church historians of the Enlightenment era, despite their endorsement of human dignity and progress, did little to thwart the ascription of early Christianity's downward slide; moreover, their static understanding of human nature left little room to chart movement. Nineteenth-century historians and philosophers, by contrast, embraced notions of historical development and human difference.

Assessing historical events in terms of their decline or development rests on ideological assumptions. *Both* notions served as ready vehicles for ideological elaboration: development was necessary to justify the emergence of Protestantism; decline, to signal the woeful state of Roman Catholicism. Yet the American Protestant professors who had studied in Germany learned to find some small redeeming moments of grace even amid the "Catholic" developments of late antiquity and the early Middle Ages. Their unsteady veering between a historiography based on decline and one based on development illustrates their own uncertain placement between traditional Protestant assumptions and newer German historiographical theories.

Development and Decline in German Historiography

Nineteenth-century German church historians countered the theme of the church's declension from apostolic purity with an appeal to a Hegelian-inspired *Geist* (rescripted as "Providence") that spiraled its way upward through time. In addition, Herder's claim that each *Volk* manifested, in its time and place, a particular genius suggested that cultural *difference* might be celebrated rather than faulted.[2] Herder's emphasis on the particularity of cultures stood against Enlightenment universalism and encouraged attention to historical specificity.[3] When these motifs were appropriated by church historians, the periods of the church's history that Protestants viewed as "dark"—namely, those from the post-apostolic era to the Protestant Reformation, with the anti-Pelagian Augustine and the proto-Protestant Waldensians providing brief intermissions—could be mined to show evidence of divine purpose.

As cited above, in 1839, Professor Friedrich August Tholuck of Halle told an American student (George Prentiss, later a professor at Union Seminary) that one word alone provided the key to understanding German thought: *"Entwicklung"* ("development").[4] The starkness of Tholuck's claim impressed itself on Prentiss. Three years later, Prentiss was still puzzling over whether the notion of historical development could find a place in American thought. He queried his friend Henry Smith: how many Americans understand the import of *Entwicklung*? Will not a long time pass before the idea takes hold of "our national, or even our literary mind"?[5]

Prentiss predicted correctly. To traditional American Protestants, historical development suggested an overly generous assessment of patristic and medieval Christianity that betokened "Catholicizing," or at the very

least, high-churchmanship. Yet a few philosophically adept professors, such
as Smith, cautiously appropriated "*Entwicklung*" to express God's providential guidance of *all* historical periods, while German-educated historian
Philip Schaff more robustly adopted the theme of the church's "organic
development."

Development, however, did not overtake decline as the reigning para-
digm for the study of early Christian history even in *German* evangelical
circles. Judging from the lecture notes that Smith took in Tholuck's courses
at Halle in the late 1830s,[6] the motif of decline was still prominent. Both
Platonic and "Judaizing" currents, Tholuck claimed, proved detrimental to
early Christianity: the former disparaged materiality, while the latter promoted an erroneous notion of "works" (*opus operatum*) and ritual law.[7]
Here, the elision of Judaism and Catholicism—a rhetoric that we shall frequently encounter—is noteworthy. "*Entwicklung*" did not find an easy
berth in Tholuck's lectures on early Christianity, even in the very years in
which he designated it the key to German thought.

Johann Mosheim and Johann Gieseler: Decline

Positive assessments of the patristic era were also slow to find a place in the
German textbooks that were first available to the American professors.[8]
Those by Johann Mosheim and Johann Gieseler incorporate a strong rhetoric of decline.[9] Only with August Neander's *Histories* does that era receive
a more positive assessment—and "*Entwicklung*" a more welcome home.
Some, in fact, deemed Neander entirely *too* accommodating in his generous
exposition of patristic Christianity.

Writing in the mid-eighteenth century, Mosheim charted the church's
decline in theology, government, worship, biblical interpretation, and
ascetic practice. When "the sacred writings" were considered "the only rule
of faith"—so goes Mosheim's tale—Christianity preserved its "native
purity."[10] But soon "the darkness of a vain philosophy" (Origen, the head
of a "speculative tribe," here stands as chief culprit) clouded the "beautiful
simplicity" of Christian teaching[11] and encouraged heretics of various
stripes (Gnostics, Manicheans, and Messalians).[12]

Decline also affected ecclesiastical orders. The original "perfect equality" among bishops degenerated by the third or fourth centuries, Mosheim
charged, when bishops of Rome began to amass greater power for them-

selves.[13] Then the clergy "abandoned themselves to the indolence and deli-
cacy of an effeminate and luxurious life," while the piety and virtue of the
laity simultaneously drooped.[14] In addition, rituals and rites increased—
probably to accommodate Jewish and heathen prejudices, Mosheim speculated. Sermons degenerated from their "ancient simplicity," and prayers
into "bombast."[15] Allegory, borrowed from Platonists, darkened Scripture
with "idle fictions" and "far-fetched" interpretations.[16] How, given these
manifestations of deterioration, could modern Christians "blindly follow
the decisions of antiquity"?[17] Although nineteenth-century evangelical professors deplored Mosheim's cool Rationalism, his views on decline sat comfortably with "pre-Neander" historiography.

Johann Gieseler, writing decades after Mosheim and in conversation
with Kantian and early Hegelian assessments of Christianity, understood
decline as the process by which Jesus' simple message had been transformed
into "positive" demands for creedal affirmation and ecclesiastical discipline.[18] Had the Greek Fathers kept to Jesus' message, the Trinitarian and
Christological controversies would have proved less detrimental.[19] Rather,
by setting a standard of "positive faith" to which all must adhere, they
injured Christian freedom and gave the hierarchy an opportunity slyly to
expand its influence.[20] Gieseler, like Mosheim, blamed both Jews and
pagans for this lapse: here, an appeal to the context in which early Christianity developed served to exonerate the church's failures. The Jews of
Jesus' time, in Gieseler's narrative, had fallen into empty ceremony and
legal fanaticism.[21] Even Jesus' disciples mistakenly construed the Messianic
kingdom as earthly and material, and the eschaton as imminent, points that
Jesus himself had never "distinctly taught."[22] And the later development of
clericalism, which styled church leaders as priests, is blamed on the influence of "Mosaic" notions of priesthood.[23]

"Externality," however, beset not only Jews. Gieseler painted a bleak
picture of the pagan religious background as well.[24] "Heathen," longing to
satisfy their moral "cravings," mistakenly sought satisfaction in "external
observances."[25] Cultivated but superstitious pagans, upon conversion to
Christianity, introduced ritual pomp to confirm their "heathenish notions
that external rites were pleasing to God."[26]

Early Christianity, Gieseler charged, adopted these unfortunate tendencies from its environment. Montanism's excesses, for example, prompted
the wider church to emphasize "external rules."[27] Yet much more went
amiss: Rome's claim to primacy (lacking divine warrant), the advent of

"state religion,"[28] the promulgation of "gross" and "absurd" depictions of hell's torments, and of misguided beliefs that saints could intercede with God and that monastic practices were meritorious. Linking Judaism and Catholicism, Gieseler claimed that "men were once more under the domination of the law and not of the Gospel."[29] Providence seems strikingly absent from Gieseler's depiction of early Christianity—and it was the appeal to Providence that would bring the otherwise dark patristic era into a more favorable light.

August Neander: Development and Decline

By the second decade of the nineteenth century, German piety was rebounding from Rationalism. Church historian August Neander, who helped to spur this revival,[30] entertained a more generous version of patristic Christianity. Henry Smith, Roswell Hitchcock, and Philip Schaff heard his lectures, and George Fisher, studying in Germany shortly after Neander's death in 1850, knew his writings. Neander was posthumously crowned "the last of the church fathers,"[31] a "Father of the Church for the church of the nineteenth century."[32] Protestant historiography's great virtue, Neander claimed, is its genial affirmation of Christianity's development, in contrast to Catholics' misguided assumption of an unchanging church tradition from the apostolic age to the present.[33]

Despite his wariness of Pantheism, Neander adopted (and adapted) the Hegelian notion that *Geist* works itself out in history.[34] Neander styled his view of historical development "organic-genetic":[35] the church developed not accidentally nor by outward force of circumstances, but through "an internally connected organism"[36] and "inwardly impelling causes."[37] Amid the varying manifestations of this development, some essence of Christianity always remained, "not in a system of Ideas, but in a tendency of the inner life."[38] Borrowing a theme from Schleiermacher, Neander claimed that Christianity was first "received into the inward experience" before it was developed as doctrine. The earliest Christians, not yet capable of reflecting on development—the necessary step for the formulation of theology—largely devoted their religious energies to polemic. Hence the early church (excepting the Alexandrian School) had no "history of dogma."[39]

For Neander, development implied that Jesus' teachings were not always best understood by his first-century audience. Eyewitnesses enjoyed no special privilege. On the contrary, time had to pass before the "inexhaustible truth" of Jesus' teaching could be understood. For example, the first Christian generations did not comprehend the significance of the Parables of the Leaven and of the Mustard Seed. These parables (when rightly understood) teach that "Christianity acting from within must pervade and ennoble all the branches of human life," its inner essence gradually penetrating the mass of humanity.[40]

This penetration, however, required human receptivity, another theme Neander borrowed from Schleiermacher. The "mental culture of the age," Neander wrote, determined the degree to and manner in which any era could "take in" Jesus' teaching. Those in later times who had most fully appropriated Jesus' message earned the right to assess *all* other religions. Poised at a "higher standpoint of religious development," these adepts (viz., learned Christians, especially Protestants) can better judge "lower" manifestations of religion, such as found in heathenism and Mohammedanism, than those religions' own devotees: "we know how to distinguish the truly religious and the sensuous." Although Neander allowed development *within* Christianity (notably, from Catholicism to Protestantism), he denied any development *beyond* Christianity, which is "the absolute Religion," alone meeting "all the religious wants of Man."[41] Development, in other words, has its limits. Hegelian and Tübingen schemes that allegedly lacked a definite end-point provoked unease even among those who otherwise espoused Christianity's inner movement through time.

Neander's understanding of Christianity's mission much influenced his American students and readers. Christianity, he taught, was meant to overcome and subject the world to itself, transforming it by abolishing the "schism between the supernatural and the natural." (Judaism had lacked this transformative power.[42]) Christianity's mission was "to take up into itself and appropriate to its own ends all that belongs to man—all that is in the world." But Christianity first had to enter into "conflict with what had hitherto been the world-subjecting principle—into a conflict with sin and the principle of heathenism." This "negative tendency," a transient stage, was needed to clear the ground and might understandably assume "an ascetic shape." Once paganism had met its downfall, however, opposition should have given way to "harmonious appropriation," including that of "the opposite element as its negative basis." But some aspects of Christianity got mired at the negative level (in the "antithesis," in Hegelian terminology) and never entered positively into the world's life.[43] Many Christians failed to be "a salt and a leaven for all human relations," burying the talent they might have used for others' benefit.[44] Yet Neander ardently hoped that Protestantism in his time would triumph over all such "negative" obstacles.

A second motif in Neander's understanding of Christianity was his stress on the inward. Christianity—*pace* Roman Catholics—was to be identified only with the inward church, "the fundamental principle" in ecclesiastical history.[45] Like the early Hegel, Neander believed that Christianity's mission was to overcome the "positivity" of religions that centered on outward obedience to commands and on external ceremonies and rituals—Judaism being the prime example in antiquity, and Roman Catholicism, in later times. For Neander, early Christianity's great error lay in its failure to suppress and take into itself (*Verinnerlichung*) this "positivity," thus defusing it; rather, nascent Christianity came to promote the outward and external.[46] Jewish "externality," in brief, was not entirely overcome.[47]

A third distinctive theme of Neander's *Histories* celebrated the manifestation of divine Providence in even seemingly negative developments. Throughout *all* ages, however "dark" and unenlightened, Christianity retained its power to sanctify.[48] Given this understanding, the patristic and medieval eras, often so despised by Protestants, might receive a more positive treatment. Neander cited the example of Julian the Apostate's attempt to supplant Christianity with paganism: divine Providence showed how impotent was his wicked scheme.[49]

To be sure, the Protestant Neander decried the church's decline in the post-apostolic period, manifested in the development of ritual, clerical hierarchy, "works righteousness," "externality," and "superstition." The Holy Spirit's operations in human history, he conceded, were frequently obscured. Yet Neander's guiding principle as a historian was to search for the rays of light amid the darkness.[50] In America, Neander's legacy fell particularly to Roswell Hitchcock and Philip Schaff.

Ferdinand Christian Baur: Development

If Neander broached the issue of development in the church's history, F. C. Baur embraced it with a vengeance, as is manifest in his *Epochen der kirchlichen Geschichtsschreibung* (1852). The American professors, who hesitatingly incorporated development into their historiographical schemes, faulted Baur for emphasizing the principle to such a degree that Christianity seemed to lose all stability. Baur, for his part, was quick to denounce church historians for their timidity.

Baur challenged historians' assumption of an essentially unchanging church.[51] He faulted Mosheim, Gieseler, and Hase for failing to perceive an "inner principle" that guided historical change toward a final purpose,[52] working through the clash of "tendencies" to a higher unity. Moreover, despite Neander's sympathetic treatment of even "repulsive" features of the church's history, Baur charged that his supranaturalistic (and hence static) approach precluded any genuine development.[53] If only human receptivity changes while the supernatural principle remains constant—as Neander believed—true development is thwarted.[54]

The Union and Yale professors appropriated Baur's commitment to the principle of development in Christian history—although they thought that he had let it run riot. For them, development must always be understood as guided—and reined in—by Providence. Neander's confessionalism rendered his approach more acceptable to the Americans than Baur's.

Church Historians in America: Decline and Development

Decline in American Protestant Ideology

Theories of development were slow to find acceptance in early and mid-nineteenth century Protestant America. Added to uncomfortable questions pertaining to the authorship and dating of New Testament books, theories of development only exacerbated fears of Infidelity. Many American Protestants saw the patristic era as the birth-moment of the Roman Catholic Church, when Christianity began its downward slide from the pure inward spirituality of Jesus' teaching into "externality," "works-righteousness," the Papacy, the Jesuits, idolatrous devotion to the mother of Jesus, and veneration of mere humans as saints and martyrs—into a church that now, its critics charged, was plaguing American cities, schools, and politics. For Protestants of *this* stripe, there had been *no* positive development in early Christianity, only decline.

Moreover, ancient pagan sources—"the classics," that staple of American college education for much of the nineteenth century—themselves favored the notion of Rome's decline, a decline that for the professors provided the context for Christianity's own downward slide. Unlike the *eigh-teenth*-century American appropriation of the classics, which (as Caroline Winterer details) aligned the virtues of Rome with those of the new American Republic,[55] and also unlike the *late* nineteenth-century praise of classical study as an uplifting antidote to the materialism of the Gilded Age ("mere getting and spending"),[56] seminary professors at mid-century favored the denunciations of ancient vice and error found in Latin satire, political invective, and moralizing literature.[57] They borrowed heavily from Sallust's rhetoric of "decline and fall,"[58] Livy's description of civic deterioration,[59] Tacitus' attack on imperial vice and praise of Germanic virtue,[60] and Juvenal's vituperative satires,[61] among other Latin writings. Aside from Ephraim Emerton late in the century, the Protestant professors engaged no hermeneutic of suspicion regarding these sources. For them, decline, begun *before* the advent of Christianity, had negatively conditioned the world in which the new religion appeared. This baggage from pagan times—negative conditioning—helped to account for the slow, often superficial adoption of Christian morals: the early church's failure to maintain Jesus' lofty spirit could be ascribed to its inheritance of "bad material" from its contemporary environment.[62] Decline was the mantra for the first centuries of the Common Era.

The historiographical presuppositions of church history professors in America shifted during the course of the nineteenth century. Those professors whose vision of early Christianity had been shaped by Neander doubted the early church's precipitous drop into darkness. Since Jesus had vowed to be with his followers until the end of the age (Matt. 28:20), *no* period of church history could completely lack divine purpose. The earliest of the professors here considered—Samuel Miller of the Theological Seminary at Princeton—remained largely innocent of German scholarship and theory, as his acerbic comments on German philosophy in his *Brief Retrospect of the Eighteenth Century* suggest.[63] From Henry Smith onward, however, American theologians who encountered in Europe a Hegelianized version of early Christian history slowly adjusted their assumptions. The course of that appropriation shows the professors indecisively veering between the newer (German) emphasis on development and the more traditional Protestant theme of decline. Conceding the hand of Providence even in dubious outcomes, they found an explanation for the latter by an appeal to context: the unfortunate influence of the Jewish and pagan environments in which Christianity arose. Quietly rearranging their *own* mental universes and taming German scholarship for their American students, they hesitantly incorporated some aspects of the new historiography.

Moreover, the American professors adopted views espoused by Continental historians regarding the providential spread of Christianity into western and northern Europe—but the patriotic Americans traced the march of Providence even further westward: had not Christianity followed the course of the sun all the way to their shores?[64] Decline was not the last word. Bishop Berkeley had presciently penned his lines,

> Westward the Course of Empire takes its Way;
> The first four Acts already past,
> A fifth shall close the Drama with the Day;
> Time's noblest Offspring is the last.[65]

Tübingen School scholarship, with its strong emphasis on development, played an ambiguous role in the American professors' discussion. Baur and his colleagues had pressed that notion too far for the comfort of most Protestant historians. In addition, Tübingen scholars had disturbingly dispensed with the boundary that had silently cordoned off the unique era of Jesus and the Apostles from that which followed. The dilemma remained for the American professors: to what extent might the theme of Christianity's development be usefully, yet piously, deployed? If the New Testament remained the standard by which all subsequent moments of Christian history were judged, could the patristic era ever escape from being marked by "lack"?

Samuel Miller: The Church's Decline

Samuel Miller, whose academic career began well before notions of historical development came into fashion, directed a litany of accusations at features of patristic Christianity's decline that he associated with high-church Episcopalianism and Roman Catholicism. To be sure, Miller told his students, ecclesiastical history is "the record of [God's] Providence"[66]—but given his largely negative assessment of patristic Christianity, Miller likely deemed her operations a bit sluggish.

Church history, Miller-the-Calvinist argued, largely manifests the "depravity of human nature." From New Testament times, through the

heresies and schisms of the patristic era, to "the holy Waldenses," there are
dark places—indeed, even the Reformers and martyrs have "spots in all
their *blaze of glory!*"[67] (Those "spots" apparently motivated the counsel of
Andover professors that instruction in church history should be delayed
until students had had time to fortify themselves.) For Miller, the church's
early decline was not counterbalanced by a theory of historical development. Even late in his career, Miller appeared to know little about developmental theories such as Neander's. In this, he joined most American
Protestants of his era.

For Miller, the church's unprovidential decline is the salient feature of
Christianity almost from its inception. Two chief manifestations of decline
were Christianity's abandonment of its original "Presbyterian" form of
church government, and the emergence of asceticism and monasticism—
tales to be told in Chapters 6 and 8. Miller's examples of early Christianity's
decline will be echoed by the later professors.

Although Miller laboriously illustrated the downward slide of the
church from the first century onward, his Calvinist confession of humans'
universal and overwhelming depravity afforded less room for genuine
movement, even of the downward variety: *all* humans in *every* era have
been fearfully corrupt. The church's history for Miller becomes the stage
on which the static "depravity of human nature" is played out—a depravity
found not only in Judas, Nero, Caligula, and Domitian.[68] The New Testament gives examples of gluttony and drunkenness among *Christians* at the
Lord's table (I Cor. 11:21)—an admission hardly to be believed, Miller
exclaimed, if not so "expressly declared in Sacred history." Heresies and
schisms among Gnostics and Ebionites arose in Christianity's very first century.[69] From the second century to the time of Augustine, no one adequately taught the doctrines of grace and justification. Miller urged students
to investigate this decline for themselves: "Read Cyprian! Read Origen!
Read Eusebius!"[70]

Miller, however, wavered on *how soon* this decline set in. His mutually
conflicting postulates suggest a strongly ideological reading of ecclesiastical
history. Even the first century, in Miller's view, offers disheartening examples. Besides the wayward Corinthians, Jesus' own disciples sinfully vied for
pride of place (Mk. 10:37; Lk. 22:24). If such disgraceful behavior was manifest while miracles were still occurring, while the memory of the Lord was
fresh and inspiration alive, what (Miller asked) could be expected a century
later? Although he cited the claim of Hegesippus, "the earliest uninspired

historian," that the "virgin purity of the church" vanished with the Apostles' deaths, Miller's rendition casts doubt on whether even *those* days were unsullied. Had not Jerome testified that the "churches were tainted with gross errors" when the "blood of Christ [was] still warm in Judea"? And Cyprian alleged that an almost "universal depravity" of clergy and laity was early on display.[71] Already in the first century, with persecution looming, "ambition, vanity, a love of novelty, and a false philosophy" disturbed the church.[72]

Elsewhere, Miller's picture of the church in the first and early second centuries was more favorable. By the close of the first century, he (sometimes) taught his students, the books of the New Testament had been collected and received, and were soon supplemented by works of Clement of Rome, Ignatius, Polycarp, Barnabas, and Hermas. Then, the church's life and its two ceremonies—the Lord's Supper and Baptism—were characterized by a "beautiful simplicity," a "humble, unaffected *spirituality*." No liturgies yet existed and pastors offered prayers "without the use of forms."[73]

In this alternative scenario, only the *second* century evinced signs of decline—although from that time, the downward slide gained momentum. Miller conceded that early patristic writers provide "respectable monuments of *piety* and *zeal*," but they by no means taught infallible truth, and some accorded "too much countenance to superstition."[74] Already in the second century, Victor of Rome's "bold and insolent" behavior prompted the Paschal Controversy, foreshadowing "the audacious claims of the *Papacy*."[75] Neither party to this dispute, in Miller's view, had apostolic warrant: it was all "a matter of *human invention*." "This, young gentlemen," Miller concluded "is a humiliating scene! . . . The Scriptural doctrine of the depravity of human nature accounts for it all." Heresies and corruptions are "the *native* product of the human heart."[76]

The human heart, however, did not account for all that had gone amiss. Another cause of Christianity's decline, in Miller's catalogue, was the mixing of "Grecian philosophy" with Christian teaching from the late second century onward: Monarchians and Patripassians mingled philosophy with the Gospel to form "a motley system."[77] Then arose the "New-Platonic" philosophy, "a source of *deep and permanent mischief*," one of whose proponents, Ammonius Saccas, dared to teach that truth was "found *equally* in *all sects*."[78] Echoing some early Christian writers, Miller charged that the "dreadful influence of unsanctified learning [philosophy]," "the pride of

science," prompted the rise of heresy.[79] Miller feared his own students
might be sucked back into Gnostic and Platonic views. "An ounce of pre-
vention," he remarked, beginning that time-honored proverb.[80]

Elsewhere, Miller marked the *third* and later centuries as the moment
of decline: texts from this era aroused his "pious indignation." Then, the
"pride and usurpation of *prelates* began to distract and divide the Church."
Those who so admire the time of Cyprian [*viz.*, Episcopalians], Miller
pointedly commented, must have a "very different criterion from that
which the Bible furnishes."[81] Origen, for his part, tarnished the luster of
Christian doctrine by mixing it with "philosophical refinements" and
inventing "fanciful, mystical, and allegorical interpretations."[82] Sinful innovations included the use of gold and silver vessels for the Lord's Supper
and its administration to infants; exorcism and other superstitious practices
connected with baptism; excessive fasting; and miraculous efficacy accorded
the sign of the cross. Now, the clergy became "very corrupt"—selfish,
voluptuous, motivated by "irregular ambition." Heresies flourished: Miller
named Manicheans, Hieracites, Noetians, Sabellians, and followers of Paul
of Samosata, along with the schismatic Novatians.[83]

Another fault resulted from Christians' desire to convert Jews and
pagans. To attract Jews, Christians began to adopt Jewish titles, ceremonies,
and vestments of "the temple service." They spoke of priests, altars, and
sacrifices, for which the New Testament gives no warrant. Likewise, to win
pagans, ministers introduced heathen ceremonies into Christian worship.[84]
The church's "vicious and irregular" adherents increased as the church
itself expanded.[85] Once more, Jews and pagans are aligned in their contribution to the development of Roman Catholicism.

The *fourth* century saw still more decline, as the religion of Jesus became
a "court religion."[86] Although Constantine possessed great talents and was
a "friend of the external church," his piety was, in Miller's view, "*doubtful.*"
With state aid, the church grew in numbers, wealth, and splendor, but its
spirituality, purity, simplicity, and "evangelical health" declined.[87] Constantine "deformed and corrupted" Christ's church: what had been "*all
glorious within*" became "all gaudy *without.*" Appropriating a sexualized
language of corruption, Miller claimed that the church decked and adorned
herself like the kingdoms of the world; she "yielded to the solicitations of
the princes of the earth, and had criminal conversation with them; and by
degrees sunk into that *mother of harlots*, which it, at present, shows itself to
be in almost every part of the world," that is, the Roman Catholic Church.[88]

This dire situation cannot be blamed *entirely* on Constantine, since decline was already present. The church's "great lights were extinguished; . . . her beauty was greatly tarnished."[89] And the fourth century saw the rise of still more heresies: Arianism, Apollinarianism, Macedonian errors concerning the Holy Spirit, and Priscillianism (a revival, Miller believed, of ancient Gnosticism).[90]

Although, on the positive side, the later fourth century saw "the destruction [by Theodosius I] of the pagan system as a public religion," and the Gospel's spread to Armenia, Ethiopia, and Georgia, to the Goths and the Gauls, it also witnessed the establishment of prelacy and the clergy's advancement in selfishness, luxury, ambition, and worldliness.[91] Deacons and elders (presbyters) forsook their assigned tasks, bishops vied to extend their power beyond their own congregations, metropolitans and patriarchs began to lord it over other clergy. At last, although the Bishop of Rome claimed supreme power over the whole church,[92] his greedy reach was checked by the elevation of Constantinople's bishop when the imperial residence was transferred eastward.[93]

Doctrine, Miller alleged, had so declined by Augustine's time that, upon his accession to the bishopric, he "scarcely found a single individual who . . . exhibit[ed] evangelical truth." The doctrine of justification by faith alone had long been forgotten. Superstition now reigned, as evidenced by the growing beliefs that the elements of the Lord's Supper undergo a change; that baptism should be postponed to the end of life as a "passport to heaven"; that Christians should worship martyrs' relics, offer prayers for the dead in purgatory, and use images and pictures in worship. To be sure, a few brave critics—Jovinian and Vigilantius in particular—opposed these practices, but were "all speedily silenced and crushed."[94]

The fifth century and beyond, in Miller's scenario, saw yet more decline. Clergy faltered further in their duties. Superstition, bizarre ascetic devotees (Stylites), unwarranted liturgical practices (auricular confession), and the multiplication of external observances all showed Christianity's degenerate state.[95] And the sixth century, filled with clerical corruption, witnessed the "Romish hierarchy slowly making progress toward the nativity of the *man of sin*" [i.e., the Pope]. The most "absurd human inventions" usurped Gospel simplicity, divine truth was ever more "obscured by human folly." Erroneous biblical interpretation was further promoted by writers appropriating "the fanciful and mystical dreams of Origen."[96]

The church after the sixth century slid further downhill.[97] The rise and flourishing of Islam (which Miller seemingly aligned with Christian heresy) entailed polygamy, denial of the divinity of Christ and other Gospel doctrines, circumcision, and the adoption of rites and ceremonies from Jewish ritual law. Miller, surprisingly, devoted more class time to Islam (he gave students seven pages of notes) than he did to any one Christian teacher, practice, or doctrine.[98]

Although a few groups in later centuries remained faithful to the primitive norm—Waldensians and "Albigenses" are predictably trotted out—only with the Reformation did some semblance of the original church order again surface. Then, Calvin restored (*not* invented, as adversaries charged) the Presbyterian form of government to its apostolic pattern.[99]

From this tale of sin and vice, Miller extracted a few positive lessons. The past woes of the church should remind contemporary Christians not to despair when divisions and heresies arise: God can bring good out of evil. Moreover, the misunderstandings of the Christological controversies (which Miller largely attributes to linguistic rather than doctrinal differences) should encourage Christians to be prudent in judgment.[100] Most important, the mass of error and corruption in the early church proves that the Bible alone contains "the religion of Protestants" and is the "only infallible rule of faith." Although the church is fallible, she nevertheless "guarded the fundamental doctrines of the Gospel."[101] Proper development, on Miller's scheme, signals reversion to Christianity's founding moments—or, what seemed the same to him, to sixteenth-century Geneva.

Henry Smith: Development and Decline in Church History

In the writings, lectures, and sermons of Henry Smith of Union Seminary, development was accorded a slightly larger role in Christianity's drama. Smith brought the notion of historical development (with caveats and modifications) from his studies in Germany to American audiences—but it lay in an unresolved tension with the traditional Protestant belief in the church's early decline.

All theological systems, Smith taught, become what they are through historic development. By studying the modifications of Christianity over time, students will gain a better understanding of their own denominations and denominational Confessions.[102] The mere word "development," he conceded, is "vague and unsubstantial." We must ask, *what* developed in the church's history, and by what criteria can development be tested? For

Protestants, the criterion is Scripture, the unique and unchanging norm. Scholars must state "fairly and fully" the subject of development and its goal in order to distinguish true developments from false. Furthermore, development should contain nothing "contrary to the demands of our moral nature" and be understood within a theistic, not a naturalistic, framework. Revelation must be accorded its place, the eternal interests of humankind claiming precedence over the temporal.[103]

What favors a theory of development? To affirm "a superintending Providence," Smith posited, we must allow for progress: "Providence" here stands in for the Hegelian *Geist*, working itself upward through historical processes. Christians also affirm development when they confess that their religion—the Absolute Religion—will in the end be victorious, despite difficulties along the way. Not only secular history manifests development: the New Testament's surpassing of the Old shows that religion, too, can advance.[104]

Appropriating the Hegelian dialectic, Smith claimed that the developmental process works through conflicts and antagonisms to a higher unity. By this process, the church arrives at "a full comprehension of God's veiled will" that reconciles Christian truth with all other truth. Each period of history has added something through its struggles, from the early Trinitarian and Christological controversies, through more recent conflicts with philosophy and Infidelity, to the present [Hegelian-inspired] desire to reconcile Christianity with all knowledge, making "one self-consistent system."[105]

Not all Christians of his era, Smith acknowledged, favor the notion of development in the church's history. Roman Catholics (John Henry Newman excepted) take a static view, imagining that their doctrines and practices were present from Christianity's beginning.[106] At the other extreme is the "ultraphilosophical" position that discounts "any stability"—a view that Smith associated with some Hegelians. Here, *all* is development. This open-ended interpretation is particularly objectionable when applied to religion, for it holds that "*all* religion is *progressive* and *naturally* grows into more and more perfect development."[107] Smith will show the error of this view.

Smith illustrated the "ultraphilosophical" approach by citing points from Hegel's philosophy of religion. He taught his students that according to this scheme, African fetishism belongs to the lowest stage of religious expression. (Smith registered two criticisms: the divine is represented by a material object, the fetish, and the object is impermanent.) Higher stands Egyptian theriomorphism (the divine reverenced in animal forms), which presents permanent images for worship. Higher still is ancient Greek religion, which worshiped the perfect human form, and Roman religion, which united church and state in a common interest—and so on. Each religion, in this scheme, is but a "different stage in the great process of development."[108] What is the fault of this scheme? It fails to consider Christianity unique, based on divinely given revelation. Unlike other religions, Christianity did not "naturally" evolve from lower forms.[109]

Smith similarly rejected an evolutionary model of true religion in his espousal of "primitive monotheism," a view more easily accommodated to the narrative of Genesis. On this model, religion does not begin at the lowest point and advance upward from fetishism through polytheism to monotheism; rather, it starts on a "high," descends precipitously to lower forms, and finds truth once more through revelation. Smith faults "the unproved hypothesis of a merely naturalistic evolution" from a lowly form of "polytheistic idolatry" to higher religions. Idolatry rather represents *degeneration* from purer religion. Early humans, when they dispersed from the Euphrates Valley, carried with them the memory of one God, the first parents, and the Flood. Materialism (disallowing the supernatural) and Pantheism ("ultraphilosophical" Hegelianism) have not disproved these "facts of history, facts of nature, and facts of human consciousness."[110] Yet for Smith, heathenism, past and present, is not devoid of all truth, for it retains remnants of "a primitive Revelation." For example, a notion of Trinity appears dimly in contemporary "Hindoo" religion.[111]

Other theories of development coming into circulation captured Smith's attention as well. In February 1860, Smith's journal published a notice of Darwin's *Origin of Species* that conveyed the current excitement over the work and registered its novelty. (Smith himself wrote a brief notice—"Man and the Gorilla"—on Thomas Huxley's debate with Richard Owen.[112]) From 1860 to the mid-1870s he frequently noted critiques of Darwin's theory in his "Theological Intelligence" column.[113] A year before his death, Smith wrote that although he conceded science its "lawful sphere," scientists erred when they attempted to construct a theory of the universe that wars against both Scripture and reason, "denying all efficient and final causes, and making a blind, unconscious force to be that in which we live and move and have our being."[114]

In a class Smith taught in 1857 ("pre-*Origin*"), he declared his opposition to a theory of humans' development from lower forms. The order of creation in Genesis 1, Smith assured his students, accords well with science.[115] It seems unlikely that *Origin of Species*, published two years later, changed his views. Although Smith was known as open-minded, his full embrace of Darwinian theory seems dubious. Various reports intriguingly claim that Smith was preparing a course on evolution at the time of his death in 1877;[116] the brief outline for the lectures that remains, I discuss in Chapter 9.

Smith did, however, countenance development in patristic Christianity, and provided several examples. Contrary to the fable that each Apostle contributed one verse to the Apostles' Creed, Smith taught students that later additions were made as a result of conflict. Clauses added to the Creed in the fourth century and beyond include Jesus' "descent into Hades" (an anti-Apollinarian addition, Smith claimed), the "communion of saints" (against Donatist criticisms of the Catholic Church), and the "forgiveness of sins" (against Novatianist and Donatist charges). Likewise, the phrase "holy Catholic Church," Smith asserted, first entered the Creed in the fourth century. The Apostles' Creed, in other words, was not given ready-made, but was formulated over time, in the midst of conflict.[117]

Smith also highlighted developments in early Christian reflection on the Holy Spirit. The inattention to the Spirit in earlier patristic creeds and doctrinal discussions, he claimed, reveals the "looseness" of theological terminology in that era. Better, more definite, formulations emerge only through discussion, elaboration, and, usually, conflict.[118]

Nevertheless, "erroneous applications" have been made of the theory of development. Students should not imagine that *any* or *every* development in Christianity is true; retrograde movements have arisen, stemming from sin and its "hindrances." Moreover, development does not mean that God's plan for the world has achieved complete realization.[119] "Mere external unity" among Christians is not the goal, nor is social well-being, political rights, or advances in freedom or intellectual culture.[120] Here, Smith's social conservatism stands in stark contrast to ideals of the Social Gospel movement a half-century later.

Despite Smith's criticisms of both Hegel and the Tübingen School, he borrowed the outlines of Baur's (and perhaps Schelling's[121]) scheme for early Christian history's development: Christianity evolved from a Jewish form (represented by Peter, the Ebionites, the Nazarenes, and the Pseudo-Clementines), through Greco-Roman forms (such as Gnosticism), to a resolution in "Catholic" Christianity after the Constantinian settlement. Only then did the Catholic Church emerge, defined as "the Apostolic Church so unfolded as to meet the wants of the Greek and Roman world."[122] In meeting those "wants," some aspects of decline became manifest.

If Smith's cautious appeal to a theory of ecclesiastical development was prompted by his encounter with recent German intellectual currents, the theory of decline he simultaneously endorsed was traditionally Protestant—although, to be sure, the German historians and philosophers who espoused theories of development were also Protestant.[123] Smith's narrative of decline does not differ significantly from Miller's, *despite* his embrace of development. Smith, however, began the downward slope later, with Constantine's era, not with the first century. In his view, the persecutions did only half as much "mischief" to true religion as had "the secularizing spirit" introduced by Constantine and later extended by the Roman hierarchy. In Constantine's day, the church's "external power and splendor" increased and its ranks swelled, yet "its grace drooped and died, its spiritual strength decayed, and true piety became almost unknown." Converts brought with them "all the corruptions of the heathen world"; their vices, delusions, and superstitions "took the garb and name of Christianity," sullying Christian life.[124] Over time, the church's appropriation of elements from the surrounding culture degraded its primitive simplicity.[125] The Constantinian church, "used as an instrument of civil government," increased both the clergy's prerogatives and ecclesiastical ritual. While the clergy degenerated, the papacy's power grew, albeit by political means.[126] Smith's appeal to context—namely, Christianity's appropriation of the surrounding culture—served to rationalize Christianity's downward slide.

By the fifth century, superstition substituted for devotion, and ritualism, for preaching. The now dim light of the church finally "went out in darkness and the long night of ages settled down upon the earth," as superstition and degeneration came to prevail in early medieval Roman Catholicism. But—Teutons to the rescue!—the mingling of races brought about by the barbarian invasions infused a "new life-blood" into Europe that would bring improvement in later centuries.[127] "Roman immorality," Smith and his successors believed, provided a reason for the Empire's defeat by sexually virtuous and spiritually minded Teutonic barbarians. Teutons, whom these Anglo-Saxon professors deem their own ancestors, served as a way-station on the road from pagan immorality to a spiritualized (and Hegelianized) modern Protestantism.[128]

Roswell Hitchcock: Development
and Decline in Church History

Roswell Hitchcock of Union Seminary, although exhibiting little interest in philosophy of history, did address decline and development. History, Hitchcock told his students, is a report of *"human evolution."*[129] All of history can be considered sacred, since God is manifest throughout.[130] Although some fear the concept of development as signaling a Hegelianized Pantheism that sinks "the finite in the Infinite," Hitchcock defended the notion that he had appropriated from Herder, Schleiermacher, and Neander. Development, he claimed, can be taken in an entirely orthodox sense and receives biblical sanction from Jesus' Parable of the Mustard Seed; in addition, the common observation that Christianity has spread over the centuries supports the notion. Against the Roman Church's view of "no development" (John Henry Newman excepted), but also against Protestant sects that affirmed the "perfection of the apostolic age" from which later eras declined, Hitchcock charted a middle course. Development, the hallmark of recent liberal Protestant historiography, Hitchcock averred, is stigmatized by Rome as a Protestant heresy.[131]

Development, a characteristic of organic life, received a distinctive treatment in Hitchcock's narration of primeval human history. He strongly rejected the "infidel theory" that the human race struggled up from "primaeval barbarism." All peoples, he claimed, derived from one set of parents, Adam and Eve, who were "primitive monotheists" and who degenerated with the Fall. Yet God providentially offered grace to the ancient Hebrews and their descendants, halting what would otherwise have been continuous decay, and enabling ascent up the developmental ladder. Providence later allowed classical civilizations to assist nascent Christianity's advance: Greece gave its language, and Rome, "roads, jurisprudence and universal empire."[132] Development of the historic races, in Hitchcock's view, has now advanced to Anglo-Saxon civilization, with a better expression yet to come.[133] As noted in Chapter 4, Hitchcock believed that history exhibited a spiral development, its upward turns manifesting progress and producing the genuinely new.

Decline is nevertheless prominent in Hitchcock's teaching and writing. He warns against exaggerating the glories of the ante-Nicene church: "We must not be deterred [from seeing the defects] by glamour."[134] He moves the locus of decline back to apostolic times, declaring that no perfect "pre-church" Christianity ever existed. Early errors include the expectation of an imminent Second Coming and Final Judgment[135] and the unseemly behavior of Corinthian Christians.[136] A century or two later, "blemishes" marked extreme ascetic self-denial, and bravery under persecution often verged on rashness. In addition, the "insipid" writings of the Apostolic Fathers show that the end of inspiration had arrived quickly.[137] Last, the ancient church expended disproportionate energy on doctrinal debate while neglecting missions: the formulation of doctrine, doubtless necessary, nevertheless impeded the more vital task of spreading the Gospel. Church councils after Nicaea (or perhaps Chalcedon) achieved nothing useful and largely confused doctrinal issues.[138]

Sacramentarian and high-church views soon ousted the primitive Christian notion of the priesthood of all believers, a change that Hitchcock blamed on Jewish and pagan converts, who expected an "outward priesthood."[139] Sacerdotalism, evident by the time of Tertullian,[140] "rivaled the pomp of Jewish hierarchy." After Christianity's triumph and the institution of the state-church, hierarchy and ritual increased, spiritual life declined. (Piety, Hitchcock remarked—one wonders whether with a touch of irony?—is "always declining."[141]) Now, "mere externalism" reigned. The union of church and state produced worldly bishops and brought the unregenerate into the church.[142] Seemingly echoing Juvenal as well as Herder, Hitchcock ascribed the weakening of Empire to the confusion of peoples and "natural boundaries." An "inherent defect of the national character," he claimed, resulted in *an entire lack of Ideality.*[143]

Symptoms of decay in patristic Christianity include the growing devotion to relics (those of the True Cross, Hitchcock joked, provide "enough wood to fill a car"[144]); the veneration of the Virgin Mary (promoted by "the excessive regard for virginity" and the lingering respect for female divinities);[145] fixed times for prayer and extensive fasting among "Oriental" Christians (to curb the "sensuality" that left them at the devil's mercy). Eastern Christianity fell to such a miserable state that, in Hitchcock's view, "Mohammedanism" served as "a terrible punishment inflicted by God upon the degenerate Christian churches of the East, destroying them rather than imparting new life."[146]

Yet amid such darkness, some rays of light shone. The persecution under Diocletian, for example, spurred the development of the canon: when edicts were issued to confiscate Christian documents, churches were forced to decide which books they considered Scripture. Providence was at work, so that the church exited the ante-Nicene period with its canon substantially formed. Even the "inevitable" but time-wasting doctrinal controversies proved useful in formulating theology.[147] Hitchcock (like Smith) conceded that fuller theological formulations are arrived at only through a process in which "antagonism" is met and given a "higher," more adequate resolution. Even in darkness and decline, some positive features emerged. Providence could not be undermined.

Philip Schaff: Development in Church History

Of the church historians here considered, Philip Schaff most warmly embraced the notion that since God had providentially guided all history, some good could be found in seemingly unfortunate events. Although he acknowledged that in the America of his own day, Europeans might see nothing but slavery, rampant materialism, political radicalism, and divisive sectarianism, this fermentation, he was sure, betokened "the necessary transition state to a higher and better condition."[148] Since Jesus had promised to be with his followers even to the end of time and send the Paraclete to guide them forever,[149] *no* period of the church's history could be devoid of God's guidance. Despite the lapses of the church, God's grace had kept the Bride of Christ from being completely sullied.

Moreover, if God has guided all of history, then no era of church history could be judged superfluous or unworthy of study.[150] That Schaff believed historical development was largely positive can be inferred from his definition of history as "a *self-evolution of God* in the course of *time.*"[151] Schaff borrowed an example from Neander: Julian's failure to reinstate paganism shows the impossibility of stopping Christianity's progress when God has ordained otherwise.[152] Providence, as always, prevails.[153]

As a student, Schaff had heard Baur's lectures on history of Christian doctrine and on the creeds ("symbolics"). He later confessed that Baur had been the first to give him the "idea of historical development, or of a constant and progressive flow of thought in the successive ages of the church."[154] His tribute to Baur, whose views on the New Testament he so strongly rejected, is notable for its generosity. Yet Schaff faulted his former professor for letting development run amok,[155] for his "pantheistic and ruinous" application of "organism" to the study of primitive Christianity.[156]

Historical development, Schaff wrote, "affords the only tenable foundation upon which to justify the Reformation and Protestantism, without doing violence to preceding history, and destroying the notion of an uninterrupted Church." The Reformation was not "a *radical* rupture" with the Catholic past; rather, Protestantism and Catholicism share the heritage of the primitive church. Yet the Protestant Reformation, Schaff feared, had unfortunately led some of its latter-day partisans to neglect tradition.[157]

In his "Principle of Protestantism" speech, given soon after he arrived in America, Schaff laid out his approach to church history. Although the normative character of Christianity was established in the New Testament, humans had experienced a progressive "*apprehension* of Christianity in the *church*"—an emphasis he imbibed from both Schleiermacher and Neander.[158] While the essence of Christianity does not change, Christians acquire a growing realization of it: the human uptake improves. The subject matter of church history, in brief, shows how successive generations of Christians *appropriated* the "life and doctrine of Christ and his apostles."[159] The church historian's task is to explicate, without "narrow prejudice," how this plan of redemption has been progressively manifested, how the church developed through an organic, "living process."[160]

In this speech, Schaff linked the development of Protestantism to its Catholic background, a view to which some of his German Reformed colleagues took strong exception. The "spiritual wealth" of the Middle Ages belongs as much to "us" (i.e., Protestants) as it does to the Roman Church, Schaff declared; Protestantism, after all, did not spring up "like a mushroom in the night." The eighteen centuries elapsing between the time of the New Testament and the present were not a "lifeless void."[161]

Schaff mocked Protestants who deemed the Middle Ages "the Dark Ages":

> O Thou light of the nineteenth century! Come call forth children of darkness, Anselm, Thomas Aquinas, Bernard, Dante, Petrarch, Leonardo da Vinci, Raphael, Francis of Assisi [et al.]. Come forth from your graves and be illuminated by the light that *now* reigns; . . . study philosophy and theology at Andover and New Haven; . . . take lessons of piety from the "camp meetings" of the Albright Brethren and sects of the same spirit.

But the mighty dead have no desire to return, Schaff concluded—and they warn us to be humble.[162]

One great contribution of early Catholicism, Schaff argued, was its conversion of the Teutonic peoples—the forefathers of Protestantism and of modern democracy. The papacy and the "Romish system", were, in Schaff's view, "eminently fitted" to convert the barbarian tribes, who needed a heavy disciplinary authority over them. Just as Judaism had been a preparation for Christianity, so the Roman Catholic Church served during these centuries as "the legitimate bearer of the Christian faith and life."[163]

Schaff's commitment to historical development spurred his critique of Christian groups who failed to appreciate this principle. In his "Principle of Protestantism" speech, for example, he faulted "Puseyites'" static understanding of the church's history. Although he considered the Oxford Movement "an entirely legitimate and necessary reaction against rationalistic and sectaristic [sic] pseudo-Protestantism, as well as the religious subjectivism of the so-called Low-Church Party," its proponents nevertheless erroneously imagined the church as a system handed down in unchanging form. "Puseyites" go utterly astray, in Schaff's view, forgetting the prime significance of the Reformation and the emergence of Protestantism from it: hence they bypass the central manifestation of development in Christianity. Newman in Tract 90 glossed over the true Protestant principle with a "Jesuitical interpretation" that lauds tradition. He and his followers wish to bind Christians to "all that has come down to us from the fathers, without any critical sifting by means of science or God's word."[164] Anglo-Catholics accord *too* much to tradition—while sectarian Protestants often accord too little. Development, in Schaff's view, requires reform and critique, not slavish devotion to the past.

Although Schaff's *Principle of Protestantism* became one of the most famous texts of American Christianity, it was received with little enthusiasm by some of his audience: indeed, he was accused of heresy.[165] His sympathetic treatment of the Middle Ages was deemed "Catholicizing," bordering on "popery."[166]

Schaff on Organic Development

Schaff borrowed (largely from Neander, with assistance from Dorner and Schelling[167]) a notion of the church's development as "organic."[168] The history of the church, he wrote, is neither a "mechanical accumulation of events" nor the product "simply of foreign influences," but stems from its own inner life. "Organic" implied to Schaff that the stages of development, "like the members of a living body, are indissolubly bound together" and "mutually complete each other."[169]

Organic development for Schaff meant that history unfolds from within; like a plant, everything is contained potentially in the germ.[170] History, he wrote, is no "heap of skeletons," but "an organism filled and ruled by a reasonable soul." Whatever lives must move and grow; "the dead only is done."[171] Organic development—in Hegelian fashion—preserves the "true and essential" elements of earlier stages, while eliminating the "untrue and imperfect."[172] At the end of his life, in the early 1890s, Schaff compared the theory of historical development to that of Darwinian evolution.[173]

Schaff claimed that the church's organic development was confirmed by Paul's imagery of the church as a body with interdependent parts (I Cor. 12, 14) and by the Parables of the Mustard Seed and the Leaven (Matt. 13: 31–32), the latter predicting the church's mysterious growth and ultimate triumph amid discouraging circumstances.[174] Growth in Christianity, he wrote, "is a process of life, which springs from within, from the vital energy implanted in the church, and which remains, in all its course, identical with itself, as man through all the stages of his life still continues man."[175]

SCHAFF ON THE CHURCH FATHERS AND DEVELOPMENT

Like other Protestant professors, Schaff favored the ante-Nicene Fathers over theologians of late antiquity: they stood, he believed, closer to the source of truth (i.e., the New Testament) and retained more of the primitive "life-force" than did their successors. He praised the pre-Nicene church for its "unworldliness," its "heroic endurance of suffering and persecution," its "strong sense of Community" and "active benevolence." Before Constantine's era, the church had retained its "grand simplicity," "spirituality," "freedom from all connection with political power or worldly splendor."[176] Based on the voluntary principle, "self-supporting and self-governing," the ante-Nicene church resembled (so Schaff believed) the church in the United States—*except* that the American government recognizes and protects, rather than persecutes, Christianity. Christianity's progress in the ante-Nicene era, amid many difficulties, testifies to its divine origin.[177]

Schaff's theory of organic development tempered traditional views of the church's corruption in the patristic era, enabling an approach to Christian history in which otherwise blameworthy occurrences could be reassessed or, at the least, redescribed more positively. For example, the persecutions of early Christians became "the seed of civil and religious liberty" and freedom of conscience.[178] Schaff's position on freedom of religion will be described more fully in Chapter 9.

Likewise, Schaff saw some benefit in the heretical developments that he attributed to the "baggage" accompanying Jews' and Gentiles' entry to the church: heresies forced greater clarification of church teaching and promoted the development of theology.[179] Whatever their errors, these "diseases" spurred progress.[180] Gnosticism—a particularly good example—stimulated intellectual activity to the extent that patristic theology, Schaff claimed, could not be understood without it.[181] Likewise, Sabellius' theology, although erroneous, "broke the way for the Nicene church doctrine, by its full coordination of the three persons."[182]

Even the growth of church hierarchy, culminating in the development of the papacy, was not an unmitigated evil. Schaff advised:

> Those who condemn, in principle, all hierarchy, sacerdotalism, and ceremonialism should remember that God himself appointed the priesthood and ceremonies in the Mosaic dispensation, and that Christ submitted to the requirements of the law in the days of his humiliation.[183]

Providence, working in silence and secrecy, used "human impulses" (i.e., popes' desire for power) to achieve a divine end, namely, to convert the barbarians.[184] The early papacy was a stage, a "necessary transitory institution," in Christianity's progress, paving the way for a higher form (i.e., Protestantism).[185] As "a training school for the barbarian nations," the papacy served God's providential purpose.[186] Yet, once Christianity came of age, this "legal schoolmaster" was no longer needed; the papacy today, Schaff claimed, has long outlived its mission.[187] Protestants, "having safely crossed the Red Sea, cannot go back to the flesh-pots of the land of bondage, but must look forward to the land of promise."[188] Acknowledging development in the church's history not only rescues patristic and medieval Christianity, it also allows Protestantism to stand as the supreme expression of the Christian faith—and of Protestants, those of the "Anglo-Saxon race," he wrote, have been the most "deeply imbued with the spirit and power of Christianity than any other people."[189] Yet Schaff, like his predecessors at

Union, also entertained a strong sense of the church's decline in the patristic era.

SCHAFF ON DECLINE IN CHURCH HISTORY

Insofar as Schaff distinguished the period of the New Testament as qualitatively different from all subsequent eras of history, he inevitably hinted at a notion of decline. God had drawn a bold line separating the apostolic church with its miracles ("the work of God") from the succeeding ages ("the work of man"). This, the most radical transition in history, Schaff wrote, is nonetheless "silent and secret." The New Testament towers above the whole of patristic literature: "the single epistle to the Romans or the Gospel of John is worth more than all commentaries, doctrinal, polemic, and ascetic treatises of the Greek and Latin fathers, schoolmen, and reformers."[190] How then could there *not* be decline?

Post-New Testament Christianity offered many examples. We should not overpraise the patristic era, Schaff warned: its faults should be expected, given the unchanging sinfulness of human nature.[191] As early as the second century, we find an (un-Protestant) "high estimate of ecclesiastical traditions, meritorious and even overmeritorious works, and strong sacerdotal, sacramentarian, ritualistic, and ascetic tendencies, which gradually matured in the Greek and Roman types of catholicity."[192] Ante-Nicene Christians poorly understood the teaching of justification by faith alone; on the contrary, they stressed sanctification and good works, sowing the seeds for the Catholic doctrine of merit.[193] Schaff rehearsed familiar charges: the development of ecclesiastical hierarchy; sacerdotalism;[194] bishops' immoral behavior;[195] the exaltation of celibacy; prayer as a meritorious work;[196] the "worship" of Mary;[197] reverence for martyrs, saints, and relics;[198] the assumption that charity garnered merit so as to cover "a multitude of sins" and assist the dead in purgatory.[199] Follow the Fathers, Schaff cautioned, only so far as they followed Christ.[200]

Patristic *literature*, as well as *practice*, should not be overrated, since it is marred by "many errors and imperfections which subsequent times [presumably since the Protestant Reformation] have corrected."[201] Writers of this period failed to promote a truly spiritual form of Christianity. Schaff cited examples. The two Pseudo-Clementine letters on virginity "show the early development of an asceticism which is foreign to apostolic teaching and practice." The *Martyrdom of Polycarp*'s "extravagant" depictions go far beyond "the sober limit of the Acts of the Apostles," revealing "the undeniable difference" between the Bible and post-biblical literature.[202] The author of the *Shepherd of Hermas* seems ignorant of the gospel of justifying faith; his Christianity is "thoroughly legalistic and ascetic."[203] Justin Martyr, also promoting a "legalistic and ascetic" theology, did not correctly distinguish between Old Testament and New, between law and gospel; his notions of sin, grace, and justification by faith are deficient.[204] Irenaeus (although "the soundest [ante-Nicene] divine"[205]) nevertheless made much of "the outward visible church, the Episcopal succession, and the sacraments."[206] And post-Nicene literature is even less edifying: Gregory of Nazianzus' depiction of the church in his era, Schaff charged, makes the later Roman Church look like an improvement![207]

Schaff offered reasons—much like Neander's—for the pre-Nicene church's corruption. First, the universality of original sin renders all Christians, early as well as late, fallible. Next, he appealed to context: the remnants—baggage—of heathenism and Judaism clouded the original Christian revelation and led to heresy, bad morals,[208] and clerical hierarchy, complete with "priesthood, altar, and sacrifice."[209] Deploying a dialectical scheme, Schaff pictured heathenism as "the starry night" and Judaism as "the dawn," both of which "lose themselves in the sunlight of Christianity."[210] Yet heathenism continues "in the natural corrupt heart" and in "many idolatrous and superstitious usages of the Greek and Roman churches," which a truer Christianity [read: Protestantism] will continue to protest until these are overcome with "the spirit and fire of the gospel."[211]

Schaff's assessment of the Constantinian era was inconsistent. On the one hand, he endorsed the traditional Protestant claim that the union of church and state injured church discipline. Assimilating the heathen upper classes, the church suffered a "loss of simplicity and spirituality."[212] Self-sacrifice, brotherly love, and strict discipline faded with the rise of fashionable Christianity. Now, "the church lost her virginity, and allied herself with the mass of heathenism."[213]

Yet Schaff sometimes took an ameliorating view. When judging Constantine, he counseled, remember that all great historical characters act under the spirit of the age—although God uses that spirit to work his providential purpose.[214] Our churches today owe Constantine a debt of gratitude for helping to forge the rights that American Christians now "justly claim as essential and inalienable," in opposition to the "heartless selfishness, and the political absolutism of the old world."[215] In addition, the degeneracy of the church was in evidence *before* Constantine, so he is not to receive sole blame. Since corruption and apostasy are "rooted in the natural heart of man," they manifest themselves, if only in germ, even in the apostolic age.[216]

Thus Schaff attempted to balance traditional Protestant views of the church's decline with more positive notions of its organic development. Providence—a Christianized version of Hegel's *Geist*—operates throughout all the highways and byways of the church's history, bringing light out of even dark moments.

George Fisher: Decline and Development in Church History

Yale's George Fisher showed less interest in the concept of historical development than did his Union colleagues. His assertion of decline, however, is rather startlingly linked to his critique of "Jewish" elements that lingered on in early Christianity, corrupting the purity of Jesus' teaching. His case suggests that there is no straightforward trajectory among the nineteenth-century American church historians toward a wholesale rejection of decline theories and a warm embrace of developmental ones: the two sit uneasily together. Fisher's account remains mixed, with a preponderance toward decline.

Fisher's strong antagonism to the Tübingen School may have dampened his enthusiasm for the theme of development. Fisher accused Baur and colleagues of carrying development too far into the patristic era and of treating it as "the movement of a great machine."[217] John Henry Newman also erred in his theory of development, which although containing a kernel of truth—Christianity was *not* "absolutely fixed" at the start—wrongly posited an infallible church to safeguard development.[218] Fisher, more than either Baur or Newman, strenuously underscored early Christianity's decline.

Fisher's account of that decline centered largely on the intrusion of "Jewish elements" into early Christianity. While Jesus himself, in Fisher's imagination, stands free of "Jewish" traits or ideas, his early followers did not similarly escape their environment: their Semitic backgrounds prompted their "attachment to forms, [a] desire for money and love of riches." Several times throughout his class lectures, Fisher indulged in seemingly gratuitous anti-Jewish caricatures, mentioning the Jews' alleged propensity for trade, attachment to portable property, and love of riches.[219] His negative view of "Jewishness" seems to dominate his account of early Christian history.

Semitic characteristics, in Fisher's view, returned to haunt the developing church, which revived "the Jewish systems of law and priesthood" (viz., the "external tendency"). An overvaluation of such religious "externals" is not, Fisher claimed, in accord with Christ's teaching.[220] Although *heathen* notions of priesthood may also have contributed to this unfortunate development, a hierarchically organized priesthood was derived chiefly from "the old Jewish economy to which the Christian system was imagined to be analogous."[221] The Jewish notion of "mediatorial priesthood" continued in Catholicism until the Reformation, abandoning the confession of Christ as the only true priest in favor of "a class of heaven-appointed intercessors, and almoners of divine grace."[222] When these Jewish elements entered Christianity, truth became "overlaid with traditions" that fostered the development of the papacy. Some centuries later, a "degenerate Judaism" (along with "Ebionitic Christianity") contributed to the development of Mohammedanism.[223]

Paganism eventually finds its place in Fisher's narrative of decline. After the conversion of Constantine, the "infection" of heathen opinions and practices became more prominent. From 312 onward, pagans entering the church encouraged an overvaluation of rites and "works."[224] Christianity's purity was further corrupted by its alliance with the state through its dependence on imperial revenues and its appropriation of the privileges formerly allowed to the pagan priesthoods (e.g., the church's being granted the right to hold property and receive legacies, and the clergy's inheriting the Vestal Virgins' right of *intercessio*).[225] Large-scale heathen conversion made for a "degenerate Christianity" with pictures, amulets, homage paid to martyrs and saints, exaltation of angels, and the "worship of Mary." Monasticism's elevation allowed Christians-in-general to content themselves with a less demanding standard. The pagan mysteries encouraged the development of ritualism in Christianity, "petrifying" the doctrine and liturgy of the Greek Church.[226]

Fisher concluded:

When Christianity was made the religion of the empire, it became also the fashion of a luxurious and decaying society. . . . Its vital principles being overlaid by ideas that were foreign to their nature, had become partially obscured. The pure and steady light of a true Christian life which should have shone abroad over the darkness and confusion of the world, was dimmed by a formal and churchly piety, or made ghostly by an unearthly asceticism.[227]

In Fisher's scheme, in contrast to Schaff's, the light is nearly overcome by the darkness.

This impure Christianity, having absorbed Jewish notions of priesthood and hierarchy, was carried to the northern "barbarians." Missionaries misguidedly portrayed the visible church as the kingdom of God that would mediate between humans and the divine. In effect, the barbarians were offered a religious training "analogous to that of the Jews under the completed hierarchical system."[228]

Considering the inferior Christianity with which the barbarians were presented, one group (at least) did well. In independence, courage, faithfulness, and purity, the Teutons surpassed other barbarian tribes. Although their religion reflected their "warlike propensities," it nevertheless eschewed the "voluptuous and effeminate" elements of classical mythology. The Teutons rapidly warmed to Christianity, despite all the shortcomings of the missionaries who, in addition to their defective message, represented a foreign power. Converts of "Teutonic blood," elevated by Christianity's spirit, were "to become the standard-bearers of modern civilization" in Europe. They felt "the softening and restraining influence of Christian teaching" as they learned "the lessons of the cross." Yet, Fisher added, the church and the clergy were "powerfully affected for the worse by the influx of barbarism and the corrupting influence of barbarian rulers in the generations after the first conquests:[229] here is a third source contributing to later decline. Still, "Christianity, an Asiatic religion by birth, finds its best home in Europe"[230]—where, in the sixteenth century, it would be purified and spiritualized.

Although Fisher expressed no explicit theory of development in early Christianity, he occasionally noted the role of Providence: God brings order and a "worthy goal," despite the "disorder introduced by human perversity."[231] Providence (i.e., God) arranged for the Roman Empire to prepare "the way for modern and Christian civilization." Likewise providential was the proliferation of synagogues throughout the regions in which early Christianity first spread, so that her first traveling missionaries found a platform ready for their use: here, Jews appear to have contributed *some-*

thing beneficial. Fisher even conceded that the papal form of Christianity was a blessing for the conversion and education of Europe, and papal rule later created an association among European states.[232] Moreover, the (otherwise despised) monks did valuable work in education among the barbarians.[233] Despite Fisher's strong narrative of decline that holds ancient Judaism responsible, he, like the other professors, agreed that God can bring good even out of seemingly recalcitrant materials.

Ephraim Emerton: Development and Decline in Church History

Although the Unitarian Ephraim Emerton, less evangelical than the other professors here studied, did not dwell on these themes, he nevertheless *assumed* that the early and medieval church "developed." Notions of the antiquity's decline, in his view, had been overstressed. For example, he faulted Gibbon's *Decline and Fall* for emphasizing "a magnificent edifice crumbling to decay," rather than "the elements of life contained in this very process."[234] Emerton read his sources with a hermeneutic of suspicion foreign to the evangelical professors. He doubted that Roman culture was so shockingly demoralized as writers of that period made out.[235] Treating late antiquity and the early Middle Ages, Emerton aimed to demonstrate how the seemingly "blind forces of destruction became agents working together in the making of a new and fairer civilization." The Germanic peoples took the best of Greece and Rome and from these elements, crafted permanent institutions. Although the early Middle Ages are often labeled the "Dark Ages," Emerton argued that men in this period were, even unconsciously, "building up a new foundation on which future culture might rest."[236]

Emerton doubted that scholars could satisfactorily trace the beginnings of Christianity's organization. Ignorance of "origins," however, left ample room for development—even if Emerton did little to link development to Providence or God. Although Roman Catholics, he told his Harvard students, believe that "the church was born fully developed," Jesus himself taught nothing about a church, nor, "as far as we know, look[ed] forward to one." Catholic writers err when they interpret the office of the early bishopric by its later instantiation: "They see no historical development of the Church," Emerton charged. Catholics argue that even if not all later features of ecclesiastical organization showed themselves at first, they "came out in the fullness of time."[237]

Unlike the evangelical professors who were keen to emphasize the universalistic message of the Jesus movement, Emerton told his students that Jesus' earliest followers imagined that Christianity was meant only for the Jews; incorporating the Gentiles was a later innovation. He recommended that students read Baur's *Church History of the First Three Centuries*[238]—a book that doubtless would reinforce the theme of early Christianity's development, its inner conflicts, and the importance of Jewish elements.

Emerton mentioned as one example of ecclesiastical development the institution of the bishopric, whose earlier form, he cautioned, cannot be identified with its later elaboration. Roman Catholic authors err on this point: either they admit *no* historical development in the church, or they argue that Catholic hierarchical organization was present *in nuce*, emerging "in the fullness of time."[239] Although Emerton strenuously disagreed with Catholic historiography on this point, he, unlike the other professors, urged students to read a Roman Catholic author on the subject, whose work he notes frequently: Blane's *Church History*.[240] Yet, conversely, evangelical Protestants who date the emergence of episcopacy as late as possible *also* get caught short, in this case, by the letters of Ignatius: if these are genuine, Emerton argued, Protestants must admit that the bishopric was formed earlier than they like to concede. He nevertheless asserted, with his fellow Protestant professors, that the "fairest period of the Church's history" occurred *before* strict clerical hierarchy developed.[241]

The church's history, Emerton believed, shows that its divine mission, while often obscured, constantly revived. He thought that as Christianity became favored by the imperial government, it "began to lose its dignity, purity and excellence of motive." When in the age of Constantine the church was granted legal status to receive property, evils grew up.[242] Although Nicaea marked an "epoch in growth" for the church, it saw the advent of "many evils," as freedom of speculation was curbed and all Christians were admonished to adhere to the same standardized belief. As a Unitarian, Emerton—clearly unlike his evangelical colleagues—held that the "contradictions" involved in Trinitarian theology were (and are) "irreconcilable"; Arius' inability to resolve them should not be attributed to a feeble intellect.[243]

Like the other professors, Emerton noted how seeming evils in early Christianity—such as the Roman primacy—contained the seeds for good.

Even if the institution of the Roman bishopric cannot be traced to Peter—Peter may never have been *in* Rome—nevertheless, it had great value in the "dark periods" of Christian history. Uniformity of doctrine, for example, required that many churches be controlled by one.[244]

As a medievalist, Emerton was especially interested in the "barbarian" groups and their Christianization: as noted earlier, he devoted twenty-seven pages of class notes to their movements and settlements. This topic lent itself to a positive assessment of the Roman bishopric's growing strength. The Roman papacy, Emerton wrote, proved to be the "most useful helper," "a great agent," in the Franks' establishment of an empire—and it was the Franks who would "give law and order to the continent of Europe."[245] Franks, in Emerton's scheme, trump Teutons as the bearers of European civilization.

Emerton ruled out appeals to the "golden thread" of Providence in historiography. For him, history is a solely human enterprise. In his presidential address to the American Society of Church History, Emerton pointedly decried church historians' propensity to identify their pet "golden thread" as the true one. Only a "tangled skein," he charged, results from their attempts to trim the divine presence to fit their own small schemes.[246] Historians, in their academic work, would do well to abandon appeals to Providence. If there has been progress in human history, it apparently did not, for Emerton, rest on divine prompting.

Conclusion

In this chapter I have detailed how traditional Protestant beliefs in the church's early and rapid decline collided with newer German theories of historical development. The professors' espousal of the church's development, however halting and unsteady, prompted them to assign a higher value to the patristic era than had been customary among American Protestants. Critics, however, charged that their views sounded "Catholicizing." Yet the professors shied from too robust an embrace of development, for fear of falling into the alleged errors of Tübingen that granted little stability to the church's early years or little privilege to the New Testament as unique. Only when Providence was eliminated as a viable historiographical category and the New Testament was studied as other works of ancient literature could the history of early Christianity find its niche in the curriculum of the (so-called) secular university.

How development and decline uneasily jostled against each other will be apparent in the professors' treatment of church polity, Roman Catholicism, and asceticism in the chapters that follow.

PART III

Topics of Early Christian History
in Nineteenth-Century Analysis

CHAPTER 6

Polity and Practice

Q: What is the distinction between the corrupt and the true church?
A: The corrupt church has so far departed from the purity of the faith and worship, that it cannot any longer be considered as a real church of Christ, but a Synagogue of Satan.

—Samuel Miller (1820/1821)

Introduction

On no topic was the Protestant professors' "quest for origins" more patent than on early Christian polity and practice. Exploring the question of when and how episcopacy developed afforded a broad opportunity for contemporary denominational apologetics and polemics. As this chapter shows, debates over the "authenticity" of various patristic writings and their authority for the present were fuelled in part by low-church Protestants'—especially Presbyterians'—need for early Christian allies in their challenge to the governmental structures of the Episcopal and Roman Catholic Churches. Moreover, preferences in models of secular government could be deployed to ideological effect: forms of ecclesiastical polity could be described in the language of monarchy (and its association with divine right), aristocracy, democracy, and republicanism.

Presbyterian and Congregationalist professors agreed that episcopacy was foreign to the New Testament: the word *episkopos* was to be translated as "pastor" or "minister." Not divinely ordained, episcopacy emerged for merely practical, even worldly, reasons. Although the professors chronicled and explained episcopacy's rise in different ways, *all* believed that clerical hierarchy was an unfortunate development, signaling the early church's decline from primitive simplicity and purity. Here, development had gone awry. Church Fathers who endorsed episcopacy, the professors claimed, carry no authority for present practice. Nevertheless, they readily appealed to the Fathers when by doing so they could gain support for their particular views: the Fathers were good to "argue with."

As the nineteenth century wore on, the professors' primary contemporary target regarding church polity changed from Episcopalianism to Roman Catholicism. That this change took place amid bourgeoning Catholic immigration at home and developments in the Vatican abroad (decrees on the Immaculate Conception of Mary [1854] and Papal Infallibility [1870], and the Syllabus of Errors [1864]) is perhaps to be expected. When Samuel Miller began teaching at Princeton in 1813, Catholicism, although especially spurned by American Protestants in the Northeast, remained a somewhat distant threat to their hegemony. By mid-century and beyond, however, professors living in New York and New England could scarcely overlook the waves of Catholic immigrants flooding into northern cities and the subsequent anti-Catholic backlash. Protestant hysteria—centered on imagined Vatican takeovers of America, Jesuits dictating school curricula, and semi-literate immigrants controlling urban governments—erupted. Philip Schaff's hope for a reunion of all Christendom, of Protestants, Roman Catholics, and Orthodox, seemed an ever-dimming prospect. Since, as the statistically minded Roswell Hitchcock informed his (largely Presbyterian) class, three-quarters of the world's Christians live under episcopacy,[1] the task of reunion would be formidable. How the professors' evangelical sympathies and only slightly veiled antipathy to the Vatican played out against their desire, spurred by their German educations and study, to affirm a progressive development in church history is a thread connecting the chapters that follow.

Appealing to the Fathers

Despite the professors' usual rejection of patristic authority, they nevertheless appealed to the early ante-Nicene Fathers and to Jerome, "Hilary" (i.e., Ambrosiaster), and John Chrysostom to argue their case against the presence of episcopacy in Christianity's first decades. That the professors believed Paul himself to have written the Pastoral Epistles lent an added urgency to their attempt to "explain away" references to bishops (*episkopoi*) in New Testament texts: what might bishops be when the Apostles still lived?

One strategy was to argue that in early Christian texts, "bishop" and "presbyter" were interchangeable terms. Here, Jerome, Ambrosiaster, and John Chrysostom proved useful allies. The professors frequently cited Jerome's *Epistle* 146 to Evangelus, in which Jerome claims that for Paul (as alleged author of the Pastorals) "presbyter" and "bishop" denote the same office, differentiated by only one function: bishops alone may ordain.[2] (On this point, they also appealed to John Chrysostom's *Homily 11 on I Timothy*.[3]) Jerome's *Epistle* 146 also offered a reason for the subsequent choice of one presbyter to rule over the rest, namely, "to remedy schism and to prevent each individual from rending the church of Christ by drawing it to himself."[4] Jerome's *Commentary on Titus* 1:5–7 also explained, to the professors' satisfaction, that the Pastor's seeming alignment of presbyters and bishops in those verses showed that in the apostolic era, the bishop was simply the head presbyter.[5]

"Hilary" (Ambrosiaster) likewise afforded valuable assistance. Seeking to explain why, in his discussion of qualifications for clerical office (I Tim. 3:8), the Pastor omitted mention of presbyters but passed directly from *episcopus* to *diaconus*, Ambrosiaster claims that bishop and presbyter have "one ordination," so that both can be styled *sacerdos*. The bishop, however, is "*primus*," so that "every bishop is a presbyter, but not every presbyter is a bishop." The bishop he describes as "*inter presbyteros primus*."[6]

Ambrosiaster's comment on another "Pauline" passage also served the Protestant professors well. Ephesians 4:11–12 differentiates Christ's gifts of various offices: apostles, prophets, evangelists, pastors, teachers. Ambrosiaster explains that Timothy, although a *presbyteros*, is nevertheless here named as *episcopus*, because the first presbyters were called bishops.[7] Patristic references such as these proved highly useful in the professors' critique of episcopacy: *episcopoi*, in the early days of the church, were merely presbyters.

Old Texts and New Finds

Into the fray over early Christian polity entered debates regarding the letters of Ignatius and the discoveries of the *Philosophumena* (*Refutation of All*

Heresies) and the *Didache* (*The Teaching of the Twelve Apostles*). The professors' special uses of these texts will be considered in detail below; here, I offer a brief introduction to the issues involved.

Ignatius' letters required careful handling by Protestant professors, given the author's frequent reference to bishops. When Samuel Miller began teaching, no agreement had yet been reached on the size of the Ignatian corpus and its "authenticity."[8] There was a "long" recension that included thirteen letters, consisting of an expanded version of the seven now considered authentic, plus six others, some bearing signs of interpolation that favored various sides of the Christological debates of late antiquity. A second option was a recension of six letters in Greek from one eleventh-century manuscript, published in 1644 by Anglican Bishop James Ussher under the title *Polycarpi et Ignatii epistulae*.[9] Toward the end of Miller's career, a third option presented itself: the "short" Syriac recension of Ignatius' letters (those to Polycarp, Ephesians, and Romans, plus a paragraph from Trallians) discovered in 1842 in Egypt and published by William Cureton of the British Museum in 1845 and thereafter.[10]

Cureton's claim that there were three "genuine" and four "ungenuine" Ignatian letters was adopted by Christian K. J. Bunsen, a German statesman and amateur scholar popular with the American professors.[11] Bunsen's assessment was hotly disputed in 1848 by F. C. Baur in *Die ignatianischen Briefe und ihr neuester Kritiker*. Baur questioned the "authenticity" of all seven letters, arguing that since they show evidence of episcopal hierarchy and Gnostic "infection," they should be dated to the late second century.[12] Baur pointedly asked why Protestants were so interested in this new Syriac manuscript find? It must go badly for Protestantism if so much rests on whether Ignatius or someone else wrote the letters! Do Spirit, Truth, and Freedom, Baur acidly queried, depend on an ancient Bishop of Antioch?[13] Several decades passed before the work of two scholars, one German and one British, laid the controversy to rest. In 1873, Theodor Zahn published *Ignatius von Antiochen* (which showed that the Cureton Syriac letters were not the "originals"), and in 1885, J. B. Lightfoot definitively established, at least to most Protestants' satisfaction, the authenticity of seven letters of the "middle" Greek recension.[14]

At mid-century, the stir over Ignatius' letters was joined by excitement over a fourteenth-century manuscript, the *Philosophumena* (*Refutation of All Heresies*) discovered on Mt. Athos in 1842. Edited by Emmanuel Miller, it was first published by Clarendon Press in 1851. Its original ascription to

Origen (as the manuscript claimed) was soon challenged, and the work re-assigned to Hippolytus.[15] The author's allegations of corruption and heresy in the early Roman bishopric were of considerable interest to both Protestant and anti-ultramontane Catholic scholars.[16] Of the Protestant professors here featured, Philip Schaff in particular was deeply intrigued by the *Philosophumena* and its implications.[17]

Last, the discovery in 1873 and publication in 1883 of the *Didache* (*The Teaching of the Twelve Apostles*) by Philotheos Bryennios, Metropolitan of Nicomedia—whom Schaff called "the Tischendorf of the Greek Church"[18] —was much heralded by American evangelical Protestants. (Indeed, even decidedly *unevangelical* Harvard Divinity School students organized a seminar on the work shortly after its publication.[19]) The *Didache*, which the professors dated as early as 90 or 100 A.D., appeared to provide evidence that the "free" state of the church had persisted longer than advocates of episcopacy claimed.[20] Volumes of commentary ensued, with both Hitchcock and Schaff producing editions, translations, and explications.

Debates over these three sets of texts, as we shall later see, were of central importance for nineteenth-century discussions of early Christian polity, particularly concerning the role of bishops. All the professors—excepting Ephraim Emerton, seemingly uninterested in the issues—were left with the question, if episcopacy had not been instituted by Jesus or the Apostles, how and why did it arise? They enlist a stock set of reasons to explain how the bishop, originally the "chief presiding officer of the Presbytery," over time gained independent status and higher rank.[21]

Episcopacy and the Professors

Samuel Miller

MILLER AND THE EPISCOPALIANS

Samuel Miller's approach to early Christian polity was strongly conditioned by his disputes, both as Presbyterian minister in New York and as seminary professor at Princeton, with Episcopalians.[22] Letters to various correspondents incorporated into the biography of Miller written by his son show his spirited attack on Episcopalian influence in New York.[23] Two of Miller's writings are particularly concerned to defend Presbyterianism and attack episcopacy. In *Letters Concerning the Constitution and Order of the Christian*

Ministry (1807; reissued in 1809 and 1830), Miller championed what he deemed the original form of church government (viz., presbyterial) against his Episcopalian adversaries. In 1840, he published *Presbyterianism; The Truly Primitive and Apostolical Constitution of the Church of Christ.* In the years between, he wrote many essays and letters on the topic.[24]

In 1803, Miller charged, New York Episcopalians for the first time became vociferous in their claim that the diocesan bishopric was a divinely appointed institution. In Miller's rendition, Episcopalians then argued that diocesan episcopacy was necessary for authorized ministry, for valid ordinations, and indeed for a true church; in consequence, Presbyterian and other Protestant ministers held no valid office. At the time, Miller had not (to his later regret) named those responsible for these claims, out of respect for the persons involved. Over two decades later, still indignant, he did: Rev. Dr. John Bowden, Professor at Columbia College, and John Henry Hobart, Episcopal Bishop of New York.[25] According to Miller, Hobart had unjustly accused him of assaulting episcopacy with arrogance, bitterness, and insidiousness. Alleging that he responded only in self-defense to Episcopalians' attacks, Miller retorted that prelacy was "an unscriptural error," "an unwarranted innovation on apostolic simplicity."[26] In 1805, he had advised every Presbyterian minister to be "particularly armed on the subject of Church Government, and the history of Presbyterian and Episcopal ordination."[27]

Later, justifying his hot critique, Miller noted that he had listed 86 pages of extracts from the writings of the Fathers—perhaps overkill?—to support his case. It was, he thought, a "fair specimen," although he had not included *every* relevant patristic text to prove erroneous the Episcopalians' claim that the diocesan bishopric was the first form of church government after the apostolic era.[28]

Once he assumed his professorial duties in 1813, Miller gave considerable attention to early ecclesiastical polity in his courses on church history and church government, as well as in his published writings. As late as 1843, Miller did not hesitate to use the classroom as a platform to rail against Episcopalians, most of whom, he alleged, are "thorough going [*sic*] Arminians, Pelagians,—even Unitarians,[29] Socinians," and, what's more, profane foxhunters, theatergoers, and card-players. As for Anglicans across the waters, Miller had heard reports of the Oxford Movement, but did not know whether it was growing or declining. In any event, he judged that about half the people of England are "perfectly heathen in life!"[30] Episcopalians in America, however, remained Miller's chief target.

Denominations that accord special authority to bishops, Miller claimed, erroneously pattern themselves on the Old Testament priesthood. The latter was intended to serve only as "a type and temporary institution," finding its fulfillment in Christ the High Priest (as the Epistle to the Hebrews attests). If episcopacy-loving groups are so enamored of the Old Testament priesthood, Miller archly asked, why do they not reinstitute sacrifices and other priestly practices?[31]

English Reformers of the sixteenth century, Miller charged, were greatly mistaken in retaining prelacy. The Reformation would have afforded them the opportune moment to cast off the spurious polity of the Catholic Church and to reinstate the original presbyterial form, a form that had continued for "two full centuries" after the apostolic era before being overtaken by episcopacy.[32] That they did not resulted in episcopacy being transferred to America.

MILLER, THE BIBLE, AND THE CHURCH FATHERS

Miller was by far the most vociferous of all the professors here considered on the issue of early church governance. That Miller faced down his opponents, alternating between prosecution and defendant as in a law court, summoning "witnesses" from the early church to provide "evidence" and "testimony," suggests not only his adversarial approach to church history, but also his notion of what the Fathers were "good for": to trounce those who enlisted them to support episcopacy.

Miller considered the textbook he used—Mosheim—highly unsatisfactory on the topic. In addition to being vague and confused, Mosheim placed the transition to prelacy too early for Miller's tastes, namely, the first century.[33] The "apostolic and primitive form of church government was Presbyterian," Miller assured his students. The Apostles, acting on the immediate direction of the "divine Master," established this form and intended it to be perpetual. All churches should have adhered to this presbyterial organization, the norm by which purity or deviation is assessed. Some deviations, Miller conceded, do not *destroy* the church—for example, (even) those associated with Episcopalianism, Congregationalism, and Independency.[34] Nevertheless, these denominations have strayed from the primitive and authoritative standard. "Origins" matter.

If episcopacy had been instituted by Christ, Miller argued, it would doubtless appear in the Gospels. Since it does not, those who affirm the rule of bishops introduce the practice to supply the Bible's alleged "lack." Miller provided his Presbyterian students with a pointed retort to those who claim that episcopacy is endorsed by the New Testament: "Impudent intruder! Whom makest thou of thyself? Art thou the supply-general of the defects of revelation?" Although Episcopalians brazenly rejoin that the *Church Fathers* witness to episcopacy, their appeal must be rejected: even if the Fathers and ten thousand other witnesses bore *"unanimous* testimony," anything contrary to Scripture should be rejected. If Christians were to follow the Fathers' "witness," as Episcopalians suggest, they would also justify the use of milk, honey, and the sign of the cross in baptism.[35] The Fathers, Miller concluded, are not a reliable, or early enough, guide to the practice of pure, primitive Christianity; they carry no authority for nineteenth-century Presbyterians on the issue of episcopacy. Authority lies in the New Testament alone.

Although chary of Anglican appeals to the Fathers, Miller, too, could summon early patristic writers to bolster his own claim.[36] In his *Letters Concerning the Constitution and Order of the Christian Ministry*, Miller cited numerous patristic sources (derived largely, it appears, from Mosheim's *Ecclesiastical History*).[37] Throughout, he summoned the Fathers as "witnesses" to the original form of church government and to its sad decline into diocesan episcopacy. Appealing to Clement of Rome, Polycarp, Papias, Irenaeus, Justin, and Clement of Alexandria, Miller concluded that nothing in their works supports the Episcopalians' claim that bishop is a distinct and higher order than presbyter.[38] Miller also called on Jerome—citing *Epistle* 146 and the *Commentary on Titus*—to testify that in apostolic times, bishop and presbyter designated the same office; the departure from this arrangement had taken place only in Jerome's own day, manifesting (according to Miller) "the decay of religion" and "the ambition of ministers."[39] Jerome also served as a useful ally for Miller to argue that in Christianity's infancy, no presbyter stood above another.[40] When Jerome distinguished bishops from presbyters, he was not (in Miller's view) citing the primitive constitution of the church, but later arrangements.[41] In an ameliorating mood, Miller cited Jerome's claim that episcopacy arose as a practical measure to remove the seeds of schism: with one man in charge, unity might better be retained.[42]

Miller also appealed to Cyprian, who—despite the latter's role in the formation of episcopacy—at least protested the growing power of the bishop of Rome. In the recitation format that he often used, Miller asked his class: Did the bishops of Rome at this time make claims that later would be deemed "monstrous and mischievous"? The correct answer (he noted) is "Yes," pointing students toward the writings of Cyprian, who resisted such claims by Rome's bishop.[43] Other Fathers could also be cited, but the truth is,

> for the first two hundred years after Christ, it is certain that neither prelacy nor Independency was known in the Church of Christ. . . . Every flock of professing Christians had its Pastor or Bishop, with its bench of Elders, by whom the government and discipline were conducted; and its body of Deacons, by whom the funds collected for the relief of the poor, were received and distributed.[44]

Given that true episcopacy is not to be found in the New Testament, when did it commence? Miller delays the onset as late as possible: although the second century showed some tendencies in this direction,[45] the institution did not develop until the fourth century. Then, bishops became distinct from presbyters. After citing yet more passages from Augustine, "Hilary," and John Chrysostom, Miller concluded that Episcopalians' appeal to Eusebius, who *did* distinguish bishops from presbyters, proves that prelacy had come to prevail only at the time of Constantine.[46]

Diocesan (as contrasted with *congregational*) episcopacy was an even later development. The New Testament, Miller argued, nowhere approves of diocesan episcopacy. Although bishops gradually extended their reach over more than one congregation, even at the time of Cyprian a bishop still ruled a single congregation, not a diocese.[47] Miller cited records from the Council of Carthage in the early fifth century: if there were then between 500 and 600 bishops in North Africa (a region "not more extensive than some of our large states"), then surely these could not have been diocesan bishops. Miller also noted Gregory of Nyssa's testimony that when Gregory Thaumaturgus served as bishop of Neo-Caesarea around 250, there were only 17 Christians in his parish[48]—a number precluding the latter's status as a diocesan bishop. In Miller's scheme, bishops were assigned a different and higher order from presbyters only late in the patristic era, as a result of humans' sinful grasp for power.

Miller offered the following explanation for episcopacy's growth. Starting in the second century, urban pastors acquired domination over "small and feeble" suburban congregations. At first, their dominance was granted as a courtesy, but later they claimed it as their "ecclesiastical right."[49] The bishops' quest for power was motivated by the human "love of pre-eminence." To be sure, Miller granted, the "desire for pre-eminence and power is natural to man"—but this does not excuse its sinfulness. That a desire for pre-eminence was manifest even in the New Testament era proves only that the primitive church itself was not entirely pure.[50]

Correlating church government with various forms of political rule, Miller wrote that the Roman Catholic papacy corresponds to a notion of "spiritual *monarchy*," episcopacy to "spiritual *prelacy*," and Independency to "spiritual *democracy*," while Presbyterianism corresponds to "spiritual *republicanism*." "Republicanism" clearly trumps "democracy" on the scale of values.

MILLER: PRESBYTERIANISM AS THE ORIGINAL
FORM OF CHURCH GOVERNMENT

Miller staunchly argued that the presbyterial form of church government was the "original," the form planned by Jesus and carried out by the Apostles: Christ "made all ministers who are authorized to dispense the word and sacraments, perfectly equal in official rank and power." Moreover, "in every Church the immediate exercise of ecclesiastical power is deposited, not with the whole mass of people, but with a body of their representatives, styled Elders [Presbyters]."[51] Finding the rudimentary forms of this "republican" structure in the "church" of the Old Testament, Miller traced its evidences in the New Testament and into early Christianity.[52]

In the presbyterial form, Miller argued, there were (1) Ministers or "Teaching Elders" who enjoyed parity with each other, taught Scripture and doctrine, and administered the sacraments; (2) Ruling Elders, who assisted in governing; and (3) Deacons. Neither Ruling Elders nor Deacons were authorized to perform the duties of the Teaching Elder. Although Miller conceded that the word "bishop" (*episkopos*) is found in the New Testament, he argued that it there denotes only the Minister or Teaching Elder of a single congregation.[53] The bishop (i.e., the Teaching Elder) and the Ruling Elder, although they shared the same *order*, differed in function.[54] *Episkopos* did not signal to Miller, as it did to Episcopalians, the chief of three distinct orders, Bishops, Elders, and Deacons.[55] Miller granted only two, namely, two forms of Elders (Teaching and Ruling), and Deacons. The perfection of the church demands that this original form of polity be retained even in the present.[56]

From his time as a minister in New York, Miller was especially keen to uphold the validity of the Ruling Eldership. He noted that New Testament passages (Acts 14:23, Titus 1:5, I Timothy 5:17, Ephesians 4:11–14) differentiate Elders from the Pastors whose function was to preach. The duty of these Elders was the exercise of discipline. Miller granted that this office (unfortunately) fell out of favor in the later patristic period,[57] but was re-established by the Protestant Reformers.[58] He summoned patristic testimony to justify the office against "Prelatists" who argued that the office of Ruling Elder was unknown until Calvin invented it in 1541. Miller heatedly discounted this charge: Calvin merely *restored* the apostolic pattern of government that had fallen into abeyance in late antiquity.[59]

Since the office of Ruling Elder is found in the New Testament, it matters not how soon after apostolic times the practice fell into disuse—although Miller summoned what evidence he could to show the office's continuance for a few centuries.[60] In fact, one sure sign of the church's decline was its abandonment of this position; after all, the officer whose duty it is to correct "aberrations" and maintain "pure and scriptural discipline" cannot be expected to be popular.[61]

In addition to biblical citations allegedly regarding Ruling Elders, Miller also cited patristic evidence, especially from Cyprian and "Hilary."[62] He summoned passages from Origen that mention elders or rulers (whom Miller takes to be Ruling Elders) who inquire into the manners and behavior of those admitted to the church and who expel the unworthy.[63] He found other references to such rulers in the writings of Hippolytus, Augustine, and Gregory the Great.[64] In effect, any time a ruler or presbyter is depicted as inquiring into a Christian's behavior, ordering someone to appear for examination, or excluding someone from the church, he is deemed a Ruling Elder. Eventually, Miller claimed, Ruling Elders were banished, probably first in large cities, where "ambition [was] the most prevalent" [bishops' ambition for precedence apparently led them to disband the office], "laxity the most indulged, and strict discipline most unpopular."[65] Miller doubtless believed that Episcopalians' refusal to acknowledge the office of Ruling Elder contributed to the worldly behavior with which he charged them.

Throughout his tenure at the Princeton Seminary, Miller continued to champion the office of Ruling Elder as necessary to the perfection of ecclesiastical polity. James Moffat, who assumed the Helena Professorship of Church History at the Seminary some years after Miller's death, quietly abandoned his fight regarding Teaching Elders and Ruling Elders. Moffat's lectures on church history contain traditional Protestant views of early church polity, but lack the fervor with which Miller engaged the subject. Moffat rejected the notion of an early episcopacy, but kept silent about the status of Elders.[66]

Henry Smith

The Union and Yale professors expressed their views on early church polity with considerably less fire than did Miller. Henry Smith granted that Jesus did not enjoin or forbid *any* particular form of church government: rather, he came to earth to found a "spiritual kingdom."[67] Smith, like Miller, named "Hilary" and Jerome as attesting the primitive condition of the church after the time of Jesus as presbyterial.[68] An originally more egalitarian system of church government was gradually displaced in favor of priesthood, hierarchy, and the belief that the sacraments, as "mysteries," were in themselves efficacious.[69]

Smith more graciously conceded an earlier development to the episcopate than had Miller: by the early second century, one of the (several) presbyters in a church had been made a president, styled bishop. From then on, greater divisions emerged between laity and clergy, as notions of priesthood developed.[70] From around 200, Smith calculated, "tradition [became] mixed with the growing hierarchical tendencies of the so-called Apostolic Churches."[71]

Cyprian of Carthage was central to Smith's discussion of episcopacy. Smith accorded Cyprian a mixed role in this development, occupying an intermediate position that marked a transition from a presbyterial to an episcopal system. Since prior to Cyprian's era, Smith wrote, there had already been a shift to episcopacy, along with the adoption of the notion of "ceremonial sanctity" and the sacraments as "mysteries," Cyprian was not responsible for these developments. An "Old Testament idea of a sacrificial priesthood" had been adopted by the church even before Cyprian's time. Cyprian, along with Firmilian of Caesarea, defended more democratic notions of ministry against the incursions and "arrogance" of the bishop

of Rome. Cyprian, Smith noted, still consulted with the presbyters, a remnant of more primitive times, and church councils of his era still included
all the clergy and "the people," not just bishops. Although "primacy of
honor" might be ceded to Rome, Cyprian had contended "for the rights of
all bishops." In Smith's reconstruction, some of Christianity's primitive
simplicity still remained in the mid-third century; a fully developed hierarchical system was not yet in place. Smith, however, did not completely
exonerate Cyprian, who stands as a symptom of the church's decline: he
imagined the Lord's Supper to constitute a sacrifice.[72]

Only in the early fourth century, in Smith's view, the era of Constantine,
was the presbyterial system suppressed and a diocesan system, "monarchical episcopacy," established, in which the clergy are "recognized as a sacerdotal class." Then, the ancient simplicity of Christianity became subverted
by union with the state.[73] Once again, more "republican" forms of church
government receive pride of place.

Roswell Hitchcock

Roswell Hitchcock likewise conceded that although episcopacy was not of
apostolic origin, it grew from apostolic times onward: the best New Testament scholars, he assured his students, hold this view. In Clement of
Rome's letter to the Corinthians, he observed, we encounter a chief presbyter who "in later time [will be] called bishop"—but in Clement's day, presbyter and bishop denoted the same office.[74] Hitchcock was adamant:
Cyprian's claim that the Apostles themselves established episcopacy is simply "not in keeping with the facts."[75] By 150, however, episcopacy as a distinct office was well established.[76]

Hitchcock's 1867 essay on the "Origin and Growth of Episcopacy" outlines points that he frequently made in his courses. He provides excerpts
from numerous ante-Nicene texts so that readers lacking access to the
"original authorities" (i.e., the primary sources) might judge the matter for
themselves. Whether they favor or reject episcopacy, they will conclude that
it is not "of Apostolic appointment, but only a growth, the principal stages
of which may be clearly traced." Hitchcock claims that (even) many knowl-
edgeable Episcopalians now concede that episcopacy was not found in the
New Testament—an alignment that left Catholics and members of "oriental churches" to argue for its apostolic origin.[77] Hitchcock's more educated

Episcopalians, it appears, are now perceived as "insiders" with evangelical Protestants, casting Roman Catholics and "oriental" Christians to the non-scholarly "outside."

In this article, Hitchcock traces his way through the writings of Clement of Rome, the accepted letters of the Ignatian corpus (detailing the status of that debate), Irenaeus, Tertullian, and Cyprian, with fourth-century corroboration provided by "Hilary" (Ambrosiaster) and Jerome. He argues that Ignatius' "excessive" appeal to bishops (at least 58 times in his letters) indicates that the word or office was an innovation that the author was doing "his utmost to recommend." Whereas Irenaeus used "wavering terminology" regarding church offices—sometimes meaning "bishop" in a "congregational sense," sometimes identifying the offices of bishop and presbyter and sometimes not[78]—Tertullian's terminology was firm. Tertullian drew a clear line between clergy and laity: here, the clergy are all priests, and the bishop a High Priest.[79] Cyprian merely solidified Tertullian's distinctions, adding "sharpness and emphasis to statements already made."[80] For Hitchcock, Tertullian is key to the development of "sacerdotalism."

Hitchcock also appealed to the writings of "Hilary" (Ambrosiaster)—whom he styles a "clear-headed and able writer"[81]—to argue that originally, the presbyter oldest in office was called bishop, who was succeeded by the next oldest. Later, however, bishops began to be elected on the basis of their ability, without regard to age. Jerome's *Letter* 146 shows that bishop and presbyter were originally one and the same; the practice of setting one presbyter over the rest emerged later. Episcopacy, according to Hitchcock, developed for merely practical considerations, not from divine ordination.[82] He cited Jerome's claim that episcopal hierarchy was devised as a practical measure to remove the seeds of schism: with one man in charge, unity might better be retained. Hitchcock also appealed to the persecutions as a factor, which (along with the threat of schism) drove the church "to a closer and more aristocratic organization."[83] "Aristocracy" was clearly not in favor with nineteenth-century American Protestants. The church should have remained a "republic."

Philip Schaff

Philip Schaff, like many Protestant scholars of his day, spiritualized the operations and organization of the early church. In the New Testament, he was sure, there was no sacerdotalism; all Christians were to offer "the sacrifice of their persons and property to the Lord, and the spiritual sacrifice of thanksgiving and praise." No post-biblical form of church government, Schaff argued, exists by divine right or commands "perpetual obligation." For Schaff, the New Testament "is the only safe guide and ultimate standard in all matters of faith and discipline."[84]

Schaff, like Hitchcock, conceded an earlier development of episcopacy than had Miller: although not of apostolic origin, it appears universally by the mid-second century,[85] and is securely established by the time of Irenaeus and Tertullian.[86] Its rise was "inseparable from the catholic principle of authority and mediation," in contrast to Protestant notions of freedom and the believer's direct relation with Christ. Episcopacy requires the notion of priesthood, sacrifice, and an "essential distinction between clergy and laity." Since this distinction did not arise in apostolic times, those styled bishops in the New Testament "must have held only a subordinate place."[87] Schaff's assignment of the Pastoral Epistles to Paul bolstered his assumption that the original disciples and Apostles were still commanding prime authority at the time bishops are mentioned in these texts; hence bishops could not have enjoyed a particularly exalted role.

Schaff sketched the development of church polity as follows: from an original, apostolical type of church organization (in which the other Apostles were independent of Peter) developed a "primitive Congregational" form, which Schaff also labeled the "Presbyterian episcopate." This in turn evolved into "metropolitan episcopacy" in the middle of the third century, into the patriarchate in the fourth, and into the papacy in the Middle Ages.[88]

Still in the mid-second century, Schaff argued, some primitive spirit remained. Even as episcopacy was taking hold, Montanists (for example) retained the notion of universal priesthood—although they manifested the principle in "an eccentric form," allowing "women to teach publicly in the church."[89] Tertullian, at the end of the century, first asserted "sacerdotal claims on behalf of the Christian ministry," and Cyprian went even further. Schaff charged Romanists and Anglicans with abusing Cyprian's writings for their own sectarian purposes; Cyprian, he argued, can be cited as much on the side of "consolidated primacy" as on that of "independent episcopacy."[90] Indeed, as we saw in the discussion of Smith, Cyprian-as-bishop could be summoned to witness *against* the claims of the bishop of Rome.

Schaff offered several reasons for the development of episcopacy. Like

Miller, he appealed to human sinfulness: the power and temporal advantage of the bishopric became "a lure for avarice and ambition, and a temptation to the lordly and secular spirit."[91] More benignly, episcopacy was a practical organizational device: Schaff refers to the statements of Jerome, John Chrysostom, and Theodoret that the episcopate arose out of practical necessity and "church usage." In addition, the sacerdotal practices of "other religions" of the Mediterranean at the time of Christianity's rise could be blamed; these religions sharply distinguished between clergy and laity, with functions of sacrifice and altar assigned to priests alone. This division swept into Christianity and promoted a priestly order, in Schaff's view, because the church was forced to adapt itself to "barbarians as well as to civilized nations,"[92] both of whom were accustomed to the institution of priests. "Barbarians," it here appears, contributed to the same development of hierarchy for which other Protestant professors had blamed aristocratic and monarchical principles.

George Fisher

George Fisher's class notes, dating from shortly after the Vatican declaration on Papal Infallibility, show an uncommon interest in the topic of episcopacy. Fisher aimed to arm students with appropriate rejoinders to proponents of episcopacy's apostolic origin. First, those proponents claim, the New Testament cites James as a head or leader (i.e., a "bishop") of Christians at Jerusalem (Fisher countered: whatever James's position, his case was unique and unrepeatable). Second, some proponents claim that the seven angels of the Apocalypse signal "bishops" (Fisher: an improbable conjecture; moreover, the Apocalypse was not written until around 70 A.D., too late to count as evidence for Christianity's first decades). Third, they appeal to Ignatius' mention of bishops (Fisher: only the shorter Greek recension of the Ignatian letters is genuine; in addition, Ignatius contends for an authority that had *not* been present earlier). In Fisher's view, bishoprics grew up "so gradually and noiselessly" that it was natural to imagine that they had always been part of church government.[93]

Late in his career, in 1899, Fisher baldly asserted that the Apostles themselves offered *no* plan for future church organization. By this date, Fisher had apparently digested recent scholarship on New Testament eschatology. Since the Apostles, he now claimed, expected a speedy return of the Savior and an end to the present order, they did not imagine *any* future church organization, whether on Episcopal, Presbyterian, *or* Congregational lines.[94] No Protestant denomination, in other words, could claim apostolic authority for itself alone. Of the American evangelical professors here surveyed, only Fisher lived long enough to witness the "eschatological turn," namely, the (belated) recognition by scholars from the 1890s on that the notion of the Kingdom of God in the Synoptic Gospels and some Pauline letters betokened an apocalyptic rending of the present world order and the institution of a different, divinely established realm.[95]

Against those who claimed a primitive establishment of episcopacy, Fisher argued that the "early Christian societies were little republics, at first under the supervision of the apostles."[96] "Bishops" and "elders" developed later, but even then, *episkopoi* and *presbyteroi* were interchangeable terms. Teaching was done in a free spirit, with the congregation moved to contribute—"as in the Methodist conference." The Apostles were in essence a "college of head pastors." No distinction existed between clergy and laity in terms of "orders," although there was a difference of functions.[97]

To explain the rise of episcopacy, Fisher appealed to the leadership vacuum left by the death of the original Apostles: replenishment of the movement's original leaders was needed. He also adopted the explanation that Christianity had been influenced by "other religions"—but the "other" *he* selected was Judaism: the church absorbed Old Testament notions of priestly mediation. This "Jewish" view, continuing until the Reformation, abandoned the original Christian belief that the only true priest is Christ. The New Testament, unlike the Old, Fisher assured his students, has no concept of a "mediatorial priesthood."[98]

Yet, Fisher conceded, even in the first three centuries, as the writings of Ignatius and Cyprian testify, there was a "gradual decline of the feeling of brotherhood" that allowed bishops to acquire a higher status than other church officers.[99] Nevertheless, the early presbyters and bishops were *laymen*—not priests—who acted on behalf of congregations. "Episcopacy in the second century was governmental, not sacerdotal," Fisher claimed, simply a means to secure "order and unity." The first manifestations of sacerdotalism (borrowed from "analogies of the Old Testament system") come with Tertullian and a half-century later were developed by Cyprian. Entering Christianity by degrees, sacerdotalism deprived the laity of its former prerogatives. The rising number of church officers reinforced the clerical-lay distinction.[100] In Fisher's view, a real development of polity—not just a continuation of earlier practices—occurred in Cyprian's era.[101]

As late as the fourth century, Fisher continued, the country-bishops retained their independence, although the bishop of the metropolis had hegemony. Bishops of non-metropolitan towns, however, gradually lost their independence before the advancing hierarchical principle. Although Cyprian entertained "sacerdotal" notions of ministry, only at the time of the Donatist controversy did "the catholic and hierarchical view" gain a "decisive victory"[102]: Fisher here implies that Augustine was the impresario of sacerdotal hierarchy. Sacerdotal theory, Fisher charged, is the ecclesiastical equivalent of the divine right of kings in political theory—a view opposed by the Protestant Reformers and by seventeenth-century Puritans,[103] not to speak of American advocates of republicanism.

Yet Fisher, like the other professors, appealed to patristic writings (e.g., to Jerome's claims that the offices of presbyter and of bishop were early identical[104]) when such an appeal appeared to assist his side of the argument. He also enlisted Irenaeus and Cyprian as allies in their protest against the developing power of the Roman bishopric: Irenaeus stood against Victor's claims, and Cyprian, against Stephen's.[105]

By the 1880s, Fisher claimed, all Protestant scholars in Europe—excepting high-church Anglicans—were in agreement that the early church held a notion of ministry, not of priesthood. Appealing to the works of J. B. Lightfoot and Edwin Hatch, Fisher affirmed:

> Historical study, conducted on the scientific method, without sectarian bias, will speedily set aside sacerdotalism so far as it leans for support on the authority and example of the Early Church. It is now apparent to what extent the Early Churches copied in their organization the models of political society and of private associations in the midst of which they were planted. Offices which have been thought to involve a mystic and inexplicable sanctity are found to have been instituted after the example of the Graeco-Roman municipal and provincial government.[106]

Fisher emphasized that the metropolitan bishops' rise to power was linked to the fact that their sees were the seats of Roman government and commanded much authority in church synods: ecclesiastical developments mirrored practices of Roman statecraft, a merely secular arrangement. To foster public order, the church borrowed models supplied by the synagogue and Greek civic institutions.[107] This claim, Fisher manifestly borrowed from Hatch's *Organization of the Early Christian Churches*.

Throughout the professors' discussions, the attempt to discount divine sanction for the institution of episcopacy is paramount. That episcopacy as later known was foreign to the New Testament is a constant theme. In the professors' appeal to purely mundane, practical motivations for episcopacy's institution, they were assisted by some passages in patristic writings themselves. And new textual discoveries and reassessments in the course of the century kept the discussion of early church polity at the fore.

The Ignatian Letters

Samuel Miller

In Miller's years as professor at Princeton, the debate over the letters of Ignatius was far from settled. Episcopalians of his day appealed to these letters to justify the three clerical "orders" they espoused.[108] In his early "defense" against advocates of episcopacy, Miller claimed that even the "shorter" Greek recension of six letters published by Ussher and Vossius[109] was "unworthy of confidence"—but conceded that he would count them as genuine in order to have a common ground for debate. Yet Miller asked, do even *these* six support diocesan episcopacy, as Episcopalians claimed? The word *bishop* in the Ignatian letters, he argued, means merely pastors of single congregations. Defective and interpolated as they are (educated Protestant divines agreeing that even *this* recension has been "tampered with"), Ignatius' letters nevertheless offer a "perfect representation" of Presbyterian government,[110] in which each church has a Bishop (i.e., a Teaching Elder or Minister), a bench of (Ruling) Elders, and Deacons. Miller here granted the "genuineness" of six Ignatian letters, only to argue that even *they* do not support diocesan episcopacy. Years later, in his book of 1840, *Presbyterianism; The Truly Primitive and Apostolical Constitution of the Church of Christ*, he confidently cited these epistles to argue that there was at Ignatius' time "a Bishop or pastor, a bench of Elders, and Deacons."[111]

Episcopalians (with considerable justification) deemed Miller's appeal to the Ignatian letters inconsistent: did he believe the letters "genuine" or not? Did not his strong differentiation of Teaching Elders from Ruling Elders call into question the notion that bishop and presbyter indicated the same office? One Episcopalian critic, John Esten Cook, complained that Miller considered the Ignatian letters "an authority on some subjects, but not on behalf of Prelacy"—only on *that* point did Miller cry "corruption."[112] Another Episcopalian writer, "N.", charged in the *Southern Churchman* that most of Miller's readers would be "entirely unacquainted" with the history of the dispute over Ignatius' letters and hence be unable to decide the issue; their ignorance gave Miller an opening to press his false views. Moreover, "N." claimed, Miller inconsistently identified Ignatius' Presbyters with *Ruling* Elders—yet since Ignatius claims *Presbyters* as successors to the Apostles, one might imagine that they ought rather to be identified with *Teaching* Elders, in Presbyterian parlance.[113]

Miller's son, Samuel Miller, Jr., devoted a section of his biography to debates in which his father was embroiled over the Ignatian letters' authenticity. Opponents, the son charged, sometimes misquoted or misconstrued his father's words. But now—the late 1860s—the theological world had become increasingly convinced that Calvin's estimate was correct, namely, "There is nothing more abominable than that trash which is in circulation under the name of Ignatius."[114] In his father's day, so the son alleged, most "learned theologians" agreed that the six-letter version was genuine, although "interpolated to favour Prelacy."[115]

The son listed passages in the Ignatian letters that his father believed would support his claims. Miller senior cited Ignatius' *Epistle to the Magnesians* 6 ("your Bishop presiding in the place of God; *your Presbytery in the council of the Apostles*; and your Deacons most dear to me") to show that Presbyters stood in the place of the original Apostles; the *Epistle to the Trallians* 3 to argue that in Ignatius' time, Presbyters constituted a "*Sanhedrin of God*"; and the *Epistle to the Smyrneans* 8, to urge that Presbyters be followed as the Apostles.[116] (Elsewhere, too, Miller quoted Ignatius' reference to the elders as a "Sanhedrin," a term that implied to Miller an ecclesiastical court.[117]) Here, the objection raised above by the Episcopalian "N." seems borne out: if Miller meant Presbyters to be analogous to the *Ruling* Elders, how could they stand in the line of the Apostles, a privilege surely reserved for *Teaching* Elders, i.e., Bishops? In the heat of controversy, however, consistency did not always prevail. For Miller, the decisive point was that Presbyterian polity constituted the "original" form of church government.

In Miller's war against Episcopalian polity, the early Church Fathers—when correctly interpreted—provide to his satisfaction the documentation to prove that the original form of church polity was Presbyterian, a polity to be retained throughout time.

Henry Smith

Like Miller, Henry Smith took a keen interest in the debate over Ignatius' letters. (Smith offers "good old Ignatius" some faint praise for his martyrdom, loosely citing Ignatius' *Epistle to the Romans* 4: with death impending, Ignatius penned the stirring words, "Now do I begin to be a disciple of my Master Christ."[118]) In 1851, when Ussher's work was long known and Cureton's manuscript (the Syriac version of the letters to Polycarp, the Ephesians, and the Romans, with a paragraph from Trallians) had recently been published, Smith told his students that Ignatius' letters are the most important of the Apostolic Fathers' writings. Smith discussed in some detail the history of scholarship regarding the Epistles and why there had there been doubts about their "genuineness." The longer corpus, he reported, has been given up as "not genuine." Since seven shorter letters were transmitted along with those that are definitely forgeries, these seven appear to be "in bad company."[119]

Another reason doubt had been cast on the authenticity of the Ignatian letters, Smith noted, was their lack of strong attestation by early patristic writers. Although Polycarp's *Epistle to the Ephesians* mentioned Ignatius' letters, Irenaeus, Tertullian, and Clement of Rome do not refer to them. Both Irenaeus and Origen report *sayings* of Ignatius, but mention no *writings*. The first Church Father who notes Ignatius' letters is Eusebius in the fourth century: this late date, Smith thought, prompts suspicion. Moreover, the internal evidence of the letters is against their being "genuine": the writer "exalts the episcopal authority far more than anyone of his time." Smith told his students, "These epistles are of special importance with reference to the episcopal controversy. The general opinion is that they are not forged but [that] the original is so extensively interpolated that no dependence can be placed on them."[120]

Smith raised so many doubts about the "genuineness" of Ignatius' letters—even of the seven that soon would be accepted—that his students doubtless concluded that the letters were not trustworthy reports about church life at the turn to the second century. In 1860–1861, the letters of Ignatius were still an issue for Smith: in his "Theological Intelligence" column, he puzzled more than once over how many were considered genuine and which recension should be accorded priority.[121] Smith did not live to see Lightfoot's definitive work later in the century.

Roswell Hitchcock

Hitchcock, who succeeded Smith at Union as Professor of Church History in 1855, was less stirred than his predecessor by Ignatius' account (in his *Epistle to the Romans*) of his impending martyrdom: in Hitchcock's view, it reveals an "utter absence of theological acumen and vigor," plainly indicating that the "end of inspiration" had arrived.[122]

Hitchcock taught his students that eight of the fifteen Ignatian letters [of the "long" Greek recension] were spurious. Since Cureton's 1845 edition of three letters of Ignatius in Syriac, "a sharp controversy" had arisen on the subject. Hitchcock supplied details for his class concerning scholars' assessments of the Greek and Syriac recensions. He cautioned students not to jump to hasty conclusions: "dogmatism [is] unseemly on this point." Hitchcock noted that in the seven-letter Greek recension, bishops are named 58 times, presbyters 23, and deacons 16, an "unnatural" emphasis upon episcopacy.[123] This "excessive" appeal, he cleverly argued, indicates that episcopacy must have been something new in Ignatius' time, which the author was doing all he could to promote.[124]

Hitchcock conceded "authenticity" to the seven-letter Greek version of Ignatius' epistles. This concession, he understood, implied that episcopacy had been established in the first quarter of the second century. Although this was not an admission designed to make many Protestants happy, Hitchcock softened the impact: even if evangelical Protestants admit that bishop became a separate office in this period, it connoted not diocesan but congregational episcopacy. Each church had one bishop, as well as elders and deacons. This arrangement is not truly "Episcopal," Hitchcock argued, but rather "Presbyterian." In any case, there was no settled polity in Ignatius' time.[125]

Hitchcock remained undecided on the geographical locale in which episcopacy first flourished: the "Orient" or the West. Given that Ignatius lived in Antioch and the Pseudo-Clementines relate to Jerusalem, we might posit an "oriental genesis."[126] Yet if "sacerdotalism" received its real impetus from Tertullian, as Hitchcock held, the "orient" might *not* be episcopacy's original home.[127] North Africa might claim this dubious prize.

Philip Schaff

Hitchcock's successor at Union, Philip Schaff, thought it remarkable that the notion of episcopal hierarchy stemmed *not* from a bishop of Rome (Clement) but from an Eastern bishop, Ignatius of Antioch. The Tübingen critics' rejection of the Ignatian letters as "inauthentic" elicited Schaff's comment, "This extreme skepticism is closely connected with the whole view of the Tübingen school in regard to the history of primitive Christianity."[128] From Schaff's perspective, Tübingen scholars doubted almost all the evidence that would let Christians affirm the historical authority of the earliest Christian texts.

Writing in 1883, Schaff deemed the Syriac manuscript of Ignatius' letters among the important finds of the nineteenth century.[129] A few years later, in the fourth edition of his *History of the Church, Volume II* (1886), Schaff announced that Lightfoot's publication of *S. Ignatius and S. Polycarp* in 1885 had definitively settled the question of the Ignatian Epistles in favor of the seven-letter Greek recension.[130] Reviewing Lightfoot's edition, Schaff praised him as the best English scholar of the ancient church since Archbishop James Ussher, that important seventeenth-century pioneer of Ignatian studies.[131] Nearly thirty years ago, Schaff recalled, Lightfoot began his study of Ignatius, at a time when Cureton's discovery of the Syriac epistles dominated the field. Lightfoot solved the question about church offices in the following manner: in the New Testament, the words *episkopos* and *presbyteros* denote the same office (a finding, Schaff added, now confirmed by the *Didache*). This conclusion suited the evangelical professors well; episcopacy, as later known, could not be traced to the apostolic age. The precise date of episcopacy's rise, Schaff continued, depended upon the dating of the Ignatian epistles, of which there are three recensions. If with Baur and the Tübingen School, all three recensions are considered later forgeries, there is no early episcopacy—but Schaff rejected this extreme view. At first, Schaff reported, Lightfoot had judged the Syriac version the earliest, but subsequently changed his mind, giving priority to the Greek and dating the letters to 110–118.[132] The significance of Lightfoot's thesis for Schaff and other evangelical Protestants lay in the concession that the episcopate was in existence by the early second century—but rendering dubious the claim that episcopacy, as later conceived, was a New Testament institution.

Schaff's own ameliorating spirit regarding the early establishment of episcopacy is revealed by an incident that his son reports regarding the work of the British and American committees on the Revision of the New Testament. The issue concerned the translation of *episkopoi* in Acts 20:28. While the British Anglicans conceded that "overseers" might stand as the main translation, relegating the alternate translation, "bishops," to the margin, Schaff generously suggested the reverse, namely, that "bishops" should be moved back into the text and "overseers" assigned to the margin.[133] Terminology, it appears, was not of prime importance to him as long as there was a properly evangelical understanding of what "bishop" meant in the first decades of Christianity's existence.

The high-church Anglican interpretation of bishops, however, was to be rejected. In an undated letter to Schaff that reveals a dispute between the correspondents, Tractarian Edward Pusey faulted Schaff's interpretation of the role of bishops and priests. For Pusey, the power of the keys (forgiveness) is tied to the priesthood:

> I mean that priests only can consecrate the Holy Eucharist or absolve; and that Priests can only be made by Bishops. I have no doubt that this was the belief of the church from S. Ignatius to Luther and Calvin and Zwingli. I cannot but think that the Lutheran doctrine that 'a man is justified because he believes himself justified' is not only untrue, but eat[s] out the doctrine of the Sacraments. I do not wish to involve you or myself in controversy. I only wish to be true and honest. . . . God bless you and guide you into his full truth."[134]

Schaff, needless to say, was not guided into Pusey's version of "full truth."

In ways such as these the Reformed Protestant professors gradually conceded that the Ignatian epistles showed the existence of episcopacy in the early second century—but surrounded that admission with explanations that deflated the power of the office and the reasons for its establishment, thus lessening the import of the Ignatian epistles for their own denominations.

Hippolytus' *Philosophumena*

Henry Smith and Philip Schaff

The *Philosophumena* (*Refutation of All Heresies*) did not come to scholars' knowledge until shortly after Samuel Miller's death.[135] The class notes in which Henry Smith of Union details early Christian doctrine, dating to February 1851, suggest that he did not know of the *Philosophumena*'s publication, an event that occurred at some point the same year.[136] In the 1860s, however—when he no longer taught church history, but theology and philosophy of religion—Smith gave frequent attention to this text in his "Theological Intelligence" column. He there noted the great excitement surrounding the text's depictions of conflicts besetting leaders of the Roman Church in the early third century, frequently citing Baron Christian Bunsen's *Hippolytus and His Age* and liberal Catholic J. J. I. Döllinger's *Hippolytus and Callistus*, which emphasized Hippolytus' criticisms of the Roman bishopric.[137] In 1868, Smith reported in his column that Volume VI of the Ante-Nicene Christian Library, containing Hippolytus' works, had been published. The *Philosophumena*, he now claimed, is one of the two most important heresiological treatises of ancient times, "one of the most remarkable remains of the third century." Known for only about 25 years, Smith reported, the treatise is now credited to Hippolytus, not Origen, by all church historians, who consider it "indispensable to a critical knowledge of the state of the church in the first part of the third century."[138]

Philip Schaff was fascinated by the discovery of the *Philosophumena*—a "sensation in the theological world," he remarked, for its alleged revelations about disputes over the Roman bishopric.[139] Like Smith, Schaff reported on Bunsen's and Döllinger's books.[140] Schaff imagined Hippolytus as the head of a disaffected and schismatic party opposed to popes Zephyrinus and Callistus. Orthodox in doctrine and rigorous in discipline, Hippolytus' type of Christianity reminded Schaff of earlier Montanist practice and foreshadowed later Novatianism. The Roman Catholic Church numbered Hippolytus as a saint and martyr, "little suspecting that he would come forward in the nineteenth century as an accuser against her." Hippolytus, he mused, has had three lives: the first as a third-century opponent of popes; the second as a fictitious canonized saint; and the third, as a literary personage after the discovery of the *Philosophumena*.[141]

Schaff stressed two points regarding Hippolytus: his contributions toward the developing doctrine of the Trinity, and his opposition to the "very lax penitential discipline of popes." The *Philosophumena*, Schaff wrote, provides information on early "Anti-Trinitarians," that is, on Monarchians, including Zephyrinus, bishop of Rome. In this work, the subordinationist Hippolytus also accuses his Roman rival Callistus of blasphemy for holding that the Son was merely a manifestation of the Father ("Sabellianism"). Readers, Schaff advised, should be aware that Hippolytus was not an objective observer, but a partisan, the leading rival to Callistus; his work must be used with caution.[142] Despite this caveat, Schaff in the years after the 1870 Vatican Council—the council that pronounced the infallibility of the Pope when speaking *ex cathedra* on issues of faith and morals—appealed to Hippolytus' testimony regarding the heretical views ("Patripassianism") of Roman Bishops Zephyrinus and Callistus to contest the dogmatic decision of his own day.[143]

Schaff reasoned that although Hippolytus was the "first great scholar of the Roman church," his polemic against Roman bishops explained why that church did not preserve his writings. Yet Schaff wondered how a schism extending through three papacies could have been so soon forgotten, "especially by Rome which has a long memory of injuries done to the chair of St. Peter and looks upon rebellion against authority as the greatest sin." Hippolytus—of whatever see he was bishop, the site being disputed—stands as "an irrefutable witness against the claims of an *infallible papacy* which was entirely unknown in the third century. No wonder that Roman divines of the nineteenth century [Döllinger excepted] deny his authorship of this to them most obnoxious book."[144] Hippolytus' *Philosophumena* proved highly useful to nineteenth-century Protestant scholars eager to fault Rome's claims to authority and infallibility in their own time.

The *Didache*

Roswell Hitchcock and Philip Schaff

The *Didache* (*The Teaching of the Twelve Apostles*), another document central to nineteenth-century polemics regarding early Christian polity and practice, was discovered in 1873 and published a decade later. The first of the professors here considered to have access to this text was Roswell Hitchcock. Although no surviving student class notes from Hitchcock's courses are dated late enough to register this event, he helped to make the discovery of the *Didache* known to the wider American reading public. With Union colleague Francis Brown, Hitchcock edited, translated, and annotated the *Didache* in 1884, thus beating his colleague Philip Schaff's edition, translation, and commentary by a year.

In the preface to their revised version of their book, published in 1885, Hitchcock and Brown state that their first edition was made in great haste so as to give "speedy circulation" to Bryennios' discovery.[145] (Indeed, Schaff claimed that his colleagues had issued their book "a few days" after Bryennios' text arrived from Constantinople via Leipzig.[146]) Hitchcock and Brown reviewed the history of the discovery, noted references to the work in early Christian writings and in modern scholarship, and described the church organization depicted in the text. They commented on a point salient for Protestant arguments over early Christian polity: that the position of bishops and deacons in this text seems "not wholly assured." Church leaders serve as prophets and teachers, with no indication of "other official acts on their part."[147] That is, "sacerdotalism" is not to be found in the *Didache*, nor any enticement to high-church practice.

Yet low-church Independents might also be chastened: no endorsement of particular baptismal practices (e.g., adult baptism, full immersion) can be gleaned from the *Didache*, Hitchcock claimed. In his accompanying notes, he stressed that the word "baptize" (*Didache* 7) itself suggests nothing about forms of practice. Searching out Hebrew and Greek words in the Bible that might be translated as "baptize," Hitchcock deemed it a "generic" term, unspecific as to the actual *form*. We need not, he told readers, conclude that the early church favored baptism by immersion ("dipping") rather than by "sprinkling." It was indeed highly improbable that the allegedly 3000 persons baptized in Jerusalem at Pentecost (Acts 2:41) could all have been "dipped."[148] Baptists, in other words, have no grounds for claiming that the *Didache* justifies adult baptism by immersion to the exclusion of other forms.

Hitchcock disagreed with Neander's claim, which had been adopted by Schaff, that baptism by immersion was practiced from earliest days in Christianity, a point that might correlate with the custom of adult baptism. Our earliest monuments do not support this view, Hitchcock bluntly stated.[149] Neander here "surrendered the citadel," he told his students. Evidence from around the year 200 for infant baptism, he claimed, makes "inconceivable that so great a change could have [occurred] without an uproar."[150] Rather, the developing preference for immersion must be deemed part of the unfortunate "externalism" creeping into church practice. The exceptions to immersion that we find in early Christian literature are "fatal to the assumption" that it was the only form of baptism.[151]

Hitchcock's classroom comments regarding immersion were made in the very year that the *Didache* appeared—and when, presumably, he began work on that text. He did not, however, discuss this point of the *Didache* with his students, according to class notes. His reference to baptism by immersion as a form of "externalism," however, suggests that Hitchcock's views of early Christian ecclesiology, so opposed to all forms of "externalism," were perhaps "lower" than Schaff's—although neither belonged to denominations that practiced baptism by immersion.

Philip Schaff was also closely involved with the *Didache*'s dissemination in America. He published an introduction, translation, and commentary on the work in 1885, one year after the Hitchcock-Brown edition and translation. Schaff's long Introduction to the work, and his fuller commentary, provided a more detailed analysis of the *Didache* than did his colleagues' edition.

Schaff had written a thirteen-page bibliographical "Appendix" of literature pertaining to the *Didache* for the Hitchcock-Brown edition. It is difficult to understand why Schaff would have edited and translated the same text the very next year unless he held different views on some aspects of the *Didache*. Although (as far as I can ascertain) he does not explicitly comment on any disagreement in his printed works or personal papers, his differing views on baptism in the early church may have provided one impetus for undertaking his own publication. His colleague Charles Briggs, in his praise for the Hitchcock-Brown version and critique of Schaff's, brings to light this disagreement, as we shall shortly see.

In the preface to the first edition (1885) of Schaff's introduction, translation, and commentary on the *Didache*, he remarked that he had spent the summer of 1884 in Europe collecting literature on that text.[152] Indeed, in his travel diary for that spring and summer, Schaff noted the professors with whom he spoke (including Driver, Hatch, Lightfoot, and Harnack) and the libraries he visited (including the Athenaeum in London, the Bodleian in Oxford, and the Royal Library in Berlin [the library of the Kaiser Wilhelm Universität]) in preparation for writing on the *Didache*.[153] Schaff also added material on this important document to the third edition of his *History of the Church, Volume II*.[154]

Schaff considered the *Didache* "the most interesting and valuable of the post-apostolic writings."[155] It fills the gap between the apostolic age and the church of the second century, "that mysterious transition period between A.D. 70 and 150," the darkest and least-known period in early church history. Although the work is "apocryphal," he assured readers, it is "no literary fraud."[156] More particularly, the *Didache* fills in the dim years between the Pastoral Epistles' description of church government (Schaff holds that the Pastorals were written by Paul) and the establishment of episcopacy, as found in the letters of Ignatius.[157] The date of the *Didache*'s composition on which Schaff settled falls between 70 and 100 A.D., with 90–100 being the favored decade.[158] To date the document to the second half of the second century, Schaff commented, would strip the *Didache* of its value "as a link in the regular chain of post-Apostolic Christianity."[159] Given that Schaff dated the New Testament books, including the Gospels and the Pastoral Epistles, earlier than is now standard (or standard with some German critics of his own time),[160] the discovery of a new document that represented the interim period was of great significance.

Schaff declared that the author of the *Didache* was "certainly a Jewish Christian and probably a companion and pupil of the Apostles." The place of composition, in his view, was either Alexandria or Palestine/Syria.[161] The *Didache* is largely lacking in dogma, dogma being a product of conflict and heresy, which (Schaff implied) had not yet developed in the form of Ebionism and Gnosticism.[162] Schaff here implicitly rejected Tübingen School theories that made "conflict" the dominant motor of early Christianity and that emphasized its Jewish base.

Schaff described the Jerusalem Monastery of the Holy Sepulchre in Constantinople in which Bryennios found the text. He claimed in passing that the Greek quarter of the city (the Phanar, whose inhabitants were employed mainly as "clerks and transcribers of documents") in which the monastery is located is cleaner and more given to thrift than the Muslim quarters.[163] Along with the *Didache* was found a new manuscript of the *Epistle of Barnabas*, now published; the only complete manuscripts of *I* and *II Clement*; the spurious epistle of Mary of Cassoboli to Ignatius ("worthless"); and twelve pseudo-Ignatian epistles. By far the most important text, however, was the *Didache,* even though numbering fewer than ten pages. Since the monks at the Jerusalem Monastery in Constantinople (in Schaff's view) were as ignorant of the documents in their midst as those at Saint Catherine's monastery had been in regard to the Codex Sinaiticus, it was fortunate for the scholarly world that Bryennios found and published the manuscript.[164] "The German divines," Schaff added, "fell upon the precious morsel with ravenous appetite."[165]

Schaff noted that an English translation of the text had also been made by C. C. Starbuck in the *Andover Review* in April 1884, one month after the publication of the Hitchcock-Brown edition.[166] Thus the *Didache* had already circulated in ministerial and scholarly circles in America by the time Schaff published his work in 1885. That the general reading public was interested in the *Didache* is suggested by the invitation Schaff received to contribute an essay on the text for the *Sunday School Times*—the editor assuring him that he would pay "the fullest price that you could expect to obtain for it from any source."[167]

In America (unlike Germany), Schaff noted, the *Didache* was immediately caught up in discussions of church polity and practice: the Baptists warmed to the notion that baptism should take place in "living water"; the Episcopalians were pleased to see that bishops and deacons were mentioned—although non-Episcopalian Protestants immediately countered that "bishop" here designated the same office as "presbyter."[168] Yet the *Didache*, Schaff countered, does not belong to any denomination, but should be placed in its historical context as marking a transition from the time of divine inspiration to that of mere human teaching, "from Apostolic freedom to churchly consolidation." The *Didache*, he concluded, provides still another example of the "infinite superiority of the New Testament over ecclesiastical literature."[169] In the "Appendix" he prepared for the Hitchcock-Brown edition, Schaff had already noted with some scorn that the American religious press seemed interested in the work only so far as it could be used to bolster particular views on baptism and episcopacy, very often "from a worthless sectarian point of view." In Schaff's opinion, the value of the *Didache* was "historical and historical only."[170]

A primary concern among Protestants occasioned by the *Didache* pertained to baptism: the document's failure to mention infant baptism led some to claim that the practice of adult baptism had been (and should be) the norm for the church. Moreover, the *Didache* advised that immersion in "living water" was the preferable mode, but that other forms could be used if no "living water" was available. Schaff addressed both points.

Despite belonging to a church that practiced infant baptism, Schaff argued that we should not expect to find this practice at such an early period. His reason: infant baptism would make no sense before the "Chris-

tian family or Christian congregation" was firmly in place to guarantee that
the child would receive "Christian nurture." Only when Christianity
became a "family religion" would infant baptism be a reasonable practice.[171] Here Schaff reveals his allegiance to a domestic, family-oriented style
of devotion popular among American Protestants in his era.[172]

As for the form of baptism, although Schaff believed (following Neander) that the early church practiced immersion, he argued that the
Didache's sense of freedom on this point suggests that a greater show of
tolerance would be advisable for present-day Christians. River-baptism,
Schaff added, went out of fashion when baptisteries began to be built in or
near churches in the age of Constantine.[173]

Schaff advised readers to remember, in any event, that as a post-
apostolic document, the *Didache* commands no more authority than do
other writings from that era. Although what truths it teaches are already
known from the New Testament, the work also contains "superstitious
notions and mechanical practices which are foreign to Apostolic wisdom
and freedom." Post-apostolic writings, in Schaff's view, "are only a faint
echo of the Gospels and Epistles, the last rays of the setting sun of a glorious
day." The great value of the *Didache* is its addition of an "irrefutable argument for the infinite superiority of the New Testament over all ecclesiastical
literature."[174]

Schaff thought that the extent to which the *Didache* contains hints of
later Catholic practice was open for debate. For example, Catholics take the
injunction in Matthew 5:26 and repeated in *Didache* I.5 ("till he has paid
the last farthing") as a reference to purgatory. Likewise, the claim that if
you can bear the whole yoke of the Lord, then you will be perfect (*Didache*
VI), foreshadows the ascetic tendency that swept the church in the Nicene
age. Schaff declined to guess how far the author favored "the higher morality," but noted that in *Didache* IV.8 the reference to a community of goods
suggests that "he included voluntary poverty in his ideal of perfection."[175]
The allusion to the "worldly mystery" (XI.11), Schaff acknowledged, has
received various interpretations. He rejects the possible meaning, "abstinence from marriage," since Paul in Ephesians used "mystery" to mean
"marriage or rather the unity of Christ with his church." Besides, the
author did not need to offer an apology for celibacy: that practice received
very early support "in opposition to the bottomless sexual depravity of the
heathen world."[176]

Schaff's book on the *Didache* received mixed reviews. In his customary fashion, he sent a copy to colleagues elsewhere. Bishop J. B. Lightfoot wrote to thank him for this "very complete and useful" book, "full of interest both from the subject and from the treatment."[177] In an advertisement for the work pasted into Schaff's Scrapbook, Harnack called the book "the most important and most comprehensive" work on the subject in English.[178] Another admirer was George Fisher of Yale, who, thanking Schaff for his copy, claimed that scholars of ecclesiastical history would value the book highly: "It is really a compendium of all the knowledge which we possess at present respecting the work to which it relates. The additions contained with the Second Appendix increase decidedly the worth of the volume."[179]

Not all scholars, however, were so favorable to Schaff's *Didache*. Schaff was hurt when in July 1885 his colleague Charles Briggs publicly attacked the book in the pages of the widely read *New-York Evangelist*. Briggs, reviewing both the revised Hitchcock-Brown edition and Schaff's edition, decidedly preferred the former—for its "minute accuracy," the "striking brevity and power" of the translation, and its better appearance as a book. On one point only does Briggs favor Schaff's interpretation: that the *Didache* probably originated in Palestine or Syria, not in Egypt (as Francis Brown, who wrote the Introduction to the Hitchcock-Brown version, had surmised).[180]

Briggs particularly faulted Schaff for bending the text to support his theory that the form of baptism described in the *Didache* must be immersion. Schaff, Briggs told readers, borrowed that idea from his teacher Neander and had pressed it in his own earlier *Church History*. In fact, Briggs countered, the *Didache* gives little support to the notion that immersion or submersion was the norm for primitive baptismal practice. In Briggs's view, Schaff had used the *Didache* as if it were "an Appendix to the first volume of his Church History."[181]

Schaff was understandably disturbed by Briggs's vehement attack. What sin have I committed, Schaff complained to his son David, that Briggs should show such "base ingratitude," and the newspaper's editor, Dr. Henry Field, should "lend his organ for my defamation!" The elder Schaff cannot refrain from letting his son know the many who *did* appreciate the work.[182] Field, the editor of the *New-York Evangelist*, indeed expressed some embarrassment over the review: in a prefatory comment, he acknowledged that the reviewer—Briggs—had criticized the work of "three of the most eminent scholars in this country," adding that the review did not necessarily represent the opinion of the editor. Yet he also assured readers that the reviewer was worthy to be reckoned on a par with the authors themselves.[183]

Conclusion

Debates over the polity of present-day churches informed arguments over that of early Christian communities. Both sets of debates were fueled by new manuscript discoveries and scholarship pertaining to them. The Protestant professors' debates over bishops and elders reveal that their world was still denominationally constructed to a significant degree. Stakes were high among Protestant groups pressing rival claims to the "original" form of church government. Yet even stalwartly Protestant professors came to accept an early attestation of bishops—although this office could be interpreted so as not to introduce hierarchy too conspicuously into more "republican" forms of church government.

The appeal to "origins" is notable in these debates. In the earlier part of the century, those advocating episcopacy as an "original" form of church government were largely Episcopalians. As the century wore on, disputes over episcopacy centered more on Roman Catholics, whose claims on early church history and whose greater presence in America became ever less easy for Protestants to discount. To them we turn.

CHAPTER 7

Roman Catholicism

Religious liberty in the sense of the Federal Constitution . . .
[is] . . . not freedom from religion, but freedom of religion
and its actual exercise.

—Philip Schaff (1857)

The representation of religious freedom as freedom *from*
rather than for Catholicism had been a staple of American
republicanism's founding documents.

—Tracy Fessenden (2007)

Introduction

While the Protestant professors here considered, like their Reformation
forebears, sharply criticized contemporary Roman Catholicism, the concept
of historical development mitigated the nineteenth-century critique: if *no*
events in history had been totally devoid of divine purpose, Catholic belief
and practice in times past might be more sympathetically registered.

The Catholic *present*, however, was a different matter. The Syllabus of
Errors (1864) and Vatican decrees on the Immaculate Conception of Mary
(*Ineffabilis Deus*, 1854) and on Papal Infallibility (*Pastor Aeternus*, 1870),
when added to Protestant unease at the swelling tide of Catholic immigrants,[1] sorely tested the professors' tolerance. The ultramontane and dog-
matically assertive Catholicism of their era, centered on pope and Jesuits,
dampened their enthusiasm for finding "good" in Catholic history.[2] The
professors variously *blamed* the Church Fathers for later Catholic develop-

ments or *enlisted* them to argue that contemporary Catholicism had devi-
ated from its ancient heritage. For Protestants who rejected theories of
historical development, however, Catholicism seemed bleak from start to
present.

All the professors here considered believed that Catholicism early had
fallen prey to "externality," materiality, and superstition. Emphasizing
"outward" devotions, Catholicism reproduced the very features of ancient
Judaism *and* paganism that Jesus and his Apostles had allegedly sought to
overcome.[3] The professors' association of Judaism and paganism with
Roman Catholicism, while not new, does not lessen the vigor with which
the charge was pressed in seminary classrooms and in print.[4] In the course
of the century, however, the heat of their attacks appears to have dimin-
ished.

This chapter describes the professors' critiques of contemporary Catholicism, how they trace present "error" to the patristic past and (conversely)
appeal to the Fathers to counter aspects of Catholicism's later development.
Then I turn to debates over Scripture and tradition, Peter's relation to papal
primacy and infallibility, and Mariology. So detailed is the professors' critique of Catholic asceticism and clerical celibacy that these topics warrant
separate treatment in Chapter 8.

On one point, however, the Union and Yale professors' German scholarship prompted them to concede the utility of the early papacy: it had
transferred Christianity to northern peoples, from whom it had imbibed
new life, recovered its inward spirituality, and continued its westward
march. By this concession, the professors countered the views of many
American Protestants of their time, for whom the papacy had never been
anything but "the synagogue of Satan."[5]

American Professors on Roman
Catholicism in the Modern World

Samuel Miller

In the first years of Samuel Miller's professorial career, Catholicism
remained a somewhat distant "threat": the waves of Catholic immigration
into northern cities and the subsequent anti-Catholic backlash were not yet
prominent features of American life.[6] By the 1830s, however, Miller's alarm

was evident. In 1834 he remarked that even a decade earlier, few would have imagined the revival of the controversy over "popery." Catholics had then constituted only about two percent of the American population and had kept (as he put it) to a "silent and inoffensive course." Now, however, "foreign" money was lavishly being provided to assist the ever-growing ranks of Catholic immigrants. Since misguided Catholics now even attempt to proselytize Protestants, the latter must "gird on their armour" to protect themselves against "these foes of God and man." Be wary, Miller warned: Catholics present their "miserable idolatry" in "an attractive, and even *bewitching* dress."[7] Against their magic, Protestants must guard.[8] In addition, Miller cautioned his students against arguing with Catholics, for whom Scripture is not the only infallible rule. For them, tradition— including the Fathers—and church authority have equal, "even paramount," influence.[9] Presbyterians who imagine that they might trounce Catholics' claims simply by quoting Scripture are deluded.

Catholicism, which Miller styled "a miserable system of Jewish ceremonial and Pagan superstition, disguised by a Christian nomenclature,"[10] appeals to those "more fond of a splendid and gaudy ritual than of a self-denying and spiritual religion." For Miller, the Church of Rome is, quite simply, the Anti-Christ,[11] an enemy to every civil and religious liberty, whose priests lust for power, pleasure, and gold. Miller denied, however, that with such words he was "persecuting" Roman Catholics, any more than Jesus' pronouncement of woes on the scribes and Pharisees constituted "persecution" of ancient Jews. Although Catholicism in North America might seem "a mild and inoffensive system," Miller advised his audience to look to Spain, Portugal, and Italy for evidence of how Catholicism manifests itself when checks on it are lacking.[12]

The inadequate and still fledgling school system in America—good public schools were scarce in many areas—prompted particular worries. Miller charged that Catholics entice the young, especially those from "the most indigent classes," with cheap or even free education. Establishing schools in sparsely populated areas where other educational opportunities are lacking, Jesuits extend their influence on the Protestant population.[13] Catering especially to the education of girls, Catholic schools appeal to the imagination and the senses so as to "dazzle and deceive." The testimony of a millennium, Miller claimed, shows that Catholic institutions in general are "sinks of deep and awful licentiousness." Protestant children who attend Catholic schools, he feared, would imbibe that "depraved" religion, perhaps even convert.[14] Catholic educators' sleight-of-hand techniques are apt to leave trusting, simple-hearted Protestants defenseless against their wiles. Miller, it is clear, had no theory of Christianity's development with which to temper his assessment of Catholicism's deadly and magical bewitchments.

Henry Smith

Unlike Samuel Miller, Henry Smith, residing in New York City from the 1850s until his death in the late 1870s, could see Roman Catholics in abundance and anti-Catholicism at full tide. Catholicism, he wrote, has "transferred millions of its most devoted adherents to this soil." In times of disorder and change (presumably such as his own), Romanism's "inflexible front and dogmatic assurance" seem attractive to many not born in that faith. Like Miller, Smith thought that Catholicism's attraction bordered on the magical: it appeals to the senses through ritual, "charms the understanding by the consistency of its system; and . . . subdues reason itself by its claims to infallibility."[15] Although Smith was not the most extreme opponent of Catholicism among his fellow Protestants—the latter of whom predicted Vatican interference in national elections, Jesuit takeover of schools, and city governments hijacked by the unwashed Catholic poor[16]— his classroom lectures and published writings exhibit only slightly more tolerance of Catholicism than Miller's. Smith did, however, argue for the validity of Roman Catholic baptism when in 1854 that view was under attack by the New-School Presbyterian General Assembly.[17] Catholicism, he thought, should at least be deemed Christian.

Yet in his inaugural lecture at Union Seminary in 1851, Smith had bluntly charged that the Roman Church was unfit to exist in the modern world. Hostile to the American spirit, Smith alleged, Catholicism is incapable of dealing with modern science, biblical scholarship, philosophy, and the great social problems of the day. Although liberal Catholics may praise republicanism and human rights, they surreptitiously seek toleration for the church they deem "sovereign and infallible." Since Catholicism has "thrown down the gauntlet," Protestant ministers should attend more closely to its real character. The remedy: the study of history, which helps Protestants to understand Rome's claims.[18] The study of early and medieval history, in other words, might render assistance to American Protestants coping with contemporary issues.

By summer 1869, the Christian world was astir with talk of a proposed Vatican Council. Smith used the journal he edited, the *American Theological Review*, especially its "Theological Intelligence" column, to critique this development. Pius IX, Smith claimed, will manipulate the council to have the *Syllabus of Errors* sanctioned and the "personal infallibility" of popes declared, despite the objections of the Italian government and liberal Catholics.[19] Smith devoted considerable space in the *Review* to criticizing ultramontane Catholicism, especially its Jesuit promoters.[20] He also highlighted the opposition wing of Catholicism: what would become the Old Catholic Church, J. J. I. Döllinger, and other Catholics of a liberal stripe.[21]

In the April 1870 issue of the *Review*, Smith featured the Council's debates over papal infallibility: he remained optimistic that Döllinger and the "anti-Infallibilists" would triumph. In the July 1870 issue, Smith (probably writing shortly before the July 18th proclamation) compared the Vatican Council—unfavorably—to a recent meeting of the Evangelical Alliance.[22] The October 1870 issue, published a few months after the Council's abrupt ending, featured an article detailing the famous "Roman Letters" by a pseudonymous "Quirinus." (These letters, originally printed in the Augsburg *Allgemeine Zeitung* while the Council was in session, had leaked reports of the Council's secret deliberations.) Smith translated in full "Letter 65 of 'Quirinus'" on the retroactive consequences of the dogma of infallibility, which listed 42 past papal pronouncements (calculated to startle Protestant readers) that now, allegedly, must be accepted as infallible.[23] Smith also printed in this issue, without comment, the text of the decree on Papal Infallibility, *Pastor Aeternus*.[24]

The year 1870 did not see the end of Smith's attacks.[25] Three years later, he published a list of books and articles treating the Vatican Council and its famous proclamation.[26] Smith also wrote a review essay covering (among other publications) German Bishop C. J. von Hefele's discussion of the famous "heretical" (Monothelite) pope, Honorius.[27] In addition, Smith either wrote or co-wrote an editorial in 1875 declaring that *Pastor Aeternus* would allow the pope to encroach on the civil sphere, demanding obedience from Catholics throughout the world.[28] Smith's "Theological Intelligence" column, in effect, not only kept American Presbyterians informed about current issues in their own denomination; it also fueled their anti-Catholic sentiments.

Smith's embrace of notions of historical development failed to temper his anti-Catholic animus. His more expansive views regarding *ancient* Catholicism rubbed uneasily against his manifest hostility toward *modern* Catholicism.

Roswell Hitchcock

In his inaugural address in 1856 as Washburn Professor of Church History at Union, Roswell Hitchcock (like his predecessor) took the opportunity to critique Roman Catholicism. Espousing a theory of ecclesiastical decline, he charged that "the Church [has] passed from Apostolic simplicity to the scarlet flauntings of the Papacy," from "unstudied prayer, to the Church of surpliced priests, and tinkling bells, and swinging censers." Today, he proclaimed, the Roman Catholic Church, encompassing half of the world's Christians, is "binding and losing on earth what is not bound or loosed in Heaven."[29]

Yet Hitchcock often took a gentler approach toward Catholicism than his Protestant contemporaries, including his predecessor Henry Smith. At the Evangelical Alliance Conference in New York in 1873, Hitchcock pointedly asked why so much of the conference program was devoted to the topic of Catholicism? Conceding that Protestants feel menaced, with "infidel bugles" blowing before them and "Papal bugles" behind them, he urged the delegates to exhibit "a larger charity." Roman Catholicism today, he claimed, is simply the church of the Middle Ages that kept on growing—whereas Protestantism, its "child," is the only branch of Christianity that has embraced the mentality of the present era. Yet if Christians hold to the three essential doctrines of incarnation, atonement, and regeneration, differences in polity and ritual do not much matter: we can afford "the largest liberty in regard to all the rest." Hitchcock urged the audience to abstain from foolish and bitter controversy with Catholics.[30]

Although opposed to Catholicism, Hitchcock appears less invested in attacking papal decrees of the era. Reviewing the historical development of the notion of papal infallibility for a class in the early 1880s, Hitchcock remarked, "July 13, 1870 [the dogma of papal infallibility] voted. July 18, 1870 proclaimed. Doctrine finished." The task of the church in the present age, he told another class, is to "outgrow the papacy and everything papal."[31] Papal Europe, he claimed, is less intelligent, industrious, enterprising, and prosperous than Protestant Europe, and less eager to educate the masses.[32] Yet Hitchcock did not dwell on the evils of Roman Catholicism as did many of his Protestant contemporaries. In his teaching, he manifested some sympathy for Irish immigrants,[33] and warmed to St. Patrick, patron saint of Ireland, so reverenced by Irish Catholics in New York.[34]

Philip Schaff

Philip Schaff took a broader view of Christianity's development than did most of his predecessors and contemporaries—and this despite his critique of Rome's reverence for martyrs, saints, and relics, her "Mariolatry,"[35] her alleged hostility to modern progress,[36] and, not least, the Jesuit Order, whose members, he claimed, write "textbooks of refined immorality."[37]

Yet in Schaff's view, since Providence worked mysteriously throughout Christian history to bring good out of apparent evil, no period of the church's history—including its early and medieval phases—was totally devoid of God's guidance. Declaring himself to be both "a child and servant of Protestantism and an admirer and friend of Catholicism," Schaff entertained a lifelong hope for the reunion of Christendom's "sundered parts."[38] George Shriver describes Schaff as a proponent of an "evangelical Catholicism" that would preserve the most valuable elements of both Catholic and Protestant traditions.[39]

Schaff decried the intolerant spirit some Protestants of his day exhibited. Members of the American Bible and Tract Societies and of the Sunday School Union, he wrote, lose their sense of charity "as soon as the Romish church is mentioned, as if she was simply an enemy of Christ."[40] After Schaff's death, Roman Catholic historian Thomas Joseph Shahan praised him for correcting misstatements about Catholicism and showing Protestants the importance of the early church—an importance (Shahan pointedly adds) that Catholics had never forgotten.[41] And Schaff, unlike many Protestants, strongly criticized what he deemed Puritanism's overly spiritualized and unhistorical approach to Christianity,[42] a fact that may have contributed to his (limited) sympathy toward Roman Catholicism—at least in its past manifestations.

Schaff spent his first nineteen years in America at the Seminary of the German Reformed Church at Mercersburg. There, he and his colleague John Williamson Nevin developed the "Mercersburg Theology," a broad version of Calvinism that was warmly appreciative of early Catholic tradition. Mercersburg's emphasis on ecclesiology and sacramentalism was foreign, indeed anathema, to mainstream American Protestants of their time.[43] Shortly after his arrival in Mercersburg, Schaff was accused of "Romanizing" on the basis of his inaugural address before the Synod of the German Reformed Church in October 1844.[44] His lengthy speech in German, translated by Nevin, was published the following year as *The Principle of Protestantism*. It is important to mark the date of this landmark speech and document: ten years before Pius IX's declaration on the Immaculate Conception of Mary, and twenty-six years before Vatican I's pronouncement of Papal Infallibility. In his 1844 address, Schaff, despite his critique of Catholicism, expressed hope that the various branches of Christendom would draw closer together.[45] The speech also gave Schaff a good opportunity to expound his views of "historical development"—views that pointed to the superiority of Protestantism, while according some worth to Catholicism in its historical manifestations.

"Protestantism," Schaff here claimed, "is the principle of movement, or progress in the history of the church." Yet Romanists must be included in this vision; the truth of *both* forms of Christianity will be realized in the "full revelation of the kingdom of God." Schaff at this time, still fresh from Germany, deemed Protestantism more endangered by Rationalism than by Catholicism: "let us expel the devil from our own temple . . . before we proceed to exorcise and cleanse the dome of St. Peter's," he cautioned.[46] Ten years later, Schaff would add that Roman Catholicism had benefited by its transplantation to North America; Americans' "spirit of enterprise" had worked its improvement. Catholicism, he then claimed, had even benefited Protestantism by serving to check the latter's "extremes" and "religious radicalism."[47] Such sentiments did not endear Schaff to conservative Protestants.

Again in 1851–1852, Schaff found himself in trouble over his allegedly "pro-Catholic" approach. He had assigned his Mercersburg students some books by Roman Catholic authors, Bellarmine and Newman among them. Such a rebellion ensued over this alleged "Romanizing" that six students who had recently come to the seminary from Germany left in protest.[48] Schaff's desire for students to read and judge for themselves apparently backfired.

In various ways, Schaff also sought to foster good—or at least civil—relations with Roman Catholics of his *own* time. He defended the validity of Roman Catholic baptism, an issue that occasioned heated debate among nineteenth-century American Protestants. In his later years, attending the meeting of the General Assembly of the Presbyterian Church in May 1885, Schaff described to his son David the Assembly's discussions. Some delegates argued that since Roman Catholicism is the synagogue of Satan, her ordinances are void. Schaff countered: despite her errors, the Catholic Church retains Scripture and ancient creeds; as a branch of Christ's visible church, she has a valid baptism. He now knows, he told David, why he was sent to this Assembly: to testify against "this unreasoning and uncharitable anti-popery fanaticism." When another speaker claimed that the pope baptized jackasses and wore petticoats, Schaff retorted (so he told David): "I proposed to stick closely with the baptism of men and women, and to leave the jackasses and petticoats alone, which created a considerable laugh."[49] If Roman Catholic baptism is invalid, he reasoned, we would have to "dig up the bones of Calvin, Knox and Luther and sprinkle them over again."[50]

Likewise in discussions of possible revision of the (Presbyterian) Westminster Confession, Schaff decried the article therein on the Pope as Anti-Christ and Catholics as idolators: those statements, he declared, are "untrue, unjust, unwise, uncharitable, and unsuitable in any Confession of Faith."[51] Presbyterians' attempts "to unbaptize or to heathenize" the Catholic Church's two million members "outpopes the Pope, who recognizes Protestant baptism." Schaff urged that the revision of this Confession omit its blatantly anti-Catholic language. In November 1889, the New York Presbytery, the largest in the United States, voted in favor of the revision.[52]

Schaff's interest in contemporary Catholicism is also revealed in his letters, memoirs, and diaries. While in his early twenties, he had served as tutor to a young Prussian nobleman and accompanied him to Italy, spending the winter and spring of 1842 in Rome. Schaff detailed the events of Passion Week (March 20–27, 1842) in the Eternal City, attending services at several Catholic churches. Although critical of many of the practices he witnessed, he declared himself deeply moved by the Good Friday service in the Sistine Chapel and by the beautiful music (much beloved by Schaff) at various churches. On Easter evening, after an exhausting week of church-attendance, he climbed Monte Pincio to view St. Peter's lighted by 1400 lamps; the obelisk in the middle of the square suggested to him "Egypt's priestly wisdom, which is as the dark night over against the bright radiance of Christianity." Apparently Roman Catholicism had not completely forfeited its power to produce some of that "bright radiance."[53]

Later in life, Schaff's curiosity regarding Roman Catholicism continued unabated. In 1870 he visited a Roman Catholic seminary in upstate New York. Journeying through Switzerland in 1877, he attended a mass celebrating Pius IX's fifty-year jubilee as a bishop. Spring 1890 found the aging Schaff in Rome, attending one lecture at the Gregorianum in the company of Jesuits and another (in Latin on "De sacram matrimonii") at the Propaganda Fidei.[54] In Rome, Schaff also visited Archbishop Corrigan of New York, to whom he had earlier sent a copy of his book, *Church and State in the United States*.[55] He had an audience with Pope Leo XIII in the company of German pilgrims and also met with Jesuits.[56] The new Catholic University of America, founded in 1889, excited Schaff's interest, and in 1892, he paid a visit.[57] John J. Keane, Catholic University's rector, in Chicago in October 1893 for the World's Parliament of Religions, read Schaff's address on "The Reunion of Christendom" and wrote to its author, declaring how much he "craves for the realization of this project." He promised to send Schaff a copy of his own speech on "Ultimate Religion."[58] Such incidents suggest an openness of mind on Schaff's part that was uncommon among American Protestants of the era, who looked with fearful, and often hateful, eyes at the swelling Catholic population.[59]

Schaff was aware of the hostility of American Protestants to their Catholic neighbors, and felt some unease himself. His deep commitment to religious liberty did not preclude his campaigning for the use of the King James Version of the Bible, Protestant prayers, and Protestant religious instruction in the public schools.[60] Like other American Protestants, he disparaged Catholics' "interference" in American politics and charged them with "aiming everywhere at political influence." In a speech to European colleagues in 1854, he reported on American Protestants' antipathy. Noting the social problems attending Catholic immigration, he characterized Irish Catholics as "ignorant, addicted to drunkenness and profanity, quarrelling and fighting." He also worried over Catholic influence on public education: Roman Catholic clergy in New York and elsewhere, he claimed, are charging the public school system with exerting "Protestant influence." Their efforts, Schaff reported, have miscarried, and have "made Romanism more unpopular, and confirmed the old charge against her of hostility to general education."[61] The Protestant majority, he told his European colleagues, fear the political despotism of the Catholic Church. He reported on some "skirmishes," as he called them: the burning of St. Augustine's Church in Philadelphia in 1844 and, a decade earlier, the "violent demolition" of the

Catholic convent at Charlestown, Massachusetts. Public insults greeted the archbishop and papal nuncio Gaetano Bedini during his visit to the United States in 1853. These incidents, Schaff alleged, reveal a "fanatical hatred" on the part of American Protestants.[62] Two years after his European address, Schaff added that although he decried the waves of anti-foreign and anti-Romanist sentiment that "swept like a whirlwind over our country" in 1855 and 1856, the "excessive immigration" of a year or two earlier had led Americans to believe that they could not digest all the "foreign food," which "threatened to decay before our doors and be poison to the atmosphere." But Schaff was sure that this reaction was only temporary: the westward movement will continue, from Europe to the United States, and in America itself, from East to West.[63]

Schaff's hope for a future reunion of Catholicism and Protestantism dimmed with Pius IX's decree on the Immaculate Conception of Mary in 1854, his Syllabus of Errors in 1864, and the Vatican Council's decree on Papal Infallibility in 1870. Schaff's essay, "The History of the Vatican Council," was included with (former British Prime Minister) William Gladstone's pamphlet, "The Vatican Decrees," published in 1875. Having reviewed Pius IX's preparation for the Council, the Council proceedings that issued in the decree on papal infallibility, and the momentous political events that led to the collapse of Napoleon III's French Empire and Vittorio Emanuele's capture of Rome in September 1870, Schaff concluded that in "reaching the summit of its power, the Papacy has hastened its downfall."[64] Schaff put in print his judgment that Pius IX was a "theological ignoramus," allegedly incapable of reading the Scriptures in Hebrew and Greek.[65] Upon Pius's death in February 1878, Schaff wrote in his *Diary*, "Infallibility suspended till the next pope is elected."[66]

In his books and articles, Schaff regularly decried the papacy, whose power, he confessed, offended him more than Catholicism's "peculiar doctrines and usages." He critiqued the False Decretals and the immorality of popes through the ages. He singled out Honorius (the "heretical" Monothelite pope of the seventh century) as case-in-point against papal infallibility.[67] Although Schaff generally refrained from identifying the papacy with Anti-Christ, yet in one of his last works, a manual for students, he wrote, "More than once he [Satan] has occupied the chair of St. Peter in Rome and changed the vicar of Christ into an Antichrist."[68] Roman Catholics may believe that the Pope is "an infallible oracle," yet, Schaff countered, alluding to the Vatican's earlier condemnation of Galileo, "the earth moves and will continue to move around the sun."[69] Toward the *modern* papacy, it is evident, Schaff exhibited less generosity than he did toward *ancient* Catholicism. Such was the mixed assessment by America's most important nineteenth-century Protestant professor of church history.

George Fisher

Despite the Protestant professors' ongoing criticism of Catholicism, the vehemence lessened. George Fisher of Yale, in an article published three years before the Vatican Council of 1870, reviewed the history of the growth of the papal estates from late antiquity to circa 1859.[70] Pius IX, Fisher thought, rightly understood that his spiritual power would be considerably damaged if he lost his temporal possessions in Italy. Catholicism's present problems, in Fisher's view, could be overcome only by the spread of Gospel-loving Protestantism to Roman Catholic territories.[71]

Writing just months before the July 1870 decree on Papal Infallibility, Fisher raised the now-familiar question of how papal infallibility could be countenanced when at least one pope (Honorius) was deemed a heretic. In the later reprint of the article, Fisher appended a long note discussing William Gladstone's pamphlet on the Vatican decrees. Here Fisher cited the responses to advance notice of the proposed decree by Archbishop (and now Cardinal) Henry Manning and John Henry Newman: even distinguished Catholics, Fisher pointedly observed, had been uneasy at the decree's possible import. Although Fisher protested that he had "no disposition to speak harshly of the Roman Catholic Church or of its prominent apologists," he nevertheless claimed that an "educated Protestant" could not escape judging Catholics as "champions of a flexible, evasive, slippery system." "Reactionary" Ultramontanism, he argued, seeks to arrest society's progress and bring it again under priestly control.[72] Yet despite the decree on papal infallibility (and the Oxford Movement's high view of priesthood), clerical authority had declined in modern society, owing to the laity's advance in intelligence since the time of the Protestant Reformation.[73] Such progress, Fisher thought, bode ill for traditional Catholicism.

In his church history class in 1870–1871, Fisher criticized Catholicism's notion of a "visible Church." The Jesuits in particular were to blame for much of what he found wrong with Catholicism: while many individual Jesuits were worthy men, the Order itself sanctioned "the great, terrible evil" of separating "the *conscience* from the religious principle." Catholicism, he told his students, was stronger in France today than before the French Revolution ("free-thinking can never supplant a religion"); if Catholicism is to be transcended, it must be "by a Luther and a *purer* religion."[74] Given that these lecture notes date to the very time of the Vatican Council and its immediate aftermath, Fisher appears more restrained than we might expect in his assessment.

At the 1873 meeting of the Evangelical Alliance in New York, Fisher (like Roswell Hitchcock of Union) addressed the question of Roman Catholicism. Taking a similarly ameliorating line in his paper, "Protestantism, Romanism, and Modern Civilization," Fisher urged Protestants not to undervalue the medieval church's contributions to society. She saved from destruction ancient literature and art, so important for "training the minds of undisciplined men" and "curbing the passions and softening the manners of rude people." For the last three centuries, however, Protestantism, not Catholicism, has been the force promoting individual rights, universal education, and civil and religious liberty.[75] Although no friend of contemporary Catholicism, Fisher was less strident in his critique than many American Protestants of his day.

As the nineteenth century wore on, the evangelical professors seemed more tolerant in their assessment of modern Roman Catholicism. Yet Vatican decrees from 1850 onward tried their tolerance and their attempt to find something of benefit in *ancient* Catholicism.

American Professors on Catholicism
in Antiquity: General Criticisms

The professors, with predictable uniformity and like their Reformation forebears, narrated how a pure primitive Christianity was overtaken by beliefs and practices that developed into a degenerate "Romanism." Here, the theme of decline often trumped their more generous impulses.

Catholics, Samuel Miller charged, exhibiting their "miserable idolatry," early substituted "deified" saints and ceremonies for Christ. By the fourth century, Catholic "superstition" affirmed a change in the elements of the Lord's Supper and advocated the postponement of baptism—imagined as a "passport to heaven"—to the end of life. Soon, Miller claimed, Catholics began to worship the relics of martyrs, offer prayers for the dead in purgatory, and introduce images and pictures to their devotions.[76] Roswell Hitchcock and George Fisher agreed: these practices, branded as "pagan," soon blemished the simplicity and purity of primitive Christianity, especially after numerous converts entered the church in the fourth century.[77]

In Philip Schaff's rendition of early Christianity's downward slide, "an idolatrous veneration of the cross of Christ or the bones and chattels of the apostles," foreign to the New Testament and Apostolic Fathers, replaced a simple reverence. This simple reverence (to which Schaff did not object) "degenerated into a form of refined polytheism and idolatry."[78] Like his colleagues and predecessors, Schaff charged early Catholicism with "paganizing": martyr-worship was merely a new form of pagan hero-worship.[79] The veneration of relics led to "pious frauds," a category that Schaff particularly abhorred. He mocked the countless splinters allegedly preserved from the True Cross—so much wood remained, "by a continuous miracle, whole and undiminished!" That the astute Ambrose could be duped by the "discovery" of the alleged relics of Gervasius and Protasius proved to Schaff that even the most enlightened men "cannot wholly divest themselves of superstition and of the prejudices of their age."[80]

Amid this degeneration, a few "choice spirits" (as Roswell Hitchcock styled them[81]) entered their protests: Jovinian, Vigilantius, Bonosus, and Helvidius, but they were "all speedily silenced and crushed," as were the brave Paulicians in the seventh century.[82] These men, "leaping centuries ahead of their time," correctly distinguished the visible from the invisible church, and opposed the "immaculate virginity of Mary, celibacy, vigils, relic-worship, and the monastic life." Such men, in effect, prefigured Protestantism.[83]

In their assessment of ancient and modern Catholicism, three topics in particular captured the professors' attention: the relation of tradition (especially in the form of appeal to the Church Fathers) and Scripture, the development of the Roman bishopric in relation to the Apostle Peter, and Mariology.

The Professors' Critiques of Catholicism, Past and Present

Tradition and Scripture

Objection to Catholicism's emphasis on the authority of the Church Fathers, unsurprisingly, forms part of the professors' critique of tradition.

Only Scripture, not the Fathers, they claimed, can settle issues of Christian truth: the New Testament must ever correct tradition.[84] The Fathers' utility lies rather in bearing witness to some aspect of Christianity's development—its adherence to or deviation from apostolic standards, its careful guarding of the New Testament canon. The professors sharply criticized Roman Catholics (and high-church Episcopalians) who accorded large authority to patristic writers.

For Samuel Miller, the mass of error and corruption that developed in Christian churches by late antiquity proved that the Bible alone, the "only infallible rule of faith," contains the religion Protestants should espouse. Henry Smith, for his part, charged that the Catholic Church had erred in confounding "testimony with authority," church authority with divine authority, and the authority of the particular Roman Catholic Church with that of the universal church.[85] The first three Christian centuries, Smith objected, were *not* "the model for all time."[86] The church of the patristic era, although a "living witness" to earlier traditions, cannot bind latter-day Christians.[87] Writing in 1861, before Schaff joined the Union faculty, Smith charged that Mercersburg theologians (i.e., Nevin and Schaff), along with Episcopalians and Catholics, conceded too much authority to the early church.[88] Those who today exalt Christians of that era, especially the martyrs, imply that "works" can win a person salvation.[89]

The Fathers, Smith alleged, given their mutual contradictions, forfeit our trust. Their disagreements empty the Vincentian Canon (what has been held "*semper ubique et ab omnibus*") of meaning. The writings on which Catholics rely to establish "tradition"—Cyprian's, for example—contain many forgeries, interpolations, and mutilations.[90]

When Catholics *do* appeal to Scripture, Smith charged, it often is to gain support for dubious beliefs and practices. For example, they cite Maccabees to justify the doctrine of purgatory and appeal to Jacob's "worshipping on his staff" to authorize devotion to relics. Catholics accept as authoritative such non-scriptural notions as the existence of an "intermediate state" or episcopal succession.[91] Catholicism implies that the Scriptures are so obscure that new revelations are needed to supplement and clarify them. It is not Scripture that is "obscure," Smith countered, but tradition.[92] Although Catholics are correct that the church is older than *written* Scripture, they are wrong not to admit that the church arose *after* the deliverance of "the Word of God—the revelation."[93] The unsettled state of the canon in Christianity's early days, Smith told his students, allowed tradition to

assume great authority.[94] Here, Smith's assumption that knowledge of revelation was available before its instantiation in a text appears to echo Catholics' appeal to unwritten "traditions."

In later centuries, Smith charged, the Catholic Church reinforced these
erroneous views. Developing "hierarchical influences" tightly linked Scripture and tradition.[95] Scholastic theologians became mired in the Fathers
rather than returning to the Bible as the norm. The Council of Trent sealed
this interpretation—so Smith taught his students—declaring tradition as
well as Scripture to come from "the mouth of Christ," "inspired by the
Holy Ghost." Thus Catholics, he averred, must accept whatever the church
demands of them, taking "everything on trust." The consequences Smith
deemed "disastrous": it "makes men slaves." "The doctrine of tradition,"
Smith predicted in the 1850s, "leads inevitably to that of Church infallibility," since tradition demands an infallible interpreter.[96]

Smith allowed some small place for tradition, but carefully circumscribed its significance. He aimed to strike a mean that avoided the (alleged)
privileging of tradition by Catholics, of illumination by Quakers, and of
reason by Rationalists. The Apostles' oral teaching does not prove "the
authority or probability of Tradition."[97] The question rather is, did the
Apostles "say anything they did not write" that can be claimed with certainty as the word of God? (For Smith, the answer is clearly "no.") By
tradition, Smith told his students, many Church Fathers meant simply what
was handed down, whether written or unwritten; reliable unwritten traditions, however, were identical to New Testament teachings. Taken in this
sense, Protestants can endorse the notion of tradition as warmly as do
Catholics.[98]

Against Catholics, Protestants were fond of claiming that they followed
the Bible alone. To this claim, Catholics had an easy response, since it was
evident that there were many biblical practices *not* adopted by Protestants.
Smith warned his students about some of these points. For example, opponents readily note that "we" [Presbyterians] have not adopted the foot-
washing that Jesus practiced in John 13:12–15, nor do we observe the seventh
day as the day of rest. Moreover, the devotees of tradition allege that Presbyterians cannot justify the practice of infant baptism from Scripture.
Smith conceded that Presbyterian views would not carry the day against
those devoted to tradition as a norm.[99] Yet, strangely, he provided no further assistance to his students in rebutting the "tradition-lovers'" arguments.

In the end, Smith declared tradition to be needless: all essential doctrines are given in Scripture. Even the earliest Fathers' writings contain no truth that is so plain as that given by the Apostles. Biblical authority outweighs all patristic teaching put together, Smith argued, since "the Fathers are not inspired, the Scriptures are." Appealing to tradition serves only to generate skepticism and an unwillingness to trust the Bible. "Custom without truth," Smith concluded, "is only the old age of error."[100]

Roswell Hitchcock similarly warned students against overvaluing the patristic era, allegedly the "heroic age of the church." The glories of the church of the first three centuries have been exaggerated by the writers of the Oxford Tracts, who consider this period the norm for all later Christianity—and Roman Catholics extend this authority as far as the fifth century. In Hitchcock's view, the patristic era ranks lower than contemporary Protestantism in its biblical exegesis, its piety regarding the Person of Christ, and its knowledge of Hebrew. Only the New Testament gives the correct rule for life.[101]

Like Smith, Hitchcock argued that by tradition, the Fathers themselves simply meant the teaching of Christ and the Apostles. Tradition acquired its role when the canon of Scripture was neither settled nor deemed as prominent as it was by later Christians. Still, Hitchcock, in line with his views that Christianity had developed, was not averse to predicting that future formulations of Jesus' message would surpass those of the creeds of the patristic era: "Better and better statements of it are in store for us."[102] Protestants, despite their opposition to tradition, can formulate new expressions of Christian theology not explicitly contained in the Bible.

Similarly, Philip Schaff criticized Catholicism's overreliance on the Fathers: they lack "normative authority."[103] Yet Schaff especially objected to Catholic writers' seeming assumption that *they* had special purchase on the Fathers. With evident distaste, he cited John Henry Newman's confession that only after he converted to Roman Catholicism could he kiss the "inanimate pages" of the Fathers and claim, "You are now mine, and I am yours, beyond any mistake." Schaff countered with a telling comparison: "With the same right, the Jews might lay exclusive claim to the writings of Moses and the prophets."[104] Schaff charged:

It betrays a very contracted, slavish, and mechanical view of history, when Roman Catholic divines claim the fathers as their exclusive property; forgetting that they taught a great many things which are as inconsistent with the papal as with the Protestant Creed, and knew nothing of certain dogmas (such as the infallibility of the pope, the seven sacraments, transubstantiation, purgatory, indulgences, auricular confession, the immaculate conception of the Virgin Mary, etc.), which are essential to Romanism.[105]

Catholicism, Schaff insisted, must be distinguished from "Romanism or Papacy." Catholicism includes the *whole* ancient and medieval church, while Romanism proper dates only from the Council of Trent. Not one of the ante-Nicene Fathers agrees with Roman doctrine on all points: they knew nothing of the dogmas of the Immaculate Conception and of Papal Infallibility. Schaff told his Protestant students that no Church Father, even the most eminent, "could stand the test of Roman orthodoxy of the Tridentine, still less of the Vatican or Ultramontane stamp, and many of them [by that standard] would have to be condemned as heretics," especially the ante-Nicene writers.[106] Except on the most general points of the Christian faith, to appeal to the "unanimous consent of the fathers" is "mere illusion."[107] On this line of argument, the ancient Catholic Church could be pitted against modern Roman Catholicism.

Schaff, however, conceded that patristic theology accords even less well with Protestant affirmations than with modern Catholic ones on points concerning the authority of Scripture, justification by faith alone, and the universal priesthood of the laity. On the contrary, as early as the second century, we find "a high estimate of ecclesiastical traditions, meritorious and even overmeritorious works, and strong sacerdotal, sacramentarian, ritualistic, and ascetic tendencies, which gradually matured in the Greek and Roman types of catholicity."[108]

Only by ignorance or "a singular delusion" could Protestants ever imagine that their own confession was "a simple restoration of the Nicene or ante-Nicene age." Rather, the "many errors and imperfections" of the Fathers' writings have been corrected in subsequent times—presumably those since the Protestant Reformation. Follow the Fathers, Schaff advised, only so far as they followed Christ: "carry forward their work in the onward march of true evangelical catholic Christianity."[109]

In these ways, the Protestant professors link Catholicism's appeal to tradition to its concession of authority to the Church Fathers: if one is faulted, so must the other be. Still, the professors sometimes could enlist the Fathers to critique *current* Catholic practices and beliefs.

The Primacy of Peter and the Development of the Papacy

German Protestant authors provided the American professors with explanations for how the bishop of Rome achieved primacy that discounted divine ordination: the precedence of the Roman see stemmed from the city's size and position as imperial capital, and by its (alleged) founding, unlike other western churches, by an Apostle. Its special position was not, in other words, due to any "peculiar rights."[110]

Regarding Petrine authority, the American professors borrowed from German sources to mount their claims. Gieseler, for example, argues that since the other Apostles had the same dignity and authority as Peter, the bishop of Rome could not "pretend" to have inherited from him any special power over other bishops. Mosheim, for his part, claims that in the primitive golden age of the church, "perfect equality" had obtained among bishops—but too soon ambition reared its ugly head and invested the bishop of Rome and his successors with larger authority than other bishops. Neander advances an argument that the American professors especially liked: that Peter was *not* the founder of the church at Rome and was never its presiding officer; rather, the city's political supremacy alone gave the Roman see its importance.[111]

Protestant professors in America largely adopted these explanations. They turned to the Church Fathers—as well as to the New Testament—to counter Catholic claims regarding Peter's primacy that were used to support confession of a divinely instituted papacy. Especially after the 1870 decree on Papal Infallibility that appealed to Peter's primacy, Protestant professors sought to undermine the historical basis for this claim. Disputing Peter's connection to Rome, they aimed to explain the rise to power of the Roman bishopric by reference to secular factors. They also placed the development of papacy relatively late, thus reinforcing its secondary status.

Samuel Miller

Scripture, Samuel Miller taught his Princeton Seminary students, is silent regarding any primacy of the bishop of Rome or even Peter's preeminence among the disciples. In fact, we do not know if Peter ever was *in* Rome, much less that he was its first bishop. In contrast to Roman Catholic teaching and practice, Jesus proclaimed, "call no man Master."[112]

Miller highlighted the conflicts and ecclesiastical politics by which the

bishop of Rome amassed power in order to show that the institution had
no divinely ordained origin or status. In the second century, Victor of
Rome acted in a "bold and insolent manner" in the Paschal Controversy,
foreshadowing "the audacious claims of the *Papacy*." The dispute, Miller
told his students, was all "a matter of *human invention*": "this, young gentlemen is a humiliating scene! . . . The Scriptural doctrine of the depravity
of human nature accounts for it all."[113] The rising esteem accorded bishops
in general, however, served one useful purpose: to check the power of
Rome. Despite these checks, by the time of Leo the Great, Roman bishops
had greatly advanced their power, "slowly making progress toward the
nativity of the *man of sin*."[114] The present papacy, Miller alleged, can be
labeled "Babylon the great—but it, unlike Babylon, does not seem to
'fall'."[115]

Henry Smith

Henry Smith of Union Seminary focused on early interpretations of Matthew 16:18 in his lectures on the development of the Roman primacy,
arguing that the Church Fathers themselves disagreed on the meaning of
the "Rock" (*petra*).[116] In any event, Jesus did not promise to give divine
guidance only to popes and bishops, but rather to the whole church. Listing
biblical passages that Catholics cite to bolster papal claims (Matt. 16:16–19;
Acts 15:25; Deut. 17:9–12), Smith charged that they indulge in a "vicious"
circular argument: they use Scripture "to prove infallibility," but then
assume infallibility for their own interpretation. He countered that Scripture provides all we need by way of infallible teaching.[117]

Only after the mid-third century, Smith claimed, did the "Roman pre-
tense" develop that Peter had been bishop of Rome and Primate; only circa
500 did bishops of Rome claim the title *"Papa"* as their exclusive right. By
the time of Leo the Great, however, who based his claims on Peter's alleged
primacy, we can speak of a "Papal empire." Along the way, not all bishops
(Cyprian, for example) bowed to Rome. Moreover, a bishop of Rome himself, Gregory the Great, held that none should claim to be universal
bishop—a point that all his successors have disregarded. Since bishops of
Rome often erred regarding doctrine, they cannot be considered authoritative teachers: one was an Arian, another a Pelagian. Even worse, one bishop
of Rome (Marcellinus) offered sacrifices to idols. Since the 1870 decree (so
Smith alleged) is intended to cover all papal decisions retroactively, the case

of the "Monothelite" Pope, Honorius I, becomes especially problematic.[118] Smith's teaching aimed to discount contemporary Catholics' appeal to early Christian history to justify the status accorded the bishop of Rome.

Roswell Hitchcock

Roswell Hitchcock also downplayed the Roman primacy, arguing that its establishment was not by divine ordination. "Primacy," he told his Union Seminary students, was not originally associated with Peter, but was first advanced by the Jewish-Christian party in Rome, the "Ebionitic church." Evidence for this lies in the "spurious Clementine Homilies," which accord the honor not to Peter, but to James. Since Protestants doubt that Peter ever was *in* Rome, he clearly had no role in establishing its bishopric. Perhaps Peter was accorded some precedence simply because of his "great age."[119]

Nevertheless, Hitchcock hinted that it was preferable for Rome and partisans of Peter to claim precedence in Christianity's development, rather than allowing Jewish Christianity to claim that prize. If, Hitchcock reasoned, more Jews had converted, Christianity would have been predominantly Jewish, centered in Jerusalem, not Rome, and primacy would have been associated with the Jewish-oriented James, not Peter.[120] For the Christian religion to have "world-wide" appeal, Hitchcock argued, it "must not be oriental;" it must be "more than Palestinian, more than Jewish."[121] Roman primacy, it appears, seemed a better option to Hitchcock than a Christianity centered on a Jewish Jerusalem.

Hitchcock listed now familiar reasons for the papacy's growing power: the excellent record of the Roman church, its legendary association with Peter and Paul, generosity to other churches, orthodox doctrine, and placement in the city that was the center of imperial government. Moreover, in late antiquity as the Empire "fell," the Roman bishop acquired further authority, strengthened by the recognition given by barbarian sovereigns. In addition, various early church councils accorded the Roman bishop special privileges, later enhanced by the "Forged Decretals." And after Leo I—the first to claim universal authority for the Roman see by virtue of inheritance from Peter—bishops of Rome gained power by their "clear purpose, towering ambition, and great craftiness."[122]

To be sure, not all ancient Christians accorded Rome highest authority. Some early bishops of Rome, such as Victor and Stephen, met with resistance. Hitchcock appealed to Cyprian, who granted only a superior "dignity" to the Roman bishopric, "precedency," not "primacy."[123] Eastern Christians also protested Rome's claims,[124] but in the end, the protests were of little avail. In sum, purely "secular" and political forces were at work in the creation of what became the papacy. God is entirely absent from Hitchcock's account.

Moreover, Hitchcock assigned the beginnings of the papacy to a relatively late date. Before the later seventh and eighth centuries, he claimed, the title "universal bishop" was accorded merely "by courtesy." Genuine "papacy" arose only with Pepin's gift of the Exarchate of Ravenna to Stephen III of Rome in 755, a gift confirmed and enlarged by Charlemagne in 774. From then on, the papal estates increased and the reign of priests flourished. Government by priests, in Hitchcock's view, is "likely to be bad"; its abysmal effects on "spiritual character" can hardly be overemphasized.[125] Since Hitchcock was delivering these comments to students in the 1870s and early 1880s, he perhaps had in mind Pius IX's campaign to reclaim his temporal possessions, the Papal Estates, of which he had been largely stripped during the unification of Italy.

Notions of "historical development," however, tempered Hitchcock's critique. He stoutly denied that the papal office was "the work of the Devil," as some Protestants claimed. Rather, the "hand of Providence" was at work: popes had provided more stable rule than otherwise might have obtained in the chaotic times of late antiquity and the early Middle Ages. As a disciplinary force over the barbarians, the papacy was a necessity, serving a "providential end." For centuries, Hitchcock concluded, the papacy, "an admirable *paidagogus*," "shaped history beneficially until the Teutonic element had been reared to manhood."[126] With this seeming praise, Hitchcock signaled that the papacy stood in the same relation to Protestantism as Paul (Gal. 3:25) had placed the Jewish Law in relation to Christianity.

PHILIP SCHAFF

"The fundamental evil of the Roman system," Philip Schaff proclaimed, "is that it identifies papacy and church, and, therefore, to be consistent, must unchurch not only Protestantism, but also the entire Oriental church from its origin down." No wonder that the Greek Church rejects the papacy and papal infallibility as heretical "because contrary to the teaching of the first

seven oecumenical councils." In Schaff's view, *no* form of church government exists by "divine right" or commands "perpetual obligation."[127]

More emphatically than his predecessors, Schaff appealed to early
Christian texts as a bulwark against present Catholic claims. Since the entire
structure of the papacy rests on acknowledging Peter's residence and martyrdom in Rome, if Peter cannot be proved to have been present in that
city, Catholic claims fail.[128] Even if we grant that Peter visited Rome late in
life, Schaff argued, the Christian congregation by then would have been
well established and cannot claim him as its founder. Since John Chrysostom knew of Peter's long residence in Antioch and named bishops in *that*
city as descendants of Peter,[129] Rome has no exclusive prerogative. Moreover, Peter (unlike Pius IX) never assumed that he was infallible; the
Fathers never heard of such a claim nor had Paul. The "*petra*" of Matthew
16:18, in Schaff's view, refers to Peter's confession, not to Peter alone, as
Roman Catholics claim. The primacy of Rome, then, began as a "purely
honorary distinction," but "gradually became the basis of a supremacy of
jurisdiction."[130]

To argue his case against the early origin of Rome's primacy, Schaff, like
his colleagues, appealed to Church Fathers who opposed the power
assumed by bishops of Rome. He noted Irenaeus' protest against Victor of
Rome in the controversy over the dating of Easter (Irenaeus stands as "a
forerunner of Gallicanism . . . against ultramontane despotism"); the opposition of Hippolytus ("an irrefutable witness against the claims of an *infallible papacy*") to Roman bishops Callistus and Zephyrinus; and Cyprian's
dispute with Stephen of Rome over what constituted valid baptism.[131] Other
ante-Nicene writers—Tertullian, Origen, and Novatian—likewise protested
Rome's claims.[132] (If Tertullian objected to a Christian's wearing the
"crown," Schaff joked, we can only imagine what he would have said about
the papal tiara![133]) Moreover, although "papistic theory" alleges that the
Pope alone can "summon, conduct, and confirm a universal council," the
fact remains that until 867 this prerogative lay with the Byzantine (i.e., East
Roman) emperor. The first to merit the name "pope," in Schaff's view, was
Leo the Great, who turned a primacy based on grace and personal qualifi-
cation into one of right and succession, threatening hell against those who
resisted his authority.[134]

Schaff's views on development within ecclesiastical history now came
to the fore. He contended that the list of Roman bishops stretching back
to the first century carries weight mainly with those who rely on external

testimonies, "without being able to rise to the free Protestant conception of Christianity and its history of development on earth." The papacy, Schaff insisted, was not "unchangeably fixed from the beginning for all times, like a Biblical article of faith," but developed through a long process of history.[135] Out of various traditions was

> built the colossal fabric of the papacy with all its amazing pretensions to be the legitimate succession of a permanent primacy of honor and supremacy of jurisdiction in the church of Christ, and—since 1870—with the additional claim of papal infallibility in all official utterances, doctrinal or moral.[136]

Despite his critique, Schaff, like Hitchcock, wove into his narrative the ameliorating theme that Providence, working in silence and secrecy, used "human impulses"—those that drove bishops of Rome to claim power—to achieve a divine end, namely, to accomplish its "disciplinary mission among the heathen barbarians."[137] Schaff advised Protestants to take a generous view of the early papacy as a stage, a "necessary transitory institution," in the progress of Christianity through time. Now, however, it has fulfilled its mission, indeed, outlived itself.[138] Once Christianity came of age, there was no need for a "legal schoolmaster," such as the papacy represented: like Judaism, the papacy paved the development for a true, more spiritual Christianity, namely, Protestantism.[139] Although the papacy had in past history served a useful function, Catholicism should now advance toward Protestantism.

GEORGE FISHER

George Fisher of Yale conceded that the Roman Church in early times was accorded a "moral ascendancy," but that this passed, "with an insensible gradation, into actual authority." He appealed to *I Clement* to support his point. Clement was alleged to be the Bishop of Rome, yet his name nowhere appears in the letter: this omission shows that "it was the Church at Rome which gave importance to the bishop, and not the bishop who exalted the Church." Perhaps Clement was granted authority due to his "superior personality," or he may simply have "assumed the precedence." In *I Clement* we see already the Roman genius for rule manifesting itself, the Latin love of order and "will to check insubordination." The old Latin spirit, Fisher declared, lives on in the papacy![140]

Moving to the third century, Fisher argued that Cyprian's insistence that the church was "one body" prompted the demand for "one head": hence, the developing emphasis on Peter's primacy. (In this case, Cyprian is cited as *contributing to*, rather than opposing, the bishop of Rome's power.) Fisher explained to his Protestant students Cyprian's line, "He has not God for his Father who has not the church for his Mother,"[141] so as to deflate Catholic claims: the Roman bishop was accorded his early preeminence for strictly pragmatic reasons. Recent converts to Catholicism have been quite mistaken on this point:

> Bellamy, Newman, Manning, etc. accept Catholicism because they accept the idea of the visible Church. If now the church as a body needed a head, Rome would naturally become that head—because (1) No city had the political claims it had. (2) Even in Diocletian's persecution, its church was very large. (3) In times of persecutions, news could be sent from Rome, and it came to be a habit to look for advice etc. Moreover several Roman bishops were martyrs, and the Christians there stood in the front ranks against paganism. (4) The Western churches were mainly founded by persons coming from Rome, and looked to it as the mother church. There is some danger however of according to it more supremacy than it really possessed.[142]

Rome's supremacy, in Fisher's narrative, did not rest on divine designation.

Fisher detailed for his students various stages in the papacy's development. He accorded the story of Peter's dying in Rome *some* foundation in fact, "because it antedates that of his primacy." In Fisher's rendition, the Clementine *Homilies*, by asserting Peter's supremacy, gave support to later Roman bishops' claim to be his successors. Fisher rehearsed the disputes between the bishop of Rome and other bishops: Irenaeus versus Victor, Cyprian (now in adversarial mode) versus Stephen. The division between eastern and western churches became "inevitable" when Rome tried to assert its supremacy over eastern bishops. Down to the Middle Ages, however, the election of the bishop of Rome required the consent of the people, although this right was gradually abridged. Fisher wavered on whether the origin of the papacy should be dated to Gregory I or Leo I.[143]

Like some of the German scholars and his German-trained professorial colleagues, Fisher conceded that the papacy was a blessing for the conversion and education of Europe. In addition, papal rule created an association that linked together various European states.[144] Religious, educational, and societal benefits attended the development of the papacy, whatever criticisms the Protestant professors leveled.

EPHRAIM EMERTON

Roman Catholics, Emerton told his Harvard students, reject the notion that the Roman see acquired its importance simply because Rome was a political center; they link the Roman Church's importance to its apostolic foundation. (Emerton, like the other professors, doubted Peter's residence in Rome.) Emerton saw the primitive church's organization as developing in stages: from a "wide-open democracy," to an "oligarchy" of the episcopate, to a "monarchy" of the papacy, the "most concrete expression of the principle of authority."[145] Emerton faulted the Roman bishopric for abandoning "spiritual *leadership*" and grasping after "a divinely appointed *authority* or right of government," based on "Petrine supremacy." On these grounds, why should not the *Jerusalem* church—founded by Jesus himself—have claimed supreme authority, rather than the *Roman*, he asked?[146]

Emerton, like his more evangelical colleagues, looked to historical explanations for how the Roman bishop achieved dominance. One factor: emperors' absence from Rome allowed its bishop a leading role. Moreover, the "great majority of the Western churches [were] founded from Rome," which contributed to that see's eminence. Emerton also detailed the controversy over Easter, in which Victor of Rome threatened to excommunicate the whole Syrian church. Rome's inability to enforce uniformity, however, eventually led the eastern and western churches to separate.[147]

Emerton particularly focused on the role of Leo I in strengthening the Roman see. Among Leo's notable actions, according to Emerton, were condemning many Manicheans to death, stamping Pelagianism as a heresy, and fighting Priscillianism. In the midst of the Christological controversy, Leo formulated "a system of doctrine" that precisely suited the occasion, his letter (the "Tome") winning approval at the Council of Chalcedon.[148] Leo also pressed the Roman primacy (as defined in Nicaea Canon 6) against those who at Chalcedon wished to make Constantinople equal to Rome (as the 28th Canon declared). Leo outlined an almost compete papal policy; he is, Emerton claimed, the first bishop of Rome fully entitled to the name "Pope." No part of future papal policy escapes clear outline in Leo's work, he concluded.[149]

By the era of Gregory the Great, Emerton continued, "the ideal of the mediaeval papacy" was nearly in place. Gregory, however, did not claim Rome's superiority to the apostolic churches, but considered himself merely an equal with their bishops. Emerton commented, "If this fair ideal of a papacy could have been maintained, its history would have been far more worthy of its high calling."[150]

Like the other professors, Emerton deemed the Roman primacy of great value "in the dark periods of the church's history." Here was a theme on which he could dwell at length, drawing on his considerable expertise regarding the barbarian invasions and settlements. Emerton especially emphasized the assistance the papacy gave to the Frankish Empire; it proved a "most useful helper" to the Franks in bringing rule and order to the European continent.[151] Franks, in Emerton's scheme, would be the primary bearers of European civilization.

In these ways the Protestant professors disputed claims to the divine origins of the Roman see and the later authority derived from that alleged origin. Yet, glimpsing light amid the darkness, they admitted that the papacy played a valuable role in establishing Christianity in northern Europe—from whence it would blossom into Protestantism and eventually be transported westward to America.

Mariology

The Protestant professors also criticized Catholic devotion to the Virgin Mary. Samuel Miller alone did not live to register the 1854 declaration on the Immaculate Conception of Mary (*Ineffabilis Deus*), an event that turned the professors' attention to patristic teaching on Mary.

Henry Smith

In his inaugural address as Professor of Church History at Union in 1851, three years before the pronouncement of *Ineffabilis Deus*, Smith noted that Catholics were excitedly discussing that subject "upon which so much can be said and so little known—the immaculate conception of the virgin."

Lecturing in the same year, he assured students that "the Pope alone cannot decide as to doctrine." That right lies with the church's ecumenical councils, whose decisions the Pope may only "sanction and enforce."[152]

Post-1854, Smith necessarily changed his line: Pius IX's proclamation of the Immaculate Conception as unassailable dogma, he told students, signals that the Pope alone is the "ultimate arbiter" of doctrine.[153] Addressing the Presbyterian General Assembly in 1855, Smith proposed that one goal of evangelical Christianity in America should be to defeat the "Anti-Christian Papacy" that rallies around "the standard of the Mary of the Immaculate Conception."[154] Soon after Vatican I's decree in 1870 on papal infallibility, Smith claimed that the earlier declaration on Mary had been instrumental in sacrificing the tradition of the church to "Infallibility." *Ineffabilis Deus*, he alleged, was the first instance of a pope pronouncing infallible dogma—in this case, "the actual deification of a woman"—on his own authority.[155]

Once again, the strategy of citing the Church Fathers *against* the present teaching of the Roman Church proved useful. The earlier Fathers, Smith told his students, accorded Mary "only honor and respect," never imagining the doctrine that now had been declared necessary to one's salvation. These Fathers and their successors all believed that Mary was conceived in sin, although some claimed that she had been sanctified by God before birth. Augustine, in Smith's view, stands as one important witness to the patristic teaching that Jesus *alone*—not Mary—should be considered sinless.[156]

Smith charted the development of Marian doctrine and practice for his class. In the fifth century, he told students, Mary was titled the "mother of God"; in the seventh, the festivals of her annunciation and purification were developed; and in the eleventh, she was named "queen of heaven." Citing medieval theologians who would, he believed, have opposed the 1854 decree, Smith appealed to Bernard's claim that Mary was for a time under original sin, and to Peter Lombard's, that Mary received grace in order to conquer sin. Only in the twelfth century, he continued, was the doctrine of the Immaculate Conception first broached, and in subsequent centuries, Franciscans and Dominicans contended for and against it. In 1447 Sixtus IV forbade debate on the heated issue, threatening excommunication to those who defied his ban. The fine distinctions that later theologians proposed were unknown to the Fathers, Smith assured his students. Smith claimed to have extracted thirteen citations from previous popes that stood against *Ineffabilis Deus.* Innocent III and John XXII, for example, believed that Mary was conceived and born in sin, although she brought forth an immaculate being, Christ.[157] By pronouncing this dogma, the present pope set himself against the church's best historians and thinkers, including John Henry Newman.[158] Even fifteen years ago, he claimed, there were not *two* Catholic theologians in Germany who would have championed the doctrine of the Immaculate Conception.[159] As is evident, an appeal to history constitutes critique for Smith. According to student notes, Smith acidly concluded his discussion, "They [Roman Catholics] are going to work on Joseph next. Good luck."[160]

Smith also charted for his students the more recent process that resulted in the 1854 decree. He noted that in 1849, Pius IX had written to bishops asking their advice on the suitability of the proposed decree; of the 602 who answered, 52 had replied that they doubted the fitness or timeliness of such a decision. Thus, Smith commented, the controversy begun in 1140 was ended and "all obstacles to the worship of the Virgin removed." *Ineffabilis Deus,* in his view, had made the Roman Church "the Church of Mary and not the Church of Christ." The decree asks Christians to worship a "creature, giving to Mary the prerogatives which Christ only can claim"—a move that renders the Catholic Church "more idolatrous" than ever.[161]

Smith also looked to political contextualization of the decree. He tightly linked the declaration on Mary with the Jesuits' power: it marks the "triumph of Jesuit theology and Papal infallibility." The Society of Jesus, he told students, from its very founding espoused the doctrine—and its members pressed for the decree "in order to create a new division in the religious world." *Ineffabilis Deus* proves to Smith that Rome's view is virtually identified with that of the Jesuits.[162] Yet the "idolatrous veneration of the Mother of our Lord," Smith pointedly remarked, was not able to deliver Rome from her political problems attending the movement for Italian unification.[163]

Obviously aroused by the topic, Smith rehearsed for his students Catholic arguments supporting the doctrine, to which Smith offered objections and rebuttals. Unsurprisingly, Smith turned to the Bible. Roman Catholic theologian Giovanni Perrone, he noted, had to "content himself" with the assertion that nothing in the Bible or the Fathers stands *against* the teaching of the Immaculate Conception—not an overwhelming recommendation *for* it, in Smith's view. The Bible, he reminded students, deems *all* humans under original sin. Defenders of the decree who appeal to Genesis 3:15 (that the offspring of Eve will bruise the head of the serpent) as a testimony to

Mary's sinlessness cite the Latin Vulgate version, interpreting the feminine *"ipsa"* ("she") to apply to Mary: yet one more instance, in Smith's view, of the misinterpretation that results when the Bible is not cited in its original languages. Catholics also wrongly cite Luke 1:28 (the angel Gabriel's greeting to Mary as the "favored one," "The Lord is with you") as if this greeting proclaimed Mary's sinlessness from the time she herself was conceived.[164]

Smith was clearly incited by the topic of the Immaculate Conception: four pages of his student's lecture notes from 1855–1856 are taken up by discussion of *Ineffabilis Deus*—more than he later devoted to the 1870 decree on Papal Infallibility. Past Catholic history, including the writings of the Church Fathers, is once more summoned to stand against present Catholic belief.

Roswell Hitchcock

Roswell Hitchcock, like Smith, provided Union Seminary students with a tour of early Christian Marian teaching. Lecturing after the 1854 decree, Hitchcock declared that the root of the doctrine lies in Irenaeus' comparison of Mary and Eve (*Against Heresies* 3.33.19). Although Hitchcock deemed Irenaeus' words in no way "idolatrous," they unfortunately led in that direction. The "good, sensible" Ephrem was chargeable with the same fault, even though he did not advocate the "worship" of Mary. Nor did early Christian prayers to the saints include Mary. Hitchcock also cited Epiphanius, who believed [presumably in his tirade against the Collyridians] that the Virgin Mary was to be held in honor, not worshipped. Debates over the ascription of the title *theotokos* to Mary during the Nestorian controversy, however, prompted further development, indeed, provided "the strongest impulse to Mariology." "Mariolatry," Hitchcock claimed, was fully established by the end of the sixth century.[165]

Hitchcock often favored arguments linking religious belief and practice to climate, but in this case, climate did not assist his explanation. It is curious, he mused, that Marian devotion was more prevalent in the "cold-blooded Occident than in the warm-blooded Orient." Instead, he attributed the spread of "Mariolatry" to the powerful preaching of its advocates, as well as to the early church's "excessive regard for virginity." Moreover, Hitchcock told students, pagans entering the church with "a lingering regard for female divinities" were enthusiastic for Marian devotion. Later,

in Teutonic nations, the reverence for womanhood [such as expressed in
Tacitus' *Germania*] also promoted the worship of Mary.[166]

Hitchcock noted that four of the later Marian feasts—Purification [February 2], Assumption [August 15], Annunciation [March 25], and Birth
[September 8]—had their origin before 800. He traced a pattern: the older
the feast, the more Mary shares honor with her Son; the later, the more she
is honored for herself. The culmination of this "spiritual decay," an even
"greater abomination," was the dogma of the Immaculate Conception: it
was, Hitchcock told students, "left for the senility of [the] R[oman] C[atholic] Church to announce this dogma in 1854, December 8th." Yet Protestants, he admitted, may lean too far in the other direction: "we are in
danger of withholding from Mary that tender interest due to her." He
reminded his Presbyterian students that even John Calvin liked to cite the
words of Luke 1:48–49 pertaining to Mary: "all generations shall call thee
blessed."[167] Hitchcock, although summoning the Church Fathers against
present doctrine, mounted a less vociferous critique than Smith.

PHILIP SCHAFF, GEORGE FISHER, AND EPHRAIM EMERTON

Philip Schaff dealt with Mary largely in writings composed some years after
the 1854 declaration, when the heat generated by *Ineffabilis Deus* among
Protestants had to some extent subsided. In addition, Schaff's views regarding Mary hint at his conservative notions of domesticity and femininity.

Surveying the New Testament representations of Mary, Schaff concluded that Mary is "true to the genuine female character" in that she
"modestly stands back throughout the gospel history." Referring to *Ineffabilis Deus*, he suggested that Jesus' rebuke to Mary at Cana should have
served as a warning to those who promoted her "future apotheosis." That
process started early: the Apocryphal Gospels of the third and fourth centuries decorated Mary's life "with fantastic fables and wonders of every kind."
To believe that Mary's womb was "closed" even after she gave birth—Schaff
alludes to the notion of Mary's perpetual virginity—requires a miracle that
he finds impossible to accept. As for the end of Mary's life, the silence of
the Apostles and the primitive church "stirred idle curiosity to all sorts of
inventions."[168]

It is natural, Schaff conceded, to associate with Mary "the fairest traits
of maidenly and maternal character." But the church of the fourth century

went beyond this, going from "veneration" to "worship," an excess fostered in the fifth century by Cyril of Alexandria. Even in the second century, Irenaeus' attempt to parallel Eve and Mary is "unscriptural," tending to "substitute Mary for Christ." Perhaps this is not unexpected: Catholicism characteristically exalts human factors as instruments or mediators of redemption, and obstructs or makes needless "the immediate access of believers to Christ." The worship of Mary, for Schaff, was "an echo of ancient heathenism." Yet we should not let the "excesses of Mariolatry, sinful as they are," keep us from recognizing the elevating influence of that "ideal of all womanhood."[169] Schaff speaks from a position of the "domestic Christianity" so popular with late nineteenth-century American Protestants. How it influenced his views on Roman Catholic asceticism and the nineteenth-century women's movement we shall see in Chapter 8.

Ephraim Emerton of Harvard, relatively uninterested in theology, went much farther than his evangelical colleagues. He mocked not only the doctrine of the Immaculate Conception, but also that of Jesus' birth from a virgin. On this point, most Protestants seem to him as credulous as Catholics. So strong is the desire to affirm Jesus' divinity, Emerton alleges, that even in our scientific times, from the teaching of the Virgin Birth, one branch of Christianity

has been able to let the logic of the situation work backward by one degree and to proclaim the "immaculate" conception of the virgin mother of Jesus! Even so-called "Protestant" churches while rejecting the worst extravagances of this Christian polytheism have retained the doctrine that makes them possible.[170]

In Emerton's view, the early Church's development of the story of the Virgin Birth contributed to the Catholic declaration on Mary: if Christians can believe one, they can believe the other.

Such is the fate of Mary in the hands of the Protestant professors. While the decree on the Immaculate Conception roused considerable opposition from Protestants at the time of its proclamation, with the passage of the years the historical development of Marian doctrine could be more coolly assessed, and Mary as a model of "true womanhood" be vaunted even by Protestants such as Philip Schaff.

Conclusion

The Protestant professors' rejection of Roman Catholic belief and practice was abundantly on display in their teaching and writing. If, as Robert Orsi notes, the discipline of religion was and is constructed by way of exclusion, by what is "cast out,"[171] then many Roman Catholic beliefs and practices were among those that Protestant professors discarded in shaping the study of early Christian history and theology. Yet those professors influenced by notions of historical development saw divine Providence at work in all of history and acknowledged that development was necessary to early Christianity: these considerations tempered their attack. The papacy, they agreed, although not a divinely ordained institution and no longer needed, had served a useful role in late antiquity and the early Middle Ages, disciplining and transforming various barbarian groups who preserved the culture of antiquity and transferred Christianity to northern and western regions. Although Catholics erred in over-valuing the Church Fathers' authority, in holding tradition equal with Scripture, and in elevating papal claims, their reverence for Mary, if suitably restrained, showed a respect for womanhood that nineteenth-century American Protestants deemed a prime manifestation of civilization.

CHAPTER 8

Asceticism, Marriage,
Women, and the Family

What is in conflict with nature and nature's God is also in
conflict with the highest interests of morality.

—Philip Schaff

Introduction

Nineteenth-century evangelical professors found the rise and development
of early Christian asceticism difficult to explain, since to their eyes the phenomenon lacked scriptural foundation.[1] If asceticism stood against the confession that Jesus' sacrifice was all-sufficient and implied that human
"works" were needed ("Pelagianism"[2]), what Protestant could not see that
it was based on a "false ideal"?[3] Yet, since the professors believed that God
had guided *all* history, early Christian asceticism must have served some
providential purpose. This dilemma plagued their teaching and writing.
They veer between "explaining" (i.e., justifying) ascetic practice in early
Christianity, and "explaining it away," largely through an appeal to the
ruinous moral context of the Roman Empire within which Christianity
developed.

Roman Catholic asceticism, however, was not alone in raising the alarm:
the Oxford Movement proved that Protestants, too, might be lured to
"renounce." That an anti-Tractarian as well as anti-Catholic animus fueled
the opening encounters of the American Protestant professors with early
Christian asceticism is evident in three articles published in 1844 by the

Professor of Ecclesiastical History at Andover Theological Seminary, Ralph Emerson, in the Seminary's newly minted journal, *Bibliotheca Sacra*.[4] To arm ignorant Protestants against the "deadly falsehoods" of early Christian asceticism, Emerson provided excerpts from the *Vitae* of Paul of Thebes, Antony, and Martin of Tours. Readers, he felt sure, would conclude that monasticism was (and is) "insidious," "baleful," and "grotesque," promoting "sacerdotal usurpation" and "the pretensions of popery." Worse yet, partisans of the Oxford Movement—Protestants!—were now "commending a return to monastic institutions." By offering readers a window onto early Christian asceticism, Emerson aimed to prevent the church's "incautious daughters" from lapsing into the very errors from which Protestantism had allegedly rescued them.[5]

Yet when the evangelical professors touted the glories of Protestant marriage as an antidote to Catholic and Tractarian recommendations of asceticism, they encountered challenges from a different quarter: partisans of the nineteenth-century women's movement. Following the Protestant Reformers, the professors decried Catholicism's alleged denigration of home and family as a corollary to its exaltation of asceticism.[6] Their pro-family argument, however, *unlike* that of the Reformers, claimed that Jesus had elevated women to be equals with their husbands in companionate marriage. Yet here, they were caught in a dilemma: the "separate sphere" to which they believed Christianity had raised these "angels of the household"—wives—was precisely the domestic arrangement now under attack by some suffrage advocates. If (such might ask) Jesus had raised women to be equals with men, why should they not vote and enter the professions, including the ministry? In response, the professors denounced feminist goals, concomitantly charging ancient paganism, Roman Catholicism, *and* feminism with women's enslavement; the Protestant (and middle-class) home, by contrast, promised emancipation. The women's movement, as James Moorhead puts it, had "endangered the last remnant of solid ground in a world convulsed by shifting terrain."[7] Faulting ancient and modern ascetic renunciation *and* modern feminist goals, the professors retreated to an idealized (and historically dubious) depiction of early Christianity's promotion of "family values." The professors' views on ascetic renunciation, I argue, fit seamlessly with their recommendations for domestic arrangements in their own era. As Protestants who esteemed marriage, family, and home among the highest goods promoted by Christianity, both Catholic asceticism and feminist aspiration unsettled their intellectual and social worlds.

In this chapter, I first survey German scholars' approach to early Christian asceticism, for the American professors borrowed their arguments wholesale. After briefly elaborating the distinctive positions of Samuel Miller, Henry Smith, Roswell Hitchcock, and George Fisher, I more fully treat Philip Schaff's discussion of these topics. Schaff's greater sympathy to early Catholic Christianity and deeper appreciation for the church's "organic development" render his assessment of asceticism particularly interesting. Only at century's end do we find the Unitarian historian, Ephraim Emerton of Harvard, taking a less confessional and apologetic approach.

German Historians on Early Christian Asceticism, Marriage, and the Family

Three textbooks by German authors—those of Mosheim, Gieseler, and Neander—used by the American professors fault early Christian asceticism on numerous fronts. Adopting the Enlightenment critique of "superstition," Johann Mosheim squarely linked early Christianity's decline with asceticism's development. Johann Gieseler's *Text-Book*, less rhetorically extravagant than Mosheim's, offered similar objections. August Neander's *Church Histories*, however, in keeping with the author's providential view of history, accorded more value to ancient Christian forms of renunciation. A brief review of the professors' German sources shows how much they borrowed.[8]

German church historians charged that since asceticism was foreign to Jesus' pure and simple teaching, its stimulus must have been imported. Mosheim blamed Platonism and the "disease" of "Oriental superstition,"[9] while Neander faulted pagan philosophy and Hellenistic Judaism.[10] Moreover, the fact that adherents of other religious groups of the present—"Mahometans," Buddhists and Indian fakirs[11]—sported ascetic practitioners proved that the phenomenon was not a special mark of Christianity.

Another source of monastic mischief, German authors alleged, stemmed from climate and the temperament of "eastern" peoples. The East, Mosheim charged, fostered "a natural propensity to a life of austerity." "Arid and burning climates" encouraged "indolent and melancholy"

"Mahometans" to seek solitude, while the "melancholy complexion" and gloomy spirits of Egyptians encouraged Christian renunciation.[12] The temperate West, lacking torrid climes, was spared ascetic excesses.[13]

Yet another explanation claimed that early Christian asceticism was a reaction against the immorality and sensuality of the pagan world. In August Neander's version, as noted earlier, Christianity's conflict with sin and heathenism, a "negative tendency," was necessary to clear the ground and might understandably assume "an ascetic shape"—but opposition to the world should have given way to appropriation once paganism was defeated. Burying the talent they should have used for others' benefit, some Christians got mired at the negative level and never progressed to the higher stage of world-appropriation. In the "glow of . . . first love," pagan converts overreacted (so Neander claimed), going beyond the "proper limits" in their rejection of the earth's goods. With the Empire's nominal passage to Christianity, monasticism stood as a rebuke to worldly, "cold and luke-warm" Christians. Here, Christians' false appropriation of the world went "hand in hand" with ascetics' false rejection.[14]

Misguided interpretation of the Bible stood as still another explanation. Monks, Gieseler claimed, appealed to the Old Testament for ancient sanction, tearing biblical passages from their context.[15] Neander—contrary to his usual criticism of *allegorical* interpretation—faulted ascetics' *overly literal* interpretation of Jesus' advice to take no thought for the morrow (Matt. 6:34) and his parable of the Rich Young Man.[16] Literalists pressed too stringently the depiction in Acts of the Jerusalem Christians sharing "all things in common"; these verses, correctly interpreted, merely counsel unselfish brotherly love.[17] Likewise, some took Paul's recommendation for celibacy in I Corinthians 7 at face value.[18] While acknowledging the ascetic import of that chapter, Neander claimed that to advance *beyond* such an interpretation, Christians needed to reach a "higher stage of historical and Scriptural knowledge"—presumably "Protestant"—than could be expected in the second or third century.[19] On this issue, Christian teaching had "developed."

.   Whatever reasons they gave for asceticism's entry into Christianity, the German scholars agreed on its noxious effects. In the place of real piety, Mosheim charged, Christian ascetics substituted "solemn looks, sordid garments, and a love of solitude." Starting up everywhere "like mushrooms," these joyless ascetics who macerated and tormented their bodies were deemed saints.[20] The "beauty and simplicity of the Christian religion" was obscured as its devotees lauded celibate priests and indulged in "unprofit-able penances and mortifications." Christian asceticism in the East, Mos-heim claimed, promoted fanaticism; in the West, profligacy.[21] Mosheim's anti-ascetic rhetoric is extreme: a "lazy set of mortals," a "gloomy institu-tion," "vicious and scandalous practices," "profligates of the most aban-doned kind," a "fanatical form of sanctity," "licentious."[22]

Mosheim emphasized the more *outré* forms of ascetic devotion—Stylites on their pillars and grass-eating "fanatics," roaming naked among the beasts—for his (Protestant) readers' titillation.[23] He also highlighted *syneisaktism*: clerics who lived with women vowed to perpetual chastity, taking "these fair saints to the participation of [their] bed." Such men were deemed holy by virtue of their bizarre behavior, "by starving themselves with a fanatic obstinacy . . . ; by running about the country, like madmen in tattered garments, and sometimes half-naked, or shutting themselves up in a narrow space." The more these fanatics abandoned reason, the more they were guaranteed "an eminent rank among the heroes and demi-gods of a corrupt and degenerate church."[24] Such was Mosheim's assessment of early Christian asceticism.

Asceticism's "wilder" manifestations, such as those practiced by Simeon Stylites, were exploited by Johann Gieseler as well. With their "self-torture," "overstrained and exaggerated views," "egregious self-conceit," and "utter want of mental discipline," Gieseler charged, monks sometimes fell into heterodoxy.[25] Indeed, some plunged into "complete madness," driven to despair by their hopeless efforts, by their excessive mortifications (per-formed under the blazing sun), and by the delusory pride such inhuman denials engendered.[26]

August Neander, too, highlighted the more extreme forms of asceticism. Standing on a pillar for years—as did Simeon Stylites—is a "frivolous" expenditure of energy that could have more been more profitably used in Christian service. Simeon might have displayed more genuine Christian piety by crafting a life in harmony with nature, rather than by "such artistic displays of a conquest over nature." Other ascetics became so dehumanized as to appear "mere brutes," wandering about like wild animals. Moreover, Neander cautioned, ascetics' spiritual pride fostered insanity.[27]

Yet, these German scholars charged, even garden-variety ascetics offered "no models of rational piety."[28] Priestly celibacy prompted immorality;[29] ascetic practice hindered "true inward self-examination," fostered spiritual pride, and masked worldliness by outward renunciation. Suppressed desires broke out, celibates indulging in "every form of sensual enjoyment."[30]

A theological point stands at the center of the German authors' critique: ascetic practices promoted an "externalizing" of Christianity, locating virtue in outward exercises rather than in "forming the heart and the affections to inward piety and solid virtue." Renunciatory practices, grounded in a Semi-Pelagian notion of "works" and human merit—salvation *"opus operatum"*—fostered a false expectation of a higher future blessedness.[31] Based on "an arbitrary set of divine rules," asceticism was legalistic, its "anxious and slavish temper" opposed to Christian freedom.[32] By introducing new "positive" precepts into a system of inward morality, a "Jewish element" entered the ascetic life: Jewish "externality" resurfaced in Catholic asceticism.[33]

Moreover, a Protestant understanding of vocation informed the litany of critiques: deserting the world and refusing their talents to society, ascetics sacrificed their utility "to the gloomy charms of a convent." Swarms of monks refused their talents and labors to society, senselessly imagining that they pursued perfection.[34] Protestants insisted, to the contrary, that vocation entailed combat against, not flight from, the world. Ascetics wrongly imagined that abandoning society was the mark of earnest Christians, for whom a "loftier virtue" was reserved.[35] "Common Christians," by contrast, were allowed a lower standard.[36] With the development of Christian asceticism, Mosheim charged, Jesus' prescription of "one and the same rule of life and manners" for all his followers degenerated into a "double rule of sanctity and virtue."[37]

Seeking allies for their view of inner-worldly vocation, the German scholars—unsurprisingly—called on the ancient critics of asceticism, Jovinian and Vigilantius.[38] Vigilantius (in Neander's imagination) reminded ascetics that the world should be the field of Christian combat; managing property well and gradually distributing its income to the needy was a fine virtue. Jovinian, appearing even more "Protestant," focused "on the inward Christian life founded in faith in the Redeemer and flowing from the new birth."[39] He fought against "the arrogant presumption which ascribed peculiar merit" to celibacy. Recapturing Paul's critique of "Jewish externality," Jovinian stressed redemptive grace alone. Neander was convinced that Jovinian, as Luther's forerunner, must have embraced a notion of the "invisible church" dear to Protestants.[40] Once more, "Jewishness" is linked to the "externality" of Roman Catholic belief and practice.

Yet Gieseler and especially Neander did find some good in early monasticism. Gieseler credited western monks for abandoning the "mechanical labor" of eastern ascetics for a more productive life. In time, Benedictines proved socially useful in reclaiming waste lands, advancing education for children, writing chronicles, and later, copying manuscripts.[41] Neander more strongly emphasized the positive contributions of early Christian asceticism: no era of Christian history was destitute of God's providence.[42] Even the world-fleeing hermits of eastern Christendom, he argued, assisted the larger society by advising important secular leaders, (allegedly) curing the sick, and chastising worldly urbanites. The cenobitic life afforded more opportunity for the exercise of brotherly love, supporting a belief in human equality that eventually led to a critique of slavery. Last, monastic cloisters became institutions of hospitality, providing for the needy and educating the young.[43]

Monasticism in the *West*, Neander emphasized, had been particularly useful. During the barbarian incursions, monasteries in southern France offered protection to refugees. As "spiritual seminaries," they sent forth bishops and missionaries to labor for humans' salvation. All in all, Neander advised his readers not to mistake ascetics' "degeneracy" for the whole monastic way of life. Its worthy points deserve credit, even if Protestants, "on evangelical grounds," oppose its overestimation of renunciation and undervaluation of married life.[44] Neander's more positive evaluation strongly influenced Philip Schaff.

These German Protestant church historians aligned their case against celibacy, past and present, with their promotion of marriage and family. Celibacy, Gieseler claimed, led Christians to the wrong view that marriage was merely a "tolerated evil."[45] Neander—himself a lifelong bachelor—argued that Christianity had sanctified and ennobled "the sacred ties of nature" in marriage, rendering them "more profound and tender." Christianity allowed a certain equality of the sexes in regard to the "higher life," yet prudently instructed woman to "remain true to the particular sphere and destination assigned her by nature"—the sphere within "the bosom of the family or some corresponding place in the administration of church affairs."[46]

Even Ferdinand Christian Baur, whose more radical New Testament criticism was rejected by the American professors, believed that primitive Christianity had elevated marriage, raising woman "above the servile position she had hitherto occupied" and gradually humanizing "the autocratic and despotic spirit" of antiquity.⁴⁷ Despite this claim, and unlike many other Protestant scholars of his era, Baur did not downplay the ascetic cast of some strands of early Christianity. For example, he admitted that in I Corinthians 7 Paul treated marriage merely as a concession to forestall *porneia*. Nor should Protestant commentators try to soften Paul's stringent recommendation for celibacy in this chapter by balancing it with the depiction of husband and wife in Ephesians 5:26–27—a book that in any event Baur did not consider Pauline.⁴⁸ Paul, Baur flatly conceded, had a deficient understanding of marriage, conditioned by the circumstances of his time.⁴⁹ Since in Baur's view Christianity was *meant* to arrive at a deeper morality through a process of historical development, Paul's inability to grasp "the inner ethical meaning of marriage" was unsurprising.⁵⁰ Even by Tertullian's era, Baur argued, "sensual" views of marriage still obtained, the essence of marriage being identified with the "act of carnal intercourse."⁵¹ Unlike many other nineteenth-century Protestant scholars, Baur did *not* read his Protestant views of marriage into early Christian texts.

The German scholars' presentation of asceticism and marriage set the tone for their American counterparts.⁵²

American Professors on Early Christian Asceticism

Samuel Miller

Samuel Miller of the Theological Seminary at Princeton had limited acquaintance with German ecclesiastical histories, judging from the catalogue of his personal library. As we have seen, at the start of his professorial career he knew and used Mosheim's works; later, he acquired a few volumes of Neander in translation.⁵³ His views regarding ancient asceticism were strongly influenced by his opposition, especially in his later years, to Roman Catholicism. Moreover, he had in his youth imbibed an Enlightenment critique of "superstition," which appeared to influence his approach to early Christian asceticism.

Miller, like other Protestants of his era, veered between accusing Catholics of gross "sensuality" in their religious practice and private lives *and* of devotion to an "unnatural" ascetic renunciation. The two charges were linked in his accusation that celibate priests, monks, and nuns indulged in "unbridled profligacy." Recent "awful disclosures" in the popular press only confirm the "testimony of a thousand years" that institutions of priesthood and monasticism were (and remain) "sinks of deep and awful licentiousness." Among the "abominations" of allegedly celibate Catholic priests, Miller charged, are those that arise from "auricular confession [that] opens a door to almost every species of licentiousness and oppression."[54] Miller's denigration of contemporary Catholic mores, assisted by his horror of "superstition," served as the backdrop for his teaching about early Christian asceticism. Catholics, lost in externals, focused either too much or too little on humans' fleshly existence.

Although Miller used Mosheim's textbook in his classes, he faulted that author for downplaying the unfortunate growth of "monkery" in early Christianity and its generation of "idleness, voluptuousness, and selfishness": Mosheim had not sufficiently emphasized the extent to which monasticism contravenes social happiness, reason, and Scripture. (One wonders what more Miller might have wanted, given Mosheim's highly stringent criticism.) Monasteries, Miller warned his students, have always been "nurseries of hypocrisy" and licentiousness, made more odious by "the garb of peculiar sanctity."[55]

Attempting to explain the origin of ascetic currents in Christianity, Miller (like the other professors) appealed to "outside influences." The chief culprit, to his mind, was Gnosticism. In the question-and-answer format he often used in class, Miller asked:

Q: "Whence did this superstition [of asceticism] arise?"
A: "From the *Gnostic* notions of the *malignity of matter*, and the best means of counteracting its influence."[56]

In Miller's rendition, Christians by the second or third century began "to imagine that *solitude, abstinence, mortification*, and *celibacy*" helped to cultivate "spiritual purity." Monasticism, that "unhappy system of delusion," appeared first in Egypt, then passed into Syria and eventually into Europe. It was fully established in the fourth century.[57] Church Fathers of that era, in Miller's view, "had drunk deep into the error concerning the merits of the monastic life." Singling out Basil, Jerome, and John Chrysostom for special criticism, Miller accused monks, "sunk into luxury and vice," of becoming "devoted friends to the unhallowed ambition of the Bishop of Rome."[58] Not even Augustine, who praised "monkery" and celibacy, escaped Miller's charge of "superstition."[59]

The East, in Miller's view, was responsible for spreading an austere form of the ascetic disease. He blamed Athanasius' *Life of Antony* (a work displaying the "grossest superstition and credulity") for introducing Egyptian monasticism at Rome, where previously it had been despised. Antony's disciple Hilarion brought the ascetic life to Palestine and Syria. Echoing Mosheim, Miller declared that within a short time "the whole East was filled with a lazy set of mortals," who by self-inflicted penalties sought to reach intimate communion with God and the angels.[60] The Stylites serve as Miller's exemplars of eastern monastic "superstition" at its most extreme.[61] In characteristic fashion, Miller responded to student questions raised during one class period in the next. A student had asked whether Simeon Stylites remained constantly on his pillar, and if so, how did he pass time? In the next class, Miller read a long extract from Theodoret that detailed Simeon's life and ascetic feats and warned students against this author's credulity. Only a few, like Vigilantius, stood staunchly against monastic superstition.[62] Western monks, Miller added, could not tolerate such severe discipline.[63]

Miller especially faulted the "superstitious" and "credulous" Sozomen as a source of knowledge for ancient Christian asceticism: bred in Palestine, Sozomen had been "educated at the feet of those Gamaliels" from whom he learned of "monkish miracles."[64] Here, Miller indulged in the now-familiar association of Jewish "legalism" with Roman Catholic practice. All in all, Miller's knowledge of early Christian asceticism appears limited. He never mentioned Pachomius; to Antony he awarded the title, the "Father of regular Monkery," the organizer of "conobitic" [*sic*] monasticism.[65] Moreover, the ascetic message of Catholicism's "miserable system" soon promoted clerical celibacy.[66] Yet, Miller stressed, still in the third century, the clergy (although highly corrupt) were allowed to marry—suggesting that clerical celibacy was not an original feature of Christianity. Forced clerical celibacy is, "as the apostle styles it, 'a doctrine of devils'" [I Tim. 4:1–3], leading to "the most enormous evils."[67] Here, Miller's belief that the Pastoral Epistles had been written by Paul provided ballast for his argument.

Henry Smith, Roswell Hitchcock, and George Fisher

The American seminary professors subsequent to Miller largely replicated the German scholars' assessment of early Christian asceticism. The first of the Union Seminary professors of church history, Henry Smith, evinced only mild interest in the subject. During his studies in Germany with August Tholuck, he had learned that second-century Christianity took a false turn in an "oriental platonic direction." A "New-Platonic" asceticism of an "Oriental" type had introduced "severity" and neglected the active life. In time, the rigorous renunciation of Christian hermits in Egypt and Stylites in Syria was modified by the monasticism that joined monks in a common life.[68]

These brief lines from Smith's notebook do not suggest that his knowledge of early Christian asceticism had been much advanced by his studies in Germany. When in the late fall of 1850 Smith began teaching church history at Union Seminary, the topic of early Christian asceticism had already been covered by a temporary instructor, Presbyterian minister Samuel Cox (father of Arthur Cleveland Coxe). Hence we lack evidence of Smith's approach to early Christian asceticism in his first year of seminary teaching.

We learn somewhat more from Smith's *History of the Church of Christ, in Chronological Tables*, published in 1861. Here, Smith listed in parallel columns the major figures, events, and writings of the church from the first century to 1858, including brief notices pertaining to early Christian asceticism. In the apostolic age, Smith noted, "Paul" warned against those who would prohibit marriage (I Tim. 4:1–5).[69] By Cyprian's era, "Christian ethics became ascetic; though celibacy is not generally enforced." As asceticism advanced, Christian writers designated virgins as "brides of Christ," Methodius (in his *Symposium*) magnified the virtue of the unmarried state, and Origen mutilated himself. Smith named several "firsts": the first ascetic hermit, Paul of Thebes, circa 250; the first law requiring clerical celibacy (the Council of Elvira in the early fourth century); the first cloisters for virgins established in Egypt. By 350, hermits were flourishing. Soon, monasticism was a "ruling influence," introducing "a false standard of virtue." Curiously, Smith in his *History* omitted Jerome's role in the promotion of ascetic values, mentioning only his work on the Vulgate.[70] In the fifth century and beyond, monasticism was increasingly favored and received further organization. Concomitant with the decline of spirituality, it came to be called "religion," pure and simple.[71] Despite the fact that Smith's *History* is merely a set of tables, his judgment on early Christian asceticism is patent.

The later Union and Yale professors adduced similar themes. Roswell Hitchcock, however, marked the mid-*second* century as the decisive period in which asceticism became "more pronounced and objectionable." In assigning the inception of celibacy as far back as the "uninspired" second century, Hitchcock claimed that he had placed it "very early"—and indeed, his dating *was* earlier than Smith's. It was then, Hitchcock alleged, that alien ascetic views and practices had "forced their way in" from sources external to Christianity.[72]

Like the German professors, Hitchcock stressed the more *outré* forms of asceticism. His claims were designed to shock simple Presbyterians. Thus he dwelt on the Stylites, a "mostly Oriental" phenomenon, a "travesty of monasticism—but an incarnation of its sterility." Hitchcock expressed amazement that so few Stylites—only six or seven on record—could have made so much "noise in history."[73] George Fisher of Yale, for his part, attempted to dissociate Christianity as much as possible from asceticism. In essence, Fisher wrote, Christianity is *not* "an ascetic system," since it favors education, culture, art, and inventions that ease human burdens.[74]

Criticisms of Christian Asceticism

The American professors adduced many objections to Christian asceticism, past and present. Asceticism, Roswell Hitchcock charged, is basically selfish, aiming at an individual's salvation rather than the extension of Christ's Kingdom. It focuses too narrowly on sins of the flesh and too lightly on pride and ambition, "Satanic sins of the spirit." Outer austerities are over-valued at the expense of the inward life. The best way to counter sins of the flesh, Hitchcock advised, is to "flank them," not exaggerate them.[75] Battle strategies may vary.

Hitchcock was quick to associate asceticism with heresy: Ebionites, Encratites, Marcionites, and Manicheans variously demanded of their adherents sexual continence and the renunciation of property, meat, and wine. But, he conceded, sometimes heretics themselves were the victims of the "monkish mob," who used their clubs—rather than their brains—to silence opponents.[76] Asceticism in general bred fanaticism, as shown in the violent behavior of Egyptian hermits.[77]

In addition, Hitchcock faulted asceticism's "aristocratic" principle. A "fine virtue for the few," asceticism forgets that the same morality is enjoined for *all*. "There are not two virtues, one for the cultured and one for the rude," Hitchcock told his students.[78] The notion of "grades of virtue" is a "false principle," introducing a "caste system" into the domain of ethics.[79] Here, Hitchcock linked Christian asceticism with a feature of Indian religion that nineteenth-century American Protestants particularly abhorred.

Perhaps worst, asceticism brought in its train new immoralities. The evidence comes early, Hitchcock claimed, alluding to Cyprian's reference (*ep.* 62) to the gynecological examination of professed virgins. (In a surprising bit of gratuitous sex education, Hitchcock informed his young male audience that it is not always possible to ascertain a woman's virginity, for some sexually inexperienced girls may *not* possess an intact hymen.) Likewise, the report of Paul of Samosata's cohabiting with virgins shows the early decline of rigorous ascetic ideals.[80] Clerical celibacy, Hitchcock claimed, has always been "followed by the shadow of immorality," "sodomy and all the rest."[81]

In this tale of asceticism's triumph, some heroic souls opposed the enforcement of asceticism. Both Smith and Hitchcock credited the desert father Paphnutius for opposing a proposal to enforce clerical celibacy that was considered at the Council of Nicaea—but to little avail, for by the end of the century, Siricius of Rome, as well as the Council of Carthage in 395,[82] had enjoined it. Jovinian (a "choice spirit" who differentiated the invisible from the visible church), Vigilantius, and Helvidius, anticipating Protestantism, all stood against "the false idea of a higher virtue."[83] Yet, Fisher conceded, many centuries would pass before "the mind of the Church would be ready for such a reformation as Jovinian would have favored."[84]

Explanations for Asceticism's Development

Like their German counterparts, the American professors cast about for reasons why asceticism had entered early Christianity. Henry Smith argued that sexual immorality in ancient Rome served as the negative foil for the development of Christian asceticism. The immoral behavior of Roman deities, Smith claimed, set a pattern for humans: "if the gods are vile so are the men."[85] He wrote:

> The unchaste deities [of Greece and Rome] made immoral devotees. Woman was everywhere debased. Unnatural lusts prevailed. . . . The

Romans had conquered the world, and nothing seemed left but to enjoy the world. They plunged into the fiercest excesses of gluttony and sensuality. . . . The mass of the people were in the deepest moral degeneracy.[86]

To underscore this point, the Protestant professors appropriated the depictions—and denunciations—of ancient immorality found in Latin satire, political invective, and moralizing literature.[87] As noted above in the discussion of early Christianity's alleged decline, they borrowed heavily from Tacitus' attack on imperial vice and praise of Germanic virtue[88] and from Juvenal's vituperative satires.[89] The classical sources provided examples of pagan depravity in contrast to which the professors sought to display the shining virtue of Christianity.

In Hitchcock's view, unchastity—"the unpardonable sin of history," "the plague spot of a decaying civilization"—was rife, following logically from pagans' assignment of women to a "lower order."[90] Although Greco-Roman civilization had the "best thought of the world," morally it was corrupt, no thanks to its gods. The "religious life of the period was conditioned by the rapid decay of Greco-Roman civilization; [it] degraded the whole tone of society."[91] Echoing Sallust, Hitchcock claimed that the "oriental conquest" broke down Roman virtue, and after the Second Punic War, morals gave way rapidly.[92] The decline could be dated as far back as Alexander the Great and became "hopeless" when Rome acquired an empire.[93]

From Juvenal, Hitchcock borrowed the line that when the Orontes emptied its vileness into the Tiber, decline set in;[94] then (he added) "every man became a paramour and nearly every woman a harlot."[95] Pederasty signaled the shocking depravity of the classical world—a depravity that entered chaste Rome from Greece.[96] Hitchcock informed his class that pederasty was not merely a practice of past degenerates; the Orient is "rotten with it today," as is manifest in the sexual behavior of the Khedive of Egypt. The corruption of society in the Muslim East, he claimed, is worse (even) than that of London, Paris, and New York.[97]

Moreover, Hitchcock condemned the fashionable entertainments of Roman antiquity—gladiatorial shows, theater—as either "cruel or vile." The "comparatively clean" plays of Terence were now superseded in popularity by those of Plautus, whose favorite characters were courtesans and pimps.[98] Hitchcock also assigned "sensuous and sensual" Greek art a central role in promoting corruption.[99]

In Hitchcock's view, Christian asceticism—a "moral miracle" in the midst of overwhelming moral decay[100]—stood as a "silent protest" against this mass of pagan corruption and licentiousness.[101] Yet some Christians overreacted. The pendulum swing toward sexual continence had the unfortunate effect not only of promoting an unbiblical renunciation, but also of hindering the development of higher notions of family life. If Christians today, Hitchcock advised, would remember that the age into which Christianity came was "most debauched and slimy . . . reeking with pollution," then they might cease to wonder at the "extravagant morality" of early Christian renunciants.[102]

George Fisher, too, set early Christian asceticism's development against the backdrop of pagan "unchastity" ("the great gentile vice"), sensuality, and "extreme worldliness." To Christians, the world seemed to be "falling to pieces morally as well as politically," Fisher claimed.[103] In phrases seemingly borrowed from Neander, Fisher argued that Christianity had a first, "negative" task to accomplish: to stand against everything in the pagan world opposed to its spirit. Next, however, it was Christianity's duty

> to take up and assimilate whatever in the world's life was truly natural. To purify and elevate, not to withstand or destroy, what was not wrong and was worth preserving, was incumbent on the Church. . . . Worldliness and asceticism were the Scylla and Charybdis between which the Church was called to steer its way.[104]

Some Christians, however, failed to advance to the stage of assimilation and purification: hence, asceticism.

Appealing to the depravity of the Greco-Roman world, however, served more than one purpose. Contextualization could also be adduced to explain the slow and uncertain progress that Christian morals made. Decline, begun *before* the advent of Christianity, negatively conditioned the world into which the new religion came. This conditioning also helped to account for the inexplicably slow progress and often superficial hold of Christian morals. The church necessarily had to work on the "material" furnished by its pagan environment, which lowered its ethical tone: "even the Holy

Spirit," Hitchcock claimed, "is conditioned in the material on which he [*sic*] works." It was hard to develop "a pure Christendom out of such a rotten heathendom." Although the dreadful moral state of the Empire provided a "capital background for Christian virtues"—"it was easy to make men better than the heathen"—it was almost impossible to bring people "up to the proper average Christian ideal." Hitchcock, in fact, cautioned his students *not* to overrate the ethical standards of the early church: the three centuries *since* the advent of Protestantism have been "infinitely higher ethically than the first three [Christian centuries]."[105] Here, nineteenth-century Protestant morality trumps that of the alleged glory days of primitive Christianity.

A second reason for asceticism's entry to Christianity was "mistaken exegesis." Jesus, Hitchcock told his class, was no ascetic. Did not Matthew 11:19 report that Jesus came eating and drinking—and was criticized as a glutton and a drunk? As for Matthew 19:12 (becoming eunuchs for the sake of the Kingdom of Heaven), this verse offers "no sufficient basis" for ascetic practice: Origen's self-castration was based on a misguided interpretation.[106]

The writings of Paul required special handling. Like most other Christians of his day, Hitchcock accepted the Pauline authorship of the Pastoral Epistles. Thus he could claim Paul's authority for the warning (I Tim. 4:3–4) that false teachers would forbid marriage and certain foods. Even I Corinthians 7 could be read so as to limit its ascetic import. Paul's demurrer that each Christian had "his own gift"—not necessarily a gift of celibacy (I Cor. 7:7, cf. I Cor. 12: 4–11)—served to counter the otherwise ascetic tone of that chapter. Paul, Hitchcock emphasized, was no advocate of asceticism, a crucifying or extirpating of the "lower appetites"; he merely encouraged "temperance," a wholesome self-restraint. Later Christians "misapplied" Paul's words.[107] Other sections of I Corinthians 7 could be read to lessen their renunciatory import. By the "impending distress" (I Cor. 7:26), Hitchcock argued, Paul signaled persecutions to come—persecutions that suggested prudence in family formation.[108]

George Fisher particularly attacked Catholics' appeal to Jesus' alleged "counsels." Their distinction between "counsels" and "precepts" had encouraged Christian renunciants to claim a morality superior to that tolerated in the common mass. This claim, Fisher charged, rests on a quantitative estimate of virtue, erroneously founded on Jesus' advice to the rich young man to sell his property in order to be "perfect," *teleios*. Although this bifurcated standard surfaced early in church teaching, it is not, Fisher assured his students, *Protestant* theology.[109]

Fisher also deemed false Renan's claim that Jesus "enjoined poverty and celibacy." Not even Roman Catholic interpreters put the matter *this* baldly, Fisher protested, but merely consider these renunciations as a "counsel." Certainly Dives in the parable of the Rich Man and Lazarus was not condemned to torment (as Renan implies) simply because he was rich. Imagining that Jesus commanded his followers to forsake parents as necessary to discipleship is "preposterous."[110] Origen's self-emasculation to eradicate sexual desire was a false application of Matthew 19:10–13: to believe that Jesus counseled castration is a "revolting absurdity."[111] The earliest followers of Jesus were *not* "a band of ascetics" and did not enjoin poverty as a "duty."[112] The picture of the Jerusalem community in Acts, in Fisher's view, should not prompt Christians to adopt extreme forms of property renunciation: Christianity rather sanctions the relations that "give rise to individual ownership."[113] Christianity, in other words, endorses capitalism as well as traditional filial piety.

Although Fisher conceded that "Oriental" influence may have left its mark on Christian asceticism, its main impetus he assigned to "that [Pauline] conflict between the flesh and the Spirit" that afflicts Christ's followers, and to early Christians' reactions "against the prevalent sensuality and worldliness" of their pagan surroundings. This conflict encouraged fasting, belief in Mary's perpetual virginity, and emulation of the celibate lives of Jesus and John the Baptist.[114] Fisher's acknowledgment that early Christianity *itself* contained elements that promoted asceticism distinguished his teaching from that of many contemporary Protestants.

Likewise distinctive is Fisher's recognition of the eschatological grounding of many New Testament passages. Paul's words on marriage in I Corinthians 7, according to Fisher, were doubtless influenced by the expectation of the world's speedy end.[115] Fisher's assumption that the Pastoral Epistles, Ephesians, and Colossians were all written by Paul, however, allowed him to downplay the ascetic trends of I Corinthians. In any event, he claimed, Paul in I Corinthians recommended celibacy not as *obligatory* but as *preferable*.[116]

A third explanation for the rise of asceticism—climate—also followed that of the German scholars. Soft, "Oriental" climates, Hitchcock claimed, invited luxury and produced enervation, for which renunciation provided an antidote. Asceticism was more at home in the heat of Egypt (and India) than in rugged northern Europe—or in the United States.[117] Jesus, Hitchcock reminded his students, came into "a semi-tropical civilization"—presumably to counsel fortitude.[118]

Fisher, for his part, argued that whenever "mystical longing" overtakes humans "in countries where the climate is mild and favorable to repose," accompanied by "a passion for self-brooding, and an unhealthy view of seclusion," some form of monasticism is apt to develop. Under the heat of the tropical sun, he alleged, hermits were driven to insanity. Cenobites managed to escape this fate, even though their more moderate mode of life drove them as well to "the wildest excesses."[119]

Still another reason for the growth of asceticism pertained to the Christianization of the Empire from the early fourth century onward. From the time of Constantine, Hitchcock taught his students, Christianity's growing acceptability fostered a lowering of standards within the church: now, opting for a life of renunciation seemed a way to preserve a purer form of Christianity. When martyrdom was no longer an option, Christians might become "life-long martyrs" by adopting ascetic practices.[120]

For Fisher, the period after 312 saw a pendulum swung between asceticism and worldliness, which fed off each other.[121] Now,

> the purity of the Church was imperiled by the influx of nominal Christianity. A feeling of alarm took possession of many serious minds. Some who lacked the courage to enter into conflict with the growing depravity looked for a secure retreat from the vanities and uncertainties of ordinary life.[122]

Those who allegedly lacked this courage misunderstood Christianity, imagining that the way to conquer an evil world was to withdraw from it.[123] At best, asceticism stood as a time-conditioned reaction to life in the Roman Empire that should be discarded when the immediate situations that called it forth no longer obtained.

In all, Fisher and Hitchcock argued, since other religions promoted asceticism, it was not unique or essential to Christianity. In the ancient world, the Vestal Virgins practiced asceticism, as did Druids, Buddhists in India, and Jews (Essenes and Therapeutae); even the Hebrew prophets had tended toward asceticism, Elijah and the Nazarites serving as cases in point. Yet asceticism had "no business to enter the Christian Church," Hitchcock brusquely added; it "forced its way in."[124] Christian asceticism, in other words, could claim no special privilege among the world's religions.

Some Benefits of Early Christian Asceticism

Following their German predecessors, especially Neander, the evangelical professors nevertheless found something to praise in early Christian renunciation. Monasticism had performed a good service in transferring Christianity from the decaying and "effete" culture of Rome to the new world of the early Middle Ages. Unlike the "fruitless" monasticism of the East, Hitchcock claimed, western monasticism had benefited the wider society up to the time of Charlemagne.[125] It stimulated the economy by its exemplary agricultural practices that restored the land, fostered learning by preserving and copying manuscripts, and served as a tool through which barbarians were Christianized.[126] Fisher added more: monks in their "self-denying devotion" provided hospitality, helped the poor, and befriended those in distress.[127] These accomplishments could be lauded, even by staunchly Protestant professors.

In the celibate missionaries who had worked to Christianize northern Europe, Hitchcock found a point of contact with his Protestant students: although self-denial, he told them, can never be an end in itself (for asceticism is heresy), there may be occasions on which celibacy is indispensable to serving the church. If necessary, it can be borne with patience and cheerfulness. Although celibacy in itself is wrong, "as a means it is right."[128] In ways such as these, early Christian asceticism could be understood as providing some—albeit limited—social benefits in a world deemed dark and desperate.

The Evangelical Professors on Women, Marriage, and the Family

The evangelical professors' praise for marriage and family, past and present, stood as the inverse of their attack on asceticism. Christianity at its inception, they claimed, had raised the status of women—although even by the patristic era, a decline had set in. The "family values" they assign to primitive Christianity, I note, seem (suspiciously) to resemble nineteenth-century middle-class American notions of domesticity.

Given Samuel Miller's attack on Christian asceticism, it is surprising to find him advising Presbyterian students who were aiming for an itinerant ministry to *avoid* marriage. He cited the unhappy marriages of Methodists John Wesley and George Whitefield: they should not have married, and when they did, they chose "strangely injudicious partners." Settled ministers, on the other hand, should consider it a duty to marry, since celibacy does not bring "perfection" and Genesis 2 stands against it.[129] Having a good family life, Miller counseled his students, is especially important for ministers.[130]

Miller, like other Protestants, charged that ascetic enthusiasts denigrate women, marriage, and family. "Man was made for society," Miller wrote, the earliest form of which was the family. He cited Job 5:24 to reinforce his point: "Thy tabernacle shall be in peace." Each family should be a little "church"—even though Miller-the-Calvinist claimed that every household is also "a little band of sinners," only "partially sanctified."[131]

Miller's praise of marriage presupposed that husband and wife had "separate spheres." In a sermon preached in 1808, Miller remarked that while he declined to judge whether women's minds are the same as men's, all could agree that the sexes are destined for different employments. Thus there should be a "species of education and a sphere of action" suited for women's capacities and for their needs as future wives and mothers. Once, he recalled—perhaps alluding to some heady moments of the Enlightenment era—people believed that all distinctions of sex should be forgotten, that females were as well suited to

> fill the academic Chair, to shine in the senate, to adorn the Bench of justice, and even to lead the train of War, as the more hardy sex. This delusion, however, is now generally discarded. The God of nature has raised everlasting barriers against such wild and mischievous speculations.[132]

Miller, however, cautioned against overly restricting women: the latter have "an immense field for the most dignified activity." Even though shut out of some offices by God or man, women still have many ways to be useful. Wives can do much to ensure a happy and well-ordered household, and their role in parenting is supreme. Education should prepare them to be wives, mothers, members of society, and Christians.[133]

Miller, to be sure, was by no means the most conservative writer on "women's sphere."[134] In his *Brief Retrospect of the Eighteenth Century*—his most acclaimed work, written before he became a professor—he praised advances in female education, repeating the familiar line that the progress of a civilization is shown by the higher worth it accords women. Since women are rational beings whom God intended as companions, not servants, for their husbands, they should be educated. Yet they should not be given the *same* education as men or be allowed the same offices and professions: such teachings are "mischievous."[135]

Miller, however, was no friend of the women's movement that was stirring in his early adult years. In his *Brief Retrospect*, he affirmed childbearing to be women's central role, a role that precludes their assumption of men's "employments and pursuits." In addition, in his call for female restriction, Miller appealed to women's smaller, weaker physical constitutions; to the immorality resulting from the "promiscuous mixing" of young women and men in educational institutions; and to biblical depictions of women's proper sphere (presumably drawn from the Pastoral Epistles). Coeducation, Miller claimed, would convert society into "hordes of seducers and prostitutes," with "universal concubinage" the rule.[136] Mary Wollstonecraft served as Miller's special target. Focusing on Wollstonecraft's alleged sexual immorality, Miller charged that "her licentious practice renders her memory odious to every friend of virtue." Her life proves that the feminist agenda destroys chastity and returns women to an abject condition.[137]

Miller, however, did not ground his arguments regarding women, marriage, and family as deeply in New Testament and early Christian teaching as did both German and later American professors. Yet his critique of early Christian asceticism, like theirs, found its corollary in nineteenth-century bourgeois notions of domesticity.

Roswell Hitchcock began his remarks on marriage and the family with an assessment of classical antiquity, whose authors he read without benefit of a hermeneutic of suspicion. Early Republican Rome, he claimed, presented a model of family life: fathers exercised authority, children obeyed their parents, and women were morally decent. But the "oriental conquest" demolished Roman virtue; after the Second Punic War, morals declined precipitously. Then, Greek views of women—an ontologically lower order, prone to evil, and fitted only to be either mothers or "toys"—sullied

Roman life. Read Euripides, Plato, and Aristotle, Hitchcock told his class! The Greek hatred of women ran so deep that men took to pederasty. Pre-Christian Rome did little better, knowing nothing of the "true domestic" condition, "of proper family life." Allegiance to the state "swallowed up," even "destroyed" the family.[138] Ancient Judaism's estimate of women, in Hitchcock's opinion, was not much better. While attempting to raise the domestic standard, Christianity was saddled with much baggage from its pagan and Jewish inheritance. Given the demoralized character of imperial Rome, the marvelous chastity proclaimed by early Christianity must be credited to divine grace.[139]

By contrast, Hitchcock deemed New Testament teaching on the family (largely derived from the Household Codes) "admirable." These teachings, he told his students, contain the proper proportion of submission and obedience on the part of wives, children, and "servants" [i.e., slaves], enjoining consideration and kindliness on the part of husbands, fathers, and masters. Unfortunately, realization of a lofty family ideal was hindered by the "higher sanctity" that was accorded to celibacy. (Hitchcock recommended to students the "beautiful sketch of married life" in Clement of Alexandria's *Instructor* [Book II].) Hitchcock freely admitted that slaves formed part of the early Christian family and that Christian writers did not attack the institution, yet, like many other Protestants of his era, he claimed that Christianity throughout its history had done much to mitigate slavery's harshness without prematurely demanding its abolition.[140]

The praise of asceticism, however, resulted in over-emphasizing the sexual dimension of life. Chastity, Hitchcock alleged, was of such supreme importance that a Christian woman would commit suicide rather than submit to "violent dishonor." Church canons (such as the Council of Elvira's) regulated the sexual lives of laypeople very rigorously; patristic writers counseled great restraint in married life, "amounting to continence." These views contributed to the belief that marriage was not the highest estate of Christian life. Catholics' (alleged) denigration of women and family life through the centuries, Hitchcock argued, remained uncorrected by the high estimate of women Paul prescribed in Ephesians 5:22–33.[141]

Was all New Testament teaching, including injunctions regarding women, still binding? Hitchcock hedged. To his classes in the 1880s, Hitchcock offered two revealing examples. One precept binding for the present, in Hitchcock's view, was the prohibition of women speaking in "promiscuous assemblies," that is, mixed audiences (women's prophesying in their own domestic circles was allowed, he added). Here, Hitchcock's belief that the Pastoral Epistles were written by Paul doubtless strengthened his conviction.[142] Yet, in contrast, the community of goods represented in Acts is *not* binding. But if it is not, why is the prohibition binding against women's speaking? Hitchcock reasoned thus: "Paul" in I Tim. 2:13–14 lays down the prohibition as a rule. His decision has "universality," not resting on "oriental reason alone." Today, Hitchcock insisted, the "instincts of [the] best men and women" agree on this point.[143] Yet he admitted that honest scholars can and will still debate this issue.[144] Hitchcock's examples illustrate once more the (relative) social conservatism of the evangelical professors: capitalism wins, movements of women's emancipation lose.[145]

George Fisher, again seemingly taking his cue from Neander, claimed that Christianity sanctifies the "natural relations" underlying the family and state. The early church, despite its growing worldliness, elevated marriage and ennobled woman far above the pagan standard. The father's absolute authority was now curtailed, the "domestic tyrant" abolished. Christianity, Fisher wrote, also opposed the pagan practice of child-abandonment, especially of female infants, that often led to the child's enslavement.[146]

Fisher argued that despite the faults of the Roman family, the Romans accorded women a higher position in the household and as companions to their husbands than did the Greeks. (Plato, by contrast, was so oblivious to "the spiritual nature of marriage" that in the *Republic* he introduced a community of wives.) Fisher reported as a fact the claim in Roman sources that there was no divorce for the first five hundred years of Roman history; it was Hellenism that led to the decline of Roman character. By Augustus' era, the demoralization of Roman society expressed itself in men's refusal to marry (Fisher cited the Augustan marriage legislation). "Unnatural vice," scarcely condemned by Greek writers, disinclined men to marry. The rumors of Julius Caesar's sexual interest in men, for example, even if false, show a measure of toleration that Fisher believed "in modern times, would render the perpetrator of them an outcast and an object of loathing."[147]

Fisher argued that Christianity, by contrast, taught that marriage was a sacred bond, dissolvable for one cause only, not at the husband's caprice. "As far as Christianity spread, respect for the rights of women extended." While later Christianity exaggerated reverence, even "unauthorized worship," for the Virgin Mary, this reverence was nevertheless "connected with a sentiment toward the wife and mother which genuine Christianity fosters."[148]

Not all early Christian women, however, met this high standard. Fisher charged that women at Corinth (as shown in I Corinthians) were fond of finery and apt to overstep the bounds of modesty set by ancient convention. Since an unseemly disposition prompted them to make themselves conspicuous in church (I Cor. 14), Paul was wise "to prohibit what would offend the sentiment of [the] world. Whether his strictures are a law for all time, may be disputed," Fisher told his students circa 1870.[149]

Hitchcock and Fisher thus praised marriage and family against Catholic asceticism, early and late. Yet while they claimed that Christianity raised the status of women, it was not in the ways that nineteenth-century suffragists usually advocated. On the topics of asceticism, women, marriage, and family, Philip Schaff provides the fullest discussion.

Philip Schaff on Christian Asceticism

Asceticism, Philip Schaff claimed, is the area that seems "most remote from the free spirit of evangelical Protestantism and modern ethics": Protestantism signaled "the end of the monastic life."[150] Christianity, he insisted, is "anything but sanctimonious gloominess and misanthropic austerity." Like Neander, Schaff believed that the Christian's role is to stand *in* the world so as to "overcome it and transform it," to "purify and sanctify" it into the Kingdom of God. From the time of his first major publication written this side of the Atlantic, *The Principle of Protestantism*, Schaff never ceased to declare that since Christianity's aim is to sanctify all spheres of natural life, "Romish monasticism," a "flight from the world," is in error.[151] The grand principle to be upheld, he taught his students at Mercersburg, is "to live in the institutions which God appointed and to keep these sacred, and here to overcome passion, desire. . . . In the family circle . . . the Christian has the greatest opportunity to develop the Christian character. Here he is to put the world under his feet."[152] Schaff warned his readers to resist the "allurements of the artificial show of ascetic hypo-holiness [sic]."[153]

Yet Schaff attempted to keep in play two seemingly contradictory notions: that all church history marked a declension from the apostolic era, but nevertheless manifested God's providential care. Although he believed that asceticism contradicted Christianity's basic principles, he also held that Providence, like Hegel's "cunning of Reason," worked in mysterious ways to bring good out of evil. Since Jesus had promised to be with his followers even unto the end of the world (Matt. 28:20), there could be *no* period of the church's history totally devoid of God's guidance. How then to explain early Christian asceticism?

Christian asceticism, Schaff claimed, was based on erroneous theological principles, "a total misapprehension and perversion of Christian morality" that exhibited a "Gnostic contempt of the gifts and ordinances of God." Substituting "an abnormal, self-appointed virtue and piety for the normal forms prescribed by God," asceticism implicitly denied that the merits of Christ are "all-sufficient." Disease metaphors embellished Schaff's description: "A mania for monasticism possessed Christendom, and seized the people of all classes like an epidemic."[154]

Ignorant of the "gospel of freedom," ascetic devotees understood Christianity as a new law, as "outward exercises" rather than an inward disposition and life of faith. Asceticism introduced a notion of "aristocracy" into Christianity; priests, monks, and nuns, in their "spiritual pride," scorned the "divinely ordained standard" of marriage. "The modest virtues of every-day household and social life" seemed to them "an inferior degree of morality."[155] Fancying themselves a little *"ecclesiola in ecclesia,"* they divorced themselves from the life of the mainstream church. They disregarded the basic Christian concept of justification by faith, practicing a quantitative calculation of "outward meritorious and even supererogatory works" that Schaff deemed "Judaizing self-righteousness." For these views, Church Fathers such as Clement of Alexandria and Origen bear much responsibility.[156]

Schaff's Explanations: Wrong Biblical Interpretation

Schaff's explanations for the development of asceticism appealed to both intra- and extra-Christian factors. Among the former, Schaff (like his German and American colleagues) blamed misguided biblical interpretation: asceticism, he claimed, has "no affinity with the morality of the Bible; and offend[s] not only good taste, but all sound moral feeling." Although Old Testament prophets are sometimes depicted as ascetically inclined, they were not bound to celibacy; Isaiah and Hosea, for example, were married, and Samuel had children.[157] Yet since ascetics appeal to the Bible to justify their practice, Schaff aimed to show that their exegesis was erroneous.

Asceticism, Schaff claimed, "starts from a literal and overstrained con-

struction of certain passages of Scripture" that exceeds "the simple and
sound limits of the Bible." Ascetic enthusiasts cite passages such as Matthew
19:12 (becoming a eunuch for the sake of the Kingdom of Heaven) and
I Corinthians 7 (Paul's recommendation for celibacy). Such passages, Schaff
suspected, had been unconsciously influenced by "foreign modes of
thought."[158]

Explaining Jesus' *own* celibacy might be harder. Jesus was not, Schaff
insisted,

> an ascetic of any kind, but the perfect pattern man for universal
> imitation. . . . His poverty and celibacy have nothing to do with
> asceticism, but represent, the one the condescension of his redeem-
> ing love, the other his ideal uniqueness and his absolutely peculiar
> relation to the whole church, which alone is fit or worthy to be his
> bride.[159]

"Not a hermit nor a saint of the desert," Jesus was "too far above all the
daughters of Eve to find an equal companion among them."[160] Since he
found no human consort of comparable lineage, he remained unmarried.[161]
Schaff's adoption of Victorian notions of companionate marriage among
partners of similar social rank here assisted his justification of Jesus' celibacy.

Moreover, Jesus' celibacy—and that (allegedly) of Paul, Barnabas, and
John[162]—could be balanced with the noncelibacy of other disciples, Peter
being an especially useful case in point.[163] That Peter was married, Schaff
inferred from the story of Jesus' cure of Peter's mother-in-law (Lk. 4:38;
Matt. 8:14) and from Paul's claim that Peter was accompanied on his travels
by a "wife" (I Cor. 9:5).[164] Peter, Schaff reported, was even held to have a
daughter.[165] Such passages led him to protest, "What right have the popes,
in view of his [Peter's] example, to forbid clerical marriage?" If "marriage
did not detract from the authority and dignity of an apostle, it cannot be
inconsistent with the dignity and purity of a minister of Christ."[166] "If the
first pope was married, [it] goes very bad for this system!" Schaff exclaimed
to his students.[167]

Passages in the Gospels referring to the brothers and sisters of Jesus
gave Schaff further opportunity to decry asceticism. Did attributing siblings
to Jesus imply his parents' impurity? Such a charge could hold only if the
marriage relation itself were "impure and unholy"—but God instituted it

in a sinless Eden, and Paul compared it to the union of Christ and the church. The Evangelists and Apostles, surer guides than the Church Fathers, never denied that Jesus had siblings. Moreover, Schaff added, Jesus' "condescending love" and "true and full humanity" was shown in his sharing of "the common trials of family life." If the claim could be *proved* that the brothers of Jesus were actually younger children of Joseph and Mary, Schaff wrote, this would "destroy by one fatal blow one of the strongest pillars of Romish Mariology and Mariolatry, and the ascetic overestimate of the state of celibacy." But, he conceded, no proof is now available.[168]

Schaff rejected what he considered "wrong readings" of other New Testament passages as well that, some alleged, promoted asceticism. For example, he construed the 144,000 *parthenoi* of Revelation 14:3–4 as those who kept themselves pure of *idolatry*; *parthenoi* should not here be translated as "virgins," he argued, both because of the vast number and because the holy disciples themselves (surely among those blessed) had married. As for Matthew 19:10–12 (becoming "eunuchs for the sake of the Kingdom of heaven"), Schaff pronounced these verses "mysterious."[169]

Schaff was much aided in his limitation of Paul's advice in I Corinthians 7 by attributing Ephesians and the Pastoral Epistles to Paul. Although Tübingen School critics had long since pruned these books from the Pauline corpus, Schaff resolutely retained them as Pauline—a necessary step to balance the ascetic message of I Corinthians 7. Although in some respects it would have been *more* convenient for Schaff and the other professors to *drop* the Pastoral Epistles from the Pauline corpus (thus eliminating those *episkopoi*, so troublesome to many nineteenth-century Protestants), the affirmation of them as Pauline served as ballast against the ascetic import of I Corinthians 7.

As a first step, Schaff hedged on whether Paul himself actually *was* celibate. The Apostle, he wrote, "*probably* never married"—although his notion [in Ephesians] of "marriage as reflecting the mystical union of Christ with his church, and his exhortations to conjugal, parental, and filial duties [in the Pastoral Epistles], seem to point to experimental [i.e., experiential] knowledge of domestic life." But, Schaff conceded, Paul probably did *not* marry: given the hardships and persecutions of his missionary work, Paul felt called to remain alone.[170] A missionary facing the dangers that Paul experienced would have found a wife a great hindrance. Freed from all domestic cares, Paul could give himself fully to spreading the gospel— just as today, Schaff added, celibacy can sometimes be recommended for missionaries, or for scholars "married" to their studies, such as Alexander von Humboldt and Schaff's own Professor Neander.[171] Or perhaps Paul was a widower, Schaff mused.[172] Yet, even if we concede that Paul *himself* preferred celibacy, "he is the most zealous advocate of evangelical freedom, in opposition to all legal bondage and anxious asceticism," Schaff assured his readers.[173]

Schaff sought to contain the ascetic import of I Corinthians 7, contriving several reasons for Paul's commendation of celibacy. First, Schaff appealed to context: the state of female education and of married life in Paul's day was "very low." Christianity had had little time to work its refining influence. Since the "frivolous heathens of dissolute Corinth"—"the most licentious city in all Greece"—could not imagine the type of marriage sketched in Ephesians 5, Paul dissuaded the Corinthian Christians from marriage, advising "a radical cure by absolute abstinence under the peculiar circumstances of the time."[174] Schaff enlisted the over 1000 *hierodouloi* in Corinth's temple of Artemis [*sic*] to indicate the corrupt state of religion in that city.[175]

Second, Schaff argued, Paul seemingly favored celibacy because he foresaw the persecutions to come. Treating the puzzling verse I Corinthians 7:37—if an unmarried man is not under "necessity" [*anagkê*], he would best refrain from marriage—Schaff explained the "necessity" as referring not to sexual desire, but to the approaching dangers of persecution. Besides, he reasoned, sexual desire presses *more* strongly on celibates than on married men, and "hence the avoidance of [sexual desire] can be no ground for recommending virginity."[176]

Third, Schaff continued, Paul's recommendation for celibacy is simply his private opinion, a human counsel, not a command from the Lord.[177] "Paul" wrote in I Timothy 4:3 that forbidding marriage is a mark of the Anti-Christ, and in I Timothy 3:2, he assumes that bishops will be married: would not Paul contradict himself if he advised celibacy in I Corinthians 7 but marriage in I Timothy?[178] The ascetic tone of I Corinthians 7, Schaff concluded, is "balanced with the Pastoral Epistles." Later writers, both orthodox and heretical, misguidedly construed Paul as an "apologist for celibacy."[179] The Catholic Church, Schaff told his students, goes beyond Scripture, indulging in a "monstrous exegesis" of I Corinthians 7 when it requires all clergy to remain celibate.[180] Monasticism is "a sad enervation and repulsive distortion of the Christianity of the Bible."[181] Misguided exegesis provides one explanation for early Christian asceticism.

Schaff's Explanations: Context

A second type of explanation presses contextualization: the "horrible licentiousness" and moral corruption of the whole heathen world—not just of Corinth—at the time of Christianity's birth, with its concomitant degrading of women and marriage, prompted Christians of "earnest mind" to seek "angelic purity" in solitude. Echoing Henry Smith, Schaff adduced the immoral behavior of pagan deities, who modeled "no restraint for vice" for their devotees.[182] All in all, Schaff deemed Greek and Roman sexual practice so disgusting that he retreated to silence: these "vices of natural and unnatural sensuality . . . decency forbids to name." The early church, however, veered to the opposite extreme, wrongly estimating virginity as "higher" than chaste married life. On this reading, Christian asceticism was an excessive reaction against "the rotten condition and misery of family life among the heathen."[183]

Schaff pressed this point when referring to the stipulations made at the Jerusalem Conference described in Acts 15:19–20. To the modern reader, he granted, connecting ceremonial prohibitions with the prohibition of fornication seems strange. He aimed to explain the passage:

> the heathen conscience as to sexual intercourse was exceedingly lax, and looked upon it as a matter of indifference, like eating and drinking, and as sinful only in case of adultery where the rights of a husband are involved. . . . In this absolute prohibition of sexual impurity we have a striking evidence of the regenerating and sanctifying influence of Christianity. Even the ascetic excesses of the post-apostolic writers [who denounce second marriage and exalt celibacy] command our respect, as a wholesome and necessary reaction against the opposite excesses of heathen licentiousness.[184]

Although Schaff in a generous mood considered monasticism "a wholesome reaction against the corruptions of heathenism," he argued that Protestantism more successfully raises the general morality of the laity. Our era, he claimed, in which the masses exhibit a much higher average level of morality than did the Nicene age, could not beget such ascetic extremes. The different effects of Catholicism and Protestantism become obvious when we compare the "intellectual and moral condition" of Roman Catholic and Protestant countries of the present.[185]

Schaff's Other Explanations

Still another reason for the development of asceticism in early Christianity, and one that Schaff borrowed from German scholars, concerns the temperament of different ethnic groups and the varying climates in which they live. The heat of Egypt and its denizens' temperament—their "sepulchral sadness"—made that country supremely suitable for renunciation.[186] Similarly, he claimed that Simeon Stylites' "heroism of abstinence" was possible only in "the torrid climate of the East," not in the West. Besides, insofar as eremitic monasticism was best suited to burning climates, but generally unsuited to women, it could not claim to be practicable on a universal scale.[187]

Still another of Schaff's explanations for monasticism's development rested on the Church's post-Constantinian status. As crowds of nominal Christians flooded into the Church, monasticism developed as a "reaction against the secularizing state-church system and the decay of discipline . . . [as] an earnest, well-meant, though mistaken, effort to save the virginal purity of the Christian church, by transplanting it in the wilderness."[188] On this reasoning, monasticism grew in opposition to the "mixed and worldly Christianity" that attended the union of church and state—the world having "rushed into the Church and swept into it all the vices of heathen Rome."[189] When Christians could no longer show their superior devotion through martyrdom, monasticism served as compensation.[190]

In the end, Schaff argued that asceticism is nothing distinctive to (and hence not an essential aspect of) Christianity. Ancient Judaism had its forms of asceticism in the Therapeutae and "paganizing Essenes." Likewise, Gnostic and Manichean sects practiced a form (albeit heretical) of asceticism; Gnosticism, Schaff alleged, perhaps influenced the Christian variety. The Encratite renunciation of the use of wine in the Lord's Supper reminded Schaff that a "certain class of abstinence men in America, in their abhorrence of all intoxicating drinks, have resorted to the same heretical practice, and substituted water or milk for the express ordinance of our Lord"[191]: still another reason to fault Protestant sectarianism.

Moreover—in a reversal of his former argument about the degeneracy of the heathen world—Schaff associated asceticism with various forms of ancient "heathenism": Greco-Roman philosophy, the Eleusinian priesthood, and the Vestal Virgins. Ascetic practice is also found further afield in Hinduism, Buddhism, Islam, and among the Persians. The desert saints of Christianity, Schaff claimed, like "Buddhist fakirs and Mohammedan dervishes," imagined that the greatest virtue lay in "bodily exercises of their own devising, which, without love, at best profit nothing, very often only gratify spiritual vanity, and entirely obscure the gospel way of salvation."[192] If asceticism *were* a superlative virtue, we would have to admit that the self-tortures of "ancient and modern Hindoo devotees" outdo anything Christianity might offer! Ascetic practice in India, Schaff argued, shows that monasticism brings no blessing: 3000 years of renunciation has not "saved a single soul, nor produced a single benefit to the race."[193]

Schaff's Criticisms of Christian Asceticism

The negative effects of asceticism, Schaff thought, were and are manifold: pride, ambition, idleness, and religious fanaticism. Under the mask of humility and self-denial, the hermit life "cherishes spiritual pride and jealousy," even lapsing into "savage barbarism, beastly grossness, or despair and suicide." Asceticism denies the "high destiny of the body and perfect redemption through Christ." It measures virtue by "the quantity of outward exercises," disseminates "self-righteousness and an anxious, legal, and mechanical religion," and favors "the idolatrous veneration of Mary and of saints, the worship of images and relics, and all sorts of superstition and pious frauds."[194] Tales of the early Christian ascetics are laden with silly and doubtless fraudulent claims—for example, that Pachomius rode over the Nile on the backs of crocodiles ("men will so believe it as may," Schaff commented to his students).[195]

Moreover, on the practical side, monasticism withdrew from society the useful forces that would have improved social, public, and family life. It hastened "the decline of Egypt, Syria, Palestine, and the whole Roman empire," and lowered the general standard of morality for ordinary Christians. Asceticism failed to cultivate those character traits that are brought out in the "school of daily family life." Rather, "for the simple, divine way of salvation in the gospel, it substituted an arbitrary, eccentric, ostentatious, pretentious sanctity. It darkened the all-sufficient merits of Christ by the glitter of the over-meritorious works of man." By teaching a two-tiered morality, monasticism lowered the general standard, as can be inferred from the complaints of Augustine, John Chrysostom, and Salvian regarding the moral laxness pervasive among Christians of their time. And it fostered a Pelagian notion of "works."[196]

Schaff also leveled a critique of ascetic hygiene. Ascetic holiness of the Egyptian variety, he argued, "is incompatible with cleanliness and decency, and delights in filth. It reverses the maxim of sound evangelical morality and modern Christian civilization, that cleanliness is next to godliness." Commenting on the advice that Jerome's friend Paula allegedly gave to her nuns (that a clean dress betokened an unclean soul), Schaff wrote, "This want of cleanliness, the inseparable companion of ancient ascetic holiness, is bad enough in monks, but still more intolerable and revolting in nuns." And Paula did a further wrong in leaving her daughter Eustochium a mass of debts: liberality should have limits. Among the reasons Schaff gave for favoring cenobitic over eremitic monasticism is that it modified harsh extremes so as to become "available to the female sex."[197]

Schaff continued:

> Many of these saints [desert fathers] were no more than low slug-gards or gloomy misanthropes, who would rather company with wild beasts, with lions, wolves, and hyenas, than with immortal men, and above all shunned the face of a woman more carefully than they did the devil.[198]

Given their "morbid aversion" to women and "rude contempt" for marriage, it is no wonder "that in Egypt and the whole East, the land of monasticism, women and domestic life never attained their proper dignity, and to this day remain at a low stage of culture."[199]

Concomitantly, monasticism brought with it the danger of "secret vices." Haunted by unchaste dreams, monks turned their excessive asceticism into "unnatural vice." A "violently suppressed" sexuality erupted in indulgence in idleness, ease, and vanity. Last, the "unnatural and shameless practice" of allegedly celibate men and women living together has "prostituted the honor of the church," and at all times "disgraced the Roman priesthood."[200]

In addition to critiquing the development of monasticism, Schaff also faulted clerical celibacy. Paul, Schaff wrote, left celibacy up to the individual, distinguishing between a divine command and a human counsel. He believed that the "oppressed condition of the Christians in the apostolic age" made celibacy a "safer and less anxious state" for those who felt called to a "special gift of grace." Yet even when that "stress" had passed, the Latin Church (although not the Greek) misguidedly made clerical celibacy an "inexorable law." The western church from the fourth century adopted "the perverted and almost Manichean ascetic principle, that the married state is incompatible with clerical dignity and holiness." Clergy now vied with monks regarding sexual purity in order to gain influence with the people. Yet since celibacy "tempted them to the illicit indulgence of appetite," these other sins damaged the clergy's influence more than "forced celibacy could compensate." The repetition of decrees against clerical marriage, Schaff claimed, shows the difficulty of carrying out "this unnatural restriction."[201]

To be sure, Schaff acknowledged, not all early Christian writers embraced the ascetic spirit. Unfortunately, the opposition of Jovinian and Vigilantius to asceticism "never acquired any importance, being confined to single individuals." Although Schaff detailed the positions of these Christian opponents of ascetic extremes, he conceded that Jovinian, Helvidius, and Vigilantius were not the only "real" Christians of the day: ascetic enthusiasts, such as Athanasius, John Chrysostom, Jerome, and Augustine can scarcely be deemed "apostates"![202] And the fact that even those early Christians who *were* married exhibit an "ascetic tendency" suggested to Schaff that there must be some link of asceticism to the apostolic church.[203]

Schaff on the Benefits of Ancient Christian Asceticism

Schaff—after these many critiques—nevertheless argued that early Christian asceticism brought some benefits: Providence used it to prepare the barbarian tribes of the early Middle Ages for Christian civilization.[204] Monasticism became "the means of converting the Heathen and advancing all the interests of civilization."[205] (Schaff described the monastery of Iona as a "lighthouse in the darkness of heathenism."[206]) In its later stages, monasticism helped to diffuse Christian teaching and ancient learning, warn against the immorality of the clergy, mitigate slavery, and level the class structure of society. Benedict, Cassiodorus, and later, the Benedictines, are to be praised for their preservation of learning and education of the laity.[207] Moreover, Schaff claimed, monasticism stood as a warning against

the worldliness, frivolity, and immorality of the great cities, and a mighty call to repentance and conversion. . . . It was to invalids a

hospital for the cure of moral diseases, and at the same time, to
healthy and vigorous enthusiasts an arena for the exercise of heroic
virtue.[208]

Here asceticism is not so much a "disease," as Schaff elsewhere stated, but
the "cure."

As a "hospital for invalids," monasticism helped to prepare the world
for a new Christian civilization among the Romanic and Germanic nations.
Yet, Schaff argued, as the Mosaic law was a *paidagogus* for Paul, so monasticism is to Protestantism: a disciplinary institution that should be cast aside
when a new era is reached. Mission accomplished, the church's "higher
duty" was to go on to transform and sanctify all divinely appointed human
relations, thus penetrating society like a leaven. This transformation
resulted, centuries later, in "the Protestant evangelical system of morality,"
which fosters the "inmost spirit of the New Testament" and the westward
march of Protestant Christianity.[209]

Philip Schaff on Women, Marriage, and the Family

Schaff, unsurprisingly, faulted monasticism for hindering the development
of edifying domestic life. Monasticism, he wrote, cannot produce "the finer
and gentler traits of character which are ordinarily brought out only in the
school of daily family life and under the social ordinance of God." Christian
virtue should be shown by enjoying God's gifts temperately in "connubial
chastity," rather than by total abstinence.[210] Monasticism, past and present,
stood against the vision of Christian domesticity that Schaff held dear—a
vision closely linked to conservative notions of "women's sphere" that were
being challenged by the suffrage movement of his day. For him, "woman"
and "home" were inextricably linked.

Schaff credited the rise of Christianity with raising the status of women.
Christianity, he claimed, unshackles woman "without thrusting her, after
the manner of modern pseudo-philanthropic schemes of emancipation, out
of her appropriate sphere of private, domestic life, and thus stripping her
of her fairest ornament and peculiar charm." "Carnal schemes" of women's
emancipation, such as those promoted by some nineteenth-century feminists, subvert "the natural and revealed order of things" and are doomed
to miserable failure. Schaff advised wives, with their "personal and moral

dignity" intact, to resign themselves trustingly to their husbands' dominance as the church submits to Christ. In the home, wives have the opportunity to show their "silent moral elevation."[211] Schaff exuberantly proclaimed, "WOMAN [in capital letters] was emancipated, in the best sense of the word, from the bondage of social oppression, and made the life and light of a Christian home."[212] Emancipation "in the best sense of the word" implies a contrast with Schaff's notion of the "worst sense": that proposed by nineteenth-century feminists.

Schaff's essay "The Influence of the Christianity on the Family," written five years after the Seneca Falls Convention, attacks pagan, Roman Catholic, Jewish, *and* feminist notions of women and the family. "Marriage, . . . the nursery of the State and the Church," Schaff began, is "a strictly divine institution" and possesses "a sacramental character" insofar as it is "a copy of the relation of Christ to his Church" (Eph. 5:22, 23). Unlike the ancient Greek deprecation of women, and the ancient Israelite and Mohammedan sanction of polygamy, Christianity raises women's status—without, however, taking "woman out of her natural sphere of subordination and domestic life, and throw[ing] her into the whirl of public activity, from which she instinctively shrinks."[213] The family, Schaff posited, constitutes a "miniature theocracy" in which the father serves as priest and king in "the sanctuary of his own house," offering his "sacrifice of thanksgiving" (prayers and Scripture reading) daily upon the "family altar." Physical procreation, in his view, is subordinate to the sanctification of character that a properly Christian marriage offers.[214] Similarly, in his book *America*, Schaff decried "the wildest excesses of ultra democracy" that Lucretia Mott had advocated (the same year as the Seneca Falls Convention, 1848), namely, "the full equalization, not only of all races, but also of both sexes." Such "overstrained spiritualism," he concluded, "ends in the flesh."[215]

Schaff's views on women's sphere are illustrated by his reflections on his favorite daughter, Meta, who tragically died of typhoid fever at age twenty. Meta had graduated third in her class from the New York Female Normal School (now Hunter College)—but upon graduation she did not become a teacher. Instead, she stayed at home, helping her father with his monumental *History of Creeds*, preparing indices for his books, and copying by hand his manuscripts for press. She continued to study modern languages, history, poetry, and music.[216] In his memorial to her, Schaff hastened to emphasize that her intellectual culture, such as was signaled by these accomplishments, did not lessen her "proper and hearty zest for domestic duties"—she always kept her room neat.[217] She was, in short, Schaff's ideal of a modern woman, educated but domestically oriented.

Schaff on Women in Antiquity

Schaff's views of women's proper roles in the present conditioned his views of women in the past. The ancient world, in Schaff's view, had failed both women and family. By elevating the state as the highest object in life, pagans had given no rights to the individual or the family, thus stalling the development of "the domestic and private virtues." Schaff contrasted Christian women with Greek *hetairai*: those "desolate characters," he indignantly protested, "were esteemed above housewives." Freeing woman from slavery to "man's lower passions," Christianity had accorded her "moral dignity and equality with man," and thus began the transformation to a "well-ordered family life."[218]

For Schaff the immoral character of the Roman world was especially revealed in the status of women, family, and home. Despite his dislike of asceticism, he conceded that dedicated virginity emancipated women "from the slavish condition under heathenism," in which she could be disposed of as an article of merchandise by parents or guardians, even in infancy or childhood. From paganism's "enslavement" of women and "Jewish" notions of their inequality, Christianity had aimed to raise the female sex—which goal, for Schaff, was identical with Christianity's elevation of family and home.[219] Primitive Christianity, Schaff wrote, "elevated woman to dignity and equality with man, upheld the sanctity and inviolability of the marriage tie, laid the foundation of a Christian family and happy home, . . . emancipated children from the tyrannical control of parents."[220] Sanctifying family life, Christianity abolished polygamy, made monogamy the proper form of marriage, condemned concubinage, and modeled marriage on the union of Christ and the church. Hence the family was "spiritualized," becoming "a nursery of the purest and noblest virtues, a miniature church," in which the father serves as shepherd and priest.[221]

Ancient Judaism's view of women did not rise much higher than paganism's, in Schaff's view. He strongly upheld Old Testament notions of the "honor and purity of the married state and the marriage bed"; any denigration of such "reflects on the patriarchs, Moses, the prophets," and God himself. Yet ancient Judaism, like heathenism, accorded woman a "slavish" position. From this abject state, Christianity raised her, giving her "true moral dignity" and making her "an heir of the same salvation with men."[222] Schaff noted that Acts 1:13–14 depicts female followers of Jesus sitting with men "in the same room as equal sharers in the spiritual blessings," not in a separate court as in the Temple, or shut off by a partition as in the synagogue—and in the "decayed churches of the East to this day," he added. This scene, he claimed, provides a "prophetic anticipation of the end," when there will be "no male and female" (Gal. 3:28). Contrasting the allegedly lax divorce legislation in ancient Judaism with Jesus' tightening of the grounds for divorce (Matt. 19:1–12), Schaff commented, "Christ restores the original law."[223]

Given Schaff's near-adulation of marriage and the family—which he nevertheless counseled should not fall into "idolatry"—he struggled to explain why the church had not always embraced this marital ideal. "The degradation of the female sex and the want of chastity" in antiquity were so great, he argued, that "this ennobling of the family, like the abolition of slavery, was necessarily a very slow process."[224] Methodius' virgin symposiasts in *The Banquet*, for example, speak of "sexual relations with a minuteness, which to our modern taste is extremely indelicate and offensive."[225] Patristic discussions of marriage and second marriage show that woman's dignity was not then what it later became after Christianity could exert its power. Only as civilization advanced would the dignity of woman become sanctified, the Protestant West now having greatly surpassed Catholic and Orthodox countries. For Schaff, the qualities Tacitus praised in Germanic women are now to be seen "most fully developed in the Anglo-Saxon race."[226] The negative conditioning provided by Roman mores thus provided a partial excuse for Christianity's limited success in rapidly improving the condition of woman and the family.

Schaff cited New Testament and early Christian examples to confirm Christianity's elevation of women and family. Jesus, unsurprisingly, stands as a model: his relation to women such as Mary Magdalene and the woman taken in adultery Schaff deemed "sublime."[227] Moreover, Jesus' "condescending love" and "true and full humanity" is shown in his sharing "the common trials of family life in all it forms." Schaff railed against those who pervert the truth of the Bible by treating the Apostles' marriages, and that of Joseph and Mary, as "empty forms" rather than as real marriages. In Ephesians 5, he noted, Paul further stresses the holiness of family, making it "a miniature of the church."[228] Yet some women in the first century, as in the nineteenth, went too far: Paul checked "this excess of democratic enthusiasm" of women speaking in public assemblies (I Cor. 14) by reminding the brethren that God is a God of peace. While Paul recognized that women possessed the gift of prophecy (I Cor. 11:4), he forbade its "exercise in the public assembly" (I Cor. 14:34; I Tim. 2:11,12).[229]

The ideal state that Schaff imagined Jesus proposing did not last for long. Schaff took at face value John Chrysostom's claim that although men and women had mingled innocently together in apostolic times, women in his own day resembled prostitutes, and men, horses in rutting. Chrysostom's words, for Schaff, provided a "sad commentary on the moral and religious condition" of that time. By the later patristic era, the church had fallen "far behind the ideal set up in the New Testament," counterbalancing biblical Christianity's elevation of woman by "an extravagant over-estimate of celibacy."[230]

Nevertheless, Schaff conceded that the patristic era saw a great advance over "heathen" morals, to which the Church Fathers' unfortunate identification of chastity with celibacy should not blind us. Ante-Nicene Christianity, all in all, promoted "well-regulated family life and a happy home," and "emancipated children from the tyrannical control of parents." Clement of Alexandria, for example, with his "reasonable" defense of marriage and wealth, sounded almost Protestant to Schaff's ears.[231]

Of the women of the patristic era whom Schaff was keen to praise, the *mothers* of noted Church Fathers stand at the forefront—more prominently than famous female ascetics.[232] He claimed that the pious mothers of Chrysostom (Anthusa), Gregory of Nazianzus (Nonna), and Augustine (Monica) "prove the ennobling influence of Christianity on the character of woman, and through her on all family relations."[233] Monica, Schaff believed, is "one of the noblest women in the history of Christianity, of a highly intellectual and spiritual cast, of fervent piety, most tender affection, and all-conquering love." A "most conscientious" housewife, Monica (in Schaff's imagination) read the Scriptures and went to church twice a day. In the *Confessions*, Augustine erected to her "the noblest monument that can never perish"; her portrayal prompts "a profounder regard for woman and a feeling of gratitude for Christianity, which raised her to so high a position."[234] Yet the writings of the Church Fathers, Schaff charged, are full of "coarse and unchristian" sayings about women: did these writers forget their own mothers? The patristic writers—Clement of Alexandria providing one of the few exceptions—so exalted virginity that in practice they neutralized or weakened their claims regarding the holiness of marriage.[235]

Schaff had less praise for women of the patristic era who committed themselves to ascetic renunciation. He faulted Jerome's friend Paula for repressing "the sacred feelings of a mother" in abandoning her young children for the ascetic life. He criticized Jerome's failure to acknowledge that the trials of married women are "a wholesome discipline for the development of Christian manhood and womanhood"—and that "celibacy also has its dangers and temptations."[236] How Roman Catholic writers love to exalt Jerome, he elsewhere complained![237]

Reflecting on Augustine's concubine, Schaff seized the opportunity to critique both the morals of the Roman world and Catholicism's preference for asceticism: "evangelical Protestant morality" is far superior. Yet, he conceded, given "the prevailing spirit of the age," Augustine would not have been so well regarded nor have accomplished so much, if he had married. "Celibacy," Schaff granted, "was the bridge from the heathen degradation of marriage to the evangelical Christian exaltation and sanctification of the family life."[238] Once again, Schaff is able to find something good even in an institution that he thought violated true Christian values.

Indeed, Augustine, seemingly so Protestant in the views of sin and grace expressed in his anti-Pelagian writings, did not endorse marriage with sufficient enthusiasm to suit Schaff's promotion of a "domestic Christianity." Thus Schaff provided some corrections. He interpreted *concupiscentia* in Augustine's writings to mean "*unlawful* sexual desire," thus presumably salvaging "lawful" sexual desire for marital domesticity. Similarly, Schaff attempted to render more palatable Augustine's ascetic regime at Hippo: although closer to Catholic than to Protestant ideals, it was at least "free from those exaggerations and elements of Pharisaical self-righteousness, which connect themselves so readily with monastic piety."[239]

In the voluminous writings of Philip Schaff, we find the fullest *apologia* of the Protestant professors here surveyed for early Christianity's alleged elevation of women, marriage, and family over the claims of asceticism. That elevation, now manifested in nineteenth-century Protestant ideals of woman, marriage, and family, also stood against the claims of suffrage advocates who wished to thrust women out of their "natural" sphere of activity, the home. Although Schaff endeavored to "explain away" early Christian asceticism, he nevertheless conceded that God could use that unChristian phenomenon to further a redeeming purpose for the world.

Ephraim Emerton on Asceticism and Marriage

With Ephraim Emerton of Harvard, we encounter a less apologetic approach to early Christian asceticism. Not an evangelical Protestant, he apparently felt less compulsion to defend or to rationalize early Christian sources. The notes that Harvard Divinity School student Earl Morse Wilbur took (sometime between 1877 and 1879) in Emerton's church history class suggest that Emerton barely touched on early Christian asceticism: the topic was apparently not of much interest to him.[240] In his textbook, *Introduction to the Study of the Early Middle Ages*, however, his discussion of early Christian asceticism aligned more closely with that of the evangelical professors. Perhaps he was catering to his presumed readers.

Emerton had a keener sense of the bias of the ancient sources than did the other professors. Addressing the state of the Roman world at the time of Christianity's advent, his evaluation differed from that of the evangelical professors. "We generally hear of the extreme depravity of Roman morals" at the beginning of the Christian era, he told his students. "But this is a great exaggeration; much of our information comes from Satirists." We also derive our notions of this period from moralists, but their points of view are not "judicial." No doubt it was an age of extremes; power was concentrated in the hands of a few, with social evils the result. The sources reveal the contrast of "great power and luxury with great poverty"—but Emerton doubted "whether Rome [was] much worse off than some modern cities."[241]

Ancient writers, Emerton warned his students, are strongly influenced by their class status. He asked, somewhat rhetorically, "Is it safe to trust what the best minds of any age say about the state of religion among the masses?" Cicero, Tacitus, and Pliny represent the latter "as in deep decay." If we took our view of Roman religion from such writers, we would "think it pretty well undermined. But there is another side, represented chiefly by monuments, inscriptions, institutions, etc." Emerton further argued that the presence of so many foreign religions in Rome showed the weakness of state religion—just as Americans today find "esoteric Buddhism" attractive.[242]

Yet Emerton, like the evangelical professors, also believed that there had been a downward slide in morals from the time of the Roman Republic, and he berated the ancients' alleged attitudes toward women. "The most terrible feature of Roman life is, to us, the relations of the sexes," Emerton told his students. "The old Roman life was rigidly pure in this respect. Girls were kept in great seclusion until marriage and then were at liberty which they too often indulged to its fullest extent."[243]

In his textbook, Emerton also sounded a more conventional note. Here he claimed that the "wickedness of life" in the great cities of world today would have to be multiplied "to get any conception of the dreadful state of Roman morals at the time when the Germans began to threaten the frontier." What "every writer from Juvenal to Sidonius" reports on the state of morals is horrifying, especially descriptions of "the wild life of the cities."[244]

Emerton positioned the development of early Christian asceticism against the backdrop of the immorality of the late Roman world. He recommended that his readers consult Charles Montalembert's *The Monks of the West*, acknowledging this Catholic author as "a warm partisan of the monastic system." Asceticism, Emerton explained to his presumably Protestant audience, was an ancient and widespread phenomenon:

> The monastic life begins almost as soon as Christianity. Indeed, ages before Christianity, in the religions of the East, in Brahminism, Buddhism, even in Judaism, we can see a tendency of men toward a form of religious life which is in all respects like the monasticism of the early Christian times. It has even been supposed that Jesus himself was a member of the Jewish sect of the Essenes.[245]

Some of Emerton's explanations for monasticism's development echo those of the other professors, although with a less apologetic bent. Psychology, he believed, offered one explanation: people with troubled souls might escape to the cloister. Climate provided another. In Egypt, Emerton wrote, "the warm climate made the hermit's existence tolerably easy and where the vast solitudes of the desert protected him from the violence of his fellow-men. But man is after all a social creature." Sociality develops when hermits gather into groups, and then form religious orders. In the West, since "the climate did not tempt men to solitary life, and the example of older religions was wanting," monasticism developed later, not much before the fifth century.[246]

Like the evangelical professors, Emerton accorded western monasticism more tolerant treatment than eastern. The "practical character" of the provisions of the Benedictine Rule made the "western system so different from the extravagant and fanatical monasticism of the East." The order of St.

Benedict, in Emerton's view, was a mean between "the brutality of masses of men" and "fanaticism of the Eastern monks." As an example of the latter, Emerton noted Simeon Stylites and commented that this type of "insane devotion," almost unknown in the West, was frowned upon. But he quickly added a sympathetic note: "We must try to learn to judge men and institutions by the use they had in the day in which they belonged, not by the use they might have for us in these better times." Yet monastic life could be dangerous: these monks often seem to us "quite as much like madmen as saints."[247]

Emerton, like the evangelical professors, found many reasons to fault asceticism. It was not socially useful: Cassian and Benedict, instead of putting "their holiness of thought into the life of the world," withdrew from society.[248] Moreover, monasteries bred immorality in the form of idleness and danger to the vows of chastity. Emerton commented,

> the instinct of nature, by which men have always been led into the highest and holiest of human relations as husbands and fathers of families, would not be kept down, and many accounts show us that the seats of learning and self-denial had become homes of ignorance and vice.[249]

Emerton, however, did add at least one original point to the critique of monasticism: the monastic enterprise was a colossal waste of money. Economic considerations have here been given a larger role in Christian history. When we see the ruins of great monastery buildings in England, Emerton wrote, we can understand "how a time must come when men would no longer bear this misuse of wealth, that had been given for the service of God, and so in a sort of wild fury tore down these homes of idleness and vice, and put the wealth where it might be of use."[250] The more violent manifestations of the English Reformation, in other words, were entirely justified.

Conclusion

For nineteenth-century Protestant scholars on both sides of the Atlantic, early Christian asceticism was a strange and discordant phenomenon that required explanation. Marriage and family, they knew, were God's plan for humanity. The American professors attacked on two fronts. Against contemporary high-Anglican and Roman Catholic proponents of ascetic renunciation, they praised biblical teachings that (allegedly) exalted marriage, women, and family. Asceticism, they charged, had allowed "Christian freedom" to be swallowed up in "Jewish externality." Yet insofar as the Protestant professors from mid-century on had been influenced by German notions of historical development, they conceded some beneficial aspects of *early*—if not *contemporary*—Christian asceticism, especially that in the West. Secondly, against the demands of some nineteenth-century suffrage advocates, they argued that women's sphere should be limited to the domestic circle—and this despite their claim that Christianity had raised women to be the equals of men. Emancipation was tied to the Christian home.

Today, when most scholars of late antiquity see asceticism as an intrinsic aspect of early Christianity and attempt to understand its function and benefits, it is salutary to remember how recently that view became current.

CHAPTER 9

The Uses of Augustine

Augustine is not the final authority on Augustine.

—James J. O'Donnell (2005)

Augustine—that is, Augustine-the-anti-Pelagian—was the chief theologian between the time of Paul and the Protestant Reformation to whom the evangelical professors warmed. Of all the Church Fathers, he had most fully professed God's electing grace and most avidly decried "works-righteousness."[1] Luther and Calvin (so the professors told their classes) had been "very thorough students" of his writings.[2]

Aspects of Augustine's theology, however, remained highly elusive— and hence offered a site for heated nineteenth-century debates. Had he taught that Adam was the "natural father" of all humans, or only their "representative"? Why had he not made clear the view of the soul that underlay his teaching of the transfer of original sin through the generations? Did his theology really imply the eternal damnation of all unbaptized persons, including newborn infants? Was his treatment of humans' proliferation in the Genesis account consonant with a "scientific" race theory? On such points, Augustine provided much ammunition for intra-Christian polemics—polemics not only between Protestants and Roman Catholics, but also among varying stripes of Reformed Protestants. Some aspects of Augustine's teaching and practice, to be sure, were simply to be condemned: among his many "errors of judgment and defects of character" was his support for religious coercion during the Donatist controversy, a view that Philip Schaff in particular found reprehensible.[3] First I will survey the professors' general comments on Augustine's theology, and then turn to the particular issues in which several of them became embroiled regarding the interpretation of Augustine's theology.

In Praise of Augustine: The Pelagian Controversy

Augustine's theology, the professors believed, centered in his opposition to Pelagianism. They faulted all the ante-Nicene (as well as the Greek-writing post-Nicene) Fathers for extolling human freedom and responsibility to the neglect of God's predestining grace.[4] Augustine's repair of that neglect had been his most important contribution. Their depiction of Pelagius, whom they saw as theological arch-villain, sometimes verged on caricature. Yet Augustine, they agreed, had not completely won this important dispute: Pelagianism had lived on to taint medieval theology in the West.[5]

Samuel Miller

Of the professors here considered, Samuel Miller was the least critical of Augustine. No other Church Father could compare: he was the first, Miller proclaimed, who had "*distinctly* understood, or taught, the Christian doctrine of *Justification*." True Christianity might have become extinct if God had not appointed Augustine as "an honored instrument" to restore (albeit partially) "the luster of divine truth," to work a great religious revival that brought "multitudes" into the Christian fold.[6] In Miller's view, Augustine "did more to restore and propagate evangelical truth than all other men of the age in which he lived."[7]

Augustine's Pelagian opponents, Miller told his class, denied original sin, accorded humans a native ability to fulfill the commandments, and understood grace not as a factor "distinguishing" one person from another, but as divine favor equally and universally available to all: the latter point was especially reprehensible to Old School Presbyterians, whose views of predestination consigned most humans, past and present, to eternal damnation. In Miller's rendition, Pelagius taught that Christians were saved by their own obedience, not by Jesus' death and resurrection. In his anti-Pelagian zeal, Miller ran into contradiction: on the one hand, he claimed that Pelagius rejected grace altogether; on the other, that Pelagius pronounced grace to be available to all, so that God would not seem "partial and unjust."[8] (Perhaps for Miller, conceding that grace was available to all was tantamount to "no grace.") To confess that Christ died for all humans, not only for the elect, Miller deemed "gross Arminianism" or "Semi-Pelagianism." Today, Miller alleged, Pelagianism has been reborn as "refined Deism." Miller warned students that their textbook's author, Johann Mosheim, a "pretty thorough-going Arminian," was far too critical of Augustine.[9]

Miller stressed Augustine's decisive influence on the Protestant Reformation.[10] God had used Augustine, the church's "great luminary," to restore sixteenth-century Christianity to purity of doctrine. Miller claimed that Augustine was the predecessor of Calvin in particular and faulted only that Father's failure to endorse "Calvinist" views strongly enough: for example, Augustine had too closely equated justification ("declaring righteous") and sanctification ("making righteous"). Yet, considering the (alleged) desolation of the late patristic era, Miller deemed Augustine surprisingly "sound"—a "soundness" evidenced by his doctrines of humans' total depravity and of "Divine Decrees," that is, predestination. In the main, Miller told his students, Augustine was "a firm Calvinist!"[11]

In contrast to the New School Presbyterians of Union and Congregationalists at Yale, Miller favored a "hard-line" reading of Augustine's views on predestination and original sin. Unlike them, as well as unlike the tender-hearted Origenists whom Augustine had reproved,[12] Miller expressed no unease at the prospect of millions of unregenerated Christians, "heathen," and unbaptized babies suffering eternal damnation. His class lectures register no disturbance at these aspects of Augustine's theology that would so distress his colleagues to the north.

Although Miller owned the collected works of Augustine,[13] he cited only two in the classroom: the *Confessions* and the *City of God*.[14] His first-hand acquaintance with most of Augustine's writings, I suspect, was slight. Although Miller claimed to his students that Augustine "spent most of his time" in combat (largely successful) with Pelagius and his followers,[15] he did not discuss Augustine's major anti-Pelagian works. Casting Augustine as a Calvinist who would have been welcome at nineteenth-century Princeton, Miller left Pelagius in the mire with (alternatively) Deists or Roman Catholics.

The Union Professors

The Union professors' estimation of Pelagius was no more sympathetic than Miller's.[16] Henry Smith, for example, spent considerable class time—25 pages of student class notes—on the topic of the Pelagian controversy. Smith conceded that both Pelagius and Augustine were learned and that both claimed the authority of earlier Church Fathers for their positions: "this," he commented, "is in the nature of all controversies, because those who go before are not sufficiently definite in their statement."[17] Pelagius mistakenly made grace appear to be "external, not internal," and implied that humans could be saved by law as well as by grace. Pelagianism, in Smith's considered judgment, simply denied that sin and guilt exist.[18] Moreover, it fostered "the monastic spirit" and a prideful reliance on "works." Smith was eager to rebut the charge that Augustine was "driven to" his theological views by Pelagian adversaries: Augustine, he claimed, had formulated his "system" before Pelagianism ever arose.[19]

On this point, Smith evinced little interest in appealing to the principle of historical development. He was especially critical of the "individualistic" emphasis of Pelagius, whom he charged with teaching an *ethic* of "self-will" that was not *religion*. (Associating Pelagius with "ethics" and Augustine with "religion" is a view Smith adopted from German church historian C. W. Niedner, whose book on church history he had recently read.) Smith contrasted Pelagius' emphasis on the individual with Augustine's generic understanding of humanity. To consider (as Smith alleged of Pelagius) the human race "a mere flock of individuals," he deemed an "infidel view." "Christian Anthropology," in Smith's opinion, should deal not with humans as an "independent beings," but as "moral beings" linked by social and racial bonds. The discussion of sin, including original sin, should be kept in this moral and "racial" framework. Smith faulted all definitions of original sin that point only to the commission of a *"particular* sin."[20]

As we shall see, Smith's emphasis on the "racial" links binding all humans accomplished several purposes in his theology and social theory. First, it supported the claim that Adam's sin was not that of an "individual": all later humans were joined in his sin and guilt. Second, it undergirded a monogenist view of human origins—all humans had descended from a first pair—that might counter the radical implications of some current anthropological and evolutionary hypotheses. Last, it promoted the "brotherhood" of all nations and peoples of color at a time when tensions in America over slavery were running high. (Smith, as noted earlier, was a strong supporter of the northern cause in the Civil War, severely chastising British friends of the American South.) How Smith pitted an Augustinian view of the unity of humanity against an alleged Pelagian "individualism" in his own theology shall be examined below.

Roswell Hitchcock's assessment of Augustine was similar to Smith's. He characterized Augustine's theology as biblical and experiential, Pelagius', as "speculative." Granting that Pelagius "had more than ordinary cleanness," Hitchcock deemed Pelagius lacking in "spiritual and intellectual depth." Hitchcock ascribed to Pelagius the seven points of the doctrines for which Coelestius was condemned at Carthage in 412. But Hitchcock disputed Augustine's claim that the "Oriental" Fathers supported *his* side of the debate: this claim, he told students, was "polemical" and largely unfounded.[21]

Philip Schaff likewise charged Pelagius with a theology centered on human endeavor. His "legal, self-righteous piety" manifested itself in an "external" morality, characteristic of asceticism. A piety of this type, in Schaff's view, promoted spiritual pride, superficiality, an individualistic theology, and, centuries later, Rationalism. Pelagius' "standard of holiness" was lower than Augustine's. Yet, Schaff conceded, Pelagius came closer to Protestantism in understanding grace as God's *declaring*—not *making*—a person righteous, the latter interpretation associated with Augustinian and Catholic teaching.[22]

Like Miller, Schaff compared Pelagianism to modern Deism. William Paley appears to have been on Schaff's mind when he wrote that the "Pelagian system is founded unconsciously upon the deistic conception of the world as a clock, made and wound up by God, and then running of itself, and needing at most some subsequent repairs." Remnants of Pelagianism also haunted contemporary Unitarianism and Universalism. To Schaff, Pelagianism seemed even "more lifeless and godless" than Pantheism, to which we have seen his strong opposition.[23]

The ideological character of Schaff's critique can be registered when we note that he *also*—in seeming contradiction to the claims just cited—blamed Pelagianism for promoting ecclesiastical hierarchy and monasticism. (Schaff's somewhat baffling assessment presumably rests on his view that Pelagianism fostered individual achievement, encouraging monkish self-restraint for all Christians.) On this point, Schaff praised Augustine for holding in check the "Pelagianizing tendencies" of ecclesiastical hierarchy and monasticism. Schaff's claim is startling, considering that Augustine, not Pelagius, was a bishop and lived in a semi-monastic community. In Schaff's view, Augustine had set the agenda for Christianity's future, namely, the reconciliation of churchly (Roman Catholic) and spiritualizing (evangelical Protestant) principles. Schaff added that the Mercersburg Theology had advanced this reconciliation by linking the evangelical notion of freedom from "Law" with a critique of "unchurchly" forms of Protestant sectarianism.[24] On other points, as we shall see, Schaff had a much stronger critique of Augustine.

Blame: Augustine's Faults

Amid their praise, the professors leveled many criticisms of Augustine's theology and practice. In his endorsement of "monkery," celibacy, relics, and "superstition," he remained too "Catholic" for Reformed Protestant tastes. He was credulous regarding miracles and the veneration of Mary.[25] Aspects of his theology lent support to the doctrines of the Immaculate Conception and Papal Infallibility.[26] His ascetic regime at Hippo did not accord with Protestant ideals. His ecclesiology too closely identified the church with the Kingdom of God.[27] His "high" ecclesiology and sacramentalism, in fact, prompted some professors to side with his schismatic opponents, the Donatists.

The Union professors in particular, who had a deeper knowledge than Miller of Augustine's literary corpus, found much overall to criticize. Granting too much weight to ecclesiastical authority, Augustine had fostered sacramentalism. His notion of baptismal regeneration was misguided. ("The unhealthful leaven of sacramental grace" in Augustine's writings, Henry Smith averred, had to be extirpated by Calvin before the Reformed Churches could "revive" Augustinianism.[28]) Augustine had not expressed a sharp enough distinction between justification ("declaring righteous") and sanctification ("making righteous").[29] He had fostered an "externalism" in the western church[30]—a fault that linked Roman Catholics to ancient Jews who had rejected Jesus' message of an inward, purely spiritual religion. Moreover, Augustine's tepid endorsement of marriage ill-suited Protestant professors keen to promote "domestic Christianity."[31]

Although all the professors stressed the anti-Pelagian aspects of Augustine's teaching, the Union professors' New School Presbyterian versions of Reformed theology accorded considerable importance to personal responsibility and holiness in the scheme of salvation: the necessity of personal holiness had not been precluded by God's electing grace. Did Augustine's theology allow for this modification? There was ample room for debate.

The Union professors sought ways to soften "hard-line" Calvinist interpretations of original sin and its imputation. To their eyes, Augustine's account of the mechanism by which original sin was transmitted and his theory of the soul's origin left much to be desired. Augustine's association of original sin with procreation seemed to imply that some evil tainted the institution of marriage. (This accusation Augustine himself had attempted to rebut in his lengthy diatribes with Julian of Eclanum.)

As for the origin of the soul, Augustine had waffled considerably.[32] If God created each soul directly ("Creationism"), was not the deity implicated in placing sin on the soul of the developing fetus? On the other hand, "Traducianism," the theory that soul was passed down by the parents along with the body, might imply that the soul was a "material" entity, a view that Augustine found repugnant. And a third option, that souls "fell" from a preexistent otherworldly condition into a physical body, as Origenists and Neo-Platonists posited, appeared in blatant contradiction to the claim of Genesis that God had created everything "very good." Augustine provided little assistance in solving the dilemma of the soul's origin, a question of great import in understanding the mechanism of the passage of original sin.

Moreover, for the Union professors, Augustine's views on predestination were too harsh. They were especially appalled by his implication that, given the transfer of original sin, most infants dying unbaptized would be damned:[33] Schaff did not hesitate to label this claim "revolting."[34] He faulted Calvin as well as Augustine for espousing a "decree of reprobation" that "sweeps whole nations *together with their infant offspring* . . . into everlasting perdition": both theologians he deemed "radically mistaken" in their reading of Paul on this point.[35]

Augustine's stress on predestination, the Union professors believed, might undercut the need for personal holiness. For Henry Smith, Augustine's theory of predestination did not sufficiently allow for the Christian's growth in holiness, as classically expressed in the doctrines of the perseverance of the saints and "unconditional election" (namely, that grace, once bestowed, cannot be lost).[36] Schaff, for his part, argued that although

Augustine "went far beyond the theology of the Oriental Church" on the doctrines of sin, grace, and redemption, his account of the transfer of the first sin to later humans left too little room for personal accountability. (Schaff went so far as to claim that on this point, Origen's theology was preferable.) Individual humans must be understood as free and responsible; they stand or fall with their *own* sins. Augustine's system, Schaff charged, *destroys* moral responsibility—but later Augustinians, "by a happy inconsistency," were always "strict moralists." Moreover, Augustine, in Schaff's view, had underplayed "the *universal* benevolence and *impartial* justice of God to all His creatures" and God's love to *all* humans.[37] On points such as these, a "gentler" form of Reformed theology is in play—so gentle, in fact, that views of Old School Presbyterians such as Miller seemed odious.

Another major critique of Augustine leveled by the Union professors centered on biblical interpretation. All three deemed wrong his interpretation of Romans 5:12, a verse decisive for their understanding of original sin. Here was yet another arena in which their views of personal responsibility for sin colored their critique. Augustine, they believed, had been led astray by the faulty Latin translation of that verse common in his day (Adam, "in whom [*in quo*] all men sinned").[38] The original Greek (*eph hō*, which could be translated as "because all men sinned") makes clear that at least some personal responsibility is involved.[39] Yet Smith added that interpreting Romans 5:12, apart from its context, to mean that individuals' *personal* sins alone occasioned their punishment did not settle the case, for the next verses (Rom. 5: 15–19) clearly implied that many were condemned by *one man's* (i.e., Adam's) offense.[40] As we shall see, Smith, more theologically adept than his colleagues, espoused a more technical discussion of sin's imputation.

Schaff judged Augustine deficient as a biblical scholar, far beyond his alleged mistake regarding Romans 5:12. Even as a young man, Augustine had entertained wrong notions of Scripture. Describing the *Confessions*,[41] Schaff reported Augustine's admission that he had considered the Bible too lowly for his cultivated literary tastes. Augustine had preferred to find truth "in a specious garb of rhetoric; he desired [truth] not as a chaste virgin, but as a voluptuous courtesan."[42] Yet in Schaff's view, even as a mature Christian Augustine had been misguided in his approach to Scripture. In knowledge of the biblical languages and in historical and grammatical exegesis, Jerome, John Chrysostom, Theodoret, and Theophylact all rank above him.[43] Schaff warned readers not to overestimate Augustine's knowledge of Greek, as had the Benedictine editors—and Augustine's ignorance of Hebrew led to "many mistakes" in his exposition of the Old Testament. Schaff gently mocked Augustine's disquiet over Jerome's Vulgate translation: "there are fogies in all ages."[44]

Further, Schaff faulted Augustine's interpretation of the opening chapters of Genesis. His allegorical interpretation of the "Mosaic cosmogony" in Books 11–13 of the *Confessions* is "foreign to our age," of value only as showing that "even abstract metaphysical subjects may be devotionally treated." Moreover, "our excellent church father" (as Schaff called Augustine) erred in reading the story of Adam and Eve as an "*empirical* delineation of paradisiacal blessedness"; he did not sufficiently distinguish the childlike innocence of Eden from the "moral maturity of manhood." He painted Adam's perfection and bliss in Eden in ways that went beyond the "sober standard" of Genesis.[45] Christian "manhood," Schaff was sure, must demand more than the bumbling ineptitude of Adam as depicted in Genesis.

The Union professors, however, defended Augustine's theology against the charge that residual Manichean tendencies sullied the anti-Pelagian writings of his mature years. Since Augustine had proved his orthodoxy by writing against the Manichees considerably *before* he entered the Pelagian debate, Smith argued, we should trust that no remnants of Manicheanism haunt his theology.[46] Hitchcock likewise denied the presence of Manichean elements in Augustine's anti-Pelagian theology: Augustine had "gone through" Manicheanism, passing on "to antagonize it."[47]

While championing many aspects of Augustine's theology and faulting others, each of the Princeton, Union, and Yale professors had his own agenda regarding Augustine's theology and practice. To these particular interests I now turn.

Special Interests: Intra-Calvinist Wars

Augustine and Original Sin

Quite apart from the utility of the anti-Pelagian Augustine in combating the alleged "works-righteousness" of contemporary Catholic teaching and practice, he served as a centerpiece of intra-Protestant debates. Old School Presbyterians, New School Presbyterians, and New Haven Congregationalists all appealed to Augustine in their interpretation of original sin. Here, Union and Yale professors aligned themselves against Princeton's Old School Presbyterianism.

Samuel Miller: Augustine Versus Episcopalians and New School Presbyterians

Claiming Augustine for Old School Presbyterianism, Samuel Miller appropriated Augustine's anti-Pelagian theories to counter not only Roman Catholics, but also Episcopalians and New School Presbyterians who had promoted a milder form of Calvinism. Pelagianism, Miller claimed, had been reborn in Catholics who trust in the efficacy of "good works" and in those Protestants, including New School Presbyterians, whose assessment of human nature he (or, he claimed, any similar "impartial judge") deemed too optimistic. Some modern Calvinists, Miller told his students, appear to ascribe "natural ability" to humans, but he trusts that they do not really accept this abhorrent Semi-Pelagian view. Old School Presbyterians who champion the doctrine of predestination (in a "judicious, rational, and Scriptural manner") are not to be slandered as "Fatalists," as modern "Arminians and Pelagians" style them.[48]

Miller (so his son reports) from his days as a minister in New York combated "Pelagian" currents circulating among some latter-day disciples of Jonathan Edwards. Some of Edwards's followers, Miller claimed, went so far as to assert that all humans are born in the same condition as Adam-before-the-Fall (i.e., not directly inheriting Adam's corrupt nature) and that Christ's Atonement might be "unlimited" (i.e., not for the elect alone). Miller's son writes that his father tolerated these aberrations, imagining that they would soon die a natural death.[49] That they did not is shown in the split between Old School and New School Presbyterians, and in ongoing disputes regarding the New England Theology, as we shall shortly see.

In addition, as late as 1843, Miller still railed against Episcopalians as "thorough going [sic] Arminians, Pelagians." In the last 150 years, Miller charged, a Pelagian or Semi-Pelagian spirit has grown up in the Church of England—and in the last 75, "almost every form of heresy has lurked under subscription to her orthodox articles." Since not only contemporary Episcopalians, Miller warned, but even the astute Augustine himself was for a time almost deceived by Pelagius, students should keep alert lest they, too, be led astray.[50]

Henry Smith: Augustine, the Origin of the Soul, and Evolutionary Theory

On several points related to the transmission of sin, Henry Smith faulted Augustine for lack of clarity—or even outright error. A first issue concerned the origin of the soul. Given the importance of this point for the question, Smith argued, Augustine was far too indecisive. Traducianism—the theory that the soul is propagated along with the body—*should* have undergirded Augustine's teaching. In favor of this theory, Scripture claims first place (e.g., Heb. 7:10; Gen. 5:3; Ps. 51:5; John 3:6; Rom. 5:12 ff.). The facts of human development also support Traducian theory: a person's mental powers are not fully formed at birth, but develop slowly (which could not be the case if Creationism were correct). Moreover, children seem to inherit the traits of their parents, moral and intellectual ones linked to "soul," as well as physical and racial characteristics (such as the "Celtic and Sclavonic").[51] "Notice," Smith urged his students, "the Anglo-Saxons, Causcasians, Africans and Celts." Natural and moral peculiarities are carried down through the nation and the race, as well as in families. Thus both Scripture and science ("the law of propagation" that "like produces like") appear to support the Traducian hypothesis. Calvinists, Smith insisted, *need* Traducian theory to ground the transmission of original sin. On the Creationist view, by contrast, God might appear as the author of sin, inserting an evil principle into the newly created soul.[52] Moreover, Creationism "tends to destroy the organic unity of the race," an essential basis for the teaching of original sin.[53] In Smith's view, Augustine had failed to develop the theory of the soul that his theology demanded. Although Smith's endorsement of Traducianism rested mainly on theological grounds, this theory of the soul's transmission benefited from what he considered its consonance with the new biology and anthropological notions of race. Augustine's reluctance to endorse Traducianism left him out of step with the views of Smith's day.

Shortly before his death in February 1877, Smith was preparing a set of lectures on evolution (of which only an outline remains) to be given under the auspices of the Ely Foundation.[54] Judging from Smith's expressed dissatisfaction with Thomas Huxley's lectures in New York in September 1876 and the subsequent discussions about evolution that occupied the New York Presbyterian ministers' discussion club (Chi Alpha) for two months, we gather that he thought that the evolutionists tried to "prove too much."[55]

In the outline that remains of his Ely Lectures, Smith veered between endorsing some points of evolutionary theory, as he understood it, and depicting Christian battles against Materialism ("Armageddon") and atheistic science ("the Anti-Christ"). On the affirming side, Smith granted that not every form of Darwinism is "Atheism," as Princetonian Charles Hodge had posited.[56] Christians, Smith argued, should appropriate all that is "proved true" in evolutionary theory. The notion that there is a continuity of earlier forms, along with the principle of development, accords with a Christian confession.[57] But a purely materialist theory that casts aside an Intelligence behind the world (a "Will directed by wisdom," "not power alone and mathematics"), a theory that deems the species "entirely arbitrary" and denies any substantial difference between man and animal, must be contested.[58] Smith, like many other Christians, resorted to the argument that evolution had not yet been "proved." Science should stick to "facts and induction," not meddle with "metaphysics and morals."[59] In claiming that evolutionary theory had no adequate notion of causality,[60] Smith's Idealist presuppositions were fully on display: "Mind is what we know nearest, most and best. The thing-in-itself, the substance which we know, and alone directly is—*Mind*."[61]

Smith apparently intended to conclude his discussion of evolutionary theory in the Ely Lectures with an appeal to Augustine: the new views of heredity "point directly to the great Christian doctrine of Original Sin." Modern science has made the questions that Christianity answers *"grander than ever."* In some respects, Smith argued, evolution can be understood as paving the way "for the view of Man's higher destiny." But a choice must be made. Will the way be that of "Augustine or Comte, Athanasius or Hegel, Luther or Schopenhauer, J. S. Mill or John Calvin?"[62] For Smith, it was surely the way of Augustine, Athanasius, Luther, and Calvin.

HENRY SMITH: ORIGINAL SIN AND ITS IMPUTATION

Smith did not merely critique Augustine's failure to develop an adequate theory of the soul's origin and sin's transfer that would resonate with modern science. He also proposed ways to speak of sin and grace that accommodated emphases of the classical Reformed tradition to nineteenth-century sensibilities. Smith faulted formulations of original sin that implied that later generations could be blamed for what was "not their fault": if Adam as an *individual* had sinned, why did not he alone suffer divine retribution? Why should the sin and guilt have been passed to all later generations?

To counter such views, Smith argued that the first sin should not be taken as an *individual's* transgression. Here, Augustine's formulation needed some modification. Although Augustine denied that a "foreign guilt" is imputed, he did not (in Smith's view) cogently set forth how the first sin and resulting guilt could affect the human race as a whole. He did not clearly distinguish the imputation of sin from "the propagation of the corrupted condition," or the "*natural*" headship of Adam as father of the race from a "*federal*" headship that understands him as a mere representative of humankind.[63] As we shall shortly see, Smith's endorsement of a "natural" headship links well with his espousal of monogenism, the theory that all humans had descended from a first pair. He wished for a formulation of Christian teaching that would (cautiously) accord with modern science and foster the brotherhood of all humans.

Smith claimed that the hereditary and "racial" character of original sin was supported by "philosophy" ("the human race is descended from one pair") and zoology (in the animal kingdom, "like begets like"). "All men are virtually, potentially, seminally" in Adam, Smith told his students, "not as the fish holds the spawn of multitudes of fishes, but as the acorn holds the acorns which are to come from its growth." [By this contrast, Smith perhaps meant to downplay the sexual and "material" passage of sin through egg and sperm.] With Adam's fall, selfishness and worldliness reigned supreme in him and became the heritage of all humans.[64]

Human experience, Smith claimed, testifies that the origin of sin is not a "deliberate *personal* choice." Adam's sin should not be viewed as the *personal* sin of the millions who are "in" him; it involves them "only so far as we have the common liabilities of the whole race." The guilt of infants cannot be understood as individual, but only as "racial." All members of the human race are brought into this condition of sin by birth before they personally transgress, as a consequence of the fall of Adam, "the head of the race." The emphasis on the "racial" quality of Adam's sin comported well with Smith's view that at the basis of the Christian life is "a common redemption provided for all":[65] both human sin and human redemption are social in nature. Considering the race before the individual, Smith argued, grounds the doctrine of redemption as well as that of sin.[66] Latter-day Calvinists, as much as they focus on sin and its transfer, should keep redemption through Christ at the forefront of their theology.

How, Christian theologians have long asked, did the guilt of that first sin find its way to the souls of developing fetuses? Princeton Old School Presbyterians espoused a theory of "Immediate Imputation," linked with a "federal" theory in which Adam is seen first and foremost as a "representative" of the human race (as in social compact theory), rather than as its "natural" head.[67] Adam's corrupt nature is imputed—"immediately made over"—to other humans, whom he "represents," independent of their own native depravity. This view, Smith charged, originally a Catholic notion, makes imputation of guilt a "forensic, outside affair" and rests on an individualistic way of conceiving humanity. It implies that sin is necessary, and sin's punishment, arbitrary. It loses the notion of the race as "a moral organic whole." This is not, Smith argued, the view of Augustine, nor does it have the weight of doctrinal history behind it.[68]

Smith and New School Presbyterians favored the view of "Mediate Imputation" of original sin (i.e., that Adam's sin was *not* immediately assigned to later humans irrespective of their participation in sin). Smith favored Jonathan Edwards's definition of original sin: "the innate sinful depravity of the heart," which includes "the liableness or exposedness of Adam's posterity, in the divine judgment, to partake of the punishment of that sin."[69] Edwards was the first theologian in America, Smith claimed, who clearly saw that "the sin is not ours because it is imputed to us, but it is imputed to us because it is ours"—a view that he believed was embodied in Augustine's position and enshrined in the Reformed Confessions. There should be no implication that sin is something pinned on later humans from "outside," a view provoking allegations that God is neither just nor benevolent. The notion of original sin's imputation, Smith argued, must always be kept in a moral framework.[70]

Smith claimed that "Mediate Imputation" considers the human race as an organic whole and teaches that Adam is the *father* of the race, not just its representative. It refers only to guilt, to the *liability* to punishment. When Adam, as the head of a race, sins, "all his descendants are born in a sinful condition, not as a punishment, but in the way of a natural connection." In the final reckoning at the Last Judgment, each person's *own* sinful acts and "ill-desert" are also counted. This view, Smith believed, keeps the teaching of original sin in a "generic" framework. Sin, he insisted, should not seem "necessary" and redemption, as transpiring without personal holiness. He claimed that the Calvinist doctrine of "divine decrees" (i.e., predestination), if correctly understood, is consistent with humans' free agency.[71] In this way, Smith presumably tried to avoid any suggestion that an unjust God punished humans for a sin they did not commit.

HENRY SMITH: THE "CHRISTOLOGIZATION" OF REFORMED THEOLOGY

Reformed teaching, Smith argued, needed reconstruction: Christology should rest at its center. Calvinists, he urged, must "Christologize predestination and decrees,"[72] i.e., the doctrines of election and reprobation should be understood through the lens of Christ's redeeming sacrifice, grace, and the forgiveness of sins. On this point, Smith faulted the New England Theology of Nathaniel Emmons. Lacking a Christological center, Emmons emphasized the fearsome sovereignty of God to the extent that he appeared to make God the "efficient cause" of humans' sin.[73] Emmons went so far as to hold that a Christian should opt to be "lost" for the glory of God; Smith considered this commitment to be no better than a "bribe," for if we were *willing* to be lost, "we never shall be."[74] Emmons wished to make a place for human freedom, action, and responsibility, but (in Smith's view) could not reconcile this wish with his strong doctrine of divine causality— and his latter-day followers' attempts to whittle down or smooth out his system to make it more compatible with modern thought had "emasculated" his theology.[75] Smith rejoined:

> The centre of Christian divinity is not in God, nor in man, but in the Godman. Christian theology is essentially a Christology, centering in facts, not deduced from metaphysical or ethical abstractions. Neither God's agency, nor man's will, can give us the whole system; but, as Calvin says, "Christ is the mirror in whom we may without deception contemplate our own election." Above the strife of the schools rises in serene and untroubled majesty the radiant form of the Son of God, the embodiment and reconciliation of divinity and humanity.[76]

Smith's Christological emphasis, with its more "optimistic" view of human salvation, distinguished his theology from Old School Presbyterianism. The Westminster Confession, he emphasized, allows a charitable reading of God's treatment of infants dying before baptism and of the "heathen" who never heard of Christ. Contrary to the harsh belief in "limited atonement" endorsed by the seventeenth-century Synod of Dort, Smith argued that "there is grace for *all* in Christ." Modifying Calvinist scholasticism's confession of human depravity and original sin, he emphasized the necessity of personal faith and obedience made possible by Christ's redeeming grace.[77] Smith's intellectual world, E. Brooks Holifield comments, unlike that of his teachers and Nathanael Taylor, was shaped by history (not "mental science"), Christology, organic (rather than mechanistic) metaphors, and attention to the "history of the progress of the kingdom of God," rather than by "the morphology of salvation."[78] In his more expansive view of Christ's salvific activity, Smith appears to have gone considerably beyond early modern Calvinist interpretations of Augustine.

Smith's "softened" Calvinism attempted to uphold simultaneously the justice of God, the unity of the human race, and the responsibility of each human for his or her own sin in the final reckoning. Sin, he insisted, should not seem "necessary" and redemption, as transpiring without personal holiness. In the end, Smith urged readers to recognize that humans cannot penetrate "the depths of the divine wisdom and sovereignty." Trying to probe too far so as to rationalize the scheme—as did some New England theologians—only muddied already troubled theological waters.[79]

George Fisher: Augustine and the New Haven Theology

Smith was not the only professor here studied who favored "Mediate" over "Immediate" Imputation. George Fisher of Yale attacked the latter interpretation with considerable vigor, arguing that the Old School Presbyterians of Princeton had wrongly claimed Augustine for *their* interpretation of original sin and its transfer. The Princeton theologians, Fisher charged, hold to a "federal" view of Adam's headship of the human race, in which his breach of the "covenant" God had made with him was immediately applied to all later humans. This federal view has no Scriptural warrant, Fisher argued, and suspiciously resembles the social contract theory of government that had been elaborated in the same era that saw the birth of federal theology. In the seventeenth century, theologians artificially, and in Fisher's view, unsuccessfully, tried to link their federalist theory with Augustine's.[80] They mistakenly took the hard-line seventeenth-century Calvinism of Francis Turretin—with its strictly federalist view and harsh confession that God does *not* desire the salvation of all—as being genuine

Calvinist theology. Turretin's is now the "text-book," Fisher charged, by which the Princetonians wage war against the New England Theology, such as was popular at New Haven. New England Theology approves Jonathan Edwards's return to the Augustinian notion that humans really participate in Adam; the latter is not simply their "representative."[81]

Augustine, Fisher claimed, unlike the Princetonians, held that "human nature as a whole was deposited in the first man," and was corrupted with him in the first transgression.[82] Today, theologians who espouse this Augustinian view are Traducians—but this was not always the case in the past: witness Augustine himself. Fisher sternly upbraids the Princetonians for their interpretation of Augustine: "We must take history as it is and not seek to read into it our reasoning and inferences. If we do not find philosophers self-consistent, we must let them remain inconsistent, instead of altering their systems to suit our ideas of logical harmony."[83] Fisher urged the Princeton theologians to abandon the attempt to link Augustine's theology to federalism, and to acknowledge Augustine's position as advocating humanity's "TRUE AND REAL PARTICIPATION IN ADAM'S SIN." What is unsatisfactory about the Princetonian position? In addition to its (allegedly) wrong reading of Augustine, it skews the notion of holiness: humans are held legally accountable for a sin in which they did not participate.[84] Sin is imputed to them from "outside."

In his essay on "Augustinian and Federal Theories" that critiques Princeton theology, Fisher in fact replicates some of Pelagius' objections to Augustine's theory: that the holiness and justice of God are impugned (God is made to seem the author of sin and not to desire the salvation of sinners), that babies are deemed sinful before they have will and knowledge. Is it not better, Fisher suggested, to adopt Augustine's concession that some questions are best left unanswered than to try to resolve them in ways that openly conflict with proper Christian conceptions of God's dealings—benevolent but just—with humans?[85]

Thus Augustine's exposition of original sin and his hesitant hypothesis of the mechanism of its transfer provided ample room for intra-Calvinist battles many centuries later. Without a clear theory of the soul's origin to support his notion of sin's transfer, Augustine had left unanswered how the human race could be "in" Adam or responsible for his sin. Nineteenth-century Reformed debates over humanity's relation to Adam, God's role in the assignment of original sin, and the fate of unregenerates, "heathen," and unbaptized infants reveal a significant modification of Calvinism as it had been formulated two centuries earlier. A "softer, gentler" Calvinism was coming to fruition, spurred by a renewed emphasis on Christology and the benevolence of God, a more optimistic view of human nature, and a desire to have biblical teaching on human origins accord with biological theory.

Special Interests: Roswell Hitchcock on Augustine

Hitchcock's appeal to Augustine had two foci: debates over high-church theology (in which he enlisted the Donatists against Augustine) and those over evolutionary and racial theory (in which he appealed to Augustine's elaboration of early human history in the *City of God*).

Against High-Churchmanship

Hitchcock's teaching on Augustine reveals the intrusion of nineteenth-century debates over ritual and sacraments associated with the Oxford Movement and Roman Catholicism: had not John Henry Newman's "defection" to Rome—ten years before Hitchcock assumed his Union professorship—shown where the Oxford Movement might lead? Hitchcock considered it a truism that as ecclesiastical ritual grows, piety decreases.[86] Here Augustine served as one culprit.

With nineteenth-century developments in mind as he taught students about Augustine, Hitchcock warned that "evangelical conceptions" should not lull them into underestimating the Fathers' strong churchly emphasis. "It seems strange to us," he declaimed, "that the New Testament idea of the universal priesthood of believers should give way [so early] to Sacramentarian and High Church views." These are *not justified* by true Christian teaching, but are *understandable* when we consider that earlier Christians envisioned the church as a "society," and that Jews and pagans of the time expected every religion to have an "outward priesthood." Moreover, in the early Christian era, persecutions, heresies, and schisms prompted the development of clerical hierarchy and more precise definitions of the true church.[87] At this point, Hitchcock turned to Augustine—or more precisely, to Augustine's Donatist opponents—to expound the development of rival theories of the church in the patristic era.

Hitchcock was sympathetic to some features of Donatism as he understood it. The Donatist schism, he believed, arose in part as a reaction to the overly close association of state and church in the fourth century—an association that American evangelicals roundly denounced. He pictured dissident Donatists objecting, "What has the Emperor to do with church matters?" Donatists, Hitchcock told his students, believed that the true church was "invisible," constituted by "the company of the really regenerated." That Donatism was not rendered wholly extinct until the Saracen invasion of 707 proves that Augustine, despite his ardent attempts, was not able to obliterate it. The assessment that evangelical Protestants make of Donatism, Hitchcock concluded, "must be very different [i.e., more favorable] from High Churchmen of all times."[88]

These "High Churchmen," such as Augustine, focus on the "external" church, fusing the visible and the invisible churches. Hitchcock called Augustine "the father of externalism in the West"—yet conceded that even *he* made some distinction between the visible and the invisible churches.[89] Hitchcock argued that at the very time that John Chrysostom and others in the East were positing that the true church was not to found in a mere outward organization but was "inward," Augustine in the West was declaring that there could be no salvation outside it.[90] The East, Hitchcock alleged, exhibited greater spirituality and fervor than the West, which stressed the practical, the "external" and the organizational. Hitchcock attributed (without elaboration) this difference to a "racial reason." Augustine, he concluded, in his ecclesiology did not carry out his own better principles; that was left for Luther.[91]

Regarding sacramental theory, Hitchcock conceded that Augustine should not be accused of the "hair-splitting distinctions of the Middle Ages"; nevertheless, he provided an impetus to sacramentarianism. During the Pelagian controversy, for example, when accused of disparaging human reproduction, Augustine so eulogized marriage that (Hitchcock alleged) he lent it "quite a sacramental cast."[92] Although much of Augustine's teaching, Hitchcock charged, was "Ritualistic," he composed other works—presumably the anti-Pelagian treatises—that "had [the] form of Protestantism in them." Despite Augustine's high-church sacramentarianism, he acknowledged when pressed that sacraments were not "absolutely indispensable" and were not a means of grace.[93]

If Augustine's ecclesiasticism favored Roman Catholicism, his anthropology—which Hitchcock called "pre-eminently Biblical and experimental" [i.e., experiential]—brought him back to Protestantism. Augustine's teaching on human nature, Hitchcock told his students, was "distasteful" to Roman Catholics. The western church, he claimed, prompted by Augustine, "surged on" in its understanding of human nature, while the East remained like the chrysalis that shows no development.[94] Here, Hitchcock appealed to the organic, ever-developing nature of Protestantism in contrast to the inorganic, allegedly static quality of eastern Christianity—and presumably, also of Catholicism.

Augustine and Race Theory

Hitchcock's most extended treatment of human origins is found in "The Laws of Civilization," an address that he delivered four times in the summer of 1860 (a half-year after the publication of Darwin's *Origin of Species*) and published in November of that year.[95] His theory is marked by its intersections with the "higher criticism" in biblical studies;[96] with science, especially geology, "climatology," and evolutionary theory; with hypotheses regarding the origins of language; and with a race theory that made Teutons the carriers of the highest human accomplishment in their move westward.[97] These contemporary interests intersected with his reading of Augustine. "The Laws of Civilization," when supplemented by course notes and Hitchcock's other writings, presents a theory of human origins consonant with Genesis and with Augustine's exposition in *City of God*, a work that Hitchcock described to students as an "able treatise."[98]

Hitchcock conceded that the opening chapters of Genesis could no longer be taken as strictly "literal," given new developments in science. For example, "fossil geology" proves that death entered the world before Adam's sin in Eden.[99] Human origins must be dated earlier than the traditional Christian view, perhaps as early as "5500 or 6000" B.C.[100] The six "days" of creation should be understood as "indefinite periods," a view Hitchcock claimed was endorsed by various Church Fathers, including Augustine.[101] Hitchcock did not relinquish Adam and Eve as "real people," but positioned them on the primeval stage somewhat awkwardly with the new science.

In Hitchcock's era, debates raged between monogenists, who ascribed a single origin to the human race, and polygenists, who posited several diverse origins. Hitchcock sided with the monogenists. For confirmation,

Hitchcock claimed the support of anatomy, comparative philology, and physiology.[102] Monogenism provided an important prop for Hitchcock's belief in the unity of the human race: united, because it had descended from an original first pair. To hold that different peoples and civilizations are "indigenous," he told his students, is an "infidel theory."[103] A few zoologists, he conceded, deny the unity of human origins—but their sphere of expertise, the animal kingdom, is not the issue at stake. (As Hitchcock put it, "from bears and wolves" one cannot reason up to man.) "Zoological analogies," he argued, are trumped by the "more potent probabilities of history," namely, that the human stock originated in Asia Minor, and the best part of it pushed westward.[104] Here, Augustine was of assistance to Hitchcock: he clearly taught the unity of the race, that "Adam stood for the race" and "whatever he did was a racial act." (Like Henry Smith, Hitchcock indirectly affirmed the point that original sin should not be imagined as a personal deed, but as a "racial" one.) Adam and Eve, in Hitchcock's scenario, carried the human race "in their loins"—and then into sin.[105]

Hitchcock rejected the theory that assigned to early humans a mere "crude capacity" that slowly evolved to something higher: the biblical and Augustinian picture of Adam and Eve trumps the implications of Darwin's theory. "It offends our moral sense," Hitchcock wrote, "to imagine the human race lying, even for a night, like a poor foundling on the cold doorsill of its future habitation." Rather, we must believe that upon its birth, humanity—"sensitive, athletic"—was taken up tenderly into the Father's arms.[106] Humanity did not originate in "barbarism," with the first man "a puling infant, staring and stammering at what he saw. We need not reckon him a philosopher, but we must believe him to have been a man; somewhat infantile, doubtless in tone, but not in capacity, nor in the method of his mental growth."[107] Humans did not rise upward from a barbarous animality, but "descended" from one first truly human pair, as Genesis and Augustine claim. "Barbarism," he wrote, "is not a youthful crudeness, but a decrepitude, of society."[108]

Evolutionary theory did, however, get limited play in Hitchcock's narrative. It was the Fall in the Garden of Eden that ushered in barbarism[109]— from which state, humans had slowly advanced. The Fall, an actual historical event, explains how humans "descended" from their original good condition. Now, deterioration, disease, and infirmity began to plague humankind.[110] By adopting this scenario, Hitchcock could affirm that humanity indeed *developed* from an earlier stage—but that stage itself was the result of a "Fall" from an original, higher condition.

Hitchcock derived still more lessons from the biblical stories of the children of Adam and Eve. To explain the origin of the foreign peoples among whom Cain wandered, Hitchcock noted that Genesis 5:4 (and later Jewish tradition) assigns "other sons and daughters" to Adam—a view also registered by Augustine.[111] Next, the corruption of humankind led to the Flood, occasioned by the "sons of God" marrying the daughters of men (Gen. 6:1–2). Who were these "sons" and "daughters"? Hitchcock preferred Augustine's explanation, that the "sons of God" were pious males of Seth's line who married daughters of the impious Cainites. This interpretation, Hitchcock told his students, shows the dangerous influence that the inferior can have over the good.[112]

How then, given the original unity of the human race that Genesis and Augustine posit, to account for distinctive *races*? Although Hitchcock was not entirely consistent, one theory of racial diversity that he elaborated appealed to the three sons of Noah. By assigning the origin of races only to the time of Noah's sons, Hitchcock avoided polygenism, but could account for "racial difference" within a framework that sanctioned the truth of Genesis. In this alternative scenario, Hitchcock posited that after the Flood, a new beginning was made. Of the three races stemming from Noah's sons, that deriving from Shem was chosen "as the special nurse and guardian of the great religions of the world" (Judaism, Christianity, and Islam).[113] It was not, however, the descendants of Shem, but those of Japheth, who would be the carriers of civilization. Hitchcock did not here explain the awkward point that those who developed civilization were not those who "guarded" the great religions of the world.

The race descending from Japheth, in Hitchcock's scheme, possessed of "dialectical intellect," "of iron muscle and iron will, stirred by a mysterious impulse, turn[ed] its back upon the seats of rising empire, pushed off northward and westward, into less hospitable climes, and there await[ed] the later call of Providence"—a call, namely, to develop the civilizations of Greece, Rome, Europe, and America.[114] Of Japheth's descendants, the Teutonic group (which settled northern Europe and early America) was morally superior to its "Pelasgic" counterpart, represented by the Greeks and Romans. Illustrating the "racial" characteristics marking those who stem from different climates and regions, Hitchcock posits that Augustine himself combined "the cleanness and sharpness and dogmatism of the North with the intensity of passion peculiar to the South."[115] Augustine in the *City of God*, "surveying the grand procession of races and nations," correctly—in Hitchcock's view—pronounced the history of the world to be "the history of redemption." Students of ancient history should follow him in seeing the "footprints" and hearing the "footfalls, of the coming Christ."[116] Particularly, it appears, they should heed those "footprints" in their westward march.

Pondering the unity of the human race led Hitchcock to speculate on theories concerning the origin of the soul and the transfer of original sin. He (like Smith) argued that the Traducian position on the origin of the soul is the most logical. Although Hitchcock disliked the term "Traducian," he conceded that if we use it simply to connote a "realism" that underscores "the unity of the race," then "it has color." Reflecting on the transmission of sin that began with the Fall, Hitchcock pondered why Augustine did not outrightly espouse Traducianism, since it would have strengthened his thesis of the unity of the human race. Hitchcock felt sure that Augustine *must* have leaned toward Traducian theory, even though he "never dared" to espouse it.[117]

Why did Augustine not "dare"? Hitchcock fixed the blame for his reticence on Tertullian, whom he considered Augustine's true forerunner. Traducianism suffered from its association with Tertullian, who gave it a "gross and crude" representation. Augustine, Hitchcock proposed, was "too politic" to embarrass himself with heretical friends such as Tertullian. (Hitchcock here interposed Tertullian's lapse into Montanism to bolster his explanation.) Yet Traducian theory best supports the notion of the organic unity of the race. Who knows, Hitchcock wrote, whether Traducianism is true? "But"—whatever the answer—"the race is one."[118] Hitchcock, we can see, attempted to accommodate Augustine's view on the single origin of humanity and the development of "races" or "nations" with the new discoveries of geology, zoology, and biology.

Special Interests: Philip Schaff,
Augustine, and Religious Liberty

Augustine as an opponent of Donatism stands as one culprit in Philip Schaff's narrative of the history of religious liberty.[119] Schaff's lifelong championship of religious freedom forms the backdrop to his critique:

since compulsion is a "fatal principle," how is it that good men such as Augustine can become "the authors of much mischief?"[120]

Schaff was an internationally recognized leader of the Evangelical Alliance, an organization that claimed to promote religious tolerance around the world.[121] Although Schaff was most vitally concerned with tolerance for Protestants living in inhospitable countries, he also protested such incidents as the expulsion of the Jesuits from Germany during the *Kulturkampf*, an action that he believed would be unconstitutional in America.[122] His sympathetic approach to the Catholic Reformer Savonarola, burned at the stake as a heretic by the papacy, likewise reveals his condemnation of violent treatment of dissenters.[123]

Schaff praised his new American homeland for its (alleged) commitment to church-state separation. (Like most other American Protestants in his day, he did not consider this separation to disallow prayer and Bible-reading in the public schools: such practices were civic exercises.) Although in his first years at Mercersburg Schaff sharply denounced the acrimonious Protestant sectarianism that focused on minute points of belief and practice, he eventually came to value the "voluntary" system of American Protestantism. That various Protestant groups must operate without financial assistance from the government he deemed a virtue: they must sufficiently value their churches to maintain them without state support.[124] European state churches, by contrast, were wracked by religious indifference and Rationalism. Despite American Protestants' light reliance on creeds and confessions, they seemed to Schaff firmer in their religious convictions than their European counterparts.[125]

Religious Liberty Before Augustine

Although Augustine's writings and practice in the midst of the Donatist controversy were Schaff's chief focus, his tale of the struggle for religious liberty extends back to ancient Rome. One feature of ancient Rome that Schaff decried was the use of religion as a tool of state policy. Whenever religion becomes a matter of state legislation and compulsion, he claimed, the educated classes fall into hypocrisy and infidelity.[126] Yet the Roman persecution of the early Christians prompted Christian Apologists to proclaim, however imperfectly, the principle of religious freedom and "the sacred rights of conscience." Schaff singled out Tertullian ("the father of evangelical Protestantism"[127]), citing *To Scapula* 2: "it is a human right, a natural capacity, that everyone should worship as he sees fit. . . . Certainly there is no place in religion to compel religion—to which we should be impelled by free will, not by force."[128] In Tertullian's time, Schaff claimed, the church was "a self-supporting and self-governing society," as it always should be. He praised Tertullian as the first Christian writer to argue for religious liberty as an inalienable, God-given right, which civil governments should not merely tolerate, but "respect and protect."[129]

Like many nineteenth-century Protestants, Schaff argued that before Constantine's accession, the church had retained its "grand simplicity" and "spirituality," free from any connection to political power or "worldly splendor." Although Schaff did not idealize the ante-Nicene church, he praised its "voluntary," "self-supporting and self-governing" character. The ante-Nicene church, he claimed, much resembles the church in the United States—*except* that the American government recognizes and protects, rather than persecutes, Christianity. Here, the separation of church and state rests on "a friendly recognition and peaceful co-operation," rather than on the "deadly opposition" that the persecuting Roman emperors mounted to Christianity.[130]

Narrating the history of religious liberty, Schaff gave Constantine a mixed assessment. A "sagacious statesman," Constantine perceived the signs of the times and went with them.[131] In generous moments, Schaff questioned whether Constantine's melding of church and state should be blamed for the church's degeneracy: rather, Constantine is owed a debt of gratitude for helping to forge the rights that American Christians now claim as "essential and inalienable."[132] Yet the toleration that Constantine granted should not be confused with modern notions of religious liberty; he merely raised Christianity to the status of heathenism.[133] The Edict of Milan, Schaff argued, did not imply the "modern Protestant and Anglo-American theory of religious liberty as one of the universal and inalienable rights of man." Rather, the Edict opened the way for "Catholic hierarchical Christianity" to become the religion of the state. Persecution of heretics was a natural consequence of the union of civil and ecclesiastical authorities. When judging Constantine, Schaff urged readers, remember that all great historical characters act under the spirit of the age—although God can use that spirit as an instrument to work his providential purpose. Not even the Protestant Reformers, he conceded, taught true religious tolerance: that awaited the eighteenth century.[134]

Despite praise for Constantine's sagacious governance, Schaff charged that church-state union injured church discipline: heresy was hated but morals were lax. The church grew more secular as Christianity became fashionable. Strict discipline, self-sacrifice, and brotherly love faded. But this decline was not *entirely* the fault of church-state union; "the corrupt heart of man" shared the blame. "In that mighty revolution under Constantine," Schaff concluded, "the church lost her virginity, and allied herself with the mass of heathenism, which had not yet experienced an inward change." Church government increasingly came to be patterned after that of the civil sphere.[135] Nevertheless, despite the corruption in the church's "bosom," Christianity was still better than heathenism, which was "sinking into hopeless ruin," or than "the conceited and arrogant schools of the Gnostics and Manicheans."[136]

Once church and state united, the spirit of Christian tolerance declined. Civil penalties were laid on heretics, an action, Schaff claimed, that violates "the spirit and example of Christ and the apostles." After Nicaea, heretics were subjected to banishment and, later, even to the death penalty. Offenses against the church were now seen as "crimes against the state and civil society."[137] As examples, Schaff mentioned the banishments of those outvoted at Nicaea: Arius and his followers stand as the first examples of the state's punishment of heresy, the beginning of "the long and dark era of persecution for all departures from the catholic or orthodox faith."[138] Lecturing to a class on this aspect of the Arian controversy, Schaff declared, "It is always a sure sign that we have no confidence in our faith when we employ violence and force to uphold and sustain it." When religion is "forced," as it was under Constantius, the "laws of history" suggest that there will be reaction, in this case, a reversion to the heathenism of Julian.[139] The interference of emperors and their courts served only to heighten the bitter contests "by adding confiscation and exile to the spiritual punishment of synodical excommunication."[140]

Later in the fourth century, Schaff continued, the Catholic persecution of Priscillianists shows the unhappy result of mixing temporal and spiritual powers. Likewise, Catholic Christians' attacks on Manicheans prompted Schaff's comment that persecuting heresy "always helps heresy unless heretics are exterminated." Yet divine Providence prevailed: "the bloody persecution of heretics . . . produced the sweet fruit of religious liberty." The blood of heretics here blends in Schaff's mind with the blood of the martyrs, whose sacrifice became "the seed of civil and religious liberty." Yet

Christianity after its triumph forgot this lesson and itself engaged in persecution of heretics, Jews, and pagans. State churches throughout time, Schaff claimed, have castigated dissenters, violating the principles of Jesus, "in carnal misunderstanding of the spiritual nature of the kingdom of heaven." Christian violence toward other Christians—as examples, the Spanish Inquisition and the massacre of Huguenots—should not cast doubt on Christianity's truth: the religion itself was not responsible for these horrors. Rather, "an unholy alliance of politics and religion" was to blame.[141]

As always, Schaff tried to find something good amid the bad. The persecution under Diocletian, for example, served a useful purpose in purifying the church of lax discipline, worldliness, and in-group fighting. And although Christians may deplore the evils that resulted from church-state union, they should not overlook Christianity's "wholesome effects," for example, its influence on the formulation of the Justinianic Code.[142]

Augustine and the Donatists

Given these views on religious liberty and the dangers of church-state union, it does not surprise that Schaff sharply criticized Augustine's sanction of the coercion of Donatists. In Schaff's (idealized) view, the Donatists had kept to the "grand simplicity" of the ante-Nicene church and "its spirituality, or freedom from all connection with political power or worldly splendor." They—not Catholic Christians—had upheld the principle of freedom from state alignment. Schaff assigned some of the blame to Augustine's misguided biblical interpretation: by a "false exegesis" of Luke 14:23 ("compel them to come in"), Augustine tried to justify coercion. The cruel suppression that Augustine endorsed led to later persecutions—and this quite apart from the "wholly anti-Protestant" views on church and sacraments that Augustine expressed in his anti-Donatist writings.[143] Although Schaff granted that Augustine sometimes recommended clemency for accused Donatists, he also cited August Neander's claim that Augustine's justification of religious coercion contributed directly to the Inquisition. Schaff, however, was confident that Augustine would have retracted his position if he could have foreseen the crusade against the Albigensians and "the horrors of the Spanish Inquisition."[144]

Yet it was not only events in the distant future for which Schaff held Augustine responsible: he must bear some blame for the unhappy fate of

Christianity in late ancient North Africa. "The result of persecution," Schaff concluded, "was that both Catholics and Donatists in North Africa were overwhelmed in ruin first by the barbarous Vandals, who were Arian heretics, and afterwards by the Mohammedan conquerors." Schaff generously imagined that in this case as well, if Augustine could have foreseen these events, he "would have shrunk back in horror."[145]

Whatever Augustine's merits, Schaff held him responsible for many errors of the Roman Church, of which the sanction of religious persecution stands in first place.[146] Despite the Protestantizing tendencies that Schaff saw in Augustine's anti-Pelagian writings, that Father, he thought, had much for which to answer.

After Schaff

By century's end, mainstream Protestant theology was busily reconceiving itself for modernity. American seminary professors soon devised new ways of interpreting Genesis 1–11 in relation to modern scientific claims. Within decades, Schaff's student and successor at Union Seminary, Arthur Cushman McGiffert, could refer to the Genesis stories as "mere poetry," advising Christians that they need not have any particular views on "the creation of the world, the origin of man, the historicity of Adam, the fall, the deluge"— any more than Christianity asked them to have particular views on "astronomy or geology or mathematics."[147] Augustine, to McGiffert's eyes, is now dismissed as "not modern,"[148] as a man who scorned astronomy and anatomy, who deemed knowledge of the physical universe unimportant, whose notion of the transfer of original sin occasioned "untold confusion."[149]

Others, however, attempted to bring Augustine into dialogue with modern thought. "Modern," however, now did not suggest debates over Mediate or Immediate Imputation, or the origin of the soul. "Modern" was now judged by attitudes toward science. Whereas in 1874, Charles Hodge of Princeton Theological Seminary had asked the question, "What is Darwinism?" and bluntly answered, "atheism,"[150] other Christian scholars soon rejoined that Augustine's theology had been a forerunner of evolutionary theory, a harbinger of Darwin: had not Augustine posited that God at creation had made the "germs" of all things and let them develop in their own good time?[151]

As the nineteenth-century professors had variously claimed Augustine for their causes, or faulted his high-church views and his collusion with governmental authority in religious persecution, so in the succeeding generations Augustine could be alternatively denounced or claimed for new causes quite unforeseen in fifth-century North Africa.

Conclusion

This book has charted the uncertain path by which early church history entered the Protestant academy in nineteenth-century America. It has shown with what scanty resources professors of the subject attempted to build a discipline, what daunting obstacles they faced. Yet, I have argued, seminary education as here described, for all its deficiencies, was the closest approximation to graduate education in the Humanities that America could boast until late in the century.

Readers today may with reason doubt whether the professors here discussed deserve the title "historian." As their class notes and publications suggest, they often appealed to early Christian writers less for their historical interest than for their provision of weapons with which to trounce "deviant" versions of Christianity in the professors' own era. Their approach to Christian history was apologetic, confessional, and moralizing. They indulged in frequent comparisons between "us" and "them"—"them" including ancient Jews and "heathens" and modern adherents of non-Christian religions, as well as other Christians of the present, both Roman Catholic and Protestant. They held the Church Fathers responsible for many aspects of later Christian belief and practice that they deemed unfortunate: for ecclesiastical hierarchy, sacramentalism, doctrinal obfuscation, and "superstition" in various forms, even (in Augustine's case) for lending sanction to religious persecution. In their view, the Fathers exemplified Christianity's downward slide from the time of Jesus and the Apostles. This theme—Christianity's early "decline"—they shared with many Protestants of their day.

A more charitable approach, however, attempts to understand these pioneers in the varying historical, religious, intellectual, and cultural contexts they so earnestly attempted to bring into harmony. Samuel Miller early in the century and Ephraim Emerton at its end—but for quite different reasons—remained largely immune from the concerns that troubled the four Union and Yale professors. The latter struggled to reconcile more radical, "German" approaches to the study of early Christianity with the pre-critical views of nineteenth-century American Protestants. However disturbing the notion of historical development seemed to their American audiences, it afforded the professors a means by which to treat the patristic and medieval eras more sympathetically—a sympathy without which the study of the Church Fathers might have been excluded from the American Protestant seminary curriculum.

The professors aligned Hegelian-influenced theories of historical development with notions of divine Providence to support their confession that God had guided human history in the past and would do so until its end. This alignment prompted them to see some beneficial features of the patristic era even in practices they denounced, such as ascetic renunciation. Their knowledge of Christian history afforded them at least a small bulwark against the radically anti-Catholic sentiments of many Americans of their era.

The professors were sure, however, that the end to which God was guiding history did not mean going "beyond" Christianity. Truth was not to be found equally in other religions and philosophies, as some forms of pantheistic Hegelianism suggested: Christianity was both the "highest" religion and the one in which truth was supremely located. Social, religious, and philosophical movements that threatened the dominance of a spiritualized and Idealistically tinged Reformed Protestantism were threats to be countered or at least "flanked" (as Rowell Hitchcock phrased it), swept into a higher synthesis. Even contemporary Roman Catholicism, so disturbing to Protestants in its doctrine, practice, and politics, might (so the professors hoped) be absorbed in a Protestantizing direction. Although James Turner argues that, by the end of the era here charted, "belief" had become "subcultural" (that is, not longer unifying and defining an entire American culture),[1] this was not the faith, or the hope, of the professors at Princeton, Yale, and Union.

The professors' version of historical development, however, cordoned off the New Testament from critical consideration: "development" pertained to Christianity only from the second century onward. A conservative approach to biblical scholarship hampered a more encompassing grasp of early Christianity's development. "Development" could not be allowed to run backward to raise disturbing questions about the New Testament. The professors imagined that the pure essence of Christianity embodied in the New Testament had remained throughout the ages, however dark the "blots" caused by human intransigence. At the time of the Protestant Reformation and in some subsequent movements, that essence again shone forth.

Despite setbacks, blamed variously on human depravity and on the remnants of "heathenism" and Judaism that clung to the early church, developing Christianity at last had found a worthy home in northern Europe and, much later, an even worthier one in North America. Indeed, the view that America was an "exceptional" nation, destined by God for a great purpose, fit easily with the Union and Yale professors' endorsement of historical development, of divine Providence, and of Romantic assertions that each "folk" had its distinctive role to fill in the world.[2] America's role was to serve as a "new Israel"[3]; she was, Philip Schaff believed, "Immanuel's land for all time to come."[4] Had not Bishop Berkeley himself, pondering the wonders of eighteenth-century America, claimed that "Time's noblest offspring is the last"?[5]

By the early twentieth century, the evangelical professors' approach to the past would not count as "history" in many academic circles. The "golden thread" of Providence, as Harvard's Ephraim Emerton wryly put it, had come unwound.[6] Only then was German biblical criticism accorded a fuller place in (even) liberal Protestant seminaries. Only then were material and economic factors in Christianity's formation given their due and Christianity's "exceptional" status among world religions challenged. And only then could the study of early Christianity enter the curriculum of allegedly secular colleges and universities.

As builders of a discipline and of institutions, however, the professors offered remarkable service. They devoted themselves tirelessly (with little monetary reward) to devising curricula in church history, founding and editing journals and book series, developing seminary libraries, contributing money and books for prizes and scholarships to encourage young scholars-in-the-making. The scholarly and institutional infrastructures they put in place, I have argued, provided the closest approximation to graduate study in Humanities in their era. Without their efforts, Princeton Theological Seminary, Harvard Divinity School, Yale Divinity School, and Union Theological Seminary would not have become the academic leaders in the study of Christian history that they soon did.

Philip Schaff had generously hoped that the next generation of historians would throw his own "preparatory labors into the shade," bringing church history into its rightful place as an important academic discipline.[7] Indeed, only after Schaff's time would a more advanced level of education in religious and theological studies flourish in America. Some decades passed before American graduate education could rival that of Germany as a suitable training ground for historians of Christianity. Along the way, many of the professors' scholarly assumptions and personal convictions would be either modified or abandoned as the discipline of early Christian studies came into sharper focus.

Henry Adams's observation with which this book began also seems a fitting conclusion: "To [the American of the year 2000] the nineteenth century would stand on the same plane with the fourth,—equally child-like,—and he would only wonder how both of them, knowing so little, and so weak in force, should have done so much."[8]

Student Notetakers

Below are brief sketches (based on available information) of the careers of students who took notes in the various professors' courses. Their notebooks constitute a major source for my study. I list in order of the dates at which the professors began their teaching careers in Church History at these institutions.

Princeton Theological Seminary
Samuel Miller

Most notes from Samuel Miller's lectures are his own.

Notes by the following students, with approximate dates of when they attended:

Allen Henry Brown (1840–1841)
Cyrenius Crosby (1820–1821)
John Finley Crowe (1813–1814)
James W. Douglas[(s] (1821)
Orson Douglass (1818–1819)
John Miller (1838)
unidentified student (1839)

Most of these students served as Presbyterian ministers, missionaries, and school educators.

Mercersburg Theological Seminary (archives at Lancaster Theological Seminary)

Philip Schaff

Student notes, with approximate dates of when they attended:

Christian C. Russell (1855)

J. W. Santee (1848–1850): Santee became a minister of the German Reformed Church.

Union Theological Seminary

Henry Boynton Smith

Some lecture notes are Smith's own.

Charles Augustus Briggs: Briggs graduated from Union Theological Seminary in 1863. He studied at the University of Berlin in the mid-to-late 1860s, became a pastor, and joined the faculty of Union Seminary to teach Hebrew Bible in 1874. He was awarded an honorary doctorate by the University of Edinburgh in 1884. Briggs's heresy trial in the early 1890s led Union to break its official ties with the Presbyterian Church.

Thomas S. Hastings: Hastings graduated from Union in 1851. He received a D.D. from New York University in 1865, and honorary degrees from Princeton and from Hamilton College, his alma mater. Hastings served as Professor of Sacred Rhetoric and Pastoral Theology at Union from 1882 to 1904, and as Union's President from 1887 to 1897.

Samuel M. Jackson (see below under Hitchcock)

James Quick: Quick graduated from the University of Michigan and was at Union from 1854 to 1856. An ordained Presbyterian minister, he spent part of his career as a missionary.

Henry A. Stimson: Stimson graduated from Yale College in 1865, and studied at Union in 1866–1867 before transferring to Andover Theological Seminary. He spent his life as a Congregationalist minister, serving as Professor of Homiletics at Hartford Theological Seminary in 1916–1917. He received honorary D.D. degrees from Ripon College and Yale College.

Roswell Dwight Hitchcock

Joseph Dunn Burrell: Burrell received a B.A. and (later) M.A. from Yale, graduated from Union in 1884, and served as a Presbyterian minister in

Iowa and later Brooklyn. He was on the Board of Directors of Union Seminary.

Samuel Macauley Jackson: Jackson graduated from Union in 1873 and studied abroad from 1873 to 1875. A Presbyterian minister in New Jersey, he was Professor of Church History at New York University from 1895 to 1912. He served as Secretary of the American Society of Church History from 1888 to 1912, and as President in 1912. Jackson worked with Philip Schaff on several editorial projects, including the *Schaff-Herzog Encyclopedia*, and the *Encyclopedia of Living Divines and Christian Workers of All Denominations in Europe and America*. On Jackson, see D. S. Schaff, "Samuel Macauley Jackson as a Co-Worker with Philip Schaff," who testifies that of the numerous young men in whom his father had taken an interest, "no one enjoyed more fully his confidence and his affection than did Dr. Jackson" (17).

Edward Caldwell Moore: Moore graduated from Union in 1884 and studied from 1884 to 1886 at Berlin, Göttingen, and Giessen. He received a Ph.D. from Brown in 1891. He held the Parkman Professorship of Theology at Harvard from 1901 to 1929, and the Plummer Professorship of Christian Morals from 1915 to 1929. Moore dedicated his book, *An Outline of the History of Christian Thought Since Kant* (1912) to Adolf von Harnack, claiming that he had been Harnack's first American pupil.

Edward B. Wright: Wright received an A.B. degree from Western Reserve and graduated from Union in 1867. In 1876, he was granted an honorary D.D. degree from Western Reserve. He served as a Presbyterian minister throughout his career.

Philip Schaff

Charles Ripley Gillett: Gillett graduated from NYU in 1874 and from Union in 1880. He studied at the University of Berlin from 1881–1883. Serving as librarian at Union from 1883 to 1908, he also taught Propaedeutics, and served as Secretary of the Faculty, as Registrar, and as Dean of Students. As librarian, he catalogued several of Union's important collections. He translated from German Adolf von Harnack's *Monasticism: Its Ideals and Its History* (1895) and Gustav Krüger's *History of Early Christian Literature in the First Three Centuries* (1897), and wrote *Burned Books: Chapters in British History and Literature* (1932). He also wrote an informative three-volume history of Union that remains in manuscript in the Union archives.

Yale
George Park Fisher

Bernadotte Perrin: Perrin attended Fisher's lectures at Yale in 1870–1871, received his Ph.D. from that institution in 1873, and studied at Tübingen, Leipzig, and Berlin between 1876–1879. He served as professor of Greek at Western Reserve and later at Yale, producing a number of editions and translations from Greek. He served as President of the American Philological Association in 1897.

Henry E. Bourne: Bourne, a student at Yale in the 1880s, assisted Fisher with his *History of the Christian Church* (1887), taken in part from Bourne's course notes. I have found no information about his later career.

Harvard
Ephraim Emerton

Earl Morse Wilbur: Wilbur was a student at Harvard in the late 1880s. He later studied in Berlin, taught courses at Meadville Seminary, and was the organizer of the Pacific Unitarian School for the Ministry at Berkeley, of which he later served as President. He wrote, among other works, *The First Century of the Liberal Movement in American Religion* (1918) and *A History of Unitarianism: Socinianism and Its Antecedents* (1946).

ABBREVIATIONS AND ARCHIVAL SOURCES

Journals

AHR	*American Historical Review*
APTR	*American Presbyterian Theological Review*
APR	*American Presbyterian Review*
AR	*Andover Review*
ATR	*American Theological Review*
BFER	*British Foreign and Evangelical Review*
BR	*Biblical Repository*
BRPR	*Biblical Repertory and Princeton Review*
BS	*Bibliotheca Sacra*
CH	*Church History*
ER	*Educational Review*
JAH	*Journal of American History*
JECS	*Journal of Early Christian Studies*
JEH	*Journal of Ecclesiastical History*
MR	*Mercersburg Review*
NAR	*North American Review*
NE	*New Englander*
PQPR	*Presbyterian Quarterly and Princeton Review*
PR	*Princeton Review*
USQR	*Union Seminary Quarterly Review*
ZKG	*Zeitschrift für Kirchengeschichte*

Institutions

GTS	General Theological Seminary
HDS	Harvard Divinity School (Theological Department, Harvard College/University)

HU   Harvard University
LTS   Lancaster Theological Seminary
MTS   Mercersburg Theological Seminary (The Seminary of the German
        Reformed Church at Mercersburg)
NYHS   New-York Historical Society
NYU   University of the City of New York (New York University)
PTS   Princeton Theological Seminary (The Theological Seminary at
        Princeton)
UTS   Union Theological Seminary
YDS   Yale Divinity School (Theological Department, Yale College/
        University)

Series

ANF   Ante-Nicene Fathers
CSEL   Corpus Scriptorum Ecclesiasticorum Latinorum
NPNF   Nicene and Post-Nicene Fathers
PG   Patrologia Graeca
PL   Patrologia Latina

Professional Organizations

AHA   American Historical Association
ASCH   American Society of Church History
SBL   Society of Biblical Literature

Archival Collections and References

The archival collections I cite are located as follows:
Harvard Divinity School (HDS)
        Joseph Henry Allen Papers (bMS 416)
        Ephraim Emerton Papers (bMS 466)
        Frederic Henry Hedge Papers (bMS 384)
        Earl Morse Wilbur Papers (bMS 119)

Lancaster Theological Seminary (LTS)
    Philip Schaff Papers (Ms.Coll. 163)
New-York Historical Society(NYHS)
    Samuel Miller Papers
New York University (NYU)
    Henry Mitchell MacCracken Papers
Princeton Theological Seminary
    Samuel Miller Papers (unless otherwise designated, all references
    to "Miller Papers" indicate those at Princeton Theological
    Seminary)
Union Theological Seminary, Columbia University (UTS)
    Charles Augustus Briggs Papers
    Francis Brown Papers
    John Crosby Brown Papers
    Evangelical Alliance Papers
    Charles Ripley Gillett Papers
    Roswell D. Hitchcock Papers
    Samuel M. Jackson Papers
    Arthur Cushman McGiffert, Jr., Papers
    Edwards Amassa Park Papers
    Philip Schaff Papers
    Henry Boynton Smith Papers
Yale Divinity School
    George Park Fisher Papers (RG 30)
Yale University, Beinecke Library
    Bernadotte Perrin Notebook

All references to archival materials are housed at the institutions at which the professors taught. Archival materials for Philip Schaff are divided between Lancaster Theological Seminary and Union Theological Seminary. In the Notes, the six professors are designated by their last names only.

Abbreviations for Archival Sources

S   Series
SS   Subseries

B   Box
F   Folder
L   Lecture
N   Notebook
Scr   Scrapbook

Introduction: Higher Education and Religion in Nineteenth-Century United States

Epigraph: H. White, "Politics of Historical Interpretation," 59.

1. The Divinity Schools at Harvard and Yale were at first designated "Theological Departments"; Princeton Theological Seminary was known as "The Theological Seminary at Princeton." The University of Chicago and Catholic University of America, both founded ca. 1890, will appear in another study.

2. Naylor, "Theological Seminary," 23, 17, 22, 27; Noll, *Between Faith and Criticism*, 14, and *Princeton and the Republic*, 293. "Humanities" was not an academic division when these schools began.

3. For nomenclature changes, see Brakke, "Early Church in North America: Late Antiquity," esp. 475–76; and Clark, "From Patristics to Early Christian Studies."

4. The original title of Kannnegiesser's article, "Fifty Years of Patristics." Yet, as Kannengiesser himself subsequently conceded, the twentieth-century European scholars he cited had not engaged "the new social dimension of patristics" that so marked the interest of North American scholars ("Future of Patristics," 133).

5. Cherry, *Hurrying Toward Zion*, 90.

6. See especially Diehl, *Americans and German Scholarship*. In 1913, the serious American student of history still went to "Berlin and Leipsic [sic]" (Gooch, *History and Historians*, 396). A school textbook from 1828, depicting a German with a book under his arm, explains, "The Germans read, write, and think a great deal" ([Eliza Robbins], *American Popular Lessons*, 22, cited in Elson, *Guardians of Tradition*, 224).

7. Robinson, "Theological Education in Germany," *BR* 1.3 (July 1831): 435. In 1868, Thomas Arnold still thought the same: Oxford and Cambridge were in reality only *hauts lycées* (*Higher Schools and Universities in Germany*, 209–13). History was not strong in eighteenth-century British universities; in Scotland, moral philosophy reigned (Iggers, "European Context," 236).

8. The peak year for Americans studying in Germany: 1895–1896 (Veysey, *Emergence*, 130). Doubters of the extent and depth of German influence on American education include Lingelbach (*Klio macht Karriere*, 673, 683), D. G. Hart ("Faith and Learning," 114), Turner and Bernard ("Prussian Road"), and (to some extent) Diehl (*Americans and German Scholarship*). None examine seminary education.

9. Marsden, *Soul*, 104, 105. Marsden notes (111n.15) that after 1850 this proportion dropped sharply. In the 1840s, at least 14 of the 47 American students in Germany were studying theology (Diehl, *Americans and German Scholarship*, 56).

10. Ringer, "German Academic Community," 415. Howard reports declining percentages of theology students in German Protestant universities: from 1/3 in 1830 to 13.6 percent in 1892. (Howard, *Religion and the Rise of Historicism*, 18, citing W. Lexis, ed., *Die deutschen Universitäten* [1893], 126).

11. Herbst, *German Historical School*, 4, 13, and see below, Chapters 1 and 3. Halle educated mostly theologians for six decades; 37 percent of American theology students in Germany, e.g., Henry Smith and Roswell Hitchcock, came from small colleges (Diehl, *Americans and German Scholarship*, 58, 62).

12. In 1857, one unnamed dissident (probably Noah Porter of Yale, himself a product of German training) decried the number of American theology students flocking to Germany—as if only Germany held the keys to knowledge. German professors do not necessarily exercise such "sound judgment" as the English ("American Student in Germany," 575, 578–80). Porter here reviews Schaff's book, *Germany* (1857); Bainton identifies Porter as the author, representing him as more favorable to German education ("Yale and German Theology," 296).

13. The professors here studied were conservative but not Fundamentalists; Fundamentalism did not spring from seminaries (Marsden, *Fundamentalism*, 61).

14. Princeton's professors did *not* adopt historicist views (Stewart, "Tethered Theology," 292).

15. On anti-Catholic bias in early modern and modern Protestant scholarship on religion, see J. Z. Smith, *Drudgery Divine*, 19–25, 34, 45, 143.

16. Given the extraordinary growth of Methodism from the late eighteenth to the mid-nineteenth century, its absence from these pages is startling. See statistics and tables in Noll, *America's God*, 165–66. Philip Schaff thought that Methodism might shrink to a sect, "if she does not cultivate the ecumenical sympathies which are congenial to her original spirit" (*Diary* [10/16/1873] UTS, B4).

17. This absence is particularly noticeable in the case of the Union Seminary professors, living in New York. My research suggests that only in the 1890s do "living Jews" (as contrasted with Old Testament "Hebrews") appear—as well as women professors at the "Seven Sisters" colleges. Before the Civil War, Jews made little impact on the national consciousness (Marty, *Righteous Empire*, 124). In 1854–1855, Schaff declared that "the Jews hardly play any part in America," having been bested in business by Yankees (*America*, 54).

18. See Noll, *American Evangelical Christianity*, 12–15, and *America's God*, 187–95, on evangelicalism's rise. For revivalism's contribution, see Marty, *Righteous Empire*, esp. 39, 60–61, 67, 138, 143. In early nineteenth-century Germany, "evangelische" connoted sympathy for the Prussian Union's attempts to unite the Lutheran and Reformed Churches (Conser, *Church and Confession*, 35). Robert Baird (*Religion in America*) makes two divisions: "evangelicals" (including Presbyterians and Congrega-

tionalists); and "unevangelicals" (Jews, Catholics, and many others); see discussion in Brekus, "Interpreting American Religion," 318. Applying supply/demand theory to religious revivals is Finke, "Illusion of Shifting Demand," 114.

19. On "Evangelical" as marking the Union of the Lutheran and Reformed Churches in Prussia under Friedrich Wilhelm III in 1813, see Penzel, *German Education*, 95–96, 109–10. "New School" Presbyterians were somewhat marked by early nineteenth-century revivalism. H. B. Smith, raised as a Unitarian, "converted" to a more orthodox Congregationalism ([E. Smith], *Henry Boynton Smith*, 13–14); he hesitated to accept a professorship at the Presbyterian Union Theological Seminary (155). Smith critiqued Unitarianism in two later book reviews: "Unitarianism of 1859"; "Unitarian Tendencies."

20. In spring 1876, Philip Schaff attended six sessions of Moody and Sankey's ten-week revival in New York. Once, the Union professors dismissed students from classes to attend (to "study practical theology at the feet of the fishermen of Galilee"). Schaff concluded, "If only Christ be preached & souls converted"; "the most remarkable revival in America" (*Diary* [2/14, 3/5, 3/10, 3/12, 3/29, 4/19, 1876] [UTS, B4]).

21. C. Johnson, *Redeeming America*, 7–8; seconded by Noll, *America's God*, 175–76, who labels the Presbyterian/Congregationalist axis as "antienthusiast formalists" (513–14n.4); this small group led in education and publishing (176, 254–55). Their respect for a formal ministry, creeds, history, and an educated interpretation of the Bible rendered them exceptional—more "European" (371). On the nineteenth-century evangelical publishing world, see C. G. Brown, *Word in the World* (although focused more on the popular press than on, e.g., *Bibliotheca Sacra* or *Princeton Review*).

22. Henry Smith marks a transition: he taught Scottish Philosophy and Baconian method at Amherst, but became one of America's experts on German philosophy; see Chapters 1 and 3. C. Johnson (*Redeeming America*, 21–22) associates the "Formalists" with Scottish Common Sense Realism, an association accurate for Samuel Miller of Princeton, but less so for Yale and Union professors. Yet, confronting Darwinian theory, Smith and others appealed to Baconian notions of verification.

23. New theories in geology and biology challenged Baconian induction. The professors' belief in development encouraged evolutionary theory up to the point at which human distinctiveness came into play. Then, they reverted to Genesis 1–3 to press human uniqueness.

24. Murphey, "On the Scientific Study of Religion," 136.

25. Ringenberg, *Christian College*, 37–38. By 1800, there were 21 colleges in America (G. Harris, *Century's Change in Religion*, 3). At mid-century, Baird reported that 45 of America's 119 colleges or universities were of Presbyterian or Congregationalist cast (*Religion in America*, 303, 304). The percentage of college students increased dramatically between 1850 and 1890, outstripping population growth. By 1890, Harvard College had 1,552 students; Yale, 1,286; Princeton, 850 (Comey, "Growth of Colleges," 129–30, statistics on 124–27). For a European perspective, see Lingelbach, *Klio macht Karriere*, chap. 2.2.

26. Roberts and Turner, *Sacred and Secular University*, 20. In 1862, Daniel R. Goodwin, provost of the University of Pennsylvania, pleaded for more religious instruction in colleges ("Religious Instruction in Colleges," 228–38). In 1890, James B. Angell, President of the University of Michigan, claimed that 22 of 24 state universities and agricultural colleges he surveyed had daily chapel services and at 12 chapel was mandatory ("Religious Life in Our State Universities," 366). By 1891, the editors of the new *Educational Review* could mock those desirous to found or fund "narrow" and "petty" sectarian universities: "Imagine a professorship of Baptist chemistry, or Methodist anatomy, or Presbyterian astronomy!" ("Editorial," 64). Marsden (*Soul*, 239) emphasizes the Low Church characteristics of American universities: pragmatic, traditionless, competitive, dependent on the market, anti-Catholic, scientific in spirit, congenial to business and advertising. They equated Christianity with "democracy and service to the nation," and understood "freedom as free enterprise for professors and individual choice for students." Marsden deems the University of Chicago the "quintessential Protestant institution."

27. See Kelley, *Yale*, 42, 80. In 1851, a seminary professor described the religious regimen at Harvard and Yale Colleges in the 1700s: morning prayers included readings from the Old Testament in Hebrew, and evening prayers from the New Testament in Greek. Freshmen read the (Westminster) Assembly's Catechism in Greek; Sophomores read Ezra and Nehemiah in Chaldee (Aramaic); Juniors read the Syriac Testament; and Seniors studied "divinity": see Smith, "Theological Encyclopedia," 1851, Hastings notes (S5, B1, F3, 231–32). On Hebrew study in early America, see Goldman, *God's Sacred Tongue*; on its strength at Harvard, see Williams, "Introduction," 4.

28. For example, at the University of Wisconsin; see Katz, "Religious Studies in State Universities," 19, citing Curti and Carstensen, *University of Wisconsin*, 1: 407— and attendance at daily prayers was required. On the religious tone of Midwestern state universities, see Longfield, "From Evangelicalism to Liberalism," 46–73.

29. College presidents were apparently deemed capable of teaching such a course: see Kelley, *Yale*, 42, 80; L. Stevenson, *Scholarly Means to Evangelical Ends*, 55; Ringenberg, *Christian College*, 67; Roberts and Turner, *Sacred and Secular University*, 21; Reuben, *Making*, 22–23. In 1857, Philip Schaff was informed that he had been elected President of Heidelberg College; his teaching duties would include courses on the Evidences of Christianity, and Mental and Moral Philosophy—and his salary, $1000 annually (M[oses] Kieffer [and Board of Trustees] to Schaff, Tiffin, Ohio, 1/19/1857 [LTS, B1, F02); I thank librarians at Heidelberg College for assistance. For Smith's description of "Evidences," see his "Theological Encyclopedia," 1851, Hastings notes (S5, B1, F3, 234).

30. Turner, "Secularization and Sacralization," 75.

31. Reuben, *Making*, 88, citing *Annual Reports of the President* for 1871 (6–7, 50–52); 1872 (4); and 1877 (19–20). President Barnard of Columbia searched in vain for someone to teach "the foundations of religion"; failing, in 1877 he hired a psychologist instead.

32. Reuben, *Making*, 89, 94. At Yale in 1890, "Evidences" was folded into a junior-year course on logic and psychology (Kelley, *Yale*, 293).

33. Veysey, *Emergence*, 2.

34. Henry Adams, *Education of Henry Adams*, 288.

35. Reuben, *Making*, 94, 95, 102 (the latter taught as Anthropology). At Yale in the 1880s or 1890s, undergraduates could enroll in Divinity School courses (Kelley, *Yale*, 294), perhaps accounting for the increase.

36. By the last third of the century, new work in philology, archeology, world religions, and text criticism had changed the discipline (Noll, *Princeton and the Republic*, 12). America did not, however, model itself on Holland, where the theological course was redesigned as "Science of Religion" (Smith, "Theological and Literary Intelligence," *PQPR* 3.11 [July 1874]: 576–77).

37. Ringenberg, *Christian College*, 69. Earlier, Harvard Divinity School's introduction of "Criticism and Interpretation of the Scriptures" was deemed radical (Solt, *Rise and Development*, 82).

38. Marsden, *Soul*, 209; Goodspeed, *William Rainey Harper*, 76; on Harper at Chicago, Wind, *Bible and the University*, 90; Harper, "Shall the Theological Curriculum Be Modified?" 56, 65.

39. Cherry, *Hurrying Toward Zion*, 118. The Society's acronym, NABI, means "prophet" in Hebrew.

40. For Roman Catholic protests over use of the "Protestant" Bible in public schools, see Chapter 7.

41. J. F. Wilson, "Introduction," 13; Roberts and Turner, *Sacred and Secular University*, 80. Although Greek and Latin language instruction declined, the study of classical "culture" thrived: see Winterer, *Culture of Classicism*, 6, 110, 121. For earlier (failed) attempts at Princeton to introduce a B.S. degree ("certificate") that exempted students from Greek and Latin, see H. Miller, *Revolutionary College*, 173, 275, 280. Samuel Miller urged his sons to concentrate on Greek and Latin in college at Princeton (*Letters from a Father*, 133). Yale's George Fisher defended the necessity of Greek in colleges; see his "Study of Greek," 63–78, urging new methods and citing Matthew Arnold's witticism, "the aorist was made for man, not man for the aorist" (76).

42. Roberts and Turner, *Sacred and Secular University*, 108. Humanities became "a secular substitute for religiously based moral education" (Reuben, *Making*, 211), as did "liberal culture" (Turner, "Secularization and Sacralization," 80–81, 89).

43. Marsden, *Soul*, 336. At the University of Chicago, Harper transferred Semitic Languages and Literatures, Biblical and Patristic Greek, and Comparative Religion from the Divinity School to the University, but they were not popular; professors complained about low enrollments (Reuben, *Making*, 99, 115, 117–18).

44. Cherry, *Hurrying Toward Zion*, 118.

45. Schools now called "universities" were "colleges" until the later nineteenth century; Yale, e.g., took the name "university" only in 1887 (Wayland, *Theological Department*, 154). Questioning whether *any* nineteenth-century American university,

with the exception of Johns Hopkins, was based on a German model are Turner and Bernard, "Prussian Road," 9.

46. Tappan, *University Education*, 48, 50, 78; on Tappan's role at Michigan, see Turner and Bernard, "Prussian Road," 12–19. At Columbia in the 1870s and early 1880s, John Burgess alleged similar conditions (see his posthumously published *Reminiscences*). Nicholas Murray Butler of Columbia also complained ("Introduction," xiv, xxiii–xxv).

47. Tappan, *University Education*, 79, 88. If the proposed university could use the Astor Library and the Brooklyn Observatory, Tappan mused, it could start up with $330,000, 50,000 books, and six fully endowed and ten partially endowed professorships (96–97, 97n.). Tappan has been called the first great "Germanizing" (or "Prussianizing") university president in America (Albisetti, "German Influence," 234).

48. Tappan, *University Education*, 95. As president of the University of Michigan (1852–1863), Tappan required students to attend a Sunday service of their parents' choice and enlisted faculty to hold daily prayer services ("Idea of the True University," 2: 515–45, at 538).

49. Naylor, "Theological Seminary," 23, 17, 22, 27. Theological education, Tappan thought, should *not* be incorporated into universities (*University Education*, 50, 30, 98, 94); for the 1880s, see Burgess of Columbia (*Reminiscences*, 203 and Appendix 1, "American University" [1884]).

50. Naylor, "Theological Seminary," 23, 27; Pranger, *Philip Schaff*, 172–73.

51. Knowles, "Importance of Theological Institutions," Appendix, Note C, 10. Princeton Seminary (founded in 1812) in two decades had educated the most divinity students (537); Andover (founded in 1808) ranked second, with 514.

52. See statistics in Baird, *Religion in America*, 322 (Andover and General Theological Seminary each had five professors; Princeton and Union four); and in Society of Clergymen, "Thoughts on the State of Theological Science," 762, 758; enrollments in European universities, which include theological faculties: approximately 2700 at Vienna, 2090 at Berlin, 1300 at Munich, 5200 at Oxford, 5530 at Cambridge, 2200 at Edinburgh, 1350 at Dublin, 7000 at Paris (762). In a report compiled in 1924, of 123 reporting seminaries, 42 percent still had fewer than five full-time faculty members (Remus, "Origins," 117n.10, citing statistics from Robert L. Kelly, *Theological Education in America* [1924]).

53. Remus, "Origins," 116–17.

54. Society of Clergymen, "Thoughts on the State of Theological Science," 764.

55. Leslie, *Gentlemen and Scholars*, 224. Kelley (*Yale*, 202) claims that by midcentury, 80 percent of Divinity School students held the B.A.

56. For information on Andover, Harvard, and Vanderbilt, see, respectively, Solt, *Rise and Development*, 70; Remus, "Origins," 92n.38; Cherry, *Hurrying Toward Zion*, 132.

57. Gillett, "Detailed History" II: 531.

58. Naylor ("Theological Seminary," 22), citing earlier statistics, dubiously claims

that at Andover in the ante-bellum era, over 90 percent of its students had completed "a course of liberal education"; at Harvard Divinity School from 1868–1871, only 14–26 percent held B.A.s (Remus, "Origins," 118n.13).

59. Naylor, "Theological Seminary," 22, 23. In 1850–1851, many more theological than medical students at Yale held the B.A. (Kelley, *Yale*, 202).

60. Kuklick, *Puritans in Babylon*, 100. His claim of "collapse" is strong; others might concede that pastoral education declined at university-based divinity schools. Tracing the development of "Oriental" studies in America, Kuklick claims that to "understand the growth of ancient Near Eastern studies is to understand the maturation of the American university and its connection to Germany" (6).

61. Remus, "Origins," 118: of 419 Ph.D.s awarded at Harvard University in 1896–1908, 36 were in religious/theological fields (Semitic philology, biblical and patristic Greek, philosophy of religion, metaphysics, ethics, and theology).

62. Schaff, "Dr. Fisher's Manual of Church History," *New-York Independent*, March 28, 1889, clipping (UTS, B6, Scr2, 161, adding that in another prominent [unnamed] seminary, modern and American church history were not mentioned until 1887).

63. Schaff, *History of the Apostolic Church*, vol. 1, in *Reformed and Catholic*, ed. Yrigoyen and Bricker, 315.

64. For discussion, see Rodgers, "Exceptionalism," 21–40.

65. Bowden, *Church History in the Age of Science*, 36, 37; Woods, *History of Andover*, 186–97, esp. 188–89.

66. For description and discussion of these texts, see Chapter 6.

67. For Schaff's Biblical conservatism, see his *Theological Propaedeutic*, Part II, 374; and Chapter 3 below.

68. Baird, *Religion in America*, 585.

69. Veysey, *Emergence*, 174–75. On specialization at Harvard, a result of the elective system, see Hawkins, *Between Harvard and America*, 68–69. Burgess, describing Columbia in the 1870s and 1880s, decries the lack of research (*Reminiscences*, 203–4, 364, 367).

70. Marsden, *Soul*, 81; Diehl, *Americans and German Scholarship*, 96.

71. Storr, *Beginning of the Future*, 19.

72. Marsden, *Soul*, 81.

73. Diehl, *Americans and German Scholarship*, 90.

74. Diehl, *Americans and German Scholarship*, 44–45, 8: a "field," Diehl reminds readers, is "a mechanism of enclosure." These differing approaches are reflected in the assumptions surrounding classical studies in nineteenth-century Germany and England; see Grafton, "Polyhistor into *Philolog*," 184.

75. Hawkins, "University Identity," 293. In nineteenth-century sources, "Department" sometimes describes an aspect of study.

76. Lingelbach, *Klio macht Karriere*, 261. In 1871, when Henry Adams took a position at Harvard, there were only two Full Professors in history; Adams was to fill the

thousand-year gap between ancient and modern history. (Some medievalists today may think that little has changed.) Adams speaks of joining the "Department of History"—but he wrote in the early twentieth century (*Education of Henry Adams*, 229, 235). At Columbia in 1876, there were only seven or eight professors and a couple of tutors for all of Arts and Sciences (Burgess, *Reminiscences*, 159, 161).

77. Higham, "Matrix of Specialization," 4.

78. On the early years of the American Historical Association, see Jameson, "American Historical Association" and "Early Days of the American Historical Association." For Harvard professors' role in the formation of the AHA and the *American Historical Review*, see Emerton [and Morison], "History, 1838–1929," 157.

79. Veysey, "Plural Organized Worlds," 73–76; Saunders, *Searching the Scriptures*, 2–3.

80. Herbst, *German Historical School*, 40. Noll argues that specialization "secularized the academy, confused the pulpit, and alienated at least large numbers in the pew" (*Between Faith and Criticism*, 14).

81. Lingelbach, *Klio macht Karriere*, 680–81; the same pattern obtains in France. For women professors' entrance to the academy, see the correspondence of H. B. Adams, with references to Smith College in particular (*Historical Scholarship*, ed. Holt). Female historians at women's colleges were often not considered the equals of male historians. On American women's colleges, see Horowitz, *Alma Mater*; on women historians, B. G. Smith, *Gender of History*. The first 90 presidents of SBL between 1880 and 1981 were all men (Saunders, *Searching the Scriptures*, 3–4).

82. Diehl, *Americans and German Scholarship*, 22. Also see Novick, *That Noble Dream*, chap. 2.

83. Rudolph, *American College*, 407. The University of Chicago Press came only slightly later (Goodspeed, *William Rainey Harper*, 111).

84. On some of the nineteenth-century journals frequently cited in this study, see Mott, *History of American Magazines*, 1: 370–74; on payment, 1: 504–5. Still in 1900, scholars were apparently paid for their essays in both professional and popular journals, e.g., A. Howard Clark to H. B. Adams, Washington, D.C., 5/22/1900, in *Historical Scholarship*, ed. Holt, 279–80.

85. The journal, in print from 1825 to 1888, often changed titles: *Biblical Repertory and Theological Review*; *Biblical Repertory and Princeton Review*; *Presbyterian Quarterly and Princeton Review*; *Princeton Review*; and finally *New Princeton Review*.

86. Selden, *Princeton Theological Seminary*, 47, 49, 50. Hodge taught "Oriental and Biblical literature" from 1822 to 1840, when he became professor of "exegetical and didactic theology" (Dulles, "Princeton Theological Seminary," 329, 330).

87. Perry Miller considered the *Mercersburg Review* the most sophisticated journal of its time ("Editor's Introduction" to Schaff, *America*, xxiv).

88. Saunders, *Searching the Scriptures*, 3–4.

89. Ryan, *Studies in Early Graduate Education*, 130. On Harper's encouragement of journals at the University of Chicago, see Goodspeed, *William Rainey Harper*, 141–

42. The now prominent *Harvard Theological Review* was not founded until 1908 (Reynolds, "Later Years," 197).

90. By 1830, the libraries at Andover, Yale Divinity, Princeton Seminary, and Gettysburg each reported more than 6000 volumes (Naylor, "Theological Seminary," 24); by 1899, Union Seminary had the most (112,000–115,000 titles), ranking tenth among libraries at all American institutions ([Librarian], "Library of the Union Theological Seminary," April 1899; Francis Brown Papers, B3, F1, 8, 11).

91. Hawkins, *Between Harvard and America*, 67–68; Lingelbach, *Klio macht Karriere*, 159. Ephraim Emerton of Harvard wrote a report on his sabbatical in Europe for university officials; see Emerton to "My dear Mr. Lane," 4/15/1900, Riva, Lago di Garda, Austrian Tyrol ("Chest of 1900," B2, HU Archives; "Mr. Lane" is perhaps Charles Chester Lane, Editor-in-Chief of the Harvard Quinquennial Catalogue and the Harvard University Directory). Emerton hopes fully paid sabbaticals will be made compulsory to forestall professors' falling deeper into "mental and physical ruts" (1b), to broaden horizons, and to "provide a reasonable amount of positive diversion and recreation" (2).

92. Oleson and Voss, "Introduction," x; Hawkins, *Between Harvard and America*, chap. 3 (although the elective system was introduced before Eliot's presidency; 92–93). By 1894, the only required courses at Harvard were rhetoric and a modern language; the latter was soon dropped (Rudolph, *American College*, 294). In his inaugural address in 1869, Eliot defended electives as traditional "in this College during the past forty years" ("President Eliot's Inaugural Address," lxv). For a description of the system, see *American Higher Education*, ed. Hofstadter and Smith, 2: 737–47. The rigor of the Harvard undergraduate curriculum might be questioned: according to a 1904 survey, the average time undergraduates spent outside the classroom per three-hour course was less than three-and-a-half hours a week (Thwing, "Should College Students Study?" 230).

93. Eliot, *University Administration* (1908), 150, cited in Rudolph, *American College*, 304–5. Under the elective system, many Harvard undergraduates enrolled in Divinity School courses (Shepard, *God's People*, 74–75).

94. Rudolph, *American College*, 305. Eliot's view was championed by President Frederick Barnard of Columbia. Harvard's commitment to the "new education," he noted, was gaining it students at the expense of other New England colleges; see Barnard, "Report: Changes in the Curriculum" (6/6/1870), 91–92. At Brown, President Francis Wayland's 1850 "Report to the Corporation of Brown University, on Changes in the System of Collegiate Education" criticized Brown's restrictive requirements (especially in classical languages), and suggested a modified elective system (Bronson, *History of Brown University*, 263–69). President Barnard in 1879 also (shockingly) advocated that women be admitted to Columbia College; amid controversy, a collegiate course for women was established in 1883, and the college bearing Barnard's name came into being in 1889: see the Report (11/4/1918) of these incidents by Butler,

"Report: The Education of Women," 190–91. At Columbia, "Germanophiles" Burgess and Butler opposed coeducation (Albisetti, "German Influence," 236, 237).

95. For one example, see Howison, "Harvard 'New Education'," 577–89.

96. McCosh, "New Departure," 22. For a sympathetic treatment of McCosh's position in the McCosh-Eliot debates, see D. G. Hart, *University Gets Religion*, 23–27.

97. Burgess, "American University," in *Reminiscences*, 352–53. College students should be able to enter advanced work in *any* branch of Arts and Sciences (365).

98. McCosh, "New Departure," 4–5, 21. Novels were also in bad favor with Samuel Miller (*Letters from a Father*, 152–57).

99. McCosh, "New Departure," 20. The American professor's role of enforcing discipline and doing "police duty" was contrasted (unfavorably) to German academia by J. M. Hart, *German Universities*, 264; in Germany, the professor lectures as "one gentleman speaking to another." Paulsen notes (*German Universities*, 203) that German university students tended to be 20 to 25 years old. Younger American students appear to have needed advice on many points: see Miller's *Letters from a Father* and *Letters on Clerical Manners*.

100. McCosh, "New Departure," 22, 23. A modified version of electives with seven undergraduate tracks was introduced in the 1880s at Johns Hopkins under the rubric of the "group system" (Gilman, "Group System," 572–74). Gilman became the first president of Johns Hopkins after serving at the University of California; on the religious tone he inculcated, see D. G. Hart, "Faith and Learning," 107–45. Cornell also had a version of the "group system" (Hawkins, *Between Harvard and America*, 84).

101. McCosh, "New Departure," 15.

102. Coulter, "University Spirit," 368.

103. On the seminar's development in Germany and the clash between ideals of research and of *Bildung*, see Grafton, "Polyhistor into *Philolog*." Caution on how "advanced" seminars were is raised by Turner and Bernard, "Prussian Road," 16, 23–24. Diehl (*Americans and German Scholarship*, Introduction, chaps. 1–4) ponders the (relative) failure of the first Americans studying Humanities in Germany to influence academic programs in America.

104. Jameson, "American Historical Association," 3; see Charles Kendall Adams's letter to H. B. Adams, Ithaca, N.Y., 2/9/1886, in *Historical Scholarship*, ed. Holt, 79; on this historian and his seminar at Michigan (with cautions), see Turner and Bernard, "Prussian Road," 22–23, 25. Henry Adams declared that he developed his seminar method only because he knew so little about his subject (*Education of Henry Adams*, 237). For other versions of the development of the seminar in languages, see Storr, *Beginnings of Graduate Education*, 24–26.

105. H. B. Adams, "New Methods," in Adams, *Methods*, 99–107; see below, Chapter 2, n. 100.

106. H. B. Adams, "New Methods," 64, 65. For the development of the seminar system in Germany, see Paulsen, *German Universities*, 157–59. Adams was offered (and rejected) the deanship of the Graduate Department at the new University of Chicago:

see William R. Harper to H. B. Adams, New Haven, 10/13/1890; and Adams to Harper, Baltimore, 5/1/1891, in *Historical Scholarship*, ed. Holt, 138, 156–57. Adams's reasons: the University of Chicago was Baptist, theological, full of "new people" rather than "society," lacked literature, was merely a "local university," and suffered from a bad climate (157).

107. H. B. Adams, "New Methods," 70, 78, 103, and passim. He praises Ephraim Emerton, who introduced the seminar method in his Harvard courses, including those at the "Harvard Annex," i.e., what became Radcliffe. Adams mentions Emerton's seminars on "the Papacy and the German Empire, the origin of mediaeval institutions, the rise of French communes, etc." (90). Emerton shared this "scientific" vision of historical work: see "Historical Seminary in American Teaching," 193–95.

108. H. B. Adams, "New Methods," 5.

109. See Turner and Bernard, "Prussian Road," 9, 33, 34, for discussion of American distinction between the undergraduate college and the graduate school.

110. Storr, *Beginning of the Future*, 20–21, 23–24, 33–35.

111. The importance of fellowships is emphasized by historian of education Rudolph, *American College*, 337. See Bristed, *Five Years in an English University*. Throughout, Bristed faults educational laxity in America and praises specialization at Cambridge (e.g., 19, 21, 23, 25, 358–59, 511–12). Burgess of Columbia, however, decried the English university system in the 1870s-1880s (*Reminiscences*, 199). H. B. Smith notes that Oxford provided for 550 Fellows, and Cambridge, for 431; "only a small minority give any instruction" ("Theological and Literary Intelligence," *ATR* 3.10 [April 1861]: 390).

112. Rudolph, *American College*, 337. Johns Hopkins gave 20 fellowships a year in its early days—a practice protested by President Eliot of Harvard, who objected to paying students to attend (so Herbst, *German Historical School*, 33, citing Hall, "American Universities and the Training of Teachers," 152). Harvard gave travel fellowships to graduates, eleven of whom in 1889–1890 went to Europe, mostly to Germany (Lingelbach, *Klio macht Karriere*, 263).

113. Naylor, "Theological Seminary," 24–25, citing amounts offered at various schools. In 1829, Samuel Miller hoped for some fellowships for men preparing for seminary teaching; he seems not to envisage study abroad ("Importance of Mature Preparatory Study," 29). At Yale, George Fisher argued that churches should contribute to divinity students' support, just as the national government pays for students at West Point (*Theological Education in Yale College*, 6–7, cited in Knoff, *Yale Divinity School*, 83–84).

114. Storr argues that the lack of fellowship aid was a chief deterrent to the development of graduate education in pre-Civil War America (*Beginnings of Graduate Education*, 28, 65–66, 105). Storr did not include theological seminaries in his study.

115. Yale *Annual Catalogue*, 1876–1877, 80, cited in Knoff, *Yale Divinity School*, 219.

116. *Prentiss, Union Theological Seminary*, 95–96; Schaff, "Reply" [to *Epistola Congratulatoria*], in *Semi-Centennial of Philip Schaff*, 18). Francis Brown is the "Brown"

of the "Brown-Driver-Briggs" Hebrew dictionary, on which generations of seminary students were raised.

117. Prentiss, *Union Theological Seminary*, 95–96.

118. Gillett, "Detailed History" II: 421, 422. For Ephraim Emerton's assignment of such topics for investigation among Harvard students later in the century, see below, 71–72.

119. Turner and Bernhard ("Prussian Road," 16) stress that for many students, "research" meant "looking up information independently," not original exploration.

120. Veysey, *Emergence*, 50; Kelley, *Yale*, 185 (the University of Pennsylvania was second, in 1871); Rudolph, *American College*, 335. By 1869, Yale had granted 12 (Eliot, "New Education I," 207; on 208, Eliot writes "13"). In 1872, the "Graduate Department" at Harvard was transmuted into a "Graduate School"; the first Ph.D.s (in History) were given in 1873 (Hawkins, *Between Harvard and America*, 55–56; Emerton [and Morison], "History, 1838–1929," 163, 156.

121. Eliot, "New Education I," 208. Those who did not hold a B.A. had to pass an admission exam.

122. Gilman, "Idea of the University," 353–67, at 358, 356: "Instruction by investigation is the key-note of university life." Gilman argued the need for university presses, sufficient professorial pay, time for attendance at conferences and for work abroad or at other venues in America, and for the security of pensions. Against technocrats, Gilman defended the idea of "liberal education," including study of French and German, principles and methods of scientific inquiry, great literatures of the world (and so on) ("Is It Worth While to Uphold Any Longer the Idea of Liberal Education?" 105–19).

123. Oleson and Voss, "Introduction," xii. Kelley (*Yale*, 257) claims that in 1870, there were only 44 graduate students in the United States, 24 of them at Yale.

124. Rudolph, *American College*, 395, citing W. H. Cowley, "European Influences upon American Higher Education," *ER* 20 (1939): 183.

125. Confirmed by Remus, "Origins," 118: for example, of the 419 Ph.D.s awarded at Harvard between 1896 and 1908, 36 dealt with topics in religion, but were given in such areas as Semitic philology, Greek, and philosophy.

126. Welch, *Graduate Education*, 230; Bainton, *Yale and the Ministry*, 210–11, 265.

127. Remus, "Origins," 120, 121; and tables in Welch, *Graduate Education*, 230–31. At Union in 1907, Francis Brown reported that more men were seeking four or five years of study, not just three ("The Seminary and Scholarship," 14). At Princeton Seminary, the Th.D. was changed to a Ph.D. in 1973: information supplied by Kenneth Henke, Reference Archivist, Princeton Theological Seminary; also see Welch, *Graduate Education*, 231.

128. Kelley, *Yale*, 340. Welch claims the Ph.D. in Religion was instituted at Yale in 1869 (*Graduate Education*, 230), but other sources disagree. Kelley (*Yale*, 254) states that only in 1879 did Yale begin offering *one* extra year of graduate work in religion/theology—not sufficient for a Ph.D.

129. The Department was allegedly to supply the spiritual tone that chapel had afforded: so Gabriel, *Religion and Learning at Yale*, 228, citing an action of the Yale Corporation in 1926.

130. Bainton, *Yale and the Ministry*, 209, 265; Keck, "Epilogue," 273; Cherry, *Hurrying Toward Zion*, 121; Remus, "Origins," 120. I thank Dean Harold Attridge for information on Yale Divinity School.

131. Remus, "Origins," 124, 125.

132. Welch, *Graduate Education*, 230–31.

133. Statistics from *Graduate Education*, ed. Welch, 205: almost twice as many lacking a seminary or other such degree than Ph.D. students in religion somewhat earlier.

134. Some medical schools (University of Pennsylvania, King's College [Columbia], and Harvard) were founded in the late eighteenth century; law schools (with the exception of Litchfield Law School) were products of the nineteenth century.

135. Grant Wacker suggests that most seminaries saw their first duty as serving churches' pastoral needs, and hence had no special concern to foster graduate education.

Chapter 1. The Institutions and the Professors

Epigraphs: Diehl, *American and German Scholarship*, 50; August Tholuck, of Henry Boynton Smith, reported in [E. Smith], *Henry Boynton Smith*, 1.

1. "Union, Andover, Harvard, Yale, and Princeton were significant academic centers, because they had the most books": so G. T. Miller, *Piety and Intellect*, 451.

2. The Union-Columbia connection came in the 1890s (qualified Union students could take courses at Columbia and NYU). See F. Brown, "Internal Development and Expansion," 340–41; Briggs, "Theological Education and Its Needs," clipping (Briggs Papers, S29, SS1, B1, Scr3, 637–38, 642). John Burgess dates the association to "soon" after 1891 (*Reminiscences*, 239).

3. The Protestant seminaries founded in the 1820s never emerged as centers of advanced theological education (Smith, *History*, 78); by 1840, there were some 30 (Selden, *Princeton Theological Seminary*, 33).

4. The Dutch Reformed Seminary at New Brunswick dates to 1784 (Selden, *Princeton Theological Seminary*, 12).

5. Trinterud, "Charles Hodge," 26–27. In 1807, Samuel Miller, then a Presbyterian minister in New York City, hoped that Andover would be "the centre of everything great and good to the eastward of New York"—a deprecation of Harvard and Yale (Miller to Mr. [Edward Dorr] Griffin, 12/28/1807, in S. Miller, [Jr.], *Life* I: 233). On Andover, G. Miller, *Piety and Intellect*, chaps. 3–4; Bendroth, *School of the Church*.

6. Smith, *History*, 78. When Stuart joined the Andover faculty in 1810, he knew no German, was deficient in Hebrew, and ignorant of Semitic languages, yet three years later published *Hebrew Grammar Without the Points* (Loetscher, *Facing the Enlighten-*

ment, 214; J. W. Brown, *Rise of Biblical Criticism*, chap. 6; Woods, *History of Andover*, 151–54). On Stuart, see Park, "Discourse Delivered at the Funeral of Prof. Moses Stuart," and W. Adams, *Discourse on the Life and Services of Prof. Moses Stuart*.

7. Fraser, *Schooling the Preachers*, 40.

8. Statistic in chap. 1, App.9 in Knoff, *Yale Divinity School*, 481, 490. In 1908, Andover reconnected (but did not merge) with Harvard Divinity School (Reynolds, "Later Years," 188–89, 192).

9. On the Seminary's development, see J. G. Wilson, *Centennial History*, 156–57; Chorley, *Men and Movements*; Mullin, *Episcopal Vision*.

10. See Chapter 2 for Coxe's editing the Ante-Nicene Fathers series.

11. DeMille, *Catholic Movement*, 22. On Bishop Hobart: Wilson, *Centennial History*, 107, 156–57; O'Brien, "Introduction," in Walworth, *Oxford Movement*, vi–x; on Samuel Miller's clash with him, Noll, *America's God*, 238–39. The high-church movement of Hobart is distinguished from the later Ritualist and Anglo-Catholic parties (Chorley, *Men and Movements*, 147, 167, 172–80, 188–90, chap. 12; Mullin, *Episcopal Vision*, xiii).

12. Walworth, *Oxford Movement*, 141, 175, 84. Episcopal bishop of New York circa 1840 and professor at General Seminary Benjamin Onderdonk advocated the Oxford Movement in America (Chorley, *Men and Movements*, 197–99); the low-church party unseated him in 1844 (Walworth, *Oxford Movement*, 127–33, 135–36).

13. Welch, *Graduate Education in Religion*, 230.

14. On Mercersburg, see Richards, *History of the Theological Seminary*, esp. chaps. 17–21, 27, 32; Binkley, *Mercersburg Theology*; Nichols, *Romanticism in American Theology*; Nichols, ed., *Mercersburg Theology*; Kuklick, *Churchmen and Philosophers*, 172–77; Shriver, "Philip Schaff: Heresy at Mercersburg," 18–55; and Conser, *Church and Confession*, 274–95.

15. The Seminary moved to Lancaster in 1871. Lancaster does not offer a Ph.D. or Th.D.

16. Allen to Russell Carpenter, Nantucket, 7/11/1880 (F62), describes Toy as a "philologue and Orientalist of some note, an enthusiast . . . in Arabic and Syriac." Educated at the University of Berlin, Toy was dismissed from Southern Baptist Seminary in Louisville in 1879 and became Hancock Professor of Hebrew and Oriental Languages at Harvard (Marsden, *Fundamentalism*, 103; Olbricht, "Intellectual Ferment," 104).

17. The College was legally renamed "Princeton University" only in 1896 (Selden, *Princeton Theological Seminary*, 83), although no graduate school was constituted until 1910 (Leslie, *Gentlemen and Scholars*, 8). By the 1820s, Presbyterians had emerged as leaders in American higher education (Marsden, *Soul*, 68); by 1860, they had 49 colleges (Tewksbury, *Founding of American Colleges*, 69, citing the 1860 U.S. Census Report).

18. Selden, *Princeton Theological Seminary*, 12, 24–25. A first effort at ministerial education at the College in 1803–1806 failed (H. Miller, *Revolutionary College*, 246–47).

19. Noll, "Founding of Princeton Seminary," 85–86. Samuel Miller's daughter

described the Seminary's founding in "Ms. of Ms. Mary Miller, Daughter of Dr. Miller, Describing His Help in Founding Princeton Theological Seminary" (B20, F54).

20. Selden, *Princeton Theological Seminary*, 22–23. Samuel Smith questioned whether polygamy was contrary to the law of nature (Loetscher, *Facing the Enlightenment*, 115, 117); on Smith's rocky career and resignation (Noll, "Founding of Princeton Seminary," 96–102).

21. Noll, *Princeton and the Republic*, 269. See letter of Samuel Miller to Dr. Ashbel Green, 3/12/1805, advocating the establishment of a theological school, cited in Loetscher, *Facing the Enlightenment*, 109; and Miller's letter to Green of 5/10/1808, in Miller, [Jr.], *Life* I: 240–41; Selden, *Princeton Theological Seminary*, 26, 27.

22. Noll, "Founding of Princeton Seminary," 83, citing *Minutes of the General Assembly of the Presbyterian Church . . . from . . . 1789 to . . . 1820*, 499–501.

23. Remus, "Origins," 124. A professor (George Thomas) was appointed in 1940 to start a department (Cherry, *Hurrying Toward Zion*, 110).

24. At Princeton, early Christian history was *not* paired with Bible/New Testament. The third appointee (in 1822) at the Seminary, Charles Hodge, was "Professor of Oriental and Biblical Literature" (Miller, [Jr.], *Life* II: 46), although he later achieved fame as a theologian. In the early 1860s, the faculty was increased to five; Ethics and Apologetics were added in 1871 (Selden, *Princeton Theological Seminary*, 56). In 1812, the College of New Jersey employed (only) two professors (Kerr, *Sons of the Prophets*, viii–ix; Loetscher, *Facing the Enlightenment*, 132).

25. Miller, "Duty of the Church to Take Measures," 41, 43 (citing Eusebius, *Church History* V.10 and Jerome, "Works" [unspecified edition], I. 105).

26. James Clement Moffat, Helena Professor of Church History from 1861 to 1888, wrote little on the subject (Dulles, "Princeton Theological Seminary," 341; see Moffat, *Outlines of Church History*). Moffat's most noted work was a *Comparative History of Religions* (1871ff.).

27. J. R. Stevenson, *Historical Position of Princeton Seminary*, 4–6, citing "Plan of the Seminary," 26.

28. Selden, *Princeton Theological Seminary*, 40. At the Seminary's semi-centennial celebration, Hodge made his celebrated remark, "I am not afraid to say that a new idea never originated in the Seminary" (*Proceedings of the Semi-Centennial Celebration*, 52, cited in Selden, *Princeton Theological Seminary*, 72). The Seminary was conservative from its inception (Noll, "Founding of Princeton Seminary," 109).

29. Kuklick, *Churchmen and Philosophers*, 79. On the early dominance of the Scottish Common Sense Philosophy, later tempered by James McCosh, see Noll, *Princeton and the Republic*, chap. 2, esp. 290–91; Hoeveler, Jr., *James McCosh and the Scottish Intellectual Tradition*, chaps. 4–6.

30. Miller to Professor [William?] Cogswell of East Windsor Theological Institute, Princeton, 7/24/1834, cited in Miller, [Jr.], *Life* II: 407. Miller was "Old School" Presbyterian.

31. Tinterud, "Charles Hodge," 33, 35; Selden, *Princeton Theological Seminary*, 45, 53.

32. Selden, *Princeton Theological Seminary*, 31, 41.

33. By 1867: see tables in Knoff, *Yale Divinity School*, App. 9, 483.

34. Leslie, *Gentlemen and Scholars*, 230. McCosh, responding to Charles Eliot's criticism of the elementary character of traditional college curricula, claimed that only one in ten undergraduates should be encouraged to take post-graduate work or special studies. Princeton, he adds, encourages such work by offering seven or eight endowed Fellowships, and always accommodates 30 to 50 post-graduate students (McCosh, "New Departure," 14–15).

In 1913, a Graduate College—a separate entity from the Graduate School—was established, modeled on the Honours Colleges of English universities (West, *Graduate College*, 24). West was Dean of the Graduate School; on his battle with Woodrow Wilson over the graduate school, see Leslie, *Gentlemen and Scholars*, 150–51; Veysey, *Emergence*, 246–47. Marsden claims the graduate school at Princeton was formed in part to oppose the favoring of undergraduate education by Francis Patton, president of the College; Patton was edged out, becoming president of the Seminary (*Soul*, 223, 229).

35. Committee of the Board of Directors [of Princeton Theological Seminary], "Modern School of the Prophets," 10, 9. Graduates of colleges other than Princeton could, while at seminary, pursue a Master's degree at the University.

36. Information supplied by Kenneth Henke, Reference Archivist, Princeton Theological Seminary; cf. Welch, *Graduate Education*, 231; Cherry, *Hurrying Toward Zion*, 110.

37. The Hollis Chair of Divinity at Harvard was the first endowed chair in the British Colonies (Ringenberg, *Christian College*, 54). Ware's prime duty was to teach the Greek New Testament. Baird, writing in 1844/1856, rues this development: For 150 years, Harvard was "a precious fountain of living water for the Church of God. But alas! For the last half century or nearly so, it has been in the hands of men who hold 'another gospel' than that held by its pious founders" (*Religion in America*, 307). Alarmed Congregationalists founded Andover Seminary three years later (C. Wright, "Early Period," 23).

38. C. Wright, "Early Period," 27. In 1916, librarian emeritus R. S. Morison cautioned against fixing just one date for the School's founding ("First Half Century," 13–14, 16, 17).

39. Eliot, "Harvard Divinity School," 209, 211; similarly, "Statement of President Eliot," 24–25. In his Centennial Anniversary speech, Eliot sharply contrasted Harvard's freedom with the control the Presbyterian Church attempted to keep over its seminaries, Princeton in particular ("Theological Education," 65–67).

40. The phrase of Ahlstrom, "Middle Period," 132–33, 104—although in 1871–1872, Divinity School students were urged to attend lectures on early Christianity given in

the University by Professor of Greek Evangelinus A. Sophocles (133n.135, citing *Annual Report* of 1871–1872, 55).

41. Jared Sparks became McLean Professor of Ancient and Modern History in 1838 (possibly 1839). Sparks began his career at Harvard as a mathematics tutor and ended as Harvard's president (H. B. Adams, "History in American Colleges, I: History at Harvard University," 535, 541–42; "II: History at Harvard University," 619). When Sparks assumed the presidency in 1849, he ceased teaching history and the subject reverted to its former torpor (Emerton [and Morison], "History, 1838–1929," 152, 153). Only in 1857 was a history professor in America assigned to modern history exclusively (Andrew Dickson White at the University of Michigan; see Roberts and Turner, *Sacred and Secular University*, 79). Although in the eighteenth century King's College (Columbia) allegedly established a chair in history, the designee probably never taught the subject (H. B. Adams, "History in American Colleges, III: History at Columbia College," 7–8).

42. C. Wright, "Early Period," 27, 37.

43. Morison, "First Half Century," 28 (funds having been raised for the purpose in 1858 [26]); Eliot, "Theological Education," 42; Ahlstrom, "Middle Period," 109–11. Hedge, who had been in Germany with Bancroft for four years, taught German in the College. On Hedge's then-radical views, see his 1864 address to the graduating class of the Divinity School, "Antisupernaturalism in the Pulpit."

44. C. Wright, "Early Period," 53; and Ahlstrom, "Middle Period," 105–6, 109–10, 132–33; Emerton [and Morison], "History, 1838–1929," 158; Allen, *Christian History in Its Three Great Periods*, iii (originally prepared as lectures at Harvard). Allen defended Auguste Comte (Cashdollar, *Transformation of Theology*, 104–9, 304).

45. Hill, "Divinity School," 219, 220. Hill was chair of the committee.

46. Hill, "Divinity School," 216–17, 222, 223.

47. Ahlstrom, "Middle Period," 134.

48. Thomas Hill, "Address at the Inauguration of Thomas Hill," 36–37, cited in Storr, *Beginning of the Future*, 39. Hill also criticized law schools and medical schools.

49. Fenn, "Charles Carroll Everett," 8. Everett, despite his German education, never advanced more "German" methods (Diehl, *Americans and German Scholarship*, 2, 71–78, 106). After Eliot, a chemist, became President of Harvard in 1869, no clergyman ever succeeded him (Turner, *Without God, Without Creed*, 121).

50. Eliot, *Annual Reports of the President [of Harvard]* (1879), 22, cited in Shepard, *God's People*, 56.

51. Reuben, *Making*, 78, citing the Eliot Papers at Harvard. In 1878, the salaries of Divinity School professors at Harvard were $4000 (Eliot, "Extract from President Eliot's Report for 1877–1878," in Bellows, *Appeal*, 30). Eliot tried to hire W. Robertson Smith in the midst of the latter's heresy trial in 1880, but Robertson Smith declined (Kuklick, *Puritans in Babylon*, 25).

52. Eliot, "Statement of President Eliot" and "Extract from President Eliot's Report for 1877–1878," in Bellows, *Appeal*, 24–25, 29–30; Eliot would like $130,000 to

be added to the endowment of the School (27); the professors want a professorship in ecclesiastical history (32). Also see Hawkins, *Between Harvard and America*, 132. For worry ca. 1880 about Harvard College's irreligion (only one of 139 missionaries of the American Board of Foreign Missions was a Harvard graduate), see Bascom, "Atheism in Colleges," 36.

53. Eliot, "Theological Education," 68.

54. Eliot, "Statement of President Eliot," 25. James McCosh of Princeton charged that Eliot encouraged students to consider religion "antiquated and effete, like the superstitions of ages past" (*Religion in a College*, 12–13). On the Eliot-McCosh debate (staged at the Nineteenth Century Club in New York in February 1886, see Reuben, *Making*, 80–82; on Eliot's importance, 78. In his forty-year presidency, Eliot developed the faculty from 60 to 600, and raised the endowment from 2 to 20 million dollars (Rudolph, *American College*, 294).

55. For how this bequest came to the "Unitarian Denomination" to fund a Chair in Ecclesiastical History at Harvard Divinity School, see Bentinck-Smith and Stouffer, *Harvard University History of Named Chairs*, 262–64.

56. Emerton's inaugural lecture: "The Study of Church History."

57. Ahlstrom, "Middle Period," 145, 147; Reynolds, "Later Years," 175, 167; Eliot, "Theological Education," 47; Emerton [and Morison], "History, 1838–1929," 158–59. On Emerton's retirement in 1919, the Winn Professorship went to Kirsopp Lake (Reynolds, "Later Years," 202).

58. See various letters of Allen to Edward Everett Hale and Russell Carpenter (F83, F84, F87). From 1877 on, Allen had urged Henry Bellows of the American Unitarian Association to intercede with Eliot for Allen to be appointed at the Divinity School (F36, F40, F46, F47, F50). Allen complained that he had been teaching church history with "a good deal less than half the pay" than a Professor would receive (Allen to Carpenter, Nantucket, 8/21/1879 [F59]). Allen believed that Eliot was undermining the Unitarian character of the Divinity School (Allen to Hale, 4/18/1881; 1/26/1882; 3/4/1882 [F69, F83, F87]).

59. Allen to Russell Carpenter, Nantucket, 7/1/1880 (F62).

60. Reynolds, "Later Years," 170–72, 178 (noting a course in church history after the Reformation). Platner, a graduate of Union Seminary, studied at the University of Berlin from 1893 to 1895. Also see Eliot, "Theological Education," 55.

61. Platner to McGiffert, Cambridge, 3/9/1897, cited in McGiffert, Jr., "Making of an American Scholar," 36.

62. Reynolds, "Later Years," 175, 200; Welch, *Graduate Education*, 230, 231.

63. H. B. Adams, "History in American Colleges, VI: History in Yale University," 335–36. Yale formally became designated a "University" in 1886 (Knoff, *Yale Divinity School*, 279, citing *Yale News*, Oct. 29, 1886).

64. Bainton, *Yale and the Ministry*, xi, 8, 79; chaps. 2–3; in 1907 the Divinity School declared itself "unsectarian" (203). Disciples of Jonathan Edwards in New England

fostered an evangelical Calvinism that critiqued the federal or covenant theology of Princeton theologians.

65. Bainton, *Yale and the Ministry*, 80; Wayland, *Theological Department*, chap. 2.

66. Kelley, *Yale*, 145.

67. Yale *Annual Catalogue*, 1857–1858, 38, and *Minutes of the Yale Corporation*, 7/16/ 1867, 222, both cited in Knoff, *Yale Divinity School*, 10, 12, 139; Wayland, *Theological Department*, 127.

68. Knoff, *Yale Divinity School*, 240.

69. For the text, written by Jeremiah Day, see "Original Papers in Relation to a Course of Liberal Education," 299–319, cited in Reuben, *Making*, 25–26; also in Hofstadter and Smith, eds., *American Higher Education*, 1: 275–91. In 1869, Yale officers were defending the classical curriculum against those who "clamor for the substitution of other branches for Greek and Latin" or (like Harvard) institute an "optional [elective] system," a change deemed "inexpedient and dangerous": see [no author listed], "Yale College and the Late Meeting of the Alumni in New York," 301. That Theodore Woolsey, a Greek scholar, was president of the University from 1846 to 1871 perhaps strengthened the stress on classics at Yale. Louise Stevenson, studying education at Yale from 1830–1890, concludes that Yale professors were modernizing "insofar as they adopted scholarship and scholarly vocation as means, but they used these means to resurrect a world infused with religious meaning" (*Scholarly Means*, 8). Stevenson argues that Noah Porter and other Yale scholars introduced the idea of education as "culture," and advocated new German methods of scholarship (10). Although the four-part essay, "American Colleges and the American Public," in four issues of *NE* 28 in 1869, is not signed, it is attributed to Porter.

70. Bainton, *Yale and the Ministry*, 161. Knoff gives the figure in 1858–1859 as 21; in 1890–1891 as 142 (*Yale Divinity School*, Summary, n.p.) Knoff (8) cites statistics from Wayland, *Theological Department*, 406. (The statistics in Wayland are not presented in a form that allows precision, but suggest that enrollment dropped considerably; see chart, 121.)

71. Knoff, *Yale Divinity School*, 8, citing statistics from Yale's *Annual Catalogue*, 1857–1858.

72. Wayland, *Theological Department*, 409–24, 444 (no financial provisions had been made for retirements). No fees were charged for instruction, room rent, or library use. In 1870–1871, weekly board was set at $5.00 (Yale *Annual Catalogue*, 1870–1871, 51, cited in Knoff, *Yale Divinity School*, 137).

73. Theology's prominence rested with Nathaniel Taylor, a leader of the New Haven Theology (Calvinism modified in an Arminian direction, or so critics charged): see Kelley, *Yale*, 146, 152, 199; L. Stevenson, *Scholarly Means*, 19; Wayland, *Theological Department*, chap. 10; Bainton, *Yale and the Ministry*, 165–66. For a spirited defense of New Haven Theology against Princeton's Charles Hodge, see [Fisher], "'The Princeton Review' on the Theology of Dr. N. W. Taylor."

74. Dwight (*Memories of Yale Life*, 282–84: many thought the school should give

up); Kelley, *Yale*, 275; Bainton, *Yale and the Ministry*, 161–62; Dwight continued to serve as Dean of the Divinity School for nine years after he assumed the presidency of the University.

75. On Harper at Yale, see Goodspeed, *William Rainey Harper*, 66, 74–78; Bainton, *Yale and the Ministry*, 178; Marsden, *Soul*, 209. Harper received his Ph.D. from Yale at eighteen, with a thesis on Latin, Greek, Sanskrit, and Gothic prepositions (Goodspeed, *William Rainey Harper*, 26).

76. Wayland, *Theological Department*, 182, 431. According to the 1857–1858 *Annual Catalogue*, there was *no* course in church history (Knoff, *Yale Divinity School*, 10–11, citing the *Catalogue*, 38). Biblical languages also were given secondary status (Wayland, *Theological Department*, 434–42). On Ezra Stiles and Hebrew at Yale, see Goldman, *God's Sacred Tongue*, chap. 3.

77. Marsden, *Soul*, 124. In this regard, Yale's seminary was behind others; Bainton blames scanty resources and "provincialism of time and place" (*Yale and the Ministry*, 186).

78. Bainton, *Yale and the Ministry*, 161–62. Church history had been taught for a few years before the professorship was established through a bequest from Augustus Street, son of Titus Street (Kelley, *Yale*, 200).

79. Knoff, *Yale Divinity School*, 63, citing *Addresses at the Inauguration of the Professors of the Theological Department of Yale College*, 26–27.

80. After a few years, the appointment of Leonard Bacon further strengthened historical studies (Bainton, *Yale and the Ministry*, 190). Bacon's proposal to teach American church history instead of doctrinal theology came as a surprise (Knoff, *Yale Divinity School*, 223, 226). Part of George Fisher's memorial tribute to Bacon is given in Knoff, *Yale Divinity School*, 92, citing *Leonard Bacon—In Memoriam*, 216.

81. Bainton, *Yale and the Ministry*, 233–35; Walker later became Provost and then Dean of the Graduate School at Yale.

82. Veysey, *Emergence*, 50; Rudolph, *American College*, 335. On graduate education at Yale, see Storr, *Beginnings of Graduate Education*, 55–58. Eliot at Harvard envisioned the creation of real "universities" in America ("New Education I," 216; here and in "New Education II," he champions scientific and technical education).

83. Yale *Annual Catalogue 1876–1877*, 80, and *Annual Report of the Theological Faculty*, 1880–1881, both cited in Knoff, *Yale Divinity School*, 219, 227–28.

84. Bainton, *Yale and the Ministry*, 209, 265; Keck, "Epilogue," 273; Cherry, *Hurrying Toward Zion*, 121. I thank Dean Harold Attridge for information on Yale Divinity School.

85. Prentiss, *Union Theological Seminary*, 8; Handy, *History*, 5, 7, 9 (the Seminary's establishment was under way before the formal split between Old School and New School Presbyterians in 1837 [83]). Friends of the Seminary wished to dispel the rumor that the Seminary had been founded to take sides in the Presbyterian strife: see [unsigned] clipping, "Extract from a Statement on Behalf of the Union Theological Seminary," *New-York Evangelist*, Feb. 13, 1841 [Briggs Papers, S29.1, B1, Scr). Old

School and New School Presbyterians reunited in 1869, with a proviso that the General Assembly of the Presbyterian Church would have the right to veto appointments if there was a majority vote to do so. This provision later stirred hot debate when Charles Briggs was transferred from one chair at Union to another: did the General Assembly have the right to veto the switch? (Handy, *History*, 44–45, chap. 4). Another issue: did the gifts earlier made to the Seminary belong to the Presbyterian Church or the Seminary? See Appendix to "Report of the Committee on Theological Seminaries to the General Assembly of the Presbyterian Church," 21–22. The original plan had been to name the institution "The New York Theological Seminary," but the State legislature incorporated it as "The Union Theological Seminary in the City of New York" (Prentiss, *Union Theological Seminary*, 22, 27). Hitchcock claimed that the founders themselves asked for the name change; the name "union" was meant as a protest against the rending of the Presbyterian Church ("Address," in *Services in Adams Chapel*, 10–11). For conversations preceding the Seminary's founding, see Hatfield, *Early Annals*, 4–11. On changes within Calvinism, see G. Harris, *Century's Change in Religion*, chap. 2.

86. Prentiss, *Union Theological Seminary*, 8, citing the original "Plan of the Seminary." After the Briggs case, Union dissolved its 1870 agreement with the Presbyterian Church, claiming that the Church had no control over either professorial appointments or the Seminary's finances, including gifts (*Report of the Committee on Theological Seminaries*, 7, 21–22). For George Prentiss's role in the negotiations, see Prentiss, *Bright Side* II: esp. 422 (Prentiss cites a letter from Union President Thomas Hastings [1/30/1892] declaring that Prentiss "saved the Seminary"). Hastings, decades earlier, was a notetaker in Smith's classes.

87. Handy, *History*, 11. The institution was meant primarily for young men "in the cities of New York and Brooklyn"—but students from various regions enrolled (Prentiss, *Union Theological Seminary*, 45). In 1864, Union's 188 students came from 17 states, with two students from abroad (*New-York Evangelist*, Jan. 7, 1864).

88. Hitchcock, "Address," in *Services in Adams Chapel*, 13; Prentiss, *Union Theological Seminary*, 25; McNamara, "Founding the Seminary," typescript, 3. McNamara emphasizes the role of the Chi Alpha society, a group of Presbyterian ministers in the New York area, in fostering the seminary's founding.

89. Hatfield, *Early Annals*, 4. (Hatfield served at Union as Recorder, Board member, and Financial Agent during the 1860s [Prentiss, *Union Theological Seminary*, 182–84]; Handy, *History*, 7–8). Theodore Woolsey of Yale railed against New York's "slavery to materialism" ("New Era," *NE* 25 [1866]: 199, cited in L. Stevenson, *Scholarly Means*, 145). On the role of the city in weakening "the evangelical empire," see Marty, *Righteous Empire*, 155. Later, Schaff extolled Union's "metropolitan position": "Theology of Our Age and Country," in Schaff, *Christ and Christianity*, 21.

90. Hatfield, *Early Annals*, 10. The plot lay between Sixth and Eighth Streets, extending from Greene to Wooster. Hatfield also sites the building on University Place, with professors' quarters behind on Greene Street (12).

91. Hatfield, *Early Annals*, 13, 15. A contemporary reports that 648 houses and stores were destroyed; banks suspended payment (Booth, *History of the City of New York*, 742–43).

92. Marty, *Righteous Empire*, 102: from 60,000 in 1800 to 600,000 by 1860. By 1894, the city's population south of 110th Street was denser than that of Paris, and lower Manhattan's population (986 people in each of the Eleventh Ward's 32 acres) exceeded that in the slums of Bombay and Prague (Gilfoyle, "Urbanization," 156).

93. Bender, *New York Intellect*, 77, 269.

94. Prentiss, *Union Theological Seminary*, 55, 94–95 (a total from James Brown of around $300,000). On the circumstances of the Roosevelt grant, see Prentiss, *Union Theological Seminary*, 30–31, and Handy, *History*, 31. In 1878, Union's six endowed professorships were the envy of President Eliot of Harvard ("Extract from President Eliot's Report for 1877–1878," in Bellows, *Appeal*, 30).

95. Handy, *History*, 56, 126. The Park Avenue real estate—10 lots—was purchased for $275,000 ("Introductory Note," *Services in Adams Chapel*, 4); four more lots were subsequently purchased. Columbia, previously downtown, moved to Morningside Heights in 1897; when Union arrived a few years later, the two institutions came into closer arrangements (Handy, *History*, 117). Artist Hughson Hawley's painting of the new Union Building on Park Avenue (as he imagines it) is the subject for the jacket of this book.

96. The first years of the Seminary, professors saw little or no pay; by the late 1840s or 1850s, salaries went up to $2500, and by 1874, to $5000 plus a $500 housing allowance (Gillett, "Detailed History" II: 334, 336, 346, 347b). In the 1860s, $2000 a year would put one in the lower middle class; Union professors were socially above that level (Burrows and Wallace, *Gotham*, 966).

97. Edwards A. Park to Smith, Andover, 6/30/1871 (S1, B1).

98. M. M. Schuyler to Smith, New York, Jan. [no year] (S1, B1), on the visit to New York of a son (foreign minister to Peru and Ecuador) of Christian K. J. Bunsen, German statesman and scholar of early Christianity.

99. George Bancroft, William Adams, and 23 other friends (including Charles Butler, Charles Scribner, William E. Dodge, Hanson Corning, and William Curtis Noyes) raised $5100 to pay off the mortgage on Smith's house at 34 East 25th Street ([E. Smith], *Henry Boynton Smith*, 246–47). In 1854, Smith's yearly salary was $1000 (Gillett, "Detailed History" I: 170b). Scribner was a leading publisher; by 1860, printing and publishing was the city's leading industry (Bender, *New York Intellect*, 156). Charles Butler was also deeply involved with New York University and hoped to link Union and NYU. He gave $100,000 to establish a chair in comparative religions at NYU; the course was popular with UTS students (Shepard, *God's People*, 27–29).

100. See newspaper articles in Schaff's Scrapbook (UTS, B6, Scr1, 154–57). Among the guests were justices of the U.S. Supreme Court and various New York courts, and assorted Harrimans, Roots, Vanderbilts, Sages, and Pierreponts. On Vanderbilt's new chateau and extravagant parties, see Burrows and Wallace, *Gotham*, 1071–72. Eliott

Shephard founded the New York Bar Association (Chamberlain, ed., *Universities and Their Sons*, 1, Part 2, 222).

101. Bender, *New York Intellect*, 139—along with William Adams (who became president of Union in 1874), F. A. P. Barnard (president of Columbia), Charles Tiffany, Luigi Cesnola (a prime donor to the Metropolitan Museum), Edwin Morgan (ex-governor of New York State), Henry Potter (rector of Grace Church and future Episcopal bishop of New York); see list of members on menu of 2 November 1878 lunch, in Schaff papers, UTS, B6, Scr1, 121) Such data suggest that Union professors were connected to men of property and cultural influence in New York. Although Sven Beckert claims that the "bourgeoisie" in New York City (by which he means propertied elites) did not include, as it did in Europe, professors (*Monied Metropolis*, 6, 8, 254), the links between Union Seminary professors such as Schaff and "higher society" are notable. On the history of the Century Club, see Duffy, *The Century at 150*.

102. The menu: Raw Oysters, Bass, Smelts, Fried Kidneys, Omelet, Lamb Chops, Beef Tenderloin, Jellied Game Pie, Broiled Partridges, Salad, Neapolitan Ice Cream, Cake, Fruit—plus Tea, Coffee, Sauterne and Claret (Schaff papers, UTS, B6, Scr1, 121).

103. Schaff, *Diary*, 10/15/1872 (UTS, B4). The dinner honored historian James Anthony Froude. On Delmonico's, see Gray, *New York Streetscapes*, 25–27.

104. Philip Schaff, *Diary*, 9/30/1873. Presumably this house was at 221 East 18th Street; see *Diary* entry for 12/15/1876. In February 1876, Schaff was seeking to buy a house priced at about $20,000; his present house (where presumably he gave the party) rented at $1700 a year (*Diary*, 2/19/1876). In March (*Diary*, 3/4/1876) he was still house-hunting; his tastes exceeded his pocketbook. On returning from Europe in August 1877, he bought a house at 15 East 43rd Street for $25,000 (*Diary*, 8/30/1877, 9/4/1877); in a year's time, he was able to reduce the mortgage by $3000 (*Diary*, 9/9/1878); all in UTS, B4. On the importance of parlors for middle-class culture, see Aron, "Evolution of the Middle Class," 186–87, discussing Richard L. Bushman's *Refinement of America* (New York, 1992), 182, 274.

105. Hatfield, *Early Annals*, 17; Prentiss, *Union Theological Seminary*, 54–55; Handy, *History*, 31–34. In 1865 came another plea to the wealthy to endow the Seminary ("Endowment of Union Theological Seminary," 6).

106. Prentiss, "Union Theological Seminary," 25, 26. Prentiss was minister of this (Presbyterian) church and later a member of the Union faculty. The man who could give $100,000 for "a theological library worthy of New-York" would build an enduring monument for himself, Prentiss told his congregation. Prentiss's wife Elizabeth was the writer of many popular children's books, including *Stepping Heavenward* and the *Little Susy* series (C. G. Brown, *Word in the World*, 130–38).

107. Prentiss, "Union Theological Seminary," 8–9, 19. On Union's teaching of Semitic languages: in 1884 President Hitchcock boasted that Union offered the whole range of Semitic studies, "including the Assyrian, which we were the first to teach on this side of the Atlantic" ("Address," in *Services in Adams Chapel*, 34).

108. Prentiss, *Union Theological Seminary*, 23–24. Professors were required to sub-

scribe to the Westminster Confession and affirm the Presbyterian form of church government (43–44). Church government was not coupled with church history, as at Princeton.

109. Albert Barnes, who chaired a committee at UTS in 1849 delegated to find a candidate for church history, conceded that "professorships [in church history] in other seminaries had not been filled in such a way as to secure the best results." The subject, he said, had been given "a subordinate place in the program of study." But knowledge of history would "tend to check vagaries in doctrine and practice" (Gillett, "Detailed History" II: 420, citing Barnes's report of 11/2/1849). Barnes had shortly before undergone a heresy trial (Prentiss, *Union Theological Seminary*, 7; Noll, *America's God*, 310–11). On the early professors of church history at Union, see Richardson, "Church History Past and Present" (Richardson's inaugural address as Washburn Professor at Union).

110. Prentiss, *Union Theological Seminary*, 49. Cox, a Presbyterian minister, was a founder of New York University, Moderator of the New School Presbyterian Assembly of 1846, on the Board of Directors of Union Seminary for 36 years—and the father of Arthur Cleveland Coxe, who early "defected" to the Episcopal Church. In 1841, William Adams was offered the Professorship of Church History, but declined (Gillett, "Detailed History" III: 417–19).

111. Gillett, "Detailed History" II: 420.

112. Smith's own testimony in "Dr. Henry B. Smith's Letter Accepting the Chair of Church History," 9/30/1850, in Appendix, Note D, in *Services in Adams Chapel*, 42.

113. Smith, "Church History," 1849 (?), Hastings notes (S5, B1, F3, 114). Whereas the eighteenth century exhibited "contempt of history," Smith alleged, the nineteenth has shown far more interest ("Problem of the Philosophy of History," 4; "Idea of Christian Theology as a System," 126). "Idea" was Smith's inaugural lecture as Professor of Systematic Theology (5/6/1855); it is noteworthy that he there refers to the Epistle to Diognetus, Lactantius, Clement of Alexandria, Augustine, John of Damascus, Origen, Athanasius, Tertullian, Cyprian, Julian the Apostate, Arius, Pelagius, the Apostles' Creed, and the Creed of Nicaea.

114. Prentiss, *Union Theological Seminary*, 68; Smith, "Relations of Faith and Philosophy," 37.

115. Gillett, "Detailed History" I: 220. The Board were at first hesitant, since they believed nobody could "fill [Smith's] place in the chair of Church History" (Prentiss, *Union Theological Seminary*, 67).

116. Mrs. Harriet Bell of New York gave the money for the chair on the condition that she could choose its first occupant; when the Union Board agreed (suspending the by-laws), she chose Hitchcock (Gillett, "Detailed History" II: 301; Prentiss, *Union Theological Seminary*, 49).

117. Handy, *History*, 37–38.

118. Prentiss, *Union Theological Seminary*, 48; Gillett, "Detailed History" II: 445.

119. In 1887, Schaff and McGiffert thought that the Board would approve McGif-

fert's appointment as assistant to Schaff. McGiffert wrote to Schaff that he wanted to introduce a historical seminar such as Harnack taught. He complained that Union's extensive Hebrew requirement was driving students away and allowing little time for church history (McGiffert to Schaff, London, 8/17/1887, cited in McGiffert, Jr., "Making of an American Scholar," 35–36).

120. F. Brown, "The Seminary and Scholarship," 11; all subjects of religious knowledge (even catechetics) were taught historically (Prentiss, *Bright Side*, 2: 381–82).

121. "Union Theological Seminary," *New-York Evangelist* 1/7/1864. In 1863–1864, three students were listed as "Resident Graduates."

122. Gillett, "Detailed History" II: 518. Most of these studied biblical theology with Charles Briggs, who championed graduate and university education ("Theological Education," 640).

123. Gillett, "Detailed History" II: 519, 520. By the turn to the twentieth century, more regulations were in place and the curriculum for graduate students was enlarged. In 1907, a further category was created, that of "graduate scholars," who received a certificate at the end of a year (II: 521).

124. Briggs, "Theological Education," 637–38, 642, adding that Union will reciprocate. Briggs favored the offering of theological education in universities (as in Europe), not in "isolated seminaries," controlled by denominational conservatives (640). Referring to the same years, John Burgess of Columbia mentioned Union's inclusion in the "university organization" at Columbia (*Reminiscences*, 239). The details remain murky.

125. Gillett, "Detailed History" II: 385. In 1912, Union President Francis Brown was attempting to secure $210,000 from John D. Rockefeller to enhance the "Graduate Department," including fellowships so that advanced students would not need to go abroad for further education (Brown to Frederick T. Gates, Esq., 3/15/1912 [Francis Brown Papers, B1, F3, 1]). Gates was Rockefeller's contact person for dealings with the Seminary.

126. (C. Butler et al.), "Proposed Basis or Terms of Voluntary Agreement between the University of the City of New York and the Union Theological Seminary of the City of New York," 4/1/1890 (MacCracken Papers, S1, B3, F 2 [Graduate School: Theological Studies]). On the early days of NYU, see Storr, *Beginnings of Graduate Education*, 33–43; and on the founding of the NYU Graduate School, Chamberlain, ed., *Universities and Their Sons*, 1: 238–40.

127. Thomas S. Hastings to Henry MacCracken, New York, 7/10/1896 (MacCracken Papers, S5, B26, F2). MacCracken complained that UTS had never published the arrangement in its *Bulletin*. Apparently the Regents granted the B.D. from 1896 to 1897 (Handy, *History*, 97). MacCracken himself taught Church History, and in 1891 published a survey of which colleges taught the subject ("Place of Church History in the College Course of Study").

128. Handy, *History*, 152, 167–68. In 1892, President Nicholas M. Butler of Columbia (discussing whether undergraduates might take courses in professional schools)

noted that at Columbia "work done in the Union Theological Seminary for graduation, is counted as part of the equipment for the higher academic degrees" ("On
Permitting Students to Take Studies in Professional Schools," 58).

129. Welch, *Graduate Education*, 231.

130. Handy, *History*, 297–98.

131. Miller, [Jr.], *Life* I: 33, 41, 57–59. Miller gave his Salutatory address in Latin,
but digressed, in English, on the neglect of female education (I: 41). Miller never got
to hear Nisbet's theological lectures; since students thought it was drudgery to take
notes, Nisbet offered the class only once (I: 59–60). On Miller's development, see John
De Witt, "Intellectual Life of Samuel Miller."

132. Miller, [Jr.], *Life* I: 173; Miller, *Brief Retrospect, Part I*.

133. Miller, [Jr.], *Life* I: 190–92, citing letters of Miller to "Mr. [Edward Dorr]
Griffin" (2/11/1805) and to Dr. [Ashbel] Green (3/12/1805); Green was elected president
of the College of New Jersey [Princeton] in 1812 (I: 336, 340). In the same period, Miller
also railed against Harvard's giving "public sanction to heterodoxy [Unitarianism]" by
appointing Henry Ware Professor of Divinity in Harvard College: see Miller, [Jr.], *Life*
I: 193, citing a letter of Miller to "Dr. Morse" [probably Samuel Morse], dated 4/13/
1805. Elsewhere, Miller excoriates Unitarianism as "nothing less than a total denial and
subversion of the Christian religion"; like "the fabled Syrens [sic] of old," Unitarians
lure so as to destroy; they should be considered "deists in disguise" (*Letters on Unitarianism*, Letter I, 19; Letter VIII, 285).

134. In 1941, Harold S. Jantz praised Samuel Miller's *Brief Retrospect* for bringing
much knowledge of German literature to America. I question whether Miller knew
many (any?) German writings in the original; neither his catalogue of books nor his
lecture notes suggest such. See Jantz, "Samuel Miller's Survey of German Literature,
1803."

135. Miller to Simeon DeWitt, New York, 12/24/1798 (Miller Papers, NYHS, Vol. I).

136. Miller, [Jr.], *Life* I: 353. He rejected presidencies at Dickinson College in 1808
(I: 245–47); at University of North Carolina (1811?); and of Hamilton College in 1812
(I: 335). In 1816, he turned down the presidency of Dartmouth (II: 22).

137. Miller, [Jr.], *Life* I: 352, citing a letter of Miller to the officers of the Church
in Wall Street, New York, 6/24/1813.

138. Miller, [Jr.], *Life* I: 348—the same salary he had received in 1805 as a minister
in New York [I: 364]).

139. Miller, [Jr.], *Life* I: 348; II: 509. To these duties were added the teaching of
"Composition and Delivery of Sermons" (II: 403).

140. Miller to Dr. [William?] Cogswell [of the East Windsor Theological Insti-
tute], 8/ 4/ 1836, cited in Miller, [Jr.], *Life* II: 407–8.

141. Miller, [Jr.], *Life* II: 409: the principles of Presbyterianism were set forth in
the New Testament.

142. Miller, [Jr.], *Life* I: 358. His list suggests that even after the Reformation, there
were "dark" periods. Miller did not have the lecture printed because (he claimed) it

would have required him to look up "numerous references and some long quotations."

143. For notices and letters pertaining to Miller's retirement, see Miller Papers, B20, F45, F47.

144. Miller, [Jr.], *Life* II: 17–18, citing comments of "Dr. Boardman," presumably Presbyterian pastor Henry Boardman, who served on the PTS Board of Directors from 1833 to 1876.

145. Miller, 9/22/1813, cited in Miller, [Jr.], *Life* I: 355–56. In a letter to Dr. [Ashbel] Green (1/16/1810) discussing the plan for Princeton Seminary, Miller declares himself "unqualified to take any part in such a seminary" (I: 280–81).

146. In a letter to Rev. James W. Moore, who had attended the Seminary and now was a minister in Little Rock, Arkansas (1/12/1825), Miller urges the need for "preliminary *literary furniture*" for the study of theology, including language study (Miller, [Jr.], *Life* II: 136–37).

147. Miller, [Jr.], *Life* I: 356; Miller to Professor [William?] Cogswell, 7/24/1834, cited in Miller, [Jr.], *Life* II: 406.

148. Miller, [Jr.], *Life* II: 12. In 1822, Alexander and Miller were joined by Charles Hodge, Professor of "Oriental and Biblical Literature"(II: 46).

149. Miller, [Jr.], *Life* II: 97. Elsewhere, Miller counts himself glad that he need not rely on the Fathers (or Tradition, or the Church) as guides; he has Scripture (*Letters on the Eternal Sonship*, 44).

150. Miller, [Jr.], *Life* II: 144, citing a lecture given by Miller in 1821 and 1829 ("Importance of Mature Preparatory Study"). Miller believed, on the evidence of the early church and later Reformers, that "Popish baptisms" should be recognized— against the view of many Presbyterians in the 1830s (II: 198, 200).

151. [Anonymous], "Notices of New Books: Life of Dr. Samuel Miller," 621. The author is probably a Congregationalist, possibly Yale's George Fisher.

152. [Anonymous], "Notices of New Books: Life of Dr. Samuel Miller," 622. The reviewer acidly comments (620) that Miller's son must have been trying to prevent the reunion of the Old and New School Presbyterians; perhaps the son should have delayed publication, since those branches just reunited.

153. [Anonymous], "Notices of New Books: Life of Dr. Samuel Miller," 623–24.

154. Before Smith was appointed, Dr. S. H. Cox instructed Union students in church history on a temporary basis. For his letter to Smith upon Smith's appointment, see below, 58.

155. For details, see [E. Smith], *Henry Boynton Smith*, 1–37. Smith started college at Bowdoin when he was fifteen (12). After one year at Andover, he transferred to Bangor Seminary (20, 22). In December 1842 or early 1843, he married Elizabeth Lee Allen, daughter of a former Bowdoin president (110–11).

156. [E. Smith], *Henry Boynton Smith*, 13–14. As a Congregationalist, he hesitated to accept a professorship at the then-Presbyterian Union Seminary (155); L. Stearns,

Henry Boynton Smith, 9–10. Smith's theology was touched by some of the "New Divinity" critiques of the older Calvinism (Conser, *Church and Confession,* 230–37).

157. L. Stearns, *Henry Boynton Smith,* 19–20; Stoever, "Henry Boynton Smith," 71–72.

158. L. Stearns, *Henry Boynton Smith,* 56–57; [E. Smith], *Henry Boynton Smith,* 39–44, 54, 269; 44–84, for vivid sketches of professors, courses, and people in Germany. For courses and professors, see below.

159. George E. Post to Elizabeth Smith, Beirut, 11/15/1880 (S1, B2). Post recalls "the simple faith which led him [Smith] to feel, what he taught so glowingly, that 'Christ is all in all'."

160. Smith, letter to his parents, n. p., 10/13/1838, cited in [E. Smith], *Henry Boynton Smith,* 56. Later, Smith remarked that Tholuck could have been a great Orientalist; he kept his private journal in Arabic (270–71).

161. Smith to his parents, Berlin (4/30/1839), in [E. Smith], *Henry Boynton Smith,* 65. (Smith's notes on Neander's *Dogmengeschichte* are in S3, Item 13.)

162. Smith to his cousins [Horatio Southgate and wife], Berlin, 5/15/1839, in [E. Smith], *Henry Boynton Smith,* 66–67. Neander was a convert from Judaism.

163. [E. Smith], *Henry Boynton Smith,* 70; Stoever, "Henry Boynton Smith," 73.

164. Prentiss, *Union Theological Seminary,* 261, on Smith's life.

165. In 1846, August Tholuck wrote to Smith, expressing regret that for two semesters there had been no American students at Halle (Halle, 6/18/1846 [S1, B1]). On Tholuck's gatherings for students in his home, see Robinson, "Theological Education in Germany," *BR* 1:3 (July 1831): 426–427.

166. [E. Smith], *Henry Boynton Smith,* 50–55, 61, 676, 69–70. Tholuck allegedly walked three hours a day, accompanied by students (Stuckenberg, "Early Life of Tholuck," 250). On Neander's influence, see Stoever, "Henry Boynton Smith," 73–74. Hegel's widow sent Smith greetings after his departure from Berlin (Prentiss, *Bright Side* I: 142). Schaff also knew Hegel's widow, and claims that she was disturbed by left-wing Hegelianism and Strauss's *Leben Jesu* ("Reminiscences of Neander," 164n.).

167. Prentiss, *Bright Side* I: 95; Stoever, "Henry Boynton Smith," 73; [E. Smith], *Henry Boynton Smith,* 47.

168. Union Seminary Archives has eleven letters of August Tholuck to Smith, and one (in excellent English) from Mathilde Tholuck (née Baroness of Gemmingen Stünegg) to Smith's wife, Elizabeth, after Smith's death. Frau Tholuck was moved by sections of Elizabeth Smith's biography that detailed Smith's conversations with Tholuck: "I seldom found that a foreigner has so thoroughly understood him" (Mathilde Tholuck to Elizabeth Smith, Halle, 8/2/1881 [S1, B2]). She includes an interesting sketch of the house that she and her husband had set up, where eight theological students were housed and provisioned. Tholuck met Smith's son in 1869 in Germany; the young man, full of "*Geist und Herz,*" made a great impression on him (Tholuck to Smith, Halle, 12/12/1869 [S1, B1]). George Prentiss claims that he taught Frau Tholuck English (*Bright Side* II: 413).

169. On Smith's untimely death in 1877, Hermann Ulrici wrote to "W.A.S." (Smith's son, William Allen Smith) thanking him for a copy of Smith's obituary from the *New-York Evangelist*; Ulrici and his wife grieve deeply at the death of his "old, dearly beloved, and highly respected friend." Ulrici wished to write a "memoir" detailing Smith's zeal in studying philosophy in Germany (Ulrici to W.A.S., Halle, 4/18/1877 [S1, B1]). After reading Elizabeth Smith's biography of her husband, Ulrici thanked her for sending him this "trefflichen Biographie meines lieben, verehrten, unvergesslichen Freundes." His memories of Smith's time in Halle are among the most treasured of his whole life (Ulrici to Elizabeth Smith, Halle, 11/12/1880 [S1, B2]).

170. Isaak Dorner to Charles Briggs, Berlin, n.d., cited in Prentiss, *Union Theological Seminary*, 263.

171. [E. Smith], *Henry Boynton Smith*, 97, 100, 103–4, 107, 115–17.

172. L. Stearns, *Henry Boynton Smith*, 86. Elizabeth Smith claims that he "wrote" eleven articles for this journal during his four years as a minister (*Henry Boynton Smith*, 132).

173. L. Stearns, *Henry Boynton Smith*, 108; [E. Smith], *Henry Boynton Smith*, 133; on 150–51 she cites a letter from Julius Seelye (later President of Amherst) reporting his courses at Amherst with Smith: philosophy, logic, moral science, constitutional law. Special topics Smith asked students to prepare included Mill's doctrine of the syllogism; Plato's *Theatetus*; Hume on cause and effect; the Baconian method; and the doctrine of Free Trade (150–51); similarly, a report from former student Francis A. March, later professor at Layfayette College, adding Reid, Hamilton, and Berkeley (151–52). W. I. Tyler, a colleague from Amherst days, reports that Smith later was offered the Presidency of Amherst, but declined (Tyler to Elizabeth Smith, Amherst College, 11/26/1880 [S1, B2]).

174. Smith to George L. Prentiss, 9/17/1850, cited in Prentiss, *Union Theological Seminary*, 65–66; also in [E. Smith], *Henry Boynton Smith*, 156, 159.

175. Smith, "Problem of the Philosophy of History," 4.

176. George Bancroft to Smith, Newport, R.I., 8/14/1854 (S1, B1).

177. George Bancroft to Elizabeth Smith, Newport, R.I., 10/15/1880 (S1, B2).

178. George Bancroft, cited in a review of [E. Smith], *Henry Boynton Smith* by Z. M. Humphrey, 477); Humphrey was Professor of Ecclesiastical History at Lane Theological Seminary. Earlier, Bancroft claimed that it would be hard to find a man in England or the United States who "excels [Smith] in comprehensiveness and exactness of knowledge, or in historical criticism and the philosophy of history" (Bancroft to William Adams, New York, 3/2/1864, cited in [E. Smith], *Henry Boynton Smith*, 244–245).

179. Smith firmly believed that his professorial duty was "to Christologize predestination and decrees" (Prentiss, *Bright Side* II: 404, citing material from Smith's papers).

180. Smith, "Report to the Evangelical Alliance," 555, 559–60, 563; and Jordan, *Evangelical Alliance*, 71.

181. [E. Smith], *Henry Boynton Smith*, 174, and Appendix B for the Resolution, 433–34. Smith's strong support for the northern cause is also shown in two articles, "Moral Aspects of the Present Struggle" and "British Sympathy with America," a scathing attack on Britain's support for the South; and in a sermon written after Lincoln's assassination ("Sermon XXI," in *Our Martyr President, Abraham Lincoln*, 359–81). Smith compares Lincoln to Moses, who brought the Israelites to the land of promise but was denied entrance (362); and to Jesus (God spared not his Son, and "spares not the best of men" [377]).

182. Schaff, *Theological Propaedeutic* II: 397. Smith wrote a number of essays on Presbyterianism, e.g., "Presbyterian Division and Reunion in Scotland."

183. Smith, "Christian Union and Ecclesiastical Reunion," warning at 274.

184. The journal was to represent an amalgamation of Congregationalist and Presbyterian views ([E. Smith], *Henry Boynton Smith*, 200–201). It became the *American Presbyterian and Theological Review* and later, the *Presbyterian Quarterly and Princeton Review*.

185. L. Stearns, *Henry Boynton Smith*, 352. Smith claimed that a third of the library's holdings, especially the Van Ess Collection, was irreplaceable; he is anxious that the Seminary get a fire-proof building for the collection (Smith to George Prentiss, Clifton Springs, 2/25/1875), in [E. Smith], *Henry Boynton Smith*, 387). Among Smith's papers are notes from his library assistants, asking for direction on shelving and cataloging.

186. For another biographical sketch, see George Prentiss's "Introductory Notice" to Smith, *Faith and Philosophy*, iii–xiv. Elsewhere, Prentiss remarks that Smith's health had "broken down" already by 1837, occasioning his trip abroad (*Bright Side* 1: 48).

187. Prentiss, *Union Theological Seminary*, 261. See Chapter 9 below.

188. For Smith's writings on the Civil War, see n. 181 above; Schaff also wrote on the topic—for a German audience, after the War had ended (*Der Bürgerkrieg* (1866 [1865]).

189. An anonymous reviewer wrote, "It is one of the encouraging signs of the times, that historical works are multiplying in our young and unhistorical country; and among the publications of the American press, we know of no one that will do more to facilitate the studies of historical students than this" ([Anonymous], *BS* 17.65 [Jan. 1860]: 232).

190. On these, see L. Stearns, *Henry Boynton Smith*, 172–74, and Chapter 2 below, nn. 133–35. The translation of the first volume, with revisions and notes, of Gieseler's *Text-Book* appeared in 1857 ([E. Smith], *Henry Boynton Smith*, 175). Smith's translation of Hagenbach's book was published in 1866: see Robert M. Landis to Smith, Danville, Kentucky, 1(?)/13/1874 (S1, B1)

191. L. Stearns, *Henry Boynton Smith*, 188.

192. Humphrey, "Henry Boynton Smith," 498.

193. Munroe Smith to Elizabeth Smith ("Aunt Lizzie"), New York, 10/19/1880 (S1,

B2). The nephew praises his aunt's biography, but criticizes the proofreading of German—he notes six mistakes on p. 50.

194. [E. Smith], *Henry Boynton Smith*, 188.

195. For other testimonies to Smith as a "workaholic," see W. I. Tyler to Elizabeth Smith, Amherst College, 12/26/1880 (S1, B2); H. G. Storer to Elizabeth Smith, Scarboro, 12/13/ 1880 (S1, B2).

196. Fisher, *History of Christian Doctrine*, 417–18.

197. Prentiss, *Bright Side* II: 401, 402, 404, citing letters he himself wrote in 1890.

198. Prentiss, *Union Theological Seminary*, 274, 276.

199. On the Chair, see Gillett, "Detailed History" II: 301; Prentiss, *Union Theological Seminary*, 279; and above, n.116.

200. Prentiss, *Union Theological Seminary*, 276–78, citing a letter of 11/9/1853 by an (anonymous) "eminent scholar," President of a New England college.

201. Prentiss, *Union Theological Seminary*, 277–78.

202. Hitchcock was still President in 1877, when he gave a lecture in Baltimore, with "stereopticon views," on "Palestine Exploration" ("Palestine Exploration," [Baltimore] *Sun*, May 11, 1877, 4).

203. Information on Hitchcock's life is supplied in various newspaper memorial notices at the time of his death in June 1887, e.g., *New-York Evangelist*, June 23, 1887; *Springfield Republican*, June 18, 1887; *New York Herald*, June 18, 1887, and from *Who Was Who in America*.

204. Prentiss, *Union Theological Seminary*, 274.

205. [Anonymous], *New-York Evangelist*, July 7, 1887, n.p.

206. [Anonymous], obituary notice, *New-York Evangelist*, June 23, 1887; Rev. Spencer S. Roche, "Roswell D. Hitchcock, D.D.," paper read to the Brooklyn [Episcopal] Clerical Club, 6/27/1887, from an unidentified newspaper; clipping folded into the back of "Memorial Notices" (Hitchcock Papers, B1). Hitchcock protested the bad effects of the "triumphant materialism" of the present (i.e., American greed) ("Modern Age," early 1880s, Burrell notes [B1, N2, 121]). In addition, Hitchcock urged the construction of an asylum for "inebriates" ("Address in Behalf of the United States Inebriate Asylum").

207. [Anonymous], Obituary notice, *Springfield Republican*, June 18, 1887, 4. In the midst of the Civil War, Hitchcock wrote to a college friend that however long the war may take, it is "for the black man" and that victory will bring "a hearty, general acknowledgment of human rights" ("Ebony War and Race," *The Friend* [Honolulu], July 3, 1863, 56).

208. Roche, "Roswell D. Hitchcock, D.D." (B1). Roche reports that Morgan, who owned the land, held out for $275,000. When Hitchcock pointed out that lots down the hill were selling for $175,000, Morgan refused to budge on his price, but gave $100,000 toward the cost. In 1880, under Hitchcock's Presidency, Morgan gave $100,000 for a fire-proof library building and library improvements; more was prom-

ised in his will (Hitchcock, "Address," *Services in Adams Chapel*, 29–30; Prentiss, *Union Theological Seminary*, 55–57, 240).

209. Prentiss, *Union Theological Seminary*, 96–97; [Anonymous], "In Memoriam—President Hitchcock," *New-York Evangelist*, Dec. 15, 1887, n..p., describing a memorial service held for Hitchcock at Union. This prize sometimes enabled advanced studies in Germany.

210. [Anonymous], "Preface," to Hitchcock, *Eternal Atonement*, vi, v. The "acquisitions" are probably books; for his library, see below, 88.

211. Hitchcock, "Cost of Service," 164.

212. *Teaching of the Twelve Apostles*, ed., trans., Roswell D. Hitchcock and Francis Brown (rev., enlarged ed.; 1885 [1884]); the Union Seminary copy is Hitchcock's.

213. Hitchcock, "Zoroastrian Religion"; "Chinese Classics" [a review of James Legge's work].

214. Hitchcock, *Socialism*; "Laws of Civilization"; *Hitchcock's New and Complete Analysis of the Holy Bible, or the Whole of the Old and New Testaments*; Smith and Hitchcock, *Life, Writings and Character of Edward Robinson*. Hitchcock also gave talks on "Christian Socialism," in which he argued for some protective legislation for workers, an eight-hour work-day, and tighter regulation of stock corporations ("Christian Socialism," *Springfield Republican* May 13, 1886, 4).

215. D. S. Schaff, *Life of Philip Schaff*. This book is especially valuable for the many letters to and from Schaff reproduced.

216. Shriver, *Philip Schaff: Christian Scholar and Ecumenical Prophet*.

217. Pranger, *Philip Schaff (1819–1893): Portrait of an Immigrant Theologian*.

218. Graham, *Cosmos in the Chaos*.

219. Penzel, "Editorial Introduction," to *Philip Schaff, Historian and Ambassador*, ed. Penzel, xvi–lxvii. Penzel reproduces Schaff's account of his early life, from Schaff's "Autobiographical Reminiscences," 15–27.

220. Penzel, *German Education of Christian Scholar Philip Schaff*.

221. Fisher, "Dr. Schaff's Volume of the German Reformation." David Brown of Aberdeen compares Schaff's work habits to those of Origen, who was dubbed "Adimantus"; "I think you are his successor in that line" (Brown to Schaff, Aberdeen, 4/2/ 1881 (?) [UTS, B1, F6]).

222. M. R. Vincent, "Address Commemorative of Philip Schaff," 1.

223. Schaff to Dr. Thompson, New York, 11/18/1876 (UTS, B2). The anonymous reviewer for *Bibliotheca Sacra* of Schaff's *History of the Christian Church, Volume I* agreed with Schaff's modest self-assessment: although Schaff "does not lay claim to any especial eminence as an independent investigator of historical problems, or as a familiar student of the church Fathers," nevertheless he is well acquainted with early Christian writings: see the anonymous "Schaff's Church History," *BS* 16.63 (1859): 454, 455. Another anonymous reviewer of the volume speculates that some may think Schaff *too* tolerant, that his Catholicism is "a little too Roman": "Schaff's Church History," *ATR* 1.2 (May 1859): 323; Schaff's views of inspiration are "hardly up to our

American standards of orthodoxy," and there are signs of "Sacramentarianism and other high-church principles" (325). The reviewer praises Schaff's long chapter on the Church Fathers (324). For a hostile review of Schaff's earlier *History of the Apostolic Church* by Princetonian Charles Hodge, see *BRPR* 26.1 (Jan. 1854): 148–192.

224. Schaff, "Autobiographical Reminiscences" (LTS, B1, F04, 1, 14). "It seems that Providence used me as a sort of mediator between the theology of churches of Germany, England, and America," Schaff wrote to his son David in 1887 (New York, 3/25/1887 [LTS, B1, F115]). That the title resonated with the names of both ancient Roman priesthoods and a title of the bishop of Rome (*pontifex maximus*) was not coincidental; Schaff may have enjoyed the joke.

225. Schaff, "Autobiographical Reminiscences for My Children" (LTS, B1, F04, 18–19). Schaff began his "Reminiscences" in New York on Dec. 31, 1871—his birthday fell the next day—and concluded it while at sea in March 1890.

226. For recent accounts of Schaff's life, see nn. 216–20 above. See Graham, *Cosmos in the Chaos*, 159–68. On the German background, see Penzel, *German Education*.

227. Shriver, *Philip Schaff*, 15–16; Graham, *Cosmos in the Chaos*, 56–57.

228. D. Schaff, *Life*, 251. Philip Schaff recounts his early years in America in "Dr. Schaff's Reply and Farewell to the Synod," 23–28.

229. Germans who enjoyed spending Sundays drinking beer posed a problem for Americans of Puritan descent (Marty, *Righteous Empire*, 126). Schaff, with his German background, probably seemed a good choice to deal with the issue; see Graham, *Cosmos in the Chaos*, 159–68.

230. For Schaff's courses before he taught church history, see Gillett, "Detailed History" II: 444–45; he conducted a course in patristic literature in 1889 "in order to encourage students in the investigation of the primary sources" (II: 424). Schaff allegedly made it a condition of his acceptance of the Church History Professorship that he might appoint A. C. McGiffert (Sr.) as his assistant—a request the Board refused (see McGiffert, Jr., "Making of an American Scholar," 35, 36). McGiffert (Sr.) got Schaff's chair after the latter's death.

231. Memorial by Adolf von Harnack, cited in D. Schaff, *Life*, 458.

232. Schaff to A. C. McGiffert, New York, 12/18/1889; 2/14/1890, cited in McGiffert, Jr., "Making of an American Scholar," 40.

233. Schaff to Dr. [Thomas S.] Hastings, New York, 3/11/1893 (LTS, B2, F01).

234. On the history of publication and later enlargement of the *Encyclopedia*, see D. S. Schaff, "Samuel Macauley Jackson," 14–15.

235. Schaff's "Reunion of Christendom" address is printed in *Evangelical Alliance Document* 33 (1893): 1–45, and reprinted in *Philip Schaff, Historian and Ambassador*, ed. Penzel, 302–40.

236. Graham (*Cosmos in the Chaos*, 102) states that Schaff originally disapproved of the Alliance, deeming it anti-Catholic. Graham cites Schaff's article, "Ein Blick in die kirchlich-religiöse Weltlage," *Der deutsche Kirchenfreund* 6 (March 1853): 107 (the organization is too narrow in its limitation to Protestantism).

237. Evangelical Alliance Constitution of 1870 (Evangelical Alliance Papers, B1, 3–4).

238. Evangelical Alliance Constitution of 1870 (Evangelical Alliance Papers, B1, 7–8). For an early and pointed critique of the Alliance, see Horace Bushnell, "Evangelical Alliance"; Bushnell faults the Alliance for dividing Christians and excluding Catholics, Quakers, and Unitarians. Other statements by the Evangelical Alliance are more anti-Catholic than its American Constitution suggests.

239. Schaff, "New York General Conference of the Evangelical Alliance," 89.

240. Minutes of the Executive Committee of the American Evangelical Alliance, 12/21/1868; 1/15/1869 (Evangelical Alliance Papers, B2, N, 8, 15).

241. Minutes of the Executive Committee of the American Evangelical Alliance, 12/26/1868 (Evangelical Alliance Papers, B2, N, 10–11). Schaff arranged with the Hamburg and Bremen line of steamers and with railroad companies for reduced fares for delegates—and also for a transatlantic backup, in case the political situation deteriorated (Minutes, 12/6/1869, 6/10 and 7/19/1870 [Evangelical Alliance Papers, B2, N, 71, 99, 110]).

242. Schaff, "Autobiographical Reminiscences" (LTS, B1, F04, 72, 84). The low point was the death of his dearly beloved, "incomparable" daughter Meta.

243. Schaff and Prime, eds., "Historical Sketch," *Evangelical Alliance Conference, 1873*, 14. At the end of the conference, delegates journeyed through Princeton and Philadelphia to Washington, D.C., and were received by President Grant (48–50).

244. Jordan, *Evangelical Alliance*, 69.

245. New York: Harper & Brothers, 1874. Post-conference, the American Committee was jubilant that it had won around 600 new American members and hoped for "hundreds of thousands" more to combat "the aggression of Romanism, the progress of infidelity, the encroachment of civil power upon the rights of conscience" (Minutes of the Executive Committee of the American Evangelical Alliance, 11/17/1873 [Evangelical Alliance Papers, B2, N, 285]).

246. Shriver, Jr., "Philip Schaff's Concept of Organic Historiography," 253, citing Schaff's opening speech to ASCH in *Papers of the American Society of Church History* (New York, 1889), 1: xv, vi–vii.

247. Schaff to D. Schaff, New York, 1/2/1889 (LTS, B1, F115).

248. Harnack, "Future of Church History," *New-York Independent*, April 11, 1889. Harnack makes interesting observations on the state of the field.

249. Emmanuel Gerhart reports to Schaff in 1890 that he has received $1000 "to complete the foundation of the 'Prize Essay' in Church History." They are organizing it in shares of $250; four people have taken it on—"elders of high standing," "gentlemen who are financially as well as morally responsible" (Gerhart to Schaff, Lancaster, 2/14/1890 [LTS, B1, F32]). Since Schaff instigated the prize and "engaged to contribute one-half of the whole amount," Gerhart wrote, the "professors decided that the name 'Schaff Prize' was the only suitable name" (Gerhart to Schaff, Lancaster, 1/2/1892 [LTS,

B1, F32]). Gerhart encloses a statement from the ASCH treasurer that the goal of $1000 for the Prize Essay had been reached.

250. "Action of the American Society of Church History," 12/28/1892, in *Semi-Centennial of Philip Schaff*, 56.

251. See Bowden, *Church History in the Age of Science*, 67, 239, 118–19.

252. Jameson, "American Historical Association," 14–15. Jameson comments on how this hurt medieval history: medieval history without the church was like Hamlet without the Prince.

253. See Bowden, *Church History*, 67, 239; and Graham, *Cosmos in the Chaos*, 119. On the later history of ASCH, see Bowden, "First Century," 294–332.

254. The Ante-Nicene Fathers series is discussed in Chapter 2 below.

255. Schaff, items in Scrapbook (UTS, B6, Scr1, 75c); also see Schaff, "Preface," Select Library of the Nicene and Post-Nicene Fathers, Ser. 1, v–vii. Fisher claimed that the NPNF translations were taken "mostly from the Anglo-Catholic Library of the Fathers" (*Notes on the Literature*, 670g); his charge is not strictly accurate.

256. Schaff, "Prospectus for *Select Library of Nicene and Post-Nicene Fathers of the Christian Church*," pasted into Schaff Scrapbook (UTS, B6, Scr1, 75c).

257. Schaff, "Preface" to NPNF Ser. 1.

258. Schaff, Scrapbook (UTS, B6, Scr1, 75c).

259. Letters concerning the project can be found in archives at Union Theological Seminary and Lancaster Theological Seminary. See letters to and from Marcus Dods and C. D. Hartrauft (regarding Augustine materials); F. J. A. Hort (declining the invitation due to lack of time) [UTS, B1). In Box 2, UTS, are letters to and from the following: J. B. Lightfoot (too busy and can't recommend anyone); H. B. Swete (asking to be let off from his promise to do Theodore of Mopsuestia; he has been ill); to M. B. Riddle (asking him to send on his translation of Augustine, *On the Harmony of the Gospels*; reports that Schaff's son David had revised the translation of Augustine's *Sermon on the Mount* and written an introduction on Augustine as an exegete; reports also that B. B. Warfield had contributed a fine introduction to Augustine's anti-Pelagian writings; remarks that Riddle's edition of Chrysostom's *Commentaries on Matthew and John* needs a "thorough essay on Chrysostom as Commentator"); from Henry Wace, reporting on a change of translator for the Theodoret material, and commenting on the progress of Dr. Robertson on Vol. 4 (Athanasius), which may appear later than Vol. 5 (Gregory of Nyssa). In his *Diary* for 8/22/1890, Schaff states that he has handed over editorial control of Vol. 3 of NPNF to Dr. Wace (Canon Venable having failed to come through) (UTS, B4).

From Lancaster Seminary archives: correspondence with W. H. Fremantle (B1, F26); Alfred Plummer (F70); S. D. Salmond (F82). Schaff reports to his son David on the progress of the edition (Donaldson is not ready with Epiphanius for Vol. 3 (Rome, 4/1/ 1890 [LTS, B1, F115]).

260. "Publisher's Agreement" for contributions to NPNF, included with letter to potential contributors (UTS, B6, Scr1, 82). The Agreement gives contributors various

options, depending on whether they were making new translations (in which case, 7½ percent of retail price of all copies sold) or revising old ones (5 percent).

261. Schaff, "Prospectus" for NPNF, pasted into Scrapbook (UTS, B6, Scr1, 75c); also in McGiffert, Jr. Papers, SIIA, B1, Correspondence).

262. "Preliminary Prospectus" for NPNF, dated 1885, pasted into Scrapbook (UTS, B6, Scr1, 75b).

263. Schaff, "Preface," pasted into Scrapbook (UTS, B6, Scr1, 82). See John Henry Newman to Schaff (LTS, B1, F66); Newman rejoices that there is "a call in the United States" for additional volumes of the Fathers, but cannot help due to his eyesight; he has "outlived the circle of friends who might have taken part in it."

264. Between 1886–1888, eight volumes of Augustine's writings had been published (Schaff, *History* III: 1039). Alfred Plummer of University College, Durham, advised Schaff that Chrysostom would have a much better sale in England than another translation of Augustine's works (Durham, 5/23/1889 [LTS, B1, F70]).

265. In September and October 1888, Schaff is engaged in writing the "Prolegomena" to the first volume of Chrysostom (Schaff to A. C. McGiffert, New York, 9/17 and 10/8/1888 [McGiffert, Jr. Papers, SIIA, B1]). Schaff's Introductions and Notes are largely free from the polemicizing that makes Coxe's footnotes and "Elucidations" so distasteful to the modern reader.

266. Schaff, "Preface," and "Prolegomena" ("Life and Work of St. John Chrysostom"), in NPNF, Ser. 1, vol. IX: "Preface," n.p.; "Prolegomena," 4. The selections were revised and annotated by W. R. W. Stephens and assistants.

267. Schaff, "Preface," n.p.

268. Schaff to D. Schaff, New York, 3/25/1887 (LTS, B1, F115). Graham (*Cosmos in the Chaos*, 101n.78) comments on Anselm Schaff's emotional and marital difficulties that rendered his work life difficult.

269. See Schaff, "For My Children" (UTS, B6, Scr1, 32 of text).

270. Schaff to A. C. McGiffert, 1885, cited in McGiffert, Jr., "Making of an American Scholar," 33.

271. Schaff, *Diary*, 5/17 and 7/15/1890 (UTS, B4); Schaff to D. Schaff, Rome, 4/1/1890 (LTS, B1, F115).

272. Schaff, *Theological Propaedeutic* Part II: 279.

273. Schaff to A. C. McGiffert, New York, 10/5/1889 (McGiffert, Jr. Papers, SII A, B1). In 1893, shortly before his death, Schaff wrote that the historical works of Eusebius, Socrates, Sozomen, Theodoret, Rufinus, Jerome, and Gennadius would be included in the Second Series (*History* III: 1040); he was pleased Gregory of Nyssa appears in English for the first time in this series (*Theological Propaedeutic*, Part II: 365). As notes above indicate, not all the authors Schaff hoped to include got included.

274. Schaff to A. C. McGiffert, London, 7/27/1888 (McGiffert, Jr. Papers, SIIA, B1).

275. C. M. Mead to Schaff, Andover/West Salisbury, Vt., 7/18/1889, claiming he had no money to invest in the company, as Schaff had requested (UTS, B2). Schaff also solicited J. Packard of Alexandria [Episcopal Theological Seminary], who likewise

regretted his inability to invest (Packard to Schaff, Alexandria, Va., 7/18/1889 [UTS, B2]).

276. Schaff to A. C. McGiffert, New York, 6/1/1889 (McGiffert, Jr. Papers, SIIA, B1).

277. Schaff to A. C. McGiffert, New York, 10/5/1889 (McGiffert, Jr. Papers, SIIA, B1).

278. (Boston) *Zion's Herald*, May 30, 1888, clipping in Schaff's Scrapbook (UTS, B6, Scr2, 148).

279. Fisher, "Dr. Schaff as an Historian," from *Papers of the American Society of Church History*, VII, 3, 4–5, 8 ("Writings C-H," B114).

280. M. R. Vincent, "Address Commemorative of Philip Schaff," 5, 7.

281. Or, as Grant Wacker has suggested, to control historicism so as to preserve it.

282. Shahan, "Dr. Schaff and the Roman Catholic Church," in *Schaff Memorial Meeting*, 26–27. Shahan expressed gratitude for Schaff's correction of misimpressions of Roman Catholicism.

283. Hurst, "Dr. Schaff as Uniting Teutonic and Anglo-Saxon Scholarship," in *Schaff Memorial Meeting*, 9, 11, 12.

284. Bainton, *Yale and the Ministry*, 187. A good example of both the Puritanism and the "mellowing" can be seen in Fisher's review of a novel, "Mr. Mitchell's Novel, 'Dr. Johns'."

285. Bronson, *History of Brown University*, 329, no reference given.

286. Williston Walker, "Professor Fisher," *Yale Divinity Quarterly*, Jan. 1910, 77, cited in Knoff, *Yale Divinity School*, 37.

287. Fisher, "Diary" (B114, 1, 60, 89). Tholuck told Fisher that when he (Tholuck) left Berlin for Halle, he had a farewell drink with Hegel, who gave the toast, "Correct the Rationalism of Halle!" (67).

288. Fisher, "Diary," 9, 10.

289. Fisher, "Introductory Note," to his translation of Augustus Neander, "The Relation of the Grecian to Christian Ethics," 477 (originally in *Zeitschrift für christliche Wissenschaft und christliches Leben*, 1850). Neander first treated Stoicism, then Platonism. He finds the ethical element of Greek philosophy fulfilled only in Christianity (482). The *Stoicorum Vetera Fragmenta* had not yet been published (Vol. 1 appeared in 1859); Neander must dig citations from the Old Stoics out of the works of Plutarch, Diogenes Laertes, and others.

290. Whereas previously few students in the Theological Department checked out books by German church historians, in 1858–1868 Neander's *History of the Christian Church* became the most frequently checked-out book (Wayland, *Theological Department*, 264–65, 278).

291. Fisher, "Diary," 63–64. Professor Müller told him that he and colleagues had tried to institute more frequent exams, but got nowhere with their proposal: there were too many students at Halle to make frequent examinations feasible for the profes-

sors. But now in Erlangen, for example, exams are more frequent—perhaps even yearly.

292. Fisher, "Diary," 51, 52. Gloomy about the prospects of the Union, Heinrich Leo did not think America was a peaceful enough country for a *wissenschaftlich* life, there being too much rush to make money and accumulate property.

293. Fisher, "Diary," 18–19.

294. August Tholuck to Fisher, Halle (?), 5/20?/1853 (B122).

295. Theodore D. Woolsey to Fisher, New Haven, 12/30/1853 (B122).

296. Bainton, *Yale and the Ministry*, 166.

297. Knoff, *Yale Divinity School*, 3–4, citing letters of Fisher to President Woolsey (6/5/ 1854), and from Noah Porter to President Woolsey (n.d.).

298. Knoff, *Yale Divinity School*, 5–6, citing Fisher's letter to Woolsey.

299. Yale *Annual Catalogue*, 1858–1859, 6, cited in Knoff, *Yale Divinity School*, 26.

300. Knoff, *Yale Divinity School*, 2; Bainton, *Yale and the Ministry*, 186.

301. Gabriel, *Religion and Learning at Yale*, 150, 174; see 148–51, 174 on tensions in the 1850s and 1860s at Yale (between 10 and 15 percent of the students were from the South).

302. Knoff, *Yale Divinity School*, 334, citing Fisher's letter of resignation from the
· Deanship and retirement from his professorial chair, from *Minutes of the Yale Corporation*, 12/13/1900, 563.

303. *Minutes of the Yale Corporation*, 12/10/1900, 569–71, cited in Knoff, *Yale Divinity School*, 335.

304. Walker, "Professor Fisher," 77, cited in Knoff, *Yale Divinity School*, 37.

305. Knoff, *Yale Divinity School*, 38.

306. Walker, "Professor Fisher," 77, cited in Knoff, *Yale Divinity School*, 37.

307. John F. Weir, "Address . . . on the . . . dedication of a Memorial Window to Professor George Park Fisher," 3, cited in Knoff, *Yale Divinity School*, 337.

308. Sir William M. Flinders Petrie to Fisher, London, 7/19/1873 (B122).

309. Wayland, *Theological Department*, 146.

310. Charles W. Eliot to Fisher, Cambridge, 10/20/1886 (B122).

311. Jameson, "American Historical Association," 11. This is the period when AHA and ASCH were fused. Reports that for several years in later life Fisher served as ASCH president presumably refer to this position (Walker, "Professor Fisher," 77–78, cited in Knoff, *Yale Divinity School*, 336). Fisher's address, *Function of the Historian as a Judge of Historic Persons*, 3.

312. From an advertisement for the journal, presumably published in 1868; no source given—perhaps from the first edition under a new name? The editors (in 1868?) announce that they will discuss church-state relations, the reconstruction of the South, "the proper sphere of legislation in repressing vices like intemperance, and the character of our laws on the subject of divorce."

313. For Fisher's attack on Positivism in this book, see Cashdollar, *Transformation of Theology*, 201.

314. Fisher compiled this introductory work (*History of the Christian Church*) in part from notes taken by his student Henry E. Bourne at Yale Divinity School in 1887 (v). Fisher notes that Bourne also added material from his own reading and submitted chapters to Fisher "for amendment."

315. James B. Angell to Fisher, Ann Arbor, 1/22/1886 (B122). (The "horse" alludes to an injury Fisher suffered in a riding accident.) Since the publishers had sent two copies of the book, Angell gave one to Michigan's "Assistant Professor of History who is most likely to be able to call the attention of students to it"; apparently there was only one Assistant Professor of History at the University of Michigan in 1886. Philip Schaff also praised Fisher's *Outlines of Universal History*. Thanking Fisher for a copy, Schaff remarked that he is glad that students in "our public schools" will have such a volume. "It will teach them the all important lesson that God is in history, and that Christianity is the greatest blessing to the human race. I am glad that a church historian of your calm, judicial and Christian temper has become a world historian" (Schaff to Fisher, New York, 2/13/1886 [B122]).

316. D. W. Gilman to Fisher, Baltimore, 6/10[?]/1896 (B122). Presumably Fairburn signals Harnack's more critical approach to church history.

317. A. M. Fairburn to Fisher, Oxford, 5/21/1896 (B122).

318. Obituary Notice [James Emerton], *Boston Journal*, June 1, 1892, 7.

319. Emerton, "Practical Method," 39.

320. Lingelbach claims that Emerton was the first professor in America appointed to a position in church history outside of a divinity school (*Klio macht Karriere*, 260).

321. Jameson, "Early Days of the American Historical Association," 3.

322. Details on Emerton's life taken from clippings in the Emerton Correspondence in the HDS Archives. His address as President of the American Society of Church History: "Definition of Church History."

323. Emerton addressed Unitarian ministers in 1888 on "Conversion of the German Tribes to Arian Christianity" ("Ministers' Institute," 5). In 1901, he spoke to Unitarians on "Rational Equipment of the Modern Minister" ("Unitarians Confer by the Sea," 12).

Chapter 2. Infrastructure: Teaching, Textbooks, Primary Sources, and Libraries

Epigraph: Turner, "Secularization and Sacralization," 78, of the nineteenth-century college curriculum. Now, "Albania" perhaps seems not so distant.

1. This shift was stimulated both by the professors' experiences of German universities and, gradually, by increased specialization.

2. Miller, [Jr.], *Life* II: 18.

3. [No author listed], *Brief Account of the Rise, Progress and Present State*, 46; Loetscher, *Facing the Enlightenment*, 158.

4. Miller, [Jr.], *Life* II: 403–4, citing Miller's letter (9/26/1834) to Professor [William?] Cogswell of East Windsor Theological Institute.

5. Miller, *Letters on Clerical Manners*, 235.

6. See Miller's class notes, "Ecclesiastical History, Second Class," 1842–1843 (B24, F4); letter of Miller to Cogswell, 7/24/1834, cited in Miller, [Jr.], *Life* II: 405).

7. Miller, "History and Pedagogy," n.d. (B8, F17, 1–3; recitation forces youth to "walk in trammels," and does not "give them *liberal* and *rich* furniture!"

8. Miller, [Jr.], *Life* II: 408.

9. Miller, *Letters on Clerical Manners*, 268; Miller, "Introductory Lecture, Ecclesiastical History" (B2, F1, 13).

10. Miller, "Literary Fountains Healed," 20–21, 28; *Letters on the Eternal Sonship of Christ*, 28.

11. Miller, "Introductory Lecture, Ecclesiastical History" (B2, F1, 3, 15, 16, 18, 20, 26).

12. Miller, "Ecclesiastical History, No. II. II and III Centuries" (B2, F4, 8). Emphasis in original; Miller often underlined and used exclamation points.

13. Miller, "Introductory Lecture, Ecclesiastical History" (B2, F1, 13, 15, 16, 18, 20, 26); also *Letters on Clerical Manners*, 231, 242.

14. Gillett, "Detailed History" II: 417, 374); middlers got two hours of church history a week, and seniors, an unspecified amount (II: 374).

15. S. H. Cox to Smith, Brooklyn, 11/18/1850, cited in [E. Smith], *Henry Boynton Smith*, 164–65. For student notes taken in Samuel Cox's Church History lectures, see Dr. Cox, "Lectures on Church History," 1849–1850 (?), Hastings notes [Smith Papers, S5, B1, F3]. Students learned some seemingly odd "facts," such as that Armenian was the original language of the world (8). For "philosophizing about history" as the goal of historical training: George Bancroft to Elizabeth Smith, Newport, R. I., 10/15/1880 (S1, B2). Similarly, Noah Porter: ministerial studies are "largely *philosophical*" ("Christian Ministry as a Profession," 349).

16. Gillett, "Detailed History" II: 421–422.

17. Smith, "Theological Encyclopedia," 1851, Hastings notes (S5, B1, F3, 231–32, 227); similarly, Miller, "Importance of Mature Preparatory Study," 15–16.

18. Smith, "Theological Encyclopedia," 1851, Hastings notes (S5, B1, F3, 235–39).

19. Smith, "Nature and Worth," 77–79.

20. Smith, "Systematic Theology," 1857? (S4, B1, F1, L1 [emphasis added]); "Systematic Theology," 3/11/1858 (S4, B1, F14).

21. Smith, "Nature and Worth," 79, 81.

22. Smith, "Systematic Theology," 1857? (S4, B1, F1, L1).

23. Smith, "Theological Encyclopedia," 1851, Hastings notes (S5, B1, F3, 227–28), possibly Thomas Reid's *Inquiry into the Human Mind on the Principles of Common Sense* (1794).

24. Smith, "Theological Encyclopedia," 1851, Hastings notes (S5, B1, F3, 230, 231).

25. Gillett, "Detailed History" III: 618; II: 421, 422.

26. Smith, "Systematic Theology," 1857? (S4, B1, F1, L1); similarly, *Introduction to Christian Theology*, 38.

27. Thomas S. Hastings, cited in [E. Smith], *Henry Boynton Smith*, 170–71.

28. [E. Smith], *Henry Boynton Smith*, 151, 152.

29. Gillett, "Detailed History" II: 422–23. Hitchcock taught medieval and modern, as well as ancient, church history (Prentiss, *Union Theological Seminary*, 90–92).

30. These courses are designated in my notes as "Church History: First Period" and "Church History: Second Period."

31. Schaff, "Roswell D. Hitchcock," *New-York Independent*, May 23, 1887 (Hitchcock Papers, B1, "Memorial Notices," N, 296).

32. Rev. Spencer S. Roche, "Roswell D. Hitchcock, D.D.," paper read to the Brooklyn [Episcopal] Clerical Club, June 27, 1887, unidentified newspaper clipping folded into "Memorial Notices" (Hitchcock Papers, B1).

33. Hitchcock, "Receiving and Giving," 234; "Cost of Service," 160.

34. [Anonymous], obituary notice, *New-York Evangelist*, June 23, 1887 (Hitchcock Papers, B1, "Memorial Notices," N, 290).

35. H. M. F., "Illustrious Dead," *New-York Evangelist*, June 23, 1887.

36. [Anonymous tribute to Roswell D. Hitchcock], *New-York Evangelist*, July 7, 1887, citing a letter to *Harper's Weekly*.

37. Schaff, "Roswell D. Hitchcock," *New-York Independent*, May 23, 1887 (Hitchcock Papers, B1, "Memorial Notices," N, 296); Inaugural Address [Washburn Chair of Church History], 9/22/1887, cited in Prentiss, *Union Theological Seminary*, 282.

38. Roche, "Roswell D. Hitchcock, D.D." (Hitchcock Papers, B1).

39. [Anonymous], "In Memoriam—President Hitchcock," *New-York Evangelist*, Dec. 15, 1887.

40. Bainton, *Yale and the Ministry*, 189, perhaps based on Williston Walker's memorial sketch, "Professor Fisher," *Yale Divinity Quarterly* (Jan. 1910): 77.

41. "Obituary Article," *Outlook*, Jan. 1, 1910, 12, cited in Knoff, *Yale Divinity School*, 337.

42. Bainton, *Yale and the Ministry*, 198.

43. Bainton, *Yale and the Ministry*, 189–90.

44. Fisher, *Brief History*, 13, v.

45. Fisher, "Church History," 1870–1871, 3.

46. D. Schaff, *Life of Philip Schaff*, 65; Pranger, *Philip Schaff*, 54, citing Schaff', "Reminiscences," 98–99.

47. Shriver, "Philip Schaff as a Teacher," 74, 78.

48. Schaff, "Autobiographical Reminiscences for My Children" (LTS, B1, F04, 129–30).

49. Schaff, *What Is Church History?* 4; reprinted in *Reformed and Catholic*, ed. Yrigoyen and Bricker; *History* I: 20 (church history is not a "curiosity shop").

50. Schaff, "Theological Encyclopedia," UTS, 1877–1878 (?), Gillett notes (UTS, B3, "Miscellaneous," N, 1).

51. Schaff, "German Universities: Berlin," *New-York Independent*, Aug. 26, 1886, clipping (UTS, B6, Scr2, 86).

52. Schaff, *Theological Propaedeutic* I: iii–iv; II: 305, 255, 256.

53. Shriver, "Philip Schaff as a Teacher," 75, 82, citing [unidentified author], "Reminiscence of Dr. Schaff," *Reformed Church Messenger* 61.46 (Nov. 16, 1893): 3.

54. Schaff, "Method of Theological Study" *New-York Independent*, Oct. 4, 1877 (UTS, B6, Scr1, 114), an address to Union students (9/20/1877).

55. Shriver, "Philip Schaff as a Teacher," 74n.1, 75, 77.

56. Schaff, *Theological Propaedeutic* II: 306, 318.

57. Schaff, "Method of Theological Study," 114.

58. Schaff, "Method of Theological Study," 114.

59. T. G. A., "Handsome Contribution to the Theological Seminary, at Lancaster, by Dr. Schaff," *[Reformed Church] Messenger*, Dec. 15, 1886, clipping (UTS, B6, Scr2, 106); E. M. Kingsley to Schaff, New York, 3/16/1889 (LTS, B1, F49). Kingsley was the Recorder at Union Seminary.

60. E. V. Gerhart to Schaff, Lancaster, Penn., 2/14/1890; 1/2/1892 (LTS, B1, F32). The "Schaff Prize" is still awarded.

61. Charles A. Briggs to Francis Brown, 2/18/1892 (letter 4411 in Briggs Papers, cited in Shriver, Jr., "Philip Schaff's Concept of Organic Historiography," 223 and n.79).

62. See letters of A. C. McGiffert to Schaff, dating from 10/25/1886, 11/28/1886, and 1/10/1887 (McGiffert, Jr., Papers, SIIA, B1).

63. Schaff to A. C. McGiffert, New York, 10/5/1889 (McGiffert, Jr. Papers, SIIA, B1).

64. Gillett, "Detailed History" III: 729.

65. U. H. Heilman, "Reminiscences of the Theological Seminary," *Bulletin of the Seminary* 3.1 (Jan. 1932): 9, cited in Shriver, *Philip Schaff's Concept of Organic Historiography*, 220–21.

66. U. H. Heilman, "Reminiscences of the Theological Seminary," *Bulletin of the Seminary* 3.1 (Jan. 1932): 9, cited in Shriver, "Philip Schaff as a Teacher," 86.

67. J. H. Dubbs to Schaff, Lancaster, Penn., 6/5/1893 (LTS, B1, F21).

68. F. A. Gast to Schaff, Lancaster, Penn., 6/12/1893 (LTS, B1, F31).

69. The views of one of these, Joseph Henry Allen, are surveyed below in Chapter 4.

70. Charles Follen was one of the earliest American students in Germany (1815 or earlier) (Follen, *Religion and the Church, Theological Tracts 1*, iii). Frederic Hedge, who had some German education (see George Bancroft to Hedge; Hedge Papers, bMS 384/2, F2), claimed himself as the first American to study German metaphysics in the original (Hedge to Caroline Dall, Cambridge, 2/1/1877, cited in Dall, *Transcendentalism in New England*, 15); Hedge details the New England Transcendentalists' interest in German philosophy (15–17). For Hedge's correspondence with Margaret Fuller, see the Hedge Papers, bMS 384.

71. See above, Chapter 1. On Allen's Unitarianism, see his *Ten Discourses on Orthodoxy*.

72. Philip Smith's *History of the Christian Church During the First Ten Centuries* is largely lifted from Schaff's *History*, usually with acknowledgment. Allen and Emerton at Harvard also used this book.

73. Allen, *On the Study of Christian History*, 1, 4, 7; similarly, *Outlines of Christian History A.D. 50–1880*, iv. Greenwood's *Cathedra Petri* is in six volumes (London, 1856–1872).

74. Allen to E. E. Hale, Cambridge, 10/15/1878 (F53); Allen to Russell Carpenter, Cambridge, 3/20/1880 [F61]).

75. Allen to Russell Carpenter, Cambridge, 10/20/1878; 3/20/1880 (F54, F 61). Allen alleged that Charles Eliot wanted ecclesiastical history taught as "a good deal of task work and mere grind" (Allen to Russell Carpenter, Cambridge, 3/4/1882 [F87]).

76. Allen speculated that by appointing Emerton, Eliot was trying to avoid "any association of the College with Unitarianism" (Allen to Russell Carpenter, Cambridge, 3/4/1882 [F87]).

77. Emerton recounts the story in "Rational Education of the Modern Minister," in *Learning and Living*, 272. He and Eliot became friends ("Remarks of Professor Ephraim Emerton," in Everett, *Theological School*, 17).

78. Emerton, "Rational Education," 272.

79. Emerton, "Academic Study," 238, 259, 242.

80. Emerton, "Academic Life," 11–13; on Emerton's assessment of Henry Adams's role in developing History at Harvard, see Emerton [and Morison], "History, 1838–1929," 154–57. For Adams's account, see *Education of Henry Adams*, 227, 229; he deems his seven years of teaching at Harvard a "Failure" (title of chap. 20).

81. Emerton, "Historical Seminary," 195, 197, 199.

82. Emerton, "Study of Church History," 2–4, 10; Harvard has done better than other schools.

83. Emerton, "Study of Church History," 6–7, 9; on archaeology (4–5).

84. Harvard Divinity School Catalogue, 1896–1897, 12.

85. Platner is listed in Harvard Catalogues up to 1902–1903. Next, Kirsopp Lake taught some courses in early Christianity, followed by George La Piana (first listed in the 1917–1918 catalogue).

86. Emerton, "Church History," 1887–1889 (10/6). A near-identical copy of Wilbur's notes from this course can be found in 466/4, F1 [labeled as Edwards Amassa Park file].

87. Emerton the Unitarian did not defend the doctrine of the Trinity; Arianism had tried to "bring man face to face with his God" without mediation (*Unitarian Thought*, 295).

88. See above, 54.

89. Emerton, "Study of Church History," 11, 8, 15–16, 18; "Definition of Church History," 68.

90. Emerton, "Place of History," 321.

91. The printed list is in a notebook labeled "Lectures in Church History by Professor Ephraim Emerton, Ph.D., Harvard University, 1887–1889, notes taken by Earl Morse Wilbur" (bMS 466/4, labeled as Edwards Amassa Park file).

92. In his paper on "Monastic Principle" (1887; Wilbur Papers, bMS 119/1, F13), Wilbur surveys asceticism in pre-Christian and extra-Christian settings; "It is inherent in the nature of man." Wilbur cites Weingarten's *Über den Ursprung des Mönchthums*, Harnack's *Das Mönchthum*, Montalembert's *Monks of the West* (in translation). He received a grade of 95 on this paper—with no comments from Emerton.

93. For another course in church history, Wilbur wrote on "The Heresy of the Adaptionists" and reviewed a book on Einhard's "Life of Charlemagne" (22 pages); for the third course, his 58-page paper is on "John Huss and the Early Bohemian Reformation." Wilbur received A or A+ on his papers (Wilbur Papers, bMS 119/1).

94. Wilbur, "Monastic Principle" (1887) (Wilbur Papers, bMS 119/1, F13).

95. Wilbur, "Life and Work of Ulfilas" (1888) (Wilbur Papers, bMS 119/1, F14).

96. E. M. Wilbur, (untitled) biographical statement (Wilbur Papers, bMS 119/2, F18 ["Biographical and Bibliographical"], 93–97). When the school at Berkeley first failed, Wilbur lost his position (but he later became President). Wilbur attempted candidacy for the Congregational ministry in 1890, but was too "unorthodox" (77–78). Wilbur's "Statement of My Religious Beliefs" shows him waffling before his examiners (bMS 119/2, F16).

97. Wilbur, "First Century of the Liberal Movement in American Religion" (1927 [1916]), centering on developments from 1815 to 1833.

98. Jameson, "American Historical Association," 3; see C. K. Adams's letter to H. B. Adams, Ithaca, N.Y., 2/9/1886, in *Historical Scholarship*, ed. Holt, 79.

99. H. B. Adams, "New Methods," in *Methods of Historical Study*, 99–107, noting seminars at Cornell and at the Universities of Pennsylvania, Wisconsin, Nebraska, and California (109). Church historian Frank Hugh Foster of Oberlin Seminary rates seminars at Johns Hopkins higher than Leipzig's (*Seminary Method*, 19n).

100. Henry Adams, *Education of Henry Adams*, 236–37; Adams and his students co-authored *Essays in Anglo-Saxon Law* (1905), dedicated to Charles Eliot.

101. Foster, *Seminary Method*, vii, 3, requiring background in metaphysics, classics, and German (23).

102. Foster, *Seminary Method*, 7, 14, 15, 16, 19–20.

103. Foster, *Seminary Method*, 96, 79–84, 120–21, 20.

104. Schaff, "German Universities: Berlin," *New-York Independent*, Aug. 26, 1886, clipping (UTS, B6, Scr2, 86).

105. In 1898–1899, McGiffert offered a seminar on the "Origin and History of the Apostles' Creed"; see Prentiss, *Union Theological Seminary . . . Its Design* (356).

106. Emerton, "Practical Method," 36–37, 39, 46–47.

107. Emerton, "Practical Method," 41, 31, 32. Emerton faults German professors who give detailed information in lectures that can easily be found elsewhere.

108. Emerton, "Practical Method," 33, 37; "Academic Study," 259; "Historical Seminary," 199.

109. Emerton, "Practical Method," 38; "Academic Study," 238; "Place of History," 317.

110. Emerton, "Historical Seminary," 199, 200.

111. Emerton, "Practical Method," 49, 56, 58.

112. Catalogues of the Harvard Divinity School for the 1880s and early 1890s. Apparently he taught the same seminar almost every year, although the list offered by H. B. Adams (Introduction, n.107) suggests other topics.

113. H. B. Adams, "New Methods," in *Methods of Historical Study*, 90; "History in American Colleges, I: History at Harvard University," 541.

114. Harnack's volumes on the history of dogma and his *Mission and Expansion of the Church* appeared later; many American Protestants thought that Harnack had capitulated too readily to destructive criticism of early Christianity.

An example of how Harnack shocked pious young Americans: Philip Schaff's son David, studying in Germany in 1888–1889 (?), reports from conversation with Harnack that he "does not believe in the coequality of the Son, and the personality of the Holy Spirit. He says, we cannot know anything about the nature of Christ's person, and it does not concern us to know." When David objected that the Apostles professed to know and that Christ made utterances concerning his person, quoting "I and the Father are *one*," Harnack replied, "I too believe that Christ uttered these words, but they may mean simply unity in will and purpose." David asked, "Suppose some man should now use such words"? Harnack replied: "Such a man would be either *verückt* or Jesus Christ" (Schaff to Julius Mann, citing a letter from David, New York, 3/31/1889 [LTS, B1, F115]).

115. Fisher, "Function of the Historian," 14–15.

116. For the assumptions of German church historians on history, see Chapter 4 below.

117. Roeber, "Von Mosheim Society," 157. The Society's founder, Justus H. C. Helmuth, feared that knowledge of German culture was fading in American life.

118. Miller, "Introductory Lecture on Ecclesiastical History" (B2, F1, 5, 6); "Introductory Address, Ecclesiastical History" (B2, F1, 11, 8).

119. Miller in *The Presbyterian*, April 11, 1832, 35, cited in Miller, [Jr.], *Life* II: 404. Miller disputes Mosheim's view that John the Baptist baptized all by immersion: How could this be? All Jerusalem and Judea? "Would *decency* admit of it? Naked? Females? If with *clothes*, how get change of raiment? Why, then, go to Jordan?" ("Notes on Mosheim, Century II, No. II" [B5, F5, 2]). Mosheim's account of the rise of prelacy is "utterly unsatisfactory" ("Notes on Mosheim, Century III" [B5, F8, 8]).

120. Miller, "Introductory Lecture on Ecclesiastical History" (B2, F1, 6); "Notes on Ecclesiastical History," c. 1843, Brown notes (B26, F5); "a pretty thorough-going Arminian" ("Ecclesiastical History, Second Class," 1842–1843 [B24, F4, 5]).

121. Miller, "Introductory Address, Ecclesiastical History" (B2, F1, 6, 7).

122. Miller, "Notes on Mosheim, Century I" (B5, F1, 5, 6, 7); "Introductory Lecture, Ecclesiastical History," Nov. 12, 1814 (B2, F2, 12).

123. [E. Smith], *Henry Boynton Smith*, 182, citing a letter of Smith to Richard H. Dana, New York, 7/1851.

124. Hitchcock, "Church History: First Period," 1872–1874, Jackson notes (Jackson Papers, B1, N1, 11–12) (perhaps thinking of the "Magdeburg Centuries"?)

125. Fisher, *Notes on the Literature*, 670e; "Church History," 1870–1871 (4).

126. Shriver, "Philip Schaff as a Teacher of Church History," 79, citing notes taken at MTS by U. H. Heilman, "Lecture Notes on Church History, 1860–1862," 24; Schaff, *Principle of Protestantism*, 207.

127. Schaff, *History* I: 39—yet Schaff praised the "easy elegance of [Mosheim's] Latin style," naming him "the father of church historiography as an *art*, unless we prefer to concede this merit to Bossuet."

128. Shriver, "Philip Schaff as a Teacher of Church History," 79, citing MTS notes taken by U. H. Heilman, "Lecture Notes on Church History, 1860–1862," 24; Schaff, *History of the Apostolic Church* I, in *Reformed and Catholic,* ed. Yrigoyen and Bricker, 305.

129. Schaff, "Dr. Fisher's Manual of Church History," *New-York Independent*, March 28, 1889, clipping (UTS, B6, Scr2, 161.)

130. Schaff, *What is Church History?* 56; also in *Reformed and Catholic*, ed. Yrigoyen and Bricker, 72.

131. Schaff, *What Is Church History?* 79; also in *Reformed and Catholic*, ed. Yrigoyen and Bricker, 95.

132. Schaff, *History* I: 50n.2. So large, in fact, that I had to stand up to see an entire page.

133. F. Cunningham, "Translator's Preface," in Gieseler, *Text-Book*, trans. Cunningham from the 3rd German edition (1836), I: iii. The fourth edition of 1844 (Volumes IV and V in German) was compiled by E. R. Redepenning after Gieseler's death in 1854, based on Gieseler's *Nachlass*.

134. Smith, "Introductory Note," in Gieseler, *Text-Book*, trans. from 4th rev. German edition by S. Davidson, rev., ed. H. B. Smith. 5 vols. (1857–1880), I: iv. Smith politely does not fault Cunningham's earlier translation ("well executed"). Smith was only partway through Volume V when he died; the rest was translated by former pupil Lewis F. Stearns (139–360) and by Mary Robinson, daughter of Edward Robinson (360–648). Union Seminary's copy of Vol. V in German is Smith's, with extensive marginal notes and inserts on slips of paper; Stearns used these in his translation.

135. Only material up to 1305 was taken from the 4th German edition. Most of Volume IV was missing in Cunningham's translation (Smith, "Introductory Note," in Gieseler, *Text-Book*, trans. Smith, I: iv).

136. Moses Stuart, "Recommendation," prefacing Gieseler, *Text-Book*, trans. Cunningham; "Recommendations" also from Charles Hodge of Princeton and Henry Ware of Harvard.

137. Fisher, "Church History," 1870–1871 (5).

138. Schaff praises Davidson's translation of Gieseler and Torey's translation of Neander ("Progress of Church History," 86).

139. Gillett, "Detailed History" II: 375; III: 606.

140. Unidentified review from the *Christian Inquirer*, praising H. J. Rose's translation of Neander's *History of the Christian Religion* (notice pasted into the front of Union's copy). Another textbook option: H. E. F. Guericke, *Manual of Church History. Ancient Church History*, trans. W. G. T. Shedd (1857 [1833]). Schaff prints Neander's accusation that Guericke plagiarized from him and others ("Recollections of Neander," 80n.1).

141. Smith to Elizabeth Smith, New York, 9/30/1860, in [E. Smith], *Henry Boynton Smith*, 226.

142. Gieseler, *Text-Book* I, trans. Cunningham, 2; trans. Smith, 14. (I give page numbers for both translations.)

143. Smith, "Introductory Note" in Gieseler, *Text-Book* I: iii-iv.

144. Gieseler, *Text-Book* I, trans. Cunningham, 10; trans. Smith, 23 ("deceit").

145. Schaff, *History* I: 42; *Theological Propaedeutic* II: 301–2.

146. Charles [Karl von] Hase, *A History of the Christian Church*, trans. from 7th ed. by C. E. Blumenthal and C. P. Wing (1855/1856 [1834]).

147. Smith, "Theology" [unspecified course], 1862, Briggs notes (Briggs Papers, S8, B34.5, N, 158).

148. E.g., Hase's discussion of early monasticism via the character of Anthony *(History*, 64–65).

149. Hase, *History*, xi–xiii;.he does not expect the "school of Neander" to like his book.

150. Hase, *History*, xiii–xv, xx.

151. Schaff, "Church History," MTS, 1855, Russell notes (LTS, B4, F03, N, 12).

152. See Shriver, *Philip Schaff's Concept of Organic Historiography*, 77n.18.

153. Schaff's "Recollections of Neander," 73–89. Neander refused to sign the Augsburg Confession (78). Schaff called Neander "a Christian Israelite without guile" ("Reply" [to *Epistola Congratulatoria*], in *Semi-Centennial of Philip Schaff*, 14).

154. See Bibliography below for Neander's works. For Schaff's glowing assessment, see *History of the Apostolic Church* I, in *Reformed and Catholic*, ed. Yrigoyen and Bricker, 264–83.

155. Dahlberg-Acton, "German Schools of History," in Dahlberg-Acton, *Historical Essays and Studies*, ed. Figgis and Laurence, 359; originally in *British Historical Review* 1 (1886).

156. Hagenbach, "Neander's Services," trans. Smith, 855, 850–51.

157. Schaff, "Dr. Fisher's Manual of Church History," *New-York Independent*, March 28, 1889, clipping (UTS, B6, Scr2, 161): Neander's and Gieseler's Church Histories were too "bulky and expensive" for student use.

158. Smith, "Theology" [unspecified course], 1861–1862, Briggs notes (Briggs

Papers, S8, B34, F5, N, 158). While a student in Berlin, Smith wrote that Neander is "the father of a new era in church history" (Smith to Mr. and Mrs. Horatio Southgate, Berlin, 5/15/1839, cited in [E. Smith], *Henry Boynton Smith*, 67).

159. "Schaff's Church History," *ATR* 1.2 (May 1859): 324. The editors wish someone would print those "common fountains" for Americans—it would take only about "a dozen good thick folios." This, Arthur Cleveland Coxe did some years later.

160. E.g., Hitchcock, "Church History: First Period," 1883, Moore notes (B2, N2, 195); Gillett, "Detailed History" II: 375; III: 606.

161. Jackson began reading on Sept. 6, 1876; stopped between Oct. 1876 and Jan. 1877; and ended on April 24, 1877: "Finished at last, thank God."

162. For Schaff's heartfelt tribute to Neander, "Reminiscences of Neander," in *Saint Augustine, Melanchthon, Neander*, 128–168. Miller also found Neander the most thorough—but apparently never tried to use Neander's books as texts ("Notes on Chronology and Ecclesiastical History," ca. 1842, J. Miller notes [B26, F3]).

163. Schaff, "Dr. Fisher's Manual of Church History," *New-York Independent*, March 28, 1889, clipping (UTS, B2, Scr2, 161); *Theological Propaedeutic* II: 301; *History* I: 40; "Reminiscences of Neander," 135.

164. Schaff, "Progress of Church History," 77; *History* I: 40–41.

165. Hitchcock, "Church History: First Period," early 1880s, Burrell notes (B1, N1, 193); Schaff, *Theological Propaedeutic* II: 301; "Progress of Church History," 77; Fisher, *Notes on the Literature*, 670e.

166. Hitchcock, "Church History: First Period," early 1880s, Burrell notes (B1, N1, 193); Schaff, *Theological Propaedeutic* II: 301; Fisher, "Church History," 1870–1871 (5).

167. Hitchcock, "True Idea and Uses," 41–42; "Church History: First Period," early 1880s, Burrell notes (B1, N1, 190–91).

168. Hitchcock, "Church History: First Period," 1872–1873, Jackson notes (Jackson Papers, B1, N1, 3); "Church History: First Period," early 1880s, Burrell notes (B1, N1, 236). Fisher also faults Gibbon ("Church History," 1870–1871 [19]). Emerton faults *Decline and Fall* for its emphasis on "decline": we see "a magnificent edifice crumbling to decay, but we are not impressed with the elements of life contained in this very process" (*Introduction to the Study*, v).

169. Schaff, "Progress of Church History," 77.

170. Schaff, "Progress of Church History," 77; Shriver, Jr., "Philip Schaff's Concept of Organic Historiography," 81, citing Schaff's articles on Neander in *MR* 3.1 (Jan. 1851): 73–90; 4.6 (Nov. 1852): 564–77.

171. Fisher, "Church History," 1870–1871 (20).

172. Schaff, "Progress of Church History," 78; letter to Julius Mann, cited in D. Schaff, *Life*, 394, 395; see Pranger, *Philip Schaff*, 195–96. In 1893, Schaff called Harnack "the chief representative of the Ritschl school among Church historians" (*Theological Propaedeutic* II: 360).

173. Schaff faults Fisher for not providing bibliography, a failure to be corrected in a new edition ("Dr. Fisher's Manual of Church History," *New-York Independent*,

March 28, 1889, clipping [UTS, B6, Scr2, 161]). Fisher subsequently wrote some extra pages on patristic scholarship (printed separately by Scribner in 1888) to be inserted into the Appendix of his *History of the Church* (671–97).

174. C. Wright, "Early Period," 53–54, citing George Moore, "Exercises with Dr. Ware on Natural and Revealed Religion," Commencing September 1836 [MS, HU Archives).

175. Milman's *History of Christianity from the Birth of Christ to the Abolition of Paganism in the Roman Empire*, 3 vols. (1840, 1866), was considered inferior to German works.

176. The list was published in "Prospectus of Our Theological Schools," *Monthly Journal of the American Unitarian Association* 10 (1869): 349–50, cited in Ahlstrom, "Middle Period," 104–5n.71. The high proportion of works by German authors is notable.

177. Emerton's predecessor at Harvard, J. H. Allen, considered Neander's volumes "heavy and confused in narrative," lacking in "perspective of political events, or the general course of Christian civilization"—but still of "highest value to the student of speculative theology and church life" (*Christian History in Its Three Great Periods*, xxiii).

178. Philip Smith acknowledges in his Preface (*History of the Christian Church*, vi) that his "manual" is not based on "original research"; whole paragraphs are lifted from Schaff's *History of the Christian Church* (usually with acknowledgment). Schaff hints that another [unidentified] writer "nearer home has made even larger, but less honest use of my book" (*History* I: 49n.1).

179. Emerton, "Church History," 1887–1889 (10/4, 10/6, 11/3). Emerton also recommends Baur and other German works in his lectures.

180. The section on America in Karl von Hase's *History of the Christian Church* was deemed so inadequate by the American translators that they asked Hase's permission to substitute their own section on the topic: see Hase's "Letter to the Translators," in the ET by Blumenthal and Wing (viii).

181. *APTR* 6.21 (Jan. 1868): 147: Germans think that "America is a Babel of sects and that its theology is a mere echo of that of Europe. But the next chapter in the History of Protestant theology will probably be written in the United States of America"; similarly, *APTR* 6.24 (Oct. 1868): 631.

182. Gieseler, *Lehrbuch* V: 377. These sections on "Neueste Kirchengeschichte von Amerika" (including Tahiti!) Smith found inadequate and erroneous.

183. Gieseler, *Lehrbuch* V: 378, 379–80.

184. Schaff, "Dr. Fisher's Manual of Church History," *New-York Independent*, March 28, 1889, clipping (UTS, B6, Scr2, 161); German authors are also ignorant of English church history.

185. Schaff, *Theological Propaedeutic* II: 294, adding that Schelling claimed Mormonism as the "only important fact" in American church history.

186. Schaff, "Preface," to Gieseler, *Text-Book* I, ed., trans. Smith, V: ii*; *Theological*

Propaedeutic II: 291–93; chairs should be established in our seminaries for this subject, Schaff (prophetically) claims.

187. Miller, "Practical Results from a Course of Ecclesiastical History" (B2, F10, 12).

188. Hitchcock, "Church History: First Period," 1872–1873, Jackson notes (Jackson Papers, B1, N1, 6).

189. "In Memoriam—President Hitchcock."

190. Hitchcock, "Church History: First Period," 1872–1873, Jackson notes (Jackson Papers, B1, N1, 7–9).

191. Hitchcock, "Church History: First Period," 1872–1873, Jackson notes (Jackson Papers, B1, N1, 2, 5); "Church History: First Period," early 1880s, Burrell notes (B1, N1, 190).

192. Schaff, *Theological Propaedeutic* II: 255, 256; *History* II: 622.

193. [Anonymous],"Schaff's Church History," *ATR* 1.2 (May 1859): 324.

194. See the letter to Schaff from J. Rendel Harris, who was preparing a new edition of the *Epistle of Diognetus*, and hoping to go on to the *Shepherd of Hermas* (Harris to Schaff, Baltimore, 10/12/1882 [UTS, B2, F39]).

195. Schaff, *Theological Propaedeutic* II: 275.

196. On Coxe, see my "Contested Bodies."

197. See discussion in Pfaff, "Anglo-American Patristic Translations," esp. 39–43. Pfaff notes the neutral tone of the Ante-Nicene Christian Library editors who, although supplementing (or "correcting") the Library of the Fathers series, keep their Calvinist assumptions largely hidden.

198. James Donaldson, one of the Edinburgh editors, was understandably miffed at Coxe's failure to send him a copy of the American edition, largely copied from the Edinburgh edition (Donaldson to Schaff, St. Andrews, 4/3/1893 [LTS, B1, F21]).

199. Pfaff, "Anglo-American Patristic Translations," 44.

200. ANF I: vi. References to Coxe's comments in the Ante-Nicene Fathers Series, ed. Roberts and Donaldson) are listed below by volume and page number.

201. I: 415, cf. V: 4; V: 159.

202. II: 4, 56, of the editors' ascription of possible Montanist tendencies to the *Shepherd of Hermas*.

203. IV: 170, of the placement of Minucius Felix.

204. VII: 529.

205. I: v.

206. II: 477, Elucidation V.

207. V: v.

208. V: 264.

209. I: v, Preface.

210. II: 605.

211. I: vii-viii, 353; II: 22, 47, 62, 79, 105, 147, 212, 279, 378, 405, 419–20, 447, 541, 543; III: 38; IV: 38, 49; V: 354, 546; VII: 93.

212. Coxe asks readers to "rejoice in the chaste marriage of the Clergy, according to the Scriptures, and in the sanctity of the Christian Family, unviolated by a compulsory Confessional and by inquisitorial casuistry alike indecent and profane" (*Criterion*, 49).

213. V: 264, 417.

214. Coxe, *Impressions of England*, viii.

215. I: 397; II: 36, 126; III: 266.

216. Already in 1831, Edward Robinson comments that a library of 50,000 volumes would be deemed small in Germany ("Theological Education in Germany," *BR* 1.3 [July 1831]: 430–31).

217. Fisher, "Diary" (B114, 6, 80).

218. *ATR* 2.7 (Aug. 1860): 531.

219. *ATR* 4.16 (Oct. 1862): 725; *APTR* 2.8 (Oct. 1864): 693; *APR* 1.1 (Jan. 1869): 208.

220. Miller Papers (B1, F1, 51).

221. Gregory's *Querela de suis calamitatibus* (*Carmen* 2.1.19), an autobiographical poem.

222. Miller regretted that the Seminary library did not own a copy of the *Magdeburg Centuries*; only two copies existed in the United States. Miller owned the three-volume abridgment ("Introductory Address, Ecclesiastical History" [B2, F1, 8, 10]).

223. Recollections of Dr. S. Irenaeus Prime, in Miller, [Jr.], *Life* II: 411 (Miller let Prime use his library while he was a student at Princeton Seminary).

224. "In Memoriam—President Hitchcock."

225. "In Memoriam—President Hitchcock." I thank Sylvia Bugbee, Assistant Archivist at the Bailey-Howe Library of the University of Vermont, for information on Samuel Emerson (1850–1939).

226. Gillett, *Detailed History* III: 729.

227. Schaff, *Diary*, 6/11/1873 (UTS, B4); perhaps the seller was a widow dispersing her husband's library?

228. Harvard *Annual Report*, 1869–1870, 30, cited in Ahlstrom, "Middle Period," 89.

229. Schaff, "Reminiscences of Neander,"148.

230. Hitchcock, "Church History: First Period," early 1880s, Burrell notes (B1, N1, 191).

231. Gapp, "Theological Seminary Library," 97.

232. Slavens, "Incidents in the Librarianship," typescript, UTS, 5 (from Slavens, *Library of the Union Theological Seminary*, chap. 3).

233. See Schaff's *Diary* entries for 12/2/1854; 9/27/1865; 7/16/1873; 7/21/1877; end page, 1890 diary (UTS, B4).

234. T. S. Hastings to Schaff, Oceanic, N.J., 6/1/1890 (UTS, B1).

235. From statistics in Knowles, "Importance of Theological Institutions," Appendix, Note C, 10.

236. Society of Clergymen, "Thoughts on the State of Theological Science," 763–

64. As late as 1914, only one-quarter of divinity libraries had 10,000 volumes: Remus, "Origins," 117, citing Anson P. Stokes, *University Schools of Religion* (1914), 5; report from *Religious Education* 9 (1914): 323–35.

237. See Chapter 1, n.184; Smith wrote a column for each issue between 1859–1877 (except when on "sick leave") entitled "Theological and Literary Intelligence." Although these columns are unsigned, we know from his wife's biography and his coeditor's comments that he was the author.

238. *ATR* 2.5 (Feb. 1860): 169, citing a report from the Smithsonian. On Joseph Cogswell's earlier collecting for the Astor Library, see Diehl, *Americans and German Scholarship*, 2.

239. Burgess, *Reminiscences*, 174, 175. Burgess was shocked at the paucity of Columbia's library when he began teaching there in 1876.

240. Gapp, "Theological Seminary Library," 91–92.

241. Miller, *Brief Retrospect, Part I*, II: 408–9.

242. Miller, "Introductory Lecture, Ecclesiastical History" (B2, F1, 11–12).

243. [No author listed], *Brief Account of the Rise, Progress and Present State*, pleading for friends of the Seminary to send books or money to buy books (58–59). On donations: Gapp, "Theological Seminary Library," 97.

244. [No author listed], *Brief Account of the Rise, Progress and Present State*, 59. In 1843, philanthropist James Lenox provided the building (Gapp, "Theological Seminary Library," 91–92).

245. Gapp, "Theological Seminary Library," 96.

246. Naylor, "Theological Seminary," 24, citing *Quarterly Register and Journal of the American Education Society* 2 (May 1830): 238–39, 247.

247. Gapp, "Theological Seminary Library," 96.

248. Gapp, "Theological Seminary Library," 93. In 1879, the librarian determined that about 73 books "per man" were being circulated, which he thought made Princeton the best-used theological library in America (94–95).

249. Lingelbach, *Klio macht Karriere*, 243: President Andrew White of Cornell secured for his institution the libraries of Charles Anthon (professor of ancient languages at Columbia), Franz Bopp (professor of "Orientalistik" and comparative linguistics at Berlin), and Jared Sparks (historian and President of Harvard), among others.

250. George Ticknor to S. Higginson, Göttingen, 5/20/1816, in *American Higher Education*, ed. Hofstadter and Smith, I: 255, 256. On Ticknor's failure to stimulate German-style education at Harvard, see Diehl, *Americans and German Scholarship*, 2, 7, 50–51, 91, 96.

251. R. S. Morison, "First Half Century," 23–24; $120 more should be appropriated annually. The new Divinity Library was completed in 1887.

252. Harvard *Annual Report*, 1869–1870, 30, cited in Ahlstrom, "Middle Years," 89.

253. "Report for the Faculty of the Boston School for the Ministry," in *Christian Register* 47 (June 19, 1869), cited in Ahlstrom, "Middle Years," 89–90.

254. Ahlstrom, "Middle Years," 90, citing Harvard *Annual Reports* from the 1870s.

255. Emerton, "Historical Seminary," 200; "Practical Method," 59–60.

256. Eliot, "Theological Education," 59.

257. Edward Robinson to Board of Directors, "Dr. Edward Robinson's Letter of Acceptance," 1/20/1837, New York, printed as Appendix, Note C in *Services in Adams Chapel*, 40.

258. Hitchcock variously reports 25,000 volumes ("Church History: First Period," 1872–1873, Jackson notes [Jackson Papers, B1, N1, 5]) and 6000 separate works and 13,000 volumes ("Church History: First Period," 1883, Moore notes [B2, N2, 191]); 430 *incunabula* and much controversial literature of the Reformation era were included (Schaff, *Theological Propaedeutic* II: 405).

259. Hatfield, *Early Annals*, 14–15; Prentiss, *Union Theological Seminary*, 73–75; Gatch, *Library of Leander Van Ess*, 10–12.

260. Hitchcock, "Church History: First Period," 1872–1873, Jackson notes (Jackson Papers, B1, N1, 5).

261. Gillett, "Detailed History" III: 708.

262. Gillett, "Detailed History" III: 710; Slavens, "Incidents in the Librarianship," 7.

263. "Interesting Relic," unidentified clipping (Schaff Papers, UTS, B6, Scr2, 143). Hatfield had served as Recorder, Board member, and Financial Agent during the 1860s.

264. Gillett, "Detailed History" III: 710. On Smith as librarian, see Slavens, *Library of the Union Theological Seminary*, chap. 3.

265. Gillett, "Detailed History" III: 722, 723. It appears that insufficient funds were raised by subscription to make a "Reference Library," as some alumni desired (III: 718).

266. Slavens, "Incidents in the Librarianship," 75. Briggs redid the Union catalogue on the scheme of "Theological Encyclopedia" (Gillett, "Library Catalogue and the Alumni," in Prentiss, *Union Theological Seminary*, 356). By 1899, the Union library had around 115,000 titles, the largest theological library in America (352). In 1904, librarian Charles R. Gillett complained to John Crosby Brown, Chair of the Board of Directors, that it would take 834 days' work for staff to catalogue titles not yet catalogued: "one full year for my entire force" (Gillett to Brown, New York, 5/2/1904 [John Crosby Brown Papers, Correspondence, B1/1]).

267. Gillett, "Detailed History" III: 703–4, 704b.

268. Slavens, "Incidents in the Librarianship," 2–4.

269. Prentiss, "Union Theological Seminary." A Discourse, 25, 26.

270. Gillett, "Detailed History" III: 707–10.

271. Slavens, "Incidents in the Librarianship," 8 (Smith's letter to G. Prentiss, 2/25/1875).

272. Hitchcock, "Address," *Services in Adams Chapel*, 29–30; Prentiss, *Union Theological Seminary*, 55. In 1907, Union's Acting President George W. Knox reported

that Union still needed about $250,000 for a library building on Morningside Heights, plus $100,000 in endowment for the library ("Review of the Year 1906–1907," 31).

273. Wayland, *Theological Department*, 229, 232.

274. Naylor, "Theological Seminary," 24, citing *Quarterly Register and Journal of the American Education Society* 2 (May, 1830): 238–39, 247. But Wayland reports that in 1829 Yale had 540 "theological titles" (*Theological Department*, 231), including 82 books in ecclesiastical history and 66 on the Fathers. The counting was clearly done differently in these reports.

275. *ATR* 3.11 (July 1861): 552; *ATR* 3.10 (April 1861): 397.

276. Wayland, *Theological Department*, 278 (between 1858 and 1868, Neander's *History of the Christian Church* was the book most frequently checked out by theology students).

277. *[Yale] College Courant*, May 29, 1869, 333; Nov. 2, 1870, 62, 59, both cited in Knoff, *Yale Divinity School*, 123–24, 84–85 (the library had about 1,400 books at its opening).

278. Henry Adams, *Education of Henry Adams*, 390.

Chapter 3. Defending the Faith: European Theories and American Professors

Epigraph: Hedge, "Antisupernaturalism in the Pulpit," 147.

1. For a classic treatment, see Welch, *Protestant Thought in the Nineteenth Century*, vol. 1, *1799–1870*.

2. Infidelity signaled deviance from orthodox Christian (usually Protestant) belief, especially that associated with Rationalism and German philosophy. Regarding biblical criticism, I here deal mainly with critical scholarship on the New (not the Old) Testament. For the development of Ancient Near Eastern studies in America, see Kuklick, *Puritans in Babylon*.

3. Colenso, *The Pentateuch and Book of Joshua Critically Examined* (1862–1879). Colenso, Anglican Bishop of Natal, denied the Mosaic authorship of the Pentateuch. For Colenso in his South African context, see *Eye of the Storm*, ed. J. A. Draper. Roswell Hitchcock, reviewing Colenso, blames English universities: Colenso probably "studied Thucydides and Aeschylus more than he studied Moses and Isaiah" ("Literary and Critical Notices of Books," 163). Some thought Colenso had "gone native."

4. The "dangers" were also illustrated in novels, e.g., Mrs. Humphry Ward's *Robert Elsmere*, whose hero loses his faith upon encountering Continental biblical scholarship.

5. See McCosh, *Scottish Philosophy*; Hoeveler, *James McCosh and the Scottish Intellectual Tradition*; Sloan, *Scottish Enlightenment and the American College Ideal*.

6. Holifield, *Theology in America*, 178.

7. See Marsden, "Collapse of American Evangelical Academia."

8. Hitchcock similarly cautioned against a (Hegelian-derived) Pantheism, "Hu-

manitarianism," and "Materialism" (Comtian Positivism) ("Laws of Civilization," 3–4, pamphlet version).

9. *New American Cyclopaedia*, ed. Ripley and Dana, X: 107–15 (Kant); IX: 51–56 (Hegel); XIV: 396–400 (Schelling); and XII: 720–21 (Pantheism). Smith was deemed a leading American authority on Pantheism (Charles A. Dana to Smith, New York, 2/6/1861? [S1, B1]); cf. [E. Smith], *Henry Boynton Smith*, 223, 124, 53. Smith wrote on Hegel and Schelling for the *Southern Quarterly* (J. H. Thornwall to Smith, "Theological Seminary" [n.p.], 9/17 and 11/20/1856 [S1, B1]); see Smith's "Schelling on the Characteristics of the Different Christian Churches."

10. J[onathan] F. Stearns, "Charge to H. B. Smith," 1–13. Stearns, a Presbyterian minister (and father of Smith's biographer Lewis Stearns), wooed Smith and Hitchcock to Union (Gillett, "Library, General Catalogue and the Alumni," in Prentiss, *Union Theological Seminary . . . Its Design*, 400). A former student testified that Smith had "destroyed" Amherst students' fascination with Pantheism (Karr, "Introductory Note," to Smith, *Introduction to Christian Theology*, iv-v).

11. Smith, "Christian Apologetics," 482–83 (Smith recommended reading ancient critics of Christianity [e.g., Celsus, Porphyry, Julian] for insight into modern Infidelity [492, 487]); "Theology" [unspecified course], 1861–1862, Briggs notes (Briggs Papers, S8, B34, F5, N1, L18, 96).

12. Smith, "Sketch of German Philosophy," 262; "Relations of Faith and Philosophy," 37–38. See L. F. Stearns, *Henry Boynton Smith*, 85: now, theology professors who have studied in German universities "have learned that all that glitters is not gold." Writing to his parents when a student in Berlin (8/15/1839), Smith hopes that God will preserve his faith from German philosophical influences (cited in [E. Smith], *Henry Boynton Smith*, 74–75).

13. Smith, "Relations of Faith and Philosophy," 24. American Transcendentalism had surprisingly little impact on the professors here studied: on the subject, see Holifield, *Theology in America*, chap. 21.

14. Smith, "Sketch of German Philosophy," 261 (written three years before the 1848 revolutions).

15. Smith, *Introduction to Christian Theology*, 10n. For Smith, that source lay in Christocentrism.

16. Smith, "Christian Apologetics," 494. See below for the controversy at Yale over Spencer.

17. Smith, "Systematic Theology," 4/23/1858 (S4, B1, F16); "Theology" [unspecified course], 1861–1862, Briggs notes (Briggs Papers, S8, B34, F5, N1, L18, 98).

18. Smith, "Systematic Theology," 4/23/1858 (S4, B1, F16); "Theology" [unspecified course], 1861–1862, Briggs notes [Briggs Papers, S8, B34, F5, N1, 154]).

19. Smith, "Pantheism," in *New American Cyclopaedia*, ed. Ripley and Dana, XII: 720, examining Spinoza, Schelling, and Hegel (720–21).

20. Although Hegelianism presents "the most complete scientific attempt" to provide a key to history, the "Author" and destiny of this historical process remain vague.

For Americans, human history does not culminate in Prussia, but in the Kingdom of Redemption (Smith, "Problem of the Philosophy of History," 24, 25).

21. Smith, "Systematic Theology," 10/25–26/1857 (S4, B1, F4); Hegel's philosophy is the most "consummate and radiant form" of the older Christian theology (*Introduction to Christian Theology*, 46–47, citing Hegel's Introduction to the *Encyclopedia*).

22. Smith, "Being and Attributes of God," 1867, Stimson notes (Edwards Amassa Park Papers, UTS, B1, N2, #3, 4). Negating the idea of spirit does not get the real world, but "o."

23. Smith, *Introduction to Christian Theology*, 171n.; "Being and Attributes of God," 1867, Stimson notes (Edwards Amassa Park Papers, UTS, B1, N2, #4).

24. Smith, "Pantheism," in *New American Cyclopaedia*, ed. Ripley and Dana, XII: 721. See Smith's translation of and comment on A. D. C. Twesten's lectures on the Trinity (*BS* 3.11 [Aug. 1846]: 499–539; 3.12 [Nov. 1846]: 760–94; 4.13 [Feb. 1847]: 25–68).

25. Smith, "Sermon" (on John 20: 30–31) (S2, B2, 25–26).

26. Smith, "Idea of Christian Theology as a System," 274–75.

27. Smith, "Being and Attributes of God," 1867, Stimson notes (Edwards Amassa Park Papers, UTS, B1, N2, #4).

28. Smith, "Being and Attributes of God," 1867, Stimson notes (Edwards Amassa Park Papers, UTS, B1, N2, #4 and 4, #2).

29. Smith, "Sermon" (on II Tim. 3:14–15) (S2, B3, 7–8).

30. On American Reformed theologians' interest in Comtian Positivism ("Materialism"), see Cashdollar, "Auguste Comte," 61, 62, 66.

31. Cashdollar, "Auguste Comte," 67. McCosh's lectures were published in 1871 as *Christianity and Positivism*.

32. Smith, "Theological System of Emmons" (1862), 240.

33. Smith, "Theology" [unspecified course], 1862, Briggs notes (Briggs Papers, S8, B34.5, N1, 74–76).

34. Smith, "Theology" [unspecified course], 1862, Briggs notes (Briggs Papers, S8, B34.5, N1, 77, 78, 80–81). See Smith's scathing review, "Draper's Intellectual Development of Europe."

35. Fisher, "Conflict: First Article," 131.

36. Fisher, *Grounds of Theistic and Christian Belief*, 77; *Beginnings of Christianity*, 392, 393.

37. Fisher, *Grounds of Theistic and Christian Belief*, 77, 78.

38. Fisher, *Beginnings of Christianity*, 5. Christianity is not an "Idea" that realizes itself through the dialectic.

39. For Porter's objection and Sumner's response, see *American Higher Education*, ed. Hofstadter and Smith, II: 849–57 (Porter claimed that Spencer attacked theism, assuming that "material elements and laws are the only forces and laws which any scientific man can recognize"); see discussion in Gabriel, *Religion and Learning at Yale*, 162–67, 182–83.

40. See Starr, *William Graham Sumner*, chap. 15 (including letters from Porter to

Sumner and Sumner to the Yale Corporation); Curtis, *William Graham Sumner*, chaps. 2–5.

41. Fisher, "Materialism and the Pulpit," 215, 208, 210, 211. Fisher perhaps knew the full French edition of Comte's *Cours de philosophie positive*, not merely the two-volume English abridgement (1853) by Harriet Martineau (Cashdollar, "Auguste Comte," 62, 63).

42. Fisher, "Rationalism," 274, 253; "Materialism," 212, 215, 213.

43. Ephraim Emerton, less philosophically and evangelically inclined, mostly avoids such discussions, while Samuel Miller seems largely unaware of the issues.

44. Noll, *Between Faith and Criticism*, 14; on debates over biblical criticism and inspiration at American seminaries, 15–30.

45. Miller's notes labeled "Biblical History" deal largely with Old Testament chronology and personages. See notes taken by students C. Crosby, J. F. Crowe, and O. Douglass (B22, F20, F16, F 4), and Miller's own notes (B8, F13).

46. See Marsden, "'Everyone One's Own Interpreter'." My research supports Marsden's claim (*Soul*, 207) that newer views of biblical criticism could not be fully accepted in America until the notion of historical development, associated with German Idealism, had been digested.

47. Wacker, "Demise of Biblical Civilization," 122. Marchand notes that although in 1873 the *Daily Telegraph* published fragments of the newly discovered Babylonian flood story, only in the 1880s did German scholars attempt to interpret it. Assyriology, she claims, "played a crucial role in the de-universalizing and demotion of the history of the Hebrews, perhaps the most momentous and ominous shift in the occidental, and especially the German, understanding of the oriental past to occur in recent times" (*Down from Olympus*, 220–23, at 221).

48. Schaff spent six weeks in England en route to Mercersburg, improving his English (Shriver, *Philip Schaff*, 15–16; Graham, *Cosmos in the Chaos*, 56–57).

49. [E. Smith], *Henry Boynton Smith*, 39–84. Smith spent some months in Paris.

50. Shriver, *Philip Schaff*, 3–12; on Berlin, Howard, *Protestant Theology*, chap. 3.

51. Williston Walker, "Professor Fisher," *Yale Divinity Quarterly* (Jan. 1910): 77, cited in Knoff, *Yale Divinity School*, 37.

52. In 1859, Halle had 465 theology students (*ATR* 3.12 [Oct. 1861]: 756). On Halle's Pietistic heritage and later developments, see Paulsen, *German Universities*, 57–61; Howard, *Protestant Theology*, 87–99.

53. Tholuck, "Evangelical Theology in Germany," 86. In 1831, Edward Robinson thought Halle still Rationalistic and of dubious piety: "Theological Education in Germany," *BR* 1.1: 20, 28–29; 1.2: 223.

54. Fisher, *Diary* (B114, 32).

55. Ullmann, "Preface," to Neander, *General History* I: x.

56. On Tholuck's generous hospitality toward students, see Robinson, "Theological Education," *BR* 1.1: 48.

57. Robinson deemed Tübingen the only German university true to Reformation doctrine ("Theological Education," *BR* 1.1: 36).

58. Edward Pusey was alleged to be one of two scholars at Oxford who knew German in the 1830s (Neil, "Criticism and Theological Use of the Bible," 278). For Renan, see the translator's "Preface" to his *Life of Jesus*, dated Dec. 8, 1863.

59. On Strauss's first version of *Leben Jesu*, see Schweitzer, *Quest*, chap. 8; on responses to Strauss, chap. 9. In 1837, Tholuck and Neander both wrote against Strauss (99–101); Schweitzer calls Neander's *Life of Jesus* the "child of despair," "a patchwork of unsatisfactory compromises" (101).

60. Hodgson, *Formation of Historical Theology*, 24. Strauss was barred from chairs elsewhere (in 1839, 40,000 people signed a petition to block his accession to the chair in dogmatics at Zurich); see Neil, "Criticism and Theological Use," in *Cambridge History*, III: 276. Although Strauss knew his approach rendered impossible his roles as minister and teacher, he thought time would tell who serves the church, humankind, and truth the best (*Life of Jesus* [1835], II: 897–901).

61. Barth, "Strauss," in Barth, *Protestant Thought From Rousseau to Ritschl*, 362.

62. Strauss, *Life* I: 61; Toews, *Hegelianism*, chap. 8.

63. Strauss, *Life* II: 897; I: 4.

64. Strauss, *Life* I: 43.

65. Schweitzer, *Quest*, 79. Strauss (*Life* I: 28) defines myth: "the representation of an event or of an idea in a form which is historical, but, at the same time characterized by the rich pictorial and imaginative mode of thought and expression of the primitive ages."

66. Strauss, *Life* I: 70–75. Among "negative" criteria: a story's irreconcilability with universal laws and its contradiction of itself or other accounts; among "positive" criteria, the appearance of characters from legend, belief that a character fulfilled a common hope.

67. Strauss, *Life* I: 43.

68. Barth, "Strauss," 381.

69. Strauss, *Life* II: 881. The story of Jesus' Transfiguration illustrates how a naturalistic interpretation (i.e., one seeking to preserve the historicity of the narrative but explain it by the laws of nature and by reason) loses the "ideal truth" contained therein (II: 615).

70. Strauss, *Life* II: 891. Since Kant's religion amounts to morals, a human historical manifestation (viz., Jesus) as bearer of moral ideas becomes unnecessary (II: 887–888). Strauss's implication that religion's chief function is to "console" distinguished his view from that of Schleiermacher, for whom religion manifests humans' feeling of "absolute dependence."

71. Strauss, *Life* I: 65.

72. Kümmel, *Introduction to the New Testament*, 197.

73. Strauss, *Life* I: 419; II: 551.

74. Strauss, *Life* I: 66–67nn., 249; Schleiermacher's picture of Christ satisfies nei-

ther science nor faith (II: 881–83). For Strauss's developed critique of Schleiermacher, see *The Christ of Faith and the Jesus of History* (1865).

75. Strauss, *Life* II: 451–54. The supernaturalistic (i.e., miraculous) interpretation of Jesus' multiplication of the loaves and the fishes is countered by the rationalistic explanation (the crowd shared their food). In contrast, the mythical interpretation shows the Evangelists' desire to represent Jesus as replicating Old Testament food miracles (e.g., Moses' provision of quails and manna on the Exodus [II: 568–82]).

76. Strauss, *Life* II: 850–51 (cf. Is. 53; Ps. 16:10); 646–47. With no resurrection, there can be no ascension (II: 861–63).

77. Strauss, *Life* I: 244, 296, 300–301; II: 895.

78. H. Harris, *Tübingen School*, 2, 249.

79. H. Harris, *Tübingen School*, v, 250, emphasizing the contributions of Eduard Zeller (4, 50, chap. 3). By the time Baur wrote *Church History of the First Three Centuries* (1853), Hegelianism had receded; Christianity is now purely ethics (158).

80. Baur, "Die Christuspartei in der korinthischen Gemeinde" (1831).

81. Baur, *Die sogennanten Pastoralbriefe des Apostels Paulus* (1835).

82. For example, Baur, *Das Manichäische Religionssystem (1831); Die christliche Gnosis* (1835); *Paulus, der Apostel Jesu Christi* (1845); *Kritische Untersuchungen über die kanonischen evangelien* (1847).

83. The School's positions had been explained for English-speaking audiences in 1863 by Mackay, *The Tübingen School and Its Antecedents*.

84. Penzel, "Editorial Introduction," to Schaff, "[General] Introduction to Church History," *History of Apostolic Christianity* I, in *Philip Schaff, Historian and Ambassador*, ed. Penzel, 123.

85. Hester, "Gedanken," 249. Hester charts Baur's development as an historian and his changing philosophical interests.

86. Baur, *Church History* I: 137.

87. Baur, *Church History* I: x–xi. Elsewhere Baur claimed that arguing from the supernatural renders correct historical estimates impossible: miracle entails "an absolutely incomprehensible beginning" (*Epochs of Church Historiography* [1852], 48, 57, 213). Hester argues that it was not Schleiermacher who gave Baur the grounds to break with supernaturalism, but his study of Schelling ("Gedanken," 249, 256, 258, 264). Also see H. Harris, *Tübingen School*, 246, 249, 251, 254.

88. Baur, *Church History* I: 1, 42, 43.

89. Baur collected some of his essays on Paul and Acts in (as translated into English) *Paul, the Apostle of Jesus Christ* (1876); see H. Harris, *Tübingen School*, 246, 181–82.

90. Baur, *Paul*, 217–18, 239; on concessions, 240. On Acts' unhistorical picture of Paul, 245; on party division at Corinth, 295–96.

91. Baur (*Epochs of Church Historiography*, 300) depicts the history of dogma as resulting from the "continual procession of Spirit in never-ending conflict with itself"; "Spirit, like Penelope, continually unravels its own web, only to begin again anew."

92. H. Harris, *Tübingen School*, 237 for Baur's dating of New Testament books.

93. H. Harris, *Tübingen School*, 184. Romans 15–16 are non-Pauline: the Roman Church was Jewish-Christian; the names listed in Romans 16 are Gentile (Baur, *Church History* I: 182–83).

94. Baur, *Church History* I: 55–76. Challenges to Paul's authority in Corinthians, Romans, and Galatians revolve around this question (I: 55–76). In Romans, Paul fully exposed Judaism's "offensive claims" (I: 73).

95. H. Harris, *Tübingen School*, 185; see Baur's *Die sogenannten Pastoralbriefe des Apostels Paulus* (1835); the opposition to heresy and the Pastor's restriction on women's activity show the Pastorals are post-Pauline.

96. H. Harris, *Tübingen School*, 210, citing Baur's *Kritische Untersuchungen über die kanonischen Evangelien* (1847). See Hodgson, *Formation of Historical Theology*, 208–20.

97. Taking the "little Apocalypse" of Matt. 24 to refer to the Bar Kokhba revolt of 132 C.E., Baur dated the final Greek version of Matthew to 130–34 (H. Harris, *Tübingen School*, 210–11).

98. Baur, *Church History* I: 25–26; and H. Harris, *Tübingen School*, 210–12, 228–29. Baur denigrates the historical authority of Mark (*Kritische Untersuchungen*, 560, cited in H. Harris, *Tübingen School*, 211). Luke overlooks the Jewish claims or represents the Jewish-oriented disciples in an "unfavourable light" (Baur, *Church History* I: 80).

99. Baur, *Church History* I: 24–25, 84–88, 153, 154–57; H. Harris, *Tübingen School*, 194–95, 261: since the apostle John is one of the "reputed [Jewish] pillars" of Gal. 2:9, he could not have written the more "universalizing" Gospel of John; dating and geographical errors also count against apostolic authorship.

100. Baur, *Church History* I: 173–77, citation at 177. Baur believed that the Quarto-decimans had the stronger claim; the Western tradition was a later adjustment (I: 175).

101. Baur, *Church History* I: 44–45. Jesus necessarily assumed the form of "the cramping and narrowing influence of the Jewish national Messianic ideal" to proclaim his moral, universalistic message (I: 49).

102. Baur, *Church History* I: 53, 55. The Paul of Acts makes concessions to Jewish Christians that "it is impossible that he should have made," while Peter looks "Pauline," e.g., he baptizes a Gentile, Cornelius (I: 133, 134, 135).

103. Baur, *Church History* I: 113, 106–8, 2–3, 4–5, 6; Jewish "particularism" is deemed "selfish" (41); allegorical interpretation helped to break it (18, 19)

104. Baur, *Church History* I: 6, 58, 8–9, 38.

105. H. Harris, *Tübingen School*, 261, 193–95, 210–12, 215–16.

106. Baur, *Church History* I: 115, 129, 122–23.

107. H. Harris, *Tübingen School*, 181–82.

108. Baur, *Church History* I: 90–97; H. Harris, *Tübingen School*, 184–85, 256–58.

109. Paul, like Simon Magus, desired the apostolic office (Baur, *Church History* I: 95–96). The Pseudo-Clementine *Homilies* attack Marcion's Gnosticism in the guise of Simon Magus (I: 236).

110. The Syriac letters were brought to the British Museum from Egypt in the early 1840s. Cureton deemed authentic only the three letters in Syriac (to Polycarp, Ephesus, and Rome), a view adopted by Baron C. C. J. Bunsen, Prussian ambassador to Britain, who wrote *Die drei ächten und die vier unächten Briefe des Ignatius von Antiochen* [1847]). Baur scathingly called Bunsen a "mere dilettante"; see Baur's letter to Robert von Mohl, 12/31/1847 (in H. Harris, *Tübingen School*, 213–14). For debates over Ignatius, see Chapter 6 below.

111. Baur, *Die ignatianischen Briefe und ihr neuester Kritiker: Eine Streitschrift gegen Herrn Bunsen* (1848), esp. 37–41, 44, 57, 60, 74, 115, 132–33. In the 1870s and 1880s, Theodor Zahn and J. B. Lightfoot independently showed the authenticity of all seven letters, arguing that the Syriac version was a crude abridgement of the original Greek; see discussion in H. Harris, *Tübingen School*, 215–16, citing Zahn's *Ignatius von Antiochen* (1873) and Lightfoot's *The Apostolic Fathers*, Part II, Vol. I (1885).

112. The Gospel of John places Jesus' crucifixion on the 14th of Nissan (Passover); the Synoptics represent it as falling on the next day; see Baur, *Church History* I: 159–75.

113. H. Harris, *Tübingen School*, 229–31. Baur wrote on John in 1844, 1847, 1848, 1854, and 1857. A trenchant criticism by Gerhard Uhlhorn pronounced the School's demise ("Die älteste Kirchengeschichte in der Darstellung der Tübinger Schule," 280–349; some passages cited in H. Harris, *Tübingen School*, 240–41). Baur's short treatise, *Die Tübinger Schule* (1859), is largely directed against Uhlhorn. Uhlhorn's criticism of Baur may have won him favor in America.

114. Baur, *Church History* I: 138, 140, 141–42, 147. Strikingly, Baur considers only Justin's *Dialogue with Trypho*, overlooking the *Apologies*.

115. Baur, *Church History* I: 148–52. The new universalism saw itself realized on the "practical" side in the church at Rome, and on the "ideal" side, in the Gospel of John, both essential to the development of the Catholic Church (I: 180).

116. Baur, *Church History* I: 181–83, 185; II: 2; II: 63. The development of the episcopate helped to "cool down" ecstatic, millenarian Montanism (*Church History* II: 30, 48).

117. Baur, *Church History* II: 229. Episcopacy bound laity closely to the clergy, yet allowed for "endless development."

118. Headlam, "Methods," 250; original lectures delivered at Trinity College, Cambridge in 1898 or early 1899.

119. Headlam, "Methods," 251.

120. Schweitzer, *Quest*, 181, 188, 190.

121. Renan, *Life*, 33, 54, 58. Miracles happen only in times and countries in which people believe in them (59).

122. Renan, *Life*, 37. Mark has a "firmer, more precise" narrative than Matthew (50); Luke carries weaker historical authority (51).

123. Renan, *Life*, 43–44, 45. Renan characterizes the speeches of Jesus in John as "pretentious tirades, heavy, badly written, and appealing little to the moral sense" (44); as "stiff and awkward discourses" (47).

124. Renan, *Life*, 46, 49. But Renan apparently opted for (at most) a one-year ministry of Jesus (125), thus rejecting John's inference of a three-year ministry.

125. Renan, *Life*, 49.

126. Renan, *Life*, 368, 121, 122, 393, 392. Among others who felt God within them: the Buddha, Plato, Paul, Francis of Assisi, and Augustine (121).

127. Renan, *Life*, 168–69, 173, 86, 250, 96, 107.

128. Renan, *Life*, 129, 269, 300, 132, 358.

129. Renan, *Life*, 235, 214, 223, 297–99, 354–55, 391. Renan calls the Pentateuch the "first code of religious terrorism"; Christianity, upon achieving power, should have abolished the regime that killed Jesus (359).

130. Renan, *Life*, 195, 197, 266, 268. Ebionism—from the Hebrew word for "the poor"—was considered a deviant early Christian sect of Adoptionist persuasion.

131. Renan, *Life*, 257, 324, 249. There was no "supernatural" for Jesus because there was no "natural" (242).

132. Renan, *Life*, 288–89, 293.

133. Renan, *Life*, 330, 294, 367, 374. The disciples understood nothing of Jesus' purpose; the apostles' writings are "full of errors and misconceptions" (335, 387).

134. Schweitzer, *Quest*, 187. Schweitzer claims that Renan had not, as a Catholic, grown up with the New Testament and hence "perfumed" biblical simplicity with sentimentality in order to feel at home with the text (192).

135. Renan, *Life*, 65.

136. On the early reception of Strauss's *Life of Jesus* in America, see J. W. Brown, *Rise of Biblical Criticism*, chap. 9.

137. Samuel Miller of Princeton Seminary did not usually teach Bible; there, the teaching of church history was linked to church polity or government. Nor did Ephraim Emerton of Harvard teach Bible. If Unitarians (such as himself) have not been leaders in biblical criticism, Emerton wrote, this is partly because they never considered "the Bible as the sole source of Christian truth." The criticism now alarming evangelical Christians, Unitarians accepted much earlier (*Unitarian Thought*, 128).

Roswell Hitchcock's views on New Testament scholarship are largely traditional. He affirms the Mosaic authorship of the Pentateuch; dates all New Testament books to the first century; upholds the priority of Matthew, the Pastoral Epistles as Pauline, and "John" as the author of the Gospel, the Epistles, and Revelation; and harmonizes the Synoptics and John (*Hitchcock's New and Complete Analysis of the Holy Bible*, 1128, 1150, 1157; "Person of Christ," 25); and Hitchcock's courses, "Life of Christ" and "Apostolic Church," mid-1860s, Wright notes (B2, N1). Despite Hitchcock's criticisms of Strauss, he deemed Strauss's *Leben Jesu* "epoch-making" ("Apostolic Church," mid-1860s, Wright notes [B2, N1, 24]). Hitchcock characterized Renan's view of Christ: "a good hardy Galilean peasant who gradually degenerated into an imposter"—rather like Mohammed. Renan's *Life of Jesus* is "at least two decades behind the time" ("Life of Christ," early 1880s, Burrell notes [B1, N1, 9, 24]).

138. Smith revisited Europe three times after his student days; see Prentiss, *Union Theological Seminary*, 261, on Smith's life.

139. Smith, "Relations of Faith and Philosophy," 38, 41–42. On Baur's death in December 1860, Smith wrote that despite his "destructive" criticism, his "writings are among the ablest in the modern German theology" (*ATR* 3.10 [April 1861]: 375).

140. Smith thought Schleiermacher's *Lectures on the Life of Jesus* would "excite fresh interest, in consequence of the recent works of Renan, Schenkl, and Strauss" (*APTR* 3.9 [Jan. 1865]: 172). Smith reported (*APTR* 3.10 [April 1861]: 327) that Strauss's forthcoming work, *The Christ of Faith and the Jesus of History*, attacked Schleiermacher's *Life of Christ*.

141. Against such views, Isaak Dorner wrote *Die Lehre von der Person Christi* (1845), which Smith warmly reviewed ("Introduction" to [I. A.] "Dorner's History of the Doctrine of the Person of Christ").

142. Smith, "Inspiration of the Holy Scriptures," 36, 4, 3.

143. Smith, "Inspiration of the Holy Scriptures," 21–22 [fourth-century "Anomoeans" denied the likeness of the Son to the Father], 23, 31, 33–34 (surveying evidence from India, China, Nineveh, and Egypt). Science does not nullify the creation narrative or "the unity of the race," humans' descent from the first pair (14–15).

144. Smith, "Inspiration of the Holy Scriptures," 17. "Remove from the Old Testament its own claims of divine authority, and it becomes a chaotic mass of superstition; concede these claims, and all is light and order" (17–18).

145. Smith, "Inspiration of the Holy Scriptures," 35.

146. Presumably Strauss's *Life of Jesus for the German People*, German original, early 1864.

147. Smith, "Renan's Life of Jesus," 403.

148. Smith, "Christian Union and Ecclesiastical Reunion," 274–75.

149. Smith, "New Faith of Strauss," 444–45. Fisher of Yale, congratulating Smith on his article, mentioned his own review of Strauss's last book for *Scribner's Magazine* (Fisher to Smith, New Haven, 4/5/1874 [S1, B1]).

150. Smith, "New Faith of Strauss," 446. Darwin's *Origin of Species* was published five years before Smith wrote. Shortly before he died, Smith was preparing lectures on evolution; see Chapter 9 below.

151. Smith, "New Faith of Strauss," 463, 466, 470, 479, 481, 486–87, 457.

152. Smith, *Introduction to Christian Theology*, 157–58, 160–62; summary of the School's teachings, 158–60.

153. *APTR* 5.19 (July 1867): 501.

154. *ATH* 2.5 (Feb. 1860): 162; *APTR* 2.5 (Jan. 1864): 192. Also reviews of Renan in *APTR* 2.6 (April 1864): 366; 6.21 (Jan. 1868): 161.

155. *APR* 1.1. (Jan. 1869): 207; *PQPR* 1.3 (July 1872): 617: Renan deems the restoration of the monarchy necessary for France's salvation.

156. *ATR* 4.14 (April 1862): 372; 4.16 (Oct. 1862): 725.

157. Smith, "Theology" [unspecified course], 1861–1862, Briggs notes (Briggs

Papers, S8, B34, F5, N, 227); Smith, "Being and Attributes of God," 1867, Stimson notes (Edwards Amassa Park Papers, UTS, B1, N2, #III).

158. Smith, "Renan's Life of Jesus," 405, 407, 403, 402.

159. Smith, "Renan's Life of Jesus," 416, 404. Critics of the Tübingen School should know its views.

160. Smith, "Renan's Life of Jesus," 404, 411, 412, 431, 416, 403–4, 435.

161. Smith, "Sermon" (John 17:17) (S2, B2, 4).

162. Smith, *Introduction to Christian Theology*, 146, 148, 147. Smith (raised as a Unitarian) objected: if the Unitarian view of Scripture were accepted, "then everything is uncertain and fluctuating," a mere human record ("Systematic Theology,"1857? [S4, B1, F1, L2]).

163. Smith, "Systematic Theology," 9/28/1857 (S4, B1, F1, L8).

164. Smith, *Introduction to Christian Theology*, 191.

165. Smith, *Introduction to Christian Theology*, 191. To be considered authoritative, biblical books must have been cited by Jesus and his Apostles, or written by the latter.

166. Smith, "Sermon" (John 17:17) (S2, B2, 17–18; in Irenaeus' *Against Heresies*, "nearly all the books of Scripture are expressly named"; "Systematic Theology," 9/28/ 1857 (S4, B1, F1, L8).

167. Smith, *Introduction to Christian Theology*, 147; "Sermon" (John 17:17) (S2, B2, 6, 18).

168. Smith apparently believed that *I Clement* was written by the "Clement" of Phil. 4:3.

169. Smith, "Sermon" (John 17:17) (S2, B2, 17); likewise for Ignatius, Polycarp, and Justin Martyr.

170. Smith, "Doctrinal History," 1851, Hastings notes (S5, B1, F3, 19).

171. Smith, "Sermon" (John 17:17) (S2, B2, 18–19).

172. Smith, *Introduction to Christian Theology*, 192; on Scripture and Tradition, see Chapter 7.

173. Smith, "Sermon" (John 17:17) (S2, B2, 6–7).

174. Smith, "Sermon" (John 17:17) (S2, B2, 8). Smith ingeniously appropriates an argument derived from Hume's critique of miracles—but to contrary purpose.

175. Smith, "Sermon" (John 17:17) (S2, B2, 10, 12, 15).

176. Smith, "Doctrinal History," 1851, Hastings notes (S5, B1, F3, 17).

177. Smith, "Church History," 1849–1850 (?), Hastings notes (S5, B1, F3, 5, 60). Smith discusses Schelling on Petrine, Pauline, and Johannine Christianity ("Schelling," in *New American Cyclopaedia*, ed. Ripley and Dana, XIV: 400). For Lectures 36 and 37 of Schelling's *Die Philosophie der Mythologie und Offenbarung*, given at the University of Berlin in 1841 and thereafter, see Penzel, "Ecumenical Vision," texts at 11–18.

178. D. Schaff, *Life of Philip Schaff*, 65; Pranger, *Philip Schaff*, 54, citing Schaff's "Reminiscences," 98–99.

179. Mercersburg boasted two professors (John W. Nevin and Schaff); when

Nevin resigned in 1850, Schaff taught the whole theological curriculum for four years (D. Schaff, *Life*, 125). At Union, Schaff taught Bible for almost twice as long—from the 1870s to 1887—as he taught Church History (Shriver, *Philip Schaff*, 49).

180. For Schaff's conservatism, see his "Plea for Primitive Christianity."

181. For a detailed discussion, see D. Schaff, *Life*, chap. 14; and Schaff, *Companion to the Greek Testament and The English Version*, chap. 8.

Harvard student Earl Morse Wilbur worked for Professor J. H. Thayer, secretary of the American Committee. His proofreading task entailed changing throughout the text, "which" to "who," or as Thayer put it, the "exorcizing of the whiches" (Wilbur, [untitled] biographical statement, in Wilbur Papers, bMS 119/2, F18 ["Biographical and Bibliographical"], 76). In the 1850s, Arthur Cleveland Coxe had worried about a "New Baptist Version" and an "American Bible Society Version" ("tampering with the English Bible" ["Apology for the Common English Bible," 14, 8]).

182. Schaff, "Is Romanism Hostile to the Bible?" clipping from [*New-York*] *Independent*, n.d. (UTS, B6, Scr1, 92). The Authorized Version best answers "the attacks and sneers of modern infidelity" (*Companion*, 406); for Schaff's reminiscences on the project, see his *Diary* (1/1/1884) (UTS, B4).

183. Revisers worked from the Westcott and Hort text, compiled mainly from the Vaticanus and Sinaiticus codices (the latter discovered only in the mid-nineteenth century). Reporting that a minority of the Committee preferred the fifth-century Alexandrinus, Schaff quipped that they "stop with the fathers, the Revisers go back to the grandfathers" ("Revised Version and Its Critics," *New-York Independent*, March 22, 1883). He assured readers that nine-tenths of the changes do not affect the sense ("Revised Version and Its Critics-II," *New-York Independent*, April 8, 1883). Not all critics approved the Revisers' choice of manuscripts to privilege or their translations.

184. The *New-York Independent* articles date from March 22 to July 5, 1883 (UTS, B6, Scr2, 2–7).

185. For the dramatic story of publication by the *Chicago Tribune* and *Chicago Times*, see Shriver, *Philip Schaff*, 75–76; D. Schaff, *Life*, 382–83. At the *Tribune* 92 compositors worked all night to produce the edition.

186. So G. Harris, *Century's Change in Religion*, 11.

187. D. Schaff, *Life*, 383. On May 21, 1881, the *New York Tribune* gave the figure as 300,000. The *New York Herald* reported that crowds of wholesalers gathered by 4 a.m. to secure as many copies as they could; single copies were available only from booksellers and street peddlers; the latter apparently did a good business on Wall Street that day (Schaff, *Companion*, 407–9).

188. Schaff, *Companion*, 405; Saunders, *Searching the Scriptures*, 13.

189. Schaff, *Companion*, 494.

190. Only in 1901, after Schaff's death, was this hoped-for edition published (Shriver, *Philip Schaff*, 77).

191. Schaff defended the traditional dating of the book of Daniel: "The moral spirit of the book is high. No fraud is to be found here." Urban Babylon could have

felt Greek influence ("General Introduction to the Old Testament Scriptures," UTS, 1877–1878 (?), Gillett notes [UTS, B3, N, 88]).

192. Schaff, "German Theology and the Church Question," 131. For Schaff, a primary significance of the discovery of Ephraem's *Commentary on [Tatian's] Diatesseron* is its support for "the genuineness of our Gospels" (*History* II: 493). The apocryphal gospels, by contrast, written by heretics, contain much that is "absurd and foolish" ("Brief Introduction to the New Testament," UTS, 1877–1878 (?), Gillett notes [UTS, B3, N, 133]).

193. Schaff, *History* I: vi.

194. Schaff, "Language of Christ," unidentified clipping (UTS, B6, Scr1, 152).

195. Schaff, "Theological Encyclopedia," UTS, 1877/1878 (?), Gillett notes (UTS, B3, "Miscellaneous," N, 36); *Companion*, 12, 15.

196. Schaff, "Language of Christ," unidentified clipping (UTS, B6, Scr1, 152); *Companion*, 15.

197. Schaff, "Brief Introduction to the New Testament," UTS, 1877–1878 (?), Gillett notes (UTS, B3, N, 123, 121).

198. Schaff, *History* III: 610–11.

199. Schaff, "Brief Introduction to the New Testament," UTS, 1877–1878 (?), Gillett notes (UTS, B3, N, 127).

200. Schaff, *History* I: 739.

201. He upheld the Pauline authorship of the Pastoral and other New Testament Epistles, 13 in all: see Schaff, "Brief Introduction to the New Testament," UTS, 1877–1878 (?), Gillett notes (B3, N, 145); *History* I: 333.

202. Schaff, "Brief Introduction to the New Testament," UTS, 1877–1878 (?), Gillett notes (UTS, B3, N, 127; the Apostles *first* preached, and *then* wrote, John composing his Gospel only at the end of the first century [122]). In his *Companion* (16, 46–54), Schaff refrained from dating the Synoptics, although he assumed that Matthew was a disciple, and that Mark and Luke lived less than a generation removed from Jesus. Also see Schaff, *History* I: 426, 605.

203. Schaff dated the finalization of the New Testament canon to the Council of Carthage in 397: "Brief Introduction to the New Testament," UTS, 1877–1878 (?), Gillett notes (UTS, B3, N, 125). The professors seem unaware of Athanasius' list in Festal Letter 39 of 367.

204. Schaff, *History* I: 28; *Theological Propaedeutic*, Part II: 326; "Brief Introduction to the New Testament," UTS, 1877–1878 (?), Gillett notes (UTS, B3, N, 221).

205. Schaff, *History* I: 106; "Christ's Testimony to Christianity," 3–4, 6, in contrast to "the crude inventions of a morbid imagination" of the Apocryphal Gospels (7).

206. Schaff, "Brief Introduction to the New Testament," UTS, 1877–1878 (?), Gillett notes (UTS, B3, N, 134).

207. Schaff, *History* I: 580, 584.

208. Schaff, *History* I: 420; "Brief Introduction to the New Testament," UTS, 1877–1878 (?), Gillett notes (B3, N, 139, 121–22, 153); similarly, *Companion*, 77–78.

209. Schaff, *History* I: 426, 605, 701, 714, 724.

210. Schaff, *Person of Christ*, 59; "Brief Introduction to the New Testament," UTS, 1877–1878 (?), Gillett notes (UTS, B3, N, 123). On the disastrous aftermath of attempts to "de-Judaize" Jesus, see Heschel, *Aryan Jesus*, especially chap. 1.

211. Schaff, *History* I: 750.

212. Schaff, "Plea for Primitive Christianity," *New-York Independent* July 8, 1880 (?), clipping (UTS, B6, Scr1, 146).

213. Schaff, "Brief Introduction to the New Testament," UTS, 1877–1878 (?), Gillett notes (UTS, B3, N, 210).

214. Schaff, *History* I: 43; *Theological Propaedeutic* II: 302.

215. Schaff, *History* I: 541n.1. Schaff added that more moderate followers of Baur admit 7 to 10 Pauline Epistles, "leaving only the three Pastoral Epistles and Ephesians in serious doubt."

216. Even Neander, in Schaff's judgment, conceded too much to modern biblical criticism: see Shriver, "Philip Schaff's Concept of Organic Historiography," 81.

217. Schaff, "Progress of Church History," 79–80, 81, 82.

218. Galatians, I and II Corinthians, and Romans minus chapter 16: Schaff, "Plea for Primitive Christianity," *New-York Independent* July 8, 1880 (?), clipping (UTS, B6, Scr1, 146).

219. Schaff, "Progress of Church History," 80–81.

220. Schaff, *History* II: 636n.2.

221. Schaff, *Theological Propaedeutic* II: 302, 374; even Baur (so Schaff reported) bowed before the miracle of Christ's resurrection and Paul's conversion.

222. Schaff, *History* I: 516. In *Companion* (77–78n.), Schaff noted that even Baur conceded the similarity between the Gospel of John and the Apocalypse, citing Baur's *Die Evangelien* (389), "Man kann mit Recht sagen, das vierte Evangelium sei die vergeistigte Apokalypse." On Schelling as a possible source for Schaff's categorization of Petrine, Pauline, and Johannine currents in Christian history, see Penzel, "Ecumenical Vision."

223. Schaff, "Autobiographical Reminiscences" (LTS, B1, F04, 116–17); Pranger, *Philip Schaff*, 29.

224. Fisher, "Christian Religion: Part III," 180–81.

225. Fisher worried, for example, about the Israelites' attempted extermination of the Canaanites, concluding the action's necessity to preserve Israelite purity ("Christian Religion: Part III," 187–88).

226. Fisher, "Christian Religion: Part III," 210, 211.

227. Fisher, "Church History," 1870–1871 (117).

228. Fisher, *Beginnings of Christianity*, 7. Even the Apostles shared "their countrymen's" hope for the coming of a visible, Messianic kingdom—not noticing the divergence of Jesus' intimations on the subject (364–65). They also erred on "the obligation of the Mosaic ceremonies" (374).

229. Fisher, *Beginnings of Christianity*, 444, 453. That Jesus did not mean an *actual*

kingdom is shown by his resisting the temptation regarding the kingdoms of the world and his advice to give tribute money to Caesar (Matt. 22:17, Mark 12:14, Lk. 20:22) (445–46, 448). Given the disciples' materialist understanding of the Kingdom, Jesus needed to teach in pictures—thus passages about drinking wine in the Kingdom (Matt. 26:29, Mk. 14:25, Lk. 22.18} or sitting on thrones judging Israel (Matt. 19:28, Lk. 22:30) are to be taken figuratively (453–54).

230. Fisher, *Beginnings of Christianity*, 25.

231. Fisher, "Christian Religion: Part III," 199.

232. Fisher, "Historical Proofs. First Article," 409, 410. No one, from the disciples onward, doubted that Jesus proclaimed himself Messiah; nor was he "dazed and deluded" (401, 403, 407).

233. Fisher, "Historical Proofs. First Article," 413 (a point Fisher probably derived from Schleiermacher), 418.

234. Fisher, "Historical Proofs. Third Article," 191, 198, claiming that "a tolerably full narrative of the life of Jesus can be put together from Justin's quotations and allusions" alone. The view that apocryphal Gospels abounded and were used in second-century churches is "groundless" (210).

235. Fisher, "Historical Proofs. Third Article," 215–16.

236. Fisher introduced himself as a "student of theology in the University at Halle": see Fisher, Introductory Note to his translation of Neander, "Relation of the Grecian to Christian Ethics," 476, 477.

237. See Schleiermacher, *Christian Faith*, 70–73, 178–84, 448–50. Schleiermacher seeks to reformulate Christian teaching to accommodate Spinoza's and Hume's critiques and the postulates of modern science.

238. Fisher, "Introductory Note," to his translation of Neander, 479, 480, emphasis added. Doctrine proves miracles, as much as miracles prove doctrine (480).

239. See Fisher, "Historical Proofs. Second Article," 35–60.

240. Fisher, "Historical Proofs. Second Article," esp. 47, 48, 56–60. Jesus declined to have his miracles broadcast to prevent a popular uprising (38–39).

241. Fisher, "Miracles," 282; Thomas Huxley is criticized for allowing only "natural causes" (278).

242. Fisher, "Historical Proofs. Second Article," 49–56; "Christian Religion: Part III," 192, 193.

243. Fisher, "Historical Proofs. First Article," 399–400. Looking to the message's incorporation in the consciousness of the believer, a Schleiermacherian theme, became popular in America in extra-academic circles, for example, through the preaching of Horace Bushnell.

244. Fisher, "Historical Proofs. Second Article," 60.

245. [Fisher], "How the New Testament Came Down to Us," 620.

246. [Fisher], "How the New Testament Came Down to Us," 611, 615, 617, 613–14. Tischendorf, through false promises, made off with the original—which he did not return.

247. Fisher, *Beginnings of Christianity*, v.

248. Fisher, "Conflict. Second Article," "genuineness" issue at 217.

249. Fisher, "Christian Religion: Part III," 193 (Jesus gave in to "Jewish" views to have his message heeded); *Beginnings of Christianity*, 464. Fisher attacked Strauss at greater length in Essays 6 and 7 in *Essays on the Supernatural Origin*, 339–420.

250. Fisher, "Conflict. Second Article," 223, 229, 252.

251. In 1871, James McCosh of Princeton, preparing a lecture, asked Fisher to send him by express mail the latest French edition of Renan's *Vie de Jesus* from the Yale library (McCosh to Fisher, Princeton, 3/24/1871 [B122, "Miscellaneous Personal Papers—Correspondence"]).

252. Fisher, "Historical Proofs. Second Article," 59.

253. Fisher, *Notes on the Literature*, 670k.

254. Fisher, "Conflict. Second Article," 261, 262–63.

255. Fisher, "Christian Religion: Part III," 178.

256. Fisher, "Conflict. Second Article," 222.

257. Fisher, "Conflict. Third Article," 420–29, 441, 452. Fisher attempted to square the testimony of Acts with that of Galatians.

258. Fisher, "Conflict. Third Article," 452; "Conflict. Second Article," 223; "Conflict. First Article," 132

259. Fisher, "Conflict. Third Article," esp. 404–6, 441, 429, 432.

260. Fisher, "Historical Proofs. Third Article," 217, 218; *Beginnings of Christianity*, v-vii.

261. Fisher, *Beginnings of Christianity*, 395; also *Essays on the Supernatural Origin of Christianity*, chap. 5 ("Baur on Ebionitism and the Origin of Catholic Christianity"); "Ebionitism and the Christianity of the Subapostolic Age," 529ff. Fisher here rejected the notion that early followers of Jesus were "humanitarians" (holding a low Christology) or inimical to Paul (551).

262. Fisher, *History of the Christian Church*, 33. Elsewhere, Fisher accorded the Jews a better place in the "preparation for Christianity" (*Outlines* I: 170–71).

263. Fisher, *Beginnings of Christianity*, 502, 503; "Ebionitism," 531–33.

264. More fully, in *Essays on the Supernatural Origin of Christianity*, chap. 2, itself a revision of an earlier essay [no date given] in *BS*. Fisher cited Irenaeus, Tertullian, Clement of Alexandria, Marcion, Valentinus, and Basilides to argue for the "genuineness" of the Fourth Gospel (39–82); a chief virtue of patristic writings is the "testimony" they give to various New Testament books.

265. Fisher, "Historical Proofs. Fourth Article," 51, that is, denying the teaching of Jesus as the incarnation of the divine Logos, as in John 1.

266. Fisher, "Some Remarks on the Alogoi," 1–9. Citing patristic sources, Fisher reviews a debate between Harnack and Zahn on what the so-called Alogoi did or did not reject. Irenaeus' testimony (*Adv. Haer.* 3.11.9) that the Alogoi set aside the Gospel of John convinced Fisher that this Gospel was not a late composition and that the

Apostle John, who spent the end of his life in Ephesus, was its author. He deemed the ascription of the Gospel by the Alogoi to Cerinthus "absurd."

267. Fisher, *Beginnings of Christianity*, 328, 535. When John wrote his Gospel, he was living in a Greek-speaking community—a point that accounts for the difference from the Apocalypse (346); also, "Historical Proofs. Fourth Article," 63.

268. Fisher, "Historical Proofs. Fourth Article," 52–55.

269. Fisher, *Beginnings of Christianity*, 321–25, citing Polycarp, *Phil. 7* (citing I John 4:3); Irenaeus, *Ep. to Florinus* 2; Irenaeus, *Against Heresies* 3.3.4; and a fragment of a letter by Irenaeus to Victor of Rome. Fisher listed Justin Martyr, *Apology* I. 61, and Ignatius, *Phil.* 7; *Rom.* 7, to argue that these authors knew the Gospel of John (330–31).

270. Fisher, *Beginnings of Christianity*, 335 (citing Celsus in Origen, *Against Celsus* 2.31, 36, 39, 55), 389; "Historical Proofs. Fourth Article," 56–61.

271. Fisher, *Beginnings of Christianity*, 335–36, 360. Fisher cited Neander (*Planting and Training of the Church*, 371) that if this Gospel was not by the Apostle John, it remains an insoluble enigma (362); cf. "Historical Proofs. Fourth Article," 79.

272. Fisher, "Historical Proofs. Fourth Article," 80, 73–74 (nor did John need to borrow the Logos-concept from Philo [63–65]); *Beginnings of Christianity*, 361, 343.

273. Fisher, *History of Christian Doctrine*, 60, 48–52, 51.

274. Fisher, *Brief History*, 12. To the present, however, the Caucasian "variety" of humankind has played the most important part in history; civilization and progress are mainly the creation of "this dominant race" (3).

275. Fisher, "Ebionitism," 564.

276. Ellis, *Seven Against Christ*, ix; within the year, the church was "convulsed" (101). Ellis emphasizes the catalytic role of Arthur Penrhyn Stanley, later Dean of Westminster. Also see Cashdollar, *Transformation of Theology*, 85–89.

277. *Essays and Reviews* (1860; I cite from the seventh edition, 1861).

278. Smith, "New Latitudinarians," 312–57. Calling the authors "New Latitudinarians," Smith signals the essayists' desire to return the Church of England to an earlier phase, a more tolerant, less high-church approach (Ellis, *Seven Against Christ*, 45, 90, 101).

279. Ellis, *Seven Against Christ*, 23–24, 36.

280. Willey analyses three divergent responses ("Septem contra Christum [*Essays and Reviews*, 1860]," 137–85, esp. 160–74).

281. A note "To the Reader" inserted as a frontispiece to the book.

282. [Smith], "Theological and Literary Intelligence," *ATR* 3.11 (July 1861): 527.

283. Ellis, *Seven Against Christ*, chap. 4 (esp. 187–89), ix, 197. The 39 Articles, formulated in the sixteenth century, were not attuned to the controversies of the nineteenth.

284. Ellis's summary, *Seven Against Christ*, 53. As for the "Germanism," Ellis claims that Christian Bunsen was "the doyen" of the essayists (53), and Kant the primary philosophical influence (301). Ellis details their knowledge of German philosophy and theology, especially Jowett's (237, 305).

285. Ellis, *Seven Against Christ*, 91, 92, 93, 95.

286. Temple, "Education of the World," in *Essays and Reviews*, 47.

287. Powell, "On the Study of the Evidences of Christianity," in *Essays and Reviews*, 105, 128, 129, 143.

288. H. B. Wilson, "Séances Historiques de Genève: The National Church," in *Essays and Reviews*, 160, 176–77.

289. Jowett, "On the Interpretation of Scripture," in *Essays and Reviews*, 334, 331, 342–43.

290. Jowett, "On the Interpretation of Scripture," 348, 349, 350, 404–5, 414, 428, 431.

291. Cairns, "Oxford Rationalism and English Christianity," 9; Gresley, "Idealism Reconsidered," 3.

292. E.g., Moberly, "Some Remarks on Essays and Reviews"; [Anonymous], *Catholicity and Reason: A Few Considerations on "Essays and Reviews"*.

293. [Smith], "Theological and Literary Intelligence," *ATR* 3.11 (July 1861): 531, 532, citing Pusey's earlier letter in the *Guardian*.

294. "S.," "Oxford Essayists,"407, 427, 408, reviewing the fifth edition of the work (1861). Jowett especially is faulted for reproducing the ideas of "his master Baur" (416n.).

295. "S.," "Oxford Essayists," 409, 410, 425, 418, 414–15, 428.

296. Smith, "New Latitudinarians," 313.

297. Smith, "New Latitudinarians," 321–23, 330, 315.

298. Smith, "New Latitudinarians," 338.

299. Smith, "New Latitudinarians," 314.

300. Smith, "New Latitudinarians," 315, 348.

301. Smith, "New Latitudinarians," 319.

302. Smith, "New Latitudinarians," 317, 318.

303. Smith, "New Latitudinarians," 353, 357.

304. Smith, "Theological and Literary Intelligence," *ATR* 2.5 (Feb. 1865): 165, and noted further (mostly negative) comments on the volume in *ATR* 2.8 (Nov. 1860): 735; 3.9 (Jan. 1861): 186; 3.11 (July 1861): 540; 4:13 (Jan. 1862): 164, 168; 4.16 (Oct. 1862): 729. Ecclesiastical court proceedings are reported in *ATR* 3.12 (Oct. 1861): 754–55; *APTR* 1.1. (Jan. 1863): 146–48.

305. As Unitarian F. H. Hedge noted, for Protestants on one side of that divide, all was "genuine historic facts"; on the other, "all figments" ("Mythical Element in the New Testament,"166).

Chapter 4. History and Church History

Epigraphs: Stanley, "Introduction to the Study of Ecclesiastical History," 47, discussed in Richardson, "Church History Past and Present," 6. Stanley continues: "We seem to be set down in the valley of the prophet's vision, strewn with bones, and behold they are 'very many' and 'very dry'; skeletons of creeds, of churches, of institutions; trodden and traversed again and again." Stanley was Regius Professor of Ecclesiastical History at Oxford (1856–1863) before becoming Dean of Westminster. Gooch, *History and Historians*, 490.

1. For an overview, see Bowden, *Church History*, chap. 1.

2. On "objectivity"'s enshrinement in the American historical profession, see Novick, *That Noble Dream*. Late nineteenth-century historians' "extraordinary degree of ideological homogeneity" (61) also well describes Protestant seminary professors.

3. H. B. Adams, "History in American Colleges, I: History at Harvard University," 538, 540. In the seventeenth century, that hour fell immediately after midday dinner ("History in American Colleges, VI: History in Yale University," 335).

4. So claimed Ephraim Emerton regarding his undergraduate days at Harvard ("Practical Method," 50); at Oxford until recently, the Professorship of History was a reward to top off a man's literary career ("Academic Study of History," 241). Henry Adams claims that in his Harvard undergraduate days no instructor ever mentioned the two most influential contemporary thinkers, Karl Marx and Auguste Comte (*Education of Henry Adams*, 46–47).

5. Jameson, "Early Days of the American Historical Association," 1. Jameson recalls that in 1882, only one of five eastern universities [presumably Harvard] employed a historian; three were considering such, and one wasn't even considering (1–2).

6. George E. Howard of the State University of Nebraska to H. B. Adams, Lincoln, Neb., 5/30/1883, in *Historical Scholarship*, ed. Holt, 65. For the link of history to classics, Lingelbach, *Klio macht Karriere*, 604–5; and the later link to political science, 606–7, 624.

7. H. B. Adams, "History in American Colleges, I," 542; Sparks helped further modern history in America (543). Late antiquity was then considered modern history. On Sparks's documentary studies of George Washington and the American Revolution, see Gooch, *History and Historians*, 376–77.

8. Emerton, "Practical Method," 50. Henry Smith at Union also advocated the study of *American* church history—then a novel proposition—but no position was authorized at Union until 1906–1907 (Gillett, "Detailed History" III: 618; II: 421, 422).

9. Schaff calls Neander "the father of the church history monograph" (*History of the Apostolic Church* I, in *Reformed and Catholic*, ed. Yrigoyen and Bricker, 274). Neander's *Kaiser Julian* (1812) was his first monograph.

10. Jameson, "American Historical Association," 2.

11. Eliot, "What Is a Liberal Education?" 207; Harvard had not done much better until recently, Eliot admits (208). Eliot's uncomplimentary reference to Princeton prompted a heated response from James McCosh, President of Princeton College. Princeton, McCosh retorted, required a short history examination for entrance; in the sophomore year, students read a textbook on universal history; in the junior and

senior years, the professor of philosophy of history gave "a historical and critical survey of the science and methods of history." In addition, each professor was expected to discuss the history of his own field (*New Departure*, 11n.1). Primary sources and seminars were not yet common at Princeton.

12. See reports to H. B. Adams from his former students in *Historical Scholarship*, ed. Holt.

13. Charles A. Levermore to H. B. Adams, University of California, 1/29/1887 (*Historical Scholarship*, ed. Holt, 94). Levermore's choice of "barbarian" groups suggests the presence of Asians in California; he also refers to the "little Jap" who helped his wife.

14. Frank W. Blackmar to H. B. Adams, University of Kansas, 12/20/1897 (*Historical Scholarship*, ed. Holt, 248–49).

15. Lingelbach, *Klio macht Karriere*, 257. The rank of Associate Professor came later.

16. Frederick Jackson Turner to H. B. Adams, Madison, Wis., 1/11/1890 (in *Historical Scholarship*, ed. Holt, 123). But in 1891 Charles Homer Haskins reported that his colleague Turner was teaching mainly American history (Haskins to H. B. Adams, Madison, Wis., 9/29/1891 [in *Historical Scholarship*, ed. Holt, 162–63]). Graduate history training at Johns Hopkins, noted for "German" influence, nevertheless required students to know all periods and regions of "universal history," a requirement, Lingelbach alleges, that curtailed students' specialized research (*Klio macht Karriere*, 253).

17. Emerton, "Academic Study of History," 256.

18. Emerton [and S. E. Morison], "History, 1838–1929," 157–58.

19. Herbst, *German Historical School*, 24.

20. For this emphasis until the late nineteenth century, see Winterer, *Culture of Classicism*. For classical history at Yale, see H. B. Adams, "History in American Colleges, VI," 336, 337. Arguing to keep Greek in the curriculum (spurred by potential changes at Harvard), see Fisher, "Study of Greek," and West, "Must the Classics Go?"

21. H. B. Adams, "History in American Colleges, II: History at Harvard University," 623. Geography was also required ("History in American Colleges, I," 544).

22. Charles Homer Haskins to H. B. Adams, Madison, Wis., 5/23/1891 (in *Historical Scholarship*, ed. Holt, 161). Students' linguistic deficiencies rendered teaching medieval history difficult.

23. H. B. Adams, "History in American Colleges, III: History at Columbia College," 8; "History in American Colleges, V: History at Amherst and Columbia Colleges," 178–79. At Columbia in 1865, President Frederick Barnard, claiming that modern history should not be taught in colleges, persuaded the trustees to abolish the professorship of history (H. B. Adams, "History in Colleges, IV: History in Columbia College," 98). See above, Chapter 1, n.41 for more information on college positions in history.

24. Lingelbach attributes the distancing from the classical curriculum that began in the second and third decades of the nineteenth century to the anti-elitism of the

Jacksonian era (*Klio macht Karriere*, 77). At elite northeastern colleges, classics remained central until late-century, amid a growing emphasis on science and modern languages. Herbert Baxter Adams emphasizes the novelty of Henry Adams's approach to medieval history: he made students do original research (in Anglo-Saxon law) and rejected the characterization of the early Middle Ages as "dark" ("History in American Colleges, II," 629–30, 631).

25. H. B. Adams, "History in American Colleges, II," 627.

26. Bowden, *Church History*, 36. At Johns Hopkins in the late 1880s, H. B. Adams taught a course on church history (including the Old Testament) that landed him in trouble (Hawkins, *Pioneer*, 313). An earnest but impolitic student, countering charges that the University was atheistic, detailed Adams's approach: miracles are traced to natural causes; the Bible is considered "the fruit of human endeavor"; "Dr. Adams sees no miraculous origin to anything": [Anonymous], "About Church History," *Baltimore American & Commercial Advertiser*, June 30, 1889. In the first half of the nineteenth century, Harvard Divinity School's introduction of a course with the Humanities-sounding title, "Criticism and Interpretation of the Scriptures," was deemed radical (Solt, *Rise and Development*, 82).

27. S. Miller [Jr.], *Life* II: 509—plus the "Composition and Delivery of Sermons" (II: 403).

28. See above, Chapter 1, n.116, for the story of this Chair's founding.

29. Knoff, *Yale Divinity School*, 2; Bainton, *Yale and the Ministry*, 186.

30. Ahlstrom, "Middle Period," 145, 147; Reynolds, "Later Years," 175, 167; Eliot, "Theological Education," 47.

31. Bowden, *Church History in the Age of Science*, 7; Woods, *History of Andover*, 188–89. Lacking meaningful theories of historical causation and process, it seemed a deadly catalog of useless facts.

32. Schaff, *History of the Apostolic Church* I, in *Reformed and Catholic*, ed. Yrigoyen and Bricker, 308–9. Schaff criticizes "Puseyites'" "undiscerning and extravagant admiration of the ancient church," which takes the patristic era as the model for the present (309–310).

33. Woods, *History of Andover*, 188.

34. The professors here surveyed, however, denied that development in history meant that Christian rites were survivals from savage practices—as might be inferred from John Lubbock's *Pre-Historic Times* (1865) and *Origin of Civilization* (1870): see Turner, *Without God, Without Creed*, 152–53.

35. On the earlier development of historical studies in German universities, see Jarausch, "Institutionalization of History," 25–48.

36. Mosheim, "Author's Preface," *Ecclesiastical History* I (original date March 23, 1755). Many manuscripts, Mosheim complains, are still not available to scholars in general, being shut up "in the collections of the curious (or the opulent, who are willing to pass for such)." Although Roman Catholic scholars have greater access to

manuscripts [presumably in the Vatican Library and elsewhere], they have fallen into greater errors than Protestant historians (xv-xvi).

37. Mosheim, *Ecclesiastical History* I: 7, 10, 11–12: for example, labeling opponents "heretics." Gieseler argued that in church history, "truth is liable to be distorted through ignorance and credulity, through narrow-mindedness and party-spirit, through a wish to accommodate it to certain ends, or even through intentional dishonesty" (*Text-Book* I, trans. Cunningham, 10; trans. Smith, 23). For Neander on impartiality, see *Lectures on the History of Christian Dogmas* I: 17.

38. Gieseler, *Text-Book* I, trans. Cunningham, 10; trans. Smith, 23; similarly, Charles [Karl von] Hase, *History of the Christian Church*, 3 (the historian may affirm Christianity as "the ultimate point and perfection of all other religions" [2]).

39. Neander, *Lectures* I: 229; *General History* I: 311–12; *History of the Planting and Training* I: 162–63.

40. Mosheim, *Ecclesiastical History* I: 7–8; Hase, *History*, 2.

41. Neander, *Lectures* I: 2 ("Die Geschichte ist etwas rein menschliches"), 3.

42. Neander, "Preface to Part III," *General History* II: v.

43. Neander, *Memorials*, 406, 415.

44. Neander, *Lectures* I: 14. The emperor Julian ("the Apostate"), for example, would be wrongly treated if the historian concentrated only on him as an individual. In his early (1812) monograph on Julian, Neander aimed to show "how little an individual can avail in a contest with providence," which guides the spirit of the times in accord with "its own everlasting decrees" (*Emperor Julian*, 18). For Neander's opposition to Socialism, see Neander, "Verworte," Alexandre Vinet, *Der Sozialismus in seinem Prinzip betrachtet*, trans. (from French) D. Hofmeister (1849), iv.

45. Baur, *Epochs of Church Historiography* (= *Ferdinand Christian Baur on the Writing of Church History*, ed., trans. Hodgson), 141, 152; Mosheim's *Commentarii de rebus Christianorum ante Constantinum Magnum* (1753) is called "epoch-making" in its treatment of Gnosticism, Neo-Platonic philosophy, Origen, and Manicheanism (149).

46. Baur, *Epochs of Church Historiography*, 43, 69, 120–21, 126, 132.

47. Baur, *Epochs of Church Historiography*, 147.

48. Baur, *Epochs of Church Historiography*, 203–5, 229, 235. Baur charges that Gieseler's *Church History* wavers between rationalistic and supernaturalistic views, while Hase's includes too much unintegrated external material (231, 235).

49. See Chapter 5. On Baur's assessment of Neander, see Hodgson, *Formation of Historical Theology*, 159–60.

50. Baur, *Epochs of Church Historiography*, 224. Baur links Neander with Schleiermacher's "immediacy of the religious consciousness" (211). Neander's emphasis on "the heart" prompted some Hegelians to dub him a "pectoral theologian"; Schaff thought the mockers should be ashamed (*History of the Apostolic Church* I, in *Reformed and Catholic*, ed. Yrigoyen and Bricker, 271n.1).

51. Baur, *Epochs of Church Historiography*, 257.

52. Hodgson, "Introduction," *Ferdinand Christian Baur*, 36. Baur, to be sure, was "pre-critical" by today's standards.

53. E.g., Hitchcock, "Church History: First Period," 1872–1873, Jackson notes (Jackson Papers, B1, N1, 3). See Chapter 5.

54. Already in 1830/1831, Edward Robinson (America's first internationally recognized theology professor) remarked that the incorporation of *Dogmengeschichte* into church history was peculiarly German ("Theological Education in Germany," *BR* 1.1 [Jan. 1831]: 5).

55. Although all the American professors here considered opposed slavery, they were not deeply involved in the abolition movement. For Hitchcock's elaboration of early human development and Caucasian race theory (a half-year after Darwin's *Origin of Species* was published), see my essay "Augustine, the Sons of Noah, and Race in Nineteenth-Century North America"; for a brief summary, see Chapter 9.

56. For a helpful explanation, see Rodgers, "Exceptionalism," 21–40.

57. Miller, "Introductory Lecture, Ecclesiastical History" (B2, F1, 1–3).

58. Miller, "Importance of Mature Preparatory Study for the Ministry," 6.

59. Miller, "Introductory Lecture on Ecclesiastical History," March 2, 1815 [and 5 other dates, up to 1839] (B2, F9, 2, 3–4, 5); emphasis in original.

60. Miller, "Ecclesiastical History" (B2, F11, 4).

61. Miller, "Introductory Lecture, Ecclesiastical History" (B2, F1, 7).

62. Smith, "Problem of the Philosophy of History," 4; "Idea of Christian Theology as a System," 126.

63. Smith studied at the University of Halle/Wittenberg in 1838–1839. The Union Seminary Archives contain Smith's lecture notes on Tholuck's *Encyclopedien* and *Christliche Sittenlehre*, and on Neander's *Dogmengeschichte* (which largely follows his discussion in his *General History*). Smith also attended lectures on Anthropology and Psychology (Erdmann); Dogmatics (Tholuck); Philosophy of Religion (Ulrici); Logic (Erdmann); Kant's Philosophy (Shaller); Introduction to Philosophy, Logic, and Metaphysics (Shaller) (S3, University Documents). In a letter (11/24/1838), he reports that he attends lectures on Schleiermacher's *Glaubenslehre* (in [E. Smith], *Henry Boynton Smith*, 59). Erdmann is described as "Hegel's representative on earth" (A. N. Wilson, *God's Funeral*, 121). In summer semester 1839 and winter semester 1839–1840, Smith studied at Kaiser Friedrich Wilhelm Universität (Berlin), attending lectures on *Apostelgeschichte* (Neander); History of Dogma (Neander); Job (Hengstenberg); History of the Kingdom of God (Hengstenberg); Introduction to Christian Ethics (Twesten); Logic and Metaphysics (professor's name undecipherable); History of the New Philosophy (Michelet); Critique of the Hegelian System (Trendelenburg); Dogmatics (Twesten); Psalms (Hengstenberg); History of the Palestinian Jews (Hengstenberg) (S3, University Documents).

64. Berlin was the largest German university in the 1840s, having over 2000 students, compared with around 700 at Halle, although Halle had more theology students: see Society of Clergymen, "Thoughts on the State of Theological Science," 762

and n.1; Schaff, *Germany*, 63, 73. In 1859, Halle still had the most theology students (465) in German-speaking Europe, although its overall numbers were dwarfed by Vienna and Berlin (*ATR* 3.12 [Oct. 1861]: 756).

65. Smith's only notes remaining from a church history course in Germany are Neander's lectures on *Dogmengeschichte* (these, however, concern the medieval period and later) and on *Apostelgeschichte* (S3, Item 13).

66. For Tholuck's own account of his career, see his "Evangelical Theology in Germany: Survey of My Life as a Teacher of Theology," 85–89. Tholuck, more radical in his youth, gave a graduation speech at his gymnasium entitled "The Superiority of the Oriental World Over the Christian" (85). Also see Park, *Sketch of the Life and Character of Prof. Tholuck* (1840) and Stuckenberg, "Early Life of Tholuck."

67. Smith, "Tholuck's *Encyclopedien*" (S3, N, Item 10 [#11, 25]).

68. Smith, "Tholuck's *Encyclopedien*" (S3, N, Item 10 [#13, 15, 16, 18, 20]).

69. Smith also reports that in June 1839, he heard Ranke lecture on Calvin and Calvinism's shaping of North America (letter to an unidentified friend, Berlin, 6/30/1839, cited in [E. Smith], *Henry Boynton Smith*, 69–70).

70. Smith, "Doctrinal History," 1851, Hastings notes (S5, B1, F3, 71).

71. Smith, "Tholuck's *Encyclopedien*" (S3, N, Item 10 [#26, 28]).

72. Smith, "Tholuck's *Encyclopedien*" (S3, N, Item 10 [#28]).

73. Smith, "Tholuck's *Christliche Sittenlehre*" (S3, N, Item 1 [division 3 ("History of Ethics"; "Ethical Anthropology," #13; Part II, #30]).

74. Smith, "Nature and Worth," 52, 54.

75. Hitchcock, sketch of Smith's life read before the New-York Historical Society (March 6, 1877) and printed in "Preface" to Gieseler, *Text-Book*, trans., ed. Smith, V: v. Yet Smith entertained the "utility" argument: only the one who has "studied the past, can know the present, and act wisely for the future" (V: vi).

76. Smith, "Nature and Worth," 85.

77. Smith to Richard H. Dana, New York, 7/1851, cited in [E. Smith], *Henry Boynton Smith*, 182.

78. Smith, "Church History: First Period," 1849–1850, Hastings notes (S5, B1, F3, 39–40, 40–41). A popular definition: history is the "biography of humanity" ("Reformed Churches of Europe and America," 5).

79. Smith, "Nature and Worth," 61: learn the facts first and then the laws by which to read the facts.

80. Smith, "Problem of the Philosophy of History," 6–7, 9. Smith compares the appeal to previously established facts with the Baconian method of going to nature.

81. For "philosophizing about history" as the goal, see Chapter 1, 39.

82. Smith, "Relations of Faith and Philosophy," 21.

83. Smith, "Historical Discourse," 3.

84. Smith, "Relations of Faith and Philosophy," 25.

85. Smith, "Problem of the Philosophy of History," 29; "Nature and Worth," 57; similarly, "Church History: First Period," 1849–1850, Hastings notes (S5, B1, F3, 46).

86. Smith, "Relations of Faith and Philosophy," 21, 34. For Smith's Christocentrism, see Chapter 9.

87. Smith, "Problem of the Philosophy of History," 27; "Historical Discourse," 3.

88. J. W. Draper, *History of the Intellectual Development of Europe* (1876 [1862]). Draper, professor of chemistry at the University of the City of New York (NYU), aimed for a scientific approach to history through physiology (iii–iv).

89. [Smith], "Draper's Intellectual Development of Europe," 616, 617, 618–19, 626, 628.

90. Smith, "Nature and Worth," 66. The "six thousand years" implies that church history includes the Old Testament: see Smith, "Church History: First Period," 1849–1850, Hastings notes (S5, B1, F3, 46).

91. Smith, "Church History: First Period," 1849–1850, Hastings notes (S5, B1, F3, 43, 42, 46, 47). The sacrifices of early peoples show that they dimly recognized that they had abandoned the worship of the one true God; on "primitive monotheism," see Smith's "Theological and Literary Intelligence" column, *ATR* 2.8 (Nov. 1860): 729; 3.10 (April 1861): 378; 3.11 (July 1861): 547; 4.13 (Jan. 1862): 164.

92. Smith, "Church History: First Period," 1849–1850, Hastings notes (S5, B1, F3, 45).

93. Smith, "Church History: First Period," 1849–1850, Hastings notes (S5, B1, F3, 118). Scripture remains the base and norm; doctrine expresses Christian truths in non-Scriptural language and forms suited to different ages (Smith, "Systematic Theology," 1857 (?) [S4, B1, F1, L1]).

94. Smith, "Systematic Theology," 10/22/1857 (S4, B1, F4); "Systematic Theology," 1857 (?) (S4, B1, F1, L1).

95. Smith, "Church History: First Period," 1849–1850 (?), Hastings notes (S5, B1, F3, 83–84).

96. Smith, "Church History: First Period," 1849–1850 (?), Hastings notes (S5, B1, F3, 114).

97. Smith, "Nature and Worth," 75; "Church History: First Period," 1849–1850 (?), Hastings notes (S5, B1, F3, 48–49, 50–51).

98. Smith, "Systematic Theology," 1855–1856, Quick notes (S5, B1, F4, NI, 4). Smith deems the New England Theology deficient in its historical aspect.

99. Smith, "Idea of Christian Theology," 126. Christianity offers "a more perfect system" than philosophy can independently: Smith, "Systematic Theology," 10/20/1857 (S4, B1, F3).

100. Hitchcock, "Laws of Civilization," 13.

101. Hitchcock, "Church History: Second Period," 1883, Moore notes (B2, N2, 412–14): in fact, Luther and Hegel in embryo.

102. Hitchcock, "Chinese Classics," 635; on race, see his "Laws of Civilization" and my essay, "Augustine, the Sons of Noah, and Race in Nineteenth-Century North America."

103. Hitchcock, "Church History: First Period," 1883, Moore notes (B2, N2, 188).

Christianity's ancient "environment" accounted for some of its unfortunate attitudes and practices.

104. Hitchcock, "Church History: First Period," 1872–1873, Jackson notes (Jackson Papers, B1, N1, 14).

105. Hitchcock, "Middle Ages: First Period," early 1880s, Burrell notes [B1, N2, 105); "Church History: First Period," early 1880s, Burrell notes (B1, N1, 177); "History of the World Before Christ," 1862, Wright notes (B2, N1, General Survey, #3).

106. Schaff, "Roswell D. Hitchcock," *New-York Independent,* June 23, 1887, 296, 298.

107. Hitchcock, "Church History: First Period," early 1880s, Burrell notes (B1, N1, 177).

108. Hitchcock's class discussion of this topic is summed up in his article, "Historical Development of Christianity," 28–54.

109. Hitchcock, "True Idea and Uses," 25–26.

110. Hitchcock, "History of the World Before Christ," 1862, Wright notes (B2, N1, General Survey, Science #2).

111. Hitchcock, "Church History: First Period," early 1880s, Burrell notes (B1, N1, 179), emphasis added.

112. Hitchcock, "History of the World Before Christ," 1862, Wright notes (B2, N1, General Survey, #2). Elsewhere Hitchcock defines Infidels as not atheists but unbelievers, "those who deny Christianity and reject the Scriptures" (*Complete Analysis of the Holy Bible,* 1121). Infidels include German or French scholars who took a critical approach to the Bible. Hitchcock also trusts that although Americans are susceptible to religious emotion, they will "refuse" German Infidelity as they once did French Infidelity ("Religion, The Doing of God's Will," 44).

113. Hitchcock, "Thanksgiving for Victories," 4 (on the occasion of northern victories at Mobile and Atlanta [1]). Hitchcock's belief that Jesus founded the Kingdom indicates that the "eschatological turn" in the study of the Synoptic Gospels was not yet current.

114. Hitchcock, "History of the World Before Christ," 1862, Wright notes (B2, N1, General Survey, Science #2).

115. Hitchcock, "History of the World Before Christ," 1862, Wright notes (B2, N1, General Survey, #3); "Church History: First Period," 1883, Moore notes (B2, N2, 210).

116. Hitchcock, "Church History: First Period," 1883, Moore notes (B2, N2, 165, 166); "Church History: First Period," 1872–1873, Jackson notes (Jackson Papers, B1, N1, 3); "Church History: First Period," early 1880s, Burrell notes (B1, N1, 182).

117. Hitchcock, "History of the World Before Christ," 1862, Wright notes (B2, N1, General Survey, #3); similarly, Hitchcock, "Laws of Civilization," 3–4. Reviewing Buckle's *History of Civilization in England,* J. G. Droysen, while appreciating Buckle's approach, faults him for underestimating the role of the "moral world" and free will (Droysen, "Elevation of History," 84, 85).

118. Buckle, *History* I: 30, 51, 106.

119. Buckle, *History* I: 136, 162, 188, 223. Literature produced by European clergy has injured society by "increasing credulity" and "stopping the progress of knowledge" (I: 223).

120. Buckle, *History* I: 154, 206, 207, 243, 250, 258. Hence his admiration for Voltaire (I: 575–586). Henry Adams, unlike Hitchcock, thought that Buckle was the only English historian not swamped in antiquarianism and who had "ideas" (*Education of Henry Adams*, 173). On Buckle's indebtedness to Comte, see Cashdollar, *Transformation of Theology*, 75–80; "Until clergy could make up their minds about positivism, they could not proceed to evolutionism or to the new biblical criticism or to the emerging social sciences or to any other intellectual problem of their time" (181).

121. Hitchcock, "Laws of Civilization," 23 (this will be so if our crimes and follies do not lead Providence to dash us to pieces [24]).

122. Hitchcock, "Address on Colportage," 4. Hitchcock rejects the term "native Americans": no continent except Asia [with the beginnings of the human race] ever had any "natives" (4–5). Elsewhere, Hitchcock writes that the "Aborigines" of North America are now perishing, Christianity having arrived too late to save them; Asian civilizations never raised themselves above thralldom to nature ("Laws of Civilization," 8, 18, 19). On depictions of American Indians in nineteenth-century textbooks, see Elson, *Guardians of Tradition*, 71–81.

123. Hitchcock, "Address on Colportage," 6.

124. Hitchcock, "Church History: First Period," 1883, Moore notes (B2, N2, 168–82 passim).

125. Hitchcock, "True Idea and Uses," 47–48.

126. Hitchcock, "Church History: First Period," 1872–1873, Jackson notes (Jackson Papers, B1, N1, 1).

127. Hitchcock, "True Idea and Uses," 22, 28–30. Hitchcock does not start with Adam-before-the-Fall.

128. Hitchcock, "True Idea and Uses," 30; the old civilizations of the "Hindoos" and Chinese are now perishing ("Laws of Civilization," 11).

129. Hitchcock, "True Idea and Uses," 33, 34–35.

130. Hitchcock, "Church History: First Period," 1872–1873, Jackson notes (Jackson Papers, B1, N1, 14). Marsden notes of nineteenth-century evangelicals, "Bias . . . was something other people had" ("Collapse of American Evangelical Academia," 242).

131. Hitchcock, "Church History: First Period," 1883, Moore notes (B2, N2, 206); "Church History: First Period," 1872–1873, Jackson notes (Jackson Papers, B1, N1, 14, 98, 99; Hitchcock remarks [122] that Origen, unlike most other Fathers, knew Hebrew; they depended on the LXX or Itala, "imperfect" translations).

132. Hitchcock, "Church History: First Period," early 1880s, Burrell notes (B1, N1, 190). Hitchcock appears to paraphrase the adage that history is philosophy teaching by examples.

133. Hitchcock, "Church History: First Period," 1872–1873, Jackson notes (Jackson Papers, B1, N1, 1); "True Idea and Uses," 44–45.

134. Hitchcock, "True Idea and Uses," 41–42.

135. Fisher, *Brief History*, 1; cf. *Outlines* I: 1.

136. Fisher, *Outlines* I: 2, 1, 4; there might also be an ethnological history describing the races of men in their movements and intermixtures (I: 10–11).

137. Fisher, *Brief History*, 1.

138. Fisher, *Outlines* I: 6.

139. Fisher, *History of Christian Doctrine*, 10, 13 (Fisher modifies the last claim: "in each of the epochs the prevailing interpretation of Christianity has corresponded to the special characteristics of time and race").

140. Fisher, *Brief History*, 1.

141. Fisher, "Church History," 1870–1871 (1). He attributes the citation to "Dr. Arnold."

142. Fisher, *Outlines* I: 1, 4.

143. Fisher, "Church History," 1870–1871 (1).

144. Fisher, "Rationalism," 257; Fisher, *Outlines* I: 4. For Fisher, science should stick to the investigation of "second causes" and to the Baconian method ("Rationalism," 268).

145. Fisher, *Outlines* I: 8.

146. Fisher, "Church History," 1870–1871 (2, 1).

147. Fisher, "Academic Career of Ex-President Woolsey," 714.

148. Fisher, "Church History," 1870–1871 (5).

149. Fisher, *Function of the Historian*, 3.

150. Fisher, "Church History," 1870–1871 (5).

151. Fisher, *Beginnings of Christianity*, 13, 12.

152. Fisher, *Function of the Historian*, 6. Fisher lists types of sources in *Outlines* I: 6–7.

153. Fisher, *Function of the Historian*, 7–14, passim; *Historical Method in Theology*, 14.

154. Fisher, *Function of the Historian*, 23; Tacitus, *Annales* 3. 65–66 gives the principle and illustrations.

155. Fisher, *Brief History*, 1, 2, 42: Fisher has heard of Ashurbanipal's library.

156. Fisher, *Brief History*, 18, 3.

157. Fisher, *Brief History*, 58, 64, 195, emphasis in original. Fisher does not stress, as did some others, that ancient Greece "corrupted" Rome.

158. Fisher, *Brief History*, 12.

159. Fisher, *Outlines* I: 3, 4.

160. Fisher, *History of the Christian Church*, 1, iii. Fisher admits (iv) that his book owes much to Neander, Gieseler, and Schaff.

161. Fisher, *History of the Christian Church*, 4.

162. Fisher, *Notes on the Literature*, 670a. This brief pamphlet was later inserted at the end of Fisher's *History of the Christian Church*, which lacked a bibliography.

163. Fisher, *Function of the Historian*, 15.

164. Fisher, *History of the Christian Church*, 2. He also appears to borrow much from Schaff regarding Christian missions, polity, doctrine, life, and worship (2–3).

165. Pranger, *Philip Schaff*, 203, adding that Schaff's student, Arthur C. McGiffert, is among the more "dispassionate" new generation of historians; on Schaff's relation to Ranke, see 219–220. Also see Pranger, "Philip Schaff: His Role in American Evangelical Education," 225. For other studies of Schaff as church historian, see Chapter 1, nn. 215–20; and Penzel, "Church History in Context: The Case of Philip Schaff"; Lotz, "Philip Schaff and the Idea of Church History."

166. Bowden, *Church History*, xiv, 54–55, 67.

167. Schaff, *What Is Church History?* 41; also in *Reformed and Catholic*, ed. Yrigoyen and Bricker, 57; *History of the Apostolic Church* I, in *Reformed and Catholic*, ed. Yrigoyen and Bricker, 231.

168. Bowden, *Church History*, 50.

169. Schaff, *What Is Church History?* 13; emphasis in original; also in *Reformed and Catholic*, ed. Yrigoyen and Bricker, 29.

170. Schaff, *History of the Christian Church* I: *Apostolic Christianity*, 2.

171. Schaff, *Theological Propaedeutic* II: 265, 255; *History* I: 24–25.

172. Schaff, "General Introduction to Church History," 410—although God works through *"living persons"* (*History of the Apostolic Church* I, in *Reformed and Catholic*, ed. Yrigoyen and Bricker, 160).

173. Schaff, "Discord and Concord of Christendom, II," *New-York Independent* [Sept. 1884], clipping [UTS, B6, Scr2, 21, 20]), given at the 1884 Evangelical Alliance Conference in Copenhagen.

174. Schaff, *Principle of Protestantism* (1845), 189 ("Revolutionary": in the spirit of the French Revolution, which Schaff considered a destructive force). This work was strongly critiqued by Charles Hodge of Princeton; see his 1845 essay, "Schaff's Protestantism," reprinted in *Princeton Theology*, ed. Noll, 155–64.

175. Schaff, *History of the Apostolic Church* I, in *Reformed and Catholic*, ed. Yrigoyen and Bricker, 157–58; similarly, *Theological Propaedeutic* II: 234.

176. Schaff, *History of the Apostolic Church* I, in *Reformed and Catholic*, ed. Yrigoyen and Bricker, 197; similarly, *Theological Propaedeutic* II: 254.

177. Schaff, *History of the Apostolic Church* I, in *Reformed and Catholic*, ed. Yrigoyen and Bricker, 266; similarly, *History* I: v, citing Tacitus, *Annales* 1.1.3. The phrase was a "convention of Greco-Roman historiography" (Momigliano, "Tacitus and the Tacitist Tradition," 113).

178. Schaff, *History* I: 209.

179. Schaff, *History* I: 3. Pranger notes that Schaff was not far from Ranke on this point (*Philip Schaff*, 219–21).

180. Schaff, *What Is Church History?* 40; also in *Reformed and Catholic*, ed. Yrigoyen and Bricker, 56.

181. Schaff, *History* I: 57; *What Is Church History?* 40; also in *Reformed and Catholic*, ed. Yrigoyen and Bricker, 56.

182. Schaff, *History* I: vi.

183. Schaff, *History of the Apostolic Church* I, in *Reformed and Catholic*, ed. Yrigoyen and Bricker, 161–62.

184. Schaff, "Theology of Our Age and Country," in Schaff, *Christ and Christianity*, 3.

185. Schaff, *What Is Church History?* 56–57, 73, 75–76; also in *Reformed and Catholic*, ed. Yrigoyen and Bricker, 72–73, 89, 91–92; emphasis in original. Brief passages on "organic development," from Herder's *Ideas for a Philosophy of the History of Mankind* [*Ideen zur Philosophie der Geschichte der Menschheit* (1784–1791)], can be found in *J. G. Herder on Social and Political Culture*, trans. Barnard, 253–326; on the ancient world and early Christianity, Herder, *Reflections on the Philosophy of the History of Mankind*, abridged Manuel.

186. Schaff, *What Is Church History?* 75–76; also in *Reformed and Catholic*, ed. Yrigoyen and Bricker, 91–92. Hegel (Schaff claims) makes evil become necessary for reaching the good; sin and moral responsibility disappear.

187. Schaff, *Theological Propaedeutic* II: 239; *History* II: 338; I: 3.

188. Schaff, "American Nationality," 3.

189. Schaff, *What Is Church History?* 39, 40, 73–74; also in *Reformed and Catholic*, ed. Yrigoyen and Bricker, 55, 56, 89–90. The scheme is reminiscent of Hegel's *Philosophy of History*.

190. Schaf [*sic*], *Anglo-Germanism*, 5–6.

191. Schaff, "American Nationality," 3. 5; America, he thought, was the "one cosmopolitan nation."

192. Schaff, "Theology of Our Age and Country," in Schaff, *Christ and Christianity*, 13. Schaff, however, disapproves of "our manifest-destinarians, who would swallow, in one meal, Cuba, all Central America, Mexico and Canada into the bargain" ("American Nationality," 22).

193. Schaff, *What Is Church History?* 91; also in *Reformed and Catholic*, ed. Yrigoyen and Bricker, 107. Schaff faults Roman Catholicism's failure to treat laypeople as a "living organism"; the hierarchy considers them only a "dependent mass" ("Christianity in America," in *Reformed and Catholic*, ed. Yrigoyen and Bricker, 385 [reprinted from Oct. 1857 *MR*]: laypeople are the "sandy plain on which the colossal pyramid of hierarchy rests."

194. Schaff, *History* I: 22, viii; "Reunion of Christendom," in *Philip Schaff*, ed. Penzel, 331; reprinted from *Evangelical Alliance Document* 33 (1893): 1–45.

195. Schaff, *Theological Propaedeutic* II: 235. The eschatological interpretation of the parables was not yet common; the two Schaff here (and frequently) cites are taken to represent the gradual growth of Christianity.

196. Schaff, *History* I: 6.

197. On church history as a *theological* discipline for Schaff, see Graham, *Cosmos in the Chaos*, 117–18.

198. Schaff, *Theological Propaedeutic* II: 234; *History* I: 20–21.

199. Schaff, *What Is Church History?* 25, 26; also in *Reformed and Catholic*, ed. Yrigoyen and Bricker, 41, 42.

200. Schaff, *History* I: 25–26; *History of the Apostolic Church* I, in *Reformed and Catholic*, ed. Yrigoyen and Bricker, 264: here, some of Hegel's "infidel followers" went astray.

201. Schaff, *Theological Propaedeutic* II: 304; Schaff, *What Is Church History?* 11; also in *Reformed and Catholic*, ed. Yrigoyen and Bricker, 27.

202. Schaff, *History* I: viii. From the perspective of 1887, Schaff deems "the extreme rationalism and skepticism" that attended German scholarship only "a temporary aberration" (I: 37). Yet he faults the Tübingen School as teaching a "modern Gnosticism"; at least "English and American theology, caring for truth, not novelty, is not likely to be extensively demoralized by these hyper-critical speculations of the Continent" (I: 209–13).

203. Schaff, *Theological Propaedeutic* II: 296; *History* I: 739.

204. Schaff, *What Is Church History?* 4; also in *Reformed and Catholic*, ed. Yrigoyen and Bricker, 20. On Schaff's critique of Puritanism, see Graham, *Cosmos in the Chaos*, 18, 25–26.

205. Schaff, "German Theology and the Church Question," in *Reformed and Catholic*, ed. Yrigoyen and Bricker, 325 (trans. C. Z. Weiser in *MR* 5.1. [Jan. 1853]: 124–44).

206. Schaff, *Theological Propaedeutic* II: 254. For historical investigation as analogous to mining, see Droysen, *Outline of the Principles of History*, 18.

207. Allen, *On the Study of Christian History* (reprint pamphlet, 1878, no bibliographical information given), 3, 4. Elsewhere Allen wrote, "Morality prescribes, with sharp emphasis, that rule of conduct which is the only pass-word into the Celestial City" ("Religion and Modern Life," in Allen, *Positive Religion*, 258).

208. See above, 26–27.

209. Strictly speaking, several of Emerton's predecessors teaching church history at Harvard Divinity School were far from "confessional." For example, J. H. Allen in the book based on his classroom lectures at Harvard, *Christian History in Its Three Great Periods*, scoffs at the Apologists' "dogma of a miraculous revival of the corpse" (64); emphasizes the unintelligibility of the Trinitarian controversy (100, 105, 106); accuses Augustine of incoherence (122); and charges that *City of God* abounds in "childish" arguments (141).

210. Emerton declined to defend doctrines of the Trinity or the divinity of Jesus. On Unitarianism's shaping of his approach, see his *Unitarian Thought*: the Unitarian's relation to Jesus is "kinship with an elder brother" (168); Jesus' perfect humanity "commends him to us as an attainable example" (164). In class, Emerton described Paul of Samosata as "one of the first propounders of Unitarianism" ("Church History," 1887–1889 [3/13]).

211. For a good introduction to Emerton's approach, see Bowden, *Church History*, chap. 4. Emerton later noted Harvard's refusal to offer a course on the "unity of

History"—suggesting a less "confessional" approach at Harvard ("Academic Study," 234).

212. Emerton, "Academic Study," 254; see Droysen, *Outline of the Principles of History*, 12 (#2.8). Throughout, Droysen stresses the moral world as the domain of history. Historians, according to Droysen, do not get the facts "as they were," for the past is always constituted in the present.

213. Emerton, "Church History," 1887–1889 (10/4); emphasis in original.

214. Emerton, "Place of History," 315, 321. One roughly contemporary commentator claimed that with the publication of the *Texte und Untersuchungen* series, headed by Harnack, "the dogmatic and speculative methods of the older German school were to be given up, and that research for the future was to begin with documents" (Headlam, "Methods," 255).

215. Emerton, "Definition of Church History," 67, 68.

216. Emerton, "Church History," 1887–1889 (10/6).

217. Described by Grant Wacker as "the recognition that the meaning of events is given not from outside history, not anterior to and independent of the process, but forged wholly from within the process" ("Demise of Biblical Civilization," 127).

218. Emerton, "Church History," 1887–1889 (10/6). Emerton stresses that *institutions* are primary shapers of human lives ("Academic Study," 250).

219. Emerton, "Church History," 1887–1889 (11/1), citing Edwin Hatch, *Organization of the Early Christian Churches* (1881).

220. Emerton, "Church History," 1887–1889 (10/6).

221. Emerton, "Church History," 1887–1889 (10/25, 10/20, 10/27).

222. Emerton, "Definition of Church History," 64, 65, 67, 68.

223. Emerton, *Introduction to the Study*, 149. For more on church historians' treatment of the Stylites—the "pillar saints"—see below, Chapter 8.

224. Emerton, "Rational Education," 295–96. Third comes the History of Religion (297).

225. Emerton, "Place of History," 310–11; emphasis in original. Pastoral studies also are historical (313).

226. Emerton, "Study of Church History," 1–18.

227. Emerton, "Study of Church History," 8, 11.

228. Emerton, "Definition of Church History," 58–59, 62, 63. Emphasis added.

229. Emerton, "Definition of Church History," 56, 57.

230. For his works on medieval and early modern history, see above, 54.

Chapter 5. Development and Decline: Challenges to Historiographical Categories

Epigraphs: Hitchcock, "Church History: Second Period," 1883, Moore notes (B2, N2, 375); both the dying Greco-Roman civilization and the "rough" Teutons are blamed. Prentiss, *Bright Side* I: 88, citing a letter to his mother from Germany (8/21/

1839). Prentiss assumed the Skinner and McAlpin Professorship of Pastoral Theology, Church Polity, and Mission Work at Union Seminary in 1872–1873 (*Bright Side* II: 252).

1. Development for Darwin was not necessarily upward, and in any case involved countless waste and slaughter along the way. Eleven or so years before Darwin's *Origin of Species*, Tennyson famously called Nature "red in tooth and claw" ("In Memoriam A.H.H.," canto 56). As J. Turner put it (*Without God, Without Creed*, 79), "It was precious little comfort to know that God watched every sparrow fall if He refused to do anything about it." The church historians here considered, however, generally understood development to connote positive advances. On the association of Spencer with Comte, see Cashdollar, *Transformation of Theology*, 145–52.

2. For some examples in Herder, see selections from his "Letters for the Advancement of Humanity," excerpted in Herder, *Philosophical Writings*, trans. and ed. Forster; Letters 114, 115, 121 (382, 384–85, 413), and Forster's "Introduction," xxv. On Herder's concept of *Volk*, see Manuel, "Editor's Introduction" to Herder, *Reflections on the Philosophy of the History of Mankind*, abridged Manuel, x–xxi; and F. M. Barnard, "Introduction," in *J. G. Herder on Social and Political Culture*, trans. and ed. Barnard, 7–40 passim.

3. For discussion of this emphasis, see Diehl, *Americans and German Scholarship*, 11–13. Diehl stresses that although Herder was not himself a "specialist," he provided an impulse for specialization. As an example of Herder's praise for a particular *Volk*, Manuel singles out his belief that Old Testament poetry was a perfect expression of the ancient Israelites' religious spirit (*Broken Staff*, 263–64, citing Herder's *Ideen zur Philosophie der Geschichte der Menschheit*, Bk. 12, chap. 3, and "Vom Geist der Ebräische Poesie"). Present-day Jews, however, were not so favored (271). Linking Herder's interest in the individuality of national cultures with wider Enlightenment concerns is Iggers, "European Context," 243. Tracing the development of Herder's notions of world history, the "genius" of various *Volk*, and his debt to his predecessors is W. Förster, "Johann Gottfried Herder," 363–87.

4. Prentiss, *Bright Side* I: 88, citing a letter to his mother from Germany (8/21/1839).

5. Prentiss, *Bright Side* I: 311, citing a letter to Smith (11/15/1842).

6. Edwards A. Park placed Tholuck in the "middle" theologically between the super-orthodox Hengstenberg and the overly accommodating Neander ("Biographical Sketch," in *Sketch of the Life and Character of Professor Tholuck*, 12).

7. Smith, "Tholuck's *Christliche Sittenlehre*" (S3, F1 [#3, "History of Ethics"; "Ethical Anthropology," #13]). Ritual law, Tholuck claimed in a Hegelianizing aside, belongs to the pedagogical aspect of Judaism, in that the rites were to be imagined as "'symbols' in which 'the Idea' was materially or sensuously contained."

8. Karl von Hase's *History of the Christian Church* offers little of interest for this discussion. Although Hase borrowed Schaff's notion of the church as progressing (1), he emphasized "decline" in the patristic era. In the Preface to the First Edition, Hase regretted his adoption of traditional opinions on the Fathers; the "Neander school"

will not like his approach (xi). In the Preface to the Third Edition, Hase declined to have his work compared to Neander's (xvii).

9. Gieseler (unlike Mosheim) refused to rule out as "Christian" any group that claimed the gospel of Christ (*Text-Book*, trans. Cunningham, 2; trans. Smith, 14).

10. Mosheim, *Ecclesiastical History* I: 5.

11. Mosheim, *Ecclesiastical History* I: 175, 183, 273.

12. Mosheim, *Ecclesiastical History* I: 134, 215, 431–32.

13. Mosheim, *Ecclesiastical History* I: 105, 179. "There remained no more than a mere shadow of the ancient government of the church" (I: 348).

14. Mosheim, *Ecclesiastical History* I: 267, 383.

15. Mosheim, *Ecclesiastical History* I: 201, 271–72, 290, 390.

16. Mosheim, *Ecclesiastical History* I: 186–87, 276–77, 368–69.

17. Mosheim, *Ecclesiastical History* I: 388–89; II: 51–52.

18. These writers used the word "positive" and "positivity" in the Kantian sense: outward expressions of religious commitment (e.g., creedal affirmations, ceremonies, obedience to religious law) were demanded—an "externality" stemming from Judaism that the developing Catholic Church inherited and maintained.

19. Gieseler claimed that Nestorius taught nothing contrary to Cyril of Alexandria's 433 confession of faith; Leo's *Epistula ad Flavianum* (the "Tome") was made the standard of faith at Chalcedon, the Council merely adding new explanations (*Text-Book* I, trans. Cunningham, 235–36, 240; cf. trans. Smith, 348–51, 353, 358).

20. Gieseler, *Text-Book* I, trans. Cunningham, 191–92; trans. Smith, 292–93.

21. Gieseler, *Text-Book* I, trans. Cunningham, 35, 27; trans. Smith, 57, 45.

22. Gieseler, *Text-Book* I, trans. Cunningham, 42–43; trans. Smith, 67 (the disciples took the "sensuous images" of Jesus' teaching and "introduced into them many more definite points").

23. Gieseler, *Text-Book* I, trans. Cunningham, 102, 151; trans. Smith, 159, 232.

24. Ethical standards; human rights; Greek art and wealth that corrupted Rome. Gieseler took Juvenal at face value on Rome's corruption (*Text-Book* I, trans. Cunningham, 16–19, 23–24; trans. Smith, 31–35, 40–41).

25. Gieseler, *Text-Book* I, trans. Cunningham, 35, 71; cf. trans. Smith, 57, 114–15.

26. Gieseler, *Text-Book* I, trans. Cunningham, 304; trans. Smith, 446, 449–50.

27. Gieseler, *Text-Book* I, trans. Cunningham, 90, 125; similarly, trans. Smith, 140, 194–95. For example, Gieseler likened the severe sentences of perpetual excommunication issued by early Spanish councils to "Montanistic rigor," and attributed the austerity of early asceticism (curtailing "Christian freedom") to Montanism (trans. Cunningham, 161–62, 169; trans. Smith, 250–52).

28. Gieseler, *Text-Book* I, trans. Cunningham, 154–55, 261–63, 192; trans. Smith, 237–38, 385–87, 293.

29. Gieseler, *Text-Book* I, trans. Cunningham, 358–59; trans. Smith, 525–26.

30. Ullmann, "Preface," Neander, *General History* I: x. Neander criticized Rationalist church historians for explaining dogma only from outward causes, rather than

from the inner impetus of Christian truth (*Lectures* I: 30); Neander saw Schleiermacher as a key figure in the war against Rationalism (I: 23).

31. Reported by Ullmann, "Preface," Neander, *General History* I: xix. Schaff claimed that the era of the Church Fathers was the period with which Neander was "most intimately familiar" ("Neander as a Church Historian," 566, 568, 572). Schaff stressed Schleiermacher's influence on Neander.

32. Hagenbach, "Neander's Services as a Church Historian," 855.

33. Neander, *Lectures* I: 73.

34. Neander, like Hegel, took Christianity as the "Absolute Religion" (*Lectures* I: 19), and appropriated Hegel's hierarchy of religions, starting with "Religions of Nature" and moving "upwards" toward Christianity (I: 4–5). Adherents of the "Absolute Religion," especially Protestants, could best assess the others (I: 17, 18).

35. Jacobi, "Preface," to Neander, *Lectures* I: viii. He acknowledged that other church historians (e.g., the Rationalist Semler) had a concept of development, but not one that was organic; focusing on the negative, it "pulled down without building up" (I: 30).

36. Neander, *Lectures* I: 12, 14. By the genetic component, Ullman explained, Neander meant that the historian should look for connecting links between events, for the "why" and the "wherefore" ("Preface," in Neander, *General History* I: xxv). Schaff appropriated this theme.

37. Ullman, "Preface" to Neander, *General History* I: xxvi; Neander did not deem Hegelianism a "necessary" movement. Pranger suggests that Neander was reacting to the "pragmatic" school of history-writing that included Gottlieb Planck, Philip Marheinecke, and Johann Gieseler, who saw *individuals* in charge of the course of history (*Philip Schaff*, 207).

38. Neander, *Lectures* I: 11, 4 ("Das Wesen des Christenthums besteht nicht in einem System von Begroffen, sondern in einer Richtung des inneren Lebens").

39. Neander, *Lectures* I: 4, 25.

40. Neander, *General History* I: 247, 1. Schaff took these parables as central to understanding the church's development.

41. Neander, *Lectures* I: 4, 18, 19.

42. Neander, *General History* I: 507, 339. Christianity could be "adapted to all stages of culture" because it "presupposed a like want in all" (I: 71).

43. Neander, *General History* I: 276; II: 161, 262; *Memorials*, 76.

44. Neander, *General History* I: 650, II: 263. The mixing of Jesus' parables is notable.

45. Neander, *General History* II: iv. Augustine, in Neander's opinion, failed to distinguish sufficiently between Christianity and the church; this incorrect view was accepted in Roman Catholicism (II: 239, 246). Schaff criticized Neander for making too strong a contrast between "the Christian" and "the ecclesiastical" (reported by Jacobi, "Preface" to Neander's *Lectures* I: x; also see Schaff, "Progress of Church History," 78).

46. Neander, *General History* I: 512. On Neander's relation to Hegelianism, see Schaff, "Recollections of Neander," 80–82 (Schaff alleged that Neander, given his dependence upon Hegel for his notion of development, was too critical of Hegelianism in general). See Hegel's early treatises, "The Positivity of the Christian Religion" (1796), "The Spirit of Christianity and Its Fate" (1798–1799) and the fragment on "Love" (1798?), in Hegel, *On Christianity: Early Theological Writings*, trans. T. M. Knox and R. Kroner; the overcoming of Jewish "heteronomy" is the basic theme. "Religious practice," Hegel writes, "is our endeavor to unify the discords necessitated by our existence and our attempt to exhibit the unification in the *ideal* as fully *existent*, as no longer opposed to reality" ("Spirit of Christianity," 206).

47. Neander, *Lectures* I: 35; *General History* I: 520.

48. Neander, *General History* I: 249.

49. Neander, *Emperor Julian*, 18.

50. Neander, *Memorials*, 415, 406.

51. Progress is "only quantitative" for the ancients, according to Baur, and for Gottfried Arnold, the real history is that of heretics, not of true, unchanging Christianity (Baur, *Epochs of Church Historiography*, 69, 120–21, 126, 132). For Baur, the church is the externalization of the internal essence of Christianity, whose true "substance" lies in dogma (254, 255).

52. Baur, *Epochs of Church Historiography*, 147, 146, 148.

53. Baur, *Epochs of Church Historiography*, 211, 213, 214. In Baur's view, Neander's "tendencies" are simply idealism versus realism, or rationalism versus supernaturalism. With no uniting synthesis, Neander is left with an unresolved dualism (220, 221).

54. Baur, *Epochs of Church Historiography*, 224, 213, 214. Baur links Neander with Schleiermacher's "immediacy of the religious consciousness" (211).

55. Winterer, *Culture of Classicism*, chap. 1, and 80, 133; also see Reinhold, *Classica Americana*.

56. Winterer, *Culture of Classicism*, 4, 83 ("chasing Mammon"), 98, 110.

57. See Lintott, "Imperial Expansion and Moral Decline in the Roman Republic," 626–38; on "moral judgement," not "economic analysis," as an approach to Rome's "decline" (626, 638).

58. Syme, *Sallust*, 56. Especially see Sallust, *Bella Catalina* 5, 10–13, 36, 52 (Cato's speech); *Bella Jugurtha* 1, 4, 41, 85 (Marius' speech); *Historiae* II, frag. 10, 12, 13, 48 (Lepidus' speech). Also see Earl, *Political Thought of Sallust*, chap. 4, and 9–15, 39–40, 64, 70, 74, 97, 109, 116–17; and Earl, *Moral and Political Tradition of Rome*, 17–19.

59. Especially seen in Book I, praef. 9–11; also see Jaeger, *Livy's Written Rome*, 10–11; Walsh, *Livy*, 18, 78; Luce, *Livy*, 230, 245, 250–84; Miles, *Livy*, 76–77, 80, 84, 94, 108, 222–23; Earl, *Moral and Political Tradition*, 74–79.

60. Tacitus, *Historiae* I.1, 5, 18, 20, 22; II. 31, 37, 38, 69, 87, 94, 95; III: 51, 72, 83; *Germania* 18–20 (on German sexual virtue); Earl, *Moral and Political Tradition*, chap. 4.

61. Especially *Satires* 2, 6, and 9.

62. Yet when touting Christianity's ethical superiority, these professors could contrast its shining virtues with pagan depravity.

63. Writing on Kant in his *Brief Retrospect of the Eighteenth Century*, Miller, after reproducing an unhelpful report of Kant's philosophy from a British journal, suggested that English scholars' complaint regarding the obscurity of Kant's philosophy shows a "strong presumption" against its rationality and truth; perhaps Kant has cloaked his thought in "enigmatic language" because his philosophy tends "to undermine all religion and morals" (*Part I*: II: 24–27). In his "Recapitulations," Miller contrasted eighteenth-century accomplishments in physical science with the "*vain speculation* and *fantastic theory*" in the philosophy of mind (416). He admitted his ignorance of "most of the languages of the continent of Europe" (xi–xii).

64. See Lingelbach, *Klio macht Karriere*, 86–87. Lingelbach sees this theme especially in the writings of George Bancroft (an admirer of Henry Smith).

65. George Berkeley, "Prospect of Planting Arts and Learning in America" in Berkeley, *A Miscellany, containing several tracts on various subjects* (Dublin: Faulkner, 1752).

66. Miller, "Introductory Lecture on Ecclesiastical History," 3/2/1815 (and 5 other dates, up to 1839) (B2, F9, 5).

67. Miller, "Practical Results from a Course of Ecclesiastical History" (B2, F10, 2, 5–6); emphasis in original.

68. Miller, "Practical Results from a Course of Ecclesiastical History" (B2, F10, 2).

69. Miller, "Ecclesiastical History. Remarks on the First and Second Centuries" (B2, F12, 8–10); "Practical Results from a Course of Ecclesiastical History" (B2, F10, 5–6).

70. Miller, "Practical Results from a Course of Ecclesiastical History" (B2, F10, 5–6, 12); similarly, "Ecclesiastical History, No. II. II and III Centuries" (B2, F14, 6). That Miller's students would have had easy access to the writings of Cyprian, Origen, and Eusebius is dubious.

71. Miller, "Ecclesiastical History. Remarks on the First and Second Centuries" (B2, F12, 5–6, 8–10); Miller does not provide references.

72. Miller, "Ecclesiastical History, No. I. I and II Centuries" (B2, F13, 27).

73. Miller, "Ecclesiastical History" (B2, F11, 21–22).

74. Miller, "Ecclesiastical History, No. II. II and III Centuries" (B2, F14, 6).

75. Miller, "Ecclesiastical History. Remarks on the First and Second Centuries" (B2, F12, 11). Miller's comments reveal his ignorance of the Quartodeciman Controversy that would so exercise the Tübingen School and their opponents.

76. Miller, "Ecclesiastical History, No. II. II and III Centuries" (B2, F14, 11–12); "Ecclesiastical History. Remarks on the First and Second Centuries" (B2, F12, 12).

77. Miller, "Ecclesiastical History, No. II. II and III Centuries" (B2, 14, 14).

78. Miller, "Ecclesiastical History, No. II. II and III Centuries" (B2, F14, 1–3). Miller claimed (22) that from the time of Ammonius until the sixth century, "New-Platonism" was almost the sole philosophy taught at Alexandria.

79. Miller, "Ecclesiastical History. Remarks on the First and Second Centuries" (B2, F12, 30). Soon, science and literature fell into decay, due to a lack of patronage, civil wars, the "incursions of barbarian nations," and the "growing taste for arms" ("Ecclesiastical History, No. II. II and III Centuries" [B2, F14, 20–21]).

80. Miller, "Ecclesiastical History. Remarks on the First and Second Centuries" (B2, F12, 32, 33, 35).

81. Miller, "Ecclesiastical History. Remarks on the First and Second Centuries" (B2, F12, 2); *Presbyterianism*, 14.

82. Miller, "Ecclesiastical History, No. II. II and III Centuries" (B2, F14, 26, 27). In his own reading notes, Miller recounted the story of Origen's castration, adding that while some hold Origen subdued his sexual desire by powerful herbs and medicines, Jerome claims that "he actually employed a *knife*!" Miller did not tell the story to his students, judging from his class notes ("Notes on Mosheim, Century III" [B5, F8, 28–29]); he also faults Mosheim's relative neglect of Origen's theological errors, e.g., the preexistence of human souls and the restoration of the damned (32). Similarly on Origen's exegesis ("Ecclesiastical History No. III. IV and V Centuries" [B2, F15, 12]).

83. Miller, "Ecclesiastical History, No. II. II and III Centuries" (B2, F14, 25, 30–36); Miller focused attention on the recondite sect of the Hieracites (32–33).

84. Miller, *Presbyterianism*, 14–15.

85. Miller, "Ecclesiastical History, No. II. II and III Centuries" (B2, F14, 9).

86. Miller, "Notes on Mosheim, Century IV," 2/18/1814 (B5, F11, 1). Here, Miller faulted Mosheim for giving an inadequate portrait of Constantine; the "infidel" Gibbon gives a much fuller picture. Constantine had no experiential knowledge and love of truth, but was a "mere professor" [of Christianity] (2–7). Miller points out Constantine's crimes and "atrocious murders," "the degrading luxury and effeminacy in which he indulged" (8). Constantine "misunderstood" Christianity, preferring to spend money on magnificent cathedrals rather than "*crucify the flesh with the affections*" (11).

87. Miller, "Ecclesiastical History, No. III. IV and V Centuries" (B2, F15, 3–4), emphasis in original. Miller elsewhere wrote, "all traces of primitive simplicity and purity were lost in the plans and splendour of worldly policy" (*Presbyterianism*, 17).

88. Miller, "Ecclesiastical History. Remarks on the First and Second Centuries" (B2, F12, 2–3), emphasis in original. With Constantine, the church "began to put on her *beautiful garments*; but it was not a *beauty of holiness*!" ("Notes on Mosheim, Century IV," 2/18/ 1814 [B5, F11, 14–15]).

89. Miller, "Ecclesiastical History, No. III. IV and V Centuries" (B2, F15, 4).

90. The orthodox persecuted the Arians "in a very unjustifiable manner," in Miller's view, although Arians persecuted the orthodox when they had power. Miller noted that the persecution of Priscillianists was the first time that Christian heretics were put to death, although this was opposed by Martin of Tours ("Ecclesiastical History, No. III. IV and V Centuries" [B2, F15, 15–17, 13–14, 18]).

91. Miller, "Ecclesiastical History, No. III. IV and V Centuries" (B2, F15, 7–9).

92. Miller, *Presbyterianism*, 15; on the decline of deacons, 58–59. Miller cites patristic evidence to document his charges (e.g., Ambrose's *Commentary on Ephesians* 4.2 [15–16, misnumbered "6"]).

93. Miller, "Ecclesiastical History, No. III. IV and V Centuries" (B2, F15, 9). Miller assumes that the Roman bishop's pre-eminence lay in Rome's being the imperial capital.

94. Miller, "Ecclesiastical History, No. III. IV and V Centuries" (B2, F15, 10, 24, 11–12; more on Augustine in Chapter 9 below). Elsewhere, Miller faults Mosheim for not mentioning Philoxenus of Hierapolis as an "iconoclast" who was "greatly abhorred by the image-mongers" ("Notes on Mosheim, Century V," 3/7/1814 [B5, F13, 22–23]). Discussing immersion and "sprinkling," Miller wrote that baptism itself does not convey salvation ("Notes on Mosheim, Century II" [B5, F4, 6]). He faulted Cyprian for believing that baptism conveys remission of sins ("Notes on Mosheim, Century III" [B5, F8, 27]).

95. Miller, "Ecclesiastical History, No. III. IV and V Centuries" (B2, F15, 19–22).

96. Miller, "Ecclesiastical History, No. IV. V, VI, and VII Centuries" (B2, F16, 4–5).

97. Miller praised seventh-century Paulicians for opposing image worship and disregarding the saints, images, holy days and worship of the Virgin Mary; for retaining only two sacraments; and for establishing the equality of the clergy. Despite persecution, they were "the light of the world" for more than 150 years ("Ecclesiastical History, No. IV. V, VI, and VII Centuries" [B2, F16, 20–21]).

98. Miller, "Ecclesiastical History, No. IV. V, VI, and VII Centuries" (B2, F16, 12–14), following Gibbon. Miller, who never visited the Middle East, was intrigued with Islam.

99. Miller, *Presbyterianism*, 18, 20, 21; not all branches even of the Reformed churches, however, adopted the primitive polity.

100. Miller, "Practical Results from a Course of Ecclesiastical History" (B2, F10, 11, 7, 9, 18). Many divines today, he added, judge that neither Nestorius' nor Eutyches' teachings were "materially erroneous, or dangerous to the orthodox faith"; the issue was one of language. Yet good came out of the struggle: the orthodox creed ("Ecclesiastical History, No. III. IV and V Centuries" [B2, F15, 26–27]). Scholars, he claims, now think Nestorius' Christology orthodox ("Notes on Mosheim, Century V," 3/7/ 1814 [B5, F13, 28]).

101. Miller, "Ecclesiastical History. Remarks on the First and Second Centuries" (B2, F12, 14–15).

102. Smith, "Systematic Theology," 1857 (?) (S4, B1, F2, L11).

103. Smith, "Nature and Worth," 64–65; "Church History: First Period," 1849– 1850 (?), Hastings notes (S5, B1, F3, 78–79).

104. Smith, "Church History: First Period," 1849–1850 (?), Hastings notes (S5, B1, F3, 75).

105. Smith, "Problem of the Philosophy of History," 12–14; "Nature and Worth," 75–76.

106. Smith, "Church History," 1849–1850 (?), Hastings notes (S5, B1, F3, 73–74); John Henry Newman as an exception. Elsewhere, Smith claimed that the Tractarian movement reshaped the parties within the English Church. The new groupings, according to Smith, are (1) the old High Church party; (2) evangelicals of a Calvinistic stripe; (3) the "catholicizing" party; (4) the Historical and Speculative party (Coleridge, Arnold, and Thayer); and (5) Independents of "higher theological culture" ("Systematic Theology," 10/9/1857 [S4, B1, F3, L14 cont.]).

107. Smith, "Church History: First Period," 1849–1850 (?), Hastings notes (S5, B1, F3, 74–75). Smith, back in America, borrowed a book by Hegel from Theodore Parker (Parker to Smith, West Roxbury, 7/2/1845 (S1, B1).

108. Smith, "Church History: First Period," 1849–1850 (?), Hastings notes (S5, B1, F3, 74–75).

109. Smith, "Recent German Works on Apologetics," 536, 537, discussing J. H. A. Ebrard's *Apologetik. Wissenschaftliche Rechtfertigung des Christenthums.* 2 Theile (Gütersloh, 1874–1875).

110. Smith, "Recent German Works on Apologetics," 536, 537.

111. Smith, "Church History," 1849–1850 (?), Hastings notes (S5, B1, F3, 101).

112. *ATR* 2.5 (Feb. 1860): 168; *APTR* 1.1. (Jan.1863): 145–46.

113. Typical criticisms: the work is "unphilosophical," "based on mere fancy instead of facts," "degrading to the dignity of human nature." Smith reported—perhaps with irony?—that Darwin was preparing a sequel to *Origin,* to be titled *On the Fertilization of British Orchids by Means of Insects* (*ATR* 4.13 [Jan. 1862]: 169).

114. Smith, "Christian Apologetics," 483, 494–95.

115. Smith, "Systematic Theology," 11/1857 (S4, B1, F6). One point of evidence: the great difference in the size of the brain in relation to the spinal cord in humans and even the "highest" mammals.

116. Prentiss, *Union Theological Seminary,* 261; [E. Smith], *Henry Boynton Smith,* 401, 404–5; [H. B. Smith], "Clergymen as Men of Science," 4; [W. Taylor],"The Late Prof. H. B. Smith," 125. In 1865, Samuel F. B. Morse gave Union Seminary funds to establish a lectureship on "Relation of the Bible to the Sciences" (Prentiss, *Union Theological Seminary,* 95n. B).

117. Smith, "Systematic Theology," 1857 (?) (S4, B1, F2, L11)"Doctrinal History," 1851, Hastings notes (S5, B1, F3, 6–7). Another example: the western church's addition to the Creed of Nicaea/Nicene Creed, that the Spirit proceeds from "the Father *and* the Son," not from the Father alone ("Systematic Theology," 1857? [S4, B1, F 2, L11); "Systematic Theology," 4/23/1858 [S4, B1, F16]).

118. Smith, "Doctrinal History," 1851, Hastings notes (S5, B1, F3, 49–50, 63).

119. Smith faulted Philip Schaff (not yet his colleague at Union) and the Mercersburg Theology for favoring the "external sacraments" as a sign of development (Schaff joined the Union faculty in 1870; Smith died in 1877.) Here, Smith's commitment to

Christianity as "inner spirituality" stood against the high-church sacramentarianism of Nevin and Schaff.

120. Smith, "Church History: First Period," 1849–1850 (?), Hastings notes (S5, B1, F3, 76–77).

121. See Penzel, "Ecumenical Vision," 8, on Petrine, Pauline, and Johannine forms of early Christianity. Smith wrote the entry on Schelling for the *New American Cyclopaedia*, ed. Ripley and Dana, XIV: 396–400.

122. Smith, "Doctrinal History," 1851, Hastings notes (S5, B1, F3, 5); "Church History: First Period," 1849–1850 (?), Hastings notes (S5, B1, F3, 60).

123. The issue is nevertheless complex: the German historians and philosophers who espoused theories of development were *also* largely Protestant, and church historians of Neander's cast believed that in some respects the church had declined in the midst of overall development. Decline as manifest in polity and in asceticism will receive separate discussions in Chapters 6 and 8 below.

124. Smith, "Sermon" (on Zechariah 4:6) (S2, B3, 8–9, 14–15); Smith also excoriated the church-state system of England; similarly, Smith, *History*, 14–15.

125. Smith, *History*, 16. Examples: "heathen rites" contributed to the development of Christmas celebration in early sixth-century Rome; the Festival of the Purification of Mary in mid-sixth century "takes the place of the Lupercalia" (22).

126. Smith, "Church History: First Period," 1849–1850 (?), Hastings notes (S5, B1, F3, 63–64).

127. Smith, *History*, 20, 23; "Sermon" (on Zechariah 4:6) (S2, B3, 8–9, 14–15).

128. The early Hegel was not so sure that the conversion of Teutons was entirely beneficial: "Christianity has emptied Valhalla, felled the sacred groves, extirpated the national imagery as a shameful superstition, as a devilish poison, and given us instead the imagery of a nation whose climate, laws, culture, and interests are strange to us and whose history has no connection whatever with our own." "Is Judea, then, the Teutons' Fatherland?" he rhetorically asks ("Positivity of the Christian Religion," in Hegel, *On Christianity*, 146, 145). For nineteenth-century Germans' (and Germanophiles') assessment of Teutonic "barbarians" as preferable to effete Romans and as positive national ancestors, see Marchand, *Down from Olympus*, 157–162; Marchand titles chapter 5, "Excavating the Barbarians."

129. Hitchcock, "Church History: First Period," early 1880s, Burrell notes (B1, N1, 177): Hitchcock adds that the term "evolution" belongs to the sphere of organic life.

130. Hitchcock, "History of the World Before Christ," 1862, Wright notes (B2, N1, General Survey, #3). Hitchcock's views on this topic are summed up in his article, "Historical Development of Christianity," 28–54.

131. Hitchcock, "Historical Development," 28 (note the non-eschatological interpretation of this parable), 30, 29 (Newman is faulted for his belief that later developments in the Roman Church were "legitimate").

132. Hitchcock, "Historical Development," 33, 34, 35–36.

133. Hitchcock, "Laws of Civilization," 15, 23; "Historical Development," 46.

134. Hitchcock, "Church History: First Period," 1883, Moore notes (B2, N2, 206)

135. Hitchcock, "True Idea and Uses," 33.

136. Hitchcock, "Church History: First Period," early 1880s, Burrell notes (B1, N1, 250).

137. Hitchcock, "Church History: First Period," 1872, Jackson notes (Jackson Papers, B1, N1, 14, 99). The Apologists show "the upward tendency of Christianity" (64), being "immensely in advance" of the Apostolic Fathers (100–101).

138. Hitchcock, "Church History: Second Period," 1883, Moore notes (B2, N2, 432); "Church History: Second Period," 1873, Jackson notes (Jackson Papers, B1, N1, 247–48).

139. For representative discussions, see Hitchcock, "Church History: First Period," 1872, Jackson notes (Jackson Papers, B1, N1, 147–49); Hitchcock, "Church History: First Period," early 1880s, Burrell notes (B1, N1, 227).

140. Hitchcock, "Church History: First Period," early 1880s, Burrell notes (B1, N1, 227 ["no sacerdotalism in the genuine Clement," however); "Church History: First Period," 1872, Jackson notes (Jackson Papers, B1, N1, 53).

141. Hitchcock, "Church History: Second Period," 1873, Jackson notes (Jackson Papers, B1, N1, 161–62); "Church History: Second Period," 1883, Moore notes (B2, N2, 375); both the dying Greco-Roman civilization and the "rough" Teutons are blamed.

142. Hitchcock, "Church History: Second Period," 1873, Jackson notes (Jackson Papers, B1, N1, 251–52); "Church History: Second Period," 1883–1884, Burrell notes (B1, N2, 39). In Hitchcock's view, the best church-state relation, the "theocracy of the future," is that in which neither absorbs the other, but where the state "shall be thoroughly pervaded by [Christianity's] spirit and shall thus bring in [the] promised golden age" (Burrell notes, 31–32). Constantine's and Theodosius' "despotisms" adapted Christianity to fit the state—unlike the situation of church and state in America, where, in Hitchcock's view, the two are "as utterly divorced as they ever can be" ("Religion, The Doing of God's Will," 41).

143. Hitchcock, "Church History: Second Period," 1873, Jackson notes (Jackson Papers, B1, N1, 180–81); emphasis in original.

144. Hitchcock, "Church History: Second Period," 1873, Jackson notes (Jackson Papers, B1, N2, 11).

145. Hitchcock added, "We [Protestants] are in danger of withholding from Mary that tender interest due to her" ("Life of Christ," 1865, Wright notes (B2, N1, 1st period, chapter 3, unpaged); cf. "Life of Christ," early 1880s, Burrell notes (B1, N1, 40–41).

146. Hitchcock, "Church History: First Period," 1872, Jackson notes (Jackson Papers, B1, N1, 67)—an unadvisable practice for the nineteenth century ("Church History: Second Period," Jackson notes [Jackson Papers, B1, N1, 197]).

147. Hitchcock, "Church History: First Period," 1883, Moore notes (B2, N2, 329); "Church History: Second Period," 1883–1884, Burrell notes (B1, N2, 40).

148. Schaff, *America* (13), summing up Europeans' presumed criticisms of

America (6–12). Providence prepared America "for the greatest work," and no earthly power can stop it if Americans remain true to their calling (20).

149. Matt. 28:20; John 14:16.

150. Schaff, *What Is Church History?* 91; also in *Reformed and Catholic*, ed. Yrigoyen and Bricker, 107.

151. Schaff, "General Introduction to Church History," 410. Similarly: history is "the evolution of God's thoughts and purposes, which have an eternal significance and power" ("Discord and Concord of Christendom, II," *New-York Independent* [Sept. 1884], clipping (UTS, B6, Scr2, 21). Schaff continued to use this Hegelianizing formula later in life.

152. Schaff, "Julian the Apostate," 17; likewise, "Church History," MTS, 1855, Russell notes (LTS, B4, F03, N9).

153. Schaff, "Julian the Apostate," 15–16n.

154. Schaff, "Autobiographical Reminiscences" (LTS, B1, F04, 116); Pranger, *Philip Schaff*, 29.

155. Schaff, *History* I: 22. Conservative Calvinist Charles Hodge of Princeton faulted Schaff's notion of "organic development" as Hegelian and pantheistic; see his review of Schaff's *History of the Apostolic Church*.

156. Schaff, *What Is Church History?* 75, 76; also in *Reformed and Catholic*, ed. Yrigoyen and Bricker, 91, 92. On the popularity of Hegel's thought during Schaff's time at Tübingen: students "thought they could reconstruct the whole universe by rethinking the thoughts of God who comes to his self-consciousness in man" ("Autobiographical Reminiscences" [LTS, B1, F04, 114]).

157. Schaff, "German Theology and the Church Question," 138, 140–41; *Principle of Protestantism*, 99 (Lutheranism had more respect for tradition than did the Reformed churches).

158. Schaff, *Principle of Protestantism*, 75. The stress on human "apprehension" appears to derive from Schleiermacher. Schaff as a *Privatdozent* in Berlin lectured on Schleiermacher.

159. Schaff, *Principle of Protestantism*, 76. Since revelation is adapted to humans' capacity to apprehend it, doctrine emerges as the consciousness of the church's life comes into sharper focus: see Meyer, "Philip Schaff's Concept of Organic Historiography," 240–42, with references to Schaff, *Theological Propaedeutic* II: 240.

160. Schaff, *Principle of Protestantism*, 176; *History* I: 22.

161. Schaff, *Principle of Protestantism*, 59–60, 118.

162. Schaff, *Principle of Protestantism*, 177. Schaff elsewhere reminded audiences that writers such as Dante were not the monopoly of the Roman Catholic communion, and that the Middle Ages were "the fertile soil of the reformation" ("Dante," 42, 46): American Protestants should adopt the liberal spirit that characterized the founders of "our Commonwealth." Narrow-minded Protestants who claim that "we *alone*" are children of Abraham are called "small pharisaical spirits."

163. Schaff, *Principle of Protestantism*, 61, 71.

164. Schaff, *Principle of Protestantism*, 158, 161, 160, 163, 164: by championing epis-copal succession, foreign to the New Testament, Tractarians deny the universal priest-hood of all believers and reintroduce "the old leaven of the Pharisees, which has never been thoroughly purged out of the Anglican Church."

165. In 1845, Schaff's *Principle of Protestantism* was attacked; see "Dr. Schaff's Reply and Farewell to the Synod," 25–26. For various charges, see Appendices F and G in Meyer, "Philip Schaff's Concept of Organic Historiography," 277–80; also in Richards, *History of the Theological Seminary of the Reformed Church*, 251–54. For dis-cussion, see Shriver, "Philip Schaff: Heresy at Mercersburg," 18–55. Schaff emerged unscathed.

In addition, the editors of the *BFER* appended a note to an article by Schaff, objecting to his views on the benefits of the early Roman bishopric. The editors remind readers that Scripture deems the papacy the work of Satan; in no way can the treach-ery, avarice, and ambition of the papacy be compared to the "Mosaic theocracy" (Schaff, "Development of the Ancient Catholic Hierarchy: II," 60n.)

166. See, for example, Janeway, "Contrast Between the Erroneous Assertions of Professor Schaf [*sic*], and the Testimony of Credible Ecclesiastical Historians," 5–37. Janeway apparently thought that he could trounce Schaff by quoting Mosheim's church histories against him. Janeway was associated with Old School Presbyterians and Dutch Reformed, as pastor and professor.

167. Shriver, "Philip Schaff's Concept of Organic Historiography," 11, 84, 106–7, 140n.162; Pranger, *Philip Schaff*, 51. Also important was Herder's theory of history as a developing, "living spirit," a theme appropriated and elaborated by Schleiermacher, Hegel, and Schelling (Schaff, *What Is Church History?* 73, 15; also in *Reformed and Catholic*, ed. Yrigoyen and Bricker, 89, 31). Schaff proclaimed Schleiermacher the "greatest theological genius" since the Reformation (77).

168. Christian history for Schaff is the story of a movement's *growth* ("Theological Encyclopedia," UTS, 1877–1878 (?), Gillett notes [UTS, B3, "Miscellaneous," N, 48]). On German scholars' contribution to Schaff's notion of organic development, see K. Johnson, "The Mustard Seed and the Leaven," 120–79; Shriver, "Philip Schaff's Con-cept of Organic Historiography," and Meyer, "Philip Schaff's Concept of Organic Historiography."

169. Schaff, *What Is Church History?* 91; also in *Reformed and Catholic*, ed. Yri-goyen and Bricker, 107. Lotz notes that the concept of organic development was to provide both stability and mobility ("Philip Schaff and the Idea of Church His-tory," 13).

170. Schaff, *What Is Church History?* 84; also in *Reformed and Catholic*, ed. Yri-goyen and Bricker, 100.

171. Schaff, *History* I: 22; *Theological Propaedeutic* II: 239.

172. Schaff, *History of the Apostolic Church* I, in *Reformed and Catholic*, ed. Yri-goyen and Bricker, 169.

173. Schaff, *Theological Propaedeutic* II: 241. Schaff, however, could not have endorsed the real import of Darwin's theory.

174. See discussion in Meyer, "Philip Schaff's Concept of Organic Historiography," 141–44; also see Shriver, "Philip Schaff's Concept of Organic Historiography," passim. Kathryn Johnson explains that Schaff borrowed the "leaven" image from Neander (expressing inward development) but that the "mustard seed" gave a greater sense of outward growth of the church ("Mustard Seed and the Leaven," 148–49).

175. Schaff, *History of the Apostolic Church* I, in *Reformed and Catholic*, ed. Yrigoyen and Bricker, 169.

176. Schaff, *History* II: 335, 122. Post-Constantine, Donatists kept to this principle. Primitive Christianity, Schaff wrote, "asserted the individual rights of man" and "raised the humble and lowly" (385).

177. Schaff, *History* II: 11, 14.

178. Schaff, *History* II: 35. State churches throughout time persecute dissenters, violating the principles of Jesus and "in carnal misunderstanding of the spiritual nature of the kingdom of heaven" (36).

179. Schaff, *History* II: 428 (as Rationalism has in modern times); cf. 509. Montanism's excessive rigor was a "fall from evangelical freedom into Jewish legalism" (425).

180. Schaff, *What Is Church History?* 99; also in *Reformed and Catholic*, ed. Yrigoyen and Bricker, 114, 115; *Principle of Protestantism*, 129–55, on the "diseases" of Protestantism.

181. Schaff, "Gnosticism," 532, 533: much patristic theology was developed in opposition to some "wrong" movement or principle; opposition fostered the development of the creeds. In the nineteenth century, German Rationalism and Pantheism similarly spurred the development of evangelical theology. Schaff elsewhere called Baur "the master spirit of modern Gnosticism," crediting him with a Valentinian system that uses Hegelian terminology (*History* II: 477 Notes).

182. Schaff, "Conflict of Trinitarianism and Unitarianism," 743, 744—although Nicene theology went beyond Sabellius to develop a Trinity of essence, with permanent, not fluctuating, manifestations of the three Persons.

183. Schaff, *History* II: 122–23.

184. Schaff, "The Latin Patriarchate," 13–14 (just as Jewish theocracy and the pagan Roman Empire, amid their errors, fostered primitive Christianity); similarly, Schaff, "Development of the Ancient Catholic Hierarchy: II," 39.

185. Schaff, "Latin Patriarchate," 29; *History* III: 289, cf. 314.

186. Schaff, *History* II: 122–23; *History* III: 314.

187. Schaff, *History* III: 314; similarly, "Development of the Ancient Catholic Hierarchy: II," 59–60.

188. Schaff, *History* I: 854. Likewise, the stagnant and superstitious Monophysite party of the Coptic Church was preserved by Providence to provide a door through which Protestants could missionize Arabs and Turks (*History* III: 772–73).

189. Schaff, "Theology of Our Age and Country," in Schaff, *Christ and Christianity*, 15.

190. Schaff, *History* II: 7, 629.

191. Schaff, *History* II: 338.

192. Schaff, *History* II: 628.

193. Schaff, *History* II: 588, 589.

194. Schaff, *History* II: 123, 125; cf. II: 247: "the idea of priesthood, sacrifice, and altar are intimately connected, and a Judaizing or paganizing conception of one must extend to all."

195. Schaff is especially offended by John Chrysostom's depiction of his deceitful escape from the priesthood, which he nevertheless thrust upon his friend Basil: the "Jesuitical maxim, 'the end justifies the means,' is much older than Jesuitism" (*History* III: 254; "Prolegomena: Life and Work of St. John Chrysostom," 8).

196. Schaff, *History* II: 363, 377 (Cyprian is here the culprit).

197. Schaff, *History* III: 410, 411.

198. Schaff, *History* III: 8, 432, 435,450, 453. Even John Chrysostom, whose preaching Schaff largely admired, fell into "extravagant laudations of saints and martyrs," thus promoting "that refined form of idolatry which in the Nicene age began to take the place of the heathen hero-worship" ("Prolegomena: Life and Work of St. John Chrysostom," 21).

199. Schaff, "Mediaeval Morals III: Mediaeval Charity," *New-York Independent*, March 19, 1885 (UTS, B6, Scr 2, 35–36).

200. Schaff, *History* III: 1017n.1; similarly, "Genius and Theology," 113.

201. Schaff, *History* III: 1017n.1; similarly, "Genius and Theology," 113.

202. Schaff, *History* II: 649–50, 668.

203. Schaff, *History* II: 681, 684: the author does not even name Christ. Moreover, the author of the *Shepherd* had a very imperfect understanding of the "free Gospel of Paul" (686 and n.1).

204. Schaff, *History* II: 722.

205. Schaff, *Theological Propaedeutic* II: 274.

206. Schaff, *History* II: 751.

207. Schaff, *Life and Labors*, 57.

208. Schaff, *History* I: 507; II: 123, 428. Schaff thought that Gnosticism in its earliest form had "Judaistic" elements, while in the second period, it emerged as a "paganizing heresy" (445); similarly, "Gnosticism," 528. Schaff accounted for Tertullian's strict morals as a response to "very lax penitential discipline of popes" (as revealed in the newly discovered *Philosophumena* of Hippolytus); this laxity drove Tertullian into Montanism ("Tertullian," 622; "Tertullian" [from an unspecified encyclopedia article] [UTS, B6, Scr2, 28]).

209. Schaff, *History* II: 123; cf. II: 247: "the ideas of priesthood, sacrifice, and altar are intimately connected, and a Judaizing or paganizing conception of one must

extend to all." For more on clerical hierarchy and sacerdotalism, see "Development of the Ancient Catholic Hierarchy: I," 667.

210. Schaff, *History* I: 58.

211. Schaff, "Church History," MTS, 1855, Russell notes (LTS, B4, Fo3, N, 11); similarly, *History* III: 125–26, 70.

212. Schaff, *History* III: 356, 630, 375, 376. Pagans, crowding into the church, brought corruption with them: see *Saint Augustine, Melanchthon, Neander*, 42; *Theological Propaedeutic* II: 430.

213. Schaff, *History* III: 125–26, 357.

214. Schaff, *History* III: 13.

215. Schaff, "Constantine the Great," 791; *History* III: 107.

216. Schaff, *History* III: 94 and n.1, 95; "Church History," MTS, 1855, Russell notes (LTS, B4, Fo3, N, 1).

217. Fisher, "Conflict: I," 131.

218. Fisher, "Old Roman Spirit," in Fisher, *Discussions*, 42–43; similarly, *History of the Christian Church*, 118; *History of Christian Doctrine*, 14–15 (Fisher disliked Baur's late dating [14]).

219. Fisher, "Church History," 1870–1871 (117, 7, 39–40).

220. Fisher, "Church History," 1870–1871 (47); *Validity of Non-Episcopal Ordination*, 30.

221. Fisher, *History of the Christian Church*, 54, 56. Gnostics are not to blame for the Judaizing "legal direction" of Christianity in this period ("Old Roman Spirit," in Fisher, *Discussions*, 42).

222. Fisher, "Church History," 1870–1871 (46); "Old Roman Spirit," in Fisher, *Discussions*, 40–41. Elsewhere in this volume ("Council of Constance and the Council of the Vatican," 132), Fisher claimed that the revival of Judaism within the Roman Catholic Church obscured for ages "an essential peculiarity of the Gospel and the Gospel dispensation."

223. Fisher, "Church History," 1870–1871 (30, 36); Mohammad at first was an "honest fanatic," but his teaching afterward became mixed with falsity and ambition.

224. Fisher, "Old Roman Spirit," in Fisher, *Discussions*, 37, 38, 39; "Church History," 1870–1871 (119). Earlier, Origen had testified to the growing worldliness of the church.

225. Fisher, *History of the Christian Church*, 90; "Church History," 1870–1871 (51–52).

226. Fisher, *History of Christian Doctrine*, 171–73.

227. Fisher, *History of the Christian Church*, 110.

228. Fisher, "Church History," 1870–1871 (30); *History of the Christian Church*, 144.

229. Fisher, *History of the Christian Church*, 145–46, 2, 92, 97.

230. Fisher, "Church History," 1870–1871 (30).

231. Fisher, *Outlines*, 3.

232. Fisher, "Church History," 1870–1871 (1, 7, 90).

233. Fisher, "Christian Religion," 13 (B114, "Writings: C-H").

234. Emerton, *Introduction to the Study*, .v.

235. Emerton, "Church History," 1887–1889 (10/20).

236. Emerton, *Introduction to the Study*, vi, 4, 142.

237. Emerton, "Church History," 1887–1889 (11/1, 11/3).

238. Emerton, "Church History," 1887–1889 (11/ 1).

239. Emerton, "Church History," 1887–1889 (11/3). Emerton detailed the development of the bishopric (without prejudicial comments) (11/8); Leo the Great was the first bishop of Rome fully entitled to the name of Pope (3/15).

240. Emerton, "Church History," 1887–1889 (11/3). As previously noted, I have not been able to trace this work.

241. Emerton, "Church History," 1887–1889 (11/8, 11/10).

242. Emerton, "Church History," 1887–1889 (10/6, 10/18, 1/10).

243. Emerton, "Church History," 1887–1889 (1/12, 1/17)—and presumably not subject him to charges of heresy. Emerton confuses points of the Trinitarian and the Christological controversies.

244. Emerton, "Church History," 1887–1889 (11/15, 11/29).

245. Emerton, *Introduction to the Study*, 93, 113, 22.

246. Emerton, "Definition of Church History," 57–58. Admittedly, Emerton gave this talk several decades after the other professors here surveyed; he had the benefit of the field's development.

Chapter 6. Polity and Practice

Epigraph: Miller, "Introduction to Ecclesiastical History," 1820 or 1821, Crosby notes (B22, F18).

1. Hitchcock, "Church History: First Period," 1872, Jackson notes (Jackson Papers, B1, N1, 41). Hitchcock recommends an article—his own—in the Jan. 1867 *APR*.

2. Jerome, *Letter* 146.1 (CSEL 56, 308; PL 22, 1194).

3. John Chrysostom, *Homily 11 on I Timothy*, 1 (on I Tim. 3:8–10) (PG 62, 553).

4. Jerome, *Letter* 146.1 (CSEL 56, 308; PL 22, 1194). Jerome's larger argument is that deacons are not equal to presbyters.

5. Jerome, *Commentary on Titus* (on Tit. 1:5–7) (PL 26, 597, 598).

6. Ambrosiaster, *Commentary on I Timothy* (on I Tim. 3:8), #1–2 (CSEL 81.3, 267): "*omnis episcopus presbyter sit, non tamen omnis presbyter episcopus.*"

7. Ambrosiaster, *Commentary on Ephesians* (on Eph. 4:11, 12), #1–5, at 5 (CSEL 81.3, 98–100): originally, when one bishop died, the next in line replaced him; but when unworthy presbyters stood next, the *episcopus* would be chosen from presbyters on the basis of merit, to avoid the scandal of an unworthy bishop.

8. On the three recensions of Ignatius' letters, see Schoedel, *Ignatius*, 3–4.

9. Ussher, *Polycarpi et Ignatii epistulae* (1644); see Schoedel, *Ignatius of Antioch*, 2–3.

10. Cureton, *Ancient Syriac Version of the Epistles of Saint Ignatius*; also see Cureton, *Vindiciae Ignatianae* and *Corpus Ignatianum*.

11. Bunsen, *Die drei ächten und die vier unächten Briefe des Ignatius von Antiochen*. Suzanne Marchand notes that Bunsen wrote his multivolumed *Aegyptens Stelle in der Weltgeschichte* (1846–1857) without ever leaving his post at Rome (*Down From Olympus*, 189).

12. Baur, *Die ignatianischen Briefe*, 14–15, 21–29, 43–44, 57, 60, 76–105, 115, 132.

13. Baur, *Die ignatianischen Briefe*, 142, 144. Baur disputes use of the categories "genuine" and "ungenuine" in analyzing early Christian literature.

14. Zahn, *Ignatius von Antiochen*; Lightfoot, *Apostolic Fathers*, Part 2: *S. Ignatius, S. Polycarp* (Lightfoot credited Zahn for dealing the fatal blow to the claims of the Cureton letters as the originals, arguing that the Syriac version represents an abridgement of the Greek Epistles in the "Middle Form" [285, 323]).

15. The reassignment was in part based on linking the text with an identical title in a list of Hippolytus' writings inscribed on a statue of that bishop rescued from the Tiber in 1551.

16. Ultramontanism is the nineteenth-century conservative Catholic movement that invested the papacy with all-encompassing powers; after the Vatican Council in 1870, a liberal "Old Catholic" Church was organized. Historian (and soon to be Old Catholic bishop) J. J. I. von Döllinger published *Hippolytus and Callistus*, detailing the scandals and very "unchristian" accusations of the rival bishops. Döllinger also attacked Bunsen's *Hippolytus and His Age*. For these debates, see Schaff, *History* II: 761–62; and "Introductory Notice to Hippolytus," ANF V: 3–7. The editor of this "Introductory Notice" claims that it is as if Hippolytus had risen up to rebuke Pius IX's "forged" doctrine of papal infallibility (4).

17. Schaff had high hopes for the Old Catholic Church, and read its letter to the Evangelical Alliance meeting in New York (*Evangelical Alliance Conference, 1873*, ed. Schaff and Prime, 487–89). Schaff contrasts the Evangelical Alliance Conference with the Vatican Council, calls Pius IX "a theological ignoramus," and chastises the Catholic bishops who had opposed the 1870 decree on papal infallibility but later submitted (485, 486).

18. Schaff, *Oldest Church Manual*, 8, 9; the University of Edinburgh awarded Bryennios a D.D. in 1884.

19. H. B. Adams, "New Methods," in *Methods of Historical Study*, 123n.1. Harvard students presumably got their copy from Prof. Ezra Abbott of Harvard, through whose auspices Egbert Smyth, editor of the *Andover Review*, acquired a copy and published a translation (by Rev. C. C. Starbuck) ("Bishop Bryennios' 'Teaching of the Twelve Apostles'").

20. *Teaching of the Twelve Apostles*, ed., trans. Hitchcock and Brown, xc–xci; the Union Seminary copy is Hitchcock's. Hitchcock was responsible for the notes, Brown

for the introduction, and both worked on the translation (iv–v). Schaff contributed a long bibliography (65–77) of works on the *Didache*.

21. Hitchcock, "Origin and Growth of Episcopacy,"153.

22. Miller's son devotes an entire chapter to "Episcopal Controversy": see Miller [Jr.], *Life* I: chap. 14.

23. See letters in S. Miller [Jr.], *Life* I: 190–94, with excerpts from letters dating from 1805 to "Mr. [Edward Dorr] Griffin" and to "Dr. [Ashbel] Green." Green was President of the College of New Jersey from 1812–1822, and a founder and President of the Seminary, serving on the board of directors from 1812–1848. Griffin taught briefly at Andover Seminary, was a founder of the American Bible Society, and became President of Williams College (1821–1836).

24. Especially notable is Miller, *Essay on the Warrant, Nature, and Duties of the Office of the Ruling Elder.*

25. Miller, *Letters Concerning the Constitution*, Part II, Letter I, 230–33. John Bowden, an Episcopal cleric, taught philosophy at Columbia (1803–1817). In 1804, Hobart published his *Companion for the Festivals and Fasts of the Protestant Episcopal Church*; lower-church Protestants objected to its claims regarding episcopacy, sacraments, and doctrine (Holifield, *Theology in America*, 245).

26. Miller, *Letters Concerning the Constitution*, Part II, Letter I, 239; Preliminary Letter, viii.

27. Miller [Jr.], *Life* I: 193, citing a letter of Miller to "Mr. Griffin" (5/16/1805). In a letter to "Dr. [Ashbel] Green" (5/13/1805), Miller rails against Episcopalians who print and distribute books that deny ministers of other denominations valid ordinations (I: 194).

28. Miller later defends his *Letters* in "The Episcopal Controversy," *Southern Religious Telegraph*, Sept. 29, 1837, 156 (B21, F7), a newspaper published in Richmond.

29. Miller abhorred Unitarians even more than Episcopalians. He depicts Unitarian (Harvard professor) Jared Sparks as "groping in darkness regarding the plan of salvation" and propagating errors leading to "eternal perdition": see [Anonymous], "Notices of New Books: Life of Dr. Samuel Miller," 624. Miller also accused Moses Stuart of Andover of leaning toward Unitarianism (*Letters on the Eternal Sonship*; Letters V and VI cite numerous patristic passages [taken largely from Bishop Bull] testifying to the "eternal generation of the Son").

30. Miller, "Lectures on Ecclesiastical History, Second Class," 1842–1843 (B24, F4).

31. Miller, "Church Government, Lectures VI, VII: Forms of Church Government: Popery and Episcopacy," 2/17/1815 (B3, F7, 8–9, 10–11).

32. Miller, *Letters Concerning the Constitution*, Preliminary Letter, xxviii-xxx, xlvii-xlviii.

33. Miller, "Notes on Mosheim, Cent. I, Apostolicum" (B5, F3, 3–4).

34. Miller, "Church Government, Lecture II: Divine Right," 7/2/1815 (B3, F5, 13–15).

35. Miller, "Church Government-Episcopal Controversy," 3/14/1816 (B3, F16).

Miller represents Episcopalians as rejoining: by your standard of judgment, how can you prove the obligation of the Sabbath on the first day of the week, and infant baptism?

36. Miller, *Letters Concerning the Constitution*, Part I, Letter IV, 80–81.

37. Miller, *Letters Concerning the Constitution*, Part I, Letter VIII, 198–99, citing Mosheim, *Ecclesiastical History* I: 101, 104–6, 348; II: 265–66.

38. Miller, *Letters Concerning the Constitution*, Part I, Letter IV, 84, 89, 97–104, 106; similarly, *Presbyterianism*, 13, 49.

39. Miller, *Letters Concerning the Constitution*, Part I, Letter V, 118–22, citing Jerome's *Commentary on Titus* and *Letter* 146 to Evangelus (misidentified as "Evagrius").

40. Miller, "Church Government-Episcopal Controversy," 3/14/1816 (B3, F16).

41. Miller, *Letters Concerning the Constitution*, Part I, Letter V, 123. Nor did Jerome consider deacons a clerical "order."

42. Miller, "Church Government-Episcopal Controversy," 3/14/1816 (B3, F16). He alludes to Jerome, *Letter* 146. If episcopal hierarchy had arisen for purely practical reasons, Miller could claim it as merely human invention, not divine ordination.

43. Miller, "Ecclesiastical History, No. II. II and III Centuries" (B2, F14, 24).

44. Miller, *Presbyterianism*, 13–14; similarly, 17.

45. Miller, "Ecclesiastical History, No. II. II and III Centuries" (B2, F14, 23).

46. Miller, *Letters Concerning the Constitution*, Part I, Letter V, 124–29. Miller cites Augustine, *Letter* 19 to Jerome (= 82.4.33); "Hilary" [Ambrosiaster], *Commentary on Ephesians* (on Eph. 4:11,12); and John Chrysostom, *Homily 11 on I Timothy* (on I Tim. 3:8–10).

47. Miller, *Letters Concerning the Constitution*, Part I, Letters I, 4–6; V, 115–16; "Ecclesiastical History, No. II. II and III Centuries" (B2, F14, 23).

48. Miller, *Letters Concerning the Constitution*, Part I, Letter V, 130 (citing statistics on Donatist and Catholic bishops at the Council of Carthage [411]); 131 (referring to Gregory of Nyssa, *On the Life of St. Gregory Thaumaturgus* [3] [PG 46, 909]).

49. Miller, "Ecclesiastical History, No. II. II and III Centuries" (B2, F14, 23).

50. Miller, *Letters Concerning the Constitution*, Part I, Letters V, 110; VIII, 184–86, citing Mk. 10:37, Lk. 22:24, and III John (the case of Diotrephes).

51. Miller, *Presbyterianism*, 7, 8. Episcopalian practices that Presbyterians reject: prescribed liturgies, the observance of holy-days other than Sunday, God-fathers and God-mothers, the sign of the cross at baptism, and the rite of confirmation (66–86).

52. Miller, *Presbyterianism*, 9–13.

53. Miller, "Ecclesiastical History" (B2, F11, 20–21); *Letters Concerning the Constitution*, Part I, Letter I, 4–6.

54. Miller, "Church Government-Episcopal Controversy," 3/14/1816 (B3, F16).

55. Miller, *Letters Concerning the Constitution*, Part I, Letter I, 4–5.

56. Miller, "Ecclesiastical History" (B2, F11, 20–21). Although the advocates of

prelacy call *presbyteroi* "presbyters," the second order of clergy [after "bishops"], Presbyterians call them "elders" (*Essay on the Warrant*, 74).

57. Miller, *Letters Concerning the Constitution*, Part I, Letter VIII, 191, referring to "Hilary's" claim that "clergy" [presumably "bishops"] were not willing to have these officers sitting with them and judging the affairs of the church.

58. Miller, "Divine Appointment, the Duties, and the Qualifications of Ruling Elders," 4–8, 11. Calvin did not invent the office (23).

59. Miller, "Duty of the Church to Take Measures" (PTS, Luce #250), 107; *Presbyterianism*, 21.

60. Miller, *Essay on the Warrant*, 73. Miller reissued this book in 1831 and 1832 (New York: Jonathan Leavitt; Boston: Crocker and Brewster).

61. Miller, *Essay on the Warrant*, 76.

62. Miller, "Divine Appointment," 15, citing Cyprian, *Letter* 29 (= 33) on Teaching Elders; and "Hilary" [Ambrosiaster], *Commentary on I Timothy* (on 5:1), #1: consulting the *seniores* (presbyters)—whose counsel formerly was necessary—fell into disuse, because ("Hilary" suspects) of the pride of "teachers." In *Essay on the Warrant*, 85, Miller cites Cyprian, *Letter* 40 (= 34), regarding Numidicus as an elder (Miller: a "ruling elder").

63. Miller, *Essay on the Warrant*, 87, citing Origen, *Against Celsus* 3 (rulers who inquire into the manners and behavior of those admitted to the church; no further reference given, possibly #51?); *Homily 7 on Joshua* (those cut off from the church by its "rulers" [Miller: "Ruling Elders"]).

64. Miller, *Essay on the Warrant*, 85–97, citing, among others, Hippolytus, *Against the Noetian Heresy* 1 (Miller: presbyters who summoned Noetus for judgment are Ruling Elders); Augustine, *On the Word of the Lord Sermon* 19; Gregory the Great, *Letter* II.19 (dubious support for the notion of Ruling Elders?)

65. Miller, *Essay on the Warrant*, 104.

66. Moffat, *Outlines of Church History*, 18–19, 46–47, 55–56. Yet Moffat rejected even the seven Ignatian letters of the shorter Greek recension as unhistorical: "The spirit . . . is that of inordinate hierarchy" (31).

67. Smith, *History*, 10.

68. Smith, "Reformed Churches of Europe and America," 19: if "superinduced hierarchy" were cut off from some present churches, presbyters and presbyteries (the form of primitive church organization described by "Hilary" and Jerome) would remain.

69. Smith, *History*, 14, 15.

70. Smith, *History*, 10: yet church officers were still elected by their own churches (no references). Smith championed Lightfoot's view that the episcopate "was formed not out of the apostolic order by localization, but out of the Presbyterial by elevation"—a claim, that might encourage Christian union ("Theological and Literary Intelligence," *PQPR* 1.1 [Jan. 1872]: 204).

71. Smith, *History*, 15.

72. Smith, *History*, 12, 14, 15. Yet only two sacraments, baptism and the Lord's Supper, were then celebrated.

73. Smith, *History*, 16.

74. Hitchcock, "Church History: First Period," 1872, Jackson notes (Jackson Papers, B1, N1, 41–42).

75. Hitchcock, "Origin and Growth of Episcopacy," 152 (no reference).

76. Hitchcock, "Church History: First Period," 1872, Jackson notes (Jackson Papers, B1, N1, 51).

77. Hitchcock, "Origin and Growth of Episcopacy," 134, 159, 133.

78. Hitchcock, "Origin and Growth of Episcopacy," 145, 146–47, citing passages in Irenaeus, *Against Heresies*, e.g., 1.27.1, 3.3.1, 3.3.3, 3.14.2, 5.20.1. This varying usage suggests "not Apostolic tradition, but . . . later genesis and growth, and that growth not yet completed" in Irenaeus' time.

79. Hitchcock, "Origin and Growth of Episcopacy," 147–148, citing Tertullian, *On the Prescription of Heretics* 41; 32; *On Baptism* 17 (the bishop as *summus sacerdos*); *On the Military Crown* 3 ("the president").

80. Hitchcock, "Origin and Growth of Episcopacy," 149.

81. Hitchcock, "Origin and Growth of Episcopacy," 155, citing Ambrosiaster, *Commentary on I Timothy*, chap. 3.

82. Hitchcock, "Origin and Growth of Episcopacy," 155–56. Hitchcock quotes from Jerome, *Ep.* 146.1, mentioning various NT verses cited by Jerome and Jerome's explanation ("afterwards one presbyter was elected to be set over the rest," "to remedy schism and to prevent each individual from rending the church of Christ by drawing it to himself"). Jerome claims that all functions of a bishop also belong to presbyters, except for ordination. Jerome thinks (*Ep.* 146.2) that "Paul" meant the word "bishop" to include presbyters as well, and hence did not mention a separate ordination of presbyters.

83. Hitchcock, "Origin and Growth of Episcopacy," 156, 154.

84. Schaff, *History* II: 125, 122, 149, 149n.1. Ignatius and Cyprian stand as early examples of the development of sacerdotalism ("Development of the Ancient Catholic Hierarchy: I," 667).

85. Schaff, *History* I: 498.

86. Schaff, "Lightfoot's Ignatius and Polycarp," clipping from unidentified newspaper, Feb. 18, 1886 (UTS, B6, Scr2, 68).

87. Schaff, *History* II: 133. Believing that Paul wrote the Pastoral Epistles, Schaff assumes that *episkopoi* date to the apostolic era but were "subordinate" to the Apostles.

88. Schaff, "Latin Patriarchate," 22, 12.

89. Schaff, *History* II: 128; cf. II: 152 (Montanism as a "democratic reaction against the episcopal hierarchy in favor of the general priesthood"); similarly, *Oldest Church Manual*, 62.

90. Schaff, *History* II: 126, 121, calling Cyprian "the proper father of the sacerdotal

conception of the Christian ministry as a mediating agency between God and the people."

91. Schaff, *History* III: 266.

92. Schaff, "Development of the Ancient Catholic Hierarchy: I," 689, 667. Schaff cites no texts; perhaps Jerome, *Letter* 146 and John Chrysostom, *Homily* 11 *on I Timothy* (on I Tim. 3:8–10).

93. Fisher, "Church History," 1870–1871 (44–45). In his later work, *History of Christian Doctrine* (35–36), Fisher deems it "probable" that seven of the Ignatian epistles in Greek are genuine.

94. Fisher, "Historical Method in Theology," 11.

95. Johannes Weiss's *Die Predigt Jesu vom Reiches Gottes* was published in 1892. Weiss delayed publication until after the death of his father-in-law, Albrecht Ritschl, whose views about early Christian ethics differed considerably from Weiss's: see Hiers and Holland, "Introduction," Weiss, *Jesus' Proclamation of the Kingdom of God*, 5–8.

96. Fisher, *Outlines* I: 191.

97. Fisher, "Church History," 1870–1871 (43); similarly, *History of the Christian Church*, 36, 51.

98. Fisher, "Church History," 1870–1871 (46–47, 87), citing Gieseler and Neander; cf. *History of the Christian Church*, 54, 56.

99. Fisher, "Church History," 1870–1871 (43, 44); *History of the Christian Church*, 51, 52.

100. Fisher, *History of Christian Doctrine*, 35–36; "Decline of Clerical Authority," 578–79; "Church History," 1870–1871 (46–47, 87).

101. Fisher, "Historical Method," 11.

102. Fisher, "Church History," 1870–1871 (47–48); *History of Christian Doctrine*, 168, 83.

103. Fisher, *Validity of Non-Episcopal Ordination*, 23, 20, 17.

104. Fisher, "Church History," 1870–1871 (46); no reference, perhaps Jerome, *Letter* 146. Fisher does not indicate why this claim is so significant (presumably because it shows the local character of the arrangement); a "bishop" was not sought from outside.

105. Fisher, "Church History," 1870–1871 (49).

106. Fisher, "Decline of Clerical Authority," 571–72. Fisher adds that now, even Anglicans Bishop Lightfoot ("Essay on the Christian Ministry") and Edwin Hatch (*Organization of the Early Christian Churches*) agree.

107. Fisher, "Church History," 1870–1871 (47–48); "Decline of Clerical Authority," 571–72 (for example, city councils and *archons*).

108. Miller, "Episcopal Controversy," 156 (B21, F7), adding that Neander, "probably the most profoundly learned antiquary now living," agrees in *History of the Church* I: 199.

109. Now, with the addition of Romans, called the "Middle Recension. See above, 208; and Schoedel, *Ignatius of Antioch*, 2–3.

110. Miller, "Episcopal Controversy," 156 (B21, F7); *Letters Concerning the Constitution*, Part I, Letter IV, 90–97.

111. Miller, *Presbyterianism*, 13; similarly, 49; Clement of Rome and Irenaeus identify "bishops" and "presbyters."

112. Miller [Jr.], *Life* II: 159, 161. Cook had left the Presbyterians for the Episcopalians; he attacked Miller's *Letters on the Christian Ministry* in "Essay on the Invalidity of Presbyterian Ordination."

113. "N.," "Dr. Miller's Opinion on Ignatius" (1837) (B21, F9). See below for illustration of this confusion.

114. Miller [Jr.], *Life* II: 439, 440, citing Calvin, *Institutes* I.13.29, referring to a point regarding Lent in (Ps.)-Ignatius' *Letter to the Philippians* 13 (now considered spurious).

115. Miller [Jr.], *Life* II: 440, noting that "the celebrated Professor Neander" was of this view.

116. Miller [Jr.], *Life* II: 441, 442, emphasis in the original.

117. Miller, *Essay on the Warrant*, 80, citing Ignatius, *Trallians* 3.

118. Smith, "Sermon" (on Exodus 3:2), given five times between 1862 and 1877 (S2, B1, 25).

119. Smith, "Doctrinal History," 1851, Hastings notes (S5, B1, F3, 12–13). In 1870, Smith visited Polycarp's alleged burial-place in Smyrna (letter to his wife, Smyrna, 5/29/1870, cited in [E. Smith], *Henry Boynton Smith*, 346).

120. Smith, "Doctrinal History," 1851, Hastings notes (S5, B1, F3, 13–14).

121. *ATR* 2.5 (Feb. 1860): 156; 3.11 (July 1861): 539.

122. Hitchcock, "Church History: First Period," 1872, Jackson notes (Jackson Papers, B1, N1, 99).

123. Hitchcock, "Church History: First Period," 1872, Jackson notes (Jackson Papers, B1, N1, 42–43); "Church History: First Period," early 1880s, Burrell notes (B1, N1, 221).

124. Hitchcock, "Origin and Growth of Episcopacy," 145.

125. Hitchcock, "Church History: First Period," 1872, Jackson notes (Jackson Papers, B1, N1, 51, 44).

126. Hitchcock, "Church History: First Period," early 1880s, Burrell notes (B1, N1, 224); "Church History: First Period," 1883, Moore notes (B2, N2, 255).

127. Hitchcock, "Church History: First Period," 1883, Moore notes (B2, N2, 255).

128. Schaff, *History* II: 660, 662. In June 1884, Schaff talked with Bishop Lightfoot at Auckland Castle about the *Didache*, the Ignatian letters, and "his new edition of Clement" (*Diary*, 6/16/1884 [UTS, B4]). Lightfoot was remembered as "the first English commentator to treat the New Testament as an historical document" (Foakes Jackson, "Work of Some Recent English Church Historians," 104).

129. Schaff, *History* II: "Preface," v–vi, along with Hippolytus' *Philosophumena*.

130. Schaff, *History* II, n.p.

131. Schaff, praising Lightfoot's work on the Apostolic Fathers, deemed him "the best patristic scholar in the Church of England" (*Theological Propaedeutic* II: 278).

132. Schaff, "Lightfoot's Ignatius and Polycarp," clipping from unidentified newspaper, Feb. 18, 1886 (UTS, B6, Scr2, 68).

133. D. Schaff, *Life*, 379–80. The RSV gives "guardians"; NEB, "shepherds."

134. E. P. Pusey to Schaff, Oxford, n.d. (LTS, B1, F75).

135. Surprisingly, Roswell Hitchcock had little to say about Hippolytus' *Philosophumena*; its chief significance lay in its inclusion of Basilides' alleged allusion to John 1:9—from which Hitchcock infers that the Gospel must have been in circulation by the late first or early second century ("Life of Christ," 1865, Wright notes [B2, N1]). Hitchcock gives the reference to *Philosophumena* 2.22; in ANF V, *Philosophumena* 7.10. Hitchcock told students that Basilides, flourishing ca. 125, stands as an early witness to the Gospel of John; cf. "Church History: First Period," 1883, Moore notes (B2, N2, 316–17).

136. Smith, "Doctrinal History," Feb. 1851, Hastings notes (S5, B1).

137. *ATR* 2.5. (Feb. 1860): 161; 2.6 (May 1860): 360; 3.10 (April 1861): 376; 3.11 (July 1861): 539; *APTR* 1.1 (Jan. 1863): 150; 1.2 (April 1863): 348; 1.3 (July 1863): 503. Bunsen's book was published in English in 1852. Also see Smith, "Introduction," to Döllinger, *Fables Respecting the Popes in the Middle Ages*, vii.

138. *APTR* 6.22 (April 1868): 309. The translator, Smith thought, aimed at "fidelity to the original rather than at a flowing version."

139. Schaff, "Conflict of Trinitarianism and Unitarianism," 741.

140. Schaff, *History* II: 757, 758. Schaff noted that although in 1853, Döllinger defended Rome against Hippolytus' charges, with the decree on infallibility in 1870 he advanced a position similar to Hippolytus' against "the error of papal infallibility" (774).

141. Schaff, *History* II: 763, 759, 758. Schaff reported that Cardinal Newman denied that Hippolytus could have written "that malignant libel on his contemporary popes" (762n.3; 774, citing Newman's *Tracts; Theological and Ecclesiastical*, 22).

142. Schaff, "Tertullian," 622; "Conflict of Trinitarianism," 738, 741; *History* II: 765.

143. Schaff, "History of the Vatican Council," 96. (Sabellianism, also called "Patripassianism" ["the suffering Father"], denoted a theological position, soon deemed heresy, that construed the Son and Holy Spirit as mere temporary "modes" of God the Father.) Schaff saw the French defeat in 1870, Italian unification, and the political disempowerment of the papacy as fostering German Protestantism's rise to "the political and military leadership of Europe"; "history records no more striking example of swift retribution of criminal ambition" (79). Material on the Vatican Council is repeated in Schaff, *Bibliotheca Symbolica Ecclesiae Universalis* I: 134–92.

144. Schaff, *History* II: 765, 773, 774. *History* II: 771n.2 lists possible sites of Hippolytus' bishopric.

145. *Teaching of the Twelve Apostles*, ed., trans., Hitchcock and Brown, iii.

146. Schaff, "Appendix" to *Teaching of the Twelve Apostles*, ed., trans., Hitchcock and Brown, 72.

147. *Teaching of the Twelve Apostles*, ed., trans., Hitchcock and Brown, lxxxix.

148. *Teaching of the Twelve Apostles*, ed., trans., Hitchcock and Brown, 43–46.

149. Hitchcock, "Church History: First Period," 1883, Moore notes (B2, N2, 304). Hitchcock cites DeRossi on the catacombs, and notes Tertullian's depiction (no reference) of a youth standing in water ankle deep, water being passed over him; and a vessel coming from Ephesus, about nine inches deep, supposedly used to hold water for baptism.

150. Hitchcock, "Church History: First Period," 1872–1873, Jackson notes (Jackson Papers, B1, N1, 96); "Church History: First Period," 1883, Moore notes (B2, N2, 306).

151. Hitchcock, "Church History: First Period," 1883, Moore notes (B2, N2, 304–6). Hitchcock also notes (305) Clement of Alexandria's reference to "sprinkling" in *Exhortation to the Greeks* 10 ("purify yourselves from custom, by sprinkling yourselves with the drops of truth").

152. Schaff, *Oldest Church Manual*, v. Schaff set his student (and successor) A. C. McGiffert a task to scrutinize the vocabulary of the *Didache* (97).

153. See entries for June-August 1884 in Schaff, *Diary* (UTS, B4).

154. Schaff, *History* II: n.p.

155. Schaff, *Theological Propaedeutic* II: 277. Not everyone agreed: a writer in the *Saturday Review* apparently commented that "this curious book is neither Catholic nor primitive"; see Alfred Plummer to Schaff, Dublin, 5/23/1889 (LTS, B1, F70), citing *Saturday Review*, April 13, 1889.

156. Schaff, *Oldest Church Manual*, vi, 12, 15.

157. Schaff, *Oldest Church Manual*, 62; 64, 66 on "bishops."

158. Schaff, *Oldest Church Manual*, 119, 122. Schaff reasoned (122) that the work would not have been called the "Teaching of the Twelve Apostles" if any Apostles were still alive; John lived into the 90s.

159. Schaff, *Oldest Church Manual*, 23; the critic is named Krawutzcky of Breslau. Schaff argued against late dating: among other points, the document shows no signs of the Ebionite heresy (24).

160. In Schaff's view, all three Synoptics pre-date 70 A.D.. (*Oldest Church Manual*, 76).

161. Schaff, *Oldest Church Manual*, 125, 123.

162. Schaff, *Oldest Church Manual*, 22. Yet, when in 1889 Schaff sent a copy of the third edition to the *Historical Times* in Cambridge (England) for review, he was rebuffed by the editor: the work is "too purely theological" (M. Creighton to Schaff, Cambridge, 3/13/1889 [LTS, B1, F18]).

163. Schaff, *Oldest Church Manual*, 1. Schaff anticipates "the end of Turkish misrule" (2).

164. Schaff, *Oldest Church Manual*, 2–5, 8, 9. Schaff here situates St. Catherine's on Mount Athos incorrectly (rather than Mount Sinai).

165. Schaff, *Oldest Church Manual*, 10, noting early citations of the work, including Harnack's in the *Theologische Literaturzeitung*, Feb. 3, 1884; published in English in the [*New-York*] *Independent*, Feb. 28, 1884.

166. Schaff, *Oldest Church Manual*, 12; see "Bishop Bryennios' 'Teaching of the Twelve Apostles'," *Andover Review*, April 1884, 426–42. Regarding issues of age of baptisands and mode of baptism, Egbert Smyth in his introduction hopes that "this testimony should lead our Baptist brethren to relax, in view of it, their doctrine of the necessity of one mode" (434–35). As noted above, Harvard students already worked on the text in early 1884.

167. H. C. Trumbull to Schaff, Philadelphia, 9/16/1889 (LTS, B1, F95).

168. Schaff, *Oldest Church Manual*, 13. Schaff concurs, adding that this identification explains why the *Didache* does not mention "presbyters" separately (73, 74); Irvingites, if any group, might find support for their church governance of [Twelve] Apostles, prophets, and Evangelists (67). George Fisher deemed the *Didache* useful in showing that episcopacy was not universally accepted at this early date (*History of Christian Doctrine*, 35, 77; "Historical Method," 11 [B114, Writings-C-H]); Irenaeus wrongly assumed that earlier there had been bishops *and* presbyters, rather than presbyter-bishops (*History of Christian Doctrine*, 78).

169. Schaff, *Oldest Church Manual*, 14.

170. Schaff, "Appendix," *Teaching of the Twelve Apostles*, ed, trans., Hitchcock and Brown, 73; *Oldest Church Manual*, 4.

171. Schaff, *Oldest Church Manual*, 31.

172. As in Horace Bushnell's *Christian Nurture* (1861).

173. Schaff, *Oldest Church Manual*, 33–34, 41. In 1855, Schaff claimed that Baptists had a better case for immersion as the original form of baptism than for denying infant baptism. He disapproves of Baptists' rebaptizing converts, "as if the operations of the Holy Ghost depended on the quantity of water and the outward form" (*America*, 172–73).

174. Schaff, *Oldest Church Manual*, 138, 140.

175. Schaff, *Oldest Church Manual*, 166, 182.

176. Schaff, *Oldest Church Manual*, 201–2.

177. J. B. Lightfoot to Schaff, 7/14 (?) /1885 (UTS, B2, F31).

178. Advertisement for Schaff's *Teaching of the Twelve Apostles* (UTS, B6, Scr2, 82).

179. Fisher to Schaff, New Haven, 2/27/1889 (UTS, B1, F17).

180. [Briggs], "Our Book Table: Teaching of the Twelve Apostles," 1.

181. [Briggs], "Our Book Table," 1. Briggs accused Schaff of deliberately misinterpreting the fresco of Jesus' baptism in the Catacomb of San Panziano, making it sound as if Jesus was "immersed."

182. Schaff to D. Schaff, Lucerne [Switzerland], 8/10/1885 (LTS, B1, F115). Schaff would soon have further troubles with Briggs's heresy trials.

183. [Field], editorial preface to [Briggs], "Our Book Table," 1.

Chapter 7. Roman Catholicism

Epigraphs: Schaff, "Christianity in America," 503; Fessenden, *Culture and Redemption*, 64.

1. By 1861, Catholicism was the single largest religious communion in America (Marty, *Righteous Empire*, 22–23). On Catholic seminaries' and bishops' influence, Holifield, *Theology in America*, chap. 20. For Catholic immigrants in New York, Dolan, *Immigrant Church*; Dunne, *Antebellum Irish Immigration*, esp. chap. 3. For Catholicism's "success," see R. Moore, *Religious Outsiders and the Making of Americans*, chap. 2. Moore questions the ubiquity of Bible-reading in public schools; northeastern schools, however, had the highest incidence ("Bible Reading and Nonsectarian Schooling," 1581–99, at 1586).

2. "Ultramontane": characterizing conservative Roman Catholics and Catholic powers of Europe who looked "beyond the mountains" (i.e., the Alps) to the Papacy as the source of supreme authority and who opposed the movement for Italian unification.

3. Hitchcock blames "externality" largely on pagan influence ("Church History: Second Period," 1883–1884, Burrell notes [B1, N2, 57]). Hitchcock and others differed from J. Z. Smith's analysis: for them, Judaism did not "insulate" early Christianity against pagan influence, but joined with it; both contributed to later Roman Catholicism (cf. *Drudgery Divine*, 83, 19–21).

4. See Neander, *Lectures* I: 35, 22, 220.

5. I omit Ephraim Emerton from much of the next discussion; he adds little to this topic.

6. Anti-Roman Catholic sentiment began to swell again in the 1830s after a reprieve following the American Revolution (McGreavy, *Catholicism and American Freedom*, 11–12), when Protestants could still remember that Catholics in the Middle Colonies had supported the Revolution (I thank Grant Wacker for this point).

7. Miller, "Introductory Essay," in "A Watchman," *History of Popery* (1834), 3–4, 8; emphasis in original. Miller characterized Catholicism as "miserable" and underlined his words for emphasis. He referred to the Bishop of Rome as the "Papal Beast" ("Notes on Church History and Church Government," 1821, J. W. Douglas notes [B25, F4, 22]). Miller rued that in comparison with the 44 million Protestants in the world—only about 6 million of whom were orthodox and evangelical—there were about 100 million Catholics ("Ecclesiastical History," ca. 1819, O. Douglass notes [B26, F4, 136–37]).

8. On the constant association of Roman Catholicism with magic, see Styers, *Making Magic*, 9–10, 26, 36–37, 100 (Weber), 125, 166 (Hume), 200 (Malinowski), 205 (Tylor).

9. Miller, "Church Government: Lectures VI, VII: Forms of Church Government: Popery and Episcopacy," 2/17/1815 (B3, F7, 3–4); "Introductory Essay," to "A Watchman," *History of Popery*, 12.

10. Miller, "Dangers of Education," 8. On religious education and the public schools, see Dolan, *American Catholic Experience*, chap. 10. For Protestant educators' brutality toward Roman Catholic pupils, see McGreavy, *Catholicism and American Freedom*, Intro. and chap. 1.

11. Miller, "Introductory Essay," in "A Watchman," *History of Popery*, 5, 15.

12. Miller, "Dangers of Education," 11, 13–14.

13. Miller, "Dangers of Education," 5–6, 7, with three-quarters of Catholic schools placed in these regions. For the success of public schools in speeding acculturation, T. L. Smith, "New Approaches to the History of Immigration," 1265–79, esp. 1272–74.

14. Miller, "Dangers of Education," 6–7, 10, 4, 9, 8. Miller assured his audience that Protestant institutions are better scholastically than Roman Catholic ones (14). On Catholicism's alleged "subversion" of young women, see Welter, "From Maria Monk to Paul Blanshard," 43–71, esp. 47–52.

15. Smith, *Introduction to Christian Theology*, 17; "Nature and Worth," 80–81.

16. For anti-Catholicism's role in the formation of the Republican Party, see M. Holt, *Political Crisis of the 1850s*, and Burton, "Civil War and Reconstruction, 1861–1867," 50. On depictions of Roman Catholicism in nineteenth-century textbooks, see Elson, *Guardians of Tradition*, 47–56.

17. See Smith, "Minority Report on Roman Catholic Baptism, 1854," Appendix A in [E. Smith], *Henry Boynton Smith*, 429–32, claiming that almost all the sixteenth-century Reformed Churches deemed Catholic baptism valid—and are we about to "unbaptize" those Protestants? The Roman Catholic Church is still a "church." We should win, not repel, the Catholic population in America. Elsewhere, Smith noted problems in assimilating the immigrant population ("Report on the State of Religion in the United States of America," 30). On Old School Presbyterians' view of Roman Catholic baptism, see Noll, *American Evangelical Christianity*, 117–18.

18. Smith, "Nature and Worth," 82–83, 79.

19. *APR* 1.3 (July 1869): 614–15. In *APTR* 4.13 (Jan. 1866): 194,; Smith reports that university students at Naples, Palermo, and Padua had burned the *Syllabus of Errors*. Several years before the 1870 decree, Smith told his students that we need an "infallible teacher," not an infallible pope, and this we have in Scripture ("Theology" [unspecified course], 1861–1862, Briggs notes [Briggs Papers, S8, B34, F5, N1, 205]). The aim of Pius IX's papacy was the pronouncement of decrees on the Immaculate Conception and Papal Infallibility—and he succeeded ("Systematic Theology, Part II," 1872–1873, Jackson notes [Jackson Papers, B1, N, 151]).

20. He exults over defections from the papal line and on stirrings toward Italian national unification. In the 1860s, he sometimes comments on the activities of the ex-Jesuit, Father Passaglia, now working for Italian nationalism against the papacy; see *ATR* 2.8 (Nov. 1860): 727; 4.16 (Oct. 1862): 724.

21. [Smith], "Passaglia, Guizot, and Döllinger," 367, 361, 362. Elsewhere, Smith praised Döllinger's *Die Papst-Fabeln des Mittelalters* ("Introduction" to Döllinger, *Fables Respecting the Popes in the Middle Ages*, ii–iii). Döllinger, Smith reported, was

inaugurated as Rector of the University of Munich, despite Ultramontanists' "warfare against science" and attempts "to falsify history" (iv). (Among the "fables" Döllinger treated are stories about Pope Joan, Constantine and Sylvester, and the Donation of Constantine.)

22. *APR* 2.2 (April 1870): 394–95; 2.3 [July 1870]: 585–86.

23. Smith, "'Roman Letters' on the Vatican Council," 667–79. The Pope might then put apostates to death, condemn charging interest on loans, and dissolve marriages.

24. *APR* 2.4 (Oct. 1870): 769–73.

25. In 1876, speaking at an international meeting of the Evangelical Alliance, Smith warned European Protestants against two dangers: "Romanism and infidelity" ("Report on the State of Religion," 38).

26. *PQPR* 2.8 (Oct. 1873): 763.

27. Honorius believed that Jesus had only one will (not one for each "nature"), a view anathematized by the Sixth Ecumenical Council in 680–681; see Smith, "Bishop C. J. von Hefele on the Case of Pope Honorius," 274–75. Schaff, ruing Hefele's submission to the 1870 decree, wrote that Bishop Hefele "has forgotten more about the history of Councils than the infallible Pope ever knew" ("History of the Vatican Council," 80).

28. Since only the pope can decide the occasions *when* he is speaking *ex cathedra*, his consultation with the larger Roman Catholic Church is not required: [Smith], "Papal Question in England," 357. The editors reprinted reactions by Archbishop Manning and John Henry Newman to the 1870 decree. While Manning insisted that it made no difference in Catholic teaching (the Pope was *already* considered infallible), Newman detailed his struggle with the decision (360–361).

29. Hitchcock, "True Idea and Uses," 34–35, 36.

30. Hitchcock, "Romanism in the Light of History," 436, 437. Hitchcock here responds to a paper by I. A. Dorner of Germany on the recent Vatican Council.

31. Hitchcock, "Middle Ages: First Period," early 1880s, Burrell notes (B1, N2, 89); "Church History: First Period," 1883, Moore notes (B2, N2, 203).

32. Hitchcock, "Staff of Life," 175; "His Last Words in Public."

33. He reminded students that Ireland had been the bright spot in Europe, "the land of the saints." He blames the misfortunes of the Irish on their "unmixed [Celtic] blood" and the peculiarities of conquest ("Church History: Second Period," 1873, Jackson notes [Jackson Papers, B1, N1, 224, 219–20]). On offensive representations of the Irish in textbooks, see Elson, *Guardians of Tradition*, 123–28.

34. Hitchcock "Protestantized" Patrick in order to array him against contemporary Catholicism: his "fervent piety [was] free from most of the Irish dogmatic features." Patrick's *Confession* promotes "no Pope, no Purgatory, no transubstantiation, no tradition, no Mariolatry" ("Church History: Second Period," 1873, Jackson notes [Jackson Papers, B1, N1, 224]).

35. Schaff, *History* III: 432; II: 78, 82 (bordering on "polytheism and idolatry"): III: 409ff.

36. Schaff, "Protestantism and Romanism," 127; *Principle of Protestantism*, 185; *Renaissance and the Reformation*, 11.

37. Schaff, *America*, 67.

38. Schaff to Prof. Oertel, cited in D. Schaff, *Life*, 200–201. Oertel was editor of the New York *Katholische Kirchenzeitung*.

39. Shriver, "Philip Schaff's Concept of Organic Historiography," iv. Here, Neander inspired (11). Schaff uses the phrase in *America*, 191–92: Catholicism stripped of the papacy, saint and relic worship, persecution, and tyranny over the conscience.

40. Schaff, *America*, 100.

41. Shahan, "Dr. Schaff and the Roman Catholic Church," 26–27.

42. Schaff criticized Puritanism's "false spiritualistic tendency and . . . utter misapprehension of the significance of the corporeal and outward" (*Principle of Protestantism*, 112); he blamed Americans' Puritan heritage for their lack of interest in history (*What Is Church History?* 4; also in *Reformed and Catholic*, ed. Yrigoyen and Bricker, 20).

43. On Mercersburg Theology, see Binkley, *Mercersburg Theology*; Nichols, *Romanticism in American Theology*; *Mercersburg Theology*, ed. Nichols; Shriver, "Philip Schaff: Heresy at Mercersburg," 18–55. Late in life, Schaff claimed that he had early retreated from some of Nevin's views (letter to "Dr. Apple" [*sic*; Theodore Appel], New York, 6/18/ 1889 (LTS, B1, F110). In his early *Principle of Protestantism*, however, Schaff expressed pleasure at his association with Nevin (211).

44. Schaff came to America with a mission to rescue American Christianity, but discovered instead that he was accused of "German infidelity" (Pranger, *Philip Schaff*, 129). For the 1845 trial, see Meyer, "Philip Schaff's Concept of Organic Historiography," Appendices F and G, 277–80; also in Richards, *History of the Theological Seminary of the Reformed Church*, 251–52, 254. In 1846, Schaff underwent examination by the German Reformed Church Synod on his dissertation, *The Sin Against the Holy Ghost*, and his *What Is Christianity?*; see Meyer, "Philip Schaff's Concept of Organic Historiography," 65.

45. Schaff's last public speech at the World's Parliament of Religions in 1893 ("Reunion of Christendom") still held out this hope. See above, 247.

46. Schaff, *Principle of Protestantism*, 196, 200, 202, 215–16, 137.

47. Schaff, *America*, 88, 180–81.

48. Penzel, *Philip Schaff, Historian and Ambassador*, 104n.5, citing James I. Good, *History of the Reformed Church in the United States* (1899), 293–95.

49. Schaff to D. Schaff, Cincinnati, 5/26/1885 (LTS, B1, F115). In 1845, all eight students in the Mercersburg Seminary debating society agreed that Roman Catholic baptism was valid (Wetzel, *Debates and Discussions in the Society of Inquiry*, 28). Wetzel notes that the votes against Catholicism increased after 1865 (57).

50. Schaff, Report on "Romish Baptism," *Cincinnati Gazette*, May 26, 1883, clip-

ping (UTS, B6, Scr2, 42). In 1845, Schaff wondered at Old School Presbyterians' vote to "unchurch the Catholic Church . . . and identify her with the kingdom of AntiChrist" ("German Theology and the Church Question," 124–25; also in *Reformed and Catholic*, ed. Yrigoyen and Bricker, 320–21).

51. Schaff, *Creed Revision in the Presbyterian Churches*, 34. See James Cardinal Gibbons's thanks to Schaff (Baltimore, 2/4/1890 [LTS, B1, F33]) for his "noble vindication" of Catholicism against charges of "idolatry." Chi Alpha discussed the validity of Roman Catholic baptism: Schaff is "pro" (*Diary* 5/27 and 6/3/1876 [UTS, B4]).

52. Schaff, *Creed Revision*, 35, 64.

53. Schaff, "Passion Week in Rome Fifty Years Ago." UTS pamphlet, n.p., n.d.; excerpted in D. Schaff, *Life*, 46–53. Schaff also attended Protestant services during Holy Week.

54. Schaff, *Diary*, 6/25/1870; 6/3/1877; 5/20 and 4/19/1890 (UTS, B4).

55. M. A. Corrigan to Schaff, New York, 3/1/1888 (LTS, B1, F09). Schaff secured a letter of introduction from James Cardinal Gibbons to the Rector of the American College in Rome, for help in gaining access to the Vatican Library (Gibbons to Schaff, Baltimore, 2/1/1890 [LTS, B1, F33]).

56. Schaff, *Diary*, 5/8 and 5/12/1890 (UTS, B4). Schaff credited Leo XIII with opening the Vatican Archives to Protestant scholars (*Theological Propaedeutic* II: 252–53).

57. Schaff to "My dear friend," New York (?), 2/7/1892 (UTS, B2).

58. John J. Keane to Schaff, Chicago (?), 10/16/1893 (LTS, B1, F48). Apparently Schaff did not receive this letter—he died on October 20—for on November 9 Keane sent condolences to Schaff's son, recalling Schaff's address.

59. Billington, *Protestant Crusade*, 33. At mid-century, Schaff told a German audience that Roman Catholics in America numbered about two million, almost one-twelfth of the population (*America*, 184). In New York City alone, there were 24 Roman Catholic churches (*America*, 78; see S. I. Prime to Schaff, New York, 6/27/1855 [UTS, B2]). Prime was editor of the *New-York Observer* and co-chair of the New York Evangelical Alliance Conference. Pot-boilers such as Maria Monk's *Awful Disclosures of the Hotel Dieu Nunnery of Montreal* sold 300,000 copies before the Civil War. The book was published in New York by "Howe & Bates" (1836), a dummy company set up by Harper Brothers, who declined to issue the book under their own name. For Protestants' fascination with this book, see Franchot, *Roads to Rome*, 154–61.

60. Billington, *Protestant Crusade*, 143. These propositions were endorsed by the Evangelical Alliance, in which Schaff was a leader. Although the Constitution of 1870 does not mention the words "Roman Catholic," the Alliance aimed "to counteract the influence of infidelity and superstition, especially in their organized forms" (Constitution of 1870, Evangelical Alliance [Evangelical Alliance Papers, B1, 3–4]).

61. Schaff, *America*, 77, 183. Schaff thought that Catholic youth attending public schools would draw closer to evangelical Protestantism (196–97). For debates, see Dolan, *American Catholic Experience*, chap. 10; on Bishop John Hughes's role, see Dunne, *Antebellum Irish Immigration*, 60–67.

62. Schaff, *America*, 77, 195.

63. Schaff, "American Nationality," 11.

64. Schaff, "History of the Vatican Council," 51–107, at 65. In November 1848, Pius IX fled Rome to escape revolutionary forces—but returned to become more conservative. In the mid-1870s, Schaff wrote that the Pope enjoys "a green old age, with the additional honor of infallibility" (*History* I: 850).

65. Schaff made this allegation at the Evangelical Alliance Conference in New York ("Introduction," "Letter from the Old Catholic Congress," Sept. 12–14, 1873, in *Evangelical Alliance Conference, 1873*, ed. Schaff and Prime, 486). His words were reported in the press: Schaff, "Vatican Council and the New York Conference," clipping from *New-York Independent* [n.d.] (UTS, B6, Scr1, 54).

66. Schaff, *Diary*, 2/7/1878 (UTS, B4).

67. Schaff, *History* III: 140; "History of the Vatican Council," 97–100; *Renaissance*, 98–108; *Bibliotheca Symbolica Ecclesiae Universalis* I: 176–80; "Vatican Council and the New York Conference," *New-York Independent* [undated; fall/early winter 1873?] (UTS, B6, Scr1, 54).

68. Schaff, *Theological Propaedeutic* II: 238.

69. Schaff alludes to Galileo's (probably apocryphal) response when asked to retract his views on the earth's circuit around the sun: "but still it moves."

70. Fisher, "Temporal Kingdoms," in Fisher, *Discussions*, 66–88 (originally in *NE*, Jan. 1867). On American Catholics' interest in the "Roman Question," see D'Agostino, *Rome in America*, Introduction and chaps. 1–2.

71. Fisher, "Temporal Kingdoms," in Fisher, *Discussions*, 91, 93, 99, 96, 98.

72. Fisher, "Council of Constance," in Fisher, *Discussions*, 124–26, 129, 138, 139–40 (originally in *NE*, April 1870).

73. Fisher, "Decline of Clerical Authority," 564–65.

74. Fisher, "Church History," 1870–1871 (49, 113, 116).

75. Fisher, "Protestantism, Romanism," in *Evangelical Alliance Conference, 1873*, ed. Schaff and Prime, 461–63.

76. Miller, "Introductory Essay," in "A Watchman," *History of Popery*, 8; "Ecclesiastical History, No. III, IV and V Centuries" (B2, F15, 11–12).

77. Hitchcock, "Church History: Second Period," 1883–1884, Burrell notes (B1, N2, 57); Fisher, "Old Roman Spirit," in Fisher, *Discussions*, 50, 53–59; *History of Christian Doctrine*, 171–72.

78. Schaff, *History* III: 453, 432, 450 ("superstitions and idolatrous excess"). Schaff notes Puritan "relics," e.g., Plymouth Rock (454).

79. Schaff, *History* III: 435, 438, 8; on saints' days, 442.

80. Schaff, *History* III: 455, 457, 461. Schaff naively failed to speculate on Ambrose's role in this "pious fraud."

81. Hitchcock, "Church History: Second Period," 1873, Jackson notes (Jackson Papers, B1, N2, 67–68).

82. Miller, "Ecclesiastical History, No. III, IV and V Centuries" (B2, F15, 11–12); "Ecclesiastical History, No. IV. V, VI, and VII Centuries" (B2, F16, 20).

83. Hitchcock, "Church History: Second Period," 1873, Jackson notes (Jackson Papers, B1, N2, 67–68); "Church History: Second Period," 1883–1884, Burrell notes (B1, N2, 57); Schaff, *History* III: 983. See Hunter, *Marriage, Celibacy, and Heresy in Ancient Christianity*.

84. Schaff, "Protestantism and Romanism," in Schaff, *Christ and Christianity*, 124.

85. Miller, "Ecclesiastical History. Remarks on the First and Second Centuries" (B2, F12, 14); Smith, *Introduction to Christian Theology*, 192.

86. Smith, "Systematic Theology," 10/9/1857 (S4, B1, F3, L14 con't.): yet the closer to the New Testament era, the more reliable was an early Christian writer.

87. Smith, "Systematic Theology," 9/28/1857 (S4, B1, F1, L8).

88. Smith, *History*, 74.

89. Smith, "Sermon" (on Rev. 14:5) (S2, B3, 15), denouncing Catholic practice.

90. Smith, "Systematic Theology," 1857 (?) (S4, B1, F1, L9 and L7); "Systematic Theology," 9/28/1857 (S4, B1, F1, L8).

91. Smith, "Systematic Theology," 1857 (?) (S4, B1, F2, L11); "Systematic Theology," 9/28/1857 (S4, B1, F1, L8). "Intermediate State": the state between death and the general resurrection, much-discussed by late nineteenth-century Protestants. See my essay, "Happiness in Hell, Virtue in the Middle State."

92. Smith, "Systematic Theology," 1857(?) (S4, B1, F1, L7); "Systematic Theology," 9/28/1857 (S4, B1, F1, L8).

93. Smith, *Introduction to Christian Theology*, 192.

94. Smith, "Doctrinal History," 1851, Hastings notes (S5, B1, F3, 20–21).

95. Smith, "Doctrinal History," 1851, Hastings notes (S5, B1, F3, 22).

96. Smith, "Systematic Theology," 1857 (?) (S4, B1, F1, L12, L7, and L9).

97. Smith, "Systematic Theology," 1857 (?) (S4, B1, F1, L2); "Systematic Theology," 9/28/1857 (S4, B1, F1, L8).

98. In the church's early history, Smith notes, both Scripture and tradition were considered sources of doctrine and "both traced back to the revelation to the Apostles" (Smith, "Doctrinal History," 1851, Hastings notes [S5, B1, 3, 15–16]; "Systematic Theology," 1857 (?) [S4, B1, F1, L7]).

99. Smith, "Systematic Theology," 1855–1856, Quick notes (S5, B1, F4, N1, 27).

100. Smith, "Systematic Theology," 9/28/1857 (S4, B1, F1, L8); "Systematic Theology," 1855–1856, Quick notes (S5, B1, F4, N1, 28); "Doctrinal History," 1851, Hastings notes (S5, B1, F3, 22).

101. Hitchcock, "Church History: First Period," 1872, Jackson notes (Jackson Papers, B1, N1, 14, 98, 99); "Church History: First Period," 1883, Moore notes (B2, N2, 206); "True Idea and Uses," 36.

102. Hitchcock, "Church History: First Period," early 1880s, Burrell notes (B1, N1, 263); "Person of Christ," 29.

103. Schaff, *Principle of Protestantism*, 113–15; likewise, "Puseyites" (161, 164, 166).

104. Schaff, *History* III: 1017n.1; similarly, "Genius and Theology," 113, citing an 1866 letter of Newman to Pusey on the latter's *Eirenicon*.

105. Schaff, *History* III: 1017n.1; similarly, "Genius and Theology," 112.

106. Schaff, *History* III: 1026, 1027; II: 628; *Theological Propaedeutic* II: 275n.2.

107. Schaff, *History* II: 628.

108. Schaff, *History* II: 628.

109. Schaff, "German Theology and the Church Question," 131 (also in *Philip Schaff, Historian and Ambassador*, ed. Penzel, 100); *History* III: 1017n.1.

110. Gieseler, *Text-Book*, trans. Cunningham, 154–55, 261–62; trans. Smith, 237–38, 385–86.

111. Gieseler, *Text-Book*, trans. Cunningham, 262–63; trans. Smith, 386–87; Mosheim, *Ecclesiastical History* I: 105, 179; Neander, *General History* I: 213, 214.

112. Miller, "Introductory Essay," in "A Watchman," *History of Popery*, 3–4.

113. Miller, "Ecclesiastical History. Remarks on the First and Second Centuries" (B2, F12, 11, 12); "Ecclesiastical History-No. II, II and III Centuries" (B2, F14, 11–12).

114. Miller, "Ecclesiastical History, No. III, IV and V Centuries" (B2, F15, 20–21); "Ecclesiastical History, No. IV. V, VI, and VII Centuries" (B2, F16, 4–5).

115. Miller, "Sermon." Delivered before the New-York Missionary Society, 27.

116. Smith, "Theology" [unspecified course], 1861–1862, Briggs notes (Briggs Papers, S8, B34, F5, N1, 202–3).

117. Smith, "Systematic Theology," 1857? (S4, B1, F2, L9, con't.).

118. Smith, *History*, 12, 14, 20, 22; "Systematic Theology," 1857 (S4, B1, F1, L7). Honorius held that in Jesus there existed only one will, a view anathematized by the Sixth Ecumenical Council in 680–681 ("Bishop C. J. von Hefele," 274–75).

119. Hitchcock, "Church History: First Period," 1872, Jackson notes (Jackson Papers, B1, N1, 46, 49, 51; by "spurious," Hitchcock meant that Clement of Rome did not write these Homilies); "Apostolic Church," 1860s, Wright notes (B2, N1, 28–32, on Peter).

120. Hitchcock, "Apostolic Church," 1860s, Wright notes (B2, N1, chap. 5, 16). That this did not happen was good: "the Jewish leaven was as strong as the Church could bear."

121. Hitchcock, "Life of Christ," early 1880s, Burrell notes (B1, N1, 90).

122. Hitchcock, "Church History: Second Period," 1873, Jackson notes (Jackson Papers, B1, N1, 238–42).

123. Hitchcock, "Church History: First Period," 1872, Jackson notes (Jackson Papers, B1, N1, 46, 49, 51, 149, citing Cyprian's *On the Unity of the Catholic Church* [presumably sections 4–5] to show that even in the mid-third century, all bishops were deemed equal).

124. Hitchcock, "Church History: Second Period," 1873, Jackson notes (Jackson Papers, B1, N1, 242), adding that easterners always turned to Rome "when in trouble."

125. Hitchcock, "Church History: Second Period," 1873, Jackson notes (Jackson

Papers, B1, N1, 243–245, 235–236); similarly, "Church History: Second Period," 1883–1884, Burrell notes (B1, N2, 36–37).

126. Hitchcock, "Church History: Second Period," 1873, Jackson notes (Jackson Papers, B1, N1, 245); "Church History," 1883, Moore notes (B2, N2, 201).

127. Schaff, *History* III: 300; "Latin Patriarchate," 21, 28; *History* II: 513–14, 122.

128. Schaff, "Latin Patriarchate," 11–12; *History* III: 303; on the *petra* of Matt. 16 (Peter or Christ? [III: 306–7]); also, "Development of the Ancient Catholic Hierarchy: II," 48–49. The Church Fathers deemed the Roman bishopric the successor to Peter on the basis of Peter's alleged martyrdom in that city (*History* I: 260).

129. Schaff, "Brief Introduction to the New Testament in General," UTS, 1877–1878 (?), Gillett notes (UTS, B3, N, 146–47); *History* III: 309, citing Chrysostom's *Homily on St. Ignatius, Martyr*, 4; *Homily 2 On the Beginning of Acts*, 6.

130. Schaff, *History* I: 850; "Brief Introduction to the New Testament in General," UTS, 1877–1878 (?), Gillett notes (UTS, B3, N, 208); *History* II: 155.

131. Schaff, *History* II: 752, 774; III: 315; II: 264.

132. Schaff, *History* II: 774.

133. Schaff, "Tertullian," 627. Tertullian took the crown of flowers worn by victorious athletes (and in *On the Military Crown*, soldiers) as a sign of idolatry.

134. Schaff, *History* III: 334, 315–19.

135. Schaff, *History* II: 166; III: 293.

136. Schaff, *History* I: 260, 261.

137. Schaff, "Latin Patriarchate," 13–14, much as Jewish theocracy and the material advantages of the Roman Empire helped prepare for Christianity; cf. "Development of the Ancient Catholic Hierarchy: II," 39.

138. Schaff, "Latin Patriarchate," 29; "Development of the Ancient Catholic Hierarchy: II," 59–60 (the editors of *BFER* inserted a note objecting to Schaff's views: the papacy is the work of Satan, whose treachery, avarice, and ambition cannot be compared to "Mosaic theocracy" [60n.]).

139. Schaff, *History* III: 289; cf. III: 314.

140. Fisher, *Beginnings of Christianity*, 556–57; "Church History," 1870–1871 (46); "Old Roman Spirit," in Fisher, *Discussions*, 45.

141. Fisher, "Church History," 1870–1871 (48–49, citing Cyprian, *On the Unity of the Catholic Church* 6).

142. Fisher, "Church History," 1870–1871 (49); similarly, *History of the Christian Church*, 57–58.

143. Fisher, "Church History," 1870–1871 (49, 3, 57).

144. Fisher, "Church History," 1870–1871 (90).

145. Emerton, "Church History," 1887–1889 (11/3; 11/15); *Unitarian Thought*, 17.

146. Emerton, *Introduction to the Study*, 107, 108; emphasis in original.

147. Emerton, "Church History," 1887–1889 (12/15; 12/17).

148. Emerton, "Church History," 1887–1889 (3/8; 3/13); similarly, Emerton, *Intro-*

duction to the Study, 106. Leo's "Tome" was the one document from a western church-man accepted by the Council.

149. Emerton, "Church History," 1887–1889 (3/15); *Introduction to the Study*, 105. At the Council of Chalcedon in 451, eastern bishops (the vast majority of those present) decreed that the Bishop of Constantinople should have the same privileges as the Bishop of Rome, since Constantinople was "the new Rome." This Canon (28) was rejected by the Bishop of Rome. At the Council of Nicaea in 325, Rome had been mentioned (Canon 6) as one of the preeminent churches that enjoyed special privileges. Constantinople did not become an imperial capital until a few years after the Council of Nicaea.

150. Emerton, *Introduction to the Study*, 109, 93.

151. Emerton, "Church History," 1887–1889 (11/15); *Introduction to the Study*, 93, 22, 113.

152. Smith, "Nature and Worth," 82–83; "Medieval History," 1851, Hastings notes (S5, B, F3, 134).

153. Smith, "Systematic Theology," 1857 (?) (S4, B1, F1, L9, L7); "Provisions of Redemption," 1859–1860 (S4, B1, F19, Part 2, #3).

154. Smith, "Reformed Churches of Europe and America," 35.

155. Smith, "Systematic Theology, Part II," 1872–1873, Jackson notes (Jackson Papers, B1, N, 155).

156. Smith, "Systematic Theology," 1855–1856, Quick notes (S5, B1, F4, N2, 264–65); "Provisions of Redemption," 1859–1860 (S4, B1, F19, Part 2, #3).

157. Smith, "Systematic Theology," 1855–1856, Quick notes (S5, B1, F4, N2, 264–66); "Systematic Theology, Part II," 1872–1873, Jackson notes (Jackson Papers, B1, N, 154–55).

158. Smith, "Provisions of Redemption," 1859–1860 (S4, B1, F19, Part 2, #3); "Systematic Theology, Part II," 1872–1873, Jackson notes (Jackson Papers, B1, N, 152).

159. Smith, "Systematic Theology," 1855–1856, Quick notes (S5, B1, F4, N2, 265).

160. Smith, "Systematic Theology, Part II," 1872–1873, Jackson notes (Jackson Papers, B1, N, 155).

161. Smith, *History*, 67; "Provisions of Redemption," 1859–1860 (S4, B1, F19, Part 2, #3); "Systematic Theology," 1855–1856, Quick notes (S5, B1, F4, N2, 266).

162. Smith, *History*, 67; "Systematic Theology," 1855–1856, Quick notes (S5, B1, F4, N2, 264–66).

163. Smith, "Passaglia, Guizot, and Döllinger," 354.

164. Smith, "Systematic Theology," 1855–1856, Quick notes (S5, B1, F4, N2, 263–65).

165. Hitchcock, "Church History: Second Period," 1872–1873, Jackson notes (Jackson Papers, B1, N2, 2–4); "Life of Christ," 1865, Wright notes (B2, N1, 1st period, chap. 3). Fisher of Yale blamed fourth-century converts from "heathenism" for fostering the "worship of Mary" ("Old Roman Spirit," in Fisher, *Discussions*, 42–43; *History of the Christian Church*, 118; *History of Christian Doctrine*, 171–72).

166. Hitchcock, "Church History: Second Period," 1873, Jackson notes (Jackson Papers, B1, N2, 3–4); "Life of Christ," 1865, Wright notes (B2, N1, 1st period, chap. 3).

167. Hitchcock, "Church History: Second Period," 1883–1884, Burrell notes (B1, N2, 44); "Life of Christ," 1865, Wright notes (B2, N1, 1st period, chap. 3).

168. Schaff, *History* III: 412, 413, 417, 426.

169. Schaff, *History* III: 410, 411, 946, 414, 411 (In Ephesus, the worship of the Virgin Mary replaced worship of "the virgin Diana" [III: 722]); *History* II: 284.

170. Emerton, *Unitarian Thought*, 167–68.

171. Orsi, *Between Heaven and Earth*, 188.

Chapter 8. Asceticism, Marriage, Women, and the Family

Epigraph: Schaff, *History* II: 413.

1. Hitchcock, "Church History: First Period," 1872, Jackson notes (Jackson Papers, B1, N1, 75).

2. Hitchcock, "Middle Ages: First Period," early 1880s, Burrell notes (B1, N2, 47); "Church History: First Period," early 1880s, Burrell notes (B1, N1, 242); "Church History: First Period," 1883, Moore notes (B2, N2, 282).

3. Hitchcock, "Church History: Second Period," 1873, Jackson notes (Jackson Papers, B1, N1, 255–56); "Church History: Second Period," 1883–1884, Moore notes (B2, N2, 468—a "false principle").

4. Emerson, "Early History of Monasticism," *BS* 1.2 (May 1844): 309–15; 1.3 (Aug. 1844): 464–525; 1.4 (Nov. 1844): 632–99. Emerson's son married Roswell Hitchcock's daughter Mary in 1881 ("Matrimony Notices," *Cincinnati Daily Gazette*, Dec. 31, 1881, 9). Emerson was a relative of the more famous Ralph Waldo Emerson.

5. Emerson, "Early History," *BS* 1.2 (May 1844): 309, 315, 316, 310, 313, 317. If Protestant ministers, "pilots in the present storm," warm to these *Vitae*, they might sacrifice their reason on "the altar of superstition" and "revert to papal institutions" ("Early History," *BS* 1.4 [Nov. 1844]: 668, 669).

6. Nineteenth-century Protestants' image of Roman Catholicism served to articulate and reinforce a "Protestant middle-class identity" (Franchot, *Roads to Rome*, "Introduction").

7. Moorhead, *American Apocalypse*, 229.

8. Joseph Bingham's eighteenth-century *Origines Ecclesiasticae*, a probable source for these professors, often seems absent. The Anglican Bingham, however, engages in little or no critique of asceticism; see *Origines Ecclesiasticae*, Book VII.

9. Mosheim, *Ecclesiastical History* I: 193.

10. Essenes and Therapeutae forsook "primitive Hebraism's" affirmation of marriage for "Oriental theosophy": Neander, *Memorials*, 72, 50–51; *General History* I: 275, 43–45, 48–49, 59–60 (an aristocratic spirit stood against true Christianity [58]); *Lectures* I: 78, 83.

11. Mosheim, *Ecclesiastical History* I: 275; Neander, *General History* II: 263, 291. Exalting an ascetic master (as Indians deify Brahmins) contradicts the true Christian view that *every* devotee of Christ is "a temple of the Holy Ghost" (*Memorials*, 194, 196).

12. Mosheim, *Ecclesiastical History* I: 193, 275, 196–97: from Egypt, ascetic practice spread to other areas.

13. Gieseler, *Text-Book* I, trans. Smith, 399–400, 510. Also see Neander, *General History* I: 274; II: 270, 294, 296 (hot climates diminish appetite; that of Egypt, Palestine, and Syria favored asceticism).

14. Neander, *General History* I: 276; II: 161, 262, 263; *Memorials*, 76, 72–73, 170, 182.

15. Gieseler, *Text-Book* I, trans. Cunningham, 272–73; trans. Smith, 402–3.

16. Neander, *General History* II: 266, 265. Antony, among others, took these passages "in too literal and outward a sense."

17. Neander, *History of the Planting and Training* I: 24–25; Christianity takes the unequal division of wealth and social inequalities as an opportunity for virtue. See Acts 2:44, 4:32–5:11 on the "primitive communism" of the early Jerusalem Christians.

18. Neander, *General History* I: 715. Neander blames the Egyptian ascetic Hieracas for wresting I Corinthians 7 out of its "proper connection," interpreting Paul's allowance of marriage *only* as a means for the "weak" to avoid "a still greater evil."

19. Neander, *History of the Planting and Training* II: 350–51.

20. Mosheim, *Ecclesiastical History* I: 346; II: 50–51.

21. Mosheim, *Ecclesiastical History* I: 197; II: 117.

22. Mosheim, *Ecclesiastical History* I: 377, 378, 381, 385; II: 32.

23. Mosheim, *Ecclesiastical History* II: 47–50.

24. Mosheim, *Ecclesiastical History* I: 269; II: 131.

25. Gieseler, *Text-Book* I, trans. Cunningham, 275–76; trans. Smith, 405–7; that women could not practice these wilder forms of asceticism shows the latter's error.

26. Gieseler, *Text-Book* I, trans. Smith, 399–400; cf. trans. Cunningham, 271.

27. Neander, *General History* II: 292–93, 274, citing Sozomen on the *boskoi* (*Ecclesiastical History* 6.33).

28. Mosheim, *Ecclesiastical History* II: 130.

29. Gieseler, *Text-Book* I, trans. Cunningham, 279, 299–300; trans. Smith, 414–15, 442–44.

30. Neander, *General History* I: 199; II: 274; *Memorials*, 74–75, 187.

31. Mosheim, *Ecclesiastical History* II: 50, 92; Neander, *General History* II: 290, 291; *Memorials*, 186.

32. Gieseler, *Text-Book* I, trans. Cunningham, 298; trans. Smith, 440–41; Neander, *General History* II: 291; *Memorials*, 199.

33. Neander, *General History* I: 520; *Lectures* I: 35. Neander was a convert from Judaism.

34. Mosheim, *Ecclesiastical History* I: 197; II: 117, 130.

35. Neander, *Memorials*, 73, 170, 189; *General History* II: 259–60.

36. Gieseler, *Text-Book* I, trans. Cunningham, 305; trans. Smith, 450.

37. Mosheim, *Ecclesiastical History* I: 192–93.

38. Mosheim, *Ecclesiastical History* I: 388–89; II: 51–52.

39. Neander, *Memorials*, 170, 199; *General History* II: 314, 304.

40. Neander, *General History* II: 305, 307, 304, 311; *Memorials*, 199. On Catholic and Protestant scholars' assessment of Jovinian, see Hunter, *Marriage, Celibacy, and Heresy in Ancient Christianity*, 5–12.

41. Gieseler, *Text-Book* I, trans. Cunningham, 278, 347–48; trans. Smith, 411, 510.

42. Neander, *General History* I: 249. Even Julian "the Apostate's" attempt to reinstate paganism shows how little human schemes can effect if they stand against Providence (*Emperor Julian*, 18).

43. Neander, *General History* II: 284–88.

44. Neander, *Memorials*, 313; *General History* II: 296, 301–2.

45. Gieseler, *Text-Book* I, trans. Cunningham, 296–97; trans. Smith, 440.

46. Neander, *General History* I: 123, 181–82, 188; presumably referring to Titus 2:3–5. Claiming the Pastoral Epistles as Pauline assists in the argument for domesticity.

47. Baur, *Church History* II: 240, 241, 243.

48. Baur, "Beiträge zur Erklärung der Korinthierbriefe-1," 14, 16, 18 (marriage and *porneia*, materially the same, are only formally differentiated), 21. Baur rejected the Pauline authorship of Ephesians.

49. Baur, *Church History* II: 251n.1.

50. Baur, "Beiträge zur Erklärung," 30, 15.

51. Baur, *Church History* II: 260, 275–76, referring to Tertullian, *Exhortation to Chastity* 9. Of the early Fathers, Clement of Alexandria (*Miscellanies*, Books 3 and 7) seems most "sensible."

52. Charles Kingsley in 1885 could offer a somewhat more positive assessment of the early Christian hermits, who, he thought, had been struggling toward light in an age of darkness—unlike the present scientific age, in which people have retreated into such "dark" practices as table-rapping to summon departed spirits (*The Hermits*, esp. 201–2).

53. [Anonymous], "Catalogue of Dr. Miller's Library," n.d. (B1, F1, n. p.).

54. Miller, "Introductory Essay" to "A Watchman," *History of Popery*, 13, 12; "Dangers of Education," 10.

55. Miller, "Lecture Notes on Mosheim, Cent. V, No. 1," 3/7/1814 (B5, F13, 24).

56. Miller, "Ecclesiastical History, No. II. II and III Centuries" (B2, F14, 8, 9).

57. Miller, "Ecclesiastical History, No. III, IV, and V Centuries" (B2, F15, 12, 13); "Lecture Notes on Mosheim: Century IV, No. 2," 2/21/1814 (B5, F12, 8, 9, 12).

58. Miller, "Lecture Notes on Mosheim: Century IV, No. 2," 2/21/1814 (B5, F12, 5, 9–10); "Ecclesiastical History, No. IV-VI. VII and VIII Centuries" (B2, F16, 3).

59. Miller, "Lecture Notes on Mosheim: Cent. V, No. 1" (B5, F14, 2–3); "Lecture Notes on Mosheim: Century IV, No. 2," 2/21/1814 (B5, F12, 9–10, 12). Given the charac-

ter of Augustine's age, we might wonder at how sound he is ("Lectures on Ecclesiastical History: Second Class," 1842–1843 [B24, F4, 5]).

60. Miller, "Lecture Notes on Mosheim: Century IV, No. 2," 2/21/1814 (B5, F12, 3, 9 [Jerome as source], 11).

61. Miller, "Ecclesiastical History, No. III, IV, and V Centuries" (B2, F15, 22).

62. Miller, "Lecture Notes on Mosheim, Cent. V, No. 1," 3/7/1814 (B5, F13, 3–4 [extract on 4–8], 20, 22)..

63. Miller, "Ecclesiastical History, No. III, IV, and V Centuries" (B2, F15, 13).

64. Miller, "Lecture Notes on Mosheim: Cent. V, No. 1," 3/7/1814 (B5, F13, 17).

65. Miller, "Ecclesiastical History, No. III, IV, and V Centuries" (B2, F15, 12, 13); "Lecture Notes on Mosheim: Century IV, No. 2," 2/21/1814 (B5, F12, 9–12).

66. Miller, "Dangers of Education," 8; "Introductory Essay," in "A Watchman," *History of Popery*, 13.

67. Miller, "Ecclesiastical History, No. II. II and III Centuries" (B2, F14, 25); *Letters on Clerical Manners*, 342.

68. Smith, "Tholuck's *Christliche Sittenlehre*" (S3, Item 1).

69. Smith, *History*, 11.

70. Smith, *History*, 10, 19, 15, 14, 16, 18.

71. Smith, *History*, 19, 20, 23; Augustinianism was supplanted by Semi-Pelagianism.

72. Hitchcock, "Church History: Second Period," 1883–1884, Burrell notes (B1, N2, 41); "Church History: First Period," 1883, Moore notes (B2, N2, 281).

73. Hitchcock, "Church History: Second Period," 1883–1884, Moore notes (B2, N2, 467); "Church History: Second Period," 1883–1884, Burrell notes (B1, N2, 41–42).

74. Fisher, "Christian Religion: III," 216.

75. Hitchcock, "Church History: Second Period," 1873, Jackson notes (Jackson Papers, B1, N1, 255); "Church History: Second Period," 1883–1884, Burrell notes (B1, N2, 47).

76. Hitchcock, "Church History: First Period," 1883, Moore notes (B2, N2, 281–82); "Church History: First Period," early 1880s, Burrell notes (B1, N1, 242); "Church History: Second Period," 1883–1884, Moore notes (B2, N2, 467).

77. Hitchcock, "True Idea and Uses," 41.

78. Hitchcock, "Church History: First Period," early 1880s, Burrell notes (B1, N1, 241, 242); "Church History: Second Period," 1883–1884, Moore notes (B2, N2, 281, 282).

79. Hitchcock, "Church History: Second Period," 1883–1884, Burrell notes (B1, N2, 42); "Church History: First Period," 1872, Jackson notes (Jackson Papers, B1, N1, 81).

80. Hitchcock, "Church History: First Period," early 1880s, Burrell notes (B1, N1, 246); "Church History: First Period," 1872–1873, Jackson notes (Jackson Papers, B1, N 1, 75).

81. Hitchcock, "Church History: Second Period," 1883–1884, Burrell notes (B1, N2, 43); "Church History: Second Period," 1883–1884, Moore notes (B2, N2, 471).

.

82. Presumably the professors refer to the Council of Carthage of 390: see Cochoni, *Origines apostoliques du célibat sacerdotal*, 23–28, 296–99 (also the Councils of Carthage in 393 and 401).

83. Hitchcock, "Church History: Second Period," 1873, Jackson notes (Jackson Papers, B1, N2, 67–68); "Church History: Second Period," 1883–1884, Moore notes (B2, N2, 508); Smith, *History*, 19. This trio, respectively, opposed "celibacy, fasting, and relics"; "superstitions, martyr-worship, pilgrimages, monastic vows and vigils"; and the perpetual virginity of Mary: "Church History: Second Period," 1883–1884, Burrell notes (B1, N2, 43); "Church History: First Period," 1872, Jackson notes (Jackson Papers, B1, N1, 74).

84. Fisher, *History of the Christian Church*, 116.

85. Smith, "Church History," 1850 (?), Hastings notes (S5, B1, F3, N, 106–7).

86. Smith, *History*, 8.

87. See Lintott, "Imperial Expansion and Moral Decline," 626–38; on "moral judgement," not "economic analysis," regarding Rome's "decline," 626, 638.

88. Tacitus, *Historiae* I. 5, 18, 20–22, 37–38; II. 31, 37–38, 69, 87, 94–95; III: 83; *Germania* 18–20; Earl, *Moral and Political Tradition*, chap. 4.

89. Especially *Satires* 2, 6, and 9.

90. Hitchcock, "Church History: First Period," early 1880s, Burrell notes (B1, N1, 243); "Church History: First Period," 1872, Jackson notes (Jackson Papers, B1, N1, 71, 76).

91. Hitchcock, "Life of Christ," early 1880s, Burrell notes (B1, N1, 25–26); "Church History, Second Period," 1883–1884, Burrell notes (B1, N2, 39).

92. Hitchcock, "Historical Development," 41; Hitchcock, "Life of Christ," early 1880s, Burrell notes (B1, N1, 27). Rome defeated Carthage in 146 B.C.E.

93. Hitchcock, "Church History: First Period," 1883, Moore notes (B2, N2, 209); "Life of Christ," 1865, Wright notes (B2, N1).

94. Hitchcock, "Church History: First Period," early 1880s, Burrell notes (B1, N1, 213); Juvenal, *Satire* 3, l. 62.

95. Hitchcock, "Church History: First Period," 1883, Moore notes (B2, N2, 178–79, 230–31); cf. "Church History: First Period," early 1880s, Burrell notes (B1, N1, 186 ["every man a gay paramour and every woman a courtezan [*sic*]"]).

96. Hitchcock, "Church History: First Period," early 1880s, Burrell notes (B1, N1, 243, 239); "Church History: First Period," 1883, Moore notes (B2, N2, 284). Poor family life is partially blamed on the notion that the state swallowed up all areas of life ("Church History: First Period," 1872, Jackson notes [Jackson Papers, B1, N1, 76]).

97. Hitchcock, "Church History: First Period," 1883, Moore notes [B2, N2, 284); "Church History: Second Period," 1883–1884, Burrell notes (B1, N2, 27). On "manliness" and "effeminacy" as watchwords of Civil War-era Protestantism, see Moorhead, *American Apocalypse*, 146.

98. Hitchcock, "Church History: First Period," 1872, Jackson notes (Jackson

Papers, B1, N1, 79); "Church History: First Period," early 1880s, Burrell notes (B1, N1, 248).

99. Hitchcock, "Church History: Second Period," 1873, Jackson notes (Jackson Papers, B1, N2, 9–10); "Church History: First Period," early 1880s, Burrell notes (B1, N1, 243, 239, 213). For a compilation of classical sources on this topic, see Pollitt, *Art of Rome*, 33–48, 64–71, for selections from, *inter alia*, Pliny, Livy, and Cicero.

100. Hitchcock, "Church History: First Period," early 1880s, Burrell notes (B1, N1, 243); "Church History: First Period," 1883, Moore notes (B2, N2, 284).

101. Hitchcock, "Church History: Second Period," 1873, Jackson notes (Jackson Papers, B1, N1, 256); also see Hitchcock, *Socialism* (1879), 110.

102. Hitchcock, "Church History: First Period," 1872, Jackson notes (Jackson Papers, B1, N1, 76); "Historical Development," 41.

103. Fisher, "Church History," 1870–1871 (118, 120); *History of the Christian Church*, 111.

104. Fisher, *History of the Christian Church*, 61.

105. Hitchcock, "Church History: First Period," 1883, Moore notes (B2, N2, 210, 231, 273). The early Church Fathers sound "childish," exhibiting "loss of stamina" ("Church History: First Period," early 1880s, Burrell notes [B1, N1, 213]).

106. Hitchcock, "Church History: First Period," early 1880s, Burrell notes (B1, N1, 242); "Church History: First Period," 1872, Jackson notes (Jackson Papers, B1, N1, 81, 73); "Church History: First Period," 1883, Moore notes (B2, N2, 285), e.g., the priests of Cybele. Anticipating his students' horrified reaction, Hitchcock assured them that the practice of castration then seemed "far less strange than now."

107. Hitchcock, "Apostolic Church," early 1880s, Burrell notes (B1, N, 148); "Church History: First Period," 1872, Jackson notes (Jackson Papers, B1, N1, 81).

108. Hitchcock, "Apostolic Church," 1882, Moore Notes (B2, N2, 112); "Apostolic Church," early 1880s, Burrell Notes (B1, N, 148). Hitchcock taught before the "eschatological turn" in New Testament scholarship: Johannes Weiss's *Preaching of Jesus Concerning the Kingdom of God* was published in 1892, and Albert Schweitzer's *Quest of the Historical Jesus*, in 1906. Only with the assimilation of these works would the eschatological import of the Synoptics and the Pauline letters—an import that formed the backdrop for the ethic of renunciation—be better understood.

109. Fisher, "Church History," 1870–1871 (120–21).

110. Fisher, "Conflict: Second Article," 261, 262, 263.

111. Fisher, "Church History," 1870–1871 (121); "Conflict: Second Article," 262–63. Jesus meant merely that celibacy is lawful when "spontaneously practiced."

112. Fisher, "Ebionitism," 551.

113. Fisher, *History of the Christian Church*, 37.

114. Fisher, *History of the Christian Church*, 78 (in contrast to Manichean asceticism, strongly influenced by Buddhism), 61–62.

115. Fisher, "Church History," 1870–1871 (118). Fisher here recognizes that the imminence of the eschaton might have been a factor.

116. Fisher, *Beginnings of Christianity*, 523; "Church History," 1870–1871 (121); "Conflict: Second Article," 262–63.

117. Hitchcock, "Church History: First Period," early 1880s, Burrell notes (B1, N1, 242); "Church History: First Period," 1883, Moore notes (B2, N2, 281).

118. Hitchcock, "Life of Christ," early 1880s, Burrell notes (B1, N1, 25). Hitchcock posits that, centuries later, Merovingian tribes moving southward into the softer climate of Gaul were rapidly "demoralized," as Greece and Rome had been earlier. Again, asceticism might seem like a suitable remedy ("Church History: Second Period," 1883–1884, Burrell notes [B1, N2, 39]).

119. Fisher, *History of the Christian Church*, 111, 114. By "mild," Fisher appears to mean "hot."

120. Hitchcock, "Church History: Second Period," 1883–1884, Burrell notes (B1, N2, 42); "Church History: Second Period," 1883–1884, Moore notes (B2, N2, 468).

121. Fisher, "Church History," 1870–1871 (120).

122. Fisher, *History of the Christian Church*, 111.

123. Fisher, *History of the Christian Church*, 111.

124. Hitchcock, "Church History: First Period," 1872, Jackson notes (Jackson Papers, B1, N1, 81, 76); "Church History: First Period," early 1880s, Burrell notes (B1, N1, 242, 246); Fisher, "Church History," 1870–1871 (120); *History of the Christian Church*, 111 (adding Serapis-worshippers).

125. Hitchcock, "Church History: Second Period," 1873, Jackson notes (Jackson Papers, B1, N1, 257); only a minority of Columba's "religious fraternity" at Iona in the sixth century were celibate (226); also see *Socialism*, 30.

126. Hitchcock, "Church History: Second Period," 1883–1884, Burrell notes (B1, N2, 42–43); "Church History: Second Period," 1883, Moore notes (B2, N2, 469–70).

127. Fisher, *History of the Christian Church*, 115–16.

128. Hitchcock, "Life of Christ," early 1880s, Burrell notes (B1, N1, 63).

129. Miller, *Letters on Clerical Manners*, 342, 343. In the mid- to late nineteenth century at Princeton, James C. Moffat claimed that Buddhism influenced the development of Christian asceticism (*Outlines of Church History* [1875], 63, 64); on Americans' fascination with Buddhism in the late nineteenth century, see Tweed, *American Encounter with Buddhism*. Moffat wrote a *Comparative History of Religions*.

130. Miller, "Importance of Domestic Happiness," 248.

131. Miller, "Importance of Domestic Happiness," 241, 245; "Means of Domestic Happiness," 250.

132. Miller, "Sermon," Preached . . . for the Benefit of the Society, 10–11.

133. Miller, "Sermon," Preached . . . for the Benefit of the Society, 11, 13, 16, 21–22.

134. Miller's salutatory address at the University of Pennsylvania scored the neglect of women's education: Miller [jr.], *Life*, I: 41.

135. Miller, *Brief Retrospect* I: 278, 280, 292, 284.

136. Miller, *Brief Retrospect* I: 285, 286, 287, 290.

137. Miller, *Brief Retrospect* I: 284, 289, 296–300; Miller opposed all utopian views based on the notion of the "perfectibility of man."

138. Hitchcock, "Historical Development," 41; "Life of Christ," early 1880s, Burrell notes (B1, N1, 27); "Church History: First Period," 1872, Jackson notes (Jackson Papers, B1, N1, 71, 76); "Church History: First Period," 1883, Moore notes (B2, N2, 288). Hitchcock again mentions the sexual behavior of the Viceroy of Egypt.

139. Hitchcock, "Church History: First Period," 1872, Jackson (Jackson Papers, B1, N1, 76, 72).

140. Hitchcock, "Church History: First Period," 1872, Jackson notes (Jackson Papers, B1, N1, 76–78).

141. Hitchcock, "Church History: First Period," 1872, Jackson (Jackson Papers, B1, N1, 72), alluding to Athenagoras, *Plea* 32–33; Clement of Alexandria, *Instructor* 2.10.

142. Hitchcock, "Apostolic Church," early 1880s, Burrell notes [B1, N1, 145).

143. Hitchcock, "Apostolic Church," early 1880s, Burrell notes (B1, N1, 96). The Pastorals' decree on once-married clergy, Hitchcock considers "binding under peculiar circumstances only" (97).

144. Hitchcock, "Apostolic Church," early 1880s, Burrell notes (B1, N1, 138). The office of deaconess *is* time-bound in that it grew out of "oriental customs." Hitchcock would not object to this form of service today (97).

145. See also Hitchcock's book, *Socialism*: acknowledging rampant social inequalities, Hitchcock asks for Christian solutions.

146. Fisher, *History of the Christian Church*, 37; "Church History," 1870–71 (118, 119); *Grounds of Theistic and Christian Belief*, 372; "Christian Religion: III," 177.

147. Fisher, *Beginnings of Christianity*, 200, 202, 205–6.

148. Fisher, *Grounds of Theistic and Christian Belief*, 372, 373.

149. Fisher, "Church History," 1870–1871 (118); *Beginnings of Christianity*, 579. A diary entry from Fisher's year in Germany (1852–1853) is of interest: German audiences were highly amused by reports of the Woman's Rights Convention in America (presumably the Seneca Falls Convention of 1848) ("Diary" [B114, 71]). Fisher does not reveal whether he too found the idea of woman suffrage amusing.

150. Schaff, *History* II: 387; III: 158. Schaff made a small exception for Methodism, claiming that "Wesley would undoubtedly have been a monk had he lived before the Reformation" ("Church History," MTS, 1855, Russell notes [LTS, B4, F03, 69–70]).

151. Schaff, *History* II: 338, 389; "Rise and Progress," 410; *Principle of Protestantism*, 173; "Protestant pietism" is also guilty.

152. Schaff, "Dogmatics," MTS, 1848–1849, Santee notes (LTS, B4, F09).

153. Schaff, "Ascetic System," 613.

154. Schaff, "Ascetic System," 600; *History* III: 189.

155. Schaff, *History* III: 220–21n.2; II: 387–88; "Principles of the Reformation," 133; "Ascetic System," 600–601; *History* III: 6.

156. Schaff, *History* II: 387–88; "Ascetic System," 601, 604, 605.

157. Schaff, *History* III: 166; "General Introduction to the Old Testament Scrip-

tures," UTS, 1877–1878 (?), Gillett notes (UTS, B3, N, 77–78). Elsewhere, Schaff wrote that the Old Testament stands against celibacy and "represents children as the greatest blessing, and sterility as a curse or misfortune" ("Brethren of Christ," 865).

158. Schaff, *History* II: 393, 397. Schaff notes probable Gnostic influence (II: 153–54).

159. Schaff, *History* III: 162. Jesus is not merely an individual man, but universal man ("Influence of Christianity on the Family," 480); "Dogmatics," MTS, 1848–1849, Santee notes (LTS, B4, F09, N).

160. Schaff, "Ascetic System," 613; *History* II: 397–98; III: 162; "Rise and Progress," 398–99; "Dogmatics," MTS, 1848–1849, Santee notes (LTS, B4, F09, N).

161. Schaff, "Influence of Christianity on the Family," 480; "Dogmatics," MTS, 1848–1849, Santee notes (LTS, B4, F09, N).

162. Schaff, "Dogmatics," MTS, 1848–1849, Santee notes (LTS, B4, F09, N). These "heroic spirits" avoided marriage in order to serve God's Kingdom.

163. Schaff, "Influence of Christianity on the Family," 480; "Rise and Progress," 398–99; *History* III: 162.

164. The RSV editors prefer "*adelphēn gunaika.*" Other readings simply have "*gunaikas.*" Also in Clement of Alexandria, *Miscellanies* 7.11.

165. In *Miscellanies* 3.52.4, Clement of Alexandria claims that Peter had "children," a tradition followed by Eusebius (*Ecclesiastical History* 3.30.1). The "daughter" figures prominently in the *Acts of Nereus and Achilles*; see McGiffert's note on Eusebius, *Ecclesiastical History* III.30, in *NPNF*, 2nd ser. I: 162n.3. Coptic papyrus Berlin 8502 containing the Acts of Peter (and the story of Peter's daughter) was not discovered and edited until 1903; see Hennecke, *New Testament Apocrypha* II: 276–78.

166. Schaff, *History* I: 262–63; II: 405.

167. Schaff, *History* I: 262–63; II: 405; "Dogmatics," MTS, 1848–1849, Santee notes (LTS, B4, F09, N).

168. Schaff, "Brethren of Jesus," 864–65, 868.

169. Schaff, "Influence of Christianity on the Family," 481n.*, 481.

170. Schaff, *History* I: 293 (emphasis mine); "Influence of Christianity on the Family," 482; "Rise and Progress," 398–99.

171. Schaff, "Dogmatics," MTS, 1848–1849, Santee notes (LTS, B4, F09, N); "Church History," MTS, 1855, Russell notes (LTS, B4, F03, N, 76). On Neander's celibacy, "Recollections of Neander," 77.

172. Schaff, *History* I: 293–94n.3. Another possibility, offered by Renan (that Schaff doubtless rejects): Paul had a spiritual union with Lydia.

173. Schaff, *History* III: 162–63.

174. Schaff, "Influence of Christianity on the Family," 483; *History* I: 758n.1.

175. Schaff, *History* I: 758n.1. The temple was to Aphrodite, not Artemis. In his summary here of the "leading thoughts" of I Corinthians 7, Schaff skips the entire chapter up to vs. 19 and after vs. 23 (760).

176. Schaff, "Influence of Christianity on the Family," 484 and note.

177. Schaff, *History* II: 242.

178. Schaff, "Influence of Christianity on the Family," 484–85; "Dogmatics," MTS, 1848–1849, Santee notes (LTS, B4, F09, N); "Rise and Progress," 398–99.

179. Schaff, "Ascetic System," 607; *History* II: 397–98.

180. Schaff, "Dogmatics," MTS, 1848–1849, Santee notes (LTS, B4, F09, N).

181. Schaff, *History* III: 163.

182. Schaff, *History* III: 155; "Ascetic System," 602, 608; *History* II: 398, 334, 335.

183. Schaff, *History* II: 315; *Saint Augustine, Melanchthon, Neander,* 80; *History* I: 444; II: 361, 386.

184. Schaff, *History* I: 348–49.

185. Schaff, *History* III: 163; *Theological Propaedeutic* II: 427.

186. Schaff, *History* II: 390 (while North African Montanists' "gloomy and rigorous acerbity" is attributed to "the Punic national character" [II: 420]); "Rise and Progress," 391, alluding to Aelian's claim that Egyptians bore torture rather than compromise truth (Aelian, *Historical Miscellany* 7.18).

187. Schaff, *History* III: 166; "Rise and Progress," 392, 393.

188. Schaff, "Rise and Progress," 390.

189. Schaff, *Theological Propaedeutic* II: 430; *History* II: 391; "Church History," MTS, 1855, Russell notes (LTS, B4, F03, N, 62).

190. Schaff, "Rise and Progress," 391; "Church History," MTS, 1855, Russell notes (LTS, B4, F03, N, 62).

191. Schaff, *History* II: 389–90, 398, 392–93, 153–54, 495. Schaff did not consider Gnosticism "Christian."

192. Schaff, "Ascetic System," 601; *History* II: 398; III: 149–51; "Influence of Christianity on the Family," 479; "Rise and Progress," 384–88, 399, 401–2.

193. Schaff, *History* III: 168 (reporting incidents from "ancient and modern travellers," including Alexander von Humboldt's encounter with Hindoos at Astracan), 173.

194. Schaff, "Rise and Progress," 407, 413; *History* III: 5, 177, 169; II: 393; *Theological Propaedeutic* II: 434.

195. Schaff, "Church History," MTS, 1855, Russell notes (LTS, B4, F03, N, 64–66).

196. Schaff, *History* III: 177, 173, 178, 202; "Rise and Progress," 409, 413, 414.

197. Schaff, *History* III: 166, 215n.2, 216 (cf. Jerome, *Letter* 108. 20, 31), 157, 196.

198. Schaff, *History* III: 167.

199. Schaff, *History* III: 171.

200. Schaff, *History* III: 169–70, 171, 249; "Ascetic System," 611, 612. On mounting concerns in the eighteenth and nineteenth centuries over masturbation, see Laqueur, *Solitary Sex.*

201. Schaff, *History* III: 242, 247, 243, 248.

202. Schaff, "Church History," MTS, 1855, Russell notes (LTS, B4, F03, N, 70); "Rise and Progress," 416–24, 388–89; *History* III: 227–33.

203. Schaff, "Dogmatics," MTS, 1848–1849, Santee notes (LTS, B4, F09, N).

204. Schaff, "Ascetic System," 612.

205. Schaff, "Ascetic System," 612; "Church History," MTS, 1855, Russell notes (LTS, B4, F03, N, 62).

206. Schaff, "Staffa and Iona," unidentified newspaper clipping, from July 25, 1877 (UTS, B6, Scr1, 94). Schaff writes from Oban, Scotland.

207. Schaff, "Rise and Progress," 394, 412, 411; *History* III: 176, 200–201, 217, 220, 225, 176–77.

208. Schaff, *History* III: 175.

209. Schaff, "Rise and Progress," 411, 394; "Ascetic System," 612, 613.

210. Schaff, *History* III: 172.

211. Schaff, *History* I: 442; "Influence of Christianity on the Family," 477, 475.

212. Schaff, *History* II: 362. On representation of women in nineteenth-century schoolbooks, including the denigration of higher education for women, see Elson, *Guardians of Tradition*, 301–12.

213. Schaff, "Influence of Christianity on the Family," 473, 474. The ancient Germans' "high regard for the female sex" and chastity in marriage prepared them well for the adoption of Christian morality (474).

214. Schaff, "Influence of Christianity on the Family," 478, 476, 475.

215. Schaff, *America*, 178.

216. Schaff, *In Memoriam*, 9, 11, 14. By 1867, there were 22,017 female teachers in New York State, but Meta did not choose this route (statistic from Smith, "Report on the State of Religion," 27). On working-class women in New York's public sphere, see Stansell, *City of Women*. Schaff deemed the large number of female elementary school teachers in America a "peculiarity" (*America*, 58).

217. Schaff, *In Memoriam*, 12. That Meta had her own room signals the Schaffs' middle-class status. Schaff's wife, by contrast, was not involved with his scholarly and professional life. On the rise of the privatized, Victorian family, see Aron, "Evolution of the Middle Class" and Laura Edwards, "Gender and the Changing Roles of Women"; for its relation to religion, see Taves, "Sexuality in American Religious History" and Braude, "Women's History *Is* American Religious History."

218. Schaff, *History* II: 354, 361; *Person of Christ*, 156n. 31.

219. Schaff, *History* II: 361–62, 399; I: 399, 442; II: 16.

220. Schaff, *History* II: 385; similarly, *History* III: 111.

221. Schaff, *History* I: 443–44.

222. Schaff, *History* II: 406; I: 441–42. The Virgin Mary marks a turning point for womanhood (442).

223. Schaff, *History* I: 230; "Brief Introduction to the New Testament in General," UTS, 1877–1878 (?), Gillett notes (UTS, B3, N, 219)—the "original law" of Gen. 2:18–24. Schaff praised Constantine's restriction of divorce: "boundless liberty" had damaged public morals (*History* III: 112–14).

224. Schaff, "Influence of Christianity on the Family," 475; *History* II: 361.

225. Schaff, "Ascetic System," 610–11.

226. Schaff, "Dogmatics," MTS, 1848–1849, Santee notes (LTS, B4, F09, N); *America*, 53, 54.

227. Schaff, "Prolegomena" ("Life and Work of St. John Chrysostom"), 17, on John Chrysostom, *Hom. 74 Matt*. Luke is the Gospel "for women" (*History* I: 662).

228. Schaff, "Brethren of Christ," 865; *History* II: 405; I: 777.

229. Schaff, *Oldest Church Manual*, 61, 71. Montanists, too, allowed women to prophesy ("like the Quakers in recent times") but "the strong tendency to order and hierarchical consolidation triumphed over freedom" (62).

230. Schaff, *History* III: 548n.1; II: 363.

231. Schaff, *History* II: 362; *Theological Propaedeutic* II: 429; "Ascetic System," 609, 610.

232. Schaff perhaps borrows from Neander, who in his *Memorials* devoted four pages to the topic (174–78).

233. Schaff, "Prolegomena: Life and Work of St. John Chrysostom," 5. Yet, Schaff wrote, Gregory Nazianzen's depiction of Nonna's piety "bore the stamp of ascetic legalism rather than of evangelical freedom, and adhered rigidly to certain outward forms" (*History* III: 911).

234. Schaff, *History* III: 990, 992; *Life and Labors*, 10; *Saint Augustine, Melanchthon, Neander*, 9.

235. Schaff, "Ascetic System," 608; *History* II: 396, 401.

236. Schaff, *History* III: 215; *Theological Propaedeutic* II: 431.

237. Schaff, *History* III: 214n.1.

238. Schaff, *History* III: 1019n.3; similarly, *Saint Augustine, Melanchthon, Neander*, 47.

239. Schaff, "Pelagian Controversy," 225; *Life and Labors*, 115; similarly, *Saint Augustine, Melanchthon, Neander*, 79. Henry Smith softened Augustine's position: Augustine believed marriage not only "good," but also seemingly "necessary" ("Church History," 1850–1851, Hastings notes [S5, B1, F3, N 1, 106]).

240. See Emerton's essays in *Unitarian Thought* (1911). His student Earl Morse Wilbur, as we saw in Chapter 2, wrote a paper on the development of monasticism.

241. Emerton, "Church History," 1887–1889 (10/20).

242. Emerton, "Church History," 1887–1889 (10/25).

243. Emerton, "Church History," 1887–1889 (10/20).

244. Emerton, *Introduction to the Study*, 17, 136.

245. Emerton, *Introduction to the Study*, 135.

246. Emerton, *Introduction to the Study*, 138, 136; similarly, *Unitarian Thought*, 241.

247. Emerton, *Introduction to the Study*, 138, 149, 144–45.

248. Emerton, *Introduction to the Study*, 138, 137.

249. Emerton, *Introduction to the Study*, 148.

250. Emerton, *Introduction to the Study*, 146.

Chapter 9. The Uses of Augustine

Epigraph: O'Donnell, *Augustine: A New Biography*, 331.

1. Miller, "Notes on Church History," 1839 (B26, F1); "Ecclesiastical History, No. III, IV, and V Centuries" (B2, F15, 24); Schaff, *History* III: 1021, 998.

2. Smith, "Medieval Church History," 1851, Hastings notes (S5, B1, F3, 168); Miller, "Ecclesiastical History, Second Class," 1842–1843 (B24, F4, 5–6); Schaff, *History* III: 1022–23n.1.

3. Schaff, *Saint Augustine, Melanchthon, Neander*, 105–6; *Life and Labors*, 133.

4. Hitchcock, "Church History: First Period," Jackson notes, 1873 (Jackson Papers, B1, N1, 125); Smith, "Theology" [unspecified course], 1861–1862, Briggs notes (Briggs Papers, S8, B34, F5, N2, Division 3, chap. 2).

5. Smith, "Doctrinal History," 1851, Hastings notes (S5, B1, F3, 63–64, 67, 115–16).

6. Miller, "Ecclesiastical History, No. II. II and III Centuries" (B2, F14, 6); "Notes on Church History and Church Government," 1821, J. W. Douglas notes (B25, F4, 4); "Miller on Mosheim, Century V, No. I," 3/7/1814 (B5, F13, 39–40); "Practical Results from a Course of Ecclesiastical History" (B2, F10, 12).

7. Miller, "Ecclesiastical History, No. III, IV, and V Centuries" (B2, F15, 24).

8. Miller, "Ecclesiastical History, V Century" (B2, F15, 23–24); "Ecclesiastical History, Second Class," 1842–1843 (B24, F4, 7); "Miller on Mosheim, Century V, No. I," 3/7/1814 (B5, F13, 37).

9. Miller, "Miller on Mosheim, Cent. V, no. II," 3/11/1814 (B5, F14, 9, 23, 22); "Ecclesiastical History, Second Class," 1842–1843 (B24, F4, 5).

10. Miller, "Ecclesiastical History, No. III, IV, and V Centuries" (B2, F15, 24); the moment when a voice from heaven had cried to the church, "Arise, shine, for your light has come" ("Introductory Lecture on Ecclesiastical History" [B2, F9, 6, citing Is. 60:1]).

11. Miller, "Fragment: Dr. Miller on the Fifth Century" (B22, F12); "Ecclesiastical History, Second Class," 1842–1843 (B24, F4, 5–6).

12. Augustine, *City of God* 21.17.

13. For a list of books in Miller's personal library, see Miller Papers, B1, F1, 51.

14. Miller, "Ecclesiastical History, Second Class," 1842–1843 (B24, F4, 5–6).

15. Miller, "Ecclesiastical History," unidentified student notes, 1839 (B26, F1).

16. George Fisher (see 329–330) attacked the Princetonian interpretation of imputation of original sin, with appeal to Augustine. Fisher is silent on Augustine's treatment of the Donatists (*History of Christian Doctrine*, 176, 179; on the Pelagian controversy, 183–97).

17. Smith, "Doctrinal History," 1851, Hastings notes (S5, B1, F3, N, 91–116; "Theology," unspecified course, 1861–1862, Briggs notes (Briggs Papers, S8, B34, F5, N2, Division 3, chap. 2).

18. Smith, "Provisions of Redemption," 1860–1861 (S4, B1, F19, chap. 3, Appendix); *System of Christian Theology*, 312 (edited by a former student, based largely on lectures from 1857).

19. Smith, "Doctrinal History," 1851, Hastings notes (S5, B1, F3, 115–16, 96).

20. Smith, "Doctrinal History," 1851, Hastings notes (S5, B1, F3, 94, 95 100); "Problem of the Philosophy of History," 5; "Systematic Theology," 12/14/1857; 3/11/1858 (S4, B1, F10, F14).

21. Hitchcock, "Church History: Second Period," 1883–1884, Burrell notes (B1, N2, 55, 54); "Church History: Second Period," 1872–1873, Jackson notes (Jackson Papers, B1, N2, 47–48); "Church History: First Period," early 1880s, Burrell notes (B1, N1, 274).

22. Schaff, "Pelagian Controversy," 206–8, 222, 234, 236; *History* III: 787, 789, 812; "Church History," MTS, summer 1855, Russell notes (LTS, B4, F03, N, 53).

23. Schaff, *History* III: 811; "Church History," MTS, summer 1855, Russell notes (LTS, B4, F03, N, 53); "Pelagian Controversy," 234–35.

24. Schaff, "Genius and Theology," 116, 120n. Schaff associated Pelagianism with a monastic, legalistic tendency ("Pelagian Controversy," 207, 243). Schaff's churchly stance contrasts with American notions of "rugged individualism" (Graham, *Cosmos in the Chaos*, 231–32).

25. Miller, "Lecture Notes on Mosheim, Cent. V, no. II," 3/11/1814 (B5, F14, 2–3); "Ecclesiastical History, Second Class," 1842–1843 (B24, F4, 5); Schaff, *History*, III: 1020–21.

26. Schaff, *Saint Augustine, Melanchthon, Neander*, 98. Schaff cited the claim perhaps wrongly attributed to Augustine, "*Roma locuta est, causa finita est.*"

27. Schaff, *Life and Labors*, 115; *History* III: 833–34, 848–49n.2, 1002, 1020; "Prolegomena: St. Augustin's [*sic*] Life and Work," 15, 17, 18. The church of Augustine's era did not exist in a "golden age of untroubled purity": that will obtain only post-resurrection (*Life and Labors*, 56; *Saint Augustine, Melanchthon, Neander*, 42).

28. Smith, "Reformed Churches of Europe and America," 17; "Calvin," *New American Cyclopaedia*, ed. Ripley and Dana, IV: 283.

29. Schaff, "Pelagian Controversy," 242.

30. Hitchcock, "Church History: Second Period," 1883–1884, Burrell notes (B1, N2, 57).

31. Smith, "Doctrinal History," 1851, Hastings notes (S5, B1, F3, 106); Schaff, "Pelagian Controversy," 225. See above, Chapter 8.

32. For discussion, see Clark, *Origenist Controversy*, 232–44 passim.

33. For the controversy between Old School and New School Presbyterians over the New Haven Theology, see above, Chapter 1. Henry Smith considered all disputants in error (*System of Christian Theology*, 309–12).

34. Schaff, "Infant Salvation,"1 (their damnation is merely a privation of bliss). Schaff softens the 418 Council of Carthage's decree on infant damnation: the clause is not present in all manuscripts ("Pelagian Controversy," 241). Schaff worked to erase

this implication from the Westminster Confession ("Plea for the Revision of the Westminster Confession," 43–44). James Turner calls infant damnation "the soft underbelly of Calvinism" (*Without God, Without Creed*, 90–91).

35. Schaff to George Prentiss, Lake Mohonk, 9/17/1891, cited in Prentiss, *Bright Side* II: 419–20.

36. Smith, "Systematic Theology," 10/1871–3/1872, Jackson notes (Jackson Papers, B1, N, 79); Calvin gave a better elaboration.

37. Schaff, *Life and Labors*, 139–40; *Theological Propaedeutic* II: 367–68 (naming Calvinists, Jansenists, and Puritans); *Saint Augustine, Melanchthon, Neander*, 105.

38. Hitchcock, "Church History: Second Period," 1873, Jackson notes (Jackson Papers, B1, N2, 46); Schaff, "Pelagian Controversy," 228; *History* III: 833–34.

39. Smith, "Systematic Theology," 2/1858 (S4, B1, F14); Schaff, "Pelagian Controversy," 228.

40. Smith, *System of Christian Theology*, 292–93.

41. Schaff considered the *Confessions* "the most interesting and edifying autobiography ever written"; "A more honest book was never written. He conceals nothing, he palliates nothing"—a comment revealing Schaff's discomfort with any hermeneutic of suspicion. See *Life and Labors*, 107, 109; "Church History," MTS, summer 1855, Russell notes (LTS, B4, F03, N, 32). Schaff notes that W. G. T. Shedd's 1860 edition of the *Confessions* is almost word for word taken from Pusey's revision of Watts's translation (*History* III: 1005 and n.3).

42. Schaff, *Saint Augustine, Melanchthon, Neander*, 20.

43. Schaff, *Life and Labors*, 129, 128; *Saint Augustine, Melanchthon, Neander*, 87; "Genius and Theology," 110.

44. Schaff, *History* III: 1001, 1001n.1, 1002; "General Introduction to the Old Testament Scriptures," UTS, 1877 or 1878 (?), Gillett notes (UTS, B3, "Miscellaneous," N, 112).

45. Schaff, "Genius and Theology," 103–4; "Pelagian Controversy," 221; *History* III: 818.

46. Smith, "Doctrinal History," 1851, Hastings notes (S5, B1, F3, 95). Augustine's theory lies midway between Manichean fatalism and Pelagian self-will ("Theology" [unspecified course], 1861–1862, Briggs notes [Briggs Papers, S8, B34, F5, N2, Division 3, chap. 2]). Briggs struggled to spell "Manicheism": "Manechae" is his best effort. Frederic Hedge of Harvard rather argued that Augustine's theory of human nature was Manichean to the end (*Atheism in Philosophy*, 188, 189).

47. Hitchcock, "Church History: Second Period," 1883–1884, Burrell notes (B1, N2, 55).

48. Miller [Jr.], *Life* II: 237; Miller, "Miller on Mosheim, Century V, No. II," 3/11/1814 (B5, F14, 30–31); Miller to Rev. John McElhenney, 4/15/1837, cited in Miller, jr., *Life* II: 228.

49. Miller [Jr.], *Life* I: 297–304. Miller's class notes do not suggest the broad tolerance that his son alleges.

50. Miller, "Ecclesiastical History, Second Class," 1842–1843 (B24, F4); *Utility and*

Importance of Creeds and Confessions, 77–78; "Miller on Mosheim, Century V, No. I," 3/7/1814 (B5, F13, 33–35).

51. Smith, *System of Christian Theology*, 168, 169; "Systematic Theology," 12/16/1857 (S4, B1, F10).

52. Smith, "Systematic Theology," 3/18 and 3/26/1858, 12/16/1857 (S4, B1, F10, F 15).

53. Smith, *System of Christian Theology*, 168.

54. The Ely Foundation was established as a gift to Union Seminary by Zebulon Stiles Ely in 1865 for lectures on "Evidences of Christianity"; he broadened the scope in 1879. For Smith's proposed lectures, see "Outline of Professor Smith's Intended Lectures on Evolution," Appendix III in Smith, *Apologetics*, 170–94. Although the sketch is not complete, Smith apparently did not cite Darwin or Thomas Huxley; his references are to German scientists.

55. See references in [E. Smith], *Henry Boynton Smith*, 401, 404–5. Smith had given a talk on evolution to Chi Alpha; one member claimed that Smith had "mastered all that had been written from Haeckel to Huxley, and that he had his own opinion upon the subject and could give good reasons for maintaining it" (404, citing Rev. William Taylor, *The Christian at Work* [Feb. 18, 1877]).

56. Smith, "Outline," 178, 175. See Charles Hodge's response to the question "What is Darwinism? Atheism" (*What Is Darwinism?* 177).

57. Smith, "Outline," 174, 175–76, 188–89.

58. Smith, "Outline," 173, 175. Is Man only "the head of the animal kingdom"? (183).

59. Smith, "Outline," 187, 186. Proponents of an older Baconian notion of science objected that the theory of evolution was merely a "hypothesis"—misconstruing what "hypothesis" meant to scientists such as Darwin. Why did Smith, so familiar with German philosophy, now resort to Bacon (whose principles he had taught at Amherst)?

60. Smith, "Outline," 186. Here Smith has a point: Mendel's demonstration of genetic transfer, some decades earlier, had not yet been appropriated by scientists.

61. Smith, "Outline," 181. The battle is one between matter and mind (177).

62. Smith, "Outline," 191, 192, 194. Christianity, not science, gives the answers.

63. Smith, "Doctrinal History," 1851, Hastings notes (S5, B1, F3, 104–5); *System of Christian Theology*, 307; "Systematic Theology," 3/19/1858 (S4, B1, F15). The "federal" view, that Adam "represented" humanity, was popular with Princetonians.

64. Smith, "Systematic Theology," 1855–1856, Quick notes (S5, B1, F4, N2, 181); *System of Christian Theology*, 299 ("Ethical" theories that emphasize the individual, not the race, lag behind natural science [320]); "Systematic Theology," 3/26/1858 (S4, B1, F15).

65. Smith, "Systematic Theology," 3/18/1858 (S4, B1, F15); *System of Christian Theology*, 319, 286, 290; "Doctrinal History," 1851, Hastings notes (S5, B1, F3, 102). This view contrasts with that of the seventeenth-century Synod of Dort (Christ came to save only the elect).

66. Smith, "Theology" [unspecified course], 1861–1863, Briggs notes (Briggs Papers, B35, F6, N2, 18).

67. Smith, *System of Christian Theology*, 284–85, 306n.1. For an encyclopedia explanation contemporary with the discussions here reported, see "Imputation," in *Cyclopaedia*, ed. McClintock and Strong, IV: 524–27. I thank Mark Noll and Grant Wacker for help with this point.

68. Smith, "Systematic Theology," 3/19/1858 (S4, B1, F15); *System of Christian Theology*, 283–85, 290, 305, 306, 307.

69. Smith, "Systematic Theology," 3/11/1858 (S4, B1, F14); *System of Theology*, 287, citing "Edwards, vol. ii, p. 309." The definition is given in Edwards's posthumously published treatise, "Christian Doctrine of Original Sin Defended."

70. Smith, *System of Christian Theology*, 308, 287; "Theological System of Emmons," in Smith, *Faith and Philosophy*, 215–63, at 222—but for Smith this moral framework does not center on "man."

71. Smith, "Systematic Theology," 3/18–19 and 3/11/1858, 11/30/1857 (S4, B1, F15, F14, F8); *System of Christian Theology*, 287, 285, 316, 290.

72. Prentiss, *Bright Side* II: 404, citing material he found in Smith's papers. "Decrees": the decrees of predestination. German evangelical theology was distinguished by its Christocentrism (Graham, *Cosmos in the Chaos*, 97).

73. Smith, "Theological System of Emmons," in Smith, *Faith and Philosophy*, 250–51, 224. For New England Theology's critique of older Calvinism, see Holifield, *Theology in America*, chap. 17; on Calvinism's decline, see Haroutunian, *Piety Versus Moralism*.

74. Smith, "Theological System of Emmons," in Smith, *Faith and Philosophy*, 226, 252–53.

75. Smith, "Theological System of Emmons," in Smith, *Faith and Philosophy*, 248, 242, 215–16. Emmons (Smith held) lacked a psychology that would give "a real human substratum to the volitions" (256). Kuklick considers Smith's essay "one of the most acute critical essays produced by a nineteenth-century American theologian," showing "the scholastic dead end to which the New England Theology had come" (*Churchmen and Philosophers*, 212).

76. Smith, "Theological System of Emmons," in Smith, *Faith and Philosophy*, 263.

77. Smith, *System of Christian Theology*, 318, 322–23, 289; emphasis added (Augustine to the contrary: *On the Soul* 3.9.14; *Against Two Letters of the Pelagians* 1.40).

78. Holifield, *Theology in America*, 368–69.

79. Smith, *System of Christian Theology*, 290, 320.

80. Fisher, "Augustinian and Federal Theories," 470–71, 511, 513, 486. In legal analogy, Adam stands as "agent" to all other humans, his "principal" (471); some seventeenth-century theologians mixed Augustinian views with a notion of covenant (491, 494). Fisher likely wrote the article defending the New England Theology against Princetonians ("'The Princeton Review' on the Theology of Dr. N. W. Taylor").

81. Fisher, "Augustinian and Federal Theories," 501–3, 507, 508. Turretin's *Insti-*

tutes of Eclectic Theology was replaced at Princeton only late in the nineteenth century by Charles Hodge's *Systematic Theology*. On New Haven Theology, see Kuklick, *Churchmen and Philosophers*, chap. 7.

82. Fisher, "Augustinian and Federal Theories," 472.

83. Fisher, "Augustinian and Federal Theories," 474–75. Fisher blames Tertullian for giving Traducianism such a materialistic turn that Augustine rejected it. Fisher cites from Augustine's letter to Jerome (*Letter* 166 [Fisher writes 165]).

84. Fisher, "Augustinian and Federal Theories," 486, 490 (capitalized in original), 513, 516.

85. Fisher, "Augustinian and Federal Theories," 514–15, 501, 477. See, e.g., Pelagius, *Letter to Demetrias* 16.

86. Hitchcock, "Church History: Second Period," 1872–1873, Jackson notes (Jackson Papers, B1, N1, 162).

87. Hitchcock, "Church History: First Period," 1872, Jackson notes (Jackson Papers, B1, N1, 147–49).

88. Hitchcock, "Church History: First Period," 1872, Jackson notes (Jackson Papers, B1, N1, 63). Hitchcock seems mistaken in stressing the "invisible" nature of the church for most Donatists (Tyconius excepted).

89. Hitchcock, "Church History: First Period," 1872, Jackson notes (Jackson Papers, B1, N1, 63); "Church History: Second Period," 1883–1884, Burrell notes (B1, N2, 57), citing *On Baptism* 5.38.

90. Hitchcock, "Church History: Second Period," 1873, Jackson notes (Jackson Papers, B1, N2, 68), no reference given.

91. Hitchcock, "Church History: Second Period," 1883–1884, Burrell notes (B1, N2, 57). On this point, the East is deemed better than the West.

92. Hitchcock, "Church History: Second Period," 1883–1884, Burrell notes (B1, N2, 58). Hitchcock failed to note that Augustine "eulogized" marriage long before he entered into debate with Pelagians; see *On Holy Virginity* and *On Holy Marriage*. Like other Protestants, Hitchcock denied the sacramental status of marriage, while—somewhat paradoxically—accusing Catholics of underestimating its sanctity. Moreover, Augustine's views on purgatory presumably gave impetus to the idea of penance as a sacrament: see Hitchcock, "Church History: Second Period," 1873, Jackson notes (Jackson Papers, B1, N2, 75: Augustine put the "purifying fire" into Hades); similarly, "Church History: Second Period" 1883–1884, Burrell notes (B1, N2, 59).

93. Hitchcock, "Church History: Second Period," 1873, Jackson notes (Jackson Papers, B1, N2, 69–70); "Church History: Second Period," 1883–1884, Burrell notes (B1, N2, 58). In anti-Donatist writings, Augustine argued that God can "make up for" the non-receipt of baptism, if that were unavoidable, e.g., the case of the thief on the cross.

94. Hitchcock, "Church History: Second Period" 1873, Jackson notes (Jackson Papers, B1, N2, 57, 68); Augustine's anthropology was not so distinctively "western" as Pelagius' was "eastern."

95. For a fuller exposition of this topic, see my essay "Augustine, Adam, and the Sons of Noah: Race Theory in Nineteenth-Century America," in *Augustine in America*, ed. Otten et al., forthcoming.

96. Hitchcock, "History of the World Before Christ," 1862, Wright notes (B2, N1). Hitchcock did not abandon the Mosaic authorship of the Pentateuch, but informed his students that a theory (the "documentary hypothesis") "denies Moses' authorship."

97. Helpful modern studies of nineteenth-century race theory: Stanton, *Leopard's Spots*; Van Riper, *Men Among the Mammoths*; Stocking, *Race, Culture, and Evolution*; Gossett, *Race*. We may speculate that Augustine himself, writing the *City of God* after the Gothic sack of Rome in 410, was less keen than Hitchcock on Teutons.

98. Hitchcock, "Church History: Second Period," 1883–1884, Burrell notes (B1, N2, 48). For Schaff, the *City of God* is "still worth reading" (*History* III: 1010).

99. Hitchcock, "Sermon Delivered at the Dedication of the New Chapel," 18. Hitchcock mentions geologist Georges Cuvier: he can construct an animal from a single bone ("History of the World Before Christ," 1862, Wright notes [B2, N1, "General Survey"]).

100. Hitchcock, "History of the World Before Christ," 1862, Wright notes (B2, N1). Elsewhere, Hitchcock told students that geology teaches that the earth is between 70 and 100 million years old ("Life of Christ," early 1880s, Burrell notes (B1, N1, 11), assuming a long period between the creation of matter and the first humans' appearance. Lengthening the "days" of the Genesis account was familiar from the late eighteenth century; see Comte de Buffon, *Des Époques de la Nature* [1778], in Buffon, *Oeuvres complètes* 9, and discussion in Haber, *Age of the World*, 114–23.

101. Hitchcock, "History of the World Before Christ," 1862, Wright notes (B2, N1). Hitchcock does not cite specific passages; see Augustine, *On Genesis According to the Letter* 4.1.1–4.2.6, 5.1.1–5.3.6; *City of God* 11.30–31.

102. Hitchcock, "Laws of Civilization" [pamphlet version], 8, 11–12, 14; "History of the World Before Christ," 1862, Wright notes (B2, N1).

103. Hitchcock, "History of the World Before Christ," 1862, Wright notes (B2, N1, "The Abode in Egypt"). Hitchcock rejected the polygenism of Harvard naturalist Louis Agassiz, which posited multiple sites for human origins. Agassiz, Hitchcock objected, would need "at least fifteen Adams" to account for human diversity. See Agassiz's essay, "Of the Natural Provinces of the Animal World and Their Relation to the Different Types of Man," prefacing Nott and Gliddon, *Types of Mankind*, lviii-lxxvi.

104. Hitchcock, "Laws of Civilization," 11, 12.

105. Hitchcock, "Church History: Second Period" 1873, Jackson notes (Jackson Papers, B1, N2, 58); "Laws of Civilization," 8; Hitchcock, "History of the World Before Christ," 1862, Wright notes (B2, N1).

106. Hitchcock, "Laws of Civilization," 5, 7.

107. Hitchcock, "Laws of Civilization," 5.

108. Hitchcock, "Laws of Civilization," 8—against Pantheists, Humanitarians, and Materialists, who consider barbarism the "primitive estate of man" (4).

109. Hitchcock, "Laws of Civilization," 8. Hitchcock urged students to reject a purely moral or symbolical interpretation of the Fall, as posited by some German scholars ("History of the World Before Christ," 1862, Wright notes [B2, N1]).

110. Cf. Augustine's claim that we cannot imagine the passionless sex that could have occurred in the Garden of Eden if Adam and Eve had not sinned (*City of God* 14.23, 26).

111. Hitchcock, "History of the World Before Christ" 1862, Wright notes (B2, N1, "Primeval Civilization": 33 sons and 27 daughters); Augustine, *City of God* 15.8.

112. For Augustine, the sons of the City of God lusted after women of the wicked, earthly city, descended from Cain (*City of God* 15.22–23); Hitchcock, "History of the World Before Christ," 1862, Wright notes (B2, N1, "The Deluge"): perhaps a warning to young men who might soon contemplate marriage?

113. Hitchcock, "Laws of Civilization," 18, 10, 8, 15. Hitchcock also believed that the Shemitic race was prone to mysticism, which eventually entered Christianity through the influence of the Orient ("History of the World Before Christ," 1862, Wright notes [B2, N1]).

114. Hitchcock, "History of the World Before Christ," 1862, Wright notes (B2, N1); "Laws of Civilization," 15. The success of Japheth's line shows that the last can be first (while the first, represented by Ham, can end last).

115. Hitchcock, "Early Church History: Second Period," 1883–1884, Burrell notes (B1, N 2, 20); "Church History: Second Period," 1873, Jackson notes (Jackson Papers, B1, N2, 54).

116. Hitchcock, "Laws of Civilization," 9.

117. Hitchcock, "Church History: First Period," early 1880s, Burrell notes (B1, N1, 274); "Church History: Second Period," 1883, Moore notes (B2, N2, 352); "Church History: Second Period," 1883–1884, Burrell notes (B1, N2, 54); "Church History: First Period," 1873, Jackson notes (Jackson Papers, B1, N1, 141).

118. Hitchcock, "Church History: First Period," 1873, Jackson notes (Jackson Papers, B1, N1, 141); "Church History: Second Period," 1883, Moore notes (B2, N 2, 355); "Church History: Second Period," 1873, Jackson notes (Jackson Papers, B1, N2, 58); "Distinguishing Features of Christianity," 97.

119. For a detailed study of Schaff's views on religious freedom in the modern world, see Graham, *Cosmos in the Chaos*.

120. Schaff argued that the term "religious liberty" (a God-given right) is preferable to "toleration," which only begrudgingly grants what it would prefer not to allow: *Progress of Religious Freedom*, 1; *Church and State in the United States*, 14 (the "progress of history is a progress of freedom" [82]); for Europe, by contrast, see Schaff, "State Church System in Europe"; also see "Genius and Theology," 115; cf. *History* III: 21: "incalculable mischief."

121. For Schaff's organization of the first conference of the Evangelical Alliance to

be held on American shores, see Minutes of the Executive Committee of the American Evangelical Alliance, 12/21/1868, 1/15/1869 (Evangelical Alliance Papers, B2, N, 8, 10–11, 15). For a detailed account, see Jordan, *Evangelical Alliance*.

122. Schaff, *Church and State*, 9, 94. Schaff was less interested in protecting Muslims' freedom: he hoped for the speedy demise of Islam, to be replaced by Protestantism. Some force might have to be exerted by Russia and England to bring down the Ottoman Empire. However selfish Russia's motives, she is Providence's agent to defeat Turkey and Islam: see *Through Bible Lands*, 258, 411–12, 121, 109; and "Eastern Conflict," *New York Observer*, June 14, 1877 (written from Istanbul, May 11, 1877).

123. Schaff, "Savonarola," 333–61.

124. These themes dominate his *Church and State*, and *Progress of Religious Freedom*, chap. 7. See J. F. Wilson, "Civil Authority and Religious Freedom in America," 148–67.

125. Schaff, *Bibliotheca Symbolica Ecclesiae Universalis* I: 20n.2; also see "State Church System in Europe," 158–59.

126. Schaff, *History* II: 41, 42.

127. Schaff, "Tertullian," 623.

128. Schaff, *History* II: 35; 825. Catholics prefer Tertullian's *On the Prescription of Heretics* as vindicating their understanding of the rule of faith against heretics (830n.1).

129. Schaff, *History* II: 829.

130. Schaff, *History* II: 122, 11; "Constantine the Great," 791.

131. Schaff, *History* II: 73–74.

132. Schaff, *History* III: 94 and 94n.1 (corruption and apostasy lurk "in the natural heart of man" [94–95]); "Constantine the Great," 791.

133. Schaff, "Church History," MTS, summer 1855, Russell notes (LTS, B4, Fo3, N, 3).

134. Schaff, *History* III: 30–31, 139, 13, 140.

135. Schaff, *History* III: 356, 125–26, 357; "Development of the Ancient Catholic Hierarchy: Part I," 693.

136. Schaff, *Saint Augustine, Melanchthon, Neander*, 43.

137. Schaff, *History* II: 515–16; III: 144–45, 630.

138. Schaff also names Eusebius of Nicomedia, Theognis of Nicaea, Theonas, Secundus; see "Arianism," in *New Schaff-Herzog Encyclopedia of Religious Knowledge*, ed. S. M. Jackson, I: 279. Jackson, a former UTS student and notetaker in Hitchcock's classes, here identifies himself as Professor of Church History at New York University.

139. Schaff, "Church History," MTS, summer 1855, Russell notes (LTS, B4, Fo3, N, 6); *History*, III: 39. Elsewhere, Schaff writes that Julian's having been forced into an "Arian-court" form of Christianity in his youth prompted his later rebellion ("Julian the Apostate," 1–2).

140. Schaff, "Arianism," in *New Schaff-Herzog Encyclopedia* I: 279.

141. Schaff, *History* III: 142; II: 502, 516, 36, 78–79.

142. Schaff, *History* II: 63, 386.

143. Schaff, *History* II: 122, 515–16; cf. III: 117, 144–45; D. Schaff, *Life*, 133 and Note.

144. Schaff, *History* II: 515–16; III: 117, 144–45.

145. Schaff, *History* III: 117; D. Schaff, *Life*, 133 and Note.

146. Schaff, *Saint Augustine, Melanchthon, Neander*, 98. After persecution come the damnation of unbaptized infants, the dogma of the Immaculate Conception, and the Vatican decree on papal infallibility. Schaff cites the phrase attributed to Augustine, "*Roma locuta est, causa finita est.*" In 1893, he writes that the phrase is not literally found in Augustine, and the general sentiment was referring only to the case of Pelagius (*Theological Propaedeutic* II: 368n. +).

147. McGiffert, "Modernism," in McGiffert, *Christianity as History and Faith*, ed. A. C. McGiffert, Jr., 81; "Theological Reconstruction," in Knox, McGiffert, and Brown, *Christian Point of View*, 46.

148. McGiffert, "Evolution of Christianity" (McGiffert, Jr., Papers, S2B, B2, F1–2, chap. 5, 3–4); McGiffert, *History* II: 120.

149. McGiffert, *History* II: 90. Other authors allude to Augustine's *On Genesis According to the Letter* 2.9.16 (scientific speculation, of no profit for those seeking religious blessing, takes time away from spiritually beneficial things). For critics: A. D. White, in *History of the Warfare of Science with Theology in Christendom* [1897], I: 375, argued that Christianity had arrested the development of science for over 1500 years; he cites Augustine's reservations in *Handbook* 3.9 about the value of physical science for religion—but White adds that in another context (*On Genesis According to the Letter* 1.19), Augustine claims that scientific knowledge should be taken from the pagan authors; see discussion in Lindberg and Numbers, "Beyond War and Peace," 341. White's earlier work, *The Warfare of Science* [1876] may have been known, at least by reputation, to theology professors of the era. Also known to Union Seminary professors were the views of John William Draper, who claimed that Augustine did more than any other Church Father "to bring science and religion into antagonism" (*History of the Conflict Between Religion and Science* [1875], 62–63).

150. Hodge, *What Is Darwinism?* 177. Hodge objects to Darwinism on the basis of the argument from design (52, 168), and appeals to the theories of Louis Agassiz (160). By 1911, Princeton theologians were accommodating evolutionary theory to some extent: see Benjamin B. Warfield, "On the Antiquity and the Unity of the Human Race" (1911), 1–24; cf. James McCosh, *Religious Aspect of Evolution* (1888; 1887), ix. Yet it was hard to see how Natural Selection could be reconciled with a God who loved the world and its peoples: see A.N. Wilson, *God's Funeral*, 188.

151. Attempting to support some form of evolutionary theory and appealing (in modern numbering of the text) to Augustine, *On Genesis According to the Letter* 5.4.11, 5.5.14, 5.23.44–46; *On the Trinity* 3.8.13, 3.9.16, see, among others, G. F. Wright, *Studies in Science and Religion* (1882), esp. chap. 5; Mivart, *On the Genesis of Species* (1871), 303–4; A. L. Moore, *Science and the Faith* (1892 [1889]), 175–76, 228. Augustine reconciles the Genesis 1 and 2 accounts (as did Philo) by arguing that God created everything first "in idea" and secondly in material form—a useful view for those who wished to

claim Augustine as a forerunner of evolutionary theory. Others attempting to reconcile Christianity and evolution include (in Britain) Frederick Temple, *Relations Between Religion and Science* (1884), esp. Lectures IV, VI, VIII.

Conclusion

1. J. Turner, *Without God, Without Creed*, 263.

2. See Moorhead, *American Apocalypse*, chap. 4.

3. Moorhead, *American Apocalypse*, 164; cf. C. D. Johnson, *Redeeming America*, 156–58.

4. Schaff, "Theology of Our Age and Country," in Schaff, *Christ and Christianity*, 13.

5. George Berkeley, "Prospect of Planting Arts and Learning in America," in Berkeley, *A Miscellany, Containing Several Tracts on Various Subjects* (Dublin: George Faulkner, 1972).

6. Emerton, "Definition of Church History," 57–58.

7. Schaff to A. C. McGiffert, New York, 12/18/1889; 2/14/1890, cited in McGiffert, Jr., "Making of an American Scholar," 40.

8. Henry Adams, *Education of Henry Adams*, 390.

BIBLIOGRAPHY
OF MODERN WORKS

For archival sources, see List of Abbreviations and Archival Sources.

"About Church History." *Baltimore American & Commercial Advertiser*, June 30, 1889.

Adams, Henry. *The Education of Henry Adams: A Centennial Version*. Ed. Edward Henry Chalfant and Conrad Edick Wright. Boston: Massachusetts Historical Society, 2007.

Adams, Herbert Baxter. "History in American Colleges, I: History at Harvard University." *Education* 6 (May 1886): 535–47.

———. "History in American Colleges, II: History at Harvard University." *Education* 6 (June 1886): 618–33.

———. "History in American Colleges, III: History at Columbia College." *Education* 6 (Sept. 1886): 7–14.

———. "History in American Colleges, IV: History in Columbia College." *Education* 6 (Oct. 1886): 92–100.

———. "History in American Colleges, V: History at Amherst and Columbia Colleges." *Education* 7 (Nov. 1886): 177–187.

———. "History in American Colleges, VI: History in Yale University." *Education* 7 (Jan. 1887): 334–344.

———. *Methods of Historical Study*. Johns Hopkins University Studies in Historical and Political Science. 2nd ser. 2: Institutions and Economics. Baltimore: Johns Hopkins University Press, Jan.–Feb. 1884.

———. *Seminary Libraries and University Extension*. Johns Hopkins University Studies in Historical and Political Science. 5th ser. 11 (Nov. 1887). Baltimore: N. Murray; Johns Hopkins University, 1887.

Adams, William. "A Discourse on the Life and Services of Prof. Moses Stuart." New York: J.F. Trow, 1852.

Agassiz, Louis. "Of the Natural Provinces of the Animal World and Their Relation to the Different Types of Man." Preface to *Types of Mankind: or, Ethnological Researches based upon the Ancient Monuments, Paintings, Sculptures, and Crania of Races*, by J. C. Nott and George R. Gliddon, lviii–lxxvi. 1854. 6th ed. Philadelphia: Lippincott, Grambo; London: Trübner, 1854.

Ahlstrom, Sydney E. "The Middle Period (1840–80)." In *Harvard Divinity School*, ed. Williams, 78–147.

Albanese, Catherine L. *A Republic of Mind and Spirit: A Cultural History of American Metaphysical Religion.* New Haven, Conn.: Yale University Press, 2007.

Albisetti, James C. "German Influence on the Higher Education of American Women, 1865–1914." In *German Education*, ed. Geitz et al., 227–44.

Allen, Joseph Henry. *Christian History in Its Three Great Periods. First Period: Early Christianity.* 1883. 5th ed. Boston: Roberts Brothers, 1894.

———. "Christian Thought of the Second Century." *Unitarian Review* (Nov. 1878): 538–53.

———. *On the Study of Christian History.* Reprint pamphlet. N.p., n.p., 1878.

———. *Outlines of Christian History A.D. 50–1880.* Boston: Roberts Brothers, 1886.

———. *Positive Religion: Essays, Fragments, and Hints.* Boston: Roberts Brothers, 1891.

———. *Ten Discourses on Orthodoxy.* 1849. 2nd ed. Boston: American Unitarian Association, 1889.

"American College Libraries." *PQPR* 3.12 (Oct. 1874): 714–23.

Angell, James B. "Religious Life in Our State Universities." *AR* 13.76 (April 1890): 365–72.

[Anonymous] [tribute to Roswell D. Hitchcock]. *New-York Evangelist*, Jul7 7, 1887.

Arnold, Thomas. *Higher Schools and Universities in Germany.* 1868. 2nd ed. London: Macmillan, 1882.

Aron, Cindy S. "The Evolution of the Middle Class." In *A Companion to 19th-Century America*, ed. Barney, 178–91.

Bainton, Roland H. "Yale and German Theology in the Middle of the Nineteenth Century." *ZKG* 4th ser. 66.3 (1954–1955): 294–302.

———. *Yale and the Ministry: A History of Education for the Christian Ministry at Yale from the Founding in 1701.* New York: Harper & Brothers, 1957.

Baird, Robert. *Religion in America; or, An Account of the Origin, Relation to the State, and Present Condition of the Evangelical Churches in the United States.* 1844. New York: Harper & Brothers, 1856.

Barnard, Frederick A. P. "Report: Changes in the Curriculum. June 6, 1870." In *The Rise of a University.* vol. 1, *The Later Days of Old Columbia College*, ed. William F. Russell, 66–92. New York: Columbia University Press, 1937.

Barney, William L., ed. *A Companion to 19th-Century America.* Malden, Mass.: Blackwell, 2001.

Barr, David L. and Nicholas Piediscalzi, eds. *The Bible in American Education: From Source Book to Textbook.* Philadelphia: Fortress, 1982.

Barth, Karl. *Protestant Thought from Rousseau to Ritschl.* Trans. Brian Cozens et al. 1947. New York: Harper & Brothers, 1959.

Bascom, John. "Atheism in Colleges." *NAR* 132.290 (1881): 32–40.

Baur, Ferdinand Christian. "Beiträge zur Erklärung der Korinthierbriefe. I: Der Zusammenhang von Kapitel 7. mit 5, 1. f.-6, 20." *Theologische Jahrbücher* 11.1 (1852): 1–40.

———."Beiträge zur Erklärung der Korinthierbriefe. VI: Die Frauen der korinthischen Gemeinde und die Schleiersymbolik des Apostels, 1 Kor. 11, 2–16." *Theologische Jahrbücher* 12.4 (1853): 535–74.

———. "Die Christuspartei in der korinthischen Gemeinde." *Tübinger Zeitschrift für Theologie* 4 (1831): 61–206.

———. *The Church History of the First Three Centuries.* 1853. Trans. Allan Menzies. 2 vols. 3rd ed. London: Williams and Norgate, 1878.

———. *The Epochs of Church Historiography.* 1852. In Baur, *Ferdinand Christian Baur on the Writing of Church History*, 43–366.

———. *Ferdinand Christian Baur on the Writing of Church History* [*The Epochs of Church Historiography*]. Trans. Peter C. Hodgson. New York: Oxford University Press, 1968.

———. *Die ignatianischen Briefe und ihr neuester Kritiker: Eine Streitschrift gegen Herrn Bunsen.* Tübingen: Fues, 1848.

———. *Kritische Untersuchungen über die kanonischen Evangelien.* Tübingen: Fues, 1847.

———. *Paul, the Apostle of Jesus Christ, His Life and Works, His Epistles and His Doctrine: A Contribution to a Critical History of Primitive Christianity.* Ed. Eduard Zeller, trans. Allan Menzies. 1845. 2nd ed. London: Williams and Norgate, 1876.

———. *Die sogenannten Pastoralbriefe des Apostels Paulus.* Stuttgart and Tübingen: J.G. Cotta, 1835.

———. *Die Tübinger Schule und ihre Stellung zur Gegenwart.* Tübingen: Fues, 1859.

Beckert, Sven. *The Monied Metropolis: New York City and the Consolidation of the American Bourgeoisie, 1850–1896.* New York: Cambridge University Press, 2001.

Beecher, Henry W. "The Progress of Thought in the Church." *NAR* 135 (1882): 99–117.

Bellows, Henry W. "An Appeal on Behalf of the Further Endowment of the Divinity School of Harvard University, To Which Are Added Statements by Charles W. Eliot . . . and By the Faculty of the School." Cambridge, Mass.: John Wilson and Son, 1879.

———. "The Break Between Modern Thought and Ancient Faith." In *Christianity and Modern Thought*, 3–31.

Bender, Thomas. *New York Intellect: A History of Intellectual Life in New York City, from 1750 to the Beginnings of Our Own Time.* New York: Knopf, 1987.

Bendroth, Margaret Lamberts. *A School of the Church: Andover Newton Across Two Centuries.* Grand Rapids, Mich.: Eerdmans, 2008.

Bentinck-Smith, William, and Elizabeth Stouffer. *Harvard University History of Named Chairs; Sketches of Donors and Donations.* Cambridge, Mass.: Secretary to the University/University Publisher, 1995.

Billington, Ray Allen. *The Protestant Crusade 1800–1860: A Study of the Origins of American Nativism.* New York: Macmillan, 1938.

Bingham, Joseph. *Origines Ecclesiasticae: The Antiquities of the Christian Church.* 1708–1722. London: Henry G. Bohn, 1846.

Binkley, Luther J. *The Mercersburg Theology*. Franklin and Marshall College Studies 7. Manheim, Pa.: Sentinel Printing House, 1953.

Bödeker, Hans Erich, et al., eds. *Aufklärung und Geschichte: Studien zur Geschichtswissenschaft im 18. Jahrhundert*. Göttingen: Vandenhoeck & Ruprecht, 1986.

Booth, Mary L. *History of the City of New York from Its Earliest Settlement to the Present Time*. New York: W.R.C. Clarke, 1860.

Bowden, Henry Warner, ed. *A Century of Church History: The Legacy of Philip Schaff*. Carbondale: Southern Illinois University Press, 1988.

————. *Church History in the Age of Science: Historiographical Patterns in the United States 1876–1918*. Chapel Hill: University of North Carolina Press, 1971.

————. "The First Century: Institutional Development and Ideas about the Profession." In *A Century of Church History*, ed. Bowden, 294–332.

Bowen, William G., and Harold T. Shapiro. "Foreword" to *The Sacred and the Secular University*, ed. Roberts and Turner, ix–x.

Brakke, David. "The Early Church in North America: Late Antiquity, Theory, and the History of Christianity." *CH* 71.3 (Sept. 2002): 473–91.

Braude, Ann. "Women's History *Is* American Religious History." In *Retelling U.S. Religious History*, ed. Tweed, 87–107.

Brekus, Catherine A. "Interpreting American Religion." In *A Companion to 19th-Century America*, ed. Barney, 317–33.

A Brief Account of the Rise, Progress and Present State of the Theological Seminary of the Presbyterian Church in the United States at Princeton. Philadelphia: A. Finley, 1822.

Briggs, Charles A. "Our Book Table: Teaching of the Twelve Apostles." *New-York Evangelist*, July 16, 1885.

————. "Theological Education and Its Needs." *Forum* 12 (Jan. 1892): 634–45.

Bristed, C. A. *Five Years in an English University*. 1852. 3rd ed. New York: G.P. Putnam, 1873.

Bronson, Walter C. *The History of Brown University, 1764–1914*. Providence, R.I.: Brown University, 1914.

Brown, Candy Gunther. *The Word in the World: Evangelical Writing, Publishing and Reading in America, 1789–1880*. Chapel Hill: University of North Carolina Press, 2004.

Brown, Francis. "Internal Development and Expansion of the Seminary Since 1886." In Prentiss, *The Union Theological Seminary*, 339–45.

————. "The Seminary and Scholarship." In *The Seminary: Its Spirit and Aims*, 9–15.

Brown, Jerry Wayne. *The Rise of Biblical Criticism in America, 1800–1870: The New England Scholars*. Middletown, Conn.: Wesleyan University Press, 1969.

Buckle, Henry Thomas. *History of Civilization in England*. 1857, 1861. 2 vols. New York: D. Appleton, 1870.

Bunsen, Christian K. J. *Die drei ächten und die vier unächten Briefe des Ignatius von Antiochen*. Hamburg: Verlag der Agentur des Rauhen Hauses, 1847.

————. *Hippolytus and His Age; or, the Beginnings and Prospects of Christianity*. 1853.

2 vols. No trans. listed. 2nd ed. London: Longman, Brown, Green, and Longmans, 1854.

Burgess, John W. *Reminiscences of an American Scholar: The Beginnings of Columbia University*. New York: Columbia University Press, 1934.

Burrows, Edwin G., and Mike Wallace. *Gotham: A History of New York City to 1898*. New York: Oxford University Press, 1999.

Burton, Vernon. "Civil War and Reconstruction, 1861–1867." In *A Companion to 19th-Century America*, ed. Barney, 47–60.

Bushnell, Horace. *Christian Nurture*. New York: Scribner's, 1861.

———. "The Evangelical Alliance." *NE* 5.17 (Jan. 1847): 102–26.

Butler, Nicholas Murray. "Introduction" to Friedrich Paulsen, *German Universities*, ix–xxxi.

———. "On Permitting Students to Take Studies in Professional Schools While Pursuing a Regular Undergraduate Course." *ER* 3 (Jan. 1892): 54–58.

———. "Report: The Education of Women." In *The Rise of a University*, ed. Edward C. Elliott, vol. 2, *The University in Action*, 189–91. New York: Columbia University Press, 1937.

Cairns, John. *Oxford Rationalism and English Christianity*. 2nd ed. London: William Freeman, ca. 1860.

Carter, Paul. *The Spiritual Crisis of the Gilded Age*. DeKalb: Northern Illinois University Press, 1971.

Cashdollar, Charles D. "Auguste Comte and the American Reformed Theologians." *Journal of the History of Ideas* 39.1 (Jan.–March 1978): 61–79.

———. *The Transformation of Theology, 1830–1890: Positivism and Protestant Thought in Britain and America*. Princeton, N.J.: Princeton University Press, 1989.

Catholicity and Reason: A Few Considerations on Essays and Reviews. London: J. and C. Mozley, 1861.

Chamberlain, Joshua L., ed. *Universities and Their Sons: New York University: Its History, Influence, Equipment and Characteristics*. 2 vols. Boston: R. Herndon, 1901, 1903.

"The Charge and Inaugural Address on the Occasion of the Inauguration of Roswell D. Hitchcock into the Washburn Professorship of Church History in the Union Theological Seminary, New York." May 6, 1856. New York: J.F. Trow, 1856.

Cherry, Conrad. *Hurrying Toward Zion: Universities, Divinity Schools, and American Protestantism*. Bloomington: Indiana University Press, 1995.

Chesnut, Glen F. "A Century of Patristic Studies." In *A Century of Church History*, ed. Bowden, 36–73.

"Christian Socialism." *Springfield Republican*, May 13, 1886.

Chorley, E. Clowes. *Men and Movements in the American Episcopal Church*. New York: Scribner's, 1950.

Christianity and Modern Thought. Boston: American Unitarian Association, 1873.

"Church History." Review of Philip Schaff, *History of the Christian Church*, vols. 2 and 3. *APTR* 5.18 (April 1867): 338–39.

Clark, Elizabeth A. "Augustine, the Sons of Noah, and Race in Nineteenth-Century North America." In *Augustine in America*, ed. Willemien Otten, Karla Pollman, and Mark Vessey. Washington, D.C.: Catholic University of America Press. Forthcoming.

———. "Contested Bodies: Early Christian Asceticism and Nineteenth-Century Polemics." *JECS* 17.2 (2009): 281–307.

———. "From Patristics to Early Christian Studies." In *The Oxford Handbook of Early Christian Studies*, ed. Susan Ashbrook Harvey and David G. Hunter, 7–41. Oxford: Oxford University Press, 2008.

———. "Happiness in Hell, Virtue in the Middle State: The Church Fathers and Some Nineteenth-Century Debates." In *Studia Patristica* 48, 403–13. Papers from 2007 Oxford International Patristics Conference. Leuven: Peeters, 2010.

———. *The Origenist Controversy: The Cultural Construction of an Early Christian Debate*. Princeton, N.J.: Princeton University Press, 1992.

Cochoni, Christian. *Origines apostoliques du célibat sacerdotal*. Paris: Lethielleux, 1981.

Colenso, John William. *The Pentateuch and Book of Joshua Critically Examined*. 7 vols. London: Longman, Green, Longman, Roberts & Green, 1862–1879.

Comey, Arthur M. "Growth of the Colleges of the United States." *ER* 3 (Feb. 1892): 120–31.

Committee of the Board of Directors [of Princeton Theological Seminary]. "A Modern School of the Prophets: The Theological Seminary of the Presbyterian Church in the United States of America, Princeton, New Jersey." Pamphlet, n.p., 1910 (?).

Conser, Walter H., Jr. *Church and Confession: Conservative Theologians in Germany, England, and America 1815–1866*. Macon, Ga.: Mercer University Press, 1984.

Coulter, John M. "The University Spirit." *ER* 4 (Nov. 1892): 366–71.

Coxe, Arthur Cleveland. *Apology for the Common English Bible and A Review of the Extraordinary Changes Made in It By Managers of the American Bible Society*. 3rd ed. Baltimore: Joseph Robinson, 1857.

———. *Christian Ballads*. 1840. Rev. ed. New York: D. Appleton, 1865.

———. *The Criterion: A Means of Distinguishing Truth from Error in Questions of the Times. With Four Letters on the Eirenicon of Dr. Pusey*. New York: H.B. Durand, 1866.

———. *Impressions of England; or, Sketches of English Scenery and Society*. New York: Dana and Company, 1856.

———. "Introduction" to John Baptist von Hirscher, *Sympathies of the Continent*. Oxford: John Henry Parker, 1852.

Cunningham, Francis. "Translator's Preface." In J. C. L. Gieseler, *Text-Book of Ecclesiastical History*, iii.

Cureton, William. *The Ancient Syriac Version of the Epistles of Saint Ignatius*. London: Rivington, 1845.

———. *Corpus Ignatianum*. London: Rivington, 1849.

———. *Vindiciae Ignatianae*. London: Rivington, 1846.

"Current Notes: Prof. Henry B. Smith as Editor, and His Successor" [Contributions by Lyman H. Atwater and J. M. Sherwood]. *PQPR* 6.22 (April 1877): 344–50.

Curti, Merle, and Vernon Carstensen. *The University of Wisconsin 1848–1925*. 2 vols. Madison: University of Wisconsin Press, 1949.

Curtis, Bruce. *William Graham Sumner*. Twayne's United States Authors Series. Boston: Twayne, 1981.

"D." "Dr. Schaff's Second Trial for Heresy." *Reformed Church Messenger* 66.40 (Oct. 6, 1898): 2–3

D'Agostino, Peter R. *Rome in America: Transnational Catholic Ideology from the Risorgimento to Fascism*. Chapel Hill: University of North Carolina Press, 2004.

Dahlberg-Acton, John Emerich Edward. "German Schools of History." 1886. In Dahlberg-Acton, *Historical Essays & Studies*, ed. John Neville Figgis and Reginald Vere Laurence, 344–92. London: Macmillan, 1907.

Dall, Caroline. *Transcendentalism in New England: A Lecture*. Boston: Roberts Brothers, 1897.

Day, Jeremiah. "Original Papers in Relation to a Course of Liberal Education." *American Journal of Science and Arts* 15 (1829): 299–319. Also in *American Higher Education*, ed. Hofstadter and Smith, 1: 275–91.

DeMille, George E. *The Catholic Movement in the American Episcopal Church*. 1941. 2nd ed. Philadelphia: Church Historical Society, 1950.

De Witt, John. "The Intellectual Life of Samuel Miller." Opening Address of the Session of 1905–1906 at Princeton Theological Seminary. Pamphlet reprint from *PTR* April 1906: 168–90.

Dickens, A. G., and John Tonkin with Kenneth Powell. *The Reformation in Historical Thought*. Cambridge, Mass.: Harvard University Press, 1985.

Diehl, Carl. *Americans and German Scholarship 1770–1870*. New Haven, Conn.: Yale University Press, 1978.

Döllinger, John J. I. von. *Fables Respecting the Popes in the Middle Ages*. Trans. Alfred Plummer. 1863. New York: Dodd and Mead, 1872.

———. *Hippolytus and Callistus; or, The Church of Rome In the First Half of the Third Century*. Trans. Alfred Plummer. 1853. Edinburgh: T & T. Clark, 1876.

Dolan, Jay P. *The American Catholic Experience: A History from Colonial Times to the Present*. Garden City, N.Y.: Doubleday, 1985.

———. *The Immigrant Church: New York's Irish and German Catholics, 1815–1865*. Baltimore: Johns Hopkins University Press, 1975.

———. "Immigration and American Christianity: A History of Their Histories." In *A Century of Church History*, ed. Bowden, 119–47.

Draper, John William. *History of the Conflict Between Religion and Science*. New York: D. Appleton, 1875.

———. *History of the Intellectual Development of Europe*. 1862(?). 2 vols. Rev. ed. New York: Harper & Brothers, 1876.

Draper, Jonathan A., ed. *The Eye of the Storm: Bishop John William Colenso and the Crisis of Biblical Interpretation*. London: Clark International, 2003.

Droysen, Johann Gustav. "The Elevation of History to the Rank of a Science: Being a Review of *The History of Civilization in England*, by H. T. Buckle." In Droysen, *Outline of the Principles of History*, 69–89 (App. I).

———. *Outline of the Principles of History* [*Grundriss der Historik*]. Trans. E. Benjamin Andrews. Boston: Ginn, 1893.

"Dr. Schaff's Works on Church History." *New Brunswick Review* 1.1 (May 1854): 1–63.

Duffy, James, ed. *The Century at 150: Excerpts from the Archives*. New York: Century Association, 1997.

Dulles, J. H. "Princeton Theological Seminary." Pamphlet reprint of *The History of Higher Education in New Jersey* (1899), chap. 15.

Dunne, Robert. *Antebellum Irish Immigration and Emerging Ideologies of "America": A Protestant Backlash*. Studies in American History 41. Lewiston, N.Y.: Edwin Mellen, 2002.

Dwight, Timothy. *Memories of Yale Life and Men 1845–1899*. New York: Dodd, Mead, 1903.

Earl, Donald C. *The Moral and Political Tradition of Rome*. Ithaca, N.Y.: Cornell University Press, 1967.

———. *The Political Thought of Sallust*. 1961. Amsterdam: Hakkert, 1966.

"The Ebony Race and the War." *The Friend* [Honolulu], 12.7, July 3, 1863.

"Editorial." *ER* 1 (Jan. 1891): 61–68.

"Editorial Notes." *New-York Evangelist*, Feb. 1, 1877.

[Editors]. "*The New Englander* for October, 1868, Art. VI." *BRPR* 41 (Jan. 1869): 144–46.

Edwards, Laura. "Gender and the Changing Roles of Women." In *A Companion to 19th-Century America*, ed. Barney, 223–37.

Eliot, Charles W. "The Harvard Divinity School." *Harvard Graduates Magazine* (Sept. 1905): 209–11.

———. *Harvard Memorials*. Cambridge, Mass.: Harvard University Press, 1923.

———. "The New Education: The Organization. I and II." *Atlantic Monthly* 23.136 (Feb. 1869): 203–20; 23.137 (March 1869): 358–67.

———. "President Eliot's Inaugural Address." October 19, 1869. In *The Development of Harvard University*, ed. Morison, lix–lxxviii.

———. "The Religion of the Future." In Eliot, *The Religion of the Future and Other Essays*, 1–40. London: British and Foreign Unitarian Association, 1911.

———. "Statement of President Eliot." In *An Appeal*, ed. Bellows, 23–30.

———. "Theological Education at Harvard Between 1816 and 1916." In *Addresses Delivered at the Observance of the 100th Anniversary of the Establishment of the*

Harvard Divinity School, Cambridge, Massachusetts, October 5, 1916, 32–68. Cambridge, Mass.: Harvard University, 1917.

———. "What Is a Liberal Education?" *Century Magazine* 28.2 (June 1884): 203–12.

Ellis, Ieuan. *Seven Against Christ: A Study of "Essays and Reviews."* Studies in the History of Christian Thought 28. Leiden: Brill, 1980.

Elson, Ruth Miller. *Guardians of Tradition: American Schoolbooks of the Nineteenth Century.* Lincoln: University of Nebraska Press, 1964.

Emerson, Ralph. "The Early History of Monasticism;—From the Original Sources." *BS* 1.2 (May 1844): 309–31; 1.3 (Aug. 1844): 464–525; 1.4 (Nov. 1844): 632–99.

Emerton, Ephraim. "Academic Life." In Emerton, *Learning and Living*, 3–44.

———. "The Academic Study of History: An Address to Students." In Emerton, *Learning and Living*, 233–68.

———. "A Definition of Church History." In *Papers of the American Society of Church History*, 2nd ser. 7, ed. Frederick William Loetscher, 55–68. New York: Putnam's, 1923.

———. "The Historical Seminary in American Teaching," In *Methods of Teaching History*, ed. G. Stanley Hall, 191–200. Pedagogical Library 1. Boston: Ginn, Heath, 1883.

———. *An Introduction to the Study of the Middle Ages (375–814).* Boston: Ginn & Co., 1896.

———. *Learning and Living: Academic Essays.* Cambridge, Mass: Harvard University Press, 1921.

———. "The Place of History in Theological Study: An Address to Theological Students." In Emerton, *Learning and Living*, 309–25.

———. "The Practical Method in Higher Historical Instruction." In *Methods of Teaching History*, ed. A. D. White et al., 31–60. Pedagogical Library 1, ed. G. Stanley Hall. 1883. 2nd ed. Boston: D.C. Heath, 1898.

———. "The Rational Education of the Modern Minister: An Address to Ministers." In Emerton, *Learning and Living*, 269–307.

———. "Remarks of Professor Ephraim Emerton." In *The Theological School in Harvard University*, ed. Everett, 16–17.

———. "The Study of Church History." *Unitarian Review and Religious Magazine* 19.1 (Jan. 1883): 1–18.

———. *Unitarian Thought.* New York: Macmillan, 1911.

Emerton, Ephraim, and Samuel Eliot Morison. "History 1838–1929." In *The Development of Harvard University*, ed. Morison, 150–77.

"The Endowment of Union Theological Seminary." *New-York Evangelist*, Jan. 19, 1865.

Essays and Reviews. London: Longman, Green, Longman, and Roberts, 1860.

Everett, Charles Carroll, ed. *The Theological School in Harvard University, 1829–1929.* Cambridge, Mass.: Harvard University Press, 1930.

Feldberg, Michael. *The Turbulent Era: Riot & Disorder in Jacksonian America.* New York: Oxford University Press, 1980.

Fenn, William Wallace, "Charles Carroll Everett as Teacher of Theology." In *The Theological School in Harvard University*, ed. Everett, 5–15.

Fessenden, Tracy. *Culture and Redemption: Religion, The Secular, and American Literature*. Princeton, N.J.: Princeton University Press, 2007.

Finke, Roger. "The Illusion of Shifting Demand: Supply-Side Interpretations of American Religious History." In *Retelling U.S. Religious History*, ed. Tweed, 108–24.

Fisher, George Park. "The Academic Career of Ex-President Woolsey." *Century Magazine* 24 (1882): 709–17.

———. "The Augustinian and the Federal Theories of Original Sin Compared." *NE* 27 (July 1868): 468–516.

———. *The Beginnings of Christianity with a View of the State of the Roman World at the Birth of Christ*. 1877. New York: Scribner's, 1889.

———. *A Brief History of the Nations and of Their Progress in Civilization*. New York: American Book Company, 1896.

———. "Catholicity—True and False." A Sermon Preached Before the National Congregational Council, at Chicago, October 13, 1886. New York: Scribner's, 1886.

———. "The Christian Religion: Part III." *NAR* 134.333 (Feb. 1882): 170–219.

———. "The Conflict with Skepticism and Unbelief: First Article: The Questions at Issue." *NE* 23.1 (Jan. 1864): 113–32.

———. "The Conflict with Skepticism and Unbelief. Second Article: The Mythical Theory of Strauss." *NE* 23.2 (April 1864): 203–64.

———. "The Conflict with Skepticism and Unbelief. Third Article: Baur's Reconstruction of the Apostolic History, and Attack Upon the Credibility of the Book of Acts." *NE* 23.3 (July 1864): 401–53.

———. "The Council of Constance and the Council of the Vatican." *NE* 29.2 (April 1870): 191–219. Also in Fisher, *Discussions in History and Theology*, 101–40.

———. "The Decline of Clerical Authority." *NAR* 135 (1882): 564–579.

———. *Discussions in History and Theology*. New York: Scribner's, 1880.

———. "Dr. Schaff's Volume of the German Reformation." *Independent*, Feb. 14, 1889.

———. "Ebionitism and the Christianity of the Subapostolic Age." *APTR* 2.8 (Oct. 1864): 529–64.

———. *Essays on the Supernatural Origin of Christianity, with Special Reference to the Theories of Renan, Strauss, and the Tübingen School*. New York: Scribner's, 1866.

———. "The Folly of Atheism." *NE* 36.1 (Jan. 1877): 76–91.

———. *The Function of the Historian as a Judge of Historic Persons*. An Inaugural Address Delivered Before the American Historical Association, at New Haven, Jan. 29, 1899. New Haven, Conn.: Tuttle, Morehouse and Taylor, 1899.

———. *The Grounds of Theistic and Christian Belief*. 1883. London: Hodder and Stoughton, 1892.

———. "The Historical Method in Theology." A Paper Read Before the Congregational Council in Boston, Sept. 21, 1899. New Haven, Conn.: Tuttle, Morehouse and Taylor, 1899.

———. "The Historical Proofs of Christianity. First Article." *PR* ser. 4, 6 (Nov. 1880): 399–418.

———. "The Historical Proofs of Christianity. Second Article: The Miracles." *PR* ser. 4, 7 (Jan. 1881): 35–60.

———. "The Historical Proofs of Christianity. Third Article: The Gospels as an Authentic Record of the Apostles' Testimony." *PR* ser. 4, 7 (March 1881): 191–220.

———. "The Historical Proofs of Christianity. Fourth Article: The Fourth Gospel: The Fourth Gospel the Work of the Apostle John." *PR* ser. 4, 8 (July 1881): 51–84.

———. *History of Christian Doctrine.* 1896. New York: Scribner's, 1899.

———. *History of the Christian Church.* 1887. New York: Scribner's, 1902.

———. "How the New Testament Came Down to Us." *Scribner's Monthly* 21.4 (Feb. 1881): 611–20.

———. "Introductory Note" to Augustus Neander, "The Relation of the Grecian to Christian Ethics." *BS* 10.39 (July 1853): 476–80.

———. "Materialism and the Pulpit." *PR* n.s. 1.1 (Jan. 1878): 207–15.

———. "Miracles, and Their Place in Christian Evidence." *Journal of Christian Philosophy* 2 (April 1883): 270–82.

———. "Mr. Mitchell's Novel, 'Dr. Johns'." *NE* 97 (Oct. 1866): 679–94.

———. "National Faults." A Sermon Delivered in the Chapel of Yale College, on Fast Day, April 6th, 1860. New Haven, Conn.: Tuttle, Morehouse and Taylor, 1860.

———. *Notes on the Literature of Church History.* New York: Scribner's, 1888.

———(?). "Notices of New Books: The Princeton Review for January." *NE* 28.2 (April 1869): 406–8.

———. "The Old Roman Spirit and Religion in Latin Christianity." *PR* ser. 4, 5 (Jan. 1880): 147–76. Also in Fisher, *Discussions in History and Theology,* 34–67.

———. *Outlines of Universal History Text-Book and for Private Reading.* 2 vols. New York: Ivison, Blakeman, 1885, 1886.

———. "The Personality of God and of Man." *PR* ser. 4, 10 (July 1882): 16–38.

———. "'The Princeton Review' on the Theology of Dr. N. W. Taylor." *NE* 27.2 (April 1868): 284–348.

———. "Rationalism." In *Christianity and Scepticism: Boston Lectures, 1870,* 240–75. Boston: Congregational Sabbath-School and Publishing Society, 1870.

———. "Sermon." In Leonard Bacon, Samuel W. S. Dutton, and George P. Fisher, *Memorial of Nathaniel W. Taylor, D.D.: Three Sermons,* 25–39. New Haven, Conn.: Thomas H. Pease, 1858.

———. "Some Remarks on the Alogoi." A Paper Read Before the American Society of Church History, in New York, December 30–31, 1889. New York: Knickerbocker Press, 1890.

———. "The Study of Greek." In D. H. Chamberlain, *Not "A College Fetish": An*

Address in Reply to the Address of Charles Francis Adams, Jr., 63–78. Boston: Willard Small, 1884; also in *PR* ser. 4, 13 (March 1884): 111–26.

———. "The Temporal Power of the Pope." *NE* 26.1 (Jan. 1867): 1–28. Also (as "The Temporal Kingdom of the Popes") in Fisher, *Discussions in History and Theology*, 68–100.

———. "Thoughts Proper to the Present Crisis." A Sermon Preached in the Chapel of Yale College, on Fast Day, January 4, 1861. New Haven, Conn.: Thomas H. Pease, 1861.

———. "The Validity of Non-Episcopal Ordination." The Dudleian Lecture Delivered in the Chapel of Harvard University on October 28, 1888. New York: Scribner's, 1888.

Foakes Jackson, Frederick John. "The Work of Some Recent English Church Historians With Special Reference to the Labors of the Late Henry Melville Gwatkin." *Papers of the American Society of Church History*, 2nd ser. 5 (1916): 103–18. New York: Putnam's, 1917.

Förster, Wolfgang. "Johann Gottfried Herder: Weltgeschichte und Humanität." In *Aufklärung und Geschichte*, ed. Bödeker et al., 363–87.

Follen, Charles. *Religion and the Church, Theological Tracts 1.* Boston: James Munroe, 1836.

Foster, Frank Hugh. *The Modern Movement in American Theology: Sketches in the History of American Protestant Theology from the Civil War to the World War.* 1939. Reprint Freeport, N.Y.: Books for Libraries Press, 1969.

———. *The Seminary Method of Original Study in the Historical Sciences Illustrated from Church History.* New York: Scribner's, 1888.

Franchot, Jenny. *Roads to Rome: The Antebellum Protestant Encounter with Catholicism.* The New Historicism: Studies in Cultural Poetics 28. Berkeley: University of California Press, 1994.

Fraser, James W. *Schooling the Preachers: The Development of Protestant Theological Education in the United States, 1740–1875.* Lanham, Md.: University Press of America, 1988.

Gäbler, Ulrich. "Philip Schaff at Chur, 1819–1834." In *Probing the Reformed Tradition: Historical Studies in Honor of Edward A. Downey, Jr.,* ed. Elsie Anne McKee and Brian G. Armstrong, 408–23. Louisville, Ky.: Westminster/John Knox Press, 1989.

Gabriel, Ralph Henry. *Religion and Learning at Yale: The Church of Christ in the College and University.* New Haven, Conn.: Yale University Press, 1958.

Gapp, Kenneth S. "The Theological Seminary Library." *Princeton University Library Chronicle* 15.2 (Winter 1954): 90–100.

Gatch, Milton McC. *The Library of Leander Van Ess & the Earliest American Collections of Reformation Pamphlets.* BSA Occasional Publications 1. New York: Bibliographical Society of America, 2007.

Geitz, Henry, Jürgen Heideking, and Jurgen Herbst, eds. *German Influences on Education in the United States to 1917.* New York: Cambridge University Press, 1995.

"Germany: Its Universities, Theology, and Religion." [Review of Philip Schaff, *Germany: Its Universities, Theology, and Religion*]. *BS* 15.58 (April 1858): 483–84.

Gieseler, J. C. L. *Lehrbuch der Kirchengeschichte.* 6 vols. Bonn: Adolph Marcus, 1844–1857.

———. *A Text-Book of Church History.* Trans. Samuel Davidson from 4th German ed. New American rev. ed., ed. Henry B. Smith. 5 vols. New York: Harper & Brothers, 1857–1880.

———. *Text-Book of Ecclesiastical History.* Trans. Francis Cunningham from 3rd German ed. 3 vols. Philadelphia: Carey, Lea, and Blanchard, 1836.

Gilfoyle, Timothy J. "Urbanization." In *A Companion to 19th-Century America*, ed. Barney, 152–63.

Gillett, Charles Ripley. "Detailed History of the Union Theological Seminary in the City of New York." 3 vols. Typescript, n.d. UTS Library.

———. "The Library." In Prentiss, *The Union Theological Seminary*, 352–60.

Gilman, Daniel C. "The Group System of College Studies in the Johns Hopkins University." *AR* 5.30 (June 1886): 565–76.

———. "The Idea of the University." *NAR* 133 (Oct. 1881): 353–67.

———. "Is It Worth While to Uphold Any Longer the Idea of Liberal Education?" *ER* 3 (Feb. 1892): 105–19.

Goldman, Shalom. *God's Sacred Tongue: Hebrew & the American Imagination.* Chapel Hill: University of North Carolina Press, 2004.

Gooch, G. P. *History and Historians in the Nineteenth Century.* 1913. Rev. ed. London: Longmans, Green, 1952.

Good, James I. *History of the Reformed Church in the United States, 1725–1792.* Reading, Pa.: D. Miller, 1899.

Goodspeed, Thomas W. *William Rainey Harper, First President of the University of Chicago.* Chicago: University of Chicago Press, 1928.

Goodwin, Daniel R. "Religious Instruction in Colleges." *ATR* 4.14 (April 1862): 228–38.

Gossett, Thomas F. *Race: The History of an Idea in America.* Dallas: Southern Methodist University Press, 1963.

Grafton, Anthony. "Polyhistor into *Philolog*: Notes on the Transformation of German Classical Scholarship, 1780–1850." *History of Universities* 3 (1983): 159–92.

Graham, Stephen R. *Cosmos in the Chaos: Philip Schaff's Interpretation of Nineteenth-Century American Religion.* Grand Rapids, Mich.: Eerdmans, 1995.

Gray, Christopher. *New York Streetscapes: Tales of Manhattan's Significant Buildings and Landmarks.* New York: Harry Abrams, 2003.

Gresley, William. "Idealism Reconsidered." London: Joseph Masters, 1860.

Guericke, Henry E. F. *A Manual of Church History: Ancient Church History, Comprising the First Six Centuries.* 1833. Trans. William G. T. Shedd. Andover, Mass.: W. F. Draper; New York: Wiley and Halstead, 1857.

Haber, Francis C. *The Age of the World: Moses to Darwin.* Baltimore: Johns Hopkins University Press, 1959.

Hagenbach, K. R. "Neander's Services as a Church Historian." *Studien und Kritiken* 3 (1851). Trans. H. B. Smith. *BS* 8.32 (Oct. 1851): 822–57.

Haldeman, I. M. *The Signs of the Times.* New York: Charles Cook, 1910.

Hall, G. Stanley. "American Universities and the Training of Teachers." *Forum* 17 (April 1894): 148–59.

Handy, Robert T. *A History of Union Theological Seminary in New York.* New York: Columbia University Press, 1987.

Harnack, Adolf von. "The Future of Church History." *Independent*, April 11, 1889.

Haroutunian, Joseph. *Piety Versus Moralism: The Passing of the New England Theology.* New York: Henry Holt, 1932.

Harper, William R. "Shall the Theological Curriculum Be Modified, and How?" *American Journal of Theology* 3 (1899): 45–66.

Harris, George. *A Century's Change in Religion.* Boston: Houghton Mifflin, 1914.

Harris, Horton. *The Tübingen School.* Oxford: Clarendon Press, 1975.

Hart, D. G. "Faith and Learning in the Age of the University: The Academic Ministry of Daniel Coit Gilman." In *The Secularization of the Academy*, ed. Marsden and Longfield, 107–45.

———. *The University Gets Religion: Religious Studies in American Higher Education.* Baltimore: Johns Hopkins University Press, 1999.

Hart, J. M. *German Universities: A Narrative of Personal Experience.* New York: Putnam's, 1874.

Hase, Charles [Karl von]. *A History of the Christian Church.* 1834. Trans. from 7th German ed. Charles E. Blumenthal and Conway P. Wing. New York: D. Appleton, 1856.

Hatch, Edwin. *The Organization of the Early Christian Churches: Eight Lectures.* Bampton Lectures, 1880. London: Rivington's, 1881.

Hatch, Nathan O., and Mark A. Noll, eds. *The Bible in America: Essays in Cultural History.* New York: Oxford University Press, 1982.

Hatfield, Edwin F. *The Early Annals of Union Theological Seminary in the City of New-York.* New York: n.p., 1876.

Hawkins, Hugh. *Between Harvard and America: The Educational Leadership of Charles W. Eliot.* New York: Oxford University Press, 1972.

———. *Pioneer: A History of Johns Hopkins University, 1874–1889.* 1960. Baltimore: Johns Hopkins University Press, 1982.

———. "University Identity: The Teaching and Research Functions." In *The Organization of Knowledge*, ed. Oleson and Voss, 285–312.

Headlam, Arthur C. "Methods of Early Church History." In Headlam, *History, Authority and Theology*, 229–77. London: John Murray, 1909.

Hedge, Frederic Henry. "Antisupernaturalism in the Pulpit." *Christian Examiner* 77.245 [5th ser.] 15.2 (Sept. 1864): 145–59.

———. *Atheism in Philosophy and Other Essays.* Boston: Roberts Brothers, 1884.

————. "The Mythical Element in the New Testament." In *Christianity and Modern Thought*, 157–76.

Hegel, G. W. F. "The Positivity of the Christian Religion" [1796], "The Spirit of Christianity and Its Fate" [1798–1799] and the fragment on "Love" [1798?]. In *Friedrich Hegel, On Christianity: Early Theological Writings*, 67–308. Trans. T. M. Knox and Richard Kroner. New York: Harper Torchbooks, 1961.

Hennecke, Edgar. *New Testament Apocrypha.* 1964. Ed. Wilhelm Schneemelcher, trans. R. McL. Wilson. 2 vols. Philadelphia: Westminster Press, 1965.

"Henry B. Smith, D.D., LL.D." [Contributions by Henry Field and William Adams]. *New-York Evangelist*, Feb. 15, 1877.

Herbst, Jurgen. *The German Historical School in American Scholarship: A Study in the Transfer of Culture.* Ithaca, N.Y.: Cornell University Press, 1965.

Herder, Johann Gottfried von. *J. G. Herder on Social and Political Culture.* Ed. and trans. Frederick M. Barnard. Cambridge: Cambridge University Press, 1969.

————. *Philosophical Writings.* Trans. and ed. Michael N. Forster. Cambridge: Cambridge University Press, 2002.

————. *Reflections on the Philosophy of the History of Mankind.* 1784–1791. Abridged with Intro. by Frank E. Manuel. Chicago: University of Chicago Press, 1968.

Heschel, Susannah. *The Aryan Jesus: Christian Theologians and the Bible in Nazi Germany.* Princeton, N.J.: Princeton University Press, 2008.

Hester, Carl. "Gedanken zu Ferdinand Christian Baurs Entwicklung als Historiker anhand zweier unbekannter Briefe." *ZKG* 84 (1973): 249–69.

Hiers, Richard H. and David Larrimore Holland. "Introduction" to Weiss, *Jesus' Proclamation of the Kingdom of God.* 1892. Trans. R. H. Hiers and D. L. Holland. Philadelphia: Fortress Press, 1971.

Higham, John. "The Matrix of Specialization." In *Organization of Knowledge*, ed. Oleson and Voss, 3–18.

Hill, Alonzo. "The Divinity School at Cambridge." *Quarterly Journal of the American Unitarian Association* 1.3 (April 1, 1854): 216–23.

Hitchcock, Roswell Dwight. "Address." In *Services in Adams Chapel at the Dedication of the New Buildings of the Union Theological Seminary, December 9, 1884.* New York: William C. Martin, 1885.

————. "An Address in Behalf of the United States Inebriate Asylum." Broadway Tabernacle, November 7, 1855. New York: M.R. Wynkoop, 1855.

————. "An Address on Colportage." Before the American Tract Society, at Their Forty-First Anniversary in Boston, May 30, 1855. Boston: American Tract Society, 1855.

————. "The Ante-Nicene Trinitarianism." *ATR* 3.9 (Jan. 1861): 161–77; 3. 11 (July 1861): 512–26; 4.13 (Jan. 1862): 54–82.

————. "The Chinese Classics." *APTR* 1.4 (Oct. 1863): 631–38.

————. "The Cost of Service." In Hitchcock, *Eternal Atonement*, 153–65.

———. "The Distinguishing Features of Christianity." In Hitchcock, *Eternal Atonement*, 91–99.

———. *Eternal Atonement*. New York: Scribner's, 1888.

———. "A Eulogy on Daniel Webster." Delivered Before the Students of Bowdoin College, Friday, Nov. 12, 1852. Brunswick, Maine: J. Griffin, 1852.

———. "His Last Words in Public: Roswell D. Hitchcock's Address at the Dedication of the Durfee High School in Fall River, Massachusetts, June 16, 1887." *New-York Evangelist*, June 30, 1887.

———. "Historical Development of Christianity." *ATR* 2.5 (Feb. 1860): 28–54.

———. *Hitchcock's New and Complete Analysis of the Holy Bible, or the Whole of the Old and New Testaments Arranged According to Subjects in Twenty-Seven Books*. New York: A.J. Johnson, 1873.

———. "The Laws of Civilization." The Substance of an Address Delivered on Several Occasions During the Summer of 1860. New York: John A. Gray, 1860.

———. "Literary and Critical Notices of Books" [Review of John William Colenso's *The Pentateuch and Book of Joshua Critically Examined*]. *ATR* 1.1 (Jan. 1863): 162–63.

———. "Origin and Growth of Episcopacy." *APTR* 5.17 (Jan. 1867): 133–59.

———. "Our National Sin." A Sermon, Preached on the Day of the National Fast, Sept. 26, 1861, South Reformed Dutch Church, New York City. New York: Baker and Godwin, 1861.

———. "The Person of Christ." Philadelphia: Presbyterian Publication Committee; New York: A. D. F. Randolph, n.d. (1860s).

———. "Receiving and Giving." In Hitchcock, *Eternal Atonement*, 225–36.

———. "Religion, The Doing of God's Will." In Hitchcock, *Eternal Atonement*, 31–51.

———. "Romanism in the Light of History." In *Evangelical Alliance Conference, 1873*, ed. Schaff and Prime, 436–37.

———. "A Sermon Delivered at the Dedication of the New Chapel of Bowdoin College." Thursday, June 7, 1855. Brunswick, Maine: George T. Barrett, 1855.

———. *Socialism*. New York: A.D.F. Randolph, 1879.

———. "The Staff of Life." In Hitchcock, *Eternal Atonement*, 169–90.

———. "Thanksgiving for Victories." Delivered at Plymouth Church, Brooklyn, Sept. 11, 1864. New York: William E. Whiting, 1864.

———. "The True Idea and Uses of Church History." In "The Charge and Inaugural Address," 21–48.

———. "The Zoroastrian Religion." *APTR* 1.2 (April 1863): 281–90.

Hitchcock, Roswell Dwight and Francis Brown, eds. *Teaching of the Twelve Apostles*. 1884. Rev. enlarged ed. New York: Scribner's, 1885.

"H.M.F." [Henry Field?]. "The illustrious Dead" [Roswell D. Hitchcock]. *New-York Evangelist*, June 23, 1887.

Hodge, Charles. "The General Assembly." *BRPR* 17 (July 1845): 428–71.

————. "Is the Church of Rome a Part of the Visible Church?" *BRPR* 18 (April 1846): 320–44.

————. Review of Philip Schaff, *History of the Apostolic Church. BRPR* 26.1 (Jan. 1854): 148–92.

————. "Schaff's Protestantism." *BRPR* 17 (Oct. 1845): 626–36. Reprinted in Noll, *The Princeton Theology*, 157–64.

————. *What Is Darwinism?* New York: Scribner, Armstrong, 1874.

Hodgson, Peter C. *The Formation of Historical Theology: A Study of Ferdinand Christian Baur.* New York: Harper & Row, 1966.

————. "Introduction." In Baur, *Ferdinand Christian Baur on the Writing of Church History*, 3–40.

Hoeveler, J. David, Jr. *James McCosh and the Scottish Intellectual Tradition: From Glasgow to Princeton.* Princeton, N.J.: Princeton University Press, 1981.

Hofstadter, Richard, and Wilson Smith, eds. *American Higher Education: A Documentary History.* 2 vols. Chicago: University of Chicago Press, 1961.

Holifield, E. Brooks. *Theology in America: Christian Thought from the Age of the Puritans to the Civil War.* New Haven, Conn.: Yale University Press, 2003.

Holt, Michael. *The Political Crisis of the 1850s.* New York: Wiley, 1978.

Holt, W. Stull. *Historical Scholarship in the United States, 1876–1901: As Revealed in the Correspondence of Herbert B. Adams.* Johns Hopkins University Studies in Historical and Political Science 56:4. Baltimore: Johns Hopkins University Press, 1938.

Horowitz, Helen Lefkowitz. *Alma Mater: Design and Experience in the Women's Colleges from Their Nineteenth-Century Beginnings to the 1930s.* Boston: Beacon Press, 1984.

Howard, Thomas Albert. *Protestant Theology and the Making of the Modern German University.* Oxford: Oxford University Press, 2006.

————. *Religion and the Rise of Historicism: W. M. L. de Wette, Jacob Burckhardt, and the Theological Origins of Nineteenth-Century Historical Consciousness.* Cambridge: Cambridge University Press, 2000.

Howe, Daniel Walker. *The Unitarian Conscience: Harvard Moral Philosophy, 1805–1861.* Cambridge, Mass.: Harvard University Press, 1970.

Howison, G. H. "The Harvard 'New Education'." *AR* 5.30 (June 1886): 577–89.

Humphrey, Zephaniah M. "Henry Boynton Smith." (Review of [E. Smith], *Henry Boynton Smith*). *Presbyterian Review* 2.7 (July 1881): 474–99.

Hunter, David G. *Marriage, Celibacy, and Heresy in Ancient Christianity: The Jovinianist Controversy.* Oxford Early Christian Studies. Oxford: Oxford University Press, 2007.

Hurst, John Fletcher. "Dr. Schaff as Uniting Teutonic and Anglo-Saxon Scholarship." In *Schaff Memorial Meeting*, 7–12.

Hutchison, William R. "Cultural Strain and Protestant Liberalism." *AHR* 76.2 (April 1971): 386–411.

————. *The Modernist Movement in American Protestantism.* Durham, N.C.: Duke University Press, 1992.

Huxley, Thomas H. "An Apologetic Irenicon." *Fortnightly Review* 311 [n.s. 52] (Nov. 1, 1892): 557–71.

Iggers, Georg G. "The European Context of German Enlightenment Historiography." In *Aufklärung und Geschichte,* ed. Bödeker et al., 225–45.

"Imputation." In *Cyclopaedia of Biblical, Theological, and Ecclesiastical Literature,* ed. McClintock and Strong, 4: 524–27

"In Memoriam—President Hitchcock." *New-York Evangelist,* Dec. 15, 1887.

Jackson, Samuel Macauley, ed. *The New Schaff-Herzog Encyclopedia of Religious Knowledge.* 1908–1914. 13 vols. Reprint Grand Rapids, Mich.: Baker Book House, 1951–54.

Jacobi, J. L. "Preface" to Augustus Neander, *Lectures on the History of Christian Dogmas,* v–xiii.

Jaeger, Mary. *Livy's Written Rome.* Ann Arbor: University of Michigan Press, 1997.

James, Edward J. "The Degree of Ph.D. in Germany." *AR* 9.54 (June 1888): 611–23.

Jameson, J. Franklin. "The American Historical Association, 1884–1909." *AHR* 15.1 (Oct. 1909): 1–20.

————. "Early Days of the American Historical Association, 1884–1895." *AHR* 40.1 (1934): 1–9.

Janeway, J. J. "A Contrast Between the Erroneous Assertions of Professor Schaf [*sic*] and the Testimony of Credible Ecclesiastical Historians, in Regard to the State of the Christian Church in the Middle Ages." New Brunswick, N.J.: J. Terhune & Son, 1852.

Jantz, Harold S. "Samuel Miller's Survey of German Literature, 1803." *Germanic Review* 16 (Dec. 1941): 267–77.

Jarausch, Konrad H. "American Students in Germany, 1815–1914: The Structures of German and U.S. Matriculants at Göttingen University." In *German Influences on Education,* ed. Geitz et al., 195–211.

————. "The Institutionalization of History in 18th-Century Germany." In *Aufklärung und Geschichte,* ed. Bödeker et al., 25–48.

Johnson, Curtis D. *Redeeming America: Evangelicals and the Road to Civil War.* Chicago: Ivan R. Dee, 1993.

Johnson, Kathryn L. "The Mustard Seed and the Leaven: Philip Schaff's Confident View of Christian History." *Historical Magazine of the Protestant Episcopal Church* 50 (June 1981): 117–70.

Jordan, Phillip D. *The Evangelical Alliance for the United States of America, 1847–1900: Ecumenism, Identity and the Religion of the Republic.* Studies in American Religion. New York: Edwin Mellen, 1982.

Jowett, Benjamin. "On the Interpretation of Scripture." In *Essays and Reviews,* 330–433.

Kane, John J. *Catholic-Protestant Conflicts in America.* Chicago: Regnery, 1955.

Kannengiesser, Charles. "Fifty Years of Patristics." *Theological Studies* 50.4 (Dec. 1989): 633–56.

———. "The Future of Patristics." *Theological Studies* 52.1 (March 1991): 128–39.

Karr, William S. "Introductory Note" to Smith, *Introduction to Christian Theology*, iii–v.

Katz, Wilber G. "Religious Studies in State Universities: The New Legal Climate." In *Religious Studies in Public Universities*, ed. McLean, 15–21.

Keck, Leander E. "Epilogue: Continuity and Change Since 1957." In Roland H. Bainton, *Yale and the Ministry: A History of Education for Christian Ministry at Yale from the Founding in 1701*, 269–81, San Francisco: Harper & Row, 1985.

Kelley, Brooks Mather. *Yale: A History*. New Haven, Conn.: Yale University Press, 1974.

Kelsey, Francis W. "Greek in the High School and the Question of the Supply of Candidates for the Ministry." In *Latin and Greek*, ed. Kelsey, 186–208.

———, ed. *Latin and Greek in American Education with Symposia on the Value of Humanistic Studies*. New York: Macmillan, 1911.

———. "The Present Position of Latin and Greek." In *Latin and Greek*, ed. Kelsey, 1–16.

Kerr, Hugh T. *Sons of the Prophets: Leaders in Protestantism from Princeton Seminary*. Princeton, N.J.: Princeton University Press, 1963.

Kingsley, Charles. *The Hermits*. New York: John B. Alden, 1885.

Knicker, Charles R. "New Attitudes and New Curricula: The Changing Role of the Bible in Protestant Education, 1880–1920." In *The Bible in American Education*, ed. Barr and Piediscalzi, 121–42.

Knoff, Gerald Everett. "The Yale Divinity School 1858–1899." Ph.D. dissertation, Yale University, 1933.

Knowles, James D. "Importance of Theological Institutions." An Address Delivered Before the Trustees, Students and Friends of the Newton Theological Institution, Nov. 14, 1832. Boston: Lincoln & Edmands, 1832.

Knox, George William. "Review of the Year 1906–1907." In *The Seminary: Its Spirit and Aims*, 30–34.

Knox, George William, Arthur Cushman McGiffert, and Francis Brown. *The Christian Point of View: Three Addresses*. New York: Scribner's, 1902.

Kuklick, Bruce. *Churchmen and Philosophers: From Jonathan Edwards to John Dewey*. New Haven, Conn.: Yale University Press, 1985.

———. *Puritans in Babylon: The Ancient Near East and American Intellectual Life, 1880–1930*. Princeton, N.J.: Princeton University Press, 1996.

Kümmel, Werner Georg. *Introduction to the New Testament*. Trans. Howard Clark Kee from 17th German ed. Nashville, Tenn.: Abingdon Press, 1975.

Laqueur, Thomas W. *Solitary Sex: A Cultural History of Masturbation*. New York: Zone Books, 2003.

"The Late Professor Smith." *New-York Evangelist*, Feb. 15, 1877

Leslie, W. Bruce. *Gentlemen and Scholars: College and Community in the "Age of the University," 1865–1917*. University Park: Pennsylvania State University Press, 1992.

"The Library of the Union Theological Seminary. Its Proper Position, Its Present Condition, Its Pressing Needs." April 1899. Pamphlet. Francis Brown Papers, UTS, S3, B1, F8.

Lichtenberger, Frédéric Auguste. *History of German Theology in the Nineteenth Century*. 1873. Trans. W. Hastie. Edinburgh: Clark, 1889.

Lightfoot, Joseph Barber. *The Apostolic Fathers*. 1885–1890. 3 vols. 2nd ed. London: Macmillan, 1889.

———. *Historical Essays*. London: Macmillan, 1895.

Lindberg, David C., and Ronald L. Numbers. "Beyond War and Peace: A Reappraisal of the Encounter between Christianity and Science." *CH* 55.3 (Summer 1986): 338–54.

Lingelbach, Gabriele. *Klio macht Karriere: Die Institutionalisierung der Geschichtswissenschaft in Frankreich und den U.S.A. in der zweiten Hälfte des 19. Jahrhunderts*. Veröffentlichungen des Max-Planck-Instituts für Geschichte 181. Göttingen: Vandenhoeck & Ruprecht, 2003.

Lintott, A. W. "Imperial Expansion and Moral Decline in the Roman Republic." *Historia* 21 (1972): 626–38.

Loetscher, Lefferts A. *Facing the Enlightenment and Pietism: Archibald Alexander and the Founding of Princeton Theological Seminary*. Contributions to the Study of Religion 8. Westport, Conn.: Greenwood Press, 1983.

Longfield, Bradley J. "From Evangelicalism to Liberalism: Public Midwestern Universities in Nineteenth-Century America." In *The Secularization of the Academy*, ed. Marsden and Longfield, 46–73.

Lotz, David W. "Philip Schaff and the Idea of Church History." In *A Century of Church History*, ed. Bowden, 1–35.

Luce, T. J. *Livy: The Composition of History*. Princeton, N.J.: Princeton University Press, 1977.

MacCracken, Henry Mitchell. "The Place of Church History in the College Course of Study." In *Papers of the American Society of Church History* 3, 217–39. New York: Knickerbocker Press, 1891.

Mackay, R. W. *The Tübingen School and Its Antecedents: A Review of the History and Present Condition of Modern Theology*. London: Williams and Norgate, 1863.

Mackenzie, William Douglas. "The Place of Greek and Latin in the Preparation for the Ministry." In *Latin and Greek*, ed. Kelsey, 154–70.

Manuel, Frank E. *The Broken Staff: Judaism Through Christian Eyes*. Cambridge, Mass.: Harvard University Press, 1992.

Marchand, Susanne L. *Down from Olympus: Archaeology and Philhellenism in Germany, 1750–1970*. Princeton, N.J.: Princeton University Press, 1996.

Marsden, George M. "The Collapse of American Evangelical Academia." In *Faith and*

Rationality: Reason and Belief in God, ed. Alvin Plantinga and Nicholas Wolters-torff, 219–64. Notre Dame, Ind.: University of Notre Dame Press, 1983.

———. "'Everyone One's Own Interpreter': The Bible, Science, and Authority in Mid-Nineteenth-Century America." In *The Bible in America*, ed. Hatch and Noll, 79–100.

———. *Fundamentalism and American Culture: The Shaping of Twentieth-Century Evangelicalism, 1870–1925*. Oxford: Oxford University Press, 1980.

———. "The Soul of the American University: A Historical Overview." In *The Secularization of the Academy*, ed. Marsden and Longfield, 9–45.

———. *The Soul of the American University: From Protestant Establishment to Established Nonbelief*. New York: Oxford University Press, 1994.

Marsden, George M., and Bradley J. Longfield, eds. *The Secularization of the Academy*. New York: Oxford University Press, 1992.

Marty, Martin E. *Righteous Empire: The Protestant Experience in America*. New York: Dial Press, 1970.

Matrimony Notices [Mary Hitchcock to Samuel Emerson]. *Cincinnati Daily Gazette*, Dec. 31, 1881.

McClintock, John, and James Strong, eds. *Cyclopedia of Biblical, Theological, and Ecclesiastical Literature*. 1867–1887. Grand Rapids, Mich.: Baker Book House, 1981.

McCosh, James. *Christianity and Positivism*. New York: Robert Carter, 1871.

———. "The New Departure in College Education." Being a Reply to President Eliot's Defence of It in New York, February 24, 1885. New York: Scribner's, 1885.

———. "Religion in a College: What Place It Should Have." Being an Examination of President Eliot's Paper, Read before the Nineteenth Century Club, in New York, February 3, 1886. New York: A.C. Armstrong, 1886.

———. *The Religious Aspect of Evolution*. Bedell Lectures of 1887. New York: Putnam's, 1888.

———. *The Scottish Philosophy*. New York: Robert Carter and Brothers, 1875.

McGiffert, Arthur Cushman. *A History of Christian Thought*. Vol. 2, *The West from Tertullian to Erasmus*. 1933. New York: Scribner's, 1954.

———. "Modernism." In McGiffert, *Christianity as History and Faith*, ed. A. C. McGiffert, Jr., 76–101. New York: Scribner's, 1934.

———. "Theological Reconstruction." An Address Given at the Union Theological Seminary Banquet, May 12, 1902. In G. W. Knox et al., *The Christian Point of View*, 31–48.

McGiffert, A. C., Jr. "The Making of an American Scholar: Biography in Letters." *USQR* 24.1 (Fall 1968): 31–46.

McGreavy, John T. *Catholicism and American Freedom: A History*. New York: Norton, 2003.

McLean, Milton D. *Religious Studies in Public Universities*. Carbondale: Southern Illinois University Central Publications, 1967.

McNamara, Mary. "Founding the Seminary." Personal communication.

Meyer, John Charles. "Philip Schaff's Concept of Organic Historiography as Related to the Development of Doctrine: A Catholic Appraisal." Ph.D. dissertation, Catholic University of America, 1968.

Miles, Gary B. *Livy: Reconstructing Early Rome*. Ithaca, N.Y.: Cornell University Press, 1995.

Miller, Glenn T. *Piety and Intellect: The Aims and Purposes of Ante-Bellum Theological Education*. Studies in Theological Education. Atlanta: Scholars Press, 1990.

Miller, Howard. *The Revolutionary College: American Presbyterian Higher Education*. New York: New York University Press, 1976.

Miller, Samuel. "Address of the Rev Dr. Miller." *Twenty-Second Annual Report of the American Bible Society*. May 10, 1838, 81–82. New York: Daniel Eanshaw, 1838.

———. *A Brief Retrospect of the Eighteenth Century. Part I: A Sketch of the Revolution and Improvements in Science, Arts, and Literature During That Period*. 2 vols. New York: T. and J. Swords, 1803.

———. "The Dangers of Education in Roman Catholic Seminaries." A Sermon Delivered Upon Request, before the Synod of Philadelphia, at Baltimore, October 31, 1837; and in New York, November 26, 1837. Baltimore: Matchett & Nelson, 1838.

———. "The Divine Appointment, the Duties, and the Qualifications of Ruling Elders." A Sermon Preached in the First Presbyterian Church in the City of New-York, May 2, 1809. New York: Samuel Whiting, 1811.

———. "The Duty of the Church to Take Measures for the Providing an Able and Faithful Ministry." A Sermon at the Inauguration of Rev. Archibald Alexander, D.D., as Professor of Didactic and Polemic [sic] Apology in the Theological Seminary of the Presbyterian Church, Princeton, August 12, 1812. Reprint Dallas: Presbyterian Heritage Publications, 1984.

———. *An Essay on the Warrant, Nature, and Duties of the Office of the Ruling Elder, in the Presbyterian Church*. 1820. 3rd ed. Philadelphia: Presbyterian Board of Education, 1840.

———. "Introductory Essay" to *History of Popery, Including Its Origin, Progress, Doctrines, Practice, Institutions, and Fruits*, by "A Watchman," 3–18. New York: John P. Haven, 1834.

———. "The Importance of Domestic Happiness: Sermon 198." *American National Preacher* 10.4 (Sept. 1835): 241–48.

———. "The Importance of Mature Preparatory Study for the Ministry." An Introductory Lecture Delivered at the Opening of the Summer Session of the Theological Seminary at Princeton, New-Jersey, July 3, 1829. Andover, Mass.: Mark Newman, 1830.

———. "A Letter to the Editor of the Unitarian Miscellany." In "Reply to an Attack, By an Anonymous Writer in That Work, on a Late Ordination Sermon Delivered in Baltimore." Baltimore: E.J. Coale, 1821.

———. *Letters Concerning the Constitution and Order of the Christian Ministry*.

Addressed to the Members of the Presbyterian Churches in the City of New York. 1807. 2nd ed. Philadelphia: Towar, J. and D. M. Hogan, 1830.

———. *Letters from a Father to His Sons in College*. 1843. Philadelphia: Presbyterian Board of Education, 1852.

———. *Letters on Clerical Manners and Habits*. Addressed to a Student in the Theological Seminary, at Princeton, New Jersey. New York: G. & C. Carvill, 1827.

———. *Letters on the Eternal Sonship of Christ*. Addressed to the Rev. Prof. Stuart, of Andover. Philadelphia: W.W. Woodward, 1823.

———. *Letters on Unitarianism*. Addressed to the Members of the First Presbyterian Church, in the City of Baltimore. Trenton, N.J.: George Sherman, 1821.

———. "The Literary Fountains Healed." A Sermon Preached in the Chapel of the College of New Jersey, March 9, 1823. Trenton, N.J.: George Sherman, 1823.

———. "The Means of Domestic Happiness: Sermon 199." *American National Preacher* 10.4 (Sept. 1835): 249–56.

———. *Presbyterianism: The Truly Primitive and Apostolical Constitution of the Church of Christ*. 1835. Philadelphia: Presbyterian Board of Education, 1840.

———. "A Sermon." Delivered Before the New-York Missionary Society, April 6, 1802. New York: T & J. Swords, 1802.

———. "A Sermon." Delivered January 19, 1812, at the Request of a Number of Young Gentlemen of the City of New-York, Who Had Assembled to Express Their Condolence with the Inhabitants of Richmond, on the Late Mournful Dispensation of Providence in That City. New York: T. and J. Swords, 1812.

———. "A Sermon." Preached March 13, 1808, for the Benefit of the Society Instituted in the City of New-York, for the Relief of Poor Widows with Small Children. New York: Hopkins and Seymour, 1808.

———. *The Utility and Importance of Creeds and Confessions: Addressed Particularly to Candidates for the Ministry*. 1824 (?). Philadelphia: Presbyterian Board of Education, 1841.

Miller, Samuel, Jr. *The Life of Samuel Miller, D.D., LL.D., Second Professor in the Theological Seminary of the Presbyterian Church, at Princeton, New Jersey*. 2 vols. Philadelphia: Claxton, Remsen and Haffelfinger, 1869.

Milman, Henry Hart. *History of Christianity: From the Birth of Christ to the Abolition of Paganism in the Roman Empire*. 1840. 3 vols. Rev. ed. New York: W.J. Widdleton, 1866.

"Ministers' Institute." *Worcester Daily Spy* 43.238 (Oct. 4, 1888).

Mivart, St. George. *On the Genesis of Species*. 2nd ed. London: Macmillan, 1871.

Moberly, George. *Some Remarks on "Essays and Reviews"*. Oxford: J.H. and Jas. Parker, 1861.

Modern, John Lardas. "Evangelical Secularism and the Measure of Leviathan." *CH* 77.4 (Dec. 2008): 801–76.

Moffat, James C. *Outlines of Church History*. Princeton, N.J.: Charles S. Robinson, 1875.

Momigliano, Arnaldo. "Tacitus and the Tacitist Tradition." In Momigliano, *The Classical Foundations of Modern Historiography*, 109–31. Sather Classical Lectures 54. Berkeley: University of California Press, 1990.

Monk, Maria [pseud.]. *Awful Disclosures of the Hotel Dieu Nunnery of Montreal*. New York: "Howe & Bates" [Harper Brothers], 1836.

Moore, Aubrey L. *Science and the Faith: Essays on Apologetic Subjects*. 1889. 3rd ed. London: Kegan Paul, Trench, Trübner, 1892.

Moore, R. Laurence. "Bible Reading and Nonsectarian Schooling: The Failure of Religious Instruction in Nineteenth-Century Public Education." *JAH* 86.4 (March 2000): 1581–99.

———. *Religious Outsiders and the Making of Americans*. New York: Oxford University Press, 1986.

Moorhead, James H. *American Apocalypse: Yankee Protestants and the Civil War 1860–1869*. New Haven, Conn.: Yale University Press, 1978.

Morison, Robert S. "The First Half Century of the Divinity School." In *Addresses Delivered at the Observance of the 100th Anniversary of the Establishment of the Harvard Divinity School, Cambridge, Massachusetts, October 5, 1916*, 5–31. Cambridge, Mass.: Harvard University, 1917.

Morison, Samuel Eliot, ed. *The Development of Harvard University Since the Inauguration of President Eliot, 1869–1929*. Cambridge, Mass.: Harvard University Press, 1930.

Mosheim, John Laurence. *An Ecclesiastical History, Ancient and Modern, from the Birth of Christ to the Beginning of the Fourth Century*. 1755 (?). Trans. Archibald Maclaine. 2 vols.. 2nd ed. London: J. Haddon, 1810, 1811.

Mott, Frank Luther. *A History of American Magazines 1741–1850*. New York: D. Appleton, 1930.

———. *A History of American Magazines 1850–1865*. Cambridge, Mass.: Harvard University Press, 1938.

———. *A History of American Magazines 1865–1885*. Cambridge, Mass.: Harvard University Press, 1938.

Mullin, Robert Bruce. *Episcopal Vision/American Reality: High Church Theology and Social Thought in Evangelical America*. New Haven, Conn.: Yale University Press, 1986.

Munroe, James P. "Certain Dangerous Tendencies in Education." *ER* 3 (Feb. 1892): 145–55.

Murphey, Murray G. "On the Scientific Study of Religion in the United States, 1870–1980." In *Religion and Twentieth-Century American Intellectual Life*, ed. Michael J. Lacey, 136–71. Cambridge: Woodrow Wilson International Center for Scholars/Cambridge University Press, 1989.

Naylor, Natalie A. "The Theological Seminary in the Configuration of American Higher Education." *History of Education Quarterly* 17 (Spring 1977): 17–30.

Neander, August. *The Emperor Julian and His Generation: An Historical Picture.* 1812. Trans. G. V. Cox. New York: J.C. Riker, 1850.

———. *General History of the Christian Religion and Church.* Vol. I, *Comprising the First Great Division of the History*; Vol. II, *Comprising the Second Great Division of the History.* 1825–1831. Trans. Joseph Torrey. 11th American rev. ed. Boston: Crocker and Brewster, 1872.

———. *The History of the Christian Religion and Church, During the First Three Centuries.* 1831. Trans. Henry John Rose. Philadelphia: James M. Campbell, 1843.

———. *History of the Planting and Training of the Christian Church by the Apostles; and Antignostikus; or, Spirit of Tertullian.* 1825. Trans. J. E. Ryland. 1832. 2 vols. London: George Bell and Sons, 1887.

———. *Katholicismus und Protestantismus*, ed. Hermann Messner. Vol. 4 of Neander, *Theologische Vorlesungen*, ed. J. Müller. Berlin: Wiegandt & Grieben, 1863.

———. *Lectures on the History of Christian Dogmas*, ed. J. L. Jacobi. Vol. 1 of Neander, *Theologische Vorlesungen.* Trans. J. E. Ryland. 2 vols. London: Henry G. Bohn, 1858.

———. *Memorials of Christian Life in the Early and Middle Ages.* 1823–1824. Trans. J. E. Ryland. London: Henry G. Bohn, 1852.

———. "The Relation of the Grecian to the Christian Ethics." *Zeitschrift für christliche Wissenschaft und christliches Leben* (1850). Trans. George P. Fisher. *BS* 10.39 (July 1853): 476–504.

———. "Verworte" to Alexandre Vinet, *Der Sozialismus in seinem Prinzip betrachtet*, iii–xii. Trans. D. Hofmeister. Berlin: Ferd. Dümmler, 1849.

Neil, W. "Criticism and Theological Use of the Bible, 1700–1950." In *Cambridge History of the Bible*, vol. 3, *The West, from the Reformation to the Present Day*, ed. S. L. Greenslade, 238–93. Cambridge: Cambridge University Press, 1963.

Nevins, William. *Thoughts on Popery.* New York: American Tract Society, 1836.

Newman, John Henry. *The Arians of the Fourth Century.* 1833. Eugene, Ore: Wipf and Stock, 1996.

———. *An Essay on the Development of Christian Doctrine.* 1845. Garden City, N.Y.: Doubleday, 1960.

———. *The Idea of a University.* 1859ff. Ed. Frank M. Turner. New Haven, Conn.: Yale University Press, 1996.

———. *Tract Ninety or Remarks on Certain Passages in the Thirty-Nine Articles.* 1841. Reprint with historical commentary by A. W. Evans. London: Constable, 1933.

Nichols, James Hastings. "John Williamson Nevin (1803–1886)." In *Sons of the Prophets*, ed. Kerr, 69–81.

———, ed. *The Mercersburg Theology.* New York: Oxford University Press, 1966.

———. *Romanticism in American Theology: Nevin and Schaff at Mercersburg.* Chicago: University of Chicago Press, 1961.

Noll, Mark A. *American Evangelical Christianity: An Introduction.* Oxford: Blackwell, 2001.

———. *America's God: From Jonathan Edwards to Abraham Lincoln.* Oxford: Oxford University Press, 2002.

———. *Between Faith and Criticism: Evangelicals, Scholarship, and the Bible in America.* San Francisco: Harper & Row, 1986.

———. "The Founding of Princeton Seminary." *Westminster Theological Journal* 42 (1979): 72–110.

———. *Princeton and the Republic, 1768–1822: The Search for a Christian Enlightenment in the Era of Samuel Stanhope Smith.* Princeton, N.J.: Princeton University Press, 1989.

———, ed. *The Princeton Theology 1812–1921: Scripture, Science, and Theological Method from Archibald Alexander to Benjamin Breckinridge Warfield.* Grand Rapids, Mich.: Baker Book House, 2001.

"Notices of New Books" [*The Life of Dr. Samuel Miller*]. *NE* 9 (July 1869): 620–25.

Novick, Peter. *That Noble Dream: The "Objectivity Question" and the American Historical Profession.* Cambridge: Cambridge University Press, 1988.

O'Brien, David. "Introduction." In Walworth, *The Oxford Movement in America*, v–xvii.

Obituary notice [James Emerton]. *Boston Journal*, June 1, 1892.

Obituary notice [Roswell Hitchcock]. *New-York Evangelist*, June 23, 1887.

Obituary notice [Roswell Hitchcock]. *New York Herald*, June 18, 1887.

Obituary notice [Roswell Hitchcock]. *Springfield (Massachusetts) Republican*, June 18, 1887.

O'Donnell, James J. *Augustine: A New Biography.* New York: HarperCollins, 2005.

Olbricht, Thomas H. "Biblical Primitivism in American Biblical Scholarship, 1630–1870." In *The American Quest for the Primitive Church*, ed. Richard T. Hughes, 81–98. Urbana: University of Illinois Press, 1988.

———. "Intellectual Ferment and Instruction in the Scriptures: The Bible in Higher Education." In *The Bible in American Education*, ed. Barr and Piediscalzi, 97–120.

Oleson, Alexandra and John Voss, eds. *The Organization of Knowledge in Modern America, 1860–1920.* Baltimore: Johns Hopkins University Press, 1979.

———. "Introduction." In *The Organization of Knowledge*, ed. Oleson and Voss, vii–xxi.

"Ordination of Professor Schaff." Trans. from Krummacher's "Palmblaetter." *Weekly Messenger* n.s. 9.51 (Sept. 4, 1844): 1–2.

Orsi, Robert A. *Between Heaven and Earth: The Religious Worlds People Make and the Scholars Who Study Them.* Princeton, N.J.: Princeton University Press, 2005.

"Palestine Exploration." *Baltimore Sun*, May 11, 1877.

Park, Edwards A. "Biographical Sketch." In *Sketch of the Life and Character of Prof. Tholuck*, 3–32. Edinburgh: Thomas Clark, 1840.

———. "A Discourse Delivered at the Funeral of Prof. Moses Stuart." Boston : Tappan & Whittemore, 1852.

Paulsen, Friedrich. *The German Universities: Their Character and Historical Development.* 1893. Trans. Edward D. Perry. New York: Macmillan, 1895.

Penzel, Klaus. "Church History in Context: The Case of Philip Schaff." In *Our Common History as Christians: Essays in Honor of Albert C. Outler,* ed. John Deschner, Leroy T. Howe, and Klaus Penzel, 217–60. New York: Oxford University Press, 1975.

———. "An Ecumenical Vision of Church History: F. W. J. Schelling." *Perkins School of Theology Journal* 17.2–3 (Winter/Spring 1964): 4–19.

———. *The German Education of Christian Scholar Philip Schaff: The Formative Years, 1819–1844.* Toronto Studies in Theology 95. Lewiston, N.Y.: Edwin Mellen, 2004.

———, ed. *Philip Schaff, Historian and Ambassador of the Universal Church: Selected Writings.* Macon, Ga.: Mercer University Press, 1991.

———. *The Private Life of Philip Schaff.* Burke Library Occasional Publication 3. New York: Union Theological Seminary, 1995.

Permanent Documents of the Society for the Promotion of Collegiate and Theological Education at the West. Vol. 1. New York: John F. Trow, 1852.

Pfaff, Richard W. "Anglo-American Patristic Translations 1866–1900." *JEH* 28.1 (Jan. 1977): 39–55.

Pfleiderer, Otto. *The Development of Theology in Germany Since Kant and Its Progress in Great Britain Since 1825.* Trans. J. F. Smith. London: Swan Sonnenschein, 1890.

Platner, John W. Review of Robert Rainy, *The Ancient Catholic Church from the Accession of Trajan to the Fourth General Council (A.D. 98–451). AHR* 8.1 (1902): 103–5.

Pochmann, Henry A. *German Culture in America: Philosophical and Literary Influences, 1600–1900.* Madison: University of Wisconsin Press, 1957.

Pollitt, J. J. *The Art of Rome c.753 B.C.–337 A.D.* Englewood Cliffs, N.J.: Prentice-Hall, 1966.

Porter, Noah (?). "The American Colleges and the American Public." *NE* 28 (Jan. 1869): 69–113; (April 1869): 319–60; (July 1869): 489–517; (Oct. 1869): 748–82.

———(?). "The American Student in Germany." [Review of *Germany: Its Universities, Theology, and Religion,* by Philip Schaff]. *NE* 15 (Nov. 1857): 574–602.

———(?). "The Christian Ministry as a Profession and a Sacred Calling." *AR* 1.4 (April 1884): 347–63.

Powell, Baden. "On the Study of the Evidences of Christianity." In *Essays and Reviews,* 94–144.

Pranger, Gary K. *Philip Schaff (1819–1893): Portrait of an Immigrant Theologian.* Swiss American Historical Society Publications 1. New York: Peter Lang, 1997.

———. "Philip Schaff: His Role in American Evangelical Education." In *German Influences on Education,* ed. Geitz et al., 213–26.

Pratt, John Webb. *Religion, Politics and Diversity: The Church-State Theme in New York History.* Ithaca, N.Y.: Cornell University Press, 1967.

Prentiss, George Lewis. *The Bright Side of Life: Glimpses of It Through Fourscore Years.* 2 vols. New York: Private printing, 1901.

————. "Charge to Roswell D. Hitchcock." In *Charge and Inaugural Address*, 5–18.

————."Introductory Notice" to Henry B. Smith, *Faith and Philosophy*, iii–xiv.

————. "The National Crisis." *ATR* 4.16 (Oct. 1862): 687–718.

————."The Political Crisis." *APTR* 4.16 (Oct. 1866): 625–46.

————. "The Political Situation." *APTR* 4.14 (April 1866): 298–334.

————. "The Union Theological Seminary." A Discourse Delivered in the Mercer-Street Church, Sunday, October 19, 1851. New York: John F. Trow, 1852.

————. *The Union Theological Seminary in the City of New York: Historical and Biographical Sketches of Its First Fifty Years*. New York: A.D.F. Randolph, 1889.

————. *The Union Theological Seminary in the City of New York: Its Design and Another Decade of Its History*. Asbury Park, N. J.: M., W. & C. Pennypacker, 1899.

"Professor H. B. Smith's System of Christian Theology." *NE* 43.180 (May 1884): 447–49.

Pusey, E. B. *An Historical Enquiry into the Probable Cause of the Rationalist Character Lately Predominant in the Theology of Germany*. London: Rivington, 1828, 1830.

Reed, Rebecca Theresa. *Six Months in a Convent, or, The Narrative of Rebecca Theresa Reed*. Boston: Russell, Odiorne & Metcalf, 1835.

Remus, Harold. "Origins." In *Graduate Education in Religion*, ed. Welch, 113–33.

Reinhold, Meyer. *Classica Americana: The Greek and Roman Heritage in the United States*. Detroit: Wayne State University Press, 1964.

Renan, Ernest. *The Life of Jesus*. 1863. New York: Modern Library, 1927.

"Report of the Committee on Theological Seminaries to the General Assembly of the Presbyterian Church in the United States of America, in Session at Washington, D.C., May 18, 1893." Pamphlet, UTS.

Reuben, Julie A. *The Making of the Modern University: Intellectual Transformation and the Marginalization of Morality*. Chicago: University of Chicago Press, 1996.

Review Essay (of Philip Schaff, *Principle of Protestantism*). *BRPR* 17 (Oct. 1845): 626–36.

Reynolds, Levering, Jr. "The Later Years (1880–1953)." In *The Harvard Divinity School*, ed. Williams, 165–229.

Richards, George Warren. *History of the Theological Seminary of the Reformed Church in the United States 1825–1934; Evangelical and Reformed Church 1934–1952*. Lancaster, Pa.: Rudisill, 1952.

Richardson, Cyril C. "Church History Past and Present." *USQR* 5.1 (Nov. 1949): 5–15.

Ringenberg, William C. *The Christian College: A History of Protestant Higher Education in America*. Grand Rapids, Mich.: Eerdmans with Christian University Press, 1984.

Ringer, Fritz. "The German Academic Community." In *The Organization of Knowledge*, ed. Oleson and Voss, 409–29.

Ripley, George, and Charles A. Dana, eds., *New American Cyclopaedia: A Popular Dictionary of General Knowledge*. 16 vols. New York: D. Appleton, 1859–1863.

Roberts, Alexander, and James Donaldson, eds.; rev. A. Cleveland Coxe. *Ante-Nicene Fathers*. 10 vols. 1885–1896. Reprint Grand Rapids, Mich.: Eerdmans, 1965.

Roberts, Jon H. and James Turner, eds. *The Sacred and the Secular University.* Princeton, N.J.: Princeton University Press, 2000.

Robinson, Edward. "Theological Education in Germany." *BR* 1.1 (Jan. 1831): 1–51; 1.2 (April 1831): 199–226; 1.3 (July 1831): 409–51; 1.4 (Oct. 1831): 613–37.

Roche, Spencer S. "Roswell D. Hitchcock, D.D., LL.D." Paper read before the Brooklyn [Episcopal] Clerical Club, June 27, 1887. Hitchcock Papers, UTS, B1, "Memorial Notices."

Rodgers, Daniel T. "Exceptionalism." In *Imagined Histories: American Historians Interpret the Past*, ed. Anthony Molho and Gordon S. Wood, 21–40. Princeton, N.J.: Princeton University Press, 1998.

Roeber, Anthony Gregg. "The Von Mosheim Society and the Preservation of German Education and Culture in the New Republic, 1789–1813." In *German Influences on Education*, ed. Geitz et al., 157–76.

Ross, Earle D. "Religious Influences in the Development of State Colleges and Universities." *Indiana Magazine of History* 46.4 (Dec. 1950): 343–62.

Rudolph, Frederick. *The American College and University: A History.* 1962. Reprint. Athens: University of Georgia Press, 1990.

Ryan, W. Carson. *Studies in Early Graduate Education: The Johns Hopkins, [sic] Clark University, The University of Chicago.* New York: Carnegie Foundation for the Advancement of Teaching, 1939.

"S." "The Oxford Essayists—Their Relation to Christianity and to Strauss and Baur." *BFER* 10.36 (April 1861): 407–30.

Saunders, Ernest W. *Searching the Scriptures: A History of the Society of Biblical Literature, 1880–1980.* SBL Biblical Scholarship in America 8. Chico, Calif.: Scholars Press, 1982.

Schaff, David S. *The Life of Philip Schaff.* New York: Scribner's, 1897.

———. "Samuel Macauley Jackson as a Co-Worker with Philip Schaff." In *Papers of the American Society of Church History*, ed. William W. Rockwell, 11–17. 2nd ser. 4. New York: Putnam's, 1914.

The Schaff Memorial Meeting. Wednesday, December 27, 1893. *Papers of the American Society of Church History* 6. Reprint. New York: Knickerbocker Press, 1894.

Schaff, Philip. "Adoptionists." In *Dictionary of Christian Biography*, ed. W. Smith and Wace, 1: 44–47.

———. *America: A Sketch of Its Political, Social, and Religious Character.* Ed. Perry Miller. 1855. Cambridge, Mass.: Belknap Press of Harvard University Press, 1961.

———. "American Nationality." An Address Delivered Before the Irving Society of the College of St. James, Md., June 11, 1856. Chambersburg, Pa.: Irving Society, 1856.

———. "The Ancient Catholic Liturgies." *APTR* 4.14 (April 1866): 230–47.

———. "The Anglo-American Sabbath." Read Before the National Sabbath Convention, Saratoga, August 11, 1863. New York: American Tract Society, 1863.

———. "Anglo-Germanism, or the Significance of the German Nationality in the

United States." Address before the Schiller Society of Marshall College, March 10, 1846. Trans. J. S. Ermentrout. Chambersburg, Pa.: Publication Office of the German Reformed Church, 1846.

———. "Arianism." In *The New Schaff-Herzog Encyclopedia*, ed. Jackson, 1: 278–81.

———. "The Ascetic System." *MR* 10 (Oct. 1858): 600–613.

———. "The Athanasian Creed." *APTR* 4.16 (Oct. 1866): 584–625.

———. "Autobiographical Reminiscences." In *Philip Schaff*, ed. Penzel, 5–27. Full version ("Autobiographical Reminiscences for My Children") in LTS, Ms. Coll. 63, Box 1, ff. 04.

———. *Bibliotheca Symbolica Ecclesiae Universalis: The Creeds of Christendom, with a History and Critical Notes*. 1877. 3 vols. Vol. 1, *The History of the Creeds*. 2nd ed. New York: Harper & Brothers, 1878.

———. "The Brethren of Christ." *BS* 21.84 (Oct. 1864): 855–69.

———. *Der Bürgerkrieg und das christliche Leben in Nord-Amerika*. 1865. 3rd ed. Berlin: Wiegandt und Grieben, 1866.

———. *A Catechism for Sunday Schools and Families*. Philadelphia: Lindsay & Blakiston; Chambersburg, Pa.: M. Kieffer, 1862.

———. *Christ and Christianity: Studies on Christology, Creed and Confessions, Protestantism and Romanism, Reformation Principles, Sunday Observance, Religious Freedom, and Christian Union*. New York: Scribner's, 1885.

———. *Creed Revision in the Presbyterian Churches*. 2nd ed., enlarged. New York: Scribner's 1890.

———. "Christianity in America." A Report Prepared for the Meeting of the Evangelical Alliance Held at Berlin in September, 1857. *MR* 9 (Oct. 1857): 493–539. Also in *Reformed and Catholic*, ed. Yrigoyen and Bricker, 345–91.

———. "Christology." In *Dictionary of Christian Biography*, ed. W. Smith and Wace, I: 489–95.

———. "Christology." In *New American Cyclopedia*, ed. McClintock and Strong, II: 277–85.

———. "Christ's Testimony to Christianity." An Apologetic Lecture Delivered in Philadelphia, January 1871. Philadelphia: Ziegler & McCurdy, 1871.

———. *Church and State in the United States or the American Idea of Religious Liberty and Its Practical Effects*. 1888. New York: Arno Press, 1972.

———. "Church History." In *The New Schaff-Herzog Encyclopedia*, ed. Jackson, II: 96–100.

———. *A Companion to the Greek Testament and the English Version*. New York: Harper & Brothers, 1883.

———. "The Conflict of Trinitarianism and Unitarianism in the Ante-Nicene Age." *BS* 15.60 (Oct. 1858): 726–44.

———. "Constantine the Great, and the Downfall of Paganism in the Roman Empire." *BS* 20.80 (Oct. 1863): 778–98.

———. *Creed Revision in the Presbyterian Churches*. 2nd enlarged ed. New York: Scribner's, 1890.

———. "Dante." In *Goethean Hall; or The Anniversary of Goethe's Birth-Day, August 28, A. D. 1846 in Mercersburg*. Chambersburg, Pa.: Office of the German Reformed Church, 1846.

———. "The Development of the Ancient Catholic Hierarchy: Part I." *BFER* 14.54 (Oct. 1865): 665–95.

———. "The Development of the Ancient Catholic Hierarchy: Part II." *BFER* 15.55 (Jan. 1866): 24–60.

———. "Dr. Schaff's Reply and Farewell to the Synod." In *The Semi-Centennial of Philip Schaff*, 23–28.

———. "The Eastern Conflict." *New York Observer*, June 14, 1877.

———. "The English Language: Heterogeneous in Formation, Homogeneous in Character, Universal in Destination for the Spread of Christian Civilization." A Lecture Delivered at Vanderbilt University, January 3, 1887. Nashville: Cumberland Presbyterian Publishing House, 1887.

———. "The Evangelical Alliance at Berlin." *MR* 9 (April 1857): 318–20.

———. "General Introduction to Church History." *BS* 6.23 (Aug. 1849): 409–41.

———. "The Genius and Theology of St. Augustine." *MR* 14 (Jan. 1867): 98–120.

———. "German Literature in America." *BS* 4.15 (Aug. 1847): 503–21.

———. "German Theology and the Church Question." Trans. C. Z. Weiser. *MR* 5.1 (Jan. 1853): 124–44. Also in *Reformed and Catholic*, ed. Yrigoyen and Bricker, 320–30; and in *Philip Schaff*, ed. Penzel, 95–115.

———. *Germany: Its Universities, Theology and Religion: With Sketches of Neander, Tholuck, Olshausen, Hengstenberg, Twesten, Nitzsch, Müller, Ullmann, Rothe, Dorner, Lange, Ebrard, Wichern, and Other Distinguished German Divines of the Age*. Philadelphia: Lindsay & Bakiston, 1857.

———. "Gnosticism." *MR* 10 (Oct. 1858): 520–33.

———. *History of the Apostolic Church with a General Introduction to Church History*. Vol. I. Trans. Edward D. Yeomans. New York: Scribner, 1853, 1858; "General Introduction" also in *Reformed and Catholic*, ed. Yrigoyen and Bricker, 149–315.

———. *History of the Christian Church*. Vol. I. *Apostolic Christianity A.D. 1–100*. 1882. New ed., rev. and enlarged. New York: Scribner's, 1887.

———. *History of the Christian Church*. Vol. II. *Ante-Nicene Christianity, A.D. 100–325*. 1883. 4th ed., new and rev. New York: Scribner's, 1887.

———. *History of the Christian Church*. 1867. Vol. III. *Nicene and Post-Nicene Christianity*. 1884. 5th ed. New York: Scribner's, 1906.

———. *History of the Christian Church*. Vol. IV. *Mediaeval Christianity. From Gregory I to Gregory VII. A.D. 590–1073*. 1885. New York: Scribner's, 1887.

———. "A History of the Vatican Council." In W. E. Gladstone, *The Vatican Decrees in Their Bearing on Civil Allegiance; A Political Exposition to which are added A*

History of the Vatican Council by Philip Schaff, 51–107. New York: Harper & Brothers, 1875.

———. "Impressions of England." *MR* 9 (July 1857): 329–58.

———. "Infant Salvation." *Independent*, May 13, 1875.

———. "The Influence of Christianity on the Family." *MR* 5 (Oct. 1853): 473–91.

———. "The Influence of the Early Church on the Institution of Slavery." *MR* 10 (Oct. 1858): 614–20.

———. *In Memoriam: Our Children in Heaven*. New York: Private printing, 1876.

———. "Julian the Apostate." *ATR* 3.9 (Jan. 1861): 1–17.

———. "The Latin Patriarchate." *APTR* 2.5 (Jan. 1864): 9–29.

———. *The Life and Labors of St. Augustine*. Trans. T. C. Porter. New York: J. C. Riker, 1854.

———. *Literature and Poetry: Studies on the English Language, the Poetry of the Bible, the Dies Irae, the Stabat Mater, the Hymns of St. Bernard, the University—Ancient and Modern, Dante Alighieri, the Divina Commedia*. New York: Scribner's 1890.

———. "The Moral Character of Christ, or The Perfection of Christ's Humanity, A Proof of His Divinity. A Theological Tract for the People." Chambersburg, Pa.: M. Kieffer., 1861.

———. "National Pride." In "Occasional Thoughts and Impressions on Religious, Moral, and Literary Topics." 1863. LTS, Ms. Coll. 163, B4, ff.12.

———. "Neander as a Church Historian." *MR* 4.6 (Nov. 1852): 564–77.

———. "The New York General Conference of the Evangelical Alliance." *APR* 3rd ser. 2.1 (Jan. 1870): 68–90.

———. *The Oldest Church Manual called the Teaching of the Twelve Apostles*. 2nd ed., rev. and enlarged. New York: Funk and Wagnalls, 1886.

———. "Passion Week in Rome Fifty Years Ago," ed. David Schaff. [Extracts from Philip Schaff's journal, Spring 1842.] Reprinted from *Homiletic Review*, n.p., n.d.(1892?). Pamphlet, UTS.

———. "The Patristic Doctrine of the Sacraments." *APTR* 4.13 (Jan. 1866): 93–100.

———. "Patristics." In *New American Cyclopedia*, ed. McClintock and Strong, VII: 779–80.

———. "The Pelagian Controversy—A Historical Essay." *BS* 5.18 (May 1848): 205–43.

———. "A Plea for Primitive Christianity from the Admissions of Skeptical Criticism." *Independent*, July 8, 1880.

———. "A Plea for the Revision of the Westminster Confession." In Schaff, *Creed Revision*, 43–51.

———. *The Person of Christ: The Perfection of His Humanity Viewed as a Proof of His Divinity*. 1862. 12th ed., rev. and enlarged. New York: American Tract Society, 1882.

———. "Preface." In *A Select Library of the Nicene and Post-Nicene Fathers of the Christian Church*, ed. Philip Schaff. Ser. I, vol. I: v–vii. 1889 (?). Reprint Grand Rapids, Mich.: Eerdmans, 1979.

———. "Preface." In *A Select Library of the Nicene and Post-Nicene Fathers of the*

Christian Church, ed. Philip Schaff. Ser. I, vol. IX: n.p. 1887 (?). Reprint Grand Rapids, Mich.: Eerdmans, 1979.

———. "Preface to the American Edition" of *A Commentary on the Holy Scriptures* by John Peter Lange, ed. Philip Schaff. Vol. I. New York: Scribner's, 1884. In *Philip Schaff*, ed. Penzel, 239–48.

———. *Principle of Protestantism*. Trans. John W. Nevin. 1845. Lancaster Series on the Mercersburg Theology, vol. 1, ed. Bard Thompson and George H. Bricker. Philadelphia: United Church Press, 1964.

———. "The Principles of the Reformation." In Schaff, *Christ and Christianity*, 135–52.

———. "The Progress of Church History as a Science." *BS* 7.25 (Jan. 1850): 54–91.

———. "The Progress of Religious Freedom as Shown in the History of the Toleration Acts." *Papers of the American Society of Church History* (1888). Vol. I: 1–126. London: Putnam's, 1889. Pamphlet reprint. New York: Scribner's, 1889.

———. "Prolegomena : The Life and Work of St. John Chrysostom." In *A Select Library of the Nicene and Post-Nicene Fathers of the Christian Church*, ed. Philip Schaff. Ser. 1, Vol. IX: 3–23. 1889? Reprint Grand Rapids, Mich.: Eerdmans, 1978.

———. "Prolegomena: St. Augustin's [*sic*] Life and Work," in *A Select Library of the Nicene and Post-Nicene Fathers*, ed. Philip Schaff. Series 1, Vol. I: 1–24. 1889. Reprint Grand Rapids, Mich.: Eerdmans, 1979.

———. "Protestantism and Romanism." In Schaff, *Christ and Christianity*, 124–27.

———. "Recollections of Neander." *MR* 3.1 (Jan. 1851): 73–90.

———. "Reminiscences of Neander." In Schaff, *Saint Augustine, Melanchthon, Neander*, 28–168.

———. *The Renaissance and the Reformation*. Address to the Ninth General Conference of the Evangelical Alliance, Florence, April 1891. Pamphlet, UTS Library.

———. *The Renaissance: The Revival of Learning and Art in the Fourteenth and Fifteenth Centuries*. New York: Putnam's, 1891.

———. "The Reunion of Christendom." A Paper Prepared for the Parliament of Religions and the National Conference of the Evangelical Alliance Held in Chicago, September and October, 1893. New York: Evangelical Alliance Office, 1893. Also in *Philip Schaff*, ed. Penzel, 302–40.

———. "The Revised Version and Its Critics." *Independent*, March 22, 1883.

———. "The Revised Version and Its Critics—II." *Independent*, April 8, 1883.

———, ed. *The Revision of the English Version of the Holy Scriptures: by a Co-operative Committee of British and American Scholars of Different Denominations*. 1873. 3rd ed. New York: Harper & Brothers, 1877.

———. "The Revision of the Westminster Confession." A Paper Read Before a Special Meeting, Nov. 4, 1889, of the Presbytery of New York.

———. "Rise and Progress of Monasticism." *BS* 21.82 (April 1864): 384–424.

———. "Roswell D. Hitchcock." *Independent*, June 23, 1887.

———. *Saint Augustine, Melanchthon, Neander: Three Biographies.* New York: Funk & Wagnalls, 1886.

———. "Savonarola." *MR* 10 (July 1858): 333–61.

———. *Slavery and the Bible. A Tract for the Times.* Chambersburg, Pa.: M. Kieffer, 1861. Also in *MR* 13 (April 1861): 288–317.

———. "The State Church System in Europe." *MR* 9 (Jan. 1857): 151–66.

———. *Die Sünde wider den heiligen Geist und die daraus gezogenen dogmatischen und ethischen Folgerungen.* Halle: Johann Friedrich Lippert, 1841.

———."Systematic Benevolence." A Sermon Presented by Appointment before the Synod of the German Reformed Church of the U.S. at Lancaster, Pa., on the 20th of October, 1851. Mercersburg, Pa.: P.A. Rice, 1852.

———. "Tertullian." *MR* 10 (1858): 621–27.

———. *Theological Propaedeutic. A General Introduction to the Study of Theology: Exegetical, Historical, Systematic, and Practical, Including Encyclopaedia, Methodology, and Bibliography. A Manual for Students.* 2 parts. Part II: New York: Scribner's, 1893.

———. "The Theology for Our Age and Country." *PQPR* 1.1 (Jan. 1872): 29–47. Also in Schaff, *Christ and Christianity*, 1–22.

———. *Through Bible Lands: Notes of Travel in Egypt, the Desert, and Palestine.* New ed., rev. and enlarged. London: James Nisbet, 1878.

———. "Ueber den Ursprung und Charakter des Mönchthums." *Jahrbücher der deutsche Theologie* 6 (1861): 555–66.

———. "The University: Past, Present, and Future." In Schaff, *Literature and Poetry*, 256–78. London: Elkin Mathews, 1890.

———. "The Vatican Council." *PQPR* 2.8 (Oct. 1873): 630–51.

———. *What Is Church History?* Philadelphia: Lippincott, 1846. Also in *Reformed and Catholic*, ed. Yrigoyen and Bricker, 17–144.

Schaff, Philip, and Roswell D. Hitchcock. "Preface" [on H. B. Smith]. In John Gieseler, *Text-Book of Church History*, trans. and ed. Smith. V: i*–vii*.

Schaff, Philip, Samuel M. Jackson, and D. S. Schaff, eds. *A Religious Encyclopaedia: or Dictionary of Biblical, Historical, Doctrinal, and Practical Theology. Based on the Real-Encyklopädie of Herzog, Plitt, and Hauck.* 1882–1884. 3 vols. Rev. ed. New York: Christian Literature Company, 1888.

Schaff, Philip, and S. Irenaeus Prime, eds. *Evangelical Alliance Conference, 1873.* History, Essays, Orations, and Other Documents of the Sixth General Conference of the Evangelical Alliance, Held in New York, October 2–12, 1873. New York: Harper & Brothers, 1874.

———. "Historical Sketch." In *Evangelical Alliance Conference, 1873*, ed. Schaff and Prime, 3–52.

"Schaff's Church History." *ATR* 1.2 (May 1859): 318–26.

"Schaff's Church History." *BS* 16.63 (April 1859): 454–56.

Schleiermacher, Friedrich. *The Christian Faith*. Ed. H. R. Mackintosh and J. S. Stewart. 1821–1822. Edinburgh: T. & T. Clark, 1936.

Schneck, Benjamin Schroeder. *Mercersburg Theology Inconsistent with Protestant and Reformed Doctrine*. Philadelphia: Lippincott, 1874.

Schoedel, William R. *Ignatius of Antioch: A Commentary on the Letters of Ignatius of Antioch*. Philadelphia: Fortress, 1985.

Schweitzer, Albert. *The Quest of the Historical Jesus: A Critical Study of Its Progress from Reimarus to Wrede*. 1906. Trans. W. Montgomery. New York: Macmillan, 1964.

Selden, William K. *Princeton Theological Seminary: A Narrative History 1812–1992*. Princeton, N.J.: Princeton University Press, 1992.

The Semi-Centennial of Philip Schaff: Berlin 1842–New York 1892. New York: Private, 1893.

The Seminary: Its Spirit and Aims. Addresses Given to the Annual Dinner of the Alumni [of Union Theological Seminary], held on May 13, 1907. New York: Irving Press, 1907.

Shahan, Thomas Joseph. "Dr. Schaff and the Roman Catholic Church." In *The Schaff Memorial Meeting*, 26–28..

Shepard, Robert S. *God's People in the Ivory Tower: Religion in the Early American University*. Chicago Studies in the History of American Religion 20. Brooklyn, N.Y.: Carlson, 1991.

Shorey, Paul. "The Case for the Classics." In *Latin and Greek*, ed. Kelsey, 303–43.

Shriver, George H., Jr., ed. *American Religious Heretics: Formal and Informal Trials*. Nashville, Tenn.: Abingdon 1966.

———. "Philip Schaff as a Teacher of Church History." *Journal of Presbyterian History* 47.1 (March 1969): 74–92.

———. *Philip Schaff: Christian Scholar and Ecumenical Prophet*. Centennial Biography for the American Society of Church History. Macon, Ga.: Mercer University Press, 1987.

———. "Philip Schaff: Heresy at Mercersburg." In *American Religious Heretics*, ed. Shriver, 18–55.

———. "Philip Schaff's Concept of Organic Historiography Interpreted in Relation to the Realization of an 'Evangelical Catholicism' Within the Christian Community." Ph.D. dissertation, Duke University, 1960.

Slavens, Thomas Paul. "Incidents in the Librarianship of Henry B. Smith." Pamphlet, UTS Library.

———. "The Library of the Union Theological Seminary in the City of New York, 1836 to the Present." Ph.D. dissertation, University of Michigan, 1965.

Sloan, Douglas. *The Scottish Enlightenment and the American College Ideal*. New York: Teachers College Press, 1971.

Smith, Bonnie G. *The Gender of History: Men, Women, and Historical Practice*. Cambridge, Mass.: Harvard University Press, 1998.

[Smith, Elizabeth]. *Henry Boynton Smith: His Life and Work.* New York: Armstrong & Son, 1881.

Smith, Henry Boynton. *Apologetics: A Course of Lectures.* Ed. William S. Karr. New York: Armstrong & Son, 1881.

———. "Bishop C. J. von Hefele on the Case of Pope Honorius." *PQPR* 1.2 (April 1872): 273–81.

———. "British Sympathy with America." *ATR* 4.15 (July 1862): 487–552.

———. "Calvin." In *New American Cyclopaedia,* ed. Ripley and Dana, IV: 281–88.

———. "Christian Apologetics." *PQPR* 5.19 (July 1876): 479–96.

———. "Christian Union and Ecclesiastical Reunion." In Smith, *Faith and Philosophy,* 265–96.

[———]. "Clergymen as Men of Science." *New-York Evangelist,* Nov. 16, 1876.

———. "Draper's Intellectual Development of Europe." *APTR* 1.4 (Oct. 1863): 615–31. Also in Smith, *Faith and Philosophy,* 337–58.

———. *Faith and Philosophy: Discourses and Essays.* Ed. George L. Prentiss. New York: Scribner's, 1886.

[———]. "Freedom Betrayed by the Evangelical Alliance of England." *APTR* 1.2 (April 1863): 233–50.

———. "Hegel." In *New American Cyclopaedia,* ed. Ripley and Dana, IX: 51–56.

———. "A Historical Discourse." Delivered in Abington, January 30, 1853, at the Close of the First Century of Abington Church and Society. Hartford, Conn.: Case, Tiffany, 1853.

———. *History of the Church of Christ, in Chronological Tables.* 1859. Rev. ed. New York: Charles Scribner, 1861.

———. "The Idea of Christian Theology as a System." In Smith, *Faith and Philosophy,* 125–66.

———. "The Inspiration of the Holy Scriptures." A Sermon Delivered before the Synod of New-York and New-Jersey in the First Presbyterian Church, Newark, New Jersey, October 17, 1855. New York: John A. Gray, 1855.

———. "Introduction" to [I. A.] "Dorner's History of the Doctrine of the Person of Christ." Trans. H. B. Smith. *BS* 6.21 (Feb. 1849): 156–67.

———. "Introduction" to J. J. I. Döllinger, *Fables Respecting the Popes in the Middle Ages.* Trans. Alfred Plummer; and Döllinger, *The Prophetic Spirit and the Prophecies of the Christian Era,* i–xii. Trans. H. B. Smith. New York: Dodd and Mead, 1872.

———. *Introduction to Christian Theology.* Ed. William S. Karr. New York: Armstrong & Son, 1883.

———. "Introductory Note" to Gieseler, *Text-Book of Church History,* trans. Davidson, iii–iv.

———. "Introductory Note by the Translator" to Ernst von Lasaulx, "The Expiatory Sacrifices of the Greeks and the Romans, and Their Relation to the One Sacrifice upon Golgotha." *BS* 1.2 (May 1844): 368–71.

———. "Kant." In *New American Cyclopaedia*, ed. Ripley and Dana, X: 107–15.

———. "The Limits of Religious Thought." *ATR* 2.5 (Feb. 1860): 1–28.

———. "Miracle." In *New American Cyclopaedia*, ed. Ripley and Dana [1870 ed.], XI: 557–60.

———. "The Moral Aspects of the Present Struggle." *ATR* 3.12 (Oct. 1861): 710–33. Reprinted in *BFER* 11.39 (Jan. 1862): 145–64.

———. "Nature and Worth of the Science of Church History." 1851. In Smith, *Faith and Philosophy*, 49–86.

———. "The New Faith of Strauss." *PQPR* n.s. 3.10 (April 1874): 259–98. Also in Smith, *Faith and Philosophy*, 443–88.

———. "The New Latitudinarians of England." *ATR* 3.10 (April 1861): 312–57. Also in Smith, *Faith and Philosophy*, 167–214.

———. "Outline of Professor Smith's Intended Lectures on Evolution." Appendix III in Smith, *Apologetics*, 170–94.

———. "Pantheism." In *New American Cyclopaedia*, ed. Ripley and Dana, XII: 720–21.

———(?) "The Papal Question in England." *PQPR* 4.14 (April 1875): 356–64.

———. "Passaglia, Guizot, and Döllinger on the Roman Question." *ATR* 4.14 (April 1862): 352–68.

———. "Presbyterian Division and Reunion in Scotland, Ireland and the United States." *APTR* 6.21 (Jan. 1868): 62–90.

———. "The Problem of the Philosophy of History." An Address Before the Phi Beta Kappa Society of Yale College, July 27, 1853. Philadelphia: Isaac Ashmead, 1854.

———. "Recent German Works on Apologetics." *PQPR* 5.20 (Oct. 1876): 720–37.

———. "The Reformed Churches of Europe and America, in Relation to General Church History." An Address Delivered by Request of the Presbyterian Historical Society before the General Assembly at St. Louis, Missouri, May 21, 1855. Philadelphia: Henry B. Ashmead, 1855. Also in Smith, *Faith and Philosophy*, 87–124.

———. "The Relations of Faith and Philosophy." An Address Before the Porter Rhetorical Society of Andover Theological Seminary, at Its Anniversary, Sept. 4, 1849. *BS* 6.24 (Nov. 1849): 673–709. Also in Smith, *Faith and Philosophy*, 1–48.

———. "Renan's Life of Jesus." *APTR* 2.5 (Jan. 1864): 136–69. Also in Smith, *Faith and Philosophy*, 401–42.

———. "Report on the State of Religion in the United States of America, Made to the General Conference of the Evangelical Alliance at Amsterdam, 1867." New York: W.C. Rogers, 1867.

———. "Report to the Evangelical Alliance." *APTR* 5.20 (Oct. 1867): 555–92.

———(?). "Roman Catholic Baptism Up Again." *New-York Evangelist*, June 6, 1876.

———(?). "Roman Catholics and Public Schools." *New-York Evangelist*, Jan. 6, 1876; Sept. 31 [*sic*], 1876.

———. "'Roman Letters' on the Vatican Council." *APR* 2.4 (Oct. 1870): 667–79.

———. "Schelling." In *New American Cyclopaedia*, ed. Ripley and Dana, XIV: 396–400.

————. "Schelling on the Characteristics of the Different Christian Churches." *APTR* 3.10 (April 1865): 283–89.

————. "Sermon XXI." In *Our Martyr President, Abraham Lincoln: Voices from the Pulpit of New York and Brooklyn*, 359–81. New York: Tibbals & Whiting, 1865.

————, trans. "A Sketch of German Philosophy" [paraphrase of articles by unidentified authors in Halle's *Allgemeine Literatur-Zeitung*, 1843–1844]. *BS* 2.6 (May 1845): 260–92.

————. *System of Christian Theology*. Ed. William S. Karr. 1884. 4th ed. New York: A.C. Armstrong, 1892.

————. "Theological and Literary Intelligence" columns. *ATR* 1859–1863; *APTR* 1863–1869; *APR* 1869–1872; *PQPR* 1872–1877.

————. "The Theological System of Emmons." *ATR* 4.13 (Jan. 1862): 7–53. Also in Smith, *Faith and Philosophy*, 215–63.

[————]. "The Unitarianism of 1859, as Officially Exhibited." *ATR* 1.4 (Nov. 1859): 730–59.

————. "Unitarian Tendencies." *ATR* 2.6 (May 1860): 259–88.

Smith, Henry Boynton, and Roswell D. Hitchcock. *The Life, Writings and Character of Edward Robinson*. 1863. New York: Arno Press, 1977.

Smith, Jonathan Z. *Drudgery Divine: On the Comparison of Early Christianities and the Religions of Late Antiquity*. Jordan Lectures in Comparative Religion 14, University of London. Chicago: University of Chicago Press, 1990.

Smith, Philip. *The History of the Christian Church During the First Ten Centuries, from Its Foundation to the Full Establishment of the Holy Roman Empire and the Papal Power*. New York: Harper & Brothers, 1879.

Smith, Timothy L. "New Approaches to the History of Immigration in Twentieth-Century America." *AHR* 71.4 (July 1966): 1265–79.

————. "Protestant Schooling and American Nationality, 1800–1850." *JAH* 53.4 (March 1967): 679–95.

Smith, William, and Henry Wace, eds. *A Dictionary of Christian Biography, Literature, Sects and Doctrines*. London: John Murray, 1877.

"Smith's Chronological Tables." *BS* 17.65 (Jan. 1860): 231–32.

Society of Clergymen. "Thoughts on the State of Theological Science and Education in Our Country." *BS* 1.4 (Nov. 1844): 735–67.

Solt, Leonard Franklin. "The Rise and Development of the Protestant Theological Seminary to 1860." M.A. thesis, Department of History, Oberlin College, 1954.

Stanley, Arthur Penrhyn. *Lectures on the History of the Eastern Church with an Introduction on the Study of Ecclesiastical History*. 1861. New York: Scribner's, 1862.

Stansell, Christine. *City of Women: Sex and Class in New York, 1789–1860*. Urbana: University of Illinois Press, 1987.

Stanton, William. *The Leopard's Spots: Scientific Attitudes Toward Race in America 1815–59*. Chicago: University of Chicago Press, 1960.

Starbuck, C. C. "Bishop Bryennios' 'Teaching of the Twelve Apostles'." *AR* 1.4 (April 1884): 426–42.

———. "Book Reviews and Notices: Papers of the American Society of Church History. Volume I." *AR* 13.74 (Feb. 1890): 233–35.

Starr, Harris E. *William Graham Sumner*. New York: Holt, 1925.

Stearns, Jonathan F. "The Charge to Henry B. Smith." In "The Charge and Inaugural Address to Henry B. Smith When Inaugurated as Chair of Systematic Theology in the Union Theological Seminary, New York, Sabbath Evening, May 6, 1855," 5–19. New York: John Wiley, 1855.

Stearns, Lewis F. *Henry Boynton Smith*. Boston: Houghton Mifflin, 1892.

Stevenson, J. Ross. *The Historical Position of Princeton Seminary*. New York: n.p., 1928.

Stevenson, Louise L. *Scholarly Means to Evangelical Ends: The New Haven Scholars and the Transformation of Higher Learning in America, 1830–1890*. Baltimore: Johns Hopkins University Press, 1986.

Stewart, John William. "The Tethered Theology: Biblical Criticism, Common Sense Philosophy, and the Princeton Theologians 1812–1860." Ph.D. dissertation, University of Michigan, 1990.

Stocking, George W., Jr. *Race, Culture, and Evolution: Essays in the History of Anthropology*. New York: Free Press, 1968.

Stoever, William K. B. "Henry Boynton Smith and the German Theology of History." *USQR* 24.1 (Fall 1968): 69–89.

Storr, Richard J. *The Beginning of the Future: A Historical Approach to Graduate Education in the Arts and Sciences*. New York: McGraw-Hill, 1973.

———. *The Beginnings of Graduate Education in America*. Chicago: University of Chicago Press, 1953.

Strauss, David Friedrich. *The Christ of Faith and the Jesus of History: A Critique of Schleiermacher's "Life of Jesus"*. 1865. Trans. Leander Keck. Philadelphia: Fortress, 1977.

———. *The Life of Jesus, Critically Examined*. 1835. Trans. Marian Evans [George Eliot]. 2 vols. St. Clair Shores, Mich.: Scholarly Press, 1970.

Stuckenberg, J. H. W. "The Early Life of Tholuck." *AR* 3.15 (March 1885): 248–67.

Styers, Randall. *Making Magic: Religion, Magic, and Science in the Modern World*. Oxford: Oxford University Press, 2004.

Syme, Ronald. *Sallust*. Sather Classical Lectures 33. Berkeley: University of California Press, 1964.

Tappan, Henry Philip. "The Idea of the True University." In *American Higher Education*, ed. Hofstadter and Smith, II: 515–45. Reprinted from Tappan, *The University: Its Constitution and Its Relations, Political and Religious* (Ann Arbor, Mich.: S.B. McCracken, 1858).

———. "Romanism and Barbarism." *American Biblical Repertory* 14 [3rd ser. 4.2] (April 1848): 252–82.

———. *University Education*. 1851. New York: Arno Press/New York Times, 1969.

Taves, Ann. "Sexuality in American Religious History." In *Retelling U.S. Religious History*, ed. Tweed, 27–56.

[Taylor, William]. "The Late Prof. H. B. Smith." *The Christian at Work*, Feb. 17, 1877.

Temple, Frederick. "The Education of the World." In *Essays and Reviews*, 1–49.

———. *The Relations Between Religion and Science. Eight Lectures Preached Before the University of Oxford in the Year 1884*. Bampton Lectures. New York: Macmillan, 1884.

Tewksbury, Donald G. *The Founding of American Colleges and Universities Before the Civil War*. 1932. New York: Arno Press/New York Times, 1969.

Tholuck, August, "Evangelical Theology in Germany: Survey of My Life as a Teacher of Theology." Trans. Leopold Witte. In *Evangelical Alliance Conference, 1873*, ed. Schaff and Prime, 85–89.

Thompson, J. Earl, Jr. "Church History Comes to Andover: The Persecution of James Murdock." *Andover Newton Quarterly* 15.4 (March 1975): 213–27.

Thwing, Charles F. "Should College Students Study?" *NAR* 180 (1905): 230–34.

Toews, John Edward. *Hegelianism: The Path Toward Dialectical Humanism*. Cambridge: Cambridge University Press, 1980.

Trinterud, Leonard J. "Charles Hodge (1797–1878)." in *Sons of the Prophets*, ed. Kerr, 23–38.

Turner, James. "Secularization and Sacralization: Speculations on Some Religious Origins of the Secular Humanities Curriculum, 1850–1900." In *The Secularization of the Academy*, ed. Marsden and Longfield, 74–106.

———. *Without God, Without Creed: The Origins of Unbelief in America*. Baltimore: Johns Hopkins University Press, 1985.

Turner, James, and Paul Bernard. "The Prussian Road to the University? German Models and the University of Michigan, 1837–c. 1895." *Rackham Reports* (University of Michigan), 1988–1989, 6–52.

Tweed, Thomas. *The American Encounter with Buddhism 1844–1912: Victorian Culture and the Limits of Dissent*. 1990. Bloomington: Indiana University Press, 1992.

———, ed. *Retelling U.S. Religious History*. Berkeley: University of California Press, 1997.

Twesten, A. D. C. "The Trinity." Trans. H. B. Smith [from Twesten's theological lectures at the University of Berlin]. *BS* 3.11 (Aug. 1846): 499–539; 3.12 (Nov. 1846): 760–74); 4.13 (Feb. 1847): 25–68.

Uhlhorn, Gerhard. "Die älteste Kirchengeschichte in der Darstellung der Tübinger Schule." *Jahrbücher für deutsche Theologie* 3 (1858): 280–349.

Ullmann, C. "Preface" to Neander, *General History of the Christian Religion and Church*, vi–xxxii.

"Unitarians Confer by the Sea." *Springfield Republican*, July 17, 1901.

Ussher, James. *Polycarpi et Ignatii epistulae*. Oxford: Lichfield, 1644.

Van Riper, A. Bowdoin. *Men Among the Mammoths: Victorian Science and the Discovery of Human Prehistory*. Chicago: University of Chicago Press, 1993.

Veysey, Laurence R. *The Emergence of the American University.* Chicago: University of Chicago Press, 1965.

———. "The Plural Organized Worlds of the Humanities." In *The Organization of Knowledge,* ed. Oleson and Voss, 51–106.

Vincent, John Martin. *Historical Research: An Outline of Theory and Practice.* New York: Holt, 1911.

Vincent, Marvin R. "Address Commemorative of Philip Schaff, D.D, LL.D." Delivered at The Century [*sic*], December 30, 1893. Schaff Papers, UTS, B1.

Wacker, Grant. "The Demise of Biblical Civilization." In *The Bible in America,* ed. Hatch and Noll, 121–38.

Walker, Williston. "Notes from a German University," *AR* 9.53 (May 1888): 491–99.

Walsh, R. G. *Livy: His Historical Aims and Methods.* Cambridge: Cambridge University Press, 1961.

Walworth, Clarence E. *The Oxford Movement in America.* 1895. Reprint. United States Catholic Historical Society Monograph Series 30. Intro. David N. O'Brien; Commentary James H. Smylie. New York: Catholic Historical Society, 1974.

Warfield, Benjamin B. "On the Antiquity and the Unity of the Human Race." *Princeton Theological Review* 9.1 (Jan. 1911): 1–24.

Wayland, John Terrill. *The Theological Department at Yale College, 1822–1858.* Ph.D. dissertation, Yale University, 1913. New York: Garland, 1987.

Welch, Claude. *Graduate Education in Religion: A Critical Appraisal.* Missoula: University of Montana Press, 1971.

———. *Protestant Thought in the Nineteenth Century.* 2 vols. Vol. 1, *1799–1870.* New Haven, Conn.: Yale University Press, 1972.

Welter, Barbara. "From Maria Monk to Paul Blanshard: A Century of Protestant Anti-Catholicism." In *Uncivil Religion: Interreligious Hostility in America,* ed. Robert N. Bellah and Frederick E. Greenspahn, 43–71. New York: Crossroads, 1987.

Wenley, R. M. "The Classics and the Elective System." In *Latin and Greek,* ed. Kelsey, 283–303.

West, Andrew F. *The Graduate College of Princeton.* Princeton, N.J.: Princeton University Press, 1913.

———. "Must the Classics Go?" *NAR* 138 (Feb. 1884): 151–62.

Wetzel, Willard W. "Debates and Discussions in the Society of Inquiry." B.D. thesis, Theological Seminary of the Evangelical and Reformed Church, Lancaster, Pa., 1954.

White, Andrew. *A History of the Warfare of Science with Theology.* 2 vols. New York: D. Appleton, 1897.

White, Hayden. "The Politics of Historical Interpretation: Discipline and De-Sublimation." 1982. In White, *The Content of the Form: Narrative Discourse and Historical Representation.* Baltimore: Johns Hopkins University Press, 1987.

Wilbur, Earl Morse. *The First Century of the Liberal Movement in American Religion.* 1918. 5th printing. Boston: American Unitarian Association, 1927.

Willey, Basil. "Septem contra Christum (*Essays and Reviews*, 1860)." In Willey, *More Nineteenth Century Studies: A Group of Honest Doubters*, 137–85. London: Chatto & Windus, 1956.

Williams, George Huntston, ed. *The Harvard Divinity School: Its Place in Harvard University and in American Culture*. Boston: Beacon Press, 1954.

———. "Introduction: The Three Recurrent Conflicts." In *The Harvard Divinity School*, ed. Williams, 3–18.

Wilson, A. N. *God's Funeral*. New York: Norton, 1999.

Wilson, Henry Bristow. "Séances Historiques de Genève: The National Church." In *Essays and Reviews*, 144–206.

Wilson, James Grant. *The Centennial History of the Protestant Episcopal Church in the Diocese of New York 1785–1885*. New York: D. Appleton, 1886.

Wilson, John F. "Civil Authority and Religious Freedom in America: Philip Schaff on the United States as a Christian Nation." In *A Century of Church History*, ed. Bowden, 148–67.

———. "Introduction" to *The Sacred and the Secular University*, ed. Roberts and Turner, 3–16.

———. *Religion and the American Nation: Historiography and History*. George H. Shriver Lecture Series in Religion in American History, University of Georgia. Athens: University of Georgia Press, 2003.

Wind, James C. *The Bible and the University: The Messianic Vision of William Rainey Harper*. Biblical Scholarship in North America 16. Atlanta: Scholars Press, 1987.

Winterer, Caroline. *The Culture of Classicism: Ancient Greece and Rome in American Intellectual Life, 1780–1910*. Baltimore: Johns Hopkins University Press, 2002.

Woods, Leonard, *History of Andover Theological Seminary*. Ed. George S. Baker. Boston: J.R. Osgood, 1885.

Wright, Conrad. "The Early Period (1811–1840)." In *The Harvard Divinity School*, ed. Williams, 21–77.

Wright, G. Frederick. *Studies in Science and Religion*. Andover, Mass.: Warren F. Draper, 1882.

"Yale College and the Late Meeting of the Alumni in New York." *NE* 28 (April 1869): 269–307.

Yrigoyen, Charles, Jr., and George M. Bricker, eds. *Reformed and Catholic: Selected Historical and Theological Writings of Philip Schaff*. Pittsburgh Original Texts and Translations 4. Pittsburgh: Pickwick Press, 1979.

Zahn, Theodor, *Ignatius von Antiochen*. Gotha: Friedrich Andreas Perthes, 1873.

INDEX

ACKNOWLEDGMENTS

Many institutions, librarians, and colleagues have helped me during the research and writing of this book. I am grateful to Duke University and my Department Chair, Richard Jaffe, for various forms of support. I was fortunate to be a Burke Scholar in Residence at Union Theological Seminary in 2004–2005, where I received excellent research assistance from archivist Ruth Tonkiss Cameron and librarians Michael Boddy and Seth Kasten. I also worked at the following university and seminary libraries and thank the principal librarians who assisted me: General Theological Seminary (Andrew Kadel); Harvard Divinity School (Frances O'Donnell); Lancaster Theological Seminary (Richard Berg, Dianne Russell); New Brunswick Theological Seminary (Tolanda Henderson); New York University (Janet Bunde); Princeton Theological Seminary (Kenneth Henke); University of North Carolina-Chapel Hill (Anne Skilton); University of Notre Dame (Kevin Cawley); and Yale Divinity School (Joan Duffy, Paul Stuehrenberg). I also thank archivists at the Catholic University of America (William John Shepherd) and the University of Chicago (Julia Gardner); material I gathered at these universities will be incorporated in a future project. Librarians at the University of Vermont (Sylvia Bugbee), Franklin and Marshall College (Michael Lear), and Heidelberg University (Nancy Rubenstein) answered particular questions. I spent five happy and profitable weeks as a Senior Research Fellow at the American Academy in Rome in spring 2008; I thank then-Director Carmela Franklin for making that experience possible.

During my research trips, I received friendly assistance from the following colleagues, whom I would like to thank: in Boston/Cambridge, Paula Fredricksen, William Graham, Karen King, Laura Nasrallah, and Robert Orsi; in Chicago, Richard Rosengarten and Margaret Mitchell; in Lancaster, Pennsylvania, Anne Thayer and Julia O'Brien; in New Haven, Harold Attridge, Dale Martin, and the late Letty Russell; in Notre Dame, Robin

Darling Young; in Princeton, Caroline Walker Bynum and Kathryn Doob Sackenfeld; in Rome, Carmela and William Franklin, Frederick Brenk, S.J., Robert Dodaro, S.J., and many Fellows at the American Academy; in New York, Alan Cameron, Euan and Ruth Cameron, David Carr and Colleen Conway, Brigitte Kahl, Natalie Kampen, John and Eileen McGuckin, Maureen and Terrence Tilley, and many friends around the city who made my visits enjoyable.

Colleagues near and far offered advice, suggestions, and criticisms: many, too numerous to count, at meetings of the American Academy of Religion, the American Society of Church History, the North American Patristics Society, the Society of Biblical Literature, and the 2003 and 2007 Oxford International Patristics Conferences. Questions, criticisms, and suggestions I received pertaining to papers I gave at the following institutions assisted my thinking and writing: Claremont Graduate University, Columbia University, Cornell University, Fordham University, Harvard Divinity School, Syracuse University, Union Theological Seminary, University of British Columbia, University of California-Riverside, University of Michigan, University of North Carolina-Chapel Hill, University of Notre Dame, University of Pennsylvania, and University of Tennessee-Knoxville. I thank all these institutions and colleagues at them.

For assistance on particular points and for bibliographical suggestions I would like to thank Carol Bleser, Frederick Brenk, S. J., Christopher Celenza, Bart Ehrman, Natalie Kampen, Bruce Mullins, Mark Noll, Albert Rabil, Gabrielle Spiegel, Maureen Tilley, Terrence Tilley, Lucas Van Rompay, Mark Vessey, and Grant Wacker.

Various Duke graduate students assisted me along the way: Stephen Carlson, Maria Doerfler, Susanna Drake, Julia Lillis, and Tola Rodrick. I also thank (then) high school student in Lancaster, Pennsylvania, Elizabeth Thayer, for assistance at the Philip Schaff Library at the Lancaster Theological Seminary.

Some stalwart souls read all of my manuscript (Mark Chaves, Bart Ehrman, Dale Martin, Randall Styers, Grant Wacker), or parts of it (Kalman Bland, Kathryn Lofton); I have incorporated some of their suggestions, but alone am responsible for any remaining errors and deficiencies. Thanks also to anonymous reviewers for the University of Pennsylvania Press, to Humanities Editor Jerome Singerman, and to Divinations Series Editors Daniel Boyarin, Virginia Burrus, and Derek Krueger, who have been encouraging throughout. Alison Anderson and Caroline Winschel at University of Pennsylvania Press were helpful throughout the production process.

I thank Betty Bolden, librarian at the Burke Library of Union Theological Seminary, Columbia University, for calling to my attention the painting of Union that graces the cover of this book.

I thank my many conversation partners at Duke, UNC, and elsewhere, who have provided pleasurable hours: Sarah Beckwith, Kalman Bland, Daniel Boyarin, David Brakke, Virginia Burrus, Averil Cameron, Stanley Chojnacki, Deborah DeMott, Bart Ehrman, Valeria Finucci, Mary McClintock Fulkerson, Barbara Harris, Tomoko Masuzawa, Patricia Cox Miller and David Miller, Janet and Albert Rabil, Randall Styers (who first suggested the title of this book), Annabel Wharton, and J. Clare Woods. To my friend of some forty years, Patricia Cox Miller, I dedicate this book with love and appreciation.